Aga Khan III

VOLUME II
1928–1955

Aga Khan III

SELECTED SPEECHES AND WRITINGS OF SIR SULTAN MUHAMMAD SHAH

Edited, Annotated and Introduced
by
K. K. AZIZ

VOLUME II
1928–1955

KEGAN PAUL INTERNATIONAL
London and New York

First published in two volumes in 1997 by
Kegan Paul International

UK: P.O. Box 256, London WC1B 3SW, England
Tel: (0171) 580 5511 Fax: (0171) 436 0899

E-mail: books@keganpau.demon.co.uk
Internet: http://www.demon.co.uk/keganpaul/

USA: 562 West 113th Street, New York, NY 10025, USA
Tel: (212) 666 1000 Fax: (212) 316 3100

Distributed by
John Wiley & Sons Ltd
Southern Cross Trading Estate
1 Oldlands Way, Bognor Regis
West Sussex, PO22 9SA, England
Tel: (01243) 779 777 Fax: (01243) 820 250

Columbia University Press
562 West 113th Street
New York, NY 10025, USA
Tel: (212) 666 1000 Fax: (212) 316 3100

© Kegan Paul International, 1997

Phototypeset in Baskerville
by Intype London Ltd
Printed and bound in Great Britain by MPG Books Ltd, Bodmin, Cornwall

British Library Cataloguing in Publication Data
Aga Khan *III 1877–1957*
The collected works of Aga Khan III.
1. India. Islam. Role of politics
I. Title
297.19770954

ISBN 0–7103–0427–7

Library of Congress Cataloging-in-Publication Data
Aga Khan III. 1877–1957.
[Works. 1991]
The collected works of Aga Khan III: speeches and writings of Sir Sultan
Muhammod Shah / edited by K.K Aziz.
p. cm.
ISBN 0–7103–0427–7
1. Ismailites. 2. Islam—20th century. 3. Muslims—India. 4. India—Politics
and government—20th century. I. Aziz. Khursheed Kamal. II. Title.
BP195.I8A5 1991
297'.822—dc20 91–12693
CIP

CONTENTS

VOLUME II 1928–1955

87   THE FUTURE OF BOMBAY 807
Message to the East India Association
Paris: 17 June 1928
The Times of India, Bombay, 19 June 1928.

88   A CONSTITUTION FOR INDIA – I 813
An Article
London: 12 October 1928
The Times, London, 12 October 1928.

89   A CONSTITUTION FOR INDIA – II 817
An Article
London: 13 October 1928
The Times, London, 13 October 1928.

90   IN DEFENCE OF FREE STATES IN INDIA 823
Letter to *The Times*
Newmarket: 17 October 1928
The Times, London, 19 October 1928.

91   LIONEL CURTIS AND INDIAN PROVINCES 825
Letter to *The Times*
London(?): 25 October 1928
The Times, London, 29 October 1928.

92   THE INDIAN ECONOMIC PROSPECTS 827
Interview with *The Times of India*
Bombay: 28 December 1928
The Times of India, Bombay, 29 December 1928.

93   NATIONHOOD FOR THE INDIAN MUSLIMS   829
Presidential Address to the All-India Muslim Conference
Delhi: 31 December 1928
*Report of the All India Muslim Conference Held at Delhi on 31 December,
1928, and 1st January, 1929,* compiled and published by authority
by Hafizur Rahman, Aligarh, n.d., pp. 20–3.

94   BRITAIN AND THE MUSLIMS OF INDIA   842
Interview with the *Daily Express*
Nice: 1 May 1929
Daily Express, London, 3 May 1929.

95   BRITISH POLICY IN INDIA   845
An Article
London: 7 November 1929
The Times, London, 7 November 1929.

96   INDIAN MUSLIM ASPIRATIONS   849
Letter to *The Times*
Antibes: 16(?) January 1930
The Times, London, 18 January 1930.

97   A FEDERATION FOR INDIA   851
Speech at the Round Table Conference
London: 21 November 1930
*Indian Round Table Conference: 12th. November 1930 – 19th. January
1931: Proceedings,* His Majesty's Stationery Office, London, 1931,
Cmd. 3778, pp. 180–1.

98   THE PRESENT OUTLOOK   856
Interview with *The Daily Herald*
London: 1 December 1930
The Daily Herald, London, 2 December 1930.

99   THE EAST THROUGH THE ORIENTAL EYES   859
Foreword to Sirdar Ikbal Ali Shah's Book on Persia
London: 8 December 1930
Sirdar Ikbal Ali Shah, *Eastward to Persia,* Wright and Brown,
London, n.d., pp. ix-x.

100   THE FUTURE OF MANKIND   860
A Speech at a Literary Gathering
London: 10 June 1931
The Times, London, 11 June 1931.

101   PROSPECTS FOR THE ROUND TABLE
CONFERENCE   861
Statement to *The Times*
London: 16 September 1931
The Times, London, 17 September 1931.

102   SAFEGUARDS FOR THE INDIAN MUSLIMS   863
Broadcast Address to the USA
London: 27 September 1931
The Times, London, 28 September 1931.

103   MY PERSONAL LIFE   866
Interview with the *Daily Sketch*
London: 2 November 1931
Daily Sketch, London, 2 November 1931.

104   IF I WERE A DICTATOR   869
A Broadcast
London: 11 November 1931
The Listener, London, 11 November 1931.

105   PROVISIONS OF A SETTLEMENT OF THE
COMMUNAL PROBLEM REGARDING THE INDIAN
CONSTITUTION   876
A Memorandum for the Round Table Conference
London: 12 November 1931
*Indian Round Table Conference (Second Session): 7th. September 1931 –
1st. December 1931*, His Majesty's Stationery Office, London, 1932,
Cmd. 3997, pp. 68–73.

106   ANGLO-MUSLIM AMITY   883
Speech at a Dinner
London: 19 November 1931
The Times, London, 21 November 1931.

107   A CALL FOR ANGLO-MUSLIM FRIENDSHIP   885
Speech to the National League
London: 24 November 1931
The Times, London, 25 November 1931.

108   THE MUSLIM OUTLOOK   886
Letter to *The Times*
Antibes: 16 December 1931
The Times, London, 18 December 1931.

109   A UNITED MUSLIM PARTY IN INDIA   890
Telegram to Sir Muhammad Yakub
London: 16 December 1931
The Times, London, 19 December 1931.

110   THE NEED FOR DISARMAMENT   892
Speech at the Conference for the Reduction and Limitation of
Armaments
Geneva: 19 February 1932
*League of Nations: Conference for the Reduction and Limitation of
Armaments: Verbatim Record (Revised) of the Fourteenth Plenary
Meeting, Friday, February 19th, 1932, at 10 a.m.*, Geneva, 1932,
pp. 2–3.

111   THE SINO-JAPANESE DISPUTE   900
Speech at the Special Session of the League of Nations
Geneva: 8 March 1932
*League of Nations Official Journal, Special Supplement No. 101: Records
of the Special Session of the Assembly Convened in Virtue of Article
15 of the Covenant at the Request of the Chinese Government*, Geneva,
Volume 1, 1932, pp. 76–7.

112   THE HINDU-MUSLIM PROBLEM IN INDIA   903
Letter to *The Times*
London: 7 June 1932
The Times, London, 9 June 1932.

113   TURKEY'S ENTRY INTO THE LEAGUE OF
NATIONS   906
Speech in the General Assembly of the League of Nations
Geneva: 6 July 1932
*League of Nations Official Journal, Special Supplement No. 102: Records
of the Special Session of the Assembly Convened in Virtue of Article
15 of the Covenant at the Request of the Chinese Government, Volume
2*, Geneva, 1932, p. 3.

114   THE WORLD LOOKS TO THE LEAGUE   908
Speech in the General Assembly of the League of Nations
Geneva: 27 September 1932
*League of Nations Official Journal, Special Supplement No. 104: Records
of the Thirteenth Ordinary Session of the Assembly, Plenary Meeting,
Text of the Debates*, Geneva, 1932, p. 36.

115 IRAQ'S ENTRY INTO THE LEAGUE OF NATIONS 911
Speech in the General Assembly of the League of Nations
Geneva: 3 October 1932
*League of Nations Official Journal, Special Supplement No. 102: Records
of the Special Session of the Assembly Convened in Virtue of Article
15 of the Covenant at the Request of the Chinese Government, Volume
2*, Geneva, 1932, p. 21.

116 MUSLIMS AND THE THIRD ROUND TABLE
CONFERENCE 912
Telegram to Sir Muhammad Iqbal
London: 12 October 1932
The Civil and Military Gazette, Lahore, 13 October 1932.

117 THE FINANCES OF THE LEAGUE OF NATIONS 914
Speech in the General Assembly of the League of Nations
Geneva: 17 October 1932
*Verbatim Record of the Thirteenth Ordinary Session of the Assembly of
the League of Nations, Twelfth Plenary Meeting, Monday, October 17th,
1932, at 10.30 a.m.*, Geneva, 1932, p. 4.

118 THE NEW CONSTITUTION FOR INDIA 918
A Statement on the Work of the Round Table Conference
London: 16 November 1932
The Times, London, 17 November 1932.

119 ON THE ROAD TO A CONSTITUTION FOR INDIA 919
Speech at the Third Round Table Conference
London: 23 December 1932
*Indian Round Table Conference (Third Session) (17th November, 1932 –
24 December, 1932)*, London, 1933, Cmd. 4238, pp. 133–5.

120 WORLD CO-OPERATION AND PEACE 924
Speech at the Conference for the Reduction and Limitation of
Armaments
Geneva: 2 February 1933
N. M. Budhwani (ed.), *The Aga Khan and the League of Nations*,
Dhoraji, 1938, pp. 39–44.

121 THE IMPORTANCE OF THE BENGALI MUSLIMS 927
Message to the Muslims of Bengal
London: 3 June 1933
Star of India, Calcutta, 12 June 1933.

122 ECONOMIC REVIVAL OF THE MUSLIM WORLD   931
A Speech to the National League
London: 29 June 1933
The Times, London, 30 June 1933.

123 COMMERCIAL PROSPECTS IN MUSLIM ASIA   934
Speech to the National League
London: 2 July 1933
The Asiatic Review, London, Vol. 29, pp. 633–7.

124 THE MAKING OF THE NEW INDIAN
CONSTITUTION   940
Speech at a Reception
London: 24 July 1933
The Times, London, 25 July 1933.

125 MUSLIMS AND THE MAKING OF THE NEW
INDIAN CONSTITUTION   943
Memorandum Submitted to the Joint Committee on Indian Constitutional Reform by the All India Muslim Conference and the All India Muslim League
London: 1 August 1933
Joint Committee on Indian Constitutional Reform (Session 1932–33), Volume 2 C, Minutes of Evidence Together with Appendix D, Government of Great Britain, London, 1934, Parliamentary Papers H.L. 79 (II C), H.C. 112 (II C), pp. 1475–81.

126 IN DEFENCE OF THE INDIAN WHITE PAPER   957
Interrogation of Winston Spencer Churchill in the Joint Committee on Indian Constitutional Reform
London: 24 October 1933
Joint Committee on Indian Constitutional Reform (Session 1932–33), Volume 2 C: Minutes of Evidence Given Before the Joint Committee on Indian Constitutional Reform (Questions 8,681–11,209, 12,055–12,720, 13,549–13,691, 14,400–15,362, 15,777–17,339) and Before Sub-Committees A, B, C and D of the Joint Committee Together with Appendix D, His Majesty's Stationery Office, London, 1934, pp. 1842–5. Parliamentary Papers H.L. 79 (II C), H.C. 112 (II C).

127 INDIAN PROPOSALS FOR THE NEW
CONSTITUTIONAL ORDER   962
Joint Memorandum Submitted to the Joint Committee on Indian Constitutional Reform by the British Indian Delegation
London: 17 November 1933

Joint Committee on Indian Constitutional Reform (Session 1933–34),
Volume 1 (Part I), Report, His Majesty's Stationery Office, London,
1934. Parliamentary Papers H.L. 6 (I, Part I), H.C. 5 (I, Part I).

128   THE INDIAN WHITE PAPER   995
Interview with the Associated Press of India
Bombay: 14 December 1933
The Times of India, Bombay, 15 December 1933.

129   THE COMMUNAL ELECTORATES   1001
Interview with the Press
New Delhi: 7 February 1934
The Times of India, Bombay, 8 February 1934.

130   ADVICE TO THE INDIAN MUSLIM LEGISLATORS 1003
Speech at a Dinner
New Delhi: 12 February 1934
Star of India, Calcutta, 14 February 1934.

131   THE MUSLIM LEAGUE AND THE NEW REFORMS 1005
Speech at a Luncheon
New Delhi: 14 February 1934
Star of India, Calcutta, 15 February 1934.

132   POLITICAL ADVANCE BY EVOLUTION   1008
Speech at a Dinner
New Delhi: 14 February 1934
The Civil and Military Gazette, Lahore, 16 February 1934.

133   COUNSEL TO THE ALL INDIA MUSLIM
CONFERENCE   1010
Address to the Executive Board
New Delhi: 15 February 1934
Star of India, Calcutta, 21 February 1934.

134   A WORD TO THE MUSLIM LEGISLATORS   1015
Speech at a Dinner
Bombay: 22 February 1934
The Civil and Military Gazette, Lahore, 23 February 1934.

135   THE MUSLIM PRESS IN BENGAL   1017
Message to the *Star of India*
Calcutta: 26 February 1934
Star of India, Calcutta, 26 February 1934.

136 THE TASK BEFORE THE MUSLIM LEGISLATORS OF
BENGAL   1019
Speech at a Luncheon
Calcutta: 28 February 1934
Star of India, Calcutta, 1 March 1934.

137 MUSLIM UNANIMITY ON INDIAN REFORMS   1023
A Statement
Calcutta: 28 February 1934
The Times, London, 1 March 1934.

138 THE IMPORTANCE OF INSURANCE   1025
Reply to the Address of Welcome by the Directors of the Eastern
Federal Union Insurance Company
Calcutta: 1 March 1934
Star of India, Calcutta, 1 March 1934.

139 COMMERCIAL RELATIONS BETWEEN INDIA AND
BURMA   1027
Reply to the Address of Welcome Presented by the Burma Indian
Chamber of Commerce
Rangoon: 6 March 1934
Ismaili, Bombay, 22 April 1934.

140 A CALL TO THE ISLAMIC WORLD   1031
A Message
London: 14 March 1934
Star of India, Calcutta, 15 March 1934.

141 PERSIAN POETS   1034
An Article
London: 22 September 1934
The Times, London, 22 September 1934.

142 AFGHANISTAN AND THE LEAGUE OF NATIONS 1039
Speech in the General Assembly of the League of Nations
Geneva: 27 September 1934
*Verbatim Record of the Fifteenth Ordinary Session of the Assembly of the
League of Nations, Twelfth Plenary Meeting, Thursday, September 27th,
1934, at 10 a.m.*, Geneva, 1934, p. 2.

143 THE PROPHET OF ISLAM   1044
A Foreword to Qassim Ali Jairazbhoy's Biography of Muhammad
Geneva: September 1934

Al-Haji Qassim Ali Jairazbhoy, *Muhammad: "A Mercy to All the Nations"*, Luzac, London, 1937, pp. 11–15.

144 THOUGHTS ON IMPERIAL DEFENCE   1047
Speech at the Navy League Dinner
London: 23 October 1934
The Times, London, 24 October 1934.

145 ON FIRDAUSI   1051
Speech to the Royal Central Asian Society
London: 31 October 1934
The Times, London, 1 November 1934.

146 INDIA AND THE REFORMS   1054
Interview with *The Times of India*
Bombay: 4 January 1935
The Times of India, Bombay, 5 January 1935.

147 THE IMPORTANCE OF RURAL DEVELOPMENT
FOR MUSLIM INDIA   1057
A Statement to the Press
New Delhi: 5 February 1935
The Times of India, Bombay, 6 February 1935.

148 A SOCIALIST PATH TO BETTERMENT   1060
Speech at a Luncheon
New Delhi: 8 February 1935
The Times of India, Bombay, 11 February 1935.

149 AN APPEAL TO THE MUSLIM LEGISLATORS
OF INDIA   1062
Speech at a Dinner
New Delhi: 9 February 1935
Star of India, Calcutta, 15 February 1935.

150 THE RENAISSANCE OF ISLAMIC CULTURE   1067
Speech to the Islamic Research Association
Bombay: 25 February 1935
The Times of India, Bombay, 26 February 1935.

151 LORD LAMINGTON'S SERVICES   1069
Speech at a Luncheon
London: 4 June 1935
The Times, London, 5 June 1935.

152   THE 1935 CONSTITUTION AND THE
MUSLIMS OF INDIA   1071
Speech at an Official Dinner
London: 6 June 1935
The Times, London, 7 June 1935.

153   THE SUFFERING IN QUETTA   1073
Speech at the Quetta Earthquake Relief Fund Meeting
London: 24 June 1935
The Times, London, 25 June 1935.

154   THE MUSLIM LANDS AND THE WEST   1086
Speech to the Council of Peers
London: 15 July 1935
The Muslim Times, London, 1 August 1935, p. 4.

155   PROSPECTS FOR THE LEAGUE OF NATIONS   1089
Speech in the General Assembly of the League of Nations
Geneva: 13 September 1935
*Verbatim Record of the Sixteenth Ordinary Session of the Assembly of the
League of Nations: Sixth Plenary Meeting, Friday, September 13th, 1935,
at 10.30 a.m.*, Geneva, 1935, p. 2.

156   THE SITUATION IN INDIA   1091
Interview with the Associated Press of India
Bombay: 10 January 1936
Star of India, Calcutta, 11 January 1936.

157   THE CHANGE IN THE BRITISH MONARCHY   1093
Interview with *The Times of India*
Bombay: January 1936
Naoroji M. Dumasia, *The Aga Khan and His Ancestors*, The Times
of India Press, Bombay, 1939, pp. 289–92.

158   A MEMORIAL FOR KING GEORGE V   1096
Speech at a Public Condolence Meeting
Bombay: 11 February 1936
Naoroji M. Dumasia, *The Aga Khan and His Ancestors*, The Times
of India Press, Bombay, 1939, pp. 292–4.

159   THE FUTURE OF THE ALIGARH UNIVERSITY   1099
Reply to the Address of Welcome Presented by the Members of
the Court of the University
Aligarh: 15 February 1936

Naoroji M. Dumasia, *The Aga Khan and His Ancestors*, The Times of India Press, Bombay, 1939, pp. 192–7.

160   RESPONSIBILITIES OF MUSLIM LEADERSHIP IN
INDIA   1105
Speech at a Meeting
New Delhi: 17 February 1936
Star of India, Calcutta, 18 February 1936.

161   THE BROTHERHOOD OF ISLAM   1110
Speech at a Dinner
New Delhi: 17 February 1936
Star of India, Calcutta, 22 February 1936.

162   THE EDUCATIONAL NEEDS OF MUSLIM INDIA   1112
Presidential Address to the All India Muhammadan Educational
Conference
Rampur: 21 February 1936
Star of India, Calcutta, 14 March 1936.

163   COMMUNAL UNITY AND REFORMS IN INDIA   1119
A Message
Bombay: 9 March 1936
The Times, London, 10 March 1936.

164   MIGRATION AND PEACE   1120
Letter to *The Times*
France: 3(?) May 1936
The Times, London, 6 May 1936.

165   THE FORTUNES OF THE LEAGUE OF NATIONS   1124
Speech in the General Assembly of the League of Nations
Geneva: 29 September 1936
*Verbatim Record of the Seventeenth Ordinary Session of the Assembly of
the League of Nations: Tenth Plenary Meeting, Tuesday, September 29th,
1936, at 3.30 p.m.*, Geneva, 1936, p. 5.

166   HAFIZ AND THE PLACE OF IRANIAN CULTURE
IN THE WORLD   1127
Inaugural Lecture Before the Iran Society
London: 9 November 1936
*The Iran Society: Inaugural Lecture: Hafiz and the Place of Iranian
Culture in the World by His Highness the Aga Khan*, The Iran Society,
London, November 1936, pp. 1–7.

167   THE ENTRY OF EGYPT INTO THE LEAGUE OF
NATIONS   1139
Speech in the General Assembly of the League of Nations
Geneva: 26 May 1937
*League of Nations Official Journal, Special Supplement No. 166: Records
of the Special Session of the Assembly convened for the purpose of con-
sidering the Request of the Kingdom of Egypt for Admission to the League
of Nations (May 26th–27th, 1937),* Geneva, 1937, p. 29.

168   FAILURES AND SUCCESSES OF THE LEAGUE OF
NATIONS   1147
Presidential Address to the League of Nations
Geneva: 13 September 1937
*Verbatim Record of the Eighteenth Ordinary Session of the Assembly of
the League of Nations, Second Plenary Meeting, Monday, September
13th, 1937, at 5.00 p.m.,* Geneva, 1937, p. 2.

169   A TRIBUTE TO DR MASARYK OF
CZECHOSLOVAKIA   1151
Speech in the General Assembly of the League of Nations
Geneva: 14 September 1937
*Verbatim Record of the Eighteenth Ordinary Session of the Assembly of
the League of Nations, Third Plenary Meeting, Tuesday, September 14th,
1937, at 10.30 a.m.,* Geneva, 1937, p. 6.

170   THE PALACE OF THE LEAGUE OF NATIONS   1153
Speech in the General Assembly of the League of Nations Inaugurating the New Headquarters
Geneva: 28 September 1937
*Verbatim Record of the Eighteenth Ordinary Session of the Assembly of
the League of Nations, Ninth Plenary Meeting, Tuesday, September 28th,
1937, at 10.30 a.m.,* Geneva, 1937, p. 1.

171   THE TASK BEFORE THE LEAGUE OF NATIONS   1155
Adjournment of the Session Speech at the League of Nations
Geneva: 6 October 1937
*Verbatim Record of the Eighteenth Ordinary Session of the Assembly of
the League of Nations, Fourteenth Plenary Meeting, Wednesday, October
6th, 1937, at 5.00 p.m.,* Geneva, 1937, p. 2.

172   ORIENTAL LITERATURE   1159
Preface to Sirdar Ikbal Ali Shah's Collection of Oriental
Literature
London: 1937
The Coronation Book of Oriental Literature, edited by the Sirdar Ikbal
Ali Shah, Sampson Low, Marston and Co., London, n.d., p.v.

173   THE RELEVANCE OF THE LEAGUE OF NATIONS 1162
Speech at the Empire Exhibition
Glasgow: 8 July 1938
The Times, London, 9 July 1938.

174   MAJOR PROBLEMS OF TODAY   1167
Interview with the Associated Press of India
Karachi: 7 December 1938
Star of India, Calcutta, 8 December 1938.

175   THE ISSUES BEFORE THE BRITISH EMPIRE   1168
Interview with the *Star of India*
Bombay: 11 December 1938
Star of India, Calcutta, 12 December 1938.

176   WAR OR PEACE   1171
A Broadcast Talk
Bombay: 17 January 1939
The Times of India, Bombay, 18 January 1939.

177   THE IMPERATIVES OF ISLAMIC RESEARCH   1173
Speech to the Islamic Research Association
Bombay: 18 January 1939
Ismaili, Bombay, 22 January 1939.

178   MUSLIMS AND THE SECOND WORLD WAR   1178
Message to the Muslims of the British Empire
Simla and London: 28 September 1939
The Civil and Military Gazette, Lahore, 30 September 1939.

179   A CONSTITUENT ASSEMBLY FOR INDIA   1180
Interview with the Press
Bombay: 8 February 1940
The Civil and Military Gazette, Lahore, 10 February 1940.

180   CONCERN FOR HUMAN VALUES   1182
Message on the Occasion of the Opening of a New Mosque in
London
Zurich: 1 August 1941
The Times, London, 8 August 1941.

181   THE RELIGIOUS REVIVAL OF ISLAM   1183
An Article (with Dr Zaki Ali)
Lahore: 1944
Prince Aga Khan and Dr Zaki Ali, *Glimpses of Islam*, Shaikh
Muhammad Ashraf, Lahore, first published 1944, 2nd enlarged
edn 1954, repr. 1961, 1965, 1973, pp. 72–83.

182   LOOKING TOWARDS THE POST-WAR WORLD   1189
Interview with *The East African Standard*
Nairobi: 26 March 1945
The East African Standard, Nairobi, 27 March 1945.

183   THE FUTURE OF ISLAM IN EAST AFRICA – I   1195
Reply to the Address of Welcome from the East African Muslim
Conference
Mombasa: 16 June 1945
Proceedings of the East African Muslim Conference, Mombasa, 1945.

184   THE FUTURE OF ISLAM IN EAST AFRICA – II   1201
Speech at the East African Muslim Conference
Mombasa: 17 June 1945
Proceedings of the East African Muslim Conference, Mombasa, 1945.

185   THE FUTURE OF ISLAM IN EAST AFRICA – III   1204
Speech at the East African Muslim Conference
Mombasa: 18 June 1945
Proceedings of the East African Muslim Conference, Mombasa, 1945.

186   THE MUSLIMS OF TANGANYIKA   1206
Reply to the Address Presented by the Tanganyika Muslim
Association
Dar-es-Salaam: 22 July 1945
The Tanganyika Standard, Dar-es-Salaam, 28 July 1945.

187   INTER-RACIAL COOPERATION IN TANGANYIKA   1208
Interview with *The Tanganyika Standard*
Dar-es-Salaam: 2 August 1945
The Tanganyika Standard, Dar-es-Salaam, 3 August 1945.

188 GUIDELINES FOR THE MUSLIMS OF
TRANSVAAL   1210
Reply to the Address of Welcome from the Transvaal Muslim
League
Johannesburg: 12 August 1945
A. J. Chunara, *Platinum Jubilee Review*, Karachi, 1954.

189 INDIANS IN SOUTH AFRICA   1215
Speech Before the Natal Indian Congress
Durban: 16 August 1945
Habib V. Keshavjee, *The Aga Khan and Africa*, Pretoria, 1946.

190 THE INDIAN SITUATION   1219
Interview with the United Press of India
Karachi: 9 November 1945
The Civil and Military Gazette, Lahore, 11 November 1945.

191 THE IMPORTANCE OF SCIENCE   1220
Reply to the Address from the Court of the Aligarh Muslim
University
Bombay: 9 March 1946
The Times of India, Bombay, 10 March 1946.

192 ADVICE TO THE EAST AFRICAN MUSLIMS   1222
Interview with the *Observer* (Nairobi)
Nairobi: June 1946
The Sunday Post, Nairobi, 2 June 1946.

193 EDUCATION AND PROGRESS OF MUSLIMS
IN EAST AFRICA   1223
Reply to the Address of Welcome from the (Second) East African
Muslim Conference
Mombasa: 27 July 1946
*Combined Report of the Second East African Muslim Conference and the
Annual General Meeting of the East African Muslim Welfare Society*,
Mombasa, 1946.

194 A UNIVERSITY FOR EAST AFRICA   1229
Speech at the (Second) East African Muslim Conference
Mombasa: 28 July 1946
*Combined Report of the Second East African Muslim Conference and the
Annual General Meeting of the East African Muslim Welfare Society*,
Mombasa, 1946.

195   WORLD PEACE AND ITS PROBLEMS   1231
A Lecture at the Dar-es-Salaam Cultural Society
Dar-es-Salaam: 3 August 1946
Special Golden Platinum Jubilee Day Number, Ismailia Association for
Tanganyika, Dar-es-Salaam, n.d. (?1956), pp. 1–14.

196   THE FOLLY OF HATE AND FEAR   1239
Speech at the Diamond Jubilee Celebrations
Dar-es-Salaam, 10 August 1946
The East African Standard, Nairobi, 12 August 1946.

197   THE FUTURE DEFENCE PROBLEM OF
SOUTH ASIA   1241
Letter to *The Times*
Lausanne: 19 July 1947
The Times, London, 23 July 1947.

198   THE CREATION OF PAKISTAN AND THE
MUSLIM WORLD   1243
Message to the People of Pakistan on the Eve of the Creation of
Pakistan
Switzerland: 17 August 1947
Message to the World of Islam by Aga Khan III, Karachi, 1977, p. 1.

199   CAN WE STOP THE NEXT WAR?   1245
An Article
October–November 1947
The Sunday Post, Nairobi, 16 November 1947.

200   GANDHI'S POLITICAL PHILOSOPHY   1250
Letter to *The Times*
France: 2(?) February 1948
The Times, London, 5 February 1948.

201   SPELLING REFORM   1252
Letter to *The Times*
Paris: 19 March 1949
The Times, London, 23 March 1949.

202   THE FUTURE OF MUSLIM STATES IN THE
BACKGROUND OF HISTORY   1254
An Address to the Pakistan Institute of International Affairs
Karachi: 8 February 1950
Pakistan Horizon, Karachi, Vol. 3, pp. 3–8.

203   WHAT PAKISTANIS SHOULD DO   1260
A Broadcast Message
Karachi: 19 February 1950
Message to the World of Islam by Aga Khan III, Karachi, 1977,
pp. 18–20.

204   A TRIBUTE TO MUHAMMAD ALI JINNAH   1262
Message to the Quaid-i-Azam Memorial Fund
Karachi: (?) February 1950
The Zanzibar Times, Zanzibar, 11 April 1950.

205   A SCHOOL OF TECHNOLOGY FOR EAST
PAKISTAN   1264
Speech at the University of Dacca
Dacca: 28 January 1951
The Pakistan Observer, Dacca, 29 January 1951.

206   PAKISTAN AS A MUSLIM STATE   1267
Speech at a Public Meeting
Dacca: 28 January 1951
Dawn, Karachi, 29 January 1951.

207   ARABIC AS THE NATIONAL LANGUAGE OF
PAKISTAN   1272
Speech Before the Motamar-al-Alam-al-Islami
Karachi: 9 February 1951
Message to the World of Islam by Aga Khan III, Karachi, 1977,
pp. 21–6.

208   CHANGING FACE OF ASIA   1276
Interview with the *Ittla'at* of Tehran
Tehran: February 1951
H.R.H. Aga Khan's Visit to Iran, Karachi, 1951, pp. 46–8.

209   THE ISMAILIS AND NATIONAL LOYALTY   1278
Speech at a Dinner of the Aga Khan Students' Union
London: June 1951
The East African Standard, Nairobi, 8 June 1951.

210   INDIA–PAKISTAN RELATIONS   1280
Letter to *The Times*
London: 1 August 1951
The Times, London, 2 August 1951.

211   THE TOLERANCE OF ISLAM   1282
Letter to *The Times*
Cannes: 3 November 1951
The Times, London, 6 November 1951.

212   ECONOMIC DEVELOPMENT IN PAKISTAN
AND OTHER MUSLIM STATES   1286
An Address to the Pakistan Institute of International Affairs
Karachi: 1 February 1952
Pakistan Horizon, Karachi, Vol. 5, pp. 3–6.

213   ISLAM AND THE MODERN AGE   1290
Letter to the President of the Arabiyyah Jamiyyat, Karachi
Marseilles: 4 April 1952
Message to the World of Islam by Aga Khan III, Karachi, 1977,
pp. 36–40.

214   INDUSTRIAL INVESTMENT IN PAKISTAN   1294
Communication to the *Dawn* of Karachi
Cannes: 16 May 1952
Dawn, Karachi, 17 May 1952.

215   THE STATUS OF WOMEN   1295
Message to the Ismaili Women's Association of Karachi
March 1953
Message to the World of Islam by Aga Khan III, Karachi, 1977,
pp. 43–4.

216   THIS I HAVE LEARNT FROM LIFE   1297
An Article
Karachi: 3 February 1954
Dawn, Karachi, 4 February 1954, "Special Supplement to Com-
memorate the Platinum Jubilee of H.H. the Aga Khan."

217   PATRIOTISM AND LOYALTY   1302
Speech at his Platinum Jubilee Ceremony
Karachi: 3 February 1954
Dawn, Karachi, 4 February 1954.

218   IN SUPPORT OF THE PAKISTAN MUSLIM LEAGUE
                                                                1304
A Message
Dacca: 3 February 1954
Dawn, Karachi, 5 February 1954.

219   THE REFUGEE PROBLEM IN PAKISTAN   1306
Interview with the *Dawn* of Karachi
Karachi: 4 February 1954
Dawn, Karachi, 5 February 1954.

220   GOOD WISHES FOR THE PAKISTAN INSTITUTE
OF INTERNATIONAL AFFAIRS   1309
A Message to the Institute
Karachi: 5 February 1954
Dawn, Karachi, 6 February 1954.

221   THE SPIRIT OF THE ALIGARH UNIVERSITY   1311
Speech to the Aligarh Old Boys' Association
Karachi: 12 February 1954
Dawn, Karachi, 13 February 1954.

222   RACIAL COOPERATION IN KENYA   1313
Letter to *The Times*
Le Cannet: 24 March 1954
The Times, London, 24 March 1954.

223   A WARNING AGAINST SECTARIANISM   1314
A Special Message to the East African Muslim Welfare Society
Evian les Bains: 10 July 1954
Souvenir of the East African Muslim Welfare Society, n.p.p., 1954, p. 3.

224   MEMOIRS: WORLD ENOUGH AND TIME   1330
Extracts from a Book
London: 10 September 1954
The Memoirs of Aga Khan: World Enough and Time, Cassell and Co.,
London, 1954.

225   THE SPIRIT OF UNITY IN ISLAM   1407
A Message to the Ismailis
Cairo: 20 February 1955
Message to the World of Islam by Aga Khan III, Karachi, 1977,
p. 33.

226   MATERIAL INTELLIGENCE AND SPIRITUAL
ENLIGHTENMENT   1408
An Address at the Platinum Jubilee Ceremony
Cairo: 20 February 1955
Ismaili, Bombay, 6 March 1955.

227 IS RELIGION SOMETHING SPECIAL?   1410
An Article
Undated
Message of H.R.H. Prince Aga Khan III, Mombasa, 1955, pp. 23–5.

228 MY PHILOSOPHY OF HAPPINESS   1413
An Article
Undated
Message of H.R.H. Prince Aga Khan III, Mombasa, 1955, pp. 26–8.

229 THE FINAL RECONCILIATION BETWEEN
SUNNI AND SHIA DOCTRINES   1416
A Declaration
Undated
*Itehad-el-Islam, Otherwise Known as the Cultural, Religious, Economic
Pan-Islamism*, Pan-Islam Series no. 5, n.p., n.p.p., n.d., pp. 1–4.

Appendices   1418
    British Monarchs
    British Prime Ministers
    Secretaries of State for India
    Governors-General and Viceroys of India

Biographical Notes   1420
Bibliography   1485

Index   1497

THE FUTURE OF BOMBAY

Message to the East India Association

Paris: 17 June 1928

Disagreement with optimistic expressions on the economic future of Bombay – protective measures for the mill industry – other remedies – the mills as the backbone of the prosperity of Bombay.

His Highness the Aga Khan writing from Paris regretting the medical interdict on his coming to preside, said he was unable to agree entirely with Sir Stanley's optimistic expressions on the economic future of Bombay. He saw little hope for the mill industry unless the Government of India, with the support of public opinion, recognised the necessity for definitely protective measures for a few years enabling the readjustments according to changed conditions to be made. Many valuable subsidiary measures could be taken, notably the development of luxury trades during winter months, so as to draw affluent people from the interior. Cheap electricity would go far to meet some of the economic difficulties of Bombay, but present prices could not be regarded as cheap. If the capital energy sunk in the mill industry were crippled, he saw no great future for the developments whether towards sea or land. The Aga Khan could see nothing to replace the mills as the backbone of the prosperity of Bombay. . . .

Source: *The Times of India,* Bombay, 19 June 1928.
    A full report of the meeting as published in *The Times of India* is as follows:
    "Sir Frederick Sykes presided over a large meeting of the East India Association when Sir Stanley Reed delivered a lecture on 'Bombay to-day and to-morrow.'
    "Sir Stanley opined that there was good reason for the complaint of step-motherly attitude of the Government of India towards the mill industry, which should be treated as a national enterprise demanding the constant support of the Government of India, the local authorities and the public. But, the share-

holders must take to heart Mr. Baldwin's advice to Lancashire, and some of the practices associated with the system of managing agents must go. Given these premises, Sir Stanley was no pessimist with regard to the mill industry.

"Sir Amberson Marten forecasted a great development for Bombay harbour as a yachting centre. His experience of the High Court and elsewhere showed that the Indian and the Englishman could work together in Bombay cordially without disagreement.

"Sir Thomas Strangman said the Bombay Customs arrangements and race meeting compared most favourably with those in England. Whatever opinions Sir Frederick Sykes held now, Sir Thomas thought he would be a warm supporter of the totalisator after the quirquemium.

"Mr. P. R. Cadell dwelt on the contribution of efficient administration of the municipality to the progress of Bombay.

"Replying to the points raised during the debate with regard to the depression in the mill industry, Sir Stanley Reed pointed out that the competition of upcountry mills could not be retarded by protective duties.

"Sir Frederick Sykes said he first saw Bombay as a subaltern in the year of Lord Lamington's assumption of the Governorship of the Presidency during the most strenuous and interest in [sic] years of his life. Then he began to realise the vastness and fascination of India. There, too, were his thoughts towards speedier communications between England and India first mouled [sic]. He had every reason to look forward to returning to Bombay and try to help in any way he could [sic]. They must agree with Sir Stanley, Sir Frederick proceeded, that with Bombay's basic advantages, there was no need to fear for the future. All knew the richness of Bombay in kindness, friendship and generosity and in what a high degree she exemplified the bond of men that exists in cities.

"Lord Lamington, referring to the Back Bay, said he always held private enterprise under Government supervision the best method, superior to the execution of work departmentally.

"[Mr. Baldwin's message to Lancashire, referred to above, is embodied in the following message dated London, May 16:– 'In view of the critical condition of the cotton industry great importance is attached to the speech of Mr. Baldwin at the luncheon given by the British Cotton-growing Association at Manchester to-day, which was attended by 500 members of the Association and representatives of the banking institutions in Lancashire and north England. Lord Derby presiding said that the whole industry must be reconstructed and new capital must be brought in. Mr. Baldwin in his speech referred to the group possibilities in South Africa and elsewhere in the Empire for cotton-growing and purchasing British goods. Referring to the depression in the steel trade, the Premier mentioned that for every shilling he had when he took office, he had something under a penny to-day. The capital of the steel trade must be reduced until it represented live assets before it could hope for better times, and every section of the cotton industry must get together somehow and cut out the dead wood and clean up the mess made in 1919 (cheers)]'."

LONDON, June 18.

"He said that in some respects Bombay was passing through a very uncomfortable stage of transition namely 'a cold fit of construction when everyone is uncomfortable with the toes being trodden on.' He pointed out the value of the reclamation in view of the scarcity of open spaces and also of 'the finest sea face in the world' hitherto unused. Sir Stanley Reed visualised a great promenade in the future stretching from Chaupatti to Colaba Point bordered by cafes and clubs where men might meet their friends in better atmosphere than 'sodden bar or heated card club.' He expressed the opinion that the dominant characteristic of Bombay to-day was 'depression,' but considered that the material future of Bombay was assured, and pointed out that signs of real economy were difficult to find. – Reuter."

The Times of London reported the lecture very briefly in the following paragraph:

"MAJOR-GENERAL SIR FREDERICK SYKES, Governor-designate of Bombay, presided at a large meeting of the East India Association yesterday at the Caxton Hall, when Sir Stanley Reed spoke on 'Bombay To-day and To-morrow.'

"Referring to the long continued depression in the Bombay mill industry, SIR STANLEY REED said the industry must be treated as a national enterprise demanding the constant support of Government, the local authorities and the public. Shareholders must take to heart the advice which Mr. Baldwin gave to Lancashire. Capital which was lost could not be regained by regarding the figures printed on share certificates as sacrosanct; and some of the practices associated with managing agents must go. He was no pessimist on the subject. The material future of Bombay, after all, was assured. What did depress him was the note of materialism in their daily life."

However, the Aga Khan's message was printed in full at the end of the report.

The most authoritative account of the history of Bombay is contained in *The Imperial Gazetteer of India*, London, 2nd. ed. 1885, Vol. 3, pp. 74–7:

"The name of Bombay was erroneously supposed to have been given by the Portuguese, on account of the geographical position of the island – *Bom-bahia* or *Boa-bahia*, '*statio fidissima nautis.*' Colonel H. Yule, however, traces it back to the latter half of the compound name Tanna-Maiamba or Mayamba, which, according to Barbosa, *circ.* 1516, was used to designate the kingdom of the Konkan in the 16th century. The name appears as Maimbi in the very early geographical *Sommario de Regni*, translated from the Portuguese in Ramudio, written probably 1520–25. There can be little doubt that this word, in its turn, was a corruption of Mamba-devi, a goddess who had a famous shrine in the neighbourhood, mentioned in Forbes' *Ras Málá, circ.* 1630. The Portuguese of the 16th century call it Mombain or Bombaim, never Bom-bahia or Boa-bahia. The Maráthá name of Bombay is Mumbaí, from Mahímá, 'Great Mother,' a title of Deví. In support of the popular etymology from Buon Bahia, 'fair haven,' it may be said that Bombay undoubtedly possesses one of the finest harbours in the world. But the evidence leaves little doubt that the true derivation is from the Maráthá Mumbaí, *i.e.* Mahímá, 'the Great Mother,' or Deví. It thus happens that both the great British capitals of India, Bombay on the western cost, and Calcutta (*q.u*) on the eastern, take their names from titles or designations of the same goddess, the wife of Siva, the lord of death and reproduction.

"The history of Bombay begins with the cession of the island by the Portuguese to Charles II. in 1651, as part of the dowry of his queen, Catherine of Braganza. The adjoining islands, however, of Salsette and Karanja still remained in the possession of the Portuguese. At this time the population was estimated at 10,000 souls, and the revenue at 75,000 *xeraphins*, or £6500. The king appears to have found his distant acquisition unprofitable, and in 1668 he transferred it to the East India Company on payment of an annual rent of £10 in gold. The Company forthwith took steps for the strengthening of the fortifications and the encouragement of European settlers. Dr. Fryer, who visited the island in 1673, describes the population as numbering 60,000 – 'a mixture of most of the neighbouring countries, mostly rogues and vagabonds.' He has left an elaborate description of the place as it then existed. The fort or castle was armed with 120 pieces of ordnance; and the town, which lay at some distance, was a full mile in length. The greater number of the inhabitants, especially of the suburb of Mazagon, were engaged in fishing. The Portuguese still had several churches on the island. Between Parel and Máhim, the sea had made a wide breach, drowning 40,000 acres of good land. But the most striking point in all the early accounts is the excessive unhealthiness of the place, which cannot be attributed solely to the mode of life of the residents. Fryer declares it as his opinion that out of every 500 Europeans who came to live on the island, not 100 left it. A current proverb affirmed that two monsoons (or rainy seasons) were the age of a man. The most fatal disease, called by the Portuguese practitioners 'the Chinese death,' has been identified with cholera. The name arose, apparently, from a fanciful French or Latin etymology for the '*mordexim*' or '*mor-de-chin*,' the old west-coast term for cholera. Garcia d'Orta (1568) distinctly states that it was an Indian word, *morxi*. It is, in fact, a corruption of the Maráthi and Konkani words *modachi* and *modshi*, meaning cholera.

"In Fryer's time (1673) the factory of Surat, established sixty years before the cession of Bombay, was the chief possession of the East India Company in western India. Bombay itself was exposed to the ill-will of the Portuguese on Salsette island, who were able to cut off all direct communication with the mainland. The most formidable enemy, however, was the Sídí or Abyssinian admiral of the Mughal fleet, whose descendants are represented at the present day by the Nawáb of Janjírá. In 1668, the Sídí wintered at Mazagon, and laid siege to Bombay castle; and the town was only saved by a direct appeal to the Emperor. During this period also, the English in India were greatly hampered by domestic dissensions. In 1684, orders were received to transfer the chief seat of the Company's trade from Surat to Bombay, and the transfer had been effected by 1687. In 1708, the two Companies privileged to trade with the East were fused into the United East India Company, and Bombay was chosen as the seat of one of the three independent Presidencies, each of which was ruled over by a Governor-in-Council. It was not till 1773 that Bombay was subjected to the control of the Governor-General. Henceforth the history of Bombay city merges into that of the Presidency. The only event that need be specially recorded is the first Maráthá war (1774–1782), which resulted, after many military vicissitudes, in the permanent occupation by the English of all the Bombay group of islands, and of the town of Tháfa on the mainland. The city had long been a refuge for the fugitives from Maráthá oppression, who could there alone find safety for their industry and commerce; but after the downfall of the Peshwá in 1818, Bombay became the capital of a large territory, and from that year may be dated her pre-eminence in Western India. She was especially fortunate in her early governors. From 1819 to 1830, she was ruled successively by the Hon. Mountstuart Elphinstone and Sir John Malcolm. The first founded the present system of administration; the second, by opening the road through the Bhor-Ghát, broke down the natural barrier that separated the sea-coast from the table-land of the Deccan. The next stage in the course of onward prosperity was reached when Bombay was brought into direct communication with Europe through the energy and exertions of Lieutenant Waghorn, the pioneer of the Overland Route. In the early years of the present century, express couriers or adventurous travellers used sometimes to make their way to or from India across the isthmus of Suez, or occasionally even through Persia. A monthly mail service was commenced by way of Egypt in

1838, and the contract was first taken up by the Peninsular and Oriental Company in 1855. Bombay is now recognised as the one port of arrival and departure for all the English mails, and also for the troopships of the Indian army. But the city could not have attained this position, if the means of communication on the landward side had not received a corresponding development. In 1850, the first sod was turned of the Great Indian Peninsula Railway, and three years afterwards the line was opened as far as Thána, the first railway in the country. By 1863, the railway had been led up the formidable Bhor-Ghát to Poona, by a triumph of engineering skill. In 1870, through communication was established with Calcutta, in 1871 with Madras. The city has a successful tramway system. There is now a prospect of more direct railway communication being established, viâ Nágpur in the Central Provinces, with Calcutta.

"But it is not only as the capital of a Presidency, or as the central point of arrival and departure for Indian travellers, that Bombay has achieved its highest reputation. It is best known as the great cotton market of Western and Central India, to which the manufacturers of Lancashire turned when the American war cut off their supplies. Even in the last century the East India Company was accustomed to export raw cotton as part of its investment, both to the United Kingdom and to China. This trade continued during the early years of the present century, but it was marked by extreme vicissitudes in quantity and price, the demand being entirely determined by the out-turn of the American crop. The war between the Northern and Southern States was declared in 1861, and the merchants and shippers of Bombay promptly took advantage of their opportunity. The exports of cotton rapidly augmented under the stimulus of high prices, until in 1864–65, the last year of the war, they reached a total value of 30 millions sterling, or nearly ten-fold the average of ten years before. Large fortunes were acquired by successful ventures, and the wild spirit of speculation thus engendered spread through all classes of the community. The scenes of the South Sea Bubble were revived. No joint-stock project seemed too absurd to find subscribers. Banks, financial associations, and land companies, each with millions of nominal capital, were started every month, and their shares were immediately run up to fabulous premiums. The crash came in the spring of 1865, when the news was received of the termination of the American war. A panic ensued which baffles description, and the entire edifice of stock exchange speculation came toppling down like a house of cards. Merchants and private individuals were ruined by hundreds, and the quasi-official Bank of Bombay collapsed along with the rest. But despite this sudden flood of disaster, honest trade soon revived on a stable basis; and the city of Bombay at the present day, in its buildings, its docks, and its land reclamations, stands as a monument of the grand schemes of public usefulness which were started during these four years of unhealthy excitement."

The history of Bombay is sketched with varying details in P. B. M. Malabari, *Bombay in the Making*, London, 1910; W. R. S. Sharpe, *The Port of Bombay*, Bombay, n.d.; S. T. Sheppard, *Bombay*, Bombay, 1932; M. D. David, *History of Bombay, 1661–1708*, Bombay, 1973; John Burneli, *Bombay in the Days of Queen Anne*, London, 1933; B. R. Banaji, *Bombay and the Sidis*, Bombay, 1932; E. C. Cox, *A Short History of the Bombay Presidency*, Bombay, 1887; J. G. de Cunha, *The Origin of Bombay*, Bombay, 1900; James Douglas, *A Book of Bombay*, Bombay, 1893; S. M. Edwardes, *The Rise of Bombay*, Bombay, 1902; G. W. Forrest, *Cities of India*, Westminster, 1903; J. H. Gense, *How Bombay was Ceded*, Bombay, n.d.; Government of Bombay, *Bombay Gazetteer, 1893–94*, 3 parts, Bombay, 1894, *Gazetteer of*

Bombay City and Island, Bombay, Vols 1 and 2, 1909, Vol. 3, 1910, *Statistical Atlas of the Bombay Presidency*, Bombay, 2nd edn, 1906 (edited by H. S. Lawrence), and its 3rd edn, 1925 (edited and corrected by H. H. Mann); B. Arunachalam, "Bombay City: Stages of Development", *Bombay Geographical Magazine*, Vol. 3 (1935); C. B. Joshi, "The Historical Geography of the Island of Bombay", *ibid.*, volume 1956; T. K. Tope, "Transfer of Bombay from the Portuguese to the British Hands", *ibid.*, Vol. 1 (1953); John Cadell, "The Acquisition and Rise of Bombay", *Journal of the Royal Asiatic Society*, volume 1958; and F. B. Tyabji, "Social Life in 1804 and 1929 amongst [the] Muslims in Bombay", *Journal of the Bombay Branch of the Royal Asiatic Society*, Vol. 6 (1930), pp. 286–300.

88

A CONSTITUTION FOR INDIA – I

An Article

London: 12 October 1928

Dominion status for India – criticism of the Nehru Report – difficulties in the way of evolving a unitary system – status of Princely States – rights of the minorities, especially Muslims – defence of India.

Now that the [Indian Statutory] Simon Commission is entering upon the most formative stage of its inquiry by a six months' tour in India, in association with the Central and Provincial Committees, I feel I should be lacking in a patriotic duty if I did not express opinions on some current proposals and offer suggestions as to the path to be pursued to reach the declared goal of British policy towards India. Though I write primarily for my own countrymen I communicate these views, not to an Indian newspaper, with its necessarily limited appeal, but to *The Times* as by far the best medium of securing attention to them in India as well as throughout the world.

Meeting at Lucknow the Congress Parties' Conference (as it may fairly be described) adopted a scheme of Dominion Government within the Empire, claiming that the time has come for India to enter the free association of nations under the King commonly known as the self-governing portion of the British Empire. No patriotic Indian can take exception to Dominion Status as an ideal to be steadfastly pursued. It is an objective to which I whole-heartedly subscribe. Indeed I may claim some measure of paternity for the idea of making this the goal of Indian political development. Many years have passed since I discussed frequently and in detail with those great leaders of political thought, Ranade, Gokhale, and Pherozeshah Mehta, the ways of attaining this ideal. At that time very few educated Indians had any clear idea of the ultimate place of their motherland in co-operation with Britain and her daughter nations.

While, however, the ideal underlying the scheme of the Nehru Report has my hearty sympathy, I find the detailed proposals open to very serious criticism, and I am confident that adoption of the lines laid down would be disastrous to the peace and security of India. The vital defect is a most inadequate recognition of the essential difficulties in the way of establishing a unitary Government for the country through a Commonwealth of India Parliament and Executive. That such a system would aggravate, instead of solving, some of the greatest problems of Indian policy is unquestionable, and we have an indication of some consciousness of this effect in the off-hand manner in which those problems are handled when they are not almost completely ignored. This failure to face the difficulties gives rise to the question whether the proposals are serious or are merely put forward to stimulate discussion and argument.

One of the problems touched in light and airy fashion is that of the Indian States. It is inconceivable that some of the signatories of the Report could have assumed that the Princes and their people would be willing to see the adoption of the unitary form of government in Swarajist India set forth in the Report. The States would in effect lose their freedom and would become little more than districts of India. The great variations in the size and importance of the principalities make it the more difficult to imagine that they will be prepared, as the Report imagines, to join a federation in which they would be subject to the legislation of the Commonwealth Parliament. The recent statements of the Maharajas of Bikaner and Patiala have made clear the non-conforming attitude of the Princes. We have to ask in the light of these statements, not whether the Nehru Report offers a good or bad solution of the problem of the relations of the States with Swaraj India, but whether it is practicable and will be accepted in the lifetime of the present generation; at least, without actual resistance.

Another major difficulty lightly handled is that of the rights of minority communities, and especially the Muhammadans. It is difficult to conceive how serious-minded people, knowing the facts of the present situation (and leaving aside all questions of whether or not a particular change is desirable), can imagine that the Muhammadans as a body are ever likely to accept the proposals of the Report. They are not prepared to give up existing guarantees for the conservation of their existence as a political force in return for vague promises for reservation of seats for Muslim minorities in proportion to their numerical percentage in the population. Expressions of Muslim opinion which have followed the publication of the Nehru Report show that the failure to find means of meeting our susceptibilities has placed needless difficulty in the way of development towards Dominion government. Other minority communities are following the lead of the Muhammadans and are asking for guarantees. The report minimises the importance of such minorities by inadequate recognition of the fact that politically they include large sections of the Hindus themselves, such as the Depressed Classes and (in some provinces) the Non-Brahmins. By playing round this question the authors have created difficulties for their scheme.

A third great issue too vaguely handled is that of defence. The unitary Dominion Government postulated in the Report could not maintain its authority without a great army. The Central Government would need enormous forces to discharge the immense responsibilities it would undertake in repelling foreign aggression and seeing its authority accepted internally. Whether or not such a force is in potential existence – as in the case of the Dominions mainly peopled by the British races – is immaterial. The question that matters is – From whence is this new unitary Government in India to find and shape such overwhelming force? Can it be imagined that it will ever have such prestige and power as to be able to gather a great army under its authority?

If it will not have that power, do its sponsors rely on the existing British Government to leave in the country a large army – to say nothing of a *personnel* for the framework of civil administration – in order that succeeding unitary Governments responsible to Indian politicians should be able to carry out their purposes? Neither party could in honour accept such an arrangement. On the one hand, it would be ruinous to the underlying principle of self-government; on the other, the British people could never honourably agree to leave an armed force, or even civil administrators, in a country for the good government of which it was no longer responsible. If the British did this in a fit of madness, of which there has been no parallel in their history, they would go down, not only in the estimation of the whole world, but in history for all time, for supplying armed force to a country wherein their responsibility had come to an end, to be administered at the beck and call of other people.

Those who advocate advance to genuine Home Rule for India, as I do, base the claim on the assumption that British force must disappear completely, and at the latest when autonomy is established. We have the precedent of Ireland, where, on the attainment of independence early in 1922, the British garrison and the British civil officials left the country and handed over undivided charge to the Free State Government. This is the only analogy that could fitly be applied to India.

Yet, if this analogy is insisted on, as the only honourable course, the task of the proposed unitary government in India becomes from the first impossible. Guarantees offered to vested interests arising from British capital and enterprise which are still doing much for the economic advancement of India, are of secondary consequence in this connection. It is not conceivable that the British people will, in the near future contemplated in the Nehru Report, embark on so stupendous an experiment as the handing over of 320,000,000 of people to a so-called Indian Commonwealth and thereupon relinquish all responsibility for their welfare.

I hope to show in the next article that the way of approach to "the progressive realization of responsible government in British India as an integral part of the Empire" (to quote the preamble of the 1919 Act) must be on quite different lines.

Source: *The Times*, London, 12 October 1928.

It contains an authoritative criticism of the Nehru Report's recommendations regarding the Indian States, the minorities, and a national army.

89

A CONSTITUTION FOR INDIA – II

An Article

London: 13 October 1928

The most serious defect of the Constitution proposed by the Nehru Report: a unitary government without safeguards – example of the Burmese people – other minorities and "self-determination" – present distribution of provinces haphazard – suitability of a federal structure – free states on basis of religion, nationality, race, language and history – a Muslim free state in the north-west – practical safeguards for the minorities – the Princely States – question of defence – analogy with the former German Confederation.

In a previous article I dwelt on the unsatisfactory treatment in the Indian Constitution proposed in the Nehru Report of the three great problems of the independent Indian States, the protection of the Muslim and other minorities, and the provision of an adequate national Army in Swaraj India. But by far the most serious, in fact the insuperable, defect of the Constitution recommended is that it predicates a unitary All-India Government, very much on the lines of the present central authority, yet without its safeguards and guarantees, moral and material, and its scope for the development of provincial autonomy and racial developments. The draft Constitution overlooks the consideration that the *raison d'être* of the call for political freedom is that peoples should govern themselves and not have an outside authority imposed upon them – whether it be that of British electorate or that of an Executive, controlled by an Indian Parliament at Delhi or Simla, inevitably accentuating the dominance in India as a whole of a particular racial or cultural portion.

The Burmese people, by faith and race and history, are so distinct from India that they could not possibly accept the dictation of a Swaraj Parliament at Delhi. The immediate result of adoption of the Left Parties' scheme would be to unite the Burmans in insistent appeals to the English people for separation and independence – appeals that could not in fairness and equity be refused.

The difficulties which would arise in India proper would hardly be smaller. It is not conceivable that, when the strong arm of Britain had disappeared, great and compact races like the Mahrattas, the Bengalis, or the Muhammadans of the north-west and Sind would accept the control of a Central Executive and Legislature. Should such an authority at Delhi, dependent on a legislative majority of the other nationalities of the sub-continent, dictate to some other of these races, or even to lesser communities like the Sikhs, the aggrieved party would be justified, at least where it is territorially preponderant, in insisting on its freedom, according to the principle of "self-determination" which has been invoked against the continuance of British rule. The demand for "self-determination" can express itself in many forms against even a Swaraj majority among strata of peoples as varied in their outlook and standards as are the peoples of India.

While not entirely unconscious of this fundamental objection to their scheme, the framers of the Commonwealth Constitution have evaded the issue, and have not proposed even half measures to meet it. Serious thinkers about the future of my country have realized that the present distribution of provinces – thrown haphazard out of British imperialism and administrative history or convenience – cannot be reconciled with a self-governing India. During his long association with India, the late Edwin Montagu (than whom no one was more responsible for making Indian autonomy a question of practical politics) often remarked to me that units like the Bombay Presidency and the Central Provinces would be impossible anomalies under self-government. But, mindful of the difficulties Lord Curzon encountered in partitioning Bengal, he wisely refused to take up the question of provincial redistribution before the inauguration of his Reforms. Determined to make a beginning with Indian responsibility, he framed the Reforms in the hope and expectation that at later stages the approach of self-government would render the present distribution not only absurd but impossible. Mr. Lionel Curtis, the real parent of dyarchy, also saw the difficulty and made the idealistic proposal of a division of British India into a considerable number of small provinces with a few million inhabitants each. Such a grouping would cut up many real nationalities and make India administratively another, if greater, France, for the provinces would be little more than the French departments. No one with practical knowledge of the various Indian nationalities, with their passion for individual expression can believe that such a scheme would go through without strife or could succeed.

The solution I urge for the consideration of my countrymen, as well as the British people (who, inevitably, whether rightly or wrongly, must be associated with the next two or three "successive stages" of advance to self-government to which they are pledged) is frankly to face the facts and boldly to accept the consequences.

India, when freed from any outside control, cannot have a unitary, non-federal, Government. The country must accept in all its consequences its own inevitable diversities, not only religious and historical, but also national and linguistic. It must base its Constitution on an association of free states, such as the German Empire was before the crash ten years ago. Each Indian province must enjoy to the full the freedom and independence of, say, Bavaria, in the years before the Great War. The Indian Free States would resemble the self-governing British Dominions in being ultimately held together by the bond of monarchy, represented by the present British Sovereign and his heirs. As a convinced monarchist I am indifferent whether the India of that day is regarded as a kingdom or as an empire. The downfall of Russia, Austria, and Germany in our time, and of the two French Empires and the Roman Empire in former generations, may be said to give to the word "Emperor" less happy associations than the word "King". But, after all, this is only a matter of fashion. In Rome "Emperor" was a popular term and the kingdom was unpopular. In our own day, the happy consequences of kingship in Great Britain, Holland, Belgium, and the Scandinavian countries have endeared the word "King" to the people immediately concerned.

By frank acceptance of the idea of an association of free states almost all the difficulties in the way of a Swaraj India would sooner or later be overcome. Each free state would be based, not on considerations of size, but on those of religion, nationality, race, and language – plus history. Thus Burma would be one state, while Bengal, with its Muhammadan East and Hindu West, would be two. The Mahratta country would be an entity in this re-grouping. Where there exists a distinct race, such as the Gujeratis, the mere fact it occupied a relatively small area would not prevent its acquisition of the status of a free state. On the other hand, the Muhammadan provinces of the North and the West would probably coalesce and make one important free state.

The burning question of the protection of minorities would in large measure be solved. The compact bodies of Muhammadans in the North-West and the East of India proper would have free states of their own. In provinces where they are a small minority they would have some guarantee of fair play in the fact of propinquity by language and residence to their Hindu neighbours, and also by being too small numerically to bid for political control. Other minorities would have similar practical safeguards. The free states would not be mere provinces with Legislatures and Executives liable to be overruled by a Central Government in which the Hindus would have a permanent majority. They would be secure from all kinds of interference, except in matters in which they would be freely associated with other states: and if the Bavarian example were taken, these would be few and far between. The Indian principalities could come into a free association of states, because in practice their semi-autonomy would be augmented and not decreased. The larger states, such as Hyderabad, Kashmir, and Mysore, could enter into the association as distinct units, while groups of smaller principalities like those of Kathiawar, Rajputana and Central India could confederate and enter the union as free and independent members. If thought desirable the states of, say, Central India could constitute two groups of free states.

To revert to the position of Burma: she would stand to gain substantially by the new system without any corresponding loss. There would be no incentive for her to separate from Eastern Dominions with which she would have close economic ties and from which she would derive commercial advantage. I have little doubt that, if the objective I have sketched is adopted, the Gujeratis or the Marhattas, or a union of the Northern Provinces and Sind, could in the relatively near future establish, within their own well-defined areas, free state administrations with good hope of success.

The popular authority would be based on national facts and have that immense asset – the nearness of the governing body in sentiment and ideas to the people. The difficulty of providing adequate defence would be overcome by stages. Initially, all that would be required would be the removal of British troops and officials from the one or two well-defined areas where the new system was taking effect. Rightly conservative and cautious, the British would be willing to start the experiment of transfer of full responsibility over one or two areas, with a view to successive extensions of the system, as it succeeded, to other units.

The success or failure of this approach to self-government would depend on the position of each unit being akin to that of Bavaria in the former German Confederation, rather than that of an American state or a Swiss canton. Anyone with a knowledge of political history must be aware of the immense difference here implied and its consequences, and must realize that it will immediately go a long way to appeal not only to the Ruling Princes, but to the various races and religions, as well as to Burma. By freeing the Muslim majorities in the North-West and East from ultimate Hindu control it will give them something worth having. Glaring injustice to any community is improbable, because nowhere in the free states of India will one nationality, race, religion or historical unit be at the mercy of a semi-foreign majority dictating its orders from a distance.

Source: *The Times*, London, 13 October 1928.

In this second and concluding part of the article, the Aga Khan takes issue with the Nehru Report's goal of a unitary India.

On the Nehru Report and its implications for Indian politics see All Parties Conference, *Report of the Committee Appointed by the Conference to Determine the Principles of the Constitution for India, together with a Summary of the Proceedings of the Conference Held at Lucknow,* All India Congress Committee, Allahabad, 1928; All Parties Conference, *Supplementary Report of the Committee,* All India Congress Committee, Allahabad, n.d.; Mirza Bashiruddin Mahmud Ahmad, *The Nehru Report and Muslim Rights,* Qadian, 1930; Haji Abdullah Haroon, *The Constitution of the Future Commonwealth of India and the Rights of the Muslim Minority: A Representation Submitted to the Members of the Nehru Committee (Allahabad) and to the All Parties Convention (Calcutta),* Karachi, 1928; William Isaac Hull, *India's Political Crisis,* Baltimore, 1930; Dhirendranath Sen, *Whither India: A Critical Study of the Nehru Report and the Exposition of the Principles of India's Future Government,* Calcutta, n.d.; *The Indian National Demand: Being a Summary of the Nehru Report and the Proceedings of the National Convention Held in Calcutta, 1928,* published by Rafi Ahmad Kidwai, Secretary, All Parties Conference, and Convention, Allahabad, 1928 (contains the final texts of the report); Punjab Information Bureau, *Selections From the Punjab Press on Simon Commission and Nehru Report,* Lahore, 1928; Talammuz Husain, *The Case of the Muslim,* Gorakhpur, 1928; G. W. Chaudhri, "The Nehru Report", in Pakistan Historical Society, *A History of the Freedom Movement (Being the Story of Muslim Struggle for the Freedom of Hind-Pakistan) 1707–1947, Volume 3, 1906–1936, Part 1, 1906–1928,* Karachi, 1961; and I. H. Qureshi, *The Struggle for Pakistan,* Karachi, 1965.

The background to the Nehru Committee and its report is as follows. In a speech in the House of Lords, asking the House to agree to the submission to the King of the names of the proposed members of the Indian Statutory (Simon) Commission, Lord Birkenhead, the Secretary of State for India, explained why no Indians had been appointed to the commission and entered into some details of the divisions of opinion and of interest in India, referring with some emphasis to the Hindu–Muslim schism. The Congress leaders in

India took deep umbrage at these words and took them as a challenge to India to produce a constitution. An All Parties Conference, which had lately been formed to bring all boycotters of the Simon Commission together, undertook to prepare a constitution to confound British official pessimism. After long discussions, the conference appointed a sub-committee to draw up a constitution. The drafting committee consisted of Pandit Motilal Nehru, Sayyid Ali Imam, Tej Bahadur Sapru, Sardar Mangal Singh, S. C. Bose, E. R. Pradhan and Shoib Qureshi. Motilal Nehru was the chairman, hence the report's popular name. The Sikh member was driven out of the Secretaryship of the Sikh League within a week of the publication of the report. The Christians, too, repudiated the principles adopted by the report in reference to the protection of the minorities. Muslim reaction to the report was a swift, uncompromising and unqualified rejection.

IN DEFENCE OF FREE STATES IN INDIA

Letter to The Times

Newmarket: 17 October 1928

Response to Sir Valentine Chirol's comments on his articles in *The Times* – Bavaria as an analogy – the future Muslim Free States and the Indian principalities would want to control their armed forces.

The objection raised by Sir Valentine Chirol to my scheme for a federation of Free States in India that there would be no strong central Government overlooks the consideration mentioned in your own comments that full details could not be given within the limits of a newspaper article. I made it clear that I selected as a constitutional model, not the pre-War German Empire, but the white Dominions of the British Crown. The analogy I drew with Bavaria (not, it should be noted, with other States of the German Union) was based in part on the consideration that under the thorough rearrangement of provinces I advocated there could be no parallel in India to the conditions which secured Prussian dominance in the German Empire. I chose Bavaria, rather than the United States of America, as an illustration because that kingdom had control of its own army in time of peace as well as of its own railways. In this connexion I had the present independent States of India and the coming Moslem Free States specially in mind. I cannot conceive that the great Indian principalities or Moslem States of the North-West and East would come into the proposed Federation on any other terms than they should control their armed forces in time of peace, as the Indian States do to-day, instead of handing them over to a distant authority.

In referring to the views of Mr. Lionel Curtis I had in mind not the joint address presented by a number of European and

Indian co-signatories in November, 1917, but some of the earlier writings of Mr. Curtis. I am glad to see that his position is nearer mine than I thought.

Source: *The Times*, London, 19 October 1928.

Sir Valentine Chirol, to whom the Aga Khan replies, had published his letter of 13 October in *The Times* of 15 October, which reads as follows:

"Sir, – The Aga Khan is singularly unfortunate in his selection of the pre-War German Empire as a constitutional model for the Federated India he contemplates, because India, he writes, 'when freed from any outside control cannot have a unitary non-federal Government.' When a Constitution was framed for the new German Empire Bismarck took care that it should be so framed as to secure for Prussia a political preponderance which no combination of the minor federated States could shake, and even to-day, after the knock-out blow dealt to Prussian militarism by the Great War, Prussia remains, in virtue of her much greater population, let alone the peculiar qualities of the Prussian people, the dominant State in the Reich. Where is a Prussia to be found in India?

"Moreover, it is generally admitted that communal differences and Hindu-Mahomedan rivalry have never been more bitter than to-day and are kept under restraint only by the existence of a strong unitary central Government. Indian political unity has been one of the greatest achievements of the British Raj, to whose educational work, by the way, the very conception of Indian Nationalism owes its birth. The lines upon which the Aga Khan would split up India into a large number of small federated States without any strong central Government to weld them together are enough to show into what a welter of confusion and strife his Highness's Federated India would quickly and inevitably be plunged."

91

LIONEL CURTIS AND INDIAN PROVINCES

Letter to The Times

London(?): 25 October 1928

Lionel Curtis's *Dyarchy* – redistribution of provinces – what the Joint Address proposed.

I have been away in Ireland and do not carry with me a copy of Mr. Lionel Curtis's "Dyarchy," published eight years ago, and hence the delay in replying to his letter published on October 20.

The course of his studies of Indian reform from the beginning of 1916 to September, 1920, the period covered by this work of 660 pages, is of interest no doubt to students of Indian constitutional history; but it cannot be expected that your correspondence columns should bear the weight of the criticism of this volume to which I am invited. Both in my article and my last letter I gave no more than illustrative reflection of the public opinion of the time in India that Mr. Curtis favoured the creation of "a considerable number of small provinces."

The Joint Address from which he quoted in his first letter proposed by way of example, that the United Provinces should be divided into four provincial states, with primitive communities, like those of the hill districts of Kumaon and Bundelkhand and of Mirzapur, reserved to the present Government of the United Provinces. Under such a scheme, apart from any federal authority, there would be five Governments in the United Provinces, which excepting Oudh, may be considered a typical Indian ethic [*sic*, ethnic], linguistic, and historical unit. Mr. Curtis, I hope, may be satisfied with the welcome I gave to his support of the principle of provincial redistribution on an ethnic and

825

linguistic basis, instead of asking for research of his voluminous writings on a point raised quite incidentally in my article.

Source: *The Times*, London, 29 October 1928.

The place from where the letter was written is not mentioned by the Aga Khan.

The letter from Lionel Curtis was written from All Souls College, Oxford, on 19 October, and published in *The Times* of 20 October. It ran as follows:

"Sir, – In your issue of October 13 your readers were told on the high authority of the Aga Khan that I had advised the redistribution of British India, regardless of national divisions, into areas comparable in status, though not in size, to French departments. On the 17th you allowed me to refer by page to published documents in which I had made proposals that have nothing in common with such ideas. His Highness now informs your readers that he had in mind some of my earlier writings. I respectfully invite him to give the references for their information."

92

THE INDIAN ECONOMIC PROSPECTS

Interview with The Times of India

Bombay: 28 December 1928

The political situation in India – the pressing economic problem
– depression in agriculture – improvements in agriculture through
scientific methods – Hindu-Muslim co-operation for India's welfare.

... the Aga Khan ... said that his views on the political situation
in India were frequently expressed and were known to all. He
would have another opportunity of restating them at the ensuing
Moslem Conference at Delhi. It was, therefore, unnecessary for
him to go into the question of the political situation which it was
their duty to handle in a statesmanlike manner with due regard
to realities. The Indian leaders should address themselves to
finding out what ails India and to remedy it. To his mind the
economic problem was one of the most pressing problems awaiting solution. On it depended the peace and progress of the
country.

After a careful study of the recent industrial activities he had
been forced to recognise that there was a great scope for improvement in the economic condition by means of improvements in
the sphere of agriculture, which was of the greatest importance
to the economic well-being of the country. No doubt India would
one day become a living industrial force, but at present the
economic depression in agriculture which was the main industry
of 80 per cent of the people, eclipsed commerce and other
industries. Indians must study scientific methods in agriculture,
give attention to the improvement in the breed of cattle and they
would not be satisfied until they were able to get a larger yield
from the soil at less cost and obtain better prices for the produce.
Prosperity in agriculture would relieve the pressure on Govern-

ment appointments and clerical and other services and this would help to solve the economic trouble which was the cause of much unrest in the country.

In Germany and Belgium, where conditions were less favourable than in India, the scientific treatment of agriculture had produced very satisfactory results and His Highness hoped the recommendations of the Agricultural Commission would give an impetus to the use of scientific methods in agriculture and the improvement of livestock. There should be greater concentration on agriculture and the Aga Khan declared that Lord Irwin during his Viceroyalty would be definitely enabled to make agriculture an attractive and profitable pursuit. . . .

Source: *The Times of India*, Bombay, 29 December 1928.

The Aga Khan arrived in Bombay on the morning of 28 December by the P. and D. mail boat *Rajputana*. He was received by the Council of the Jama'at of the Ismailis and a deputation of the All India Muslim Conference led by Fazal Ibrahim Rahimtulla. From the port he drove first to the *Jama'atkhana* and then to his residence at Walkeshwar. He left on the following day for Delhi in order to preside over the first session of the newly-formed All India Muslim Conference.

93

NATIONHOOD FOR THE INDIAN MUSLIMS

Presidential Address to the All-India Muslim Conference

Delhi: 31 December 1928

Concern about the King-Emperor's health – the future of Muslims in India – importance of general consensus of views and opinions of the people – examples from Europe – Muslim leaders and aspirations of Muslim masses – necessity of good relations with Hindus – protection of Muslim cultural entity – dependence on the British for defence of India – desires of the Indian Muslims – Muslim leaders and the general interests – Muslim education – language of instruction – Muslims of India are a nation – Muslim representation – relations between Hindus and Muslims – public slaughter of cows.

Gentlemen,

I thank you for the great honour you have done me in asking me to preside over your deliberations. Before proceeding with business, I am sure the Muslim community will join me unanimously in wishing His Majesty the King-Emperor complete restoration to health and strength. The deep anxiety which the world has shown for His Majesty's health, which had been undermined by overwork in the zealous discharge of his multifarious and onerous duties, shows that they all appreciate his solicitude for the welfare of humanity at large. It has been an anxious time not only for His Majesty's subjects but for the whole world who have watched with keen anxiety one who had been regarded as a great pillar on which depends the progress of the world. Happily our anxiety is nearly, if not wholly, over. The illness drew sympathy for the Queen Empress, the Prince of Wales and the Royal family, and it must have been some comfort to them that their trouble was shared not only by every individual in the

Empire but by the people of other countries. May His Majesty live long to continue to shower the blessings of his beneficent rule on his subjects.

Now, I will at once come to the immediate business before us which is to consider the future of our co-religionists and their interests in the body-politic of India. The views and opinions I express are based on long experience of public affairs as well as the study of the past and present history of other nations. The lessons of the Great War have further strengthened these convictions and the conclusions which I have arrived at after mature consideration.

The great lesson of modern history, to my mind, is that only those nations succeed and only those policies lead to national greatness, which are based not on ideas or ideals of a few leaders, however eminent, or of a few thinkers, but on the general consensus of views and opinions of the people. I will give one or two examples in support of this argument. The policy of Imperial Germany was shaped by the leaders of that nation as a class. The pre-war policy of Russia was not that of the Russian people, but inspired by the Panslavists, Kat Kof and his disciples. The policies of England and France were, indeed, based on the desires of the English and French people. Similar examples are to be found on every page of recent history. When in my manifesto last year, I appealed to the Muslims of India to replace the old self-constituted political bodies that had served their day and purpose by an organisation of all Muslim members in touch with their electorates, I wished to place the guidance of our people in their own hands. The time has come when the leaders should keep their ears to the ground and ascertain the views and wishes of the masses. Gentlemen, make no mistake. The changes that must come over India profoundly affecting our future, will not come in a day. They will not come as in Russia like a thief in the night. Had the result of this War been different, we might have suddenly found ourselves in that position, but the attitude of the overwhelming mass of the Indian public during the War showed to the world that they were not in favour of such a hurried solution. Whatever our wishes may be, this Conference is but the first of many more that will have to evolve a truly representative body to look after and further the desires of Muslims of India. The greatest service you can render to your people would be to organise all the Muslim members of each and every Council into a body where exchange of views and ideas and communication of the same to the electors as well as the reception of the general desires of the masses, would remain the main purpose and object. In politically successful countries, from the Premier or the President to the humblest voter, it is but one succession of nerve lines of communication. If we had such a body, I for one should sleep in peace; for I would know that many political theories would most certainly be made by them and not by anybody else for them. From now onwards we must ever remember, even in this Conference, not what are our own individual political preferences but what are the aspirations of the Muslim masses in this country.

Then there are certain obvious truisms which are necessary forms of thoughts for political activity just as certain mental truisms are the basis of natural science and intellectual life. In this connection, I may give you several examples of those obvious facts that may be forgotten at times. Here is one. It is impossible for Muslims to live happily and peacefully in India if friction and suspicion are to prevail between them and the Hindus. Another vivid instance. India as a whole cannot be a prosperous or self-governing country if such a large and important section of the community as the Muslims remain [sic] in doubt as to whether their cultural entity is safe or not. Here is a third and most important one. As long as we are dependent for protection against external aggression and internal security and for peace upon Great Britain and the British garrison occupies the land and the air and naval forces survey us from above and watch the coasts, Great Britain will naturally claim a dominant share and voice in the governance of India. It is essential that these and similar other truisms should not be lost sight of. The Muslim masses are, I am sure, sufficient realists to know and appreciate them. Gentlemen, you come from them; you are in touch with them; you know their views.

Another point to be kept before us is that our desires must not be mere ideas and ideals. You are part of them. It is your duty to interpret as far as you can their wishes, their aspirations and their ideals, till such time as our political organisation is sufficiently advanced to let the people carry out their own wishes. Another point to be kept in view is that our wishes or ideals are not necessarily realities.

You must avoid forcing your own preferences when they clash with what we believe to be the real wishes of the mass of the people. The policy to be pursued during the immediate years, I would once more emphasize, must not be based on our personal views and predilections, but on what you know to be the general desires of the people to whom you belong. What are the desires of the Indian Muslims? I can safely say that the overwhelming majority of Muslims are determined to maintain their cultural unity (hear, hear) and remain culturally interrelated with the Muslims of the world. How that can best be accomplished, it is for you to think out.

But that does not mean that the general welfare of the whole commonwealth is to be ignored by us. It does not mean that the Muslim representatives' activities are to be confined to their own sectional interests. That would be wrong. The Muslim members should consider it their duty to look after the interests of India as a whole or of a Province as a whole and advocate the promotion of general interests at every opportunity. I will illustrate what I mean by giving a concrete example. Now, take the question of education, primary, secondary and higher. For more than a generation, I have urged that a national educational policy for India is impossible unless financed by large educational grants raised by the State as loans and not from current revenue. Such loans should be as much a legitimate object as any public work as they will, through improvement in intelligence, add to the economic welfare of the country. In regard to Muslim education, especially, one striking fact is that there exists a sort of gauge between primary and secondary education in the universities and technological and other institutions. It is incumbent on us all to find a solution of this most important Muslim problem. Our secondary educational institutions specially need further support from the State.

Another great difficulty which has been ineffectually tackled in the past is the question of language as medium for instruction. We must bear in mind that the acquisition of knowledge is quite a different thing from the medium of acquiring it. Our linguistic traditions are mainly based on Persian and Urdu. Urdu is one of the most important and widespread languages in the world. It serves as a medium of communication between Muslims of different parts of India as well as between Muslims and other communities of a district. The foundation of the Oosmania University, which owes its existence to the magnificent generosity of His Exalted Highness the Nizam of Hyderabad, is bound to give a great impetus to the educational activities of our people. It is adapted to higher culture. But both Urdu and Persian scripts present serious difficulties in the primary stages of education, and it is a matter for deliberation how we can improve and simplify the change of script.

Now, whether in education or politics, I would beg of you to consider the realities and not to throw away the substance for the shadow. Whether in education or in politics, build on a solid foundation. Do not be carried away by catchwords; nor hanker after ideals that may not be within your grasp but concentrate your minds on what is practicable and useful under pressing economic and political needs of the country and strive after actualities to promote the higher happiness of mankind.

In recent times, no question seems to have aroused so much controversy as the question of separate electorates for the protection of the right[s] of minorities.

The merits and demerits of separate or so-called communal electorates have been discussed so often that it is unnecessary to re-examine them in detail. In regard to the implications of the term "communal", I may remark in passing that the Muslims of India are not a community, but in a restricted, special sense a nation composed of many communities and population totally out-numbering the total even of the pre-war German Empire [*sic*].

The vital and dominant consideration which underlies [*sic*] is the real representation of Muslims in all legislatures and self-governing bodies. How that can be secured is a problem for the Muslim population of this country to consider and solve without any prejudices.

Gentlemen, I have specially at your request come to this Conference and felt it more than ever my duty to draw attention to the urgent problems that can be dealt with rather than to discuss doubtful questions of an uncertain future. If through your elected representatives you can further the practical solution of these problems, a great step forward will have been taken.

I cannot allow my speech to close without making a passing reference to a subject of constant friction between the two sister communities and making a fervent appeal, with all the earnestness that I command, to remove that friction as far as possible so that Muslims may live in amity with their Hindu brethren. While referring to the cause of friction, I take this opportunity of expressing profound admiration and gratitude of Indians to His Excellency the Viceroy for his earnest endeavour to bring about harmonious relations between the Hindus and Mahomedans.

Cow-killing has unfortunately been a perpetual source of bitter feelings between Muslims and Hindus. It is incumbent on us all to find a remedy. It may help us to do this, if we trace the origin of sacrificial rites. We are all agreed that we celebrate the historical sacrifice by Ibrahim. But it must be remembered that Ibrahim, one of our great Prophets, did not sacrifice a cow, nor is the sacrifice of a bovine especially enjoined anywhere. One [sic] the contrary, the camel or the sheep is more frequently mentioned in connection with sacrificial rites. How many of our Hajis have sacrificed cows in Arabia, the home of Islam?

The Emperor Baber, who was as Mr. Edwards has pointed out, the greatest monarch of his age, enjoined his son Humayun to respect the religious sentiments and even the prejudices of the Hindus and he specially mentioned the cow as an animal venerated in India. The late Ameer Habibullah Khan, who was a good Muslim, discountenanced the practice. If other Muslim leaders share their views, they will certainly not be acting against any Islamic injunction.

You no doubt know our religious dictum that "the flesh and blood of animals do not reach God". This is a humanitarian view entirely in accord with our conception of the Deity and His creation.

I am open to be enlightened on this point by our Ulama, but am certain that not one of them will countenance the parade of sacrificial rites in public places. There are many other communities who eat beef, but they do not hurt the susceptibilities of their neighbours by parading the sacred and adored animals for slaughter.

In the light of these facts, which I have mentioned, it is a matter for your serious consideration whether we should re-examine our views on this particular sacrifice and test its true significance. If by doing so, we can readjust our relations with our Hindu friends, we shall indirectly render a service of incalculable value and importance to the cause of peace and prosperity and even perhaps satisfactory political readjustment.

Source: *Report of the All India Muslim Conference Held at Delhi on 31 December, 1928, and 1st January, 1929,* compiled and published by authority by Hafizur Rahman, Aligarh, n.d., pp. 20–3. An account of the Conference was also published in *The Times of India,* Bombay, 1st January, 1929.

On the All India Muslim Conference see John Coatman, *Years of Destiny: India 1926–1932,* London, 1932; Khaliquzzaman, *Pathway to Pakistan,* Lahore, 1961; Mian Muhammad Shafi, *Some Important Indian Problems,* Lahore, 1930; "Shamloo" (comp.), *Speeches and Statements of Iqbal,* Lahore, 1945; Abdul Hamid, *Muslim Separatism in India: A Brief Survey 1858–1947,* Lahore, 1967; Waheeduzzaman, *Towards Pakistan,* Lahore, 2nd ed, 1969; and K. K. Aziz (ed.), *The All India Muslim Conference, 1928–1935: A Documentary Record,* Karachi, 1972.

The first resolution which the conference passed between 31 December 1928 and 1 January 1929 became the bill of rights of the Muslims of India. Throughout the three sessions of the Round Table Conference and the Joint Committee on Indian Constitutional Reform the Aga Khan was stressing the importance of the demands made in it and fighting for them. The resolution ran as follows:

"1. Whereas, in view of India's vast extent and its ethnological, linguistic, administrative and geographical or territorial divisions, the only form of government suitable to Indian conditions is a federal system with complete autonomy and residuary powers vested in the constituent states, the Central Government having control only of such matters of common interest as may be specifically entrusted to it by the constitution;

And whereas it is essential that no bill, resolution, motion or amendment, regarding inter-communal matters be moved, discussed or passed by any legislature, central or provincial, if a three-fourths majority of the members of either the Hindu or the Muslim community affected thereby in that legislature oppose the introduction, discussion or passing of such bill, resolution, motion or amendment;

And whereas the right of Muslims to elect their representatives on the various Indian legislatures through separate electorates is now the law of the land and Muslims cannot be deprived of that right without their consent;

And whereas in the conditions existing at present in India and so long as those conditions continue to exist, representation in various legislatures and other statutory self-governing bodies of Muslims through their own separate electorates is essential in order to bring into existence a really representative democratic government;

And whereas as long as Musalmans are not satisfied that their rights and interests are adequately safeguarded in the constitution, they will in no way consent to the establishment of joint electorates, whether with or without conditions;

And whereas, for the purposes aforesaid, it is essential that Musalmans should have their due share in the central and provincial cabinets;

And whereas it is essential that representation of Musalmans in the various legislatures and other statutory self-governing bodies should be based on a plan whereby the Muslim majority in those provinces where Musalmans constitute a majority of population shall in no way be affected and in the provinces in which Musalmans constitute a minority they shall have a representation in no case less than that enjoyed by them under the existing law;

And whereas representative Muslim gatherings in all provinces in India have unanimously resolved that with a view to provide [*sic*] adequate safeguards for the protection of Muslim interests in India as a whole, Musalmans should have the right of $33^1/_3$ per cent representation in the Central Legislature and this Conference entirely endorses that demand;

And whereas on ethnological, linguistic, geographical and administrative grounds the province of Sind has no affinity whatever with the rest of the Bombay Presidency and its unconditional constitution into a separate province, possessing its own separate legislative and administrative machinery on the same lines as in other provinces of India, is essential in the interests of its people, the Hindu minority in Sind being given adequate and effective representation in excess of their proportion, as may be given to Musalmans in the provinces in which they constitute a minority of population;

And whereas the introduction of constitutional reforms in the North-West Frontier Province and Baluchistan along such lines as may be adopted in other provinces of India is essential not only in the interests of those provinces but also of the constitutional advance of India as a whole, the Hindu minorities in those provinces being given adequate and effective representation in excess of their proportion in population as is given to the Muslim community in provinces in which it constitutes a minority of the population;

And whereas it is essential in the interests of Indian administration that provision should be made in the constitution giving Muslims their adequate share along with other Indians in all services of the State and on all statutory self-governing bodies, having due regard to the requirements of efficiency;

And whereas, having regard to the political conditions obtaining in India, it is essential that the Indian constitution should embody adequate safeguards for protection and promotion of Muslim education, languages, religion, personal law and Muslim charitable institutions, and for their due share in grants-in-aid;

And whereas it is essential that the constitution should provide that no charge in the Indian constitution shall, after its inauguration, be made by the Central Legislature except with the concurrence of all the states constituting the Indian federation;

This Conference emphatically declares that no constitution, by whomsoever proposed or devised, will be acceptable to Indian Musalmans unless it conforms with the principles embodied in this resolution."

"2. The All India Muslim Conference invites the attention of the Musalmans of India that it is high time the different schools of thought amongst them should put forth their joint efforts and undertake all or any of the following items for the well-being of the community:

(1) Promotion of primary education among Muslim boys and girls.
(2) Provision of qualified teachers.
(3) Introduction of up-to-date curriculum in national institutions.
(4) Establishment of night schools for the secular and religious education and instruction of Muslim adults.
(5) Revival of Islamic spirit by utilizing mosques as centres for social, moral and economic activities.
(6) Adoption of means whereby Muslims may be saved from following un-Islamic customs and habits.
(7) Encouragement of trade, arts and industries to combat unemployment.
(8) Establishing or encouraging Muslim newspapers for creating public opinion in favour of the scheme."

> *The Main Resolution of the All India Muslim Conference*, published by Muhammad Shafee Daoodi, Patna (Bihar and Orissa), Working Secretary, All India Muslim Conference, n.d. (? 1930) (printed at the Army Press, Simla), pp. 3–6.

The background of the making of this resolution was that:

On 1 January 1929, at 10 a.m. an informal conference of leaders met near the Conference *pandal* (stage) in a separate *shamiana* (tent) to discuss the whole situation facing the Conference. Maulana Muhammad Ali and Maulana

Shaukat Ali, who had arrived from Calcutta, were present. Among the principal speakers were Sir Muhammad Shafi, Maulana Muhammad Ali, and Maulana Mufti Kifayatullah. After a long discussion, the general principles on which the resolutions were to be drafted were agreed upon.

At 11 a.m. the Subjects Committee met in the Conference *pandal* with the Aga Khan in the Chair. The proceedings of this meeting were not published, but it was greatly understood that the main difference of opinion centred round the question whether separate electorates were to be demanded unconditionally or joint electorates were to be accepted if certain conditions, like those embodied in the Delhi Proposals of March 1927 were fulfilled. Sir Muhammad Shafi defended the former position; Maulana Muhammad Ali and Maulana Muhammad Shafee Daoodi supported the latter suggestion.

At the opening of the regular session, Sir Muhammad Shafi moved the first resolution (No. 1 in the text). Maulana Muhammad Ali seconded it. Speeches in its support were delivered by Sir Abdul Karim Ghuznavi, Maulana Muhammed Shafee Daoodi, Dr. Sir Muhammad Iqbal, Sharfuddin, Hafiz Hidayat Husain, Maulvi Muhammad Yakub, Dr. Shafa'at Ahmad Khan, Abdul Aziz, Daoodbhoy Salehbhoy Tayebji, Seth Haji Abdullah Haroon, Maulana Abdul Majid Badayuni, Maulana Mufti Kifayatullah, Naweb Mehdi Husain, Maulana Azad Sobhani, Shaikh Muhammad Sadiq, and Maulana Muhammad Ali, in this order. It was put to the house and unanimously carried.

Maulana Shaukat Ali announced at this stage that as the President (the Aga Khan) wanted to leave, he (the Maulana) desired to move a resolution of thanks to him and other functionaries of the Conference. The resolution was moved, seconded by Zahur Ahmad and passed without dissent.

The Aga Khan briefly spoke in reply to the vote of thanks, and then proposed that Sir Ibrahim Rahimtoola should occupy the Chair. Sir Muhammad Shafi seconded it.

The proceedings continued under the presidentship of Sir Ibrahim Rahimtoola. Maulana Shaukat Ali moved the second resolution (No. 2 in the text), and Syed Habib seconded it. The supporting speakers included Mir Muhammad Baloch, Maulvi Anees Ahmad, Maulvi Mazharuddin, Mufti Muhammad Sadiq, Sahibzada Muhammad Rashiduddin, Gulsher Khan, and Muhammad Sadiq. It was unanimously passed.

Another resolution (the text of which is not available) condoled the death of the Rt. Hon. Sayyid Ameer Ali and that of Hakim Ajmal Khan. It was moved from the Chair.

Among the parties and groups officially represented at the Conference were: All India Muslim League (Lahore Section), Central Khilafat Committee, Jamiat-ul-Ulama-i-Hind, Central Muslim Legislative Assembly Party, Ahmadiyya Community, Jamiat-ul-Quraish, Bazm-i-Sufia, Zia-ul-Islam (Bombay), All India Muslim Federation, All India Shia Conference, Young Men's Muslim Association, Roohaniat Movement, Bombay Khilafat Committee, and Sind Khilafat Committee.

The conference of December 1928 to January 1929 was by far the most representative gathering of the Muslims of India that ever met. The following delegates were present:

Khilafatists

Khwaja Abu Ahmed Iqbal Saheb Ansari, Khwaja Muhammad Ayyub Saheb Ansari, Abdul Wahab Usmani, Gulsher Khan, Maulana Muhammad Ali,

Maulana Shaukat Ali, Maulana Muhammad Irfan, Hafiz Muhammad Usman, Haji Muhammad Moosa Khan Sherwani.

Members of the Jamiat-ul-Ulama
Maulana Mufti Kifayatullah, Maulana Abul Mohasin Muhammad Sajjad (Behar), Maulana Abdul Haleem Siddiqi, Maulana Ahmed Saeed, Maulana Umar Daraz Baig, Maulana Husain Ahmed Madani.

Delhi
Shams-ul-Ulama Maulana Syed Ahmad (Imam, Jame Masjid), Maulana Muhammad Siddiq, Muhammad Aminuddin, Muhammad Rashiduddin, Nawab Abul Hason, Nawab Shaikh Fariduddin, Maulvi Mazharuddin, Khwaja Ghulam-us-Sibtain, Khan Saheb Master Fazluddin, Mirza Ejaz Husain.

The United Provinces
Khan Bahadur Syed Jafar Husain, M.L.C.; Khan Bahadur Maulvi Fasi-huddin, M.L.C.; Khan Bahadur Hafiz Hidayat Husain, M.L.C.; Dr. Shafaat Ahmed Khan, M.L.C.; Khan Bahadur Masud-ul-Hasan, M.L.C.; Khan Bahadur M. Ziaul Haq, M.L.C.; Matinuddin, M.L.C.; Syed Habibullah, M.L.C.; Abdul Bari, M.L.C; Shaikh Abdullah, M.L.C.; Raja Syed Ahmed Ali Khan Alavi, Raja of Salempur, M.L.C.; Mushir Hosain Kidwai; Zahoor Ahmad, M.L.C.; Haji Abdul Qayyum, M.L.C.; Khan Bahadur Shaikh Syed Muhammad, M.L.C.; Nawab Jamshed Ali Khan of Bhagpat, M.L.C.; Nawabzada Abdus Sami Khan, M.L.C.; Honourable Nawab Muhammad Yusuf, M.L.C.; Shaikh Khaliluddin, M.L.C.; Dr. Ziauddin Ahmad; Muhammad Yamin Khan, M.L.A., Nawab Muhammad Ismail Khan, M.L.A.; Dr. L. K. Hyder, M.L.A.; Maulana Abdul Majid Badayuni; Hakim Moazzam Ali Khan; Khan Bahadur Nawab Shaikh Wahiduddin; Muhammad Bashir; Muhammad Amin; Maulana Hasrat Mohani; Begum Hasrat Mohani; Rao Abdul Hameed Khan; Kanwar Haji Ismail Ali Khan; Nawab Muhammad Mehdi Hasan Rizvi; Maulvi Muhammad Yaqub (Deputy President, Central Assembly); Dulay Bhai; Maulvi Obaidur Rahman Khan Sherwani, M.L.C.; Maulana Azad Sobhani; Kazi Masood Hasan; Khan Bahadur Nawab Muhammad Ibrahim Khan; Ahsan Ali Khan; Mahmmod Ahmad Abbasi; Sahibzada Shaikh Rashiduddin; Hasan Mohayyuddin Abbasi; Kazi Maqbool Husain; Hafizur Rahman; Muhammad Aminullah; Maulvi Haji Muhammad Muqtada Khan Sherwani; Abdul Basit Khan; Shaikh Abdul Hamid; Muhammad Faruq; Abdus Samad Muqtadari; Chaudhri Muhammad Swaleh; Haji Muhammad Swaleh Khan Sherwani; Syed Zakir Ali; Muhammad Mahmud Ahmad; Kazi Ghiasuddin; Syed Mujtaba Ali; Muhammad Hafizur Rahman; Ali Maqsood; Abdul Kadir; Shaikh Zuber Hasan.

The Punjab
Muhammad Hasan Qureshi, M.L.C.; Shaikh Muhammad Sadiq, M.L.C.; Maulvi Mahboob Alam; Shaikh Niaz Muhammad; Shaikh Muhammad Bukhsh; Maulana Ghulam Mohayyuddin; Syed Mohsin Shah; Maulana Syed Habib; Qazi Nazir Ahmed; Khan Saheb Khwaja Gul Muhammad Khan; Khan Bahadur Nawab Muhammad Ibrahim Ali Khan; Nawabzada Muhammad Ihsan Ali Khan of Maler Kotla; Dr. Khalifa Shujauddin; Mian Sir Muhammad Shafi; Honourable Malik Firoz Khan Noon; Dr. Sir Muhammad Iqbal; Ghulam Rasul Meher; Abdul Majid Salik; Mian Muhammad Shah Nawaz, M.L.A.; Mian Muhammad Rafi; Sir Rahim Bukhsh, M.L.C.; Nawab Sir

Zulfiqar Ali Khan, M.L.C.; Nawab Ahmed Jan Khan Daultana, M.L.C.; Zahur Ahmed Bugvi; Rashid Ahmed; Manzoor Ali Bin Taib; Afzal Ali Hasan; Shaikh Muhammad Sadiq.

Bombay
Sir Ibrahim Rahmatullah, Maulvi Abdur Rauf, Fateh Muhammad Munshi, I. S. Haji, Ali Muhammad Chunera, Haji Ahmed Muhammad Bhindiwalla, Maulvi Anis Ahmed, Maulana Nazir Ahmed, Muhammad Zakria Maniar, Muhammad Ali Maniar, Sabze Ali, Abbas Bhai Abdul Ali, Musaji Imamji, Varas Daya Bhai Velji, Khan Saheb Mansuri, Daood Khan Saleh Bhai Tayebji, M.L.C.; Hosain Ali M. Rahmatullah, Haji Ahmed Saheb, Hashem Moldina Saheb, Abdur Rauf Khan, Mir Muhammad Baloch.

Sind
Seth Haji Abdullah Haroon, Shaikh Abdul Majid, Abdul Hameed Khudadad Khan, Nawab Khaliqdad Khan, Alijah Mukhi Husain Mukhi Allahrakhi.

Central Provinces
Sharfuddin, Khan Bahadur Mirza Rahman Beg, M.L.C.; Kazi Hifazat Ali M.L.C.; Siraj Ahmed.

Madras
Hamid Hasan Schamnad, Khan Bahadur Haji Abdullah Haji Kasim, M.L.A.

North-West Frontier Province
Abdul Aziz, Azizullah Khan of Toru, Fateh Muhammad Khan Khattak, Nawab Khaliqdad Khan Bhaya, Abdul Hameed Khan.

Assam
Abdul Hameed (President, Assam Legislative Council).

Bihar and Orissa
Maulana Muhammad Shafi Daudi, M.L.A.; M. Shah Masood Ahmed; Maulvi Manzoor Ahsan Ejazi; Hakim Khalil Ahmed; Sir Sultan Ahmed; Khan Bahadur Khwaja Muhammad Nur (President, Legislative Council, Behar and Orissa); M. Ismail Muhammad Khan; Maulvi Muhammad Ishaq; Sirajuddin; Muhammad Siddiq; Muhammad Illahi Bukhsh; Maulana Mehdi Saheb.

Bengal
Sir A. K. Ghuznavi, Bedar Bakht, Honourable Mahmood Suhrawardy (Member, Council of State), Abul Kasim.

Qadianees
Mufti Muhammad Sadiq, Chaudhry Zafarullah Khan, Hakim Abu Tahir Muhammad Ahmed, Babu Ijaz Husain.

Miscellaneous
Inamullah, Siraj Ahmed, Ijaz Husain, Ibrahim Usuf Ali.

Subsidiary List
Khan Bahadur Haji Maulvi Ziayuddin Muhammad (Madras); Syed Ghulam Bhik Nairang (Ambala); Hakim Habibur Rahman (Dacca); Syed Muhammad

Ashraf (Kohat); S. A. Hadi (Jubblepore); Honourable Sir Ebrahim Haroon Jaffer (Bombay); Mir Noor Muhammad Khan (Jacobabad); Muhammad Rafiq, M.L.A. (Calcutta); Syed Muttalabi Faridabadi (Faridabad); M. I. Khuro, M.L.C. (Sind); Chaudhry Din Muhammad (Lahore); Pir Akbar Ali, M.L.C. (Ferozepur); Azimullah (Lahore); Mian Muhammad Hayat Qureshi, M.L.C. (Panjab); Maulvi Masudur Rahman Nadvi; Honourable Ali Bukhsh Muhammad Husain (Member Council of State) (Sind); Hakim Syed Ali Ahmed Zaidi (Faridabad); Kazi Muhammad Aslam (Peshawar); Khan Bahadur Makhdoom Syed Rajan Bukhsh Shah Jilani, M.L.A. (Multan); Sardar Naharsingji alias Nasrullah Khan Thaor [sic. Thakur of Amod]; G.A.D. Wazif, M.L.C. (Malegaon); Abdul Hameed Khan, M.L.C. (Behar and Orissa); Khan Sahib Bashir Ahmed Khan (Gurdaspur); Abdul Latif Haji Hajrat Khan, M.L.C. (Sholapur); Abdullah Haji Isa (Bhagat-Godhra); Mian Abdul Haye, M.L.A. (Ludhiana); Kazi Syed Ishaq Syed Hason, Kazi of Wai and Mahableshwar (Bombay Presidency); H. Shaheed Suhrawardy (Calcutta); Muhammad Sadique (Jalpaiguri); Khan Saheb A. A. Deshmukh (Pochora);

Report of the All India Muslim Conference held at Delhi on 31st December, 1928, and 1st January, 1929, compiled and published (by authority) by Hafizur Rahman, Aligarh, n.d., p. 6–8, xvii. The compiler's note to the first list reads: "The following are names of some of the prominent delegates who attended the Conference and whose names could be noted down in a haphazard way by volunteers while it was actually sitting. Many names must surely be missing in this list'. He prefaces the subsidiary list with this gloriously nonchalant statement: "The following gentlemen communicated their intention of attending the Conference to its authorities and were most probably—nay, almost certainly—present in it. Somehow their names escaped being noted down by volunteers."

The conference was organized on the following lines:

OBJECTS

The Objects of the Conference are:–

(a)   To safeguard and promote the rights and interests of the Indian Musal-mans at all stages of constitutional advance towards full responsible government in India.

(b)   To organize the Indian Musalmans and to co-ordinate the existing Muslim Organizations having an All-India character for the purpose of giving expression to Muslim opinion on questions affecting the Musal-mans of India, without interfering with the special features which distinguish such organizations.

CONSTITUTION PARTS

(i)   The elected Muslim Members of the Central and Provincial Legis-latures, who subscribe to the National Muslim Creed.

(ii)   Twenty Members each of:

(a)   The Central Khilafat Committee;

(b)   The Jamiat-ul-Ulama-i-Hind; and

(c)   The All India Muslim League (Lahore Section), elected respectively by these organizations who subscribe to the Muslim National Creed; and

(iii) The other prominent Indian Musalmans who have subscribed to the National Muslim Creed and been elected by the Working Committee.

OFFICE BEARERS

President : His Highness Sir Aga Khan
Secretaries : Nawab Muhammad Ismail Khan, M.L.A.
    Fazal Ibrahim Rahimtoola, M.L.A.
Financial Secretary : Khwaja Ghulam-us-Sibtain
Working Secretary : Muhammad Shafee Daoodi, M.L.A.
Members of Working Committee:

1. Mian Sir Muhammad Shafi
2. Dr. Sir Muhammad Iqbal, M.L.C. (Panjab)
3. Hon'ble Malik Feroz Khan Noon, Minister of the Punjab Government
4. Maulana Muhammad Ali, President-elect All India Muslim Conference, 1930
5. Maulana Mufti Muhammad Kifayatullah, President, Jamiat-ul-Ulama-i-Hind
6. Hakim Jamil Khan, Chairman, Reception Committee of All-India Muslim Conference, Delhi, 1929
7. Maulana Shaukat Ali, Secretary, Central Khilafat Committee
8. Sir Ibrahim Rahimtoola
9. Seth Haji Abdullah Haroon, M.L.A.
10. Maulana Hasrat Mohani
11. Hon'ble Muhammad Yusuf, Minister of the United Provinces Government
12. The Hon'ble Maulvi Muhammad Yaqub, President, Legislative Assembly
13. Nawab Habibullah of Dacca
14. Mr. A. H. Ghuznavi, M.L.A.
15. Mr. Husain Shaheed Suhrawardy, M.L.A.
16. Maulana Syed Murtaza Saheb Bahadur, M.L.A., Secretary, Central Khilafat Committee
17. Mr. Syed Abdul Aziz, M.L.C., Bar-at-Law
18. Mr. Abdul Qadir Siddiqi, M.L.A.
19. Nawab Sahibzada Sir Abdul Qayyum, M.L.A.

The Main Resolutions of the All India Muslim Conference, published by Muhammad Shafee Daoodi, Patna (Bihar and Orissa), Working Secretary, All India Muslim Conference, n.d. (? 1930) (printed at the Army Press, Simla), pp. 1–2.

Between 1928 and 1935 the conference had the following presidents:

December 1928	Delhi	The Aga Khan
November 1930	Lucknow	Nawab Muhammad Ismail Khan
April 1931	Delhi	Maulana Shaukat Ali
March 1932	Lahore	Sir Muhammad Iqbal
December 1932	Calcutta	Abdullah Yusuf Ali
Decembe 1933		Dr. Shafa'at Ahmad Khan
December1934		Nawab Sir Ahmad Said Khan of Chattari
December 1935		Seth Haji Abdullah Haroon

94

BRITAIN AND THE MUSLIMS OF INDIA

Interview with the Daily Express

Nice: 1 May 1929

The Simon Commission – Muslims of India united politically – association of free Indian States – comparison with pre-war Germany – Hindu-Muslim relations – solution to poverty in India – tribute to King George V.

"What is the future of British rule in India, your highness?" I asked.

"British rule at present is too centralised and too powerful," replied the prince, weighing each phrase carefully. "Of course I do not know what will be found in the report which the Simon Commission will eventually draft, but unless the findings of the commission are based on an association or federation of Indian free States – which I shall explain to you in a moment – then, God help them! They will simply be reaping more Dead Sea fruit.

"As you know, I recently returned from India, where I succeeded in uniting seventy million Moslems on a political basis. It was not a new Moslem party which I created, but rather a reuniting of the old party.

"Our aims are purely political. The religious differences separating the various sects of Mohammedanism exist and will exist for all time as far as we can foresee.

"The time has come for India to be organised on national lines. We want to see the creation of free Indian States within the framework of the British Empire – but an association which will be equal to the other units of the British Empire as it exists at present.

"There would be between twenty and thirty Indian free States, each one with economic and military freedom – do you follow me? – but each of these States with a British Governor and with a British Viceroy directing the association or federation, whichever you like to call it.

"I cannot do better to explain my meaning than to ask you to remember the German Empire as it was before the great war, when Bavaria, although part and parcel of that empire had perfect military and economic freedom. I know and realise that it will require a man of great courage and resource to bring about this change of government, and perhaps Edwin Montagu might have been able to do this had it not been for his untimely death. But even Montagu was scared by what happened in Bengal.

"The majority of the Indian people wholeheartedly desire the change which I have outlined, but there is a certain amount of inertia in India which will have to be overcome. The present trouble in India between the Moslems and Hindus will eventually disappear if they, as well as other Indian nationals, are organised as nationalistic free States on historical and linguistic foundations."

"What is the feeling in India towards Communist agitation, your highness?"

"Communism only fishes in troubled waters. One must distinguish between legitimate agitation and that which is being sponsored by the Communists. We have very great poverty in India but this poverty cannot be overcome by charity, however well meant; nor by lord mayors' funds, no matter how laudable their offering. But it can be overcome by the development of agricultural colleges and the assistance and encouragement of agriculture."

H.H. the Prince Aga Khan is a realist in Indian affairs, and a most devoted friend of the British Empire. During and since the war I have had many conversations with him concerning Indian affairs, but I can remember no occasion when the prince has himself not brought into the conversation the name of the King. This afternoon was no exception.

After stating how glad he was that the King had made such a splendid and wonderful recovery his highness said:–

"Do you know, I think the King is the most hard-working man in the British Empire. I have known scores of other rulers and the heads of big business concerns, but I know of no other man who regards his job with such attachment and devotion.

"It should never be forgotten that the person of the British

Sovereign is the bond of union not only between the great white Dominions and England, but between all the non-British races in the Empire and the white section.

"Bismarck used to say that he could get through his job by working five minutes a day. Perhaps that was a boast, but King George reads every line and every word of every document brought to him for signature."

Source: *Daily Express*, London, 3 May 1929.

The interviewer was Harry James Greenwall, who later wrote a biography of the Aga Khan (*His Highness the Aga Khan: Imam of the Ismailis*, Cresset Press, London, 1952, with a Foreword on Racing by the Aga Khan himself), and who was at this time a special correspondent of the *Daily Express*. The newspaper prefaced the report of his interview with the statement that the Aga Khan was "the greatest figure in the Moslem world". The report of the interview was published on the front page under a three-column headline.

95

BRITISH POLICY IN INDIA

An Article

London: 7 November 1929

History of British rule in India – the will of the British nation to establish dominion status – problems to be solved – adjustment of relations between the Indian States and a Dominion India – freedom for Burma – federalism as a solution of the Hindu-Muslim question – withdrawal of the British Army – need for Indian statesmanship.

The announcement made by the Viceroy last week cannot be considered by any serious student of the history of the British connexion with India as anything more than a natural and inevitable development in this marvellous episode in world history, designed to remove doubts which have arisen in India as to the ultimate aim of British policy.

Clive and Hastings, and those associated with them, were little concerned with the final destiny of the Empire in the East they were creating. But soon afterwards Sir John Malcolm thought deeply regarding the ultimate goal of Britain's work in India, and came to certain definite conclusions. From this time onwards there have always been prominent Englishmen, either in India or in Parliament, who have held whether consciously or subconsciously, to the views of Malcolm and Mountstuart Elphinstone. Those great administrators realized that permanent dominion of a foreign people was an impossibility. The question they propounded was whether India should be prepared to take her place united to England by ties of political alliance and cultural and commercial pupilage, or whether a new era of chaos and invasion such as they had themselves witnessed was to succeed the British connexion.

845

Then came a long period when the declaration of equality of opportunity in the Act of 1833, confirmed by Queen Victoria's Proclamation of 1858, came to be regarded by political-minded Indians as the charter of their liberty. They asked for equality of opportunity in the service of the Crown, for administrative improvements, such as the separation of judicial and executive functions, for the spread of education, and for reforms in land tenure and assessment, rather than for political freedom and power to govern.

A disastrous break took place when Lord Dufferin, after at first encouraging the newly-formed Indian National Congress, turned his back on this policy. From that day to the end of Lord Curzon's rule there was little understanding and sympathy between the British rulers and the Indian *intelligentsia*. As a member of the Viceroy's Legislature during Lord Curzon's time, I saw at close quarters how foreign the Government was in spirit and atmosphere, and how, on the other side, dissatisfied at not having succeeded in obtaining the earlier demands, Indian leaders began to clamour not so much for administrative reform as for the control of their political destiny.

A little later Lord Morley and Lord Minto came to realize that the spirit of dominance had done its work in India and that it was impossible to stand still. Accordingly they introduced their reforms. Lord Hardinge's Viceroyalty was the continuation in letter and in spirit of the Morley-Minto regime. Though his constitutional powers were retained under the reforms, he was most successful in his efforts to govern with the people at his back.

There is a widespread idea in England that the declaration of August 20, 1917, was due to the initiative of statesmen in White-hall. This is not correct. Like the declaration of last week, it was made at the instance of the Viceroy, then Lord Chelmsford. The British officials who were members of the Government of India considered it necessary and inevitable, as did the British heads of Provinces. The declaration and the preamble of the Act of 1919 leave no doubt that it is the will of the British nation to bring about the establishment of what is now known as Dominion status – which is, in truth, actually nothing more or less than autonomy and alliance under a common Sovereign.

Dominion status cannot be anything more than an ambition and a goal till a great many practical problems have been settled. Indian leaders have now to show the courage, the forbearance, and the fundamental liberalism that the highest type of British statesmanship has shown towards India. The problems which have to be settled are many, and I can mention only some of the outstanding considerations.

For instance, the adjustment of the relations of the Indian States to a Dominion India will need the patience, courage, and tact that are essential to true statesmanship. It cannot be successfully undertaken without British guidance. Again, is Burma to be India's Ireland? I hope that our statesmanship will repair the injustice of the absorption of Burma in British India, and allow that nation the fullest freedom which its leaders may desire. I, for one, would encourage her becoming a Dominion within the British Commonwealth.

The trans-Indus question is as delicate and difficult as that of Burma. In a famous phrase Mr. Lloyd George spoke of Austria-Hungary as "a ramshackle Empire". It had grown as a personal estate of the House of Hapsburg. British India today is ramshackle in its grouping: great nations like the Marhattas are divided, small ones like the Sindhis are submerged. I cannot conceive of any final and satisfactory solution of the Hindu-Muslim question except by the establishment of federalism on nationalistic, racial, and linguistic principles throughout the self-governing provinces.

Of one thing I am convinced: if Indian statesmen will take as their models Malcolm and his successors down to Willingdon and Irwin rather than the men who lost the American colonies, they will ultimately be able to dispense with the British Army in India. Without its withdrawal there can be no real Dominion status: the term is not consistent in the full sense with dependence on Great Britain for protection from internal chaos and external invasion.

Thus a dispassionate survey of the history of the British connexion compels the conclusion that the Viceroy's announcement is an affirmation of facts made at the time when Lord Irwin (who after all is the most responsible authority and in the best position to judge) considered it necessary that the ultimate aim should be restated to the whole world. As a practical step towards Dominion status no settlement and no resolution of those in authority can take India farther. The declaration in itself, though it has removed any doubts that may have been entertained as to the goal of British intentions, cannot bring Dominion status any nearer unless Indian statesmanship rises to the occasion.

Source: *The Times*, London, 7 November 1929.

The trend of this article bears a very interesting comparison with the ideas running throughout the text of *India in Transition* published eleven years earlier.

INDIAN MUSLIM ASPIRATIONS

Letter to The Times

Antibes: 16(?) January 1930

Position of India's Muslims – All India Muslim Conference of 1928 – a federal system for India and separate Muslim electorates – Sind as a separate province – reforms in the North-West Frontier Province and Baluchistan.

In his letter published on January 14 Sir Arthur Conan Doyle, complaining of lack of effort to counter the Indian National Congress agitation for independence, suggests *inter alia* that the Mohamedans of India should say what they want. Those who follow closely Indian affairs will not have forgotten that the wishes of the community were expressed clearly and emphatically at the All-India Moslem Conference held at Delhi under my presidency on December 31, 1928, and the following day. The Conference was composed of an overwhelming majority of the elected representatives of the community in the Central and Provincial Legislatures and the leaders and influential men of every section from the extreme Left to the extreme Right. In the words of *The Annual Register*, 1928, the gathering was "remarkably representative."

A manifesto, in the form of a long resolution passed unanimously, states the full case of the Indian Moslems. Postulating a federal system for India, it insists on the necessity for the continuance of separate Moslem electorates as essential, under existing conditions, for the evolution of really representative democratic government. It asks that Sind should be constituted a separate province, and that constitutional reforms should be introduced in the North-West Frontier Province and Baluchistan. The minimum safeguards required against communal legislation and unfavourable amendment of the Constitution are indicated. The final paragraph declares that no Constitution, by whomsoever proposed or devised, will be acceptable to the Moslems unless it conforms to the principles laid down in the resolution.

The events of the past 12 months have strengthened rather than weakened Moslem adherence to this considered declaration. It was reaffirmed again and again in evidence submitted to the Joint Free Conference under Sir John Simon's chairmanship, and is the basis of a closely reasoned minute of dissent to the Report of the Indian Central Committee signed by two Moslem members.

Source: *The Times*, London, 18 January 1930.

The letter, written from Antibes in France, is undated. It is reasonable to assume that it was written on 16 January, received by the journal on the 17th and published in the issue of the 18th.

97

A FEDERATION FOR INDIA

Speech at the Round Table Conference

London: 21 November 1930

Practically every school of Indian thought has expressed its views
– unanimity on self-government – assurances to British commercial
interests – a federal scheme could lead to full self-government and
responsibility.

Mr. Prime Minister, I did not intend speaking here either to-day
or at any stage of these proceedings but some of the members
of the British India Delegation have told me, as recently as last
night and this morning, that it was my duty to express my views.
I have come quite unprepared, but the best preparation of all
has been the proceedings of this Conference. You, Sir, and the
British representatives of the three Parties of the State have heard
practically every school of Indian thought. From the Hindus to
the Muslims, coming down across the centre, nearly every school
has spoken. Their Highnesses, the Princes, have spoken. If we
eliminate all differences, there is on one point complete unanimity. We all ask for a full measure of self-government. I think,
as Chairman of the British India Delegation, working in co-
operation with the two other Delegations, I can say that we are
all unitedly asking for that. We ask you to promise us the framework. If the picture that we are to paint on it is unsatisfactory to
any of the important minorities, or to the Princes, or to a small
section of the minorities, we will try again – and if we fail we will
try again: and we will continue trying till we produce something
that will be generally satisfactory. I, for one, am particularly
anxious that it shall be in a form which will ensure that, not only
every Indian minority, but the British commercial element in
India shall be satisfied that their interests are safe in our hands.
As to the interests of this country, a united India could offer her

851

a far greater security as to her commercial interests than anything she has at present; could offer her a long-dated treaty on the lines of the German-Russian Treaty of 1904. For many years that would ensure your commerce fair and equitable treatment, and that would give your people a sense of security. The same applies to debt and to other interests, which would be infinitely safer than merely relying, as at present, on the strength of this country and not on a consented agreement with India.

Mr. Prime Minister, there is no reason why, if we can produce a federal scheme that will please the Princes, that will please the Hindus, that will please the Muslims, that will please the smaller minorities and that will satisfy all the legitimate commercial interests, and at the same time for a period reserve certain objects, there is no reason why we should not at this moment start on the basis of full self-government and responsibility.

Source: *Indian Round Table Conference: 12th. November 1930–19th. January 1931: Proceedings*, His Majesty's Stationery Office, London, 1931, Cmd. 3778, pp. 180–1.

For those interested in the audience which heard the Aga Khan make this speech I give below a complete list of the delegates to the first session of the Round Table Conference:

British Delegation
J. Ramsay MacDonald (President of the Conference)
Lord Sankey (Deputy President of the Conference)
Wedgwood Benn
Arthur Henderson
J. H. Thomas
Sir William Jowitt
H. B. Lees Smith
Earl Russell
Earl Peel (Chairman of the Conference)
Marquess of Zetland
Sir Samuel Hoare
Oliver Stanley
Marquess of Reading (Chairman of the Conference)
Marquess of Lothian
Sir Robert Hamilton
Isaac Foot

Indian States' Delegation
Maharaja of Alwar
Gaekwar of Baroda (Chairman of the Conference)
Nawab of Bhopal (Chairman of the Conference)
Maharaja of Bikaner (Chairman of the Conference)
Maharaja Rana of Dholpur
Maharaja of Jammu and Kashmir
Maharaja of Nawanagar

Maharaja of Patiala
Maharaja of Rewa
Chief Sahib of Sangli
Sir Prabhashankar Pattani
Sir Manubhai Mehta
Sardar Sahibzada Sultan Ahmad Khan
Nawab Sir Muhammad Akbar Hydari
Sir Mirza Muhammad Ismail
Colonel K. N. Haksar (Secretary General to the Indian States' Delegation)

British Indian Delegation
The Aga Khan (Chairman of the Conference)
Sir C. P. Ramaswami Aiyar
Maulana Muhammad Ali (died during the Conference session)
Dr. B. R. Ambedkar
Sarijut Chandradhar Barooha
J. N. Basu
Sir Muhammad Shah Nawaz Khan Bhutto
Sir Hubert Carr
C. Y. Chintamani
Nawab Sir Ahmad Said Khan Chchattari
Maharajaadhiraj of Darbhanga
Captain Raja Sher Muhammad Khan
A. K. Fazlul Haq
A. H. Ghuznavi
Lt.-Col. H. A. J. Gidney
Sir Ghulam Husain Hidayatullah
Hafiz Hidayat Husain
B. V. Jadhav
M. R. Jayakar
Sir Cowsaji Jehangir
Muhammad Ali Jinnah
T. F. Gavin Jones
N. M. Joshi
Dr. Narendranath Law
Sir B. N. Mitra
Sir P. C. Mitter
H. P. Mody
B. S. Moonje
Ramaswami Mudaliar
Raja Narendra Nath
A. T. Pannir Selvam
Raja of Parlakimedi
Sir A. P. Patro
K. T. Paul
Sahibzada Nawab Sir Abdul Qaiyum
M. Ramachandra Rao
Sir Sayyid Sultan Ahmad
Sir Tej Bahadur Sapru
B. Shiva Rao
Sir Mian Muhammad Shafi
Sardar Sampuran Singh

Srinivasa Sastri (Chairman of the Conference)
Sir Chimanlal Setalvad
Kanwar Bisheshwar Dayal Seth
Sir Phiroze Sethna
Dr. Shafa'at Ahmad Khan
Begum Shah Nawaz
M. R. Rao Bahadur Srinivasan
Mrs. Subbarayan
S. B. Tambe
Sardar Ujjal Singh
Sir C. E. Wood
Zafrullah Khan

Officials Attending in Consultative Capacity
Sir W. M. Hailey
Sir C. A. Innes
Sir A. C. MacWatters
H. G. Haig
L. W. Reynolds

Indian States' Advisers
Hyderabad: Sir Richard Chenevix-Trench
          Nawab Mehdi Yar Jang
          Sir Ahmad Husain, Amin Jang
          Sir Reginald Glancy
South Indian States: T. Raghaviah
Gaekwar of Baroda: Krishnama Chari
Orissa States: K. C. Neogy
Chamber of Princes: L. F. Rushbrook-Williams
                   Qazi Ali Haider Abbasi
                   Sardar Jarmani Das
                   A. B. Latthe
                   D. A. Surve

On the Round Table Conferences see the White Papers bearing the command numbers Cmd. 3772 (1931), 3778 (1931), 3972 (1931), 3997 (1932), 4069 (1932), 4147 (1932), 4238 (1933), 4268 (1933); *India: The Commission and the Conference: A Reprint of Leading Articles from "The Times" on Indian Question from the Return of the Statutory Commission from India to the Conclusion of the Round Table Conference in London*, London, 1931; N. Gangulee, *The Making of Federal India*, London, n.d. (?1937); D. Madhava Rao, *The Indian Round Table Conference and After*, London, 1932; R. Coupland, *The Indian Problem 1833–1935: Report on the Constitutional Problem in India, Part 1*, London, 1942; Lord Halifax, *Fullness of Days*, London, 1957; Chimanlal H. Setalvad, *Recollections and Reflections*, Bombay, n.d. (?1946); Lord Simon, *Retrospect: the Memoirs of the Rt. Hon. Viscount Simon, G.C.S.I., G.C.V.O.*, London, 1952; Lord Templewood, *Nine Troubled Years*, London, 1954; R. Craddock, "After the Round Table Conference", *English Review*, February 1931; "India After the Conference", *Round Table*, June 1931; Lord Meston, "Round Table Difficulties", *Fortnightly Review*, January 1933; Hugh Molson, "The Third Round Table Conference", *Journal of the East India Association*, vol. for 1933; Muhammad Yakub, "Indian Muslims and the Reforms", *Asiatic Review*, October 1933; "India: Conference on Intransigence", *Round Table*,

December 1930; Lord Meston, "The Indian Conference", *The Nineteenth Century and After,* October 1930; W. P. Barton, "India: A Federation", *Empire Review,* January 1931; J. R. MacDonald, "The Round Table Conference", *Listener,* 28 January 1931; Lord Meston, "Round Table and After", *The Nineteenth Century and After,* March 1931; "Round Table Problems", *Manchester Guardian,* 8 September 1931; "The Round Table Conference", *Economist,* 17 October 1931; Earl Winterton, "The Conference and After", *Fortnightly Review,* February 1931; Marquess of Zetland, "The Round Table Conference and After", *Asiatic Review,* July 1931; John Coatman, "The Round Table Conference", *The Nineteenth Century and After,* January 1932; J. M. Kenworthy, "Some Thoughts on the Round Table Conference", *The Review of India,* February 1932; Shafa'at Ahmad Khan, "Muslims in the New India", *Asiatic Review,* January 1932; "The Results of the Round Table Conference", *Round Table,* March 1932; and Marquess of Zetland, "The Indian Round Table Conference: The Second Phase", *Asiatic Review,* July 1932.

THE PRESENT OUTLOOK

Interview with The Daily Herald

London: 1 December 1930

Conversation with Mrs. Asquith – interest in horses – personal concern for India and its welfare – citizen of the world – the First World War – English literature – mistakes of the Treaty of Versailles – prevent another war.

One of the things that made an immense difference to me is that twenty years ago I sat next at table to Lady Oxford – Mrs. Asquith as she was then.

It must always matter supremely to a man that he sits next to that admirably witty lady. But this was something out of the ordinary.

She told me of a medicine. And that medicine has made all the difference to me physically. Otherwise I should have probably been a hopeless neurasthenic.

Oh yes, I was in a fair way to become that, I know the extent of my debt. There can scarcely be a greater one.

Now, as to my racing. Plainly, that has mattered a good deal to me. But, then, racing has always been part of my natural life. My father and my grandfather raced. I was always among horses. I loved them.

I rode a pony when I was two. Probably before that I rode a wooden horse in a nursery. Yes, racing is a great game. And more than a game, when you remember what horses have meant to man.

Some people wonder why, with Turkey against us, I could be on the side of the Allies during the war.

I was able to do it because I belong to two worlds, and I am a link between them. There is my Arabian and Persian descent.

My descent from the Prophet has mattered supremely.

But I was born in India. And I regard myself as a member of that community. India and her welfare are very dear to me. India matters very much. The problem of her destiny occupies my mind to-day.

But for many years now I have been a citizen of the world, above all of Europe. And let me say here how much it matters that I should know well the languages of Europe.

It is not merely a new speech that is open to you, but a new culture and a new world. To have your own race, your own country, and then to have all these other countries. To be able to live the life of many nations, not as an outsider, but as one of themselves.

Yes, that is a tremendous privilege that has mattered very much indeed.

You will understand, then, how dreadful to me was the outbreak of the war. That, I think, has mattered to me more than anything else in my life.

You see, I had been convinced that such a war was impossible. I had said so.

And then the whole world went to pieces. My whole world went to pieces.

I had believed in the hereditary principle. But now I was forced to say that if the ruling classes could bring us to this they had failed, they were no longer fit to rule.

I don't say that England could have avoided the war. The Germans were not evil men. But they were – impossible. They had their obsession. Which was symbolised by the goosestep. They were impossible. But . . . . anyhow, I concluded that hereditary rule, class rule, was discredited.

And that, to me, was a catastrophic conclusion to be forced to. It changed my whole scheme of things.

What of the native States of India? Well, they are on their trial. They must prove themselves – now. This Round-Table Conference is of great importance.

It matters much to me, more to India, and most of all to the native princes. They have to prove themselves. I sincerely trust that they will do so.

English literature has mattered very much to me. Shakespeare, of course. The greatest of them all. But before the war I'd read many novels.

After re-reading them all, I found that none of them – Dickens, Thackeray, Eliot – were so much to my mind as three of the moderns, first of all Conrad, and then Wells (I love all of Wells) and Arnold Bennett.

But that is past. Since the war I have read nothing but books about it. I have read everything – on the causes of it, the course of it, and the lamentable things that happened after it, beginning with the most lamentable event of all – the Treaty of Versailles.

I think that, next to the war, the Treaty was the most shocking thing that has happened to the world in modern times.

The opportunities that were missed! The old animosities that were maintained, and the new ones that were aroused!

Yes, if the war discredited the ruling classes, what shall be said of the Peace?

And now I use my opportunities of mixing with people of influence to tell them that another war like the last would finish us, would abolish civilisation, would plunge us into barbaric chaos; and that the world is drifting steadily towards that war.

It is! It is! And the rulers of the civilised world obstinately shut their eyes to it.

Nothing matters to me now as much as this: to use all my influence – in Europe and in Asia – to prevent another war.

Source: *The Daily Herald*, London, 2 December 1930.
The interviewer was W. R. Titterton. The report was published under the headline "The Aga Khan . . . My Life Moulded by Religion, Racing and the War," in the series "Things That Matter to Me".

99

THE EAST THROUGH THE ORIENTAL EYES

Foreword to Sirdar Ikbal Ali Shah's Book on Persia

London: 8 December 1930

At the height of Islamic civilization Muslim scholars wrote books of travel – similar works being written today – the value of Sirdar Ikbal Ali Shah's books.

At the height of its civilisation and glory there were many distinguished Moslems of learning, who visited every part of the Islamic world, and wrote books of travel that have remained classics even to this day.

One of the signs of the renaissance of learning and art in the East is the fact that men like Sirdar Ikbal Ali Shah have travelled over such little-known countries as Afghanistan, Arabia and Persia, and are now writing books of travel which will differ from those of Western scholars by their angle of vision.

It is a well-known fact that works of art are differently interpreted by experts from the East or West. The same applies to the culture, habits and institutions of countries.

For these reasons, I think Sirdar Ikbal Ali Shah's books – and especially this latest book on Persia – should be read by those in the West who want to see the East through Oriental eyes.

Source: Sirdar Ikbal Ali Shah, *Eastward to Persia*, Wright and Brown, London, n.d., pp. ix–x.

The Aga Khan's Foreword is dated London, 8 December 1930. The book carries no date of publication, but must have appeared in early 1931. The text carries the following heading: "Foreword by His Highness Sir Agha Sultan Mohamed Shah, G.C.I.E., G.C.S.I., G.C.V.O., K.C.I.E., LL.D., better known in Europe as the Aga Khan". The author's own Preface is signed from Tehran without a date. Sirdar Ikbal Ali Shah, an Indian resident of Britain, was the son of Sirdar Amjad Ali Shah of Sardhana.

THE FUTURE OF MANKIND

A Speech at a Literary Gathering

London: 10 June 1931

The objective of life – freedom for the individual – optimism for the future of mankind – the value of sports.

He was optimistic about the future of the race provided the individual had an opportunity for free development. If the world in the future were to avoid past shortcomings and a repetition of the pain and sorrow through which the race had been evolved, it was essential that the mind as well as the body of the individual should be free to act according to its own independence, its inner conviction and nature for the welfare of all other individuals. He was optimistic as to the future of mankind, and would place no limit to human development, provided the elements out of which they had developed to the present stage were not crushed.

Alluding to a reference by Sir Ernest Benn to his attachment to "the finest of British sports," the Aga Khan added that he was convinced that the day when the Englishman became less of a sportsman than now would set a great barrier to the development of the higher and better world and the greater and more happy humanity of which he had spoken. Sport could be pursued without interference with the happiness of others, and he thought there was no other single propensity which more promoted, not only our physical and mental well-being, but also our sense of responsibility towards others.

Source: *The Times*, London, 11 June 1931.
This was a philosophic address (*The Times'* description) entitled "The One and the Many" delivered at the monthly luncheon of the Individualist Bookshop held at the Hotel Victoria, Northumberland Avenue, London.

101

PROSPECTS FOR THE ROUND TABLE CONFERENCE

Statement to The Times

London: 16 September 1931

India and the world-wide desire for peace – difficulties before the Round Table Conference – grounds for optimism.

In a statement to *The Times* the Aga Khan said that he came to the Conference, at which all Indian political parties were now represented, in a hopeful spirit.

India, he continued, must make her contribution to the world-wide desire for peace. When so large a part of the globe was unsettled and disturbed, the peace and prosperity of the whole world were injured. He knew only too well that the Conference had formidable difficulties to face; but much depended on the settlement of some of the more complicated and intractable questions. Human experience showed that when, in a many-sided problem, two or three outstanding points were settled the adjustment of the many others calling for solution was greatly facilitated. These were among the grounds on which he based his hopes.

Asked if he was more hopeful than he was when the Conference assembled late last autumn, his Highness replied, "I am always an optimist."

Source: *The Times*, London, 17 September 1931.

The statement was given at the Victoria Railway Station in London in the late evening of 16 September on his arrival in Britain. As he was at this time chairman of the British-Indian Delegation to the forthcoming Round Table Conference, he was received at the station by a number of delegates and officials of the Conference. Among those present on the platform were the Nawab of Bhopal, the Chancellor of the Chamber of Princes, who left a meeting of the

States' Delegation to greet him, Mian Sir Muhammad Shafi, Sir Sultan Ahmad, Sir Geoffrey Corbett, Sir Umar Hayat Khan, Sir Maneckji Dadabhoy, Dr Shafa'at Ahmad Khan, Mr Bajpai, Alma Latifi, Dr Ambedkar, Chaudhri Muhammad Zafrulla Khan, the Imam of the London Mosque, P. K. Dutt, Mr Qureshi, and John Coatman, who conveyed a message of welcome from Lord Reading.

102

SAFEGUARDS FOR THE INDIAN MUSLIMS

Broadcast Address to the USA

London: 27 September 1931

Numerical strength of Muslims in India – how they differ from Hindus – dreadful events at Cawnpore and the Muslim anxiety – Muslims and usury – Indian Muslims are patriotic – they want their interests to be safeguarded – Muslims will join Hindus for achieving a democratic government.

He pointed out that the Muslims – more numerous than the 62,000,000 people of Germany – number 78,000,000 of India's population of 335,000,000. Fifty years ago the Muslims were one-fifth of the population of India, but they have been steadily increasing until today, His Highness said, they are one-fourth; "they will be one-third before our children are middle-aged men".

"Do not think", the Aga Khan continued, "that the Indian Muslims are aliens in India. For centuries they have been there, and nine-tenths have been in India at least as long as the Normans have been in England. But the Muslims of India differ from the Hindus in most matters which can divide one set of people from another. They differ in customs, in habits, in laws, and, above all, in their food and in their clothes. They also differ in cultural and economic ideals. In India there is such a thing as the untouchable. The Muslim religion teaches that all men are created equal. To them it is a sin to consider any human being as untouchable. We believe that one man has as good a right to walk erect on God's earth as any other man. Our religion gives equal rights to both men and women – in this world as in the next ... [... in the original – Ed.] The difference between the Muslims and the Hindus of India is, therefore, more than religious. It is greater than the difference of Protestant and Catholic in Ireland, or even of French Canadians and English Canadians in Canada.

We all regret that India should be a house divided against itself. Alas! recent events in India show that some people fly at the throats of others on the least excuse. The dreadful events of Cawnpore and elsewhere in India in March of this year made the Muslims more than ever nervous as to their future.

The Muslim religion forbids usury. The rule was made to save the poor man from economic enslavement by the rich. In India the Hindu is permitted to take interest on capital, while in most cases Muslims still do not. The result is that in the course of ages the Hindu has become the capitalist and the Muslim the labourer or the tiller of the soil.

So there has been an unfortunate wrangle between the "haves" and the "have nots" for a place in the sun, particularly where there is an overwhelming majority of Hindus, as majorities are likely to tyrannize and oppress the minorities unless proper safeguards are provided. We have been accused of looking beyond the frontiers of India and not concentrating all our political patriotism on our Motherland. This is an unfounded accusation. While we are a world-wide brotherhood, while we share the joys and sorrows of Muslims throughout the world, while our spiritual brotherhood is complete with them, politically we have no other country and no other patriotism except that of India. We would resent any intervention in Indian affairs from any outside Muslim as much as any other Indian would. Politically we have no other loyalty except as Indian members of the British Commonwealth of Nations.

But the Muslims want such a Federal Constitution for India as will safeguard their legitimate interests. They want something that will save them [sic] their ideals from being submerged. They ask for an adequate share in the Federal Legislature, as also in the Federal administration of India, and they claim self-determination, as well as fully autonomous administrations, for all racial and linguistic areas – and particularly for those areas which have a majority Muslim population. They want to decide freely for themselves whether they will keep the institution of separate electorates for their protection or not. They do not want this right, borrowed by India from the experience of some European Constitutions, to be forcibly taken from them. They will resist to the last any attempt which, under colour of democracy, places them at the mercy of any other section.

The Muslims will, however, fight shoulder to shoulder with their Hindu brothers for a Constitution which will give India a stable Government of the people, by the people, for the people, for the equal good and advancement of all – and not for the advantage of any particular caste or creed, which would hold the others in its grasp.

Source: *The Times*, London, 28 September 1931.

103

MY PERSONAL LIFE

Interview with the Daily Sketch

London: 2 November 1931

Spiritual happiness – glories of nature – the English landscape – painting – literature – poetry – sports – horses – marriage – responsibilities of life.

First I would place spiritual happiness. A man must be at one with God. This may sound old-fashioned to some people. A few may think that they do not believe in God, and some others that it matters little to the individual in his daily life how he stands with regard to Him.

Ruling out the atheist, with whom a believer can no more argue than he can discuss colour with a blind man, it is surely strange that a believer in an omnipotent and ever-present Deity should fail to realise that how we stand this instant and every instant toward Him matters to us more than anything else in the universe.

That is the fundamental question:– Are you in harmony with God? If you are – you are happy.

Next I would place appreciation and enjoyment of the glories of nature. All those sunrises and sunsets – all the intricate miracle of sky colour, from dawn to dusk. All that splendid spendthrift beauty . . . . As a very rich man treasures the possession of some unique picture, so a man should treasure and exult in the possession – his individual possession – of the sights of this unique world.

Those glories are his from dawn to dusk, and then – and then comes night – "a night of stars – all eyes." The fact that Mr. So-and-So has weighed Orion in a scale and mapped beyond a peradventure the path of the Pleiades does not destroy their magic. I look up at night and I know – I *know* the glory of the stars. It is then that the stars speak to us – and the sense of that mystery is in our blood.

There are other more homely delights in an English landscape – twisting lanes with living leafy walls, villages clustered in a nook of the hills, the soft undulation of down or moorland, no more than emphasised by the occasional bold scarp of a rocky peak. But you have grandeur enough in the tall cliffs that look down so proudly on your encircling seas. All that is yours, and mine – ours for the seeing.

With nature I would link painting. Pictures are very useful. If a man cannot get to the countryside, a picture will remind him of it. And the man who has been blind to the beauty of nature may have his imagination quickened by seeing the visions of great artists. He may come to see that dawn and dusk make glorious even the drab pavement of a town.

Then comes literature – above all poetry. Poetry is the voice of God speaking through the lips of man. If great painting puts you in touch with nature, great poetry puts you in direct touch with God. It is not a soft indulgence, you need to be wide awake, with all your wits about you, to share the poet's joys. And, indeed, happiness is never a negative affair; it is to be won by men who are fully alive, full of the joy of living.

Next I would place the joys of rapid movement such as you get from games like golf, tennis, football, and, they tell me, cricket. As with literature the mind, so with games the body feels itself vividly, happily alive.

Of all sports of rapid movement the riding of a horse is the best.

The legend of the centaur – half man, half horse – was no idle dream; for you and the splendid creature are one. As its limbs gather and stretch out in perfect rhythm, electricity passes from the animal to you. It is a joy of the spirit as of the body. Through us speak the souls of our ancestors, who have ridden horses from the beginning of time. Yes, we may well believe that the horse was with man from the beginning.

No doubt we who have ridden horses get a touch of that great happiness when English thoroughbreds, the exiles of Arabia, fly down the course like winged messengers of speed.

Of course you cannot get a comparable feeling from the utmost Horse-Power (save the mark!) of a machine. No! No!

These are the independent means of happiness. Any man may worship God, wonder at the miracles of nature, exult when he hears (in literature) the sons of God shouting for joy, and give praise for the perfection of his body in rapid movement. But there is a dependent means of the first importance.

When I speak of marriage, I need not emphasise the joys of a happy marriage and fortunate parentage. They are inextricably interwoven – warp and woof of the same pattern, and the pattern is the whole of life in miniature.

He who refuses that venture because of the risk is refusing life. No. I have no liking for hermits and other solitaries who refuse all responsibilities. They may live in a town as likely as in a desert, and their avowed purpose may be to lead holy lives; but, in fact, if they have ecstasies, they are the ecstasies of self-indulgence. My concern is not with them.

Those who accept the normal responsibilities of life, with all the chances of minor annoyance and utter catastrophe, may know many small griefs and much great sorrow – that is why I called their joys dependent – but, if they are at one with God and have lived manfully, behind the mask of sorrow, bitter though it may be, their souls will be at peace.

Source: *Daily Sketch*, London, 2 November 1931.
The report of the interview was preceded by the following pen-picture of the Aga Khan:
"A large, eager, mobile face. The skin lit up rather than darkened by the glow of the Eastern sun. The eyes like blazing jewels. The body in continual easy movement! The hands active in their eloquence. Every inch of the man, every atom of him, vehemently, joyously alive. A happy man! As the talk turns from point to point of the argument, a flash of the joys he speaks of radiates from his face. A kingly man – so absolute in his kingship that he would talk with the least of his subjects as an equal. Yet for all his ease and charm, you feel that he could be an edged sword when in command.
"This is His Highness the Aga Khan Aga Sultan Mahomed Shah, Indian by birth and attachments, Persian and Arab by immemorial descent, the religious chief of one vast section of the Muslim world – the Ismaili Mohammedans – with countless followers in Central Asia, India and East Africa, and great race-horse-owner, who did what no other man could have done in the Great European war – kept it from being the universal Armageddon and final twilight of the world.
"At his ease in a London hotel, the happy philosopher told the *Daily Sketch*, what, to his mind, a man needs to be happy."

104

IF I WERE A DICTATOR

A Broadcast

London: 11 November 1931

Prevention of another war – abolition of national armies and navies
– an international force and a super-national government –
national autonomy – readjustment of national groupings – federation in India and Arabia – bi-culturalism an essential feature of
education – broad education – spiritual values – freedom and
equality of religious opinion – physical culture – science and economic policy – forces of nature – freedom of trade – currency –
private property – loans to industrialists – freedom of communication and travel – leisure for every consumer.

It is a common place [*sic*] of contemporary history that the Great
War opened the flood gates of the troubles from which we still
suffer. So I should deem it my first duty as Dictator to make, as
nearly as can be, impossible the overwhelming calamity of
another world war, and to rectify the acknowledged errors of the
peace concluded twelve years ago. To this end the demilitaris-
ation of the world by the abolition of national armies and navies
would be a first essential. I know that authority must in the final
resort rest upon force, but the force I would provide would be
internationally owned. For purposes of internal peace, national
police and gendarmerie would be ample. Ordinary voluntary
forces could be established for aiding the police on occasions of
sudden necessity. These might be enrolled and placed under the
local authorities who would co-operate with the police if any
abnormal need arose through internal disturbances. There would
be freedom of the air and of the seas with international aerial
and naval patrol to prevent air raids and any return to the piracy
of former days. Thus the real army, the air and sea forces, the
striking arm of the land forces through light cavalry, mobile

infantry, smaller tanks and various other technical improvements would remain at the disposal only of the supernational government whose members would represent a free choice of all the nationalities that would go to make the League which would take up the succession of my dictatorship after the twenty years in which I had organised the national and super-national government.

My dictatorship would uphold, rather than break down, national autonomy within a super-national world. Excessive centralisation would be avoided by the maintenance of local Parliaments, but with a World Parliament at Geneva or Lausanne, the heart of civilisation, to advise and assist the Dictator, and to replace the present League of Nations.

It would be essential to the satisfactory working of the new order to readjust national groupings, where they form a source of irritation and unrest. From long and close study of world affairs I am driven to the conclusion that few things are more inimical to peace and goodwill between neighbours than the tearing asunder of ethnic and linguistic groups at the dictate whether of a Napoleon or a President Wilson, to serve the ends of larger and more powerful competing interests. A general world-wide recasting of existing political units would not be necessary. The New World could be left untouched, for neither in North America nor South America is there any sense of serious grievance. On the Continent of Europe there need be no territorial reshaping of Great Britain, Spain, Portugal, France, Muscovy and the Scandinavian countries. This is also broadly true of Italy, except that she might be asked to surrender some acquisitions along the Alps which, in my view, are essentially German and not Italian.

The danger zones are Central Europe, the Balkans and Asia. I would make of Germany and Austria one nation, restoring to them such truly Germanic territory as has been acquired by others. In districts essentially Hungarian in population I should return to that unjustly maimed but generous and talented race such territories as desired by a free plebiscite to join her. In the Balkans, which have undergone so many transformations in national groupings as a result of ten years' almost continual fighting, I would have a properly conducted and free plebiscite for all doubtful zones. Where racial and cultural unity existed in the past I would let the peoples concerned unite or remain united. In a word, aggressor States would be compelled to disgorge, and the map of Europe would be re-made on cultural and voluntary lines.

I would pursue the same policy in the Middle East and Central Asia, by aiming at re-uniting, each under one strong Government, the Persian and Turkish races. The Central Asian regions I would form into States on cultural and racial lines.

The present clumsy and ill-assorted provincial groupings in India are the issue of historical or administrative accident and not of planned design. They would be replaced by more homogeneous provinces bringing together to the fullest extent permitted by inexorable circumstance groups of the same linguistic tribe.

I advocated such remaking of the map of India in a book published in 1916, when the Montagu-Chelmsford Reforms were being shaped, and I remain convinced today that this policy would provide one of the keys to an effective All-India Federation. The Arabs are to-day an unjustly treated race. They are under different governments and different mandatories. I would make a federal but united Arabia something on the lines of the old Germanic Empire, leaving here and there to hereditary principalities their internal autonomy, but uniting the whole peninsula and the adjacent Arab lands by a central federal government at some central place on the lines of Washington or Canberra. Japan can retain unimpaired her island nationality. In China there is linguistic affinity and a tradition of centuries of unity, but, in view of the course of events in our day, I should be inclined to give large provinces the opportunity for contracting out – if they wished to do so.

In Africa the tendency would be toward aggregation rather than division. For instance, I would make of the North-West one State. Egypt and the Sudan would be left as at present. The South African Union would be retained, excepting that Natal, being so preponderatingly British, might be given the option to contract out. . .

The re-groupings made as a means to cultural progress would need to be safeguarded from an excess of particularism. Today the two main streams of civilisation are fed from two widely divided cultures – the Asiatic and the European. Every Asiatic of education is brought face to face with European culture in a variety of ways; but, broadly speaking, the European who has not lived in the East (and nine hundred and ninety-nine out of a thousand of his fellow-countrymen who have sojourned in Asia) does not know Eastern culture in any real sense. I would, therefore, make bi-culturalism an essential feature of education. I should aim at the ideal of every European child being taught an Eastern language, and every Asiatic child a European language. It is scarcely necessary to say that under my dictatorship compulsory education would be world-wide and kept up till, say, eighteen or twenty years of age. I should certainly give to education a wider meaning than that which it now has in the public mind. The system would include teaching on health, on the laws of sex and parenthood, and on art and the life of the soul in the widest sense. The broad aim would be to give the workers a recognition of the value of their leisure in providing opportunities for spiritual, aesthetic and intellectual pursuits, for delight in nature and art in their manifold forms and, above all, for direct communion with the Unseen. The effort would be to enrich life through many channels. Travel, like staff rides in the army, would be regarded as a normal part of education. Spiritual values would be given the pre-eminence which is their inherent right. By spiritual experience I must make it clear that nothing in the nature of asceticism or monkery or renunciation of the responsibilities, as well as of the enjoyment, of life is meant. Good and beautiful thoughts, kindliness and gentleness towards others as well as a constant feeling of communion with the obvious soul in the universe around us – these, rather than absurd inhibitions and taboos, would be the meaning of religious education. The value and importance for happiness and contentment of reflection over the fruits of knowledge and the direct reactions to outer nature would be taught to the young. The habit of contemplation would be as general during moments of leisure as is today the wastage of precious time. There would be full freedom and equality of religious opinion, and also of practice so long as it did not trench upon the rights of others. Poetry and imaginative literature of all countries, especially of the neglected Moslem world, would be brought within the reach of each and all. The promotion of the public health would be sought both by education thereon and by the encouragement of physical culture, hiking, sports and games.

The time and money now foolishly wasted by sections of the public in overclothing and over-feeding would be replaced by rational diet and dress and the use of golf courses, tennis courts, cricket, football and hockey grounds and other sports for which widespread provision would be made. In these ways the people would be encouraged to divert the mind and exercise the body.

There would be no regimentation in the use of amusements, as each individual would be left free to choose his own form of recreation.

The dictatorship would recognise that there is no standing still in human affairs and that both science and economic policy must serve the ends of progress. As Sir J. J. Thomson showed in his presidential address to the Section of Mathematical and Physical Sciences at the centenary meeting of the British Association a few weeks ago, there is too much mass production in university science teaching. Far too many unsuitable men are turned to laboratory work in various branches of research. The best results can be achieved, I am confident, by providing the fullest means for investigation to men of proved power and achievement. I would give a Faraday, a Ross and an Einstein adequate resources and let him choose his own assistants. In this way scientific research and progress would be revitalised with the fire of individual genius. The higher prizes would be offered – not only from the material, but from the social and honorific points of view – for scientific discoveries; while those who showed natural inclinations and promise by original thought and work would be placed in positions where they could carry forward their researches, not only in all the inductive sciences, but in history, literature and economic studies.

From all that has been said it might appear that the necessity for man to face danger and adversity, to develop his mental resources for sudden decisions in the face of unforeseen events, for constant and hard effort, for preparation and foresight might be weakened. Peace, a higher development of contemplation and reflective education and more general possession and variety of goods might, one would think, in the long run sap the foundations from which progress comes. But I maintain, on the contrary, that the twenty years of my dictatorship would go a long way to strengthen these qualities, and change their direction. Instead of having to combat man, to face danger from neighbouring States, instead of making the effort for a painful production of goods, instead of years of spending and service in order to save a little, in order to buy a little, the society I should have prepared (for the super-national States that would take up the continuation of my work) would have learned that the greatest of all conquests, and the greatest of all struggles, and the greatest of all triumphs will be over the forces of nature. Through the constant encouragement of individual effort to overcome the impediment that nature has placed in the way of man's progress a new mentality would be gradually formed. The draining and reclaiming of Africa, of Siberia, of the deserts of Central Asia; the development of the vast sub-Himalayan forests by means intensely more powerful than those now at man's disposal, by even the conquest through science of the coldest North and the warmest areas of the Equator, the qualities now wasted in fratricidal wars would be turned to the preparation of such organisations as would render a retrograde reaction after my twenty years' dictatorship came to an end, if not impossible, at least most improbable.

Recent events have shown how great are the reactions of economic policy upon the welfare of the world. As Dictator I would break down high Tariff walls and promote a real freedom of trade, subject only to the proviso that the circumstances of any given area of production might make it beneficial for the world (and not merely for the country itself) to secure temporary protection for the proper development of a given industry. The uncertainty and speculation which hold the world in thrall so long as the value of goods depends entirely upon the precious metals would be replaced by a fixed unvarying exchange, whereby both gold and silver tokens and paper money (based upon the guarantees of the dictatorship) would balance goods. Private property in the holding of shares would be encouraged; and for purposes of production and development the State might make advances to industrialists at nominal rates. With freedom of trade I would restore the freedom of communication and travel which now suffer from so many post-war restrictions. It would be in accordance with the spirit of the policy I have outlined to reduce the volume of legislation in all countries.

The fact that, owing to scientific discovery, more and more goods can be placed on the market should not lead to such depreciation of general values as to render men workless and poor. On the contrary, money values would be so adjusted to goods as to make it the object of the world State to place at the disposal of each consumer (for very little money value) as large and as varied a quantity of materials as to make a position of leisure possible for him. He would thus benefit from the intellectual and physical advantages of the higher culture brought to his door not only by his proper education in youth, but by courses of lectures, private but voluntary tuition, and intellectual and explanatory series of visits to important cities and the countryside.

You will see that the broad general principles of the exercise of my dictatorship would be to secure the prevention of war, to break down the animosities and barriers to goodwill, to provide scope for both national and individual self-expression, and to seek to give each citizen capacity and opportunity to share in the rich heritage which the human race as a whole and not merely some portions of it, should receive, by reason of the toil, the teaching and the sacrifice of past generations.

And then, when my twenty years' dictatorship was over, I should hope and believe that the better world for which I had prepared would not so easily fall back into the state of spiritual, intellectual, social, political and economic anarchy which has been the fate of mankind up till to-day.

Source: *The Listener*, London, 11 November 1931.
It was a talk broadcast on the British radio.

105

PROVISIONS OF A SETTLEMENT OF THE COMMUNAL PROBLEM REGARDING THE INDIAN CONSTITUTION

A Memorandum for the Round Table Conference

London: 12 November 1931

Safeguards for individuals and communities – inclusion of Muslims and other minorities in the Central Government – separate electorates – fair representation on the Public Services Commission – legislation affecting minority interests – special claims of Muslims, the depressed classes, the Anglo-Indians and the European community.

No person shall for reason for his origin, religion, caste or creed, be prejudiced in any way in regard to public employment, office of power or honour, or with regard to enjoyment of his civic rights and the exercise of any trade or calling.

Statutory safeguards shall be incorporated in the constitution with a view to protect against enactments of the Legislature of discriminatory laws affecting any community.

Full religious liberty, that is, full liberty of belief, worship, observances, propaganda, associations and education, shall be guaranteed to all communities subject to the maintenance of public order and morality.

No person shall merely by change of faith lose any civic right or privilege, or be subject to any penalty.

The right to establish, manage and control, at their own expense, charitable, religious and social institutions, schools and other educational establishments with the right to exercise their religion therein.

The constitution shall embody adequate safeguards for the

protection of religion, culture and personal law, and the promotion of education, language, charitable institutions of the minority communities and for their due share in grants-in-aid given by the State and by the self-governing bodies.

Enjoyment of civic rights by all citizens shall be guaranteed by making any act or omission calculated to prevent full enjoyment an offence punishable by law.

In the formation of Cabinets in the Central Government and Provincial Governments, so far as possible, members belonging to the Mussulman community and other minorities of considerable number shall be included by convention.

There shall be Statutory Departments under the Central and Provincial Governments to protect minority communities and to promote their welfare.

All communities at present enjoying representation in any Legislature through nomination or election shall have representation in all Legislatures through separate electorates and the minorities shall have not less than the proportion set forth in the Annexure but no majority shall be reduced to a minority or even an equality. Provided that after a lapse of ten years it will be open to Muslims in Punjab and Bengal and any minority communities in any other provinces to accept joint electorates, or joint electorates with reservation of seats by the consent of the community concerned [sic]. Similarly after the lapse of ten years it will be open to any minority in the Central Legislature to accept joint electorates with or without reservation of seats with the consent of the community concerned.

With regard to the Depressed Classes no change to joint electorates and reserved seats shall be made until after 20 years' experience of separate electorates and until direct adult suffrage for the community has been established.

In every Province and in connection with the Central Government a Public Services Commission shall be appointed, and the recruitment to the Public Services, except the proportion if any reserved to be filled by nomination by the Governor-General and the Governors, shall be made through such Commission in such a way as to secure a fair representation to the various communities consistently with the considerations of efficiency and the possession of the necessary qualifications. Instructions to the Governor-General and the Governors in the Instrument of Instructions with regard to recruitment shall be embodied to give effect to this principle, and for that purpose – to review period-ically the composition of the Services.

If a Bill is passed which, in the opinion of two-thirds of the members of any Legislature representing a particular community affects their religion or social practice based on religion, or in the case of fundamental rights of the subjects if one-third of the members object, it shall be open to such members to lodge their objection thereto, within a period of one month of the Bill being passed by the House, with the President of the House who shall forward the same to the Governor-General or the Governor, as the case may be, and he shall thereupon suspend the operation of that Bill for one year, upon the expiry of which period he shall remit the said Bill for further consideration by the Legislature.

When such Bill has been further considered by the Legis-lature and the Legislature concerned has refused to revise or modify the Bill so as to meet the objection thereto, the Governor-General or the Governor, as the case may be, may give or withhold his assent to it in the exercise of his discretion, provided, further, that the validity of such Bill may be challenged in the Supreme Court by any two members of the denomination affected thereby on the grounds that it contravenes one of their fundamental rights.

The North-West Frontier Province shall be constituted a Gover-nor's Province on the same footing as other Provinces with due regard to the necessary requirements for the security of the Frontier.

In the formation of the Provincial Legislature the nominations shall not exceed more than 10 per cent of the whole.

Sind shall be separated from the Bombay Presidency and made a Governor's Province similar to and on the same footing as other Provinces in British India.

Mussulman representation in the Central Legislature shall be one-third of the total number of the House, and their represen-tation in the Central Legislature shall not be less than the proportion set forth in the Annexure.

The constitution shall declare invalid any custom or usage by which any penalty or disadvantage or disability is imposed upon or any discrimination is made against any subject of the State in regard to the enjoyment of civic rights on account of Untouch-ability.

Generous treatment in the matter of recruitment to Public

Service and the opening of enlistment in the Police and Military Service.

The Depressed Classes in the Punjab shall have the benefit of the Punjab Land Alienation Act extended to them.

Right of Appeal shall lie to the Governor or Governor-General for redress of prejudicial action or neglect of interest by any Executive Authority.

The Depressed Classes shall have representation not less than set forth in the Annexure.

Generous interpretation of the claims admitted by sub-Committee No. VIII (Services) to the effect that in recognition of the peculiar position of the community special consideration should be given to the claim for public employment, having regard to the maintenance of an adequate standard of living.

The right to administer and control its own educational institutions, i.e., European education, subject to the control of the Minister.

Provisions for generous and adequate grants-in-aid and scholarships on the basis of present grants.

Jury rights equal to those enjoyed by other communities in India unconditionally of proof of legitimacy and descent and the right of accused persons to claim trial by either a European or an Indian jury.

Equal rights and privileges to those enjoyed by Indian-born subjects in all industrial and commercial activities.

The maintenance of existing rights in regard to procedure of criminal trials, and any measure or bill to amend, alter, or modify such a procedure cannot be introduced except with the previous consent of the Governor-General.

Agreed by:

HIS HIGHNESS THE AGA KHAN (Muslims),

DR. AMBEDKAR (Depressed Classes),

RAO BAHADUR PANNIR SELVAM (Christians),

SIR HENRY GIDNEY (Anglo-Indians),

SIR HUBERT CARR (Europeans).

Source: *Indian Round Table Conference (Second Session): 7th. September 1931 – 1st. December 1931*, His Majesty's Stationery Office, London, 1932, Cmd. 3997, pp. 68–73.

The most difficult issue before the Conference was the communal divisions in India. The Minorities Committee was almost all the time in session, but no agreement was in sight. At last, as his contribution to the solution of the problem, Gandhi tabled the Congress scheme for a settlement which was a reproduction of the Nehru Report. This brought all the minorities together, just as the publication of the Nehru Report in 1928 had united all non-Hindu groups against its recommendations. As a counter to the Congress scheme the Muslims, the Untouchables, the Indian Christians, the Anglo-Indians and the Indian Europeans presented a joint statement of claims which, they insisted, must stand or fall as an independent whole. It is generally believed that the Aga Khan was the chief architect of this formula.

The second session of the Round Table Conference lasted from 7 September to 1 December 1931. The delegates who composed the Conference were:

British Delegation
J. Ramsay MacDonald
Lord Sankey
Wedgwood Benn
Arthur Henderson
J. H. Thomas
H. B. Lees Smith
Sir William Jowitt
F. W. Pethick-Lawrence
Lord Snell
Earl Peel
Marquess of Zetland
Viscount Hailsham
Sir Samuel Hoare
Oliver Stanley
Marquess of Reading
Marquess of Lothian
Sir Robert Hamilton
Isaac Foot
H. Graham White

Indian States' Delegation
Maharaja of Alwar
Maharaja Gaekwar of Baroda
Nawab of Bhopal
Maharaja of Bikaner
Maharaja Rana of Dholpur
Maharaja of Jammu and Kashmir
Maharaja of Nawanagar
Maharaja of Patiala
Maharaja of Rewa
Chief Sahib of Sangli
Raja of Korea
Raja of Sarila
Sir Prabhashankar Pattani
Sir Manubhai Mehta
Sardar Sahibzada Sultan Ahmad Khan
Nawab Sir Muhammad Akbar Hydari
Sir Mirza Muhammad Ismail
T. Raghavia
K. N. Haksar

British Indian Delegation
The Aga Khan
Sir C. P. Ramaswami Aiyar
Sir Sayyid Ali Imam
Dr. B. R. Ambedkar
Sirijut Chandradhar Barroah
J. C. Basu
E. C. Benthall
Sir Muhammad Shah Nawaz Khan Bhutto
Sir Hubert Carr
C. Y. Chintamani
Nawab Sir Ahmad Said Khan Chchattari
Sir Maneckji Dadabhoy
Maharajadhiraja of Darbhanga
Mawlawi Muhammad Shafee Daoodi
Dr. S. K. Datta
Raja Sher Muhammad Khan
A. K. Fazlul Haq
M. K. Gandhi
A. H. Ghuznavi
Sir H. A. J. Gidney
Sir Padanji Ginwala
V. V. Giri
Sir Ghulam Husain Hidayatullah
Hafiz Hidayat Husain
Sir Muhammad Iqbal
Rangaswami Iyengar
B. V. Jadhav
M. R. Jayakar
Sir Cowasji Jehangir
Muhammad Ali Jinnah
T. F. Gavin Jones
N. M. Joshi
Dr. Narendra Nath Law
Pandit Madan Mohan Malaviya
Nawab Sir Sayyid Mehr Shah
Sir P. C. Mitter
H. P. Mody
B. S. Moonje
Ramaswami Mudaliar
Mrs. Sarojini Naidu
Raja Narendra Nath
Sayyid Muhammad Padshah
A. T. Pannir Selvam
Raja of Parlikimedi
Sir A. P. Patro
Sahibzada Nawab Sir Abdul Qaiyum
M. Ramachandra Rao
B. Shiva Rao
Sir Sayyid Sultan Ahmad
Sir Tej Bahadur Sapru
Sir Mian Muhammad Shafi

Sardar Sampuran Singh
Srinivasa Sastri
Sir Chimanlal Setalvad
Kanwar Bisheshwar Dayal Seth
Sir Phiroze Sethna
Dr. Shafaat Ahmad Khan
Begum Shah Nawaz
Mawlana Shaukat Ali
M. R. Roy
Rao Bahadur Srinivasan
Mrs. Subbarayan
S. B. Tambe
Sir Purshotamdas Thakurdas
Sardar Ujjal Singh
Sir C. E. Wood
Zafrullah Khan.

106

ANGLO-MUSLIM AMITY

Speech at a Dinner

London: 19 November 1931

Tributes to Sir Tej Bahadur Sapru and the Maharao of Cutch –
relations between Great Britain and the Muslim world.

I am happy to say that there are still men, like Sir Tej Bahadur
Sapru, whom I can claim as representatives not only of Hindu
civilization but of Moslem interest, and who know so much about
Islam, and the Maharao of Cutch, who is a real father to his
Moslem subjects. You have said that England and the Moslem
world have in the past quarrelled; but as the world gets older
and grows up school-boy quarrels are outgrown. So I, for one,
sincerely hope that, with greater maturity, security will come
throughout the world and that we may learn more and more to
understand each other.

Source: *The Times*, London, 21 November 1931.
"The Secretary of State for India made a statement on Anglo-Moslem
relations at a dinner given in his honour at Park Lane Hotel on Thursday night
by Dr. Shafa'at Ahmad Khan, a member of the Moslem Delegation to the
Round-Table Conference. The guests included members of the Conference
belonging to all the delegations.
"The toast of the Secretary of State and Lady Maud Hoare was proposed by
the Aga Khan, who said that Sir Samuel Hoare had won the esteem and
affectionate regard of the delegates.
"Sir Samuel Hoare, in the course of his speech, said:–
" 'Whatever the future may bring to me in politics, however long or short
the period may be that I occupy my present office, I can say I shall always look
back with pleasure to this present period of my life and to the many friendships
that I have been privileged to make with Indians in these last few weeks, not
least among the Moslems. During centuries past the paths of Islam and the
British Empire have crossed; century after century we have been brought into
close contact with each other. We have very often carried those difficulties to
the sword. But, upon the whole, looking back over this long period of many

centuries, I think I may say without fear of contradiction that we have understood each other very well and, in spite of mistakes, it may be on both sides, we have remained very good friends. I assure you that as an Englishman I look back with the most sincere admiration at the great history of Islam during the 1,400 years of its existence; I think of your great record as conquerors, I think of your high standard in the world of art and poetry – your poets, one of the most distinguished of whom is among your delegation to day.

" 'I am glad to think that almost all the causes of difference that may in the past have divided us are now removed. With Turkey we are in the most friendly relations. Going farther towards the East I see there the recreation – for it is no new creation – of the Arab civilization. I am glad to think that during the years I was at the Air Ministry I was able to help in the re-creation of the Arab Army. Passing nearer to India I see the best of relations in existence between the King of Afghanistan and the King-Emperor. I have said enough to show that there is no reason so far as I see that any threatening clouds that may have existed in the past between the British Empire and Islam exist now. I look to you, the representatives of the Moslem world in India, to play an invaluable part in the new India which is to come. I pray that communal differences that may at present hold up so much of the progress that we wish to see in India may be once for all removed. Of one thing I am certain, whatever may be the changes in store, we and the Moslem world have so much in common that we shall always remain friends, and with all your great history behind you you will play a great part in the history of India.' "

"The Aga Khan spoke after Sir Samuel Hoare, and was followed by Sir Tej Bahadur Sapru who said that, knowing '. . . Moslem history and culture as he did, he thought it would be a great mistake to say that the Moslem community in India was an outside body. He did not think that any one of those present, Moslem or Hindu, could look to a future for India when India would be ruled either by Hindus or by Moslems. He wanted every community to be placed in a position of equality one with the other, and no community could feel that it had not an ascertained and definite place under the Constitution and that it had to seek favour at the hands of others.' "

A CALL FOR ANGLO-MUSLIM FRIENDSHIP

Speech to the National League

London: 24 November 1931

Muslim attitudes to Great Britain.

... The Aga Khan said that the Moslems offered the right hand of friendship, and it was for the people of England to decide whether or not they would grasp it. The Moslems desired to live in conditions of amity – self-respecting amity – and on terms of equality of friendship of other peoples and races.

Source: *The Times*, London, 25 November 1931.
These words were said by the Aga Khan at a farewell reception given by the National League at the Hyde Park Hotel in London to the Muslim delegates to the Round Table Conference. Lord Lamington presided. After the Aga Khan's brief speech Sir Ahmed Said, Nawab of Chchattari, said that it was to the mutual advantage of the British Empire and of the Moslems of the world that thoroughly friendly relations should be kept between them. Of 210,000,000 Moslems in the world no fewer than 100,000,000 lived within the confines of the British Empire, which was thus the largest Moslem Power in the world. The Indian Moslems had cemented their relations with the Empire by shedding the blood of their young men during the Great War on the battlefields of Flanders, Palestine, and Iraq.

THE MUSLIM OUTLOOK

Letter to The Times

Antibes: 16 December 1931

Developments in the Muslim world – their influence on the
Muslims of India – nationalism – preservation of Muslim individuality and culture – Muslims are united – All India Muslim League
and All India Muslim Conference should reach the masses – the
Muslim press – provincial autonomy – the next two years.

The position of the Moslems of India calls for examination now
that the second session of the Round-Table Conference has
closed and the statement of the National Government thereon
has been fully debated and approved in both Houses of Parliament. A survey of the kind is the more desirable since India,
unhappily, is faced with the prospect of a revival of the subversive
non-cooperation movement, at least in the United Provinces and
Bengal.

Moslem India is now at the parting of the ways. It cannot be
oblivious to the fact that Moslem countries are undergoing a
process of spiritual and political reconstruction. Islam is in
a ferment, and Moslems all over the world are awake and conscious of the need for adaptation to the requirements of modern
life. It was neither possible nor desirable for the Moslems of
India, kept in touch with modern currents of thought by the
close contact of their country with Great Britain and the Western
world in general, to remain uninfluenced by these new conditions. On the one hand, they are profoundly affected by that
current of nationalism which has swept over India with a
momentum and force that would have seemed impossible a few
years ago. On the other hand, they are conscious of a need which

in the past was but dimly comprehended: that of the preservation of their political individuality and cultural existence.

If Moslem India has not yet attained the level of political knowledge or economic influence which would qualify it to play a leading part in the shaping of the new Constitution, it has made progress at a pace surprising even to those who had formed the most sanguine estimates of its political capacity. We are now a compact and homogeneous body, united by a programme which has brought Moslems of different Provinces and varying interests on to a common platform, and has provided them with an instrument for united political expression.

The All-India Moslem League, founded a quarter of a century ago, did a most useful service by training our young men in political work, and inculcating in them a deep and abiding purpose to assist the development of their community. It focused the attention of the Moslem *intelligentsia* on matters of crucial importance to our people, and developed among them a desire for constitutional advance on sound lines. A later organization, constituted on a different basis and doing useful work, is the All-India Moslem Conference.

Conflict between the two bodies has been avoided hitherto by the good sense, tact, and reasonableness of the leading members of both organizations. But I am confident that it is not in the best interests of the community to maintain two organizations. They should be amalgamated and together form an organization to be called the United Moslem League Conference. I have pressed this view in a manifesto sent to India by the last air mail for publication.

The proposed amalgamation should serve to focus Moslem political thought and concentrate within itself the energy, ability, wealth, and influence of the community throughout India. I have written to my fellow Moslems that we cannot afford to dissipate our energies at a time so critical in our history: that division and disunion may ruin the prospects of a lasting settlement of the claims of Indian Moslems. I may here quote textually from the manifesto:–

Islam in India can exist and advance only if and when all its sons are willing and eager to follow the lead of their political organizations. I am therefore most strongly of the opinion that Moslem leaders should immediately hold a joint meeting of the working committees of the two bodies, frame rules for a common organization, and organize branches in every part of

India. Unless we do this, we shall never be able to achieve what we have been striving so anxiously to realize. So far as the programme is concerned, there is, in my opinion, no material difference in the political purpose of either body.

The amalgamated political organization of which I have written must not be content with a central executive committee. The work of organizing branches should be taken in hand, and every effort should be made to keep in constant touch with the feeling and desires of the masses. In these days of extended franchise, work among the *intelligentsia* is not in itself sufficient. A centre, and possibly two or three centres, should be established for training young men for political work. There is urgent need also for the improvement and extension of the Moslem Press.

I have expressed very decided opinions in the manifesto on a great question of procedure, of which much was heard in the closing weeks of the Round-Table Conference. I have urged that the Moslems, while not abating in any way their desire for Government to implement their pledges regarding federal responsibility, should uphold the absolute necessity for provincial autonomy as an intermediate stage. Provincial autonomy was envisaged in the dispatch of Lord Hardinge's Government on the changes to be announced by the King-Emperor at the Delhi Durbar. The provinces have waited 20 years; they can wait no longer than may be required for the necessary adjustments to be made. Indian Moslems should press for this advance with all the influence at their command. Other political parties in India have been clamouring for it since the early days of the introduction of the Montagu-Chelmsford reforms. It should be emphasized, of course, that there should be no slackening of the measures to which Government is pledged for the establishment of an All-India Federation with central responsibility.

I believe the next two years will be the most critical in the history of India that we of the present generation have known. If Moslems remain solid and well organized, if they act as disciplined soldiers and follow the policy of their main organization with cheerful zeal, they will succeed in maintaining their due position in the Indian body politic, and will play a part in the development of their country that is consonant with their great past and their present importance as by far the largest of the Indian minorities.

888

Source: *The Times*, London, 18 December 1931.
   The letter was written from Antibes, France.

109

A UNITED MUSLIM PARTY IN INDIA

Telegram to Sir Muhammad Yakub

London: 16 December 1931

Muslims cannot afford two organisations – amalgamate Muslim League and All India Muslim Conference – party branches – provincial autonomy.

Muslim India is at the parting of the ways. Islam is in a ferment. The Muslims stand united by the resolutions of the Muslim Conference of 1929, which was a landmark in their political development.

The Muslim League has done and is doing great work in creating political consciousness and it is impossible to exaggerate its work in political development. I have done my best for the Muslims through both organisations and I believe that the Moslems cannot afford two organisations with identical programmes. Conflict between the two organisations has hitherto been avoided by the tact of the leaders. I am convinced that the time has now come for the amalgamation of the two organisations and that amalgamation is absolutely imperative. I suggest that the amalgamated body be called the United League Conference and that it should focus political life by serving real Muslim interests.

Any conflict between the two organisations at this juncture is suicidal and I strongly urge upon the Muslim leaders to hold a joint meeting of the working committees of both bodies with a view to framing rules for a common organisation. Branches should be organised immediately everywhere for carrying on a common programme formulated by leaders. The Muslim Conference resolution is satisfactory and has stood the test of experience.

I hold that the Government must implement its pledges for federal responsibility. The Muslims must urge the introduction of provincial autonomy, since they are convinced that the Provinces cannot wait. This has been advocated by all political parties for the last eight years. There is a need for political training among Muslims in order that all their demands may be secured.

Source: *The Times*, London, 19 December 1931.

Yakub received this telegram from the Aga Khan when he (Yakub) was in Bombay in connection with the work of the Army Retrenchment Committee. The news is datelined Bombay, 17 December. I presume that the telegram was sent by the Aga Khan on 16 December.

110

THE NEED FOR DISARMAMENT

Speech at the Conference for the Reduction and Limitation of Armaments

Geneva: 19 February 1932

The problem of disarmament after the Great War – ideal of peace in India – the Hague Conferences – the First World War and its consequences for India – in spite of hopes for peace, insecurity persists – remove fear – reduce armaments – the army in India – the American example – India's maritime interests – protection of civilian population – the draft convention – consolidate the establishment of peace – Treaty of Locarno – regional fraternity between Canada and USA – French proposals – Soviet and American aloofness from the League – a world authority with its own forces – an international police force and a judicial organization – a series of world conferences – work to be accomplished – desire of the citizens of every country for peace – the League must forge ahead.

Almost all of us here are preoccupied with the pressing problems that have arisen as a consequence of the great war. Among these, the most urgent is that of disarmament, with all that it implies. But let us not forget that for many years before the war this problem was insistent. The general burden of armaments had created alarm among those who were able to look ahead, and widespread dissatisfaction among the vast masses of the populations in all continents and countries – eastern and western alike – and India was no exception.

I am speaking here for many millions of my fellow-countrymen, who place the love of peace and the repudiation of violence among the first of the human virtues. With them, the ideal of peace is no mere economic expedient; it is an element deep-rooted in their very nature. That is the spirit which it is my task to reflect in making what contribution I can to the proceedings of this Conference.

The striving of mankind after some more organic development than the mere clash of nations and States is nothing new. Many of us who are taking part in this Conference will remember the hopes raised in our hearts by the first Peace Conference at The Hague; and we remember the grievous disappointment that followed its meagre results. The second Hague Conference was also a failure and, even from the beginning, little was ever expected from it.

Since then we have had the terrible lessons of the world war. Confined in the first place by historical and other causes to one continent, it gradually spread its devastating effects throughout the world. In distant India, as in Europe, it created a host of mourners and left a legacy of bitter tragedy. Over a million of my fellow-countrymen were called to arms, of whom more than 50,000 laid down their lives. The ravages of war, in its toll of humanity, its social and economic disturbances, have left their mark on India as on the other countries which were drawn into its vortex.

With the coming of peace, new hopes were raised that at last we had learned our lesson; that we could look to a better world in which force would be replaced by disarmament and arbitration, by the adjustment of national differences and difficulties through methods of peaceful co-operation; and that the reign of law was now to be firmly established.

Alas! We have found that armaments still hold sway, and that the feeling of insecurity persists. It is by no means certain that the war to end war has been fought and won.

To-day social and economic conditions throughout the world make it imperative that, unless the fabric of organised human society is to collapse, vigorous steps must be taken forthwith. In this work, the present Conference is called to play a leading part. On the moral side, we must set ourselves to remove the paralysing effects of fear, ill-will and suspicion. On the material side, it is absolutely essential that the non-productive effort devoted to warlike preparations should be reduced to the bare minimum. That minimum has already been stressed by the spokesman of the United States of America. In India, we have constantly borne in mind the underlying principle – namely, the maintenance of forces that shall be no more than adequate to guarantee peace and order on and within her borders.

893

India's own scale of armaments allows no margin for aggressive uses. The size of her forces has to be measured with reference to the vastness of her area and the diversity of her conditions. The fact is so often forgotten that I will venture to recall it here, that the area of India is more than half that of the whole of Europe, and her population nearly one-fifth of that of the entire globe. May I also recall that within India herself more than one-third of the total area is under the jurisdiction of Rulers of the Indian States? Many of these maintain forces of their own, in part for the preservation of the order within the States' boundaries, and to some extent also for co-operation in the task of guaranteeing the defence of India against the possibility of aggression from without. The remoteness of India is my excuse, if I need one, for alluding to these facts.

A happy augury of our proceedings – and I can say, with experience of various conferences, that it is indeed a happy augury – is that we have already at this early stage heard and bent our minds to a number of concrete proposals. This is the more helpful and fortunate since the time for detailed study in commissions of the Conference is fast approaching. Before we met here, expectations ranged between the high hopes of idealists and the scepticism of those who looked for little or no result. The very atmosphere of our meetings and the earnest attention paid on all sides to fruitful suggestions give us confidence that we can now work for positive results. Would anyone have ventured to say three weeks ago that so much practical ground-work could be accomplished within so short a time?

I think I am right in saying that there is already a general body of support for detailed suggestions of the kind that have been put before us by the representative of that great country, the United States of America, and may I say that America's long record of success in combining peace with prosperity is one that fitly entitles her to take the active part she has already taken in our deliberations? I look with hope and confidence to a continuance of her efforts.

Her suggestions are fresh in our minds. In dealing with them, I might seem to be travelling away from the more immediate problems of my country if I refer to the larger questions of naval defence. But I would recall that India is essentially interested in these matters. Her coast-line extends over 5,500 miles – a length comparable perhaps with that of any of the States here represented. Though in the main an agricultural country, she possesses five great centres of industry that, from their situation, are exposed to attack from the sea, and her volume of sea-borne trade is a vital factor in her prosperity. She acknowledges the immeasurable advantages given to her by the protecting power of the British Navy. In saying this, I have in mind not only defence in war but the policing of the seas for the benefit of all who go about their lawful occasions. If not a maritime Power, India has maritime interests that entitle her to share in the discussion of all measures for relieving the burden of naval armaments.

Then, again, we will co-operate to the full in devising means for protecting the civil population against ruthless methods of warfare. Thus we support such proposals as that for the total abolition of the submarine, and of lethal gas and bacteriological warfare, and the use of poison generally.

Again, we would pay special attention to any suggestions for limiting the destructive power of air bombardment, and generally for restricting weapons of warfare which may broadly be classed as aggressive in their purposes. I know well the difficulty of marking off these weapons with any degree of logical precision. But there is already a great body of sentiment which considers that such a distinction can, and demands that it should, be made, and that no merely technical obstacles should be allowed to stand in the way.

To focus discussion on all these matters we have before us the draft Convention. We whole-heartedly recognise the patient thought and work out of which it has been constructed, and we readily accept it as the starting-point of our new activities. Its detailed provisions deserve, and will receive, the closest examination. We shall have to consider whether the principle of budgetary limitation may not provide an invaluable cross-check on the limitation of armaments. We shall have to face the intricacies of the problem fully and frankly. We must meet the difficulty, for instance, of comparing the very different facilities for production that exist in different countries. We must deal with the problem of relating the cost of highly paid members of a voluntary force to that of the lower paid members of a force recruited by conscription. And here let me say, on behalf of my country, that India would welcome anything that can be done to limit the burden of conscription and so to release human energy for the purely peaceful activities for which it was destined.

The authors of the draft Convention, however, themselves urge that it should be supplemented wherever possible by any further constructive proposals that at present lie outside its scope. For the work of peace that we have in view, we must not concentrate a powerful frontal attack on warfare on one or two points only. We must attack warfare all along the line. We must consolidate the establishment of peace. We must make peace invulnerable by the limitation of armaments, by the development of arbitral methods, by each and every means of giving to weak and strong alike an abiding sense of security.

The basis of all security is a foreign policy rooted in mutual goodwill and co-operation; a foreign policy in which no country covets its neighbour's possessions or seeks to infringe its moral and spiritual rights. Strides have already been taken in this direction, notably in the Treaty of Locarno. Those four great statesmen (Briand, Chamberlain, Mussolini and Stresemann), whose names will always be associated with that agreement, have placed not only their own countries, but the whole world, under a lasting debt of gratitude. The spirit of Locarno is, however, no fitful spark. For many years it has governed the relations between the States that compose the two great continents of North and South America – and here the case that comes most readily to the mind of a member of the British Commonwealth of Nations is that of the United States of America and Canada, where the very idea of aggression has been so completely banished that, whatever other calamities may threaten or befall their citizens, the calamity of mutual warfare never enters into their lives or thoughts. May there not still be ample room to develop regional fraternities which could in course of time come to cover the whole globe, to act as a reinforcement to the common instrument that already exists in the League of Nations with all its varied activities?

For shaping the work of future world peace, France, which has so often led the world in brilliant ideas, has put forward far-reaching proposals which have already arrested our attention. We must approach them from two sides. We must bear in mind the practical problems to which they may give rise, the vast and formidable adjustment of machinery that they may involve. But let us not lose sight of the ideal by which they are inspired. Let us keep before us the possibility of a better world organisation, created not for sectional interests or for self-assertion, but for the single purpose of freeing each one of the many millions on this planet from the fear of war and from the burden of guarding against war in time of peace. The ideal, distant though it may be, will, I venture to say, carry an intimate appeal to my own fellow-countrymen, for whom the greatest good is that each individual should go about his daily task in peaceful and ordered co-operation with his neighbour.

I have placed this ideal in the forefront to show the spirit in which I would approach the practical problems underlying these proposals. We shall neither exaggerate nor evade them. For India, the first problem would be how a supreme world authority could be constructed so long as great and powerful countries like the United States of America, the Union of Soviet Socialist Republics and several States which are India's neighbours remain outside the League of Nations.

India has only one desire – to live in goodwill and amity with her neighbours. She is watching with friendly interest the processes to which they are now devoting themselves or readjusting their national and economic life, and she is not unhopeful that in the event they may find themselves able to assume the full rights, duties and responsibilities of Members of the League of Nations.

I will mention briefly some other problems to which the proposals would give rise. For instance, would it be possible to compose an organisation to direct the forces under the command of the world authority? Can it be formed out of the nationals of the various countries; and, if so, how can it function if the international force has at any time to be employed against one of those countries? Again, the central body of the world authority would have to be equipped with the power to take prompt and decisive action. Experience, so far, has unfortunately shown the extreme difficulty of assuring this condition, which nevertheless would be essential to the prestige, and, indeed, the existence, of a world authority possessing the final power to enforce its will upon recalcitrants. Further, the function of the forces maintained by the world authority, if they should ever have to be set in action, will largely be to defend the weaker against the more powerful; yet both will be represented on an equal footing in the League. Here we encounter the thorny question whether decisions would be taken by a majority or by a unanimous vote alone. There is, moreover, the problem – which may be of special interest to India – whether the forces maintained by the world authority should be stationed at some central spot or distributed regionally in areas where the possibility of conflict may have to be taken into account. Beyond all this, the establishment of a world authority would call for a vast and complex adjustment of the manifold provisions of international law. That may well be a stupendous problem, no less than the others I have indicated.

However, I do not wish to dwell on the difficulties. I instance them to show that a vast amount of ground has yet to be traversed before we can confidently say that this, that or the other solution will terminate the problems and perplexities in which we are now living. But once again let us bear in mind what may be implied in the ideal which I have sketched. In the organisation of States, a universal feature is the maintenance of a police force which commands respect just because it embodies the authority of the State; but behind it is a judicial organisation which equally represents that authority. The one is dependent on the other. Both these bodies would have to find a parallel if humanity should work its way towards an all-embracing world organisation. The judiciary would have to draw on the best representatives of the ability of nations, and of mankind. The central authority, acting as a whole, would have to exercise more than merely judicial or advisory functions. If confronted in various areas with vast internal forces of discontent, it might in its ultimate state be called upon to carry out rectifications, re-alignments and re-adjustments in accordance with the wishes of the peoples most vitally concerned. Its duty would be to give effect to those wishes without ill-will and without risk of conflict between the nations. Above all, it should be a living and developing organism and not the dead hand of the past trying to prevent the full and healthy development of the future.

Clearly this ideal will demand all our best thought and our most patient study before it can come near fulfilment. Let us face the facts and agree that only a series of world conferences can lead us to the achievement of this happy end for mankind.

Meanwhile, we must concentrate on the work that lies immediately to our hand. There is no excuse for us to sink back in despair and abandon ourselves to cut-throat competition and the ceaseless rivalry of armaments. Rather we must use and develop to the full the instruments that are already in our hands. In particular, we cannot afford to cast aside the practical results achieved at the cost of such long and careful discussion by the Preparatory Commission. And to look further afield, it is inconceivable that the League of Nations as it now exists, with the immense and worldwide moral prestige that it has already won for itself, should not forge ahead. Let us devote our best energies to this great purpose. Above all, let us seize the occasion which has now called us together. Disarmament in its widest sense – the neutralisation of war, the security and peace of mankind – can and must be taken in hand. Let us go forward with it here and now.

There is a cry going up from the heart of all the peace-loving citizens of every country for the lessening of their military burdens, for a decrease in the financial load which those burdens impose, for the security of civil populations against indiscriminate methods of warfare, and, above all, for security against the very idea of war. It is their growing hope and demand that all the moral authority of the League should be used now and strengthened in every case to prevent aggression and to support and establish the reign of peace, law, arbitration and international goodwill. My countrymen, to whom the cause of peace is sacred since time immemorial, will anxiously follow our endeavours and wholeheartedly pray for their success.

Source: *League of Nations: Conference for the Reduction and Limitation of Armaments: Verbatim Record (Revised) of the Fourteenth Plenary Meeting, Friday, February 19th, 1932, at 10 a.m.*, Geneva, 1932, pp. 2–3.

The Right Honourable Arthur Henderson of Great Britain was in the chair. The first speaker of the day was Mahmoud Fakhry Pasha of Egypt, and he was followed by the Aga Khan; the third and last speaker was M. Castillo Najera of Mexico.

On the Disarmament Conference, as it was generally known, see H. M. Swanwick, *Collective Insecurity*, London, 1937; J. T. Shotwell and Marina Salvin, *Lessons on Security and Disarmament from the History of the League of Nations*, New York, 1949; W. Arnold-Forster, *The Disarmament Conference*, London, 1931; R. E. Dell, *The Geneva Racket, 1920–1939*, London, 1940; Clarence A. Berdahl, "Disarmament and Equality", *Geneva Studies*, April 1932; Norman H. Davis, "Disarmament Conference", *International Conciliation*, December 1932; and Henri Bouché, "La guerre moderne et la sécurité collective", *World Affairs*, September 1938.

111

THE SINO-JAPANESE DISPUTE

Speech at the Special Session of the League of Nations

Geneva: 8 March 1932

The universality of the League and the diversity within it – patience and understanding required for dealing with the Sino-Japanese dispute – history of India's intimate relations with China and Japan – the commercial ties – appeal to both the parties to seek peace – the primary duty of the General Assembly is to mediate – India's hope for a true friendship between China and Japan – abide by the principles of the Covenant of the League.

It has already been said that the universality of the League of Nations is at once its weakness and its strength. We might equally say that its universality creates problems as well as solves them, because the League comprises a diversity which is hard for any individual mind to grasp. That diversity is even more marked in Asia than in Western countries; but the fundamental laws of justice and fair play, forebearance and goodwill apply in the East just as much as in the West. Our need in approaching the grave task before us is, above all, patience and understanding. I come from a country which, like other countries whose representatives have spoken here, has a tradition of friendship with both the Parties to the case that is before the Assembly; but much more than that, China is our good neighbour in the north and in the east, and with her province of Turkestan we have had, since time immemorial, friendly cultural and economic relations. India has behind her a long history of intimate association with China and Japan. The mutual influence of the three countries in religion, in art and in literature has endured since time immemorial. There is a town in my country which I know well and which contains one of the most sacred shrines of Buddhism. There you will find, side by side in common worship, Buddhist pilgrims, not only from Burma, where that great and ancient religion holds firm sway, but from the more distant homes of the Buddhist both in China and Japan.

So too in art and thought, in literature and creative work, we find the living traces of that mutual influence. Just as the Indian Buddha has influenced Chinese and Japanese thought, so the great Confucius has left his living and eternal mark on India. Equally we have been drawn together by the ties of commerce that have grown stronger and more complex with the march of modern civilisation. Memories are long in the East, and India will have memories of all she has given and received in interchange with Further Asia, and cannot now be backward in pressing earnestly the cause of reconciliation in the spirit of the thought which has inspired the three countries alike.

The facts of history give me a platform from which I can rightly and earnestly appeal alike to my friends of China and Japan to seek the road to peace, reconciliation, adjustment and friendship, and to economic and intellectual co-operation in the permanent interests of both. The leaders of China and Japan must realise that, without this friendship and co-operation, the future can never be as happy and as peaceful for either of those great countries. We are here to help them by undertaking the work of mediation and to help to lay the foundation of a surer conciliation for the future.

Mediation is the first duty laid upon this Assembly by the terms of the Covenant. It is true that the Covenant prescribes other courses of action to be followed as circumstances develop, but, if we are faithfully to perform our first duty of friendly mediation, we must not let ourselves be deflected by thoughts of any other duties that may later devolve upon us.

If we do not concentrate with a single mind upon mediation, we shall not only be prejudging the issues; we shall fall into a far greater error. No mediator can hope to succeed unless he sets himself to win and hold the confidence of both parties. He may too easily forfeit their confidence if he allows himself to be influenced by the knowledge that he may later have to form other conclusions. Yet if once the parties lose confidence in him, he will not only have failed completely in his first duty, but will have raised formidable obstacles in the path of further progress.

Therefore I would urge the Assembly, not only to concentrate on its first and vital immediate task of mediation, but to hold fast to the principles which alone can guarantee its success.

Is it too much to ask that the two Parties on their side should co-operate by placing themselves freely in the hands of the mediators, confident that the mediation will be carried out in a spirit of complete fairness and impartiality for the permanent peace and friendship of the Far East?

India hopes earnestly that mediation will be but the first step towards true friendship between China and Japan. To achieve its aim, mediation must be based, not on methods of expediency, but on clear guiding principles. Where else are we to seek these principles but in the Covenant itself, which is the mainspring of all our efforts here? All the signatories have fully weighed and understood the obligations which it lays on them; but that fact is perhaps not sufficiently appreciated. Let us make it clear beyond dispute to the world as well as to ourselves. I gladly support the suggestion made by the representative of the United Kingdom that we should seize the opportunity to reaffirm in all their bearings the fundamental principles that underlie the Covenant. If that suggestion can win united support, we shall lay a sure foundation on which an edifice of lasting peace, friendship and co-operation in the Far East can be constructed.

Source: *League of Nations Official Journal, Special Supplement No. 101: Records of the Special Session of the Assembly Convened in Virtue of Article 15 of the Covenant at the Request of the Chinese Government,* Geneva, Vol. 1, 1932, pp. 76–7.

The speech was made in the fifth meeting of the General Commission on Tuesday, 8 March, at about 4.30 p.m.

On the Sino-Japanese conflict see W. W. Willoughby, *The Sino-Japanese Controversy and the League of Nations,* Baltimore, 1935, and S. R. Smith, *The Manchurian Crisis, 1931–32: A Tragedy in International Relations,* New York, 1948.

THE HINDU–MUSLIM PROBLEM IN INDIA

Letter to The Times

London: 7 June 1932

Recent Hindu–Muslim outbreak in Bombay should not be used as a pretext for stopping constitution-making – causes of recent communal riots – provisional settlement and claims of Muslims and the minority communities – minorities and the civil disobedience campaign – position of Sind – Muslim claim for one-third seats in the federal legislature – representation in the native states – Muslim demands not recent.

In some quarters the recent lamentable Hindu-Moslem outbreak in Bombay has been used as an argument for closing down the work, begun on the appointment of the Simon Commission nearly five years ago, of preparing India for a new Constitution. In other quarters it is suggested that the riots provide one more terrible proof that the realities of the communal problem lie wholly outside any political settlement, by whomsoever devised, and are simply a question of the level of civilization attained by the vast majority of the inhabitants of British India.

Neither view can be accepted by any informed observer of Indian conditions. Intense indignation would sweep through articulate India if the work of Constitution-building were brought to an abrupt end. That Hindu-Moslem differences existed and found occasional manifestation in pre-War days is not to be denied; but such conflicts were infrequent and altogether negligible in comparison with the many sanguinary conflicts of the last few years. These latter have been due largely to the action of the dominant Hindu political organization in endeavouring to force its will upon the Musulmans, in obstructing the Administration, and in raising the standard of civil-disobedience, whereby political ill-will has been created. Moslem citizens who have resisted the tyranny of boycotts and *hartals* have been attacked and have suffered severe loss in trade and property. The so-called "non-violent" civil disobedience cult has spread to urban masses unable to appreciate the subtle distinction between passive and active constraint in imposing duress upon fellow citizens.

The real moral of the unhappy events in Bombay is that of the deteriorating effect of continued uncertainty as to the future. All the world knows that efforts to settle the rival political claims of the communities by agreement have failed; and that his Majesty's Government, at the instance of the Consultative Committee of the Round-Table Conference sitting in Delhi, is pledged to impose a provisional settlement "with no avoidable delay". I am well aware that the preoccupations of the Cabinet at this difficult phase in Empire and international affairs are grave and constant, but I trust that the provisional settlement will be announced at the earliest practicable date so as to allay the growing suspicion and restiveness of minority communities.

Nothing is more obvious than that such an award must meet in a generous spirit the claims of the Moslems and the minorities associated with them for the safeguarding of their rights and interests. These minorities have consistently held aloof from the civil disobedience movement; they have no sympathy with the efforts of some misguided sections to bring about anarchy. The Red Shirt movement is a thing apart, having its roots in local frontier conditions, which it would take too much of your space to expound. The attachment of the minorities to the British connection is unquestioned. They are working not merely in their own interest, but in the interest of law and order, security and stability. It is obvious that no new Constitution can be made a success without Moslem cooperation. In respect to Bengal and the Punjab, the Moslems ask for no more than that their comparatively small numerical majority in these two provinces shall be given due weight, since they will be in an overwhelming minority at the Centre and in no fewer than six other provinces. How is an overwhelming natural majority better than a statutory bare majority under the prevailing conditions?

Two further claims of great importance must be mentioned. The Central Government should undertake responsibility for any deficit in the separated province of Sind. Provision is not made in the rough forecast of the Federal Finance Committee for a subvention to the province, for the reason that it has not yet been established that a deficit exists. The question should be lifted out of the rut of party warfare by a Government announcement of readiness to pay the deficit if one should arise.

Further, the settlement must provide for Moslems to constitute one-third of the British India membership of the Federal Legislature. In claiming such "weightage" the Moslems are asking for less than they agreed to at the Kashmir Conference in respect to the Hindu minority of the State under the proposed Constitutional Reforms, as outlined in your columns of June 1, although their interests are more vital and the percentage of Moslems in British India is much higher than those of the Hindus in Kashmir. In regard to the Moslem share in the allotment of seats to the Indian States, it would be sufficient for the Princes themselves to arrive at a convention whereby a proportion may be secured satisfactory to Moslem India, making it one-third of the whole Federal Legislature.

The allegation that the renewal of civil disobedience has led the Moslems to advance their demands is contrary to the fact. There is nothing in the claims I have outlined which goes a step beyond the resolutions which for years past have secured enthusiastic adoption at the meetings of the main Moslem organizations. But there is a danger of increasing tension so long as the issues are clouded by uncertainty. Nothing can be clearer than that the announcement of a provisional settlement by his Majesty's Government as soon as the necessary material for the purpose is completed is a matter of pressing necessity.

Source: *The Times*, London, 9 June 1932.

The letter is undated, and the place from where it was written not mentioned by the Aga Khan. An interval of two days between its writing and posting and its publication is a reasonable assumption.

TURKEY'S ENTRY INTO THE LEAGUE OF NATIONS

Speech in the General Assembly of the League of Nations

Geneva: 6 July 1932

Welcome to Turkey on behalf of India – historical bonds between India and Turkey – both countries will promote world peace.

I am most happy to support the draft resolution on behalf of the delegation of India. The history of India has been linked for countless centuries with that of Turkey, sometimes in the clash of rivalry, but more often with ties of culture and friendship. We rejoice that these are now to be given lasting form in common membership of the world organisation for peace and goodwill. There is a saying that those who have fought each other hardest make the best friends. We are proving the truth of that saying. We are happy to claim that no bitterness has been left, but rather a feeling of mutual respect on which true friendship can most surely be built.

India thus gives Turkey a triple welcome to the League – as age-long neighbours and co-operators in culture and civilisation, as recent opponents, and now we can say, with confidence, as life-long friends. We hope to march forward together as firm allies in the cause of world peace.

Source: *League of Nations Official Journal, Special Supplement No. 102: Records of the Special Session of the Assembly Convened in Virtue of Article 15 of the Covenant at the Request of the Chinese Government*, Vol. 2, Geneva, 1932, p. 3.

The draft resolution supporting the candidature of Turkey was submitted by Spain and supported by several countries. Its text and sponsors were the following:

ENTRY OF THE TURKISH REPUBLIC INTO THE LEAGUE OF NATIONS: ADOPTION OF THE DRAFT RESOLUTION PROPOSED BY THE DELE-

GATIONS OF ALBANIA, AUSTRALIA, AUSTRIA, THE UNITED KINGDOM, BULGARIA, COLOMBIA, CUBA, CZECHOSLOVAKIA, DENMARK, ESTONIA, FINLAND, FRANCE, GERMANY, GREECE, GUATEMALA, HUNGARY, ITALY, JAPAN, LATVIA, NETHERLANDS, NEW ZEALAND, PANAMA, PERSIA, POLAND, RUMANIA, SPAIN, SWEDEN, SWITZER-LAND, AND YUGOSLAVIA.

The President:
Translation: You will remember that, at our previous meeting on July 1st, the Assembly decided to place on the agenda of its special session a draft resolution submitted by the Spanish delegation, and supported by several other delegations, proposing that the Turkish Republic be invited to become a Member of the League of Nations.

The text of that resolution is as follows:

"The delegations of Albania, Australia, Austria, the United Kingdom, Bulgaria, Colombia, Cuba, Czechoslovakia, Denmark, Estonia, Finland, France, Germany, Greece, Guatemala, Hungary, Italy, Japan, Latvia, Netherlands, New Zealand, Panama, Persia, Poland, Rumania, Spain, Sweden, Switzerland and Yugoslavia,

"Recognising that the Turkish Republic fulfils the general conditions laid down in Article 1 of the Covenant for a State to become a Member of the League of Nations:

"Proposes to the Assembly that the Turkish Republic should be invited to enter the League of Nations and give it the benefit of its valuable co-operation."

In conformity with the decision taken at its last meeting, the Assembly is called upon to examine this proposal.

The Rules of Procedure of the Assembly provide that:

"The Assembly may, in exceptional circumstances, place additional items on the agenda . . ."

In virtue of this provision, you decided last week to place this proposal on the agenda of the present session. Paragraph 4 of Rule 4 continues as follows:

"But all consideration of such items shall, unless otherwise ordered by a two-thirds majority of the Assembly, be postponed until four days after they have been placed on the agenda, and until a committee has reported upon them."

In the first place, therefore, we must know whether the Assembly consents, by a two-thirds majority, to study the proposal immediately, without referring it to a committee for a report.

Since no one objects to this proposal, I consider it adopted unanimously.
The proposal was adopted.

The session was presided over by M. Hymans. The first speaker was Sir Granville Ryrie of Australia who was followed by M. Gwiazdowski of Poland, the Aga Khan of India, Lester of the Irish Free State, M. Pflügl of Austria, M. Dupré of Canada, and M. Restrepo of Colombia. The meeting lasted from 10 to 11.35 a.m.

114

THE WORLD LOOKS TO THE LEAGUE

Speech in the General Assembly of the League of Nations

Geneva: 27 September 1932

Constructive foundations laid by the Disarmament Conference – problem of shaping a convention – world economic depression – solution to meet needs of all countries – hopes from the League – concentration on European problems – the World Economic and Monetary Conference – dispute between China and Japan – dispute between Paraguay and Bolivia – welcome to representatives of Turkey – Iraq's application.

Among the outstanding work of the League during the last year has been the Disarmament Conference, in which I myself have been privileged to take part. We all know the great difficulties which that Conference has had to encounter in undertaking its formidable task, yet we are all confident that, with patience, goodwill and co-operation, these difficulties can be overcome. The Conference has now laid the foundations upon which its constructive works can be raised. It is approaching the most critical part of its labours, the problem of shaping a Convention that shall embody, in the form of definite obligations, the principles laid down in the resolution adopted by the General Commission on July 23rd. On its success may depend nothing less than the peace of the world. That alone should inspire us to go forward whole-heartedly in the supreme endeavour to consolidate peace and disarmament and banish that fear which is the enemy of peace.

But upon the success of the Disarmament Conference depends also, in increasing measure, the prosperity of the world.

The Assembly meets again under the shadow of the economic depression which in the past year has become more intense and

908

presents its problems to-day in a form more urgent and no less baffling than on the occasion of the last Assembly. India, at once a great industrial nation and a great producer of primary products, has not escaped the blast. The crisis is widespread and, with every day that passes, it becomes more evident that no solution will be fruitful which does not embrace the needs of all countries, and that in the co-operation of nations lies the only sure hope of the world's salvation.

The world therefore looks to the League, and it is essential alike for the credit of the League as for the welfare of the world that these hopes should not be disappointed. A propitious beginning has indeed been made at Lausanne, but it is a beginning only, and here again we cannot fail to observe the intimate relation that the problem of peace and goodwill may be found to bear to our economic and financial difficulties.

I need not disguise a certain measure of disappointment, on reviewing the activities of the League in this field during the past year, that the energies of the League, and in particular of its technical organisations, have been concentrated, as it seems to me, perhaps in an undue degree upon the solution of purely European problems. I do not, however, wish to dwell upon this at the moment. The World Economic and Monetary Conference will, I hope, be subject to no such limitation. In that Conference, India hopes to participate, and will make to it, for the general good, such contribution as her position in the sphere of finance, commerce and industry dictates or allows.

The unhappy dispute between China and Japan, which is a matter of such deep concern to us all, must, since the report of the Commission appointed by the Council is not yet before the Assembly, be regarded at this stage as *sub judice*. I will say no more than that the Government and the people of India deeply deplore the relations at present subsisting between these two great Eastern and Asiatic nations, which, whether in their religious, cultural, geographical or commercial aspects, present so many points of contact with India, and they earnestly hope that a solution satisfactory to all parties to the dispute and consistent with the principles to which we are pledged will be found.

We are also unfortunately confronted with a dispute between two other members of our society. I refer to Paraguay and Bolivia. It is the earnest hope of us all that the good offices of the League will lead to a speedy settlement which may redound at once to the credit of the League and to the goodwill and restraint of everybody concerned.

I cannot let this opportunity pass without saying once again how gladly India welcomes the presence of representatives of the Republic of Turkey.

We have also before us the application of the Government of Iraq for admission to the League. The League is a worldwide organisation and it is of first importance that the universality of its obligations, extending to all countries and to both hemispheres, should never be obscured. The admission of each new State to our membership is another milestone on the road to the attainment of that co-operation between all the nations of the world for which we cannot cease to strive, and to which indeed the admission of these two Asiatic States will bring us sensibly nearer.

Source: *League of Nations Official Journal, Special Supplement No. 104: Records of the Thirteenth Ordinary Session of the Assembly, Plenary Meeting, Text of the Debates,* Geneva, 1932, p. 36.

The Assembly met at 4 p.m., under M. Politis, for the general discussion of the report on the Work of the League of Nations since the twelfth session of the Assembly. The Aga Khan was the second speaker after the Right Honourable W. M. Hughes of Australia.

The text of the Aga Khan's speech is also available in *Verbatim Records of the Thirteenth Ordinary Session of the Assembly of the League of Nations, Third Plenary Meeting, Tuesday, September 27th, 1932, at 4 p.m.,* Geneva, 1932, p. 5.

On the League of Nations see C. Howard Ellis, *The Origin, Structure and Working of the League of Nations,* Boston, Mass., 1928; Robert A. Cecil, *A Great Experiment,* London and New York, 1941; Gilbert Murray, *From the League to the United Nations,* London, 1948; John I. Knudson, *A History of the League of Nations,* Atlanta, 1938; E. P. Walters, *A History of the League of Nations,* London, 1960; C. K. Webster and S. Herbert, *The League of Nations in Theory and Practice,* London, 1933; and V. S. Ram and B. Sharma, *India and the League of Nations,* Lucknow, 1932.

115

IRAQ'S ENTRY INTO THE LEAGUE OF NATIONS

Speech in the General Assembly of the League of Nations

Geneva: 3 October 1932

Felicitations on independence – welcome to the League member-ship – old ties with India.

On behalf of the Government and peoples of India, I wish most heartily to congratulate Iraq on her independence and to welcome her entry into the League.

The whole world knows the long and intimate spiritual, cultural and economic relations between India and the lands that to-day form the Kingdom of Iraq. We sincerely hope and pray that a future of great prosperity and peace, worthy of its great history, awaits Iraq as a Member of the League of Nations.

Source: *League of Nations Official Journal, Special Supplement No. 102: Records of the Special Session of the Assembly Convened in Virtue of Article 15 of the Covenant at the Request of the Chinese Government, Vol. 2*, Geneva, 1932, p. 21.
This was the seventh plenary meeting held at 3.30 p.m. The first speaker was Tevfik Rüstü Bey of Turkey, the second M. Bérenger of France, the third the Aga Khan of India, and the fourth M. Foroughi of Persia.

MUSLIMS AND THE THIRD ROUND TABLE CONFERENCE

Telegram to Sir Muhammad Iqbal

London: 12 October 1932

Call for a full session of the All India Muslim Conference – Muslim representation in provinces – instructions to the Muslim delegates to the Round Table Conference – a party to safeguard Muslim interests.

"I think the time has come," His Highness says, "when a full session of the All-India Muslim Conference should be held and, in the permanent interests of the community, give definite instructions to Muslim representatives regarding their attitude in the coming Round Table Conference.

"It should insist upon their taking this opportunity of getting the problem of the separation of Sind finally solved.

"In Bengal, I suggest, attention should be concentrated on reasonable possibilities of Muslims getting a majority by having the seats of labour and landlords allotted in a way which will not exclude Muslims but will make it possible for us to get in practice 51 per cent of the total number of seats as in the case of the Punjab. However forlorn the prospects may be, the door will not be permanently closed to a solution of this problem.

"On general constitutional problems Muslim representatives who are coming to the Round Table Conference should not be left in the lurch but receive reasonable instructions which can be carried out and at the same time safeguard the future of Muslims. It might be advisable tactics to invite the Muslim League leaders to the conference.

"I entirely approve of the idea of running a party essentially for

Muslim interests during the first few elections till constitutional development is further advanced.

"I also expect that you will all work together on the lines of my former cables and get a fair allotment of seats for labour and landlords so that Muslims may also get a chance.

"The next few months are all-important. Please get the leaders to understand this. I am doing my utmost."

Source: *The Civil and Military Gazette*, Lahore, 13 October 1932.

The report said that "a cable containing instructions from him to Muslim leaders in India has been received by Sir Muhammad Iqbal and circulated among members of the All India Muslim Conference." Iqbal was then the current president of the All India Muslim Conference.

117

THE FINANCES OF THE LEAGUE OF NATIONS

Speech in the General Assembly of the League of Nations

Geneva: 17 October 1932

The problem of retrenchment – the financial position of the League demands serious consideration – two options: reduction in salaries or a curtailment of activities – India's views on the solution.

Certain questions of vital importance for the world have this year fallen outside the scope of the Assembly. Nevertheless, one question remained, upon which, if it were to discharge its responsibilities, it was incumbent upon the Assembly to take resolute action. I refer to retrenchment, which the League in common with the rest of the world must face. I do not wish to give countenance to the somewhat alarmist views which have found expression in certain quarters, but the financial position of the League is unquestionably such as to demand its most serious consideration.

I should like to hope that the appeal to those States which are in arrears with their contributions will bear fruit. But, as the delegate for India said in the Fourth Committee, there is no escaping the conclusion that there are only two practicable alternatives before us – either a reduction in salaries on such a scale as to secure really substantial economies, or a curtailment of the activities of the League.

It has now become clear that no decision of the Assembly can secure a reduction of salaries on anything approaching the scale that the situation demands. We must therefore face the alternative, a curtailment of the League's activities. When I use the word "curtailment" I do not mean necessarily an actual cessation of work already undertaken – a desperate expedient to which I do

914

not think we need yet have recourse – but a check in the progressive expansion of the sphere of its undertakings.

I deeply regret that it should be necessary to have recourse to this expedient. Growth is as natural to the League in the early stages of its existence as to the adolescent child, and a check to that development is as unnatural and harmful as is the check to the growth of the child. This all Members of the League will recognise with equal concern.

But there is a special aspect of the question, on which, on behalf of India, I feel I should speak very frankly. I deplore the necessity for any curtailment of the League's activities, but especially do I deplore, from the point of view of India, the failure to secure a reduction of salaries, which would have saved us from that necessity.

I cannot contemplate without anxiety the effect upon opinion in India of the knowledge that, alone of public administrations, the League Secretariat may remain almost unaffected by the universal stringency.

Source: *Verbatim Record of the Thirteenth Ordinary Session of the Assembly of the League of Nations, Twelfth Plenary Meeting, Monday, October 17th, 1932, at 10.30 a.m.,* Geneva, 1932, p. 4.

The Assembly was debating the report of the fourth committee on the financial questions. After a short discussion under the presidentship of M. Politis, the following draft resolutions proposed by the fourth committee were put to the vote and adopted:

I. GENERAL QUESTIONS.

1. The Assembly, in virtue of Article 38 of the Regulations for the Financial Administration of the League of Nations, finally passes the audited accounts of the League of Nations for the thirteenth financial period, ending on December 31st, 1931.

2. The Assembly,
In virtue of Article 17 of the Regulations for the Financial Administration of the League of Nations:
Passes for the financial period 1933 the budget of the League of Nations to the total sum of 33,429,132 gold francs;
And decides that the aforesaid budget shall be published in the Official Journal.

3. The Assembly, in conformity with the recommendation of the Committee on the Allocation of Expenses, fixes at ten the number of units assigned to Turkey in 1933, and at three that assigned to Iraq, in the scale for the allocation of the League's expenditure.

4. The Assembly adopts the conclusions of the various reports of the Supervisory Commission submitted for its consideration, except in regard to the question referred to in Chapter V of the present report.

5. The Assembly appoints to the Supervision Commission for the period ending on December 31st 1935: as regular member, His Excellency M. C.

915

Parra-Pérez; and as substitute members, M. G. de Ottlik and His Excellency M. Jean de Modzelewski.

6. The Assembly adopts the present report of the Fourth Committee.

II. Rationalization and Concentration
of the Services of the Secretariat
and of the International Labour Office.

The Assembly, on the basis, among others, of the proposals submitted to it by the Supervisory Commission, requests the latter to proceed to a detailed study of the possibilities of effective economies in the expenditure of the League of Nations by means of a technical concentration of its activities and by any other means of reorganisation and rationalisation in the services of the Secretariat and of the International Labour Office, on condition, however, that these measures should in no way hamper the essential functions of the League.

The Assembly requests the Governing Body of the International Labour Office, which has already undertaken studies and adopted measures in the direction, to lend its assistance with a view to the study as regards the International Labour Office and its co-operation with the Secretariat.

For the purposes of this examination, the Supervisory Commission may enlist the assistance of special experts.

The Supervisory Commission is requested to submit to the next ordinary session of the Assembly a report on the results of this examination.

It is understood that posts which, as a result of this examination, may be regarded as superfluous may be abolished by the Secretary-General and before the said session.

Nevertheless, in the case of larger readjustments the Secretary-General should first submit the question to the Council for approval.

The Assembly requests the Secretary-General to examine, in each case in which an existing contract comes to an end or a post becomes vacant for any other reason, whether it is possible to postpone the appointment of new officials in order to permit of a detailed examination of the necessity to the League's activities of the duties in question.

III. Reduction of Salaries as regards
Future Contracts.

The Assembly decides that, for a period of two years from October 15th, 1932,

(1) All future contracts, whether contracts for the retention of the services of officials of the Secretariat, the International Labour Office or the Registry of the Permanent Court of International Justice whose appointments expire or contracts with new officials, shall be made on the basis of a 10 per cent reduction of the existing salary scales of the categories of officials in question (such reduction applying also to the increments) and shall provide that the Assembly shall be entitled unilaterally to change the salaries fixed thereby;

(2) Members of the staff of these organisations, on promotion to a higher grade, shall be placed upon rates or scales of salary lower by 10 per cent than those now payable to the grades in question, except that the initial salary payable after such promotion shall not be less than the salary received prior to promotion;

(3) It is understood that the above provisions will apply neither to tem-

porary staff engaged on short-term contracts and serving on rates of pay already reduced, nor to officials who receive a salary equal to, or less than, 6,500 francs per annum.

IV. STAFF PENSIONS FUND.

The Assembly,

Takes note of the report of the Administrative Board of the Staff Pensions Fund for the year 1932;

Sanctions the admission, in accordance with the recommendation of the Board, of eight officials of the Secretariat whose applications for membership are received after December 31st, 1931;

Adopts the report on the valuation of the Fund as submitted by the Fund's consulting actuary;

And decides:

That the assets of the Provident Fund shall be transferred to the Pensions Fund subject to leaving with the Provident Fund a sum in cash equal to the balances of the accounts of its members and an appropriate share of the Death and Invalidity Fund;

That any shortage due to the depreciation of the assets taken over from the Provident Fund shall be amortised, if necessary, after the period of thirty years fixed by Article 7 (b) of the Regulations;

That the contribution of the League to the Pensions Fund for 1933 shall be 9 per cent of the pensionable emoluments of the members of the Fund;

That its contribution in respect of arrears due for service prior to January 1st, 1931, shall be at the same rate of contribution as was fixed for 1931;

That no credit shall be inserted in the budget for 1933 to supplement the contributions paid by officials of branch offices in depreciated currencies;

And that the League's contribution to the amortisation, in accordance with Article 7 (b) of the Regulations, of the deficit in the Pensions Fund due to the application of the Regulations to officials already in the service on January 1st, 1931, shall be 400,000 Swiss francs for 1933.

118

THE NEW CONSTITUTION FOR INDIA

A Statement on the Work of the Round Table Conference

London: 16 November 1932

Indians coming nearer to each other – the new Constitution – India's place among the Dominions.

... His Highness said that, as chairman of the British Indians, he was happy to think that as time had gone on the Indians had drawn nearer to each other. He sincerely hoped and believed that the Constitution they had assisted to frame would be such as would satisfy Indian opinion and would be capable of being worked as a Federal system through the transition stage to the time when India took her full place in the great federation of Dominions which made up the British Empire.

Source: *The Times*, London, 17 November 1932.
This statement was given to *The Times* in London a little before his departure for France after the completion of his work as chairman of the British Indian Delegation to the Joint Select Committee on Indian Constitutional Reform. At Victoria railway station, from where he departed, he was garlanded by A. H. Ghuznavi, a fellow delegate, on behalf of the Orient Club of London, and presented with an address. The address stated that the club was composed of men of all creeds and castes of India and that it greatly appreciated the fact that in the last three years the Aga Khan had combined, for the first time in modern history, Hindus, Muslims, Sikhs and other delegates. In reply, the Aga Khan said that "he looked to his young friends to take their part in the work of building up a better and happier India" (*The Times*, 17 November 1932).
The Aga Khan was scheduled to sail for Bombay on 1 December.

119

ON THE ROAD TO A CONSTITUTION FOR INDIA

Speech at the Third Round Table Conference

London: 23 December 1932

Progress made by the Conference – the unresolved issues – need for future unity – Lord Irwin's declaration of Dominion status – tasks before the British Prime Minister – the road ahead.

Mr. Secretary of State, My Lords and Gentlemen, now we have come to the close of this third session of the Round Table Conference we may congratulate ourselves upon the fact that a great step forward has been taken towards our goal, than which none more difficult or more splendid has ever been envisaged by statesmen. I am confident I speak the general mind when I say that we have come closer together. The three main groups of which the Conference is composed, British public men, representatives of the Princes, and British Indian delegates, have been working on the whole in a businesslike and matter of fact way, a fine example indeed of inter Imperial co-operation in the achievement of a great end. I was going to join my friend, Sir Tej [Bahadur] Sapru, in making an appeal to the representatives of the Princes, and, through them, to the Princes, for an early decision, but the happy speeches made by Sir Akbar Hydari, Sir Manubhai Mehta, Nawab Liaqat Hyat-Khan and Raja Oudh Narain Bisarya have made that unnecessary. In our discussions there have been differences of opinion, but always, in all sections of the Conference and, I am glad to say, including all the British delegates, the good of India as a whole has been the dominant consideration. Some matters of importance, such as the distribution among various sections of representation in the Central Legislature, and other similar questions remain unsettled and

919

must be decided by His Majesty's Government before placing their scheme before the Joint Select Committee. It is our earnest hope that, by such decisions and by the formulation of broad agreements, the remaining differences will be settled and that those who may be called upon to co-operate with the Joint Committee will be united, irrespective of whether they are British, British Indian or States representatives. I should like to see a Round Table Party, a party consisting of all of us who have worked together here, to meet the Joint Select Committee of the two Houses of Parliament. Unity is needed for giving the final touches to the great work of which the foundation stone was laid when Lord Irwin, with the full consent of the Prime Minister, made his historic declaration in respect of Dominion status.

I have heard it said – and I think this point ought to be cleared up once for all – that that declaration of Lord Irwin's was the result of the announcement of 1917. Such an interpretation is a very wrong and misleading reading of history. The declaration of Lord Irwin was inevitable the moment that destiny brought England and India together in the seventeenth and eighteenth centuries. In view of the historic character of the English people and the peoples of India, without some such development their association would be historically meaningless. We find the very seeds of this declaration already in the speeches and writings and thought of Burke and Fox and all the leading statesmen of the late eighteenth century. In India already in the nineties men like Gokhale and Mehta and others with my humble self, were speaking and writing on this subject. Before the first Durbar some of us represented this to Lord Curzon as a happy occasion on which to give an indication of the ideal that should unite the two peoples.

I hope you will pardon me for going into these questions of the past, but I feel that it is necessary to make it clear that this was not a sudden departure from past history. May I say in this connection that while we deeply regret the absence of the Prime Minister, we well understand how pressing and continuous are the demands upon him, particularly in the midst of his great work for world recovery. I am convinced that if he succeeds in his great ambition of helping forward disarmament, peace, and world economic recovery, that will be the shortest cut to bring about the happiest results desired for the general welfare and prosperity of India.

We have had the continued good fortune of the Chairmanship of the Lord Chancellor, to whose courteous patience, sympathy and friendliness in guiding our proceedings we owe no small measure of the harmony that has prevailed. We are fortunate also, most fortunate indeed, in the fact that so large a share in deciding His Majesty's Government's policy has fallen to the present Secretary of State for India. Sir Samuel Hoare [later Lord Templewood] has impressed us deeply by his unswerving loyalty to the Federal idea and to the creation of true Federal units in the autonomous Provinces and in co-operation with the great self-governing States.

I have no doubt that when the Constitution has been framed we shall then consider how to give effect to it. I have also no doubt that the living forces of India will find reasonable and satisfactory methods of procedure. It is as well in politics, while we should always have the goal and object in view, to get over obstacles as we meet them and as we go along, and not unnecessarily tie our own hands in advance. I cannot possibly finish this evening without first of all thanking the English people for all the hospitality which for three consecutive sessions they have shown us. I must also thank the British Secretariat, the India Office staff, the various people associated with the work of this Conference as well as the British Indian Secretariat which has helped us on every occasion, whose work under difficult circumstances I admire and for which I feel most grateful.

We have come now to the close of this stage in the gratifying assurance that we have after all made an advance under the guidance of the Secretary of State towards India's attainment of full political status, and to sincere and devoted co-operation as a partner in the Commonwealth of Nations of which His Majesty the King-Emperor is the Sovereign.

Source: *Indian Round Table Conference (Third Session) (17th November, 1932–24 December, 1932)*, London, 1933, Cmd. 4238, pp. 133–5.

This last session of the conference was attended by the following delegates:

British Delegation
J. Ramsay MacDonald
Lord Sankey
Sir Samuel Hoare
Viscount Hailsham
Sir John Simon
Lord Irwin
J. C. C. Davidson
R. A. Butler
Earl Peel
Earl Winterton
Marquess of Reading
Marquess of Lothian

Indian States' Delegation
Raja of Sarila (small States)
Raja Oudh Narain Bisarya (Bhopal)
Krishnama Chari (Baroda)
Nawab Liaquat Hayat Khan (Patiala)
Wajahat Husain (Kashmir)
Nawab Sir Muhammad Akbar Hydari (Hyderabad and Rewa)
Sir Mirza Muhammad Ismail (Mysore)
Sir Manubhai N. Mehta (Bikaner)
Sir Sukhdeo Prasad (Udaipur, Jaipur and Jodhpur)
D. A. Surve (Kolahpur)
L. F. Rushbrook-Williams (Nawanagar)

British Indian Delegation
The Aga Khan
Dr. B. R. Ambedkar
Sir Hubert Carr
Pandit Nanak Chand
A. H. Ghuznavi
Sir Henry Gidney
Hafiz Hidayat Husain
Sir Muhammad Iqbal
M. R. Jayakar
Sir Cowasji Jehangir
M. N. Joshi
N. C. Kelkar
Raja of Khallikote
Ramaswami Mudaliar
Begum Shah Nawaz
Sir A. P. Patro
Sir Tej Bahadur Sapru
Dr. Shafaat Ahmad Khan
Sardar Tara Singh
Sir Nripendra Nath Sircar
Sir Purshotamdas Thakurdas
Zafrullah Khan

Indian States' Delegation Staff
R. Z. Abbasi (Khairpur)
Sahibzada Mumtaz Ali Khan (Malerkotla)
Pandit Amar Nath Atal (Jaipur)
Sir Richard Chenevix-Trench (Hyderabad)
C. L. Corfield (Rewa)
K. V. Godbole (Phaltan)
C. G. Herbert (Cochin)
M. S. A. Hydari (Hyderabad)
Nawab Mehdi Yar Jang (Hyderabad)
Pandit Ramchandra Kak (Kashmir)
Digvijaya Sinhji of Limbdi (Nawanagar)
Mir Maqbool Mahmood (Patiala and Jhalawar)
K. C. Neogy
Major Pande (Ochcha)

K. M. Panikkar
Pandit P. N. Pathak (Sarila)
Sir Prabhashankar Pattani (Bhavnagar)
G. P. Pillai (Travancore)
B. I. Powar (Kolahpur)
S. Qureshi (Mysore)
Madhava Rao (Mysore)
R. K. Ranadive (Baroda)
C. N. Seddon (Sangli)
R. K. Sorabji (Datia)
J. W. Young (Jodhpur)
B. H. Zaidi (Rampur)

120

WORLD CO-OPERATION AND PEACE

Speech at the Conference for the Reduction and Limitation of Armaments

Geneva: 2 February 1933

Love of peace among Indians – call to the member nations to resolve their differences – goal of security and disarmament – Western superiority in science and invention but not in spirit and morals – Asian countries' appeal to use science for beneficial purposes – the positive effort of co-operation – Ramsay MacDonald's plan for disarmament – the draft convention.

The Aga Khan (India) supported whole-heartedly the appeal from the Prime Minister of the United Kingdom to all parties to the Conference to make what contribution they could towards the promotion of the spirit of peace and the will to pursue peace. At one of the plenary meetings over a year ago, he had ventured to use the following words:—

"I am speaking here for many millions of my fellow-countrymen, who place the love of peace and the repudiation of violence among the first of the human virtues; with them, the ideal of peace is no mere economic expedient; it is an element deep-rooted in their very nature. That is the spirit which it is my task to reflect in making what contribution I can to the proceedings of this Conference."

In the same spirit, he appealed to his fellow-delegates and to the Governments they represented to make the supreme effort called for at the present moment to resolve differences between them and to face the crisis in the deliberations of the Conference with a firm resolution to avert the great risk – indeed, the certainty – of disaster to international relations and to world peace which would be involved in the Conference's failure or even in its adjournment without conclusive results achieved in the twin spheres of security and disarmament.

In making these remarks, he was thinking in particular of the continent of Europe. To-day, in India, and probably in other parts of Asia, all sections of society were convinced that in science and invention, Western culture had reached a far higher standard than Asiatic, but the peoples of Asia did not admit any superiority of the West in the realms of spirit and morals. Nevertheless, the Indians and their friends in Asia were grateful for the practical lessons they had learned from Europe.

They wished to absorb the methods of applied science, with all the benefits they offered to mankind in the mass and in the individual. But they had seen, too, how science and civilization could be shaped to the purposes of warfare and destruction of culture. Could they not fairly appeal to Europe to show a still better way, the way to harmonious co-operation and international unity in the new command of natural forces for the benefit rather than the destruction of fellow-men? Europe must face her responsibility – whether she would go down before history as the one who had taught Asia how to improve the material conditions of men, or how to destroy them.

In the present Conference, and outside it, the theory of insuring against war by armed preparation had been given too prominent a place. To think, to speak, or to act as though war was not only a possibility, but an imminent probability, was the surest way of bringing about that indescribable disaster. Let men talk of peace, let them think in terms of peace, and they would achieve, not only the success of the Conference, but peace as well, that peace which was not merely the absence of war, but a positive effort of co-operation amongst the nations of the world towards a Society of Nations.

With regard to the procedure for attaining the successful issue of the Conference, he fully agreed with Mr. MacDonald that the time had come to face the facts, however unpalatable, and to pass, for the time being, from the study of details in compartments to the consideration of a complete plan of disarmament. He particularly welcomed the plan put forward by Mr. MacDonald because it brought the Conference face to face with concrete proposals based on specific facts and figures, to which delegations must give a definite answer. Further, it had the great merit of bringing together the different issues involved, and seeking an answer to each in relation to the rest. While it was true that the Conference was thus confronted with numerous proposals, not all of which were likely to be acceptable to anyone, the project nevertheless assumed a certain rough balance which made it possible to view it as a whole and which should facilitate a decision on each part thereof. On some such basis as the document before the commission he hoped and believed that common agreement would be possible, if all the nations were determined to approach the problem in a mood of conciliation and compromise. The draft convention represented no more than a first draft of the instrument the signature of which by the representatives of all States would be the happy conclusion of the Conference's work. There might be adjustments which could and must be made in the draft if the legitimate needs of various countries were to be met, in accordance with Article 8 of the Covenant. There were, without doubt, points of detail which would require careful consideration and concerning which he, and no doubt others, would wish to speak in due course. But in its general outline, the draft convention was a document which, on behalf of India, he welcomed most warmly as a means of enabling the delegations to co-ordinate their efforts and to reach an early conclusion of their work.

Source: N. M. Budhwani (ed.), *The Aga Khan and the League of Nations*, Dhoraji, 1938, pp. 39–44.

THE IMPORTANCE OF THE BENGALI MUSLIMS

Message to the Muslims of Bengal

London: 3 June 1933

Importance of the Muslims of Bengal – the state must provide education for all – Muslim representatives are working for the interests of Bengali Muslims.

The importance of Bengal Muslims has only recently come to be fully appreciated. I have always held that the Muslims there are equal in importance for the cause of the Faith that they profess to the Muslims of all the Provinces put together. Bengal Muslims have now a very great opportunity to prove to the world that the efforts we, as their spokesmen, have made in this country have not been in vain and that they are alive to the needs of modern times. Let them take the fullest advantage of the position.

The Bengal Muslims have been maligned as backward in education. Now is the time for them to use the power in the government that the reforms are bound to give them to remove the stigma of being backward in education. Private efforts can never combat illiteracy. In this country the right of every man for a free and useful education is recognised and respected. And in Bengal, too, there must be education by the State for all, and not restricted to those who can afford to pay.

Bengal is the brightest Islamic jewel and it is up to the Bengali Muslim to prove that it is so still, and will continue to be. I have been always keenly interested in the welfare of the Bengali Muslims.

When the Muslims are properly equipped with education, there will be no power that can impede them in their march to their rightful place. The Bengal Muslims, I have found, are hardworking, honest, and sincere. Their backwardness, if there is any, is the result of circumstances and not their fault.

The Bengal Muslims hold the key to the entire Islamic problem. If they can come out successful and strong, the difficulties of the whole of Muslim India will be solved. They are at the far-end of India and theirs is a great responsibility.

We are all bound by our honour not to give any interviews or to divulge in any other way the working of the Joint Select Committee. All I can say is that the Bengal Muslims can rest satisfied that the delegates of the whole of Muslim India are working for them and will not leave any stone unturned to get them their just rights. And yet what use are delegates if the people who are our mainstay do not themselves continually vindicate us by their actions afterwards and now?

Source: *Star of India*, Calcutta, 12 June 1933.
The message formed a part of a lengthy dispatch from the newspaper's "own correspondent" from London. The whole dispatch gives a good contemporary picture of the Aga Khan's popularity and prestige, besides furnishing some minor but little known details about the Aga Khan's life style. For these reasons I reproduce the entire dispatch here.
"It is an unpardonable sin to fall back upon proverbs and hackneyed phrases. And hardly any saying has been worn so threadbare by repetition as the one about some people are born great, some become great and some have greatness thrust upon them.
"And yet I cannot find anything better to describe His Highness the Aga Khan than to say that in his case His Highness has been born great and that he has become great and that greatness has been thrust upon him. It is a unique position that His Highness occupies in the world. His name is a household word in the three Continents. Go to Zanzibar in Africa, lose yourself in the wilds of Turkestan, wander about in the rosy land of Persia, the bright star of Aga Khan's popularity is seen ever shining.
"And this adulation is not confined to the followers of the Aga Khan to whom, of course, he appears in a far more divine light. Many must have pondered over the sway that His Highness has exercised over men of various religious, political and social classes. Many have envied him his wealth, his intelligence, and his learning, but few can wholly account for his eminence through any of these qualities.
"It was not, therefore, in a confident mood that I presented myself to His Highness at the Ritz Hotel. The tempers of smaller men than the Aga Khan are known to be erratic. It was Sadi who said that the princes exalt the humble one day only to abase him the next. Caprice dictates their every act. The thing about the Aga Khan is that though he is a Prince, he is not capricious; though he is wealthy, he is not arrogant or extravagant; though he is [a] religious head, he is not fanatic; though he has power, he meets a humble man on equal terms.
"The Ritz Hotel to the Indians is known as the place where the Aga Khan stays. His Highness has a suite which is permanently associated with his name. As I sat waiting the call to his suite, I could see why it was that His Highness

was so popular with the hotel staff. The porters looked upon him as their special charge, I was almost going to say as a member of their own family. Every mention of his name, and mostly it was in French, was allied with something affectionate, something human.

"The Aga Khan was not just a client staying at the hotel, like so many hundreds of others. He was one who was interested in them and who was as solicitous of their welfare as they were in duty bound to be of his.

" 'The Aga Khan has sent my boy to a college', confides one to me.

" 'The Aga Khan always asks about my wife who has been ill so long', says the other.

"And how many men in much humbler walks of life can find time for such things, or have the inclination to bother about them?

"Treading on silken Persian carpets, my feet sinking into their softness and my heart sinking into my shoes, I left the gorgeous vestibule of the hotel in company with a perky young man, smartly dressed, who called himself a page. The lift went up gracefully. There was no vulgar hurry in that palatial building.

"Still following the gentle hints as to the direction from my confident guide, I found myself lost in the maze of corridors, where hung crystal chandeliers and soft lights peeped in from the concealed lighting system.

"His Highness's suite was ultimately reached and my reverie ended. The charm seemed, however, to grow more potent, and the nearness of His Highness seemed to exude from the place. Unostentatious and simple was the furniture of the place. It was decorated with that care which, by its very simplicity, is all the more impressive. The Islamic severity and austerity was imprinted on the spareness of the rich colours.

"The drawing room in which His Highness received me looked more like the work-room of a busy philosopher than the room of the Prince whose name is to be conjured with in the racing and sporting world. On a table were piled documents and books, and at the moment of my hesitating entrance, I noticed His Highness busy with his correspondence. But that engrossment did not prevent him from rising from his seat and greeting me, true Muslim-wise, with As-Salaam-u-Alaikum, and from his offering me most courteously a seat near him. I was lucky in finding His Highness alone. Not more than a minute had elapsed before I was at my ease and talking to him with a freedom of thought and expression I had not imagined possible.

"As His Highness sat there, I cast a glance at him. Here was a massive head, broad shoulders and a strong frame. He was if anything more serious than at the other occasions I had caught a glimpse of him. And yet in his eyes was a glow of satisfaction as if he had, though after a great deal of effort, at last achieved results that satisfied him. I asked His Highness to give me a message to the Muslims of Bengal."

Then followed the text of the message I have reproduced as the document. The dispatch continued:

"Let no one run away with the idea that His Highness spoke continually. There were pauses; there was emphasis laid; there were my questions and there was, above all, the calm mind of a clear-thinking and wise man behind these words. It shows how much His Highness moves with the times for him to exhibit the true value of journals in modern life [*sic*]. Here in this country one sees so many examples of the might and the power of the press that one wonders how it was ever possible in days gone by to do without newspapers.

"A man who can personally see to his enormous racing studs, write articles and books, deliver speeches, and conduct the affairs of one of the most wealthy communities in India, West Indies, Java, Turkestan, Palestine, Mesopotamia, and his own enormous personal estates, and all of them with great success must be possessed of an exceptionally active brain and a great fund of human sympathy and understanding."

ECONOMIC REVIVAL OF THE MUSLIM WORLD

A Speech to the National League

London: 29 June 1933

The rise and decline of Muslim power – the need for expanding commerce with the Muslim world – improvements in communications – the strategic position of Muslim India – practical suggestions for improving Anglo-Muslim relations.

The Aga Khan pointed out that in the golden age of Islamic civilization, reaching down to the sixteenth century, the Moslem countries were in the van of the world's economic life; but with the discovery of America and of the Cape route to the East, seaborne trade to the Far East and India took the place of trade through the Moslem countries. What could be conveniently called the big Moslem square from Samarkand to Sind and from Egypt to Constantinople diminished in economic importance for the world in general and for Europe in particular. In the end it was almost ignored by the general trend of British and other European commercial enterprise. In the post-War world the old and familiar sources of trade and commerce were proving insufficient. New sources must be found; new economic worlds must be conquered. Fortunately now the opening up of the economically backward Moslem countries was most needed, science had placed at our disposal means and methods by which the end could be achieved. Motor traffic – for which vast quantities of petrol could be found in the very heart of Islamic lands – had made it possible with the development of roads once more to bring commercial prosperity to the farthest interior of these countries. Every part of them would be easy of access by means of the aeroplane, which was taking the place of the camel as "the ship of the desert." The immense importance of this transformation to all concentrated and quick forms of trade was obvious. The world depression, which had shown the insufficiency of markets for West and East alike, would lead every manufacturing country to turn its eyes to this revived field of commercial enterprise.

The Aga Khan went on to show that the political and territorial adjustments following the War have placed Great Britain and her Empire in a peculiarly advantageous position to benefit to the full from these developments. The Moslems of India were happily placed in being the link alike in friendship and in trade between the people of Great Britain on one side and those of Islamic lands on the other, and also between the vast Hindu population of India and the Moslem countries to their west. He desired to place some practical suggestions before his British fellow-subjects for expediting the process of the economic regeneration of Moslem countries and the improvement of British export trade. Might it not be possible for at least some of the younger English people to learn Persian or Arabic or Urdu? In addition to the stimulus knowledge of these languages would give to the mental and spiritual understanding between East and West, the practical and commercial advantage would be great. Anyone with a knowledge of one of these languages could easily familiarize himself with the other two, since they were closely related linguistically. Another need was a supply of commercial travellers suited to the conditions now obtaining. Speaking as one who knew the sentiments of Moslems generally, he could say that they showed not only willingness but anxiety for political, cultural, and, above all, financial, economic, and commercial co-operation with the people of this land.

Source: *The Times*, London, 30 June 1933.

The report of the newspaper gave the background to the speech:

"The contribution Islam may make to the solution of world problems was the subject of addresses at a meeting held at the House of Commons yesterday afternoon. It was arranged by the National League, and was attended by many members of both Houses. Lord Derby was in the chair, and paid a warm tribute to the Aga Khan for his efforts to strengthen the economic links between India and this country."

Mr (later Sir) A. H. Ghuznavi, in supporting the Aga Khan's views said that it could not be doubted that "... the characteristic doctrine of Islam which prohibited the practice of usury by pious Moslems had acted as a brake on the economic progress of Moslem countries. Finance, with its necessary feature of an economic rate of interest, was the life-blood of all economic activities, and the flow of this vital stream had been blocked as far as Moslems themselves were concerned by their religion. But he might be permitted to observe that an approximation on the part of certain Western countries to the Islamic view of interest would greatly facilitate the settlement of the vexed question of War debts."

Dr (later Sir) Shafa'at Ahmed Khan and Chaudhri (later Sir) Muhammad Zafrullah Khan also spoke at the meeting.

COMMERCIAL PROSPECTS IN MUSLIM ASIA

Speech to the National League

London: 2 July 1933

Islam and commerce – economic dominance of Muslim countries up to the 16th century – decline thereafter – post-First World War situation – absence of cheap transport in Muslim countries – consequences of the transport revolution, particularly for trade – new geo-political situation – public debt in Muslim countries – Britain's relations with the Islamic world – pivotal position of Muslims of north-western India – importance of insurance business – the younger Britons working in India should learn Oriental languages – need for an efficient corps of commercial travellers – Muslim desire to co-operate with the British in all fields.

It is perhaps not generally known that our Holy Prophet started life as a trader and merchant, and up to the moment when he received the divine call he was active as one of the leading merchants of Mecca. In numerous passages of the Koran not only the vital importance but the blessedness of commerce, industry, and trade are impressed upon the faithful. Many passages deal with trade by sea and land, with agriculture, with mining, with all the wonders that Nature has placed at the disposal of man for his material comfort and enjoyment.

In the golden age of Islam's civilization, reaching down to the sixteenth century, the Muslim countries were in the van of all that we consider the world's economic life. But a great change came with the discovery of the Americas and the Cape route to the East. Sea-borne trade to the Far East and India replaced trade through the Muslim countries. It developed and became the great source of wealth for the world in general. This process went on with ever-increasing momentum till the outbreak of the Great

War. The vast millions of China and India were brought into touch with the advanced countries of Western Europe and America by direct communication. What can be conveniently called the big Muslim square from Samarkand to Sind and from Egypt to Constantinople diminished in economic importance for the world in general and for Europe in particular. This process went so far that, although here and there attention was paid to those countries by houses that had hereditary and historic connection with them, they were ignored by the general trend of commercial enterprise in Great Britain.

Then came the War with its immediate reaction of fictitious prosperity, but with its present consequences of worldwide depression and economic languor. The old and familiar sources of trade and commerce are proving themselves insufficient to meet the productive activity of the post-war world. New sources must be found; new economic worlds must be conquered. It is fortunate that, now the opening-up of the economically backward Muslim countries is most needed, science has placed at our disposal means and methods by which that end can be achieved. We have only to consider the conditions which have led to the World Economic Conference to see that the fulfilment of the task is imperative for the welfare, not only of Islamic countries, but of the world at large.

One of the main causes of the diminished economic import-ance of Muslim lands before the war was the absence of cheap means of transport. They were essentially land-locked continental areas with – here and there – a window to the sea. Bays and channels and inland seas were rare, if not wholly absent. The great rivers such as the Nile, the Indus, and the Euphrates were far apart and were separated by vast continental areas. When railways came in other countries the initial cost of that form of communication made it difficult, if not impossible, to build and equip sufficient lines to give Islam a due share in the nineteenth century prosperity of the West.

Today new and cheap forms of communication have revolu-tionized the outlook upon the geographical and economical conditions of these undeveloped lands. Motor traffic – for which vast amounts of petrol can be found in the very heart of the land of Islam, in Persia, and Arabia – has made it possible, with the development of roads, once more to bring commercial prosperity to the furthest interior of these countries.

The aeroplane is replacing the camel as "the ship of the desert," and cheap aviation will make every part of these countries easy of access. Overland travel from Europe to the heart of Asia is far quicker, safer, and more convenient, and is held to be much more pleasant and interesting than the sea voyage.

Thus the process started after the sixteenth century is being reversed, and once more the great and populous lands of Eastern and Southern Asia can communicate with Europe over land rather than by sea. The immense importance of this transformation to all concentrated and quick forms of trade is obvious. The world depression, which has shown the insufficiency of markets for West and East alike, will lead every manufacturing country to turn its eyes to this new world of Islam which again, after 400 years, takes its place among the great markets of the world.

Political and territorial adjustments that followed the war have placed Great Britain and her Empire in a peculiarly advantageous position to benefit to the full from these developments. The old bureaucratic Ottoman Empire has been broken up and replaced by the nationalistic States of Iraq and Arabia and by Turkey. Persia has been freed from the political dominance of Russia. The old Empire of the Czars which – with the help of protective tariffs – hoped to dominate the markets of Western Asia with dumped goods has disappeared. The new Communist Socialist Soviet Republic has not so far shaped an industrial and economic system by which it can seriously compete with the export trade of a highly organized and experienced commercial community such as exists in this country.

It may be argued by some of my readers that the countries of Western Asia are poor. But I would point out that since the war there has been a radical change in this respect. Afghanistan has no public debt. The capital debt of Persia is less than the receipts of the Shah's Government in one year from the Anglo-Persian Oil Company. Arabia has no external debt, and in Iraq the debt commitments are very small. The bearing of these facts on the question of trade relations is obvious. The countries I have named are not among the nations which must export goods for the purpose of paying debt and interest charges. Consequently they can buy our British and Indian goods by the mutually beneficial method of exchange of commodities.

Great Britain has today very friendly relations with Egypt, and her moral influence in that part of the world is greater than ever in the past. I think this can be said with equal truth about all Arab lands, and I have every hope that a fair and equitable adjustment of conflicting claims will be made in Palestine. With the new kingdom of Iraq and her ruler this Empire is happily not only on terms of friendship, but of intimate co-operation. There are no serious political differences with Persia or Afghanistan. Of the 80 millions of Indian Muslims a large proportion inhabit the borders of these very States, and thus come within the geographical limits of the solid Muslim economic block to which I have referred. The Muslims of North-Western India can become the great bridge-head for further trade development, economic improvement, and healthy, peaceful, commercial rivalry both for the manufacturers of this country and for the producers of India and Burma.

There used to be a saying when I was young that "trade followed the flag." Today we can go further and say "Trade follows friendship." The Muslims of India are happily placed in being the link alike in friendship and in trade between the people of Great Britain on one side and those of Islamic lands on the other, and also between the vast Hindu population of India and Muslim countries to their west. But this friendship can hardly grow as quickly as the economic needs of the world require today, nor can it be built without a full and complete understanding of each other's mentality.

I desire to place some practical suggestions before you as my British fellow-subjects for expediting the process which we should all welcome. It is urgent because it will go far towards the economic regeneration of Muslim countries on the one hand and the improvement of export trade and employment in this country on the other.

I could give many practical illustrations in respect of the opportunities for business which are available. But I will mention only one of these. We all know how great a place insurance fills in modern business life. The development of this branch of business in South America enured to the benefit of well-established insurance companies in Great Britain and the United States. But it does not seem to be realized that in the Islamic countries to which I have referred the insurance business is non-existent. In all these lands there is hardly a house, or life, or packet of merchandise owned by the inhabitants which has been insured. In this field alone there are enormous possibilities which have never been touched. It is not an over-estimate to put the potential capital value of insurances to be effected in these countries at £200,000,000.

Some years ago it was usual to hear fathers of families of nearly all classes in Britain say that they would like their children to learn Spanish and Portuguese so as to be prepared to take advantage of the economic development of South America then in sight. But the Muslim countries to which I refer have potential wealth and trade possibilities which can favourably compare with those vast regions of South America, the development of which has proved insufficient for the business enterprise of the people of this country. Might it not be possible for at least some of the younger English people to learn Persian, or Arabic, or Urdu? In addition to the stimulus knowledge of these languages would give to mental and spiritual understanding between East and West, the practical and commercial advantages would be great. Incidentally, anyone with a knowledge of one of these languages can easily familiarize himself with the other two, since they are intimately related. As a knowledge of Spanish is necessary for those who go out for trade in South America, so for trade with Islamic countries a knowledge of at least one of the three principal languages there spoken is essential for the realization of all the possibilities.

Another thing which has so far been neglected in Muslim lands (perhaps through the want of cheap and easy communications hitherto) is the supply of commercial travellers suited to the conditions of today. Such men ought to be able to sell the goods that are required and for which markets are needed and, on the other hand, to buy the local goods for this country.

Many of you know the regular commercial traveller on the Continent and in America. I have seen him in wayside inns all over Europe and found him both modest and efficient. A great many not only sell, but also buy, and a number bring back news as to the kind of material needed and the kind of manufacture required. The same methods applied to Muslim countries by an efficient corps of commercial travellers would, I am sure, give most satisfactory results. In this great work the Muslims of India can become coadjutors and partners, they can become the helpmates of their British fellow-subjects of the King as well as of their co-religionists throughout the rest of the Middle and Near East.

There is no wish on our part for exclusiveness, and no jealousy, but an intuitive yearning after an understanding and co-operation for mutual benefit. I know very well the feelings and sentiments not only of my Muslim countrymen, but of Muslims generally. Everywhere they show not only willingness, but a sincere desire for political, cultural, and, above all, financial, economic, and commercial co-operation with the people of this land.

Source: *The Asiatic Review*, London, Vol. 29, pp. 633–7.

The article is based on an address delivered on 2 July 1933 at a meeting of members of both Houses of Parliament and visitors convened by the National League at the House of Commons during the sittings of the Joint Select Committee on Indian Reforms.

The meeting at which this speech was delivered was organized by Miss Margaret Farquharson, the President of the National League, to enable members of the House of Lords and the House of Commons to hear the Muslim delegates to the Joint Select Committee on Indian Constitutional Reform on the subject of an Islamic solution of world problems. Lord Derby presided. The meeting was very well attended. The Aga Khan was the principal speaker.

After the Aga Khan's address, Zafrullah Khan outlined the Islamic principles which brought about an equal distribution of wealth, making millionaires rare but spreading prosperity generally. The purification tax (presumably the *zakat*)helped the rich to give their support to the poor. It was not charity, but the right of the poor to be supported out of the income of the rich, especially as the ultimate source of man's wealth was land and nature's gifts were meant for the whole community. Islam recognized individual effort, but the portions of God's free gifts were fairly divided.

Dr. Shafa'at Ahmad Khan was the next speaker, and he emphasized the stability that Islam brought to a society and also the democracy that it emphasized. Then Sir A. K. Ghuznavi gave a discourse on Islam and the world's economic problems.

Among the Indian Muslims present on the occasion were Malik Sir Umar Hayat Khan Tiwana, Abdullah Yusuf Ali, Nawab Mehdi Yar Jang, and Begum Abbas Ali Baig.

This account of the meeting is taken from the *Star of India* of 17th July 1933, the same date on which it published the Aga Khan's address.

124

THE MAKING OF THE NEW INDIAN CONSTITUTION

Speech at a Reception

London: 24 July 1933

The occasion a source of pride and satisfaction – Indians are united on the historical changes taking place – the experience of British statesmanship – tribute to Sir Samuel Hoare – an appeal to Indians for unity.

The Aga Khan, who was received with hearty cheers, said that there had been no occasion in his life – not even when he won the Derby – on which he could look back with more pride and satisfaction. They heard much, especially from quarters which were slow to recognize the great changes taking place in India, of the differences in that sub-continent of caste, race, creed, language and outlook. But he defied any informed thinker to point to any part of the world of the same vast extent and the scene of so many historical developments in which there was so much essential unity. Nothing could afford stronger proof of that unity than that they had been able to bring their discords into the remarkable measure of harmony which was summed up in the White Paper policy. They had been helped in this task by the experience of British statesmanship, now moving with deliberate purpose toward that proudest day of British destiny of which Macaulay spoke so eloquently a century ago – the day when India would not only seek but secure the management of her own affairs.

As a loyal British subject and a life-long believer in the British connexion, he appealed to the British public to be guided on this great issue by statesmen like Sir Samuel Hoare who in his examination by the Joint Select Committee had shown such mastery of every detail of this complicated issue and whose steady patriotism as an Englishman could not for one moment be questioned. He appealed even more strongly to his own countrymen to set aside jealousies and exclusively sectional aims, and to keep away from the sterile fields of fault-finding and mere destructive criticism. They should make the best use of the powers and responsibilities they were to be given in the confidence that by this means, and when they showed themselves capable of it, India would ultimately attain to the full attributes of a dominion.

Source: *The Times*, London, 25 July 1933.

According to the *Times*' report:

"A reception in honour of the Aga Khan was given at the Dorchester Hotel, Park Lane, yesterday afternoon by all his fellow delegates to the Joint Select Committee on Indian Reforms, and their regard for him was expressed by Sir Akbar Hydari on behalf of the States Delegation, and by Sir Tej Bahadur Sapru on behalf of the British Indian Delegation.

"Sir Akbar Hydari said that it had always been the endeavour of His Highness to adapt communal claims and communal policies to the interests of India as a whole. Though he was the leader of the Moslem Delegation from the first session of the Round Table Conference he was also elected from the beginning Chairman of the entire British Delegation. When committees ceased from troubling and conferences were at rest His Highness was still a most acceptable ambassador of India in this country. His varied interests included not only politics but sport, and it was not too much to say that he could not have done a greater service to India than when he won the Derby. (Cheers.) In the constitutional discussions of the last three years His Highness had played a great, but unobtrusive part. He had not made many speeches, but had been behind the scenes directing with all the wise judgment which he had, all those who had been working for an honourable settlement between England and India in the matter of the future governance of India.

"Sir Tej Bahadur Sapru associated himself with these tributes. He said the Aga Khan's great influence had been used in the direction of moderation of view on matters which had divided one section from another. He exemplified the best culture of both the East and the West.

"There were 26 hosts, and those who accepted invitations were: –

"The Brazilian Ambassador, the Polish Ambassador, the Portuguese Ambassador, the Austrian Minister, the Cuban Minister, the Czechoslovak Minister, the Estonian Minister, the Finnish Minister, the Greek Minister, the Lithuanian Minister, the Paraguayan Minister, the Swiss Minister, the Yugoslav Minister, the Albanian Chargé d'Affaires, the Columbian Chargé d'Affaires, the Danish Chargé d'Affaires, the Persian Chargé d'Affaires, the Peruvian Chargé d'Affaires, General-Major Nyssens, the Archbishop of Canterbury, the Lord Mayor and Lady Mayoress, the Maharajah of Morvi, General Smuts, Prince Aly Khan, Syed Amjad Ali, Mr. and Mrs. Amery, the Duke and Duchess of Atholl, Sir Adrian and the Hon. Lady Baillie.

"Mr. R. B. Bennett, Sir Henry and Lady Betterton, Lord Blanesburgh, Sir Denys and Lady Bray, Mr. and Mrs. R. A. Butler, Major Edward Cadogan, Lady Carr, Sir Austen and Lady Chamberlain, Mrs. Neville Chamberlain, Sir Atul and Lady Chatterjee, Mr. and Mrs. Winston Churchill, Mr. Tom Clarke, Sir Reginald

Craddock, Sir Philip and Lady Dawson, Mr. and the Hon. Mrs. J. C. C. Davidson, the Earl of Derby, the Hon. Violet Douglas-Pennant, Lord and Lady Ebbisham, the Earl and Countess of Ellesmere, Major Elliot, Mr. Isaac Foot, Sir Reginald and Lady Glancy, Sir Padamji and Lady Gunwala, Sir Ernest and Lady Graham-Little, Sir Maurice Gwyer, Mr. H. A. Gwynne, Major and Mrs. G. Lloyd George, Sir Malcolm Harley, Mr. H. Wilson Harris, Sir Dennis and Lady Herbert, Sir Samuel and Lady Maud Hoare, Lady Horridge, Lady Hydari, Lord and Lady Irwin, Sir Henry and Lady Jackson, Mr. and Miss Jinnah, Mr. Morgan Jones, Sir Louis and Lady Kershaw.

"Sir Clement and Lady Kinloch-Cooke, Sir Cecil and Lady Kisch, Lord Leigh, the Marquess and Marchioness of Londonderry, the Marquess of Lothian, Mir and Begum Maqbool Mahmood, Sir Reginald and Lady Mant, Sir Homi Mehta, Lord Mildmay of Plete, Sir Bhupendra Nath Mitra, Mr. H. P. Mody, Lord and Lady Hutchison of Montrose, Colonel Sir Joseph and Lady Nail, Sir Stewart and Lady Patterson, Lady Pattani, Lord and Lady Eustace Percy, the Hon. Mary Pickford, Sir John and Lady Power, Lord Rankeillour, Miss Eleanor Rathbone, the Marquess and Marchioness of Reading, Viscount Sankey and Miss Sankey, Sir Herbert and Lady Samuel, Sir Nairne Stewart-Sandeman, Sir Henry Strakosch, Sir Findlater and the Misses Stewart, Viscount Templetown, Mr. and Mrs. J. H. Thomas, Sir John and Lady Thompson, Sir Richard and Lady Trench, Colonel Nawab Sir Umar Hayat Khan, the Kumara Rajah of Venkatagiri, Mr. and Mrs. Vincent, Sir T. Vijayaraghavacharya, Sir John Wardlow-Milne, Sir Henry and Lady Wheeler, Sir Mohammad Yakub, Sir Hilton and Lady Young, the Marquess and Marchioness of Zetland, and Dr Zia-ud-din Ahmad."

MUSLIMS AND THE MAKING OF THE NEW INDIAN CONSTITUTION

Memorandum Submitted to the Joint Committee on Indian Constitutional Reform by the All India Muslim Conference and the All India Muslim League

London: 1 August 1933

The origins of the All India Muslim League – the Nehru Report of 1928 and the All India Muslim Conference – the resolution of the conference in January 1929 – the White Paper and Muslim rights – no delay in the introduction of provincial autonomy – residuary powers for the provinces – one-third of the seats in the "whole" Lower House for Muslims – Muslim representation in the Upper Chamber – women's franchise – effective representation for labour – powers of the Governor-General and the Governors – law and order and the provinces – Muslim representation in the provinces – women's franchise – representation of special interests – the control of provincial governments over the services – suggestions regarding Baluchistan, Delhi and Ajmere-Merwara – relations between the federation and the provinces – the judiciary – the railway board – Muslim share in the public services – suggestion for a declaration of fundamental rights – resolutions of the All India Muslim Conferences of 1929 and 1933.

1. The political awakening among the Indian Muslims took definite shape in 1906 when a deputation of leading representative Muslims waited on Lord Minto under the leadership of H. H. the Agha Khan in connection with the contemplated reforms which afterwards came to be designated the Minto-Morley Reforms. This was the nucleus from which was formed the influential body known as the All India Muslim League. This body played an important part in the evolution of the Montford

Scheme and generally guided the political policy of the Indian Muslims.

2. The publication of the Nehru report in 1928 caused widespread dissatisfaction amongst the Muslims of India and it was considered desirable to organise all the existing All India Muslim political associations into one compact body representing all shades of Muslim opinion including the Ulama so as to provide a common political platform. This body was named the All India Muslim Conference. Its first meeting was held in Delhi under the presidency of H. H. the Agha Khan and was attended by delegates from all over the country representing all shades of Muslim political thought.

3. The Muslim Conference as well as the Muslim League aim at safeguarding the legitimate rights and interests of the Muslims of India and co-operating with other communities for the political advancement of India. These rights are embodied in the fundamental Resolution of the All India Muslim Conference passed at Delhi on January 1st, 1929. The Muslim attitude towards the system of government to be established in India may be summed up in the following extract from the first paragraph of that Resolution: –

"The only form of government suitable to Indian conditions is the Federal system with complete autonomy and residuary powers vested in the constituent States, the central government having control only of such matters of common interest as may be specifically entrusted to it by the constitution."

4. This Resolution embodies the political programme of the Muslims of India, and the Muslim community has adhered to it in overwhelming strength. In India it is the creed of an overwhelming number of Muslims in every Province, while in England, at the three Round Table Conferences which were held in the years 1930–1932, the Muslim delegates regarded it as the most authoritative and representative expression of Muslim feelings and aspirations.

5. The attitude of the community towards the White Paper will be made perfectly clear by the Resolution passed by the Executive Board of the Conference, held at Delhi on March 26th, 1933.

6. As the White Paper does not embody a number of rights which the Muslims deem to be vital to their political interests, they urge that it should be modified to that extent.

7. The Muslims have consistently discouraged unconstitutional action, and believe in co-operation with all the elements of the Indian population for the purpose of making the new Reforms a success. They think, however, that the scheme outlined in the White Paper will not be a complete success until the Muslim community is assured of those rights which the White Paper has ignored. The Muslims earnestly request His Majesty's Government to modify the White Paper along the lines indicated in the Resolution of the Executive Board of the Conference passed on March 26th, 1933, at Delhi. If the suggestions made in the Resolution are adopted, the Muslim community throughout India will render substantial help in making the new scheme a success, and in heartily working the new Constitution.

8. Copies of the fundamental Resolution of the Conference passed at Delhi on January 1, 1929, and the Resolution of the Executive Board of the Conference on the proposals of His Majesty's Government embodied in the White Paper, passed at Delhi on March 26, 1933, are enclosed herewith.

9. We would lay particular stress on the following points:–

I. – INTRODUCTION OF REFORMS.

There should be no delay in the introduction of Provincial Autonomy. If the pre-requisites for the setting up of Federation as laid down in the White Paper (Introduction 12, 13 and 32) are likely to take a few years, the Muslims are strongly of opinion that Provincial Autonomy should not be held up.

II. – THE FEDERATION OF INDIA.

We feel that there are great difficulties in working out an All-India Federation in which the Indian States must necessarily influence British Indian policy while British India will be precluded from interfering in the internal affairs of the States. We therefore urge that as many subjects as possible should be transferred to the Provinces, and as few retained for the Federal Centre as possible. It should be specifically laid down in the Constitution that the residuary powers should be vested in the Provinces.

III. – FEDERAL LEGISLATURE.

A. – *The Lower Chamber or House of Assembly.*

Muslim representation in the House of Assembly must be effective and adequate. The demand of the Mussalmans for one-third representation in the Central Legislature was made at a time when an All-India Federation comprising both the States and the British Indian Provinces was not within the range of practical politics. When, as at present, it is intended to give considerable representation to the States, one-third of the seats of the British Indian Provinces, if reserved for Muslims, will give them about 22 per cent. of the whole House. In order to rectify this and to give the Muslims their due influence in the Legislature, the Mussalmans should be guaranteed one-third of the total number of seats in the whole House. The seats awarded, namely, 82 out of 250, are even less than one-third of the British Indian seats.

B. – *Upper Chamber or Council of State.*

(i) The election to this Chamber should not be through joint electorates by the method of the single transferable vote, but through separate electorates, the Muslim members of the provincial legislature forming a separate constituency for each Province.

(ii) The Muslims should be specifically guaranteed one-third of the seats of the whole House as in the lower chamber.

(iii) No seats should be filled by nomination.

C. – *Franchise for the Legislature.*

Women should not be given the vote in the right of their husbands.

D. – *Labour Representation.*

We should like to see Labour being effectively represented. Special representation should be given to maritime Labour (Seamen) in as much as maritime shipping and navigation are proposed to be an exclusively federal subject. Similarly inland mariners working on mechanically propelled ships on inland rivers (also proposed to be made an exclusively federal subject) should be given special representation.

E. – *Ministers' Salaries.*

These should be a votable item.

IV. – GOVERNOR-GENERAL'S RELATIONS
WITH THE LEGISLATURE.

There is no reason why the Governor-General should be given the extraordinary power of making Acts, a power which is fundamentally subversive of all principles of responsible government and would have the effect of depriving the elected representatives of the people of their exclusive right to legislate.

V. – Special Responsibilities of the Governor-General and Governors.

It should be clearly laid down in the Constitution that the special powers vested in the Governor-General for safeguarding the financial stability and credit of the Federation and the prevention of commercial discrimination and in the Governors for the latter purpose, should not be used in such a way as to prejudice the growth of Indian commerce and industry, nor should the special powers with regard to peace and tranquillity be used unless there is widespread danger.

VI. – Governors' Provinces.

(a) *Provincial Autonomy.*

The principle of giving full autonomy to all the Provinces having been admitted, it is not necessary to say anything further under this head. But as it has been suggested in some quarters that law and order should be reserved in some Provinces, we would like to stress the extreme inadvisability of making any invidious distinction in this matter, as between the Provinces.

(b) *Governors' Acts.*

Consistently with the principle of provincial autonomy, the provincial legislature alone should have the power of making Acts, and the Governor should have no special powers in that behalf.

VII. – Provincial Legislatures.

(a) *Muslim representation in the Provinces.*

While we realise that the Communal decision has been necessitated by the inability of the communities in India to come to an agreement with each other, and while we are in general agreement with the principles underlying that decision and are prepared to work the Constitution on that basis, we feel it our duty to point out that the Muslims have not been fairly treated.

In the first place, the well-recognised principle that no majority should be reduced to the position of a minority, or even to that of equality, has been departed from in the case of Bengal.

Again, the weightage enjoyed by the Muslims in the Provinces where they are in the minority has been reduced in nearly all cases.

As regards the new province of Orissa, which was not dealt with by the communal decision, the weightage given to Muslims is inadequate and ineffective. Their position ought to be recognised.

(b) *Upper Chambers.*

There should be no Upper Chamber in Bengal. The Legislative Council and public opinion have declared themselves to be emphatically against it.

Further, there should be no nominations in the Upper Chamber.

(c) *Provincial franchise.*

(i) Re Women: The same remarks as in the case of federal franchise. The women should vote in the separate communal electorates of the communities to which they belong.

(ii) Universities: The electorate should consist of the members of the Senate or the Court as the case may be.

(iii) Commerce: Muslim Chambers of Commerce, wherever existing, should form separate electoral units in their respective Provinces.

(iv) Landholders: The electoral qualifications of landholders in Bengal and Bihar should be reduced and instead of there being several single-seated constituencies, there should be only one many-seated constituency for each of the two Provinces, the election taking place by the method of the single transferable vote.

(d) Ministers' salaries should be made votable and the Ministers should be fully responsible to the Legislature, and should hold office only so long as they enjoy the confidence of the House.

(e) *Muslim Ministers.*

There should be at least one Muslim Minister in every Province in which the Muslims are in a minority.

(f) *Control of Provincial Governments over the Services.*

Provincial Governments should have effective control over the existing All-India Service officers, and should have complete control over future All-India Service officers and over all existing and future Provincial and other Services.

(g) *Miscellaneous.*

(i) A substantial measure of Reform should be immediately introduced in Baluchistan.

(ii) Delhi: Delhi as the ancient capital and the present metropolis of India, has a special importance of its own, and this importance is likely to grow more and more. It should have a franchise analogous to the franchise in the Presidency towns.

The one seat allotted to Delhi in the Upper Chamber should go to Muslims and non-Muslims by rotation.

(iii) Ajmere-Merwara: Ajmere-Merwara should, like Delhi, have a Muslim seat in the Lower House by separate election and a Muslim and non-Muslim seat by rotation in the Upper House of the Federal Legislature.

VIII. – RELATIONS BETWEEN THE FEDERATION AND THE UNITS.

(a) Residuary powers should vest in the federating units (see II above).

(b) Division of subjects: As many subjects as possible should be allotted to the Provinces (see II above). With special reference to White Paper, Appendix VI, List I: –

"17. *Shipping and Navigation* on Inland Waterways as regards mechanically propelled vessels" should be entirely a Provincial subject where the operations are confined to a single Province: where more than one Province is concerned this jurisdiction should be concurrent.

49. *Income Tax.* – This should be made a Provincial subject.

50, 51, 52. *Death Duties, Taxes on Mineral Rights, Terminal Taxes, etc.* – These should be allotted to the Provinces from which they are derived, and not merely distributed.

54. *Imposition and Administration of Taxes not otherwise specified in List I or II.* – This should be provincial.

There are some subjects which may, with advantage, be made concurrent, e.g. 14, Inland waterways passing through two or more units, and 15, Maritime shipping.

As regards item No. 2, in List III, Civil Procedure Code, no modification made by the Central Legislature should be enforced in any particular Province unless the Local Legislature of that Province has itself adopted that modification by a vote of the House.

IX. – THE JUDICATURE: HIGH COURTS.

The High Courts should be entirely a Provincial subject. The judges should be appointed by His Majesty on the recommendation of the Governor. There should be no additional judges. Temporary judges may be appointed as may be necessary by the Governor.

Every judge should retire at the age of 60.

The Provincial Legislature and not the Federal Legislature should regulate the powers of superintendance to be exercised by the High Courts over the subordinate judiciary in the Province.

X. – STATUTORY RAILWAY BOARD.

The Railway Board should have an Advisory Body on which all Provinces should be fully represented.

XI. – SERVICES.

Provincial Governments must have full control over all who serve under them. The rights and privileges of the present incumbents of the All-India Services should be guaranteed, but future recruitment for the Provinces should be placed in the hands of the Provinces. If necessary, the minimum qualifications of candidates may be laid down, and they should be recruited by Provincial Public Services Commissions, on the same lines as in England.

While we welcome Indianization, we strongly urge that the Muslims should have a full and adequate share in all grades of the Public Services, including the Army and other forces of the Crown. The inclusion of the large Muslim community under the general heading of Minorities has very much prejudiced the interests of the Muslims, as they have been treated on the same plane as numerically insignificant minorities.

To ensure the due representation of Muslims, we urge that the proportion of Muslims in the Services should reflect their proportion of representation in the several legislative bodies.

We would call special attention to the wholly inadequate representation of Muslims in the All-India Services, particularly the Railways, the Posts and Telegraphs, and the Accounts and Audit Departments. The Muslim employees should, in view of the fact that their rights have frequently been ignored, be accorded the right of being heard through their own recognised Trades Unions and Associations, as they have failed to secure the redress of their grievances through general Trades Unions and Employees' Associations. We ask that specific reference should be made to this matter in the Instruments of Instructions.

XII. – FUNDAMENTAL RIGHTS.

We regret to note that no provision has been made for incorporating in the Constitution Act a declaration of Fundamental

Rights. It is stated (Introduction 75) that "His Majesty's Government see serious objections to giving statutory expression" to large declarations of this kind but no objections have been specified and it is therefore not possible to meet them. It must however be stated that Muslim opinion in India is strong about the necessity of providing proper safeguards for the protection of Muslim religion and culture, education, languages and law, and this can only be ensured if a provision to that effect is embodied in the Constitution Act.

APPENDIX I.

Resolution of the All-India Muslim Conference, Delhi, 1st January, 1929.

"Whereas, in view of India's vast extent, and its ethnological, linguistic, administrative and geographical or territorial divisions, the only form of Government suitable to Indian conditions is a federal system with complete autonomy and residuary powers vested in the constituent States, the Central Government having control only of such matters of common interest as may be specifically entrusted to it by the Constitution;

"And whereas it is essential that no Bill, resolution, motion or amendment regarding inter-communal matters be moved, discussed or passed by any legislature, central or provincial, if a three-fourth majority of the members of either the Hindu or the Muslim community affected thereby in that legislature oppose the introduction, discussion or passing of such Bill, resolution, motion or amendment;

"And whereas the right of Moslems to elect their representatives on the various Indian Legislatures through separate electorates is now the law of the land and Muslims cannot be deprived of that right without their consent;

"And whereas in the conditions existing at present in India and so long as those conditions continue to exist, representation in various Legislatures and other statutory self-governing bodies of Muslims through their own separate electorates is essential in order to bring into existence a really representative democratic Government;

"And whereas as long as Musalmans are not satisfied that their rights and interests are adequately safeguarded in the constitution, they will in no way consent to the establishment of joint electorates, whether with or without conditions;

"And whereas, for the purposes aforesaid, it is essential that

Musalmans should have their due share in the central and provincial cabinets;

"And whereas it is essential that representation of Musalmans in the various legislatures and other statutory self-governing bodies should be based on a plan whereby the Muslim majority in those provinces where Musalmans constitute a majority of population shall in no way be affected and in the provinces in which Musalmans constitute a minority they shall have a representation in no case less than that enjoyed by them under the existing law;

"And whereas representative Muslim gatherings in all provinces in India have unanimously resolved that with a view to provide adequate safeguards for the protection of Muslim interests in India as a whole, Musalmans should have the right of 33 per cent. representation in the Central Legislature and this Conference entirely endorses that demand;

"And whereas on ethnological, linguistic, geographical and administrative grounds the province of Sindh has no affinity whatever with the rest of the Bombay Presidency and its unconditional constitution into a separate province, possessing its own separate legislative and administrative machinery on the same lines as in other provinces of India is essential in the interests of its people, the Hindu minority in Sindh being given adequate and effective representation in excess of their proportion in the population, as may be given to Musalmans in provinces in which they constitute a minority of population;

"And whereas the introduction of constitutional reforms in the N.W.F. Province and Baluchistan along such lines as may be adopted in other provinces of India is essential not only in the interests of those provinces but also of the constitutional advance of India as a whole, the Hindu minorities in those provinces being given adequate and effective representation in excess of their proportion in population, as is given to the Muslim community in provinces in which it constitutes a minority of the population;

"And whereas it is essential in the interests of Indian administration that provision should be made in the constitution giving Muslims their adequate share along with other Indians in all services of the State and on all statutory self-governing bodies, having due regard to the requirements of efficiency;

"And whereas, having regard to the political conditions obtaining in India it is essential that the Indian Constitution should embody adequate safeguards for protection and pro-motion of Muslim education, languages, religion, personal law and Muslim charitable institutions, and for their due share in grants-in-aid;

"And whereas it is essential that the constitution should provide that no change in the Indian constitution shall, after its inauguration, be made by the Central Legislature except with the concurrence of all the States constituting the Indian federation;

"This Conference emphatically declares that no constitution, by whomsoever proposed or devised, will be acceptable to Indian Musalmans unless it conforms with the principles embodied in this resolution."

APPENDIX II.

Resolution No. 11, passed at Delhi on March 26th, 1933. This meeting of the Executive Board of the All-India Muslim Confer-ence expresses its profound disappointment with the schemes of reforms outlined in the White Paper. In the opinion of the Board the said scheme fails to meet the demand of the Muslim community as embodied in the various resolutions of the All-India Muslim Conference.

In view of the extreme dissatisfaction of the Muslim community with the proposals of His Majesty's Government, the Board demands radical changes on the following lines: –

(1) The Provinces should be granted the largest measure of fiscal, administrative and legislative autonomy;

(2) The Governors' powers are excessive and should be cur-tailed.

(3) The provincial Ministers should be fully responsible to the Legislature, and should hold office only so long as they enjoy the confidence of the House.

(4) The provincial Governments should have effective control over imperial and complete control over provincial and other services.

(5) The powers of the Governor-General should be curtailed.

(6) The High Court should be an exclusively provincial subject. The appointment of High Court Judges should be made by His Majesty on the recommendation of the Provincial Governors and of the Provinces in which the High Courts are situated. The provincial legislature (and not the federal legislature as noted in section 175 of the White Paper) should regulate the power of

superintendence exercised by the High Court over the subordinate courts in the Province.

(7) No weightage or other discriminatory privileges should be given to the Indian States.

(8) Fundamental safeguards for the protection of personal law, education and culture of the Muslims should be incorporated in the constitution.

(9) Provision should be made for the effective representation of the Muslims in the public services of the country and the army. Effective steps should be taken to Indianize the army within a fixed period.

(10) As the Muslims claim one-third representation of the whole House in the Upper House of the Federal Legislature, and have been definitely promised one-third of the British Indian share of the seats in the House and cannot see any effective way of securing sufficient seats among the representatives of the States to make up their proportion to one-third of the whole House, it is their considered opinion that slightly increased proportion of their seats in the British Indian share over the one-third is essential.

The Muslims further disapprove of the principle of joint electorate in the elections to the Upper House of the Federal Legislature, and urge the adoption of separate electorate by direct method.

(11) A substantial measure of reforms should be immediately introduced in Baluchistan.

(12) The one seat allotted to Delhi in the Upper House should go to the Muslims and Non-Muslims by rotation.

(13) The population of Delhi and Ajmere being equal, Ajmere should have the same measure of representation in both Houses of the Federal Legislature as Delhi, and such representation should be regulated by the same principle as in Delhi, and when one is represented by a Muslim the other should be represented by a Non-Muslim in the Upper House.

(14) That inasmuch as His Majesty's Government's decision promised to give Muslims of Bihar and Orissa 42 seats out of 175 seats, i.e. 24 per cent. of whole House by separate electorates. This meeting of the Executive Board demands that the proportion then fixed should on no account be changed and the seats should be so allotted to Muslims in the Province of Bihar

and Orissa in both the Provincial Legislatures that the total proportion of 24 per cent. should not be disturbed.

(15) That representation awarded to commerce should include the Muslim Chamber of Commerce of Bengal and Bihar as electoral units in their respective Provinces.

(16) That the electoral qualifications of the landholders constituency should be reduced in Bengal and Bihar and single-seated constituencies should be changed into one multi-seated constituency in each Province by single transferable votes.

(17) The Indian States should be given no privileges of competing for All-India Service such as the I.C.S., I.M.S. and commissions in the Indian Army until the States agree to extend the same privileges to British Indian subjects in their territories.

Source: *Joint Committee on Indian Constitutional Reform (Session 1932–33), Volume 2 C, Minutes of Evidence Together with Appendix D*, Government of Great Britain, London, 1934, Parliamentary Paper H.L. 79 (II C), H.C. 112 (II C), pp. 1475–81.

The Committee met at 10.30 a.m. with the following members present:

Lord Archbishop of Canterbury.
Marquess of Salisbury.
Marquess of Zetland.
Marquess of Linlithgow.
Marquess of Reading.
Earl Peel.
Lord Ker (Marquess of Lothian).
Lord Irwin.
Lord Rankeillour.
Lord Hutchison of Montrose.
Major Attlee.
Mr. Butler.
Major Cadogan.
Sir Austen Chamberlain.
Mr. Cocks.
Sir Reginald Craddock.
Mr. Davidson.
Mr. Isaac Foot.
Sir Joseph Nall.
Lord Eustace Percy.
Miss Pickford.

The following Indian Delegates were also present:–

Indian States Representatives.
Rao Bahadur Sir Krishnama Chari.
Nawab Sir Liaqat Hayat-Khan.
Sir Akbar Hydari.
Sir Mirza M. Ismail.
Sir Manubhai N. Mehta.
Mr. Y. Thombare.

British Indian Representatives.
His Highness The Aga Khan.
Dr. B. R. Ambedkar.
Sir Hubert Carr.
Mr. A. H. Ghuznavi.
Lt.-Col. Sir H. Gidney.
Sir Hari Singh Gour.
Mr. M. R. Jayaker.
Mr. N. M. Joshi.
Begum Shah Nawaz.
Sir A. P. Patro.
Sir Abdur Rahim.
Sir Phiroze Sethna.
Dr. Shafa'at Ahmad Khan.
Sardar Buta Singh.
Sir N. N. Sircar.
Sir Purshotamdas Thakurdas.
Mr. Zafrulla Khan.

The Marquess of Linlithgow in the Chair.

On the same day the All India Muslim League and the All India Muslim Conference submitted this memorandum, and the following gentlemen representing the two organizations were called in and examined: Abdullah Yusuf Ali, c.b.e., Sir Muhammad Yakub, Kt., m.l.a., H. S. Suhrawardy, m.l.c., Dr Khalifa Shujauddin, ll.d., and Khan Sahib Haji Rashid Ahmad.

I have included this memorandum among the works of the Aga Khan because, as the late Sir Muhammad Zafrullah Khan told me in a conversation in 1967 in London, His Highness virtually dictated the broad principles on which it was drafted, and also because he had been, in his time, the founder and president of both the parties submitting the document.

The Times of 7 December 1933 carried a full summary of the memorandum (the White Paper in which it appeared was released on 6 December).

126

IN DEFENCE OF THE INDIAN WHITE PAPER

Interrogation of Winston Spencer Churchill in the Joint Committee on Indian Constitutional Reform

London: 24 October 1933

The White Paper scheme a result of discussions at the Round Table Conferences and consultations between representatives of Indian opinion and the British – those behind the proposals are responsible to millions of people in India – the main goal of the scheme – the autonomy of the provinces – the federal system – the attitude of the Princes.

15,024. Mr. Churchill, you are aware that the White Paper Scheme is the result, not only of many discussions at the Round Table Conferences between the Princes, their Representatives, Indians of all sections of opinion, Hindus of every important school of thought, the official representatives of the Muslims, who have behind them the overwhelming support of the Muslim Community, the Sikhs, and the Representatives of the Depressed Classes and Labour, but that the White Paper Scheme has come out of a long series of public and private discussions between them, the Secretary of State, the Prime Minister, the Lord Chancellor, ex-Viceroys like Lord Irwin and Lord Reading, and that the authorship of this White Paper is really the result of the experience of people drawn from all conceivable elements that could represent India. On the other hand, your scheme has behind it for authorship a small number probably of experts whose knowledge of India is not up-to-date, none of whom has had recent experience of responsibility, and yourself who, in the midst of your many very important activities and so on, could not have given except very slight attention to it; and you have what I may call a cursory knowledge. Now of the two schemes, if you were alone asked by Parliament as a responsible individual which one you were going to recommend, which one would you recommend? – I do not think this matter can be settled at all by trying to pile up expert authority on one side or the other. This is a decision which is sought from the British Parliament, and the British Parliament does not consist of experts upon India; a great many of them have not had the opportunity of serving out there or of serving in high positions. It is a decision which is asked from the Sovereign Assembly under the Crown in this country, and I do not think it is to be settled apart from a free use by the Members of both Houses of their own good judgment. They have to weigh the different assertions that are made by the experts and high authorities on the one hand or on the other, and I certainly do not feel myself bound because two ex-Viceroys are in favour of the scheme to suspend the discharge of my duty as a Member of the House of Commons.

15,025. You have not really understood my question, I think, Mr. Churchill. Those behind the White Paper Proposals are not merely experts: they are, many of them, responsible to millions of people in India. The Princes are not experts. They are rulers of vast States, and they think that this scheme is likely to work as well as any scheme can work for India, as far as we can see. That is the Indian side of it, and they have convinced responsible British opinion. Are you ready to tell Parliament that this scheme has not any support behind it other than that of two ex-Viceroys? – If that argument is valid, why is the Joint Select Committee sitting?

15,026. The Joint Select Committee is sitting to sift it as far as it can, but it must pay some attention to the fact that the authorship of a scheme for a Constitution for India should have some Indian responsibility behind it as well? – I think all opinion should be weighed as far as possible, but I am not prepared in any way to admit that because these consultations took place at the Round Table Conference and because a lot of discussions have gone on between the Secretary of State and various gentlemen and notabilities and Princes, the function of Parliament is in any way impaired or the responsibility of Parliament in any way diminished, and I, of course, base myself upon the recent statement of the Secretary of State that we are uncommitted.

15,027. Would you say that it would be a good thing for India to have a Constitution in the authorship of which no important section of Indian opinion or Princes or classes or communities took any kind of moral responsibility? – It would not be a good thing, but neither would it be a good thing to establish prematurely a Federal system before the units which are to compose it have come into being and without regard to the solution of a great many difficulties attendant upon it. When I am told that there is a great body of Indian opinion gathered behind this scheme it is quite true that a large number of Indian gentlemen and statesmen are moving along in support of the scheme, but with very different purposes and with a very different voice, and a very large number of those who accept this scheme for the time being accept it only as an instrument of machinery to lead to something very much larger.

15,028. That is inevitable, of course. No scheme that had not the possibilities of a future development in it would be accepted. This scheme has those possibilities; it is not being accepted. The kind of people who are advocating this are not the people who want to use this only as a step forward for agitation. It is only a scheme out of which the country's commercial and agricultural prosperity could be developed further and general peace gained during the next decade? – I must take exception to my friend the Aga Khan's use of the expression that I have a scheme – that it is my scheme.

15,029. The alternative scheme? – The basis of the proposals with which I associate myself is the Report of the Statutory Commission which did not establish the Federal system at the Centre, but which did in fact, under some reservations, propose to transfer Law and Order in the Provinces. All I do is that I suggest that that transference should be effected only in the manner which I have ventured to define. Then there was this additional point about inspectorates which is intended to be helpful and to co-ordinate the working of the transferred services in the different Provinces, but that does not constitute a scheme at all. In the main, all that I have said rests entirely within the scope of the recommendations of the Statutory Commission, and so you have not a right to brush it aside and say these are only the opinions of one man, with a few aged Indian administrators whom he may have consulted. On the contrary, this is a Commission of Parliament appointed for the purpose; it went to India for three years, and saw everybody, on which the three Parties were represented, and on which the three Parties gave a unanimous Report. You cannot brush it aside like that.

15,030. There is another question. According to the scheme of which you approve there will be autonomous Provinces, will there not? – Yes.

15,031. Do you think that the present Centre, as it is now, with a sort of isolated Viceroy and Executive drawn half and half from Indian and from British officials, with a huge Assembly, always criticising, without responsibility, is a better Centre to meet these Provinces than a Federal Centre in which the Princes and all the important sections of Indian thought and opinion are represented and who are behind the Viceroy and in which he has got a much larger influence? – I have not the slightest doubt that the proposals at the present time to establish a Federal system for India will be fertile of friction and in inconvenience and that the existing system, in spite of its disadvantages is far more likely to enable us to get through this period, when the Provinces are being brought into existence as autonomous entities. It would be, in my opinion, a most dangerous thing to introduce a principle of dyarchy at the Centre and summit of India at this time. Surely it would be only reasonable to carry out one great forward step in the Provinces by itself and await the result of that step before the Federal solution is taken.

15,032. You think that the Government of India as at present constituted will be better able to deal with autonomous Provinces than a Government which has behind it the support of the Princes and the new elements that are being brought in? – You say the support of the Princes. I do not wish to go into that in very great detail, but I have heard a great deal one way and another about the support of the Princes and about misgivings on the part of the Princes and about pressure put upon the Princes. I have heard a great deal about that, and I am not at all prepared to assume that there is a fierce demand on the part of the Princes of India for this departure. When this matter comes to be debated in Parliament we shall then have a proposal before us, no doubt for a Federal Constitution. It will be presented in the precise language of a Statute. I have not the slightest doubt that it will be possible to apply to that proposal far more damaging criticisms than any that can be laid against the present system which, with all its defects, is at the present moment functioning and working.

15,033. Without the autonomous Provinces. With regard to the Princes, I will leave it to my friends here, but do you know of any individual Prince who would give way to pressure of that kind and would not speak up? Do you happen to think that there are any among your acquaintances who would do anything like that? – I was very much pained to see that the Jam Sahib was silenced by the Viceroy when he was unfolding arguments which seemed to me very right and worthy to be stated as a contribution to this discussion. It grieved me very much, and I may say the grief was widespread throughout this country – especially, when that episode was so swiftly succeeded by his untimely death.

The *Aga Khan.*] I do not wish to ask anything more.

Sir *Samuel Hoare.*] Perhaps I might clear up the misunderstanding that Mr. Churchill's last observation may leave in the minds of some Members of the Committee. The incident to which he referred was very different in actual practice from what he actually seems to think.

The *Aga Khan.*] Hear, hear!

Sir *Samuel Hoare.*] The Jam Sahib was under the impression that it was the moment at which to make a speech about Federation. That was not the case. The Viceroy stopped him because the particular speech was obviously out of order upon the occasion, which was the reception of the report of the Princes delegation at the Round Table Conference. I am not disclosing any confidence when I say that the Jam Sahib himself fully realised that fact and afterwards assured the Viceroy that he fully accepted his ruling, and he thought that in the circumstances it was a very good ruling.

Mr. *Isaac Foot.*] Is not it right, too, that at the Round Table Conference the Jam Sahib was one of the strongest advocates of the Federal system?

Sir *Samuel Hoare.*] Certainly.

Witness.] But, after all, this speech which was not delivered on that occasion because it was out of order had already been published, and no one who reads it can possibly contend that it did not contain very grave words of warning, falling from one of the best known of the Princes of India, and I believe at that time the President – is it not so? – of the Princes Association.

Source: *Joint Committee on Indian Constitutional Reform (Session 1932–33), Volume 2 C: Minutes of Evidence Given Before the Joint Committee on Indian Constitutional Reform (Questions 8,681–11,209, 12,055–12,720, 13,549–13,691, 14,400–15,362, 15,777–17,339) and Before Sub-Committees A, B, C and D of the Joint Committee Together with Appendix D,* His Majesty's Stationery Office, London, 1934, pp. 1842–5. Parliamentary Paper H.L. 79 (II C), H.C. 112 (II C).

127

INDIAN PROPOSALS FOR THE NEW CONSTITUTIONAL ORDER

Joint Memorandum Submitted to the Joint Committee on Indian Constitutional Reform by the British Indian Delegation

London: 17 November 1933

The declaration of policy made by the British Prime Minister at the end of the First Round Table Conference – the preamble to the Constitution Act should mention the ultimate goal of "dominion status" – a definite date for the inauguration of the federation – the psychological effect of such a provision – give greater opportunities to Indians to influence the army policy – suggestions for achieving the goal – the provision of more than two counsellors for the three Reserved Departments not necessary – the debt position of India – India's contribution to the First World War – there should be no severe financial restrictions on the Indian Legislature – modifications suggested for the financial section of the White Paper – freedom to safeguard India's commercial interests – the question of tariffs – the prevention of unfair discrimination against British business and at the same time the Indian desire to develop indigenous industries – suggestions for the modification of the White Paper – the Constitution should provide for the establishment of a railway board – proposals regarding the Lower Federal Chamber – direct elections – general approval for the scheme of provincial responsibility – specific suggestions for modifications to the White Paper – observations on federal finance – objections in India to the scheme in the White Paper for recruitment to the Indian Civil Service and the India Police – specific suggestions – the role of the Governor in protecting the rights and privileges of officers – the powers of the ministers – appointment of governors of the provinces – the principle of automatic growth of the Constitution – transfer of responsibility to Indians should be continuous.

PART I.

INTRODUCTION.

1. The Memorandum in which we submit our views on the various issues raised by the White Paper scheme has been prepared in two sections. In the first section we have stated the principal modifications that should in our opinion be made in the scheme in order to satisfy moderate public opinion in India and have indicated very briefly the reasons justifying them. In the second section we have attempted to answer the chief criticisms directed against the basic principles of the White Paper proposals.

We have throughout kept in view the declaration of policy made by the Prime Minister at the end of the first Round Table Conference on behalf of the last Labour Government and endorsed by the present National Government and the present Parliament. The salient sentences of that declaration are as follows:–

> "The view of His Majesty's Government is that responsibility for the government of India should be placed upon Legislatures, Central and Provincial, with such provisions as may be necessary to guarantee, during a period of transition, the observance of certain obligations and to meet other special circumstances, and also with such guarantees as are required by minorities to protect their political liberties and rights.
>
> In such statutory safeguards as may be made for meeting the needs of the transitional period, it will be a primary concern of His Majesty's Government to see that the reserved powers are so framed and exercised as not to prejudice the advance of India through the new constitution to full responsibility for her own government."

It is in the light of this declaration of policy that we have examined the White Paper proposals. The modifications we suggest do not affect the basic structure of the scheme. They are intended to ensure that the reserved powers are so framed and exercised as not "to prejudice the advance of India to full responsibility", and to secure that the period of transition is not indefinitely extended.

Preamble to the Act.

2. We consider that the preamble to the Constitution Act should contain a definite statement that the "natural issue of

India's constitutional progress is the attainment of Dominion Status". This declaration, as Lord Irwin explained in the announcement he made on behalf of His Majesty's Government on October 31, 1929, is in accordance with previous public declarations of Ministers of the Crown and also with the directions given in the Instrument of Instructions by His Majesty the King "that it is His will and pleasure that the plan laid down by Parliament in 1919 should be the means by which British India may attain its due place among His dominions." That the expression "Dominion Status" was not used in a ceremonial or honorific sense is clear from the following extract from the message conveyed to India by His Majesty the King-Emperor, through H.R.H. the Duke of Connaught, on the solemn occasion of the inauguration of the new Central Legislatures in 1921:–

"For years, it may be for generations, patriotic and loyal Indians have dreamed of *Swaraj* for their Motherland. To-day you have beginnings of *Swaraj* within my Empire, and widest scope and ample opportunity for progress to the liberty which my other Dominions enjoy."

Indian public opinion has been profoundly disturbed by the attempts made during the last two or three years to qualify the repeated pledges given by responsible Ministers on behalf of His Majesty's Government. Since it is apparently contended that only a definite statement in an Act of Parliament would be binding on future Parliaments, and that even the solemn declaration made by His Majesty the King-Emperor on a formal occasion is not authoritative, we feel that a declaration in the preamble is essential in order to remove present grave misgivings and avoid future misunderstandings.

Date and conditions for the inauguration of the Federation.
3. We consider that, following the precedent of some of the Dominion Constitutions, a definite date after the passing of the Act should be fixed by the Constitution Act for the inauguration of the Federation. We have been assured that no serious difficulty is now anticipated in the way of an early establishment of the Reserve Bank, and we have also been authoritatively informed by the witnesses who appeared on behalf of the Princes' Chamber that a period of one year would be sufficient for the negotiations in connection with the Treaties of Accession. If it is feared that unforeseen difficulties might delay the inauguration

of the Federation, power might be given to His Majesty's Government to postpone the date by means of a Royal Proclamation.

In making this suggestion we have in view the psychological effect of such a provision on the political parties in India. The uncertainty that must necessarily result from the absence of any definite date in the Constitution Act for the inauguration of the Federation and the possibility of further delay arising from the procedure of an address in both Houses for the issue of a Proclamation would seriously prejudice the formation or realignment of political parties in India. On the other hand, we have reason to suppose that if a definite date were fixed, even the parties which are dissatisfied with the White Paper Constitution would probably cease to carry on an agitation on the present lines and would be encouraged to concentrate their attention on the new elections. We attach very great importance to this development, since the satisfactory working of the new scheme must necessarily depend on the existence of well-organised parties, prepared to work the scheme.

The Reserved Subjects.

The Army.

4. We have accepted the necessity for the reservation, during a period of transition, of Defence, Foreign Affairs, and the Ecclesiastical Department. We regret to note, however, that in spite of the insistent demands of the Indian Delegates at the Round Table Conference for greater control over Army administration and the promise contained in the Prime Minister's declaration that the reserved powers will not be so framed and exercised as to prejudice the advance of India to full responsibility, the White Paper provisions relating to the Army, so far from giving Indians greater opportunities for influencing Army policy, actually make the constitutional position in some respects worse than at present. While at present the Governor-General and his Council, three Members of which are Indians, "superintend, direct and control"* the military government of India, the Governor-General, assisted by a Counsellor appointed at his discretion, will in future solely determine Army policy. A direction in the Instrument of Instructions to encourage joint consultation between the Ministers and Counsellors is obviously no satisfactory substitute for the opportunities which the present statute affords to the Indian public of expressing its views through the Indian Members of the Executive Council. Past experience of the actual

* Government of India Act, Section 33.

working of a similar direction to Provincial Governors as regards joint consultation between Executive Councillors and Ministers justifies this statement. In Madras under Lord Willingdon joint consultation was invariably the practice, while in some other provinces separate meetings of the two sections of the Executive were the rule rather than the exception. Nor were these variations due to local circumstances, for in the same province under different Governors the practice has been different.

5. We summarise below the modifications that should, in our opinion, be made in the White Paper provisions relating to Defence:–

(1)* (*a*) The Army Counsellor should be a non-official Indian, preferably an elected member of the Federal Legislature, or one of the representatives of the Indian States in the Federal Legislature.

(*b*) There should be a definite programme of Indianization with reference to a time limit of twenty or twenty-five years, and one of the primary duties of the Indian Army Counsellor should be the provision and training of Indian officers for the programme of Indianization.

The position of the Army Counsellor, we may point out, will be fundamentally different from that of any responsible Minister. Army policy will, in all vital matters such as discipline, strategy, equipment, etc., be determined by the Commander-in-Chief. The principal functions of the Army Counsellor will be "to express the views of the Governor-General on defence matters in the Legislature, since these will impinge upon strictly Federal matters",† and to co-ordinate policy in all matters in which the activities of the Army Department bring it into contact with the civil administration. We consider that for the discharge of these very limited functions it would be more appropriate and desirable to have a non-official Indian Counsellor, chosen by the Governor-General at his discretion. The Counsellor will, of course, merely advise the Governor-General who will be free to reject his advice.

---

* Sir Henry Gidney considers that the Army Counsellor should be a non-official but not necessarily a non-official Indian.

† Para. 12 of the Second Report of the Federal Structure Committee.

(2) The Treasury control now exercised in respect of Army expenditure by the Finance Member and the Finance Department should be continued under the new constitution. We fully recognise that in cases of differences of opinion the decision of the Governor-General, who is ultimately responsible for defence, should be final.

(3) All questions relating to Army policy and the annual Army budget estimates should be considered by the entire Government, including all the Counsellors and the Ministers. We again recognise that if the united Cabinet should fail to arrive at an agreement regarding the expenditure to be included in the budget or on other questions referred to it, the Governor-General's decision should be final. This is the minimum that would satisfy the Indian public, especially as the White Paper scheme involves the abolition of the Governor-General's Council, the Indian members of which have not only influenced Army policy, but have actually participated in the determination of that policy.

(4) There should be a statutory Committee of Indian Defence constituted on the lines of the Committee of Imperial Defence. The Committee should consist of the Commander-in-Chief and other Army experts, the principal Federal Ministers and any other Ministers including representatives of the Indian States whom the Viceroy may at his discretion select.

(5) The cost of defence is primarily an administrative issue, but the scale of Army expenditure is a dominant factor in the financial situation and seriously reduces the margin available for the nation-building services. Our views on this subject are well known to His Majesty's Government. We merely repeat our request that an endeavour should be made further to reduce the military expenditure very substantially and that the provisions we have suggested above to ensure economy in Army administration should be given effect to in the Constitution Act.

(6) There should be a provision in the Statute requiring the consent of the Federal Legislature to the employment of the Indian Army outside India, except, of course, for the purpose of the defence of India itself. At the third Round Table Conference His Majesty's Government agreed to consider the suggestion how far the Legislature might be given a voice as to the loan of Indian forces to the Imperial Government "on

occasions when the interests of India within the sphere of defence were not involved."*

Other Reserved Subjects.

6. We consider that it is unnecessary to provide for more than two Counsellors for the three Reserved Departments, since the administration of Ecclesiastical affairs does not involve any appreciable work and can easily be entrusted to the Army Counsellor. We have been assured that it is not the intention to appoint more than two Counsellors, but the provision for a third Counsellor in Proposal 12 has created some misapprehension in India, for it is feared that if a third Counsellor is appointed and is placed in charge of the special responsibilities of the Governor-General, there is considerable danger of his developing into a super-Minister, whose activities must necessarily take the form of interference with the work of the responsible Ministers.

Financial Safeguards.

7. In view of the great importance that has been attached at the Round Table Conferences to the sterling obligations of India and of the attempts that have been made in this country to exploit the nervousness of the investor for political purposes, we have analysed in the second part of our Memorandum in some detail the debt position of India. Three conclusions emerge from this analysis:–

(1) In the first place, five-sixths of India's debt is covered by productive assets, which are mainly State railways and irrigation works.

(2) In the second place, the internal rupee debt of India is nearly one and a half times the sterling debt and an appreciable portion even of the latter is held by Indian investors.

(3) In the third place, a considerable portion of the rupee debt is held by millions of small investors belonging to the upper and lower middle classes who are politically the most vocal section of the population and among whom nationalist feeling finds expression in its most intense form.

The significance of these conclusions lies in the fact that any factors that affect the stability of India's finances or its credit in

* Page 47, Indian Round Table Conference Proceedings, Third Session.

England would have serious repercussions on India's internal credit.

8. We must also draw the attention of the Committee to another feature of India's debt. The total expenditure incurred by India on the Great War was £207.5* millions or about Rs. 311 crores at the rate of exchange prevailing at the time. Of this sum the *direct* contribution from Indian revenues towards Great Britain's War expenditure was £146.2 millions or Rs. 220 crores, nearly two-thirds of which was found by borrowing. These figures include the gift of £100 millions but *not*, of course, the numerous private gifts or the contributions of Indian States. If British India's total contributions towards Great Britain's war expenditure and the interest paid on War borrowings had been utilised for wiping out the sterling debt of India, the sterling debt to-day would have been very small; for a substantial portion of the amount was borrowed before the War at low rates of interest and until recently the securities were quoted at rates very much below par. We fully recognise that these enormous contributions were made by the Indian Legislature and we also recognise that whatever the circumstances connected with the composition of India's sterling debt the position of the British investor is not affected. We have not referred to this subject at any of the Round Table Conferences, and we refer to it now with great reluctance for the last thing we desire to do is to exploit for political purposes a gift made with the full assent of Indian representatives. Nevertheless when attempts have been made in this country to exploit the nervousness of the British investor for purposes of political propaganda, it is necessary to bring to the notice of the British public and of Parliament the fact that, if India had utilised the money which she contributed towards the expenditure on the Great War to wipe out her sterling obligations, the sterling debt to-day would have been very small. We must appeal to the British sense of fair play to see that the financial sacrifices which India made in order to assist Great Britain in her hour of need do not result in the imposition of severe restrictions on the powers of the Legislature and the responsible Finance Minister in the administration of the country. Nothing would exasperate Indian public opinion more than the realisation of the fact that the enormous sacrifices that India had made have actually become the justification for impediments in the way of her constitutional advance.

* The figures in this paragraph are taken from the publication "India's contribution to the Great War" published by the authority of the Government of India.

9. We now proceed to indicate the modifications we suggest in the White Paper provisions.

(1) The fact that a large number of Indians have invested in Indian sterling securities in this country and that an appreciable portion of the Rupee debt is held by a large class of small investors who will be in a position to wield considerable political influence under the new constitution constitutes in our opinion an effective safeguard for the security of India's finances and of her credit abroad. A special responsibility in respect of financial stability and credit has, however, been imposed on the Governor-General. At the Third Round Table Conference attempts were made by several delegates to define this responsibility precisely and to restrict its application to specific cases such as borrowings to beet [sic] budgetary deficits. While considerable sympathy was expressed for this latter demand, the difficulty of drafting a clause that would cover all such cases has apparently been the principal consideration that has influenced His Majesty's Government in retaining the wording adopted in the White Paper. If the difficulties of drafting are found to be insuperable, we consider that the intentions of His Majesty's Government should be made clear by means of appropriate directions in the Instrument of Instructions.

(2) We recognise that if the Governor-General is to have a special responsibility in respect of financial stability and credit, it will be necessary for him to have a Financial Adviser on the spot, for it is better that he should be guided by an adviser who is stationed in India and is in touch with local conditions than that he should be obliged to invoke the aid of experts in England who have had no direct or recent contact with India. We have, therefore, no objection to the appointment of an adviser for a limited period under the new constitution, but it should be made clear either in the Statute or in the Instrument of Instructions, that the intention is that he should not interfere in any way in the ordinary day-to-day administration.

We are further of opinion that there are considerable advantages in designating him Adviser to the entire Government, i.e., the Governor-General as well as the Ministry. It is also very important that the Financial Adviser should be a financier approved by and acceptable to the Finance Minister. The success of the Financial Adviser will depend not merely on his experience and knowledge but upon his personality and his political outlook. His duties under the Constitution will be to advise the Governor-General when he considers that the financial stability or credit of the Federation is in danger: but a financial crisis is often due to the cumulative effect of a series of acts which individually are not of such consequence as to justify interference. It is obvious that the utility of a Financial Adviser would be gravely diminished if he could deal only with the consequences of a crisis and had no opportunities of preventing it by giving his expert advice at the appropriate moment. It is, therefore, of the utmost import- ance that the Minister, while retaining fully his right to reject the advice of the Financial Adviser, be encouraged to consult him as frequently as possible. We request the Committee to take the psychological factors into consideration. If the Financial Adviser were chosen without the agreement of the Minister and did not enjoy his confidence, the latter would probably never consult him, however able and experienced he might be. The inevitable tendency would be for the Finance Minister to isolate himself, as far as constitutional provisions would permit, from the Financial Adviser, and the main object for which the appointment is con- sidered necessary would be frustrated. On the other hand, if the selection were made with the approval of the Minister, he would probably get into the habit of consulting him and of accepting his advice without any prejudice to his constitutional right to reject it in cases in which he considered it necessary to do so.

(3) We have recognised the importance on financial grounds of the constitution of a Reserve Bank. We do not propose to offer any detailed observations on a subject which has been discussed by a special committee here and is now before the Indian Legislative Assembly. We wish, however, to emphasize here that it is of the utmost importance that the principal officers of the Bank, namely, the Governor and Deputy Governor, should not be under the influence either of Whitehall or of the City. In the course of the discussion which some of the Delegates to the Round Table Conference had last year with representatives of the City, very great emphasis was laid on the importance of estab- lishing a Bank which had the confidence of the Indian public. Nothing would shake public confidence in India more than the suspicion that the Governor and the Deputy Governor were acting under the influence of Whitehall or the City.

(4) The legislation in respect of currency and coinage and of the Reserve Bank should not, as proposed in paragraph 119 of the White Paper, be subject to the previous assent of the Governor-General. (Two Members dissent from this proposal.)

These provisions and the establishment of a Reserve Bank, independent of the Federal Executive, would in effect mean that the Finance Minister would not, in respect of currency and exchange policy, be responsible to the Indian Legislature. We draw the attention of the Committee to a statement made by the Secretary of State on December 24th, 1932, at a meeting of the Round Table Conference, that "the British Government have fully accepted the fact that there can be no effective transfer of responsibility unless there is an effective transfer of financial responsibility."* We do not see how Finance can be regarded as a transferred subject unless and until the Finance Minister is also responsible for the currency and exchange policy of the country and is in a position to determine that policy solely in the interests of India. Indeed, as we have shown in the second part of the Memorandum, so long as the currency and exchange policy of the country is reserved it would be difficult for the Ministers in charge of Industry and Agriculture to accept full responsibility for the development of these Departments. It is unnecessary, especially at present, to emphasize the fact that the prosperity of industry and agriculture is very closely connected with the level of commodity prices, which, of course, is dependent on the currency and exchange policy of the country.

(5) Future Indian sterling loans should be raised on behalf of the Government of India by the High Commissioner or some other suitable agency. The Secretary of State in his evidence before the Committee recognised the justification for a change in the present procedure. The question has a political aspect, since the necessity for securing the position of the British investor is one of the principal justifications for the financial safeguards. We realise that any change of procedure might result in a higher rate of interest for Indian loans, but this possibility must be faced by India at some time or other.

Fiscal Convention.

10. Under the White Paper provisions, Commerce will be a transferred subject, in charge of a responsible Minister, and fiscal policy will be determined solely by the Ministry and the Legislature. Since the special responsibilities of the Governor-General do not include fiscal policy or the other matters at present dealt with under the Fiscal Convention, the Governor-General will, in regard to such matters, be guided by the advice of his responsible Minister. We have no modifications to suggest as regards the provisions of the White Paper, but in view of statements that have been made in this country, we wish to draw the attention of the

* Page 79, Round Table Conference Reports, Third Series.

Committee to the following passage in the Report of the Joint Select Committee of 1919:–

"Whatever be the right fiscal policy for India, for the needs of her consumers as well as for her manufacturers, it is quite clear that she should have the same liberty to consider her interests as Great Britain, Australia, New Zealand, Canada, and South Africa."

The further declaration based on this passage made by Mr. Montagu in 1921 in reply to a deputation from Lancashire cannot be too often noted. He said:–

"After that Report by an authoritative Committee of both Houses and Lord Curzon's promise in the House of Lords, it was absolutely impossible for me to interfere with the right which I believe was wisely given and which I am determined to maintain – to give to the Government of India the right to consider the interests of India first, just as we, without any complaint from any other parts of the Empire, and the other parts of the Empire without any complaints from us, have always chosen the tariff arrangements which they think best fitted for their needs, thinking of their own citizens first."

The confidence inspired by this declaration of policy and the policy of discriminating protection (which, it may be noted, is a far more diluted form of protection than the system in force in the Dominions) have led to the remarkable industrial development in India during the last decade, to which reference was made by the witnesses who appeared on behalf of the Manchester Chamber of Commerce. Any departure from this policy would cause dissatisfaction of the very gravest character in India and the consequences might be most disastrous even from the point of view of British commercial interests.

11. At a very late stage of our deliberations a suggestion has been made that while complete freedom in the matter of tariff arrangements should be definitely recognised by Statute, there should be a clause prohibiting discriminatory tariffs penalising British imports as compared with those of other countries, imposed with the object of exercising political pressure on Great Britain. It was explained that such a clause would not prevent discrimination against Great Britain if it was necessary in the economic interests of India, nor would it restrict in any way

the right of India to conclude trade agreements with foreign countries in the interests of Indian commerce and industry. For instance, it was made clear that a reciprocal agreement with Japan as regards the purchase of Indian cotton by Japan and the purchase of Japanese cotton goods by India would not come within the scope of this clause even if it involved a certain measure of discrimination against Great Britain.

12. The possibility of the tariff being utilised as an instrument of political pressure is remote. Our fear is that misunderstandings are bound to arise if the Governor or the Governor-General is the authority that will decide whether there is a political motive underlying the economic policy of the Ministers. If British politicians have been alarmed by some of the statements of the Congress and some of the implications of Congress policy, we venture to point out that Indian commercial interests have also been very disturbed by statements in a section of the British press that in the economic interests of Great Britain there should be no relaxation of Parliamentary control.

13. We would like in this connection to refer briefly to the tariff developments in the past and to their psychological reactions on Indian public opinion. The efforts of Lancashire to interfere with the tariff arrangements of India in the latter half of the last century, the abolition of the whole of the import duties in 1881 after a memorial by the Manchester Chamber of Commerce and a prolonged controversy between the Secretary of State and the Government of India, and finally the imposition of excise duties on cotton goods in 1896, again under pressure from Lancashire, had had very serious political repercussions on Indian public opinion, which are familiar to all who are acquainted with the fiscal and political history of India during the last 50 years. The excise duty on cotton goods became a grave political issue and the demand for its abolition continued long after the levy of heavy import duties on cotton goods. The grant of freedom in respect of tariff arrangements under the Fiscal Convention of 1919 and the abolition of the excise duties in 1925 have had a remarkable effect on the fiscal outlook of India and in particular on its attitude on the question of Imperial preference. In 1926 India had refused to accept the full policy of Imperial preference; but a Bill for the grant of preference to British steel was carried through the Legislature in 1927 though by a small majority. The Ottawa agreement was ratified by the Legislature last year by a very large majority, and the Indian tariff now provides for preference for several classes of British goods. The reason for the

change has been explained in the evidence of Sir Charles Innes, who was a member of the Viceroy's Council in charge of Commerce for five years and is undoubtedly one of the greatest authorities on Indian commercial matters. The following is his reply to Mr. Davidson's question No. 5007:–

"I think it was mainly due to the fact that the Indians realised that it was for themselves to decide whether or not they would ratify that agreement. In the old days, before we introduced this principle of discriminating protection, every Indian thought that Britain kept India a free-trade country in the interest of her own trade. When the Fiscal Convention was introduced, and when we passed a Resolution in favour of discriminating protection, and the first Steel Bill was passed, we at once transferred all that from the political sphere to the economical sphere, and in recent years in the Indian Legislative Assembly more and more we have been creating a strong Free-Trade party. It was getting more and more difficult for me to pass Protection Bills. I think that is all to the good; it shows the value of responsibility, and I am perfectly sure that if we had not taken that action, you would never have got the Indian to agree to preference on British steel, or to the Ottawa agreement, and it seems to me a very good example of the stimulating effect of responsibility."

14. In these circumstances we request the Committee definitely to recognise by Statute India's freedom to regulate her fiscal policy without any reservations or qualifications. Such a course, we are convinced, would be fully justified by the results. In our opinion, so far as the fiscal relations between Great Britain and India are concerned, the question is not whether there will be any tariff discrimination against Great Britain but but to what extent *preference* will be given to Great Britain. A constitutional provision which might never have to be applied in practice but which would tend to offend public opinion in India might seriously prejudice the development of any preferential arrangements as regards Great Britain. India desires to shake hands with Great Britain in token of friendship based on a recognition of equality. A proposal that she should be hand-cuffed before she is allowed to shake hands, lest she be tempted to strike, is hardly the most expedient method of beginning a new era of cordiality and mutual understanding.

975

Commercial Discrimination.

15. The question of Commercial Discrimination has been the subject of prolonged negotiations and discussions for many years. Throughout these discussions and negotiations, the expression "Commercial Discrimination" was used in a very limited sense. It had reference solely to internal restrictions on trade and commerce. It was never intended to include tariff arrangements and the other matters dealt with under the Fiscal Convention. In fact, the only reference to the subject in the reports of the first Round Table Conference is found in the Report of the Minorities Sub-Committee.

16. On the question of principle there has always been a substantial measure of agreement. The All Parties Conference which met in India in 1928 and which was presided over by that eminent leader of the Congress, the late Pandit Motilal Nehru, stated in their report (commonly known as the Nehru Report) that "it is inconceivable that there can be any discriminatory legislation against any community doing business lawfully in India". The statement was endorsed in even more emphatic terms by Mr. Gandhi at the second Round Table Conference. It has been accepted on the one hand that there shall be no unfair discrimination against British companies operating in India, while it is equally agreed on the other side that the Indian Government should have all the powers which Great Britain and the Dominions possess to develop indigenous industries by all legitimate methods. The difficulty throughout has been to define by legislation the expressions "legitimate" and "unfair" and also the term "indigenous".

17. The question was considered by the authors of the Montagu-Chelmsford Report and also by the Simon Commission. The former in paragraph 344 of their report made an appeal to Europeans "to be content to rest like other industries on the new foundation of government in the wishes of the people" and to Indians "to abstain from advocating differential treatment aimed not so much at promoting Indian as at injuring British commerce". The Simon Commission considered that it was not feasible to prevent discriminatory legislation by attempting to define it in a constitutional instrument. Any such provision would, in their opinion, have to be drawn so widely as to be little more than a statement of abstract principle, affording no precise guidance to courts which would be asked to decide whether the action complained of was discriminatory. The Parliamentary draftsmen, however, considered otherwise, and attempts have

been made in the White Paper in Proposals 122, 123 and 124 to deal with this highly complicated question. The view of the Simon Commission has, however, been justified, for the draft has already been found to be unsatisfactory and a complete redraft has been suggested in the memorandum circulated by the Secretary of State. We must point out that if the clauses are drawn so widely as to prevent legitimate discrimination, the Government would be driven to State socialism as the only method by which the provisions of the Act could be circumvented.

18. Before we deal with this revised draft, we must state very frankly the apprehensions of Indian commercial and industrial interests in this matter. A protective tariff, as regards which complete freedom has been given and is to be continued under the White Paper scheme, is the most common and perhaps the most effective method by which indigenous industries can be fostered and developed. The clauses relating to commercial discrimination also recognise that in the case of bounties, subsidies, or other payments of grants from public funds, discrimination even in the case of British companies operating in India would be legitimate under certain circumstances. These, however, do not exhaust the methods by which other countries, including Great Britain, have attempted to develop indigenous industries or to counteract attempts made by foreign companies to frustrate the objects of a protective tariff. The particular difficulty which is disturbing the minds of Indian commercial men is the possibility of powerful foreign trusts establishing themselves in India and making it impossible for Indian industries to develop, not necessarily by methods which in ordinary commercial practice would be regarded as unfair, but by their superior resources, powers of organisation, political influence, etc. It is immaterial from the Indian point of view whether these trusts are British or international, nor do we see how legislation can differentiate between a foreign company which is registered in Great Britain and a British company.

The question has already arisen in the case of the match industry. As a result of the heavy revenue imposed on matches in 1922, a big indigenous industry has developed, and the Swedish Match Company has also established several factories in India. When the question whether the revenue duty should be definitely recognised as a protective duty was considered by the Tariff Board in 1928 one of the points which it examined was whether the Government should introduce any special measures to curtail the activities of the Swedish Match Company in the interests of the Indian companies. The Board, which was presided over by an Indian and had a majority of Indians, recommended that a no-discriminatory action was necessary, though the situation required careful watching; but it is interesting to note that the Tariff Board did not consider itself precluded from considering the question of discrimination and examined several possible methods, such as the establishment of a quasi-monopoly under Government control, State control of sales and prices, and a differential excise duty.*

19. In dealing with the revised draft, it would probably be better for us to state clearly on what lines the draft should, in our opinion, be modified rather than to suggest specific modifications of the draft. We summarise below in the form of propositions our views on this subject:—

(a) We have no objection to the general declaration as to British subjects in regard to the holding of public offices or to the practising of any profession, trade or calling. We would, however, very strongly object to any provision which makes it impossible for India to discriminate against subjects of the Dominions and Colonies which impose disabilities on Indian subjects. We do not wish to elaborate the point further, for His Majesty's Government are aware of the strength and intensity of Indian feeling on this question.

(b) Proposal 124 of the White Paper and the revised draft fully recognise that in respect of bounties, subsidies, or other payments from public funds, discrimination would be legitimate. We would, however, like to point out that the Report of the External Capital Committee of 1924, on which the draft is based, is not the last word on this subject. The conditions imposed in accordance with the recommendations of this Committee have so far been found to be satisfactory, but it is not improbable that altered circumstances will necessitate other conditions or modifications of these conditions with a view to the encouragement of Indian trade or industry. The clause should not, therefore, restrict the right of the Government and the Legislature to impose further conditions, if necessary.

(c) The clauses relating to the special provisions for persons who are British subjects domiciled in the United Kingdom are based on the principle of reciprocity. In the course of the discussions we have referred to several methods by which

* Appendix A, Report of the Indian Tariff Board regarding grant of protection to the Match industry, 1928.

Western countries have attempted to foster and develop national industries and which might in certain circumstances be held to contravene one or other of these provisions. We have two alternative proposals to make.

20. We strongly hold the view that a friendly settlement by negotiation is by far the most appropriate and satisfactory method of dealing with this complicated matter. Any statutory safeguards given to British commercial interests would irritate public opinion and would operate as impediments to be a friendly settlement [*sic*]. We therefore earnestly suggest the omission of clause 123 of the White Paper and the corresponding clauses in the re-draft. If any legislation which subjects to unfair discrimination any class of His Majesty's subject protected by this clause is passed by the Federal Legislature, the Governor-General has already the right under clause 39 to reserve the Bill for the significance of His Majesty's pleasure. Any such action on the part of the Governor-General would itself put the rival parties in the proper frame of mind for a satisfactory agreement. The fear on the one hand of the exercise of the ultimate veto and on the other the possibility of assent being given in view of the strongly expressed public opinion in the matter would probably induce the parties to arrive at a satisfactory compromise. (Sir Henry Gidney dissents from this proposal.)

21. A less satisfactory alternative (though in our opinion much better than the White Paper proposals) would be the inclusion of legislation, which discriminates against any class of His Majesty's subjects in India, in the list of legislation which, under Proposal 119, requires the previous assent of the Governor-General given at his discretion. It should, however, be made very clear by means of a provision in the Statute itself or by means of appropriate directions in the Instrument of Instructions that the assent should not be refused unless the object of the legislation is "not so much to promote Indian commerce as to injure British commerce."

We consider that a clause drafted generally on these lines would be preferable, though it is open to the objection referred to in paragraph 12.

In the first place a provision of this sort would be more elastic than the White Paper provision, for the Governor-General or the Governor, as the case be, would be in a position to decide with reference to the merits of each individual case whether the measure was a legitimate attempt, intended to promote Indian industries, or whether its aim was primarily to injure British commerce in India.

In the second place it would avoid a reference to the Courts to which there are obvious objections, some of which have been given by the Simon Commission in paragraph 156, Volume II of their Report. We do not think that the Courts should be placed in a position in which they might have to give a decision contrary to strongly expressed public opinion in the Legislature. Indeed, any attempt to test the legality of popular legislation by a foreign company would at once raise political issues and would tend to mobilise the forces of public opinion against the company concerned. European companies have during the last four years realised how extremely effective a boycott, supported by public opinion, can be in India.

In the third place a reference to the Federal Court with the right of appeal would mean considerable uncertainty and delay, which might in certain circumstances frustrate the very object of the legislation. Moreover, if the legality of the legislation is challenged, not immediately, but some years after the passing of the Act, a decision of the Federal Court declaring the legislation *ultra vires* on the ground of discrimination would inflict heavy losses on the companies, which in the meanwhile had invested capital and commenced operations.

22. We see grave practical objections to any constitutional provisions against administrative discrimination. Indian Ministers in charge of Transferred Departments in the Provinces have exercised unrestricted powers in respect of contracts and the purchase of stores for the last twelve years and there has been no complaint from any British companies that the powers have been abused. Apart from the fact that any provision in the new constitution which would enable the Governor-General or the Government to interfere with the discretion of the Indian Ministers in these matters would be very strongly resented as an encroachment on the rights already granted by convention, we are convinced that administrative interference would, in practice, seriously affect the relations between the Governor-General or the Governor and his Ministers. In practice no such discrimination against British companies in India is likely to take place, especially as the vast majority of the shareholders in many of the so-called European companies in India, such as the jute companies of Bengal, are Indians. The Indian shareholders, like the shareholders of any other country, do not concern themselves very much with political or racial issues so long as they get

their dividends regularly. Although the shareholders in the jute companies have been predominantly Indian, the management and direction has, as is well known, been almost exclusively European.

Railway Board.

23. The question of the constitution of a Statutory Railway Board was never discussed at the Round Table Conferences but was considered by the Consultative Committee of the Round Table Conference in India. This Committee, while recognising the advantages of the establishment by Statute of a Railway Board for the administration of the Indian Railway system on commercial lines, considered that the Constitution should merely contain a clause requiring the establishment of such a body and that the constitution, functions and powers of the Board should be determined by an Act of the Federal Legislature. We agree with this recommendation.

Federal Legislature.

24. We generally accept the proposals in the White Paper both as regards the composition of the Lower Federal Chamber and as regards the method of election to it.* The representatives of some of the bigger Indian States have urged the desirability of smaller Legislatures and also the adoption of an indirect system of election. The arguments that have been advanced against direct election are familiar to those who have taken part in the constitutional discussions of the last five years, but since the matter is of such vital interest we propose to deal with the principal objections which are as summarised below:–

(1) Direct election, even with Legislatures of the size contemplated by the White Paper scheme, would necessitate extensive constituencies, and with the comparatively undeveloped state of communications in India it would be impossible for the individual member to maintain that personal contact with the electorate which is the essence of the democratic system.

(2) The vast mass of the electors who are to be enfranchised under the White Paper scheme are illiterate, and in the absence of a well-organised party or press, it would be difficult for the

* Some members of the Delegation would much prefer smaller legislatures though they are in favour of direct election to the Lower Chamber. One member considers that in view of the special circumstances of his community at present, indirect election would be preferable.

illiterate voter to understand the complicated and in some cases highly technical issues which the Federal Government would deal with under the new constitution.

(3) India has not sufficient men with the necessary qualifications to fill Provincial and Central Legislatures of the size provided for in the White Paper scheme, and a large Federal Legislature is unnecessary for the purposes of the Federal scheme, since the functions of the Federal Government under this scheme will be very restricted.

25. The first two arguments have been answered in the following passage from the Government of India's despatch on a similar proposal made by the Statutory Commission:–

"First, the central elector has exercised the franchise with increasing readiness and at least as freely as the elector to provincial councils. A great deal of the business of the central legislature is as intimate to the elector, and is as fully within the scope of his understanding as the business of the provincial councils. We need cite only such matters as the Sarda Act, the income-tax, the salt tax, the railway administration, and postal rates. Even more abstruse matters, such as the exchange ratio and tariffs, interest large sections of the electorate. Second, the electoral methods natural to the social structure of India may be held to some extent to replace personal contact between candidate and voter, a contact which adult suffrage and party organizations make increasingly difficult in western countries. The Indian electorate is held together by agrarain [sic], commercial, professional and caste relations. It is through these relations that a candidate approaches the elector, and in this way political opinion is the result partly of individual judgment, but to a greater extent than elsewhere of group movements. These relations and groups provide in India a means of indirect contact between voter and member, reducing the obstacles which physical conditions entail. Moreover, we are impressed by the further consideration that ten years ago Parliament of its own motion set up for the first time a directly elected Assembly, representative of the whole of India. That Assembly, in part perhaps because it is directly elected, has appealed to the sentiment of India, and sown the seeds, as yet only quickening, of real representation. Accordingly, unless new considerations of greater importance have to be taken into account, we feel reluctant as yet to condemn an experiment undertaken so recently in a country awakening to political consciousness."

Apart from the other weighty arguments which have been urged by others in favour of a system of direct election, we wish to draw the attention of the Committee to the possibility, almost amounting to certainty, of Provincial elections being fought on All-India issues if the Federal Legislatures were indirectly elected by the Provincial Councils. The result would be that none of the advantages claimed for the indirect system could be secured, since All-India issues would be voted upon by an electorate of 35 millions instead of by the more restricted electorate recommended by the Lothian Committee for the Federal Assembly.

26. As regards adequacy of qualified men to fill the legislatures, whatever the conditions in the Indian States, no-one who is in touch with conditions in British India doubts that, except perhaps in the case of the depressed classes, men with the necessary qualifications will not be available. Our fear, on the other hand, is that the number of candidates will be embarrassingly large.

27. We consider that there should be a definite provision regulating the procedure for the participation by representatives of Indian States in matters of exclusively British Indian interest. The following formula indicates the procedure which in our opinion should be followed:–

(1) In a division on a matter concerning solely a British Indian subject, the representatives of the Indian States will not be entitled to vote.

(2) Whether a matter relates solely to a British Indian subject or not will be left to the decision of the Speaker of the House, which will be final.

(3) If a substantive vote of "No Confidence" is proposed in the House on a matter relating solely to a British Indian subject, the representatives of the Indian States will be entitled to vote since the decision on such a question will vitally affect the position of a Ministry formed on the basis of collective responsibility.

(4) There should be a definite provision in the Constitution regarding the procedure on this important point, since the issues raised affect the status and rights of the representatives of the Indian States on a question of voting in the Legislature.

(5) If the Ministry is defeated on a vote of the Legislature on

a subject of exclusively British Indian interest, it will be for the Ministry to decide whether it should continue in office. It will not necessarily resign as a result of the vote.

Provincial Constitutions.

28. We approve generally the scheme of Provincial responsibility provided for in the White Paper proposals, and our observations and suggestions are confined to matters of detail.

(1) We are very strongly opposed to the proposal that Law and Order or any section of the Police Department should be reserved. In the first place, the isolation of this Department would result in the intensification of the hostility to this Department which would be increasingly recognised as the agency of an alien Government. In the second place, the maintenance of Law and Order is very closely connected with the administration of the other departments, since the Police are the agency through which in the last resort the policy of the other departments is enforced. For instance, the periodical Moplah outbreaks in the south, the tenancy agitation in the U.P., and the Gurudwara agitation in the Punjab were due to agrarian or religious movements which necessitated action in the Transferred Departments. To give another instance, the enforcement of prohibition, which has the sympathy of a large section of the population in India, is, as has been demonstrated by the American experiment, primarily a question of Law and Order.

(2) Any special provision for dealing with the terrorist activities in Bengal and elsewhere, which would involve a restriction of ministerial responsibility in respect of Law and Order, would, apart from its political reactions, defeat the object in view. It is well-known that the terrorist activities have been aggravated by social and even religious influences, unemployment among the University graduates, and by economic conditions of the Province in general. Absence of any strongly expressed public opinion against the movement has also been one of the principal factors that has contributed to its growth. Only an Indian Minister who is very closely in touch with the classes of the population from which the terrorists are drawn can mobilise the forces of public opinion against the movement and deal effectively with the social and the other factors that have influenced its growth. (Sir Henry Gidney dissents.)

(3) There is nothing in the White Paper scheme which could prevent the Governor-General from carrying out the suggestion

984

that, while Law and Order would be completely transferred in the Provinces, there should be a small organisation directly under the Governor-General which would, in co-operation with the provincial authorities, supply him with information relating to movements of a subversive character which extend over more than one Province and which raise questions relating to the defence and security of the country. The military section of the C.I.D. does, as a matter of fact, discharge this function.

(4) The Instrument of Instructions should definitely contain a direction to the Governors that the collective responsibility of the Cabinet with a Prime Minister should be introduced from the very inception of the provincial constitutions.

(5) *Special responsibilities of the Governor.**

While we recognise that certain special responsibilities would have to be imposed on the Governor in view of the demands of the Minorities and other circumstances, we consider that the following modifications should be made in Proposal 70 of the White Paper:–

(i) In respect of the prevention of grave menace to the peace and tranquillity of the Province, the Governor's action should be confined to the Department of Law and Order. In other words, these special powers should not be exercised so as to interfere with the administration of the other Departments. It is suggested that the special responsibilities should be restricted to cases in which the menace arises from subversive movements or the activities of a person or persons tending to crimes of violence.

(ii) In the case of Minorities, the expression "legitimate interests" should be more clearly defined and it should be made clear that the Minorities referred to are the racial and religious minorities which by usage are generally included in this expression.

(iii) In the case of the Services, the expression "legitimate

---

* Sir Abdur Rahim is of the opinion that the special responsibilities and special powers of the Governor as proposed in the White Paper will make it extremely difficult for responsible Governments in the Provinces to function and considers that the provision made to meet cases of breakdown of the Constitution should suffice to meet all serious contingencies. He is convinced that if the rights and interests of the Minorities and the Services are properly defined in the Constitution Act itself that will afford more effective protection to them. The Governor should, however, be responsible for carrying out the orders of the Federal Government and protecting the rights of Indian States.

interests" should be clearly defined. The Governor's special responsibility should be restricted to the rights and privileges guaranteed by the Constitution. (The other special responsibilities of the Governor will be dealt with in the appropriate sections of this memorandum to which they relate.)

(6) The power of issuing ordinances should be given only to the Governor-General as at present. The Governor should have no difficulty in getting ordinances issued even in emergencies as at present. (Some members of the Delegation dissent from this proposal and support the White Paper proposal.)

(7) We are opposed to the creation of second Chambers in Bengal, Bihar and the U.P. The opinion of the present Legislative Councils in these Provinces is not conclusive in the matter.

If, however, in spite of our opinion a second Chamber with a nominated element is to be constituted in these Provinces, we consider that it should be definitely recognised that persons appointed Ministers must be or become within a stated period elected members of one of the two Chambers. (One member of the Delegation considers that in the case of the United Provinces a Second Chamber is necessary, while another would like to have it in all the three Provinces.)

(8) In respect of the Governor's Act, referred to in Proposals 92 and 93 of the White Paper, most of us would prefer that, if any legislation were required for the discharge of the special responsibilities imposed on the Governor, he should take the entire responsibility for such legislation and should not be required to attempt to secure the assent of the Legislature.

Federal Finance.

29.—(1) The allocation of the sources of revenue between the Federation and the units, which follows with slight modifications the recommendations of the Peel Committee of the Third Round Table Conference, is the result of a compromise and we do not, therefore, suggest any change.

(2) In regard to the division of income-tax, however, we observe that the contentions of the British Indian members of the Peel Committee have not been accepted. These members, realising the importance of strengthening the financial position of the Federal Government by the permanent allocation of a portion of the income-tax, agreed, as a compromise, to the suggestion that the proceeds of the income-tax which are not derived solely

from residents in British India should be allotted to the Federal Government, in addition to the Corporation Tax which would be definitely classed as a Federal source of revenue. According to the figures placed before the Peel Committee, the amount of income-tax so allotted was roughly about $2^1/_2$ to 3 crores of rupees, or only about 20 per cent. of the balance remaining after the allocation of the Corporation Tax to the Federal Government.

Under the White Paper scheme, the portion of the income-tax to be assigned to the Federation has been fixed at not less than 25 per cent. and not more than 50 per cent. of the net proceeds, the exact percentage to be fixed by a committee just before the inauguration of the Federation.

Since the Percy Committee have definitely found that the pre-Federation debt of India is covered by the assets to be transferred to the Federal Government, there is no justification in theory for the assignment to the Federal Government of any portion of the personal income-tax paid by the residents of the Provinces, since no corresponding tax on incomes will be paid by the States. Any such proposal would have serious political repercussions, for an economic issue of this sort might determine the line of party cleavage in the Federal Legislature. It would be very deplorable if at the very inception of the new constitution the representatives of British India and those of the Indian States were ranged in opposite camps in the Federal Legislature.

(3) In Proposal 137, it is stated that the Federal Legislature will be empowered to assign the salt duty, the Federal excises and the export duties "in accordance with such schemes of distribution as it may determine". It should be made clear that the system of distribution should be on the basis of population or according to some other method that would not render possible the exercise of administrative control over the units of the Federation. In other words, the scheme of distribution should not be interpreted as including grants-in-aid as an instrument of control.

(4) There should be a provision in the Constitution Act for the appointment by the Governor-General of a committee (say, three years after the Federation has begun to function) to institute an inquiry into the financial conditions of the Federation and of the British Indian Provinces and to make recommendations for the allocation of the income tax to the Provincial units according to a time-table.

*Public Services.**

30. No part of the White Paper proposals has caused more dissatisfaction in India than the provisions relating to the Public Services. Before we indicate our views on these provisions, we may draw the attention of the Committee to certain features of the duties and conditions of service, particularly with reference to the key Service, namely, the Indian Civil Service. The Covenant or contract signed by a member of the Indian Civil Service imposes many obligations on him, but confers hardly any rights or privileges, which have all been granted either by Statute or by rules, such as the Devolution Rules and the Classification Rules. The salaries and other conditions of service have been varied from time to time and are still subject to variation by the Secretary of State in Council. The duties and functions of this Service have also undergone considerable changes. Originally the Collector and Magistrate was a fiscal officer, a revenue and criminal judge, the local head of the police, jails, education, municipal and sanitary departments. Owing to the increase of specialisation by the creation of new departments, transfer of certain departments to the direct control of the Imperial Government, de-officialis-ation of local authorities and other administrative changes due to the introduction of the Montagu-Chelmsford reforms, his duties have been considerably restricted, but he continues to be the administrative head of the district, whose principal functions, apart from the collection of revenue, are the maintenance of law and order and the co-ordination of the work of the different departments of Government in the district. Many of the higher administrative appointments and almost all the higher secretariat appointments in the Provincial Governments and in the Government of India are reserved for the members of this Service under the present Constitution.

31. According to the White Paper scheme, the Secretary of State will continue to recruit on the present basis for the two key Services, namely, the Indian Civil Service and the Indian Police. There is to be a statutory inquiry after a period of five years after which Parliament will determine on what basis future recruitment should be made.

Very strong objection has been taken in India to this part of the scheme which is, it may be noted, not in accordance with the recommendations of the Services Sub-Committee of the Round Table Conference. We consider that, after the passing of the Constitution Act, recruitment for the Central Services should

* Wherever the word "Indian" is used, it includes "Statutory Indians."

be by the Federal Government and for the Provincial Services, including the Indian Civil Service and the Indian Police, should be by the Provincial Governments, who should have full power to determine the pay and other conditions of service for future recruits and also the proportion of Europeans that should be recruited.* We give below some statistics, necessarily based on certain assumptions, as to the number of European officers that would remain in service even if recruitment were completely stopped in 1935:–

	Indian Civil Service.	Indian Police.
(1) Total sanctioned strength	1,225	683
(2) Present strength (on 1st January, 1932, latest figures available)	1,308	680
(3) Number of European officers at present (1st January, 1932)	843	528
(4) Number of European officers if recruitment were stopped in 1935—		
(a) in 1935	762	498
(b) in 1940	632	443
(c) in 1945	502	388

There would thus be a very substantial European element in the two key Services for another generation, even if European recruitment were completely stopped after the passing of the Act. The proposal that a statutory inquiry should be instituted after a period of five years is open to very strong objection. The problem of European recruitment cannot be considered in isolation. It is very closely connected with standards of administration, the state of communal feeling and other factors which are of a very controversial nature and raise political issues. Any such inquiry even of an informal nature would, therefore, have a grave disturbing effect on the political atmosphere and would seriously affect the relations between the Services and the Legislatures.

32. We now proceed to deal with the existing rights of officers appointed by the Secretary of State in Council which are to be guaranteed by Statute. We may say at once that we have no objection to the proposal that the pensions, salaries, and the privileges and rights relating to dismissal or any other form of punishment or censure should, in the case of the existing

* Sir Henry Gidney dissents from this proposal.

members of the All-India Services, be fully safeguarded by the Constitution. We consider, however, that the Governor-General in his discretion is responsible to the Secretary of State, and that constitutionally there would be very little change. Indian public opinion, however, attaches great importance to this formal change, which would be more in keeping with the rest of the Constitution.

To meet the reasonable demands made by the Services Association we are prepared to go further and agree to the following concessions:–

(1) Although the members of the All-Indian Services, appointed after the commencement of the Government of India Act of 1919, are not entitled to the "existing and accruing rights or to compensation in lieu thereof" referred to in Section 96B (2) of the Government of India Act, we have no objection to the proposal that these rights should be extended to the officers appointed before the passing of the Act.

(2) We agree to the proposal that the right of retiring on proportionate pension should be extended to all European members of the All-India Services, appointed up to the passing of the Act.

33. Our objection is mainly to the rights and privileges which operate as restrictions on ministerial responsibility. We foresee many administrative developments. We therefore consider that there should be no restriction on the Ministers as regards postings, allocation of work, reorganisation of services and functions, and other matters which relate to the enforcement of policy and the efficiency of administration. The Ministers should also have the power of abolishing individual appointments now held by members of the All-India Services, subject to right of compensation in certain cases on the lines indicated in the evidence of the Secretary of State.

34. We see no justification for the proposal to exempt from income-tax the pensions of retired officers of the All-India Services. Any such exemption would not benefit the retired officials resident in Great Britain or Northern Ireland who are subject to the British income-tax and who come within the scope of the double income-tax arrangements. Whether India levied an income-tax on pensions or not, they would continue to pay income-tax at the British rate. The only persons who would be protected are the retired officials who have settled in foreign countries in order to evade the British income-tax. We do not

think that these officers deserve the sympathy of Parliament or that any special constitutional provision should be made for their benefit.

The question is not, in fact, connected with service rights or privileges, for retired British officials in India are subject to Indian income-tax. The matter is one for adjustment between the British Treasury and the Indian Government, if the latter decided to remove the present exemption.

It is possible that, owing to the fact that under the Indian income-tax provisions no exemptions are given for families, in a few cases the British rate might be lower than the Indian rate of income-tax and that a few retired officials in Great Britain and Northern Ireland would therefore become subject to a higher rate of tax. To avoid any hardship in this comparatively small number of cases, we would have no objection to any arrangements under which retired officials in Great Britain and Northern Ireland would continue to pay income-tax at the same rate as at present.

Appointment of Governors.

35. We strongly feel that the Governors of all the Provinces should under the new Constitution be selected from amongst public men in Great Britain and in India. Members of the permanent services in India, whether retired or on active service, should be excluded from these high appointments.

Automatic Growth of the Constitution.

36. The Simon Commission declared that one of the most important principles which should be borne in mind in considering the constitutional proposals was that the new Constitution should as far as possible contain within itself provision for its own development. As the Commission observed –

"It has been a characteristic of the evolution of responsible government in other parts of the British Empire that the details of the constitution have not been exhaustively defined in statutory language. On the contrary, the constitutions of the self-governing parts of the British Empire have developed as the result of natural growth, and progress has depended not so much on changes made at intervals in the language of an Act of Parliament as on the development of conventions and on the terms of instructions issued from time to time to the Crown's representative."

The Prime Minister's declaration which we have quoted in the introductory paragraph of this memorandum also states clearly that –

"In such statutory safeguards as may be made for meeting the needs of the transitional period, it will be a primary concern of His Majesty's Government to see that the reserved powers are so framed and exercised as not to prejudice the advance of India through the new constitution to full responsibility for her own government."

We recognise, however, that Parliament cannot now, once for all, completely divest itself of its ultimate responsibility. We make no detailed proposals as regards this subject, but indicate our views in the following propositions:–

(*a*) The machinery to be provided in the new Act for the further constitutional advance of India should not involve an inquiry such as that conducted by the Simon Commission.

(*b*) The Constitution Act should definitely give the power of initiating proposals for constitutional changes to the Indian Legislatures. Such proposals should be required by Statute to be placed before Parliament in appropriate form through the Secretary of State.

(*c*) The constitutional procedure required for implementing these proposals should not, except in a few strictly limited cases, involve Parliamentary legislation.

(*d*) Provisions analogous to those of Section 19A of the present Government of India Act should be inserted in the new Act for the purpose of facilitating the devolution of authority by Parliament to the Indian Legislatures.

Our proposals are intended to secure that the process of further transfer of responsibility shall be continuous. We recognise that during an initial period, which in our opinion should not exceed ten years, certain provisions of the new Constitution must remain unaltered. We cannot, however, too strongly impress upon the Committee that unless the new Constitution brings the realisation of a Government fully responsible to the Legislature within sight and its provisions are so framed as to render possible further constitutional progress by the action of the Indian Legislatures, political activity outside the Legislatures will continue to absorb important sections of the politically-minded classes in India.

37. We have not in this memorandum attempted to exhaust all the issues which the White Paper proposals raise. On the points, which we have not specifically dealt with in the preceding paragraphs, we have expressed our opinion either individually or collectively in the course of the discussion or in the course of the cross-examination of the Secretary of State.

AGA KHAN.
ABDUR RAHIM.
M. R. JAYAKAR.
H. S. GOUR.
SHAFAAT AHMAD KHAN.
A. H. GHUZNAVI.
PHIROZE SETHNA.
BUTA SINGH.
HENRY GIDNEY.
B. R. AMBEDKAR.
ZAFRULLA KHAN.
N. M. JOSHI.

B. RAMA RAU,
Secretary,
British Indian Delegation.
17th November, 1933.

Source: *Joint Committee on Indian Constitutional Reform (Session 1933–34), Volume 1 (Part 1), Report,* His Majesty's Stationery Office, London, 1934. Parliamentary Paper H.L. 6 (I, Part 1), H.C. 5 (I, Part 1).

The Joint Committee was appointed on 11 April 1933 and met over seventy times. It was empowered to call into consultation representatives of the Indian States and of British India, and accordingly invited the following to attend its deliberations:

Delegates from the Indian States
Rao Bahadur Sir V. T. Krishnama Chari, C.I.E.
Nawab Sir Liaqat Hyat-Khan, O.B.E.
Nawab Sir Muhammad Akbar Hydari.
Sir Mirza Muhammad Ismail, C.I.E., O.B.E.
Sir Manubhai Nandshanker Mehta, C.S.I.
Sir Prabhashankar Dalpatram Pattani, K.C.I.E.
Mr. Y. Thombare.

Delegates from Continental British India
His Highness the Right Honourable Sultan Sir Mohamad Shah,
    Aga Khan, G.C.S.I., G.C.I.E., G.C.V.O.
Sir C. P. Ramaswami Aiyar, K.C.I.E.
Dr. B. R. Ambedkar.

Sir Hubert Carr.
Mr. A. H. Ghuznavi.
Lieut.-Colonel Sir Henry Gidney.
Sir Hari Singh Gour.
Mr. A. Rangaswami Iyengar.
Mr. M. R. Jayakar.
Mr. N. M. Joshi.
Mr. N. C. Kelkar.
Begum Shah Nawaz.
Rao Bahadur Sir A. P. Patro.
Sir Abdur Rahim.
The Right Honourable Sir Tej Bahadur Sapru, K.C.S.I.
Sir Phiroze Sethna.
Dr. Shafa'at Ahmad Khan.
Sardar Bahadur Buta Singh.
Sir Nripendra Nath Sircar.
Sir Purshotamdas Thakurdas, C.I.E., M.B.E.
Mr. Zafrullah Khan.

Delegates from the Province of Burma
Sra Shwe Ba.
Mr. C. H. Campagnac, M.B.E.
Mr. N. M. Cowasji.
U Kyaw Din.
Mr. K. S. Harper.
U Chit Hlaing.
U Thein Maung.
Dr. Ba Maw.
U Ba Pe.
Dr. Ma Saw Sa.
U Shwe Tha.
Mr. S. A. S. Tyabji.

All the above were able to attend with the exception of Mr. Kelkar, who was prevented by illness from coming to England.

On the work of the Joint Committee see its reports, proceedings and minutes of evidence in the Parliamentary Papers H.C. 112 (I) of 1933, and H.C. 5 (I), H.C. 5 (II) A, H.C. 5 (II) B, H.C. 112 (II) A, H.C. 112 (II) B, H.C. 112 (II) C and H.C. 112 (II) D of 1934; and Eustace Percy, *Some Memories*, London, 1958.

128

THE INDIAN WHITE PAPER

Interview with the Associated Press of India

Bombay: 14 December 1933

Tribute to members of the Delegation to the Joint Committee – the White Paper – tribute to Sir Samuel Hoare – the road to Dominion Status – the need for constructive discussion – avoid recrimination – an appeal for co-operation and unity – the Communal Award – economic progress – the new Governor of Bombay – the task before Indians.

Interviewed by a representative of *The Times of India,* His Highness the Aga Khan first paid a tribute to the disinterested and enlightened labours of the leaders of British India, especially Sir Tej Bahadur Sapru, Mr. [M. R.] Jayakar, Sir Phiroze Sethna, Dr. Sir Barisingh Gour, Sir Abdur Rahim and the representatives of the States, like Sir Akbar Hydari.

He said that the members of the British Indian and Indian States Delegation created a most favourable impression by the fact that they acted not as Hindus, Moslems, Parsis, Sikhs or Christians, but as Indians, and their constructive work was conceived in the interests of India as a whole.

There was no sectional or separatist tendency and everyone was animated by a genuine desire to promote the constitutional advance of India, which is ensured. The joint memorandum presented by the British Indian delegation who collaborated with the Joint Select Committee and which represented the views of the delegation as a whole is a testimony to the unity of purpose and agreement among the members, and moreover it follows the line of the able and illuminating memorandum of Sir Tej Bahadur Sapru.

"Our case has been ably presented, and I have no fear whatsoever that the principle embodied in the White Paper will be whittled down, for I can say from my personal experience that every member of the National Government in England is determined to carry through the proposals," said the Aga Khan.

"The principles enunciated in the White Paper may be regarded as a preliminary to and a step forward towards the realisation of India's aspirations towards Dominion Status. We know the opposition that is offered to the principles of the White Paper by a powerful section of the Conservatives, but in the Secretary of State, Sir Samuel Hoare, India has found a staunch friend, who remained unshaken in his determination to stand by India.

"I do not know what to admire most, his liberalism or his tenacity of purpose, or his steadiness and stand against the fire of the enemies. I do not say we have got the Dominion Status, but now that we are on the high road to it, it is for us, Indians, to impede or accelerate the journey. I have always emphasised one fact that there is no short cut to constitutional advance and that if we prove ourselves capable of progress by enlightened and sustained effort, no power in the world can arrest our onward march towards progress: but if we fritter our energies by futile quarrels among ourselves for monopoly of power or the form of Government, we shall be held guilty of holding up the progress of the country.

"More than one country in Europe is now learning the lesson that it is difficult to find an efficient substitute in place of the sudden deposition of her experienced sons with traditions of ruling authority. But I earnestly appeal to my countrymen not to throw away the substance for the shadow. By all means urge amendments of the proposals, stand up for your constitutional rights, and where you consider the proposals in the White Paper deficient, point it out in a firm and dignified manner and meet argument by argument and urge on the authorities to supply the deficiency.

"But for God's sake if you love India, if you have her interests at heart, do not hold up the progress and do not try to slay each other. Persevere in the path of peaceful progress. Forget the past and look to the future. There are weak points, there are defects in the Federal plan placed before the country, but please remember that it is the most momentous and unparalleled political transition in the history of India.

"It is a gigantic task and such a novel experiment in democracy in a continent like India cannot be perfected without experience and tremendous constructive effort. But a false start should, and could, be avoided at any rate. It is no use indulging in recrimination. I am prepared to give credit to the critics of the proposed constitutional advance for honesty of purpose, but I would beseech them to extend to us the same courtesy.

"All my life, I have fought for unity in India and for constitutional advance of India on the lines of least resistance under the aegis of the Crown, in whose vast dominions a real League of Nations can be found – I claim that my labours extending over 30 years for the advance of India have not been in vain. Federation has received blessings from Indian Princes who have not been slow to sacrifice such of their sovereign powers as are essential for the establishment of the Federal Government, and the way in which the representatives of His Exalted Highness the Nizam, and the rulers of Mysore, Baroda, Bikaner, Kashmir, Patiala, Udaipur, Jodhpur, Jaipur and others stood by India in her hour of need was indeed a marvellous revelation to the friends as well as the critics of the Government plan.

"Equally gratifying was the great forensic ability and devotion to the cause of the motherland by that Indian patriot, Sir Tej Bahadur Sapru, and by Mr. Jayakar, Sir Harising Gour, Sir Pheroze Sethna and Sir Abdur Rahim and other leaders of political thought.

"While realising the essential need of compromise as an expediency in politics, Sir Tej Bahadur refused to receive anything less than responsibility in the centre as a first and important measure towards Dominion Government, subject to safeguards in the interests of India during the period of transition.

"I have always appealed for co-operation between Indians and Indians and between Indians and Englishmen. I thankfully acknowledge a very large measure of support I have received from my countrymen as well as my co-religionists and even Englishmen of all the political parties in England. I have always worked for unity and peace and I hope my Hindu and Muslim brethren will realise that at no time there was a greater necessity for co-operation and unity to solve great political problems of stupendous magnitude and dispel the dark cloud of depression that has been running over India.

"The unity for which I earnestly appeal is not the unity of a pious paper resolution but unity of heart, achieved through its promptings and cemented by bonds of mutual affection, mutual goodwill pointing to common interests of the country and the Empire."

Asked as to the Communal Award he said emphatically that it has come to stop [*sic*] unless both parties come to a mutual agreement. No leader and no party had a right to change it. That controversy should be considered as closed.

Continuing the Aga Khan said: – "We did our best to come to an honourable agreement without the help of the third party. We who worked for the good of the country, have a clear conscience as we have a clear duty towards our countrymen as our co-religionists. We cannot betray our trust. Our people and they alone as a body can change the plan. We have shown accommodating spirit in every direction and if larger sacrifices were required for our dear country's cause we would not have hesitated to make those sacrifices but we were all convinced and were able to convince others that in the ignoring or belittling of our just demands there was not safety but danger for Indian nationalism.

"I am not tired of reiterating," said the Aga Khan, "that politics are only an avenue and a means for securing our economic and social regeneration. Our first and paramount duty should be to stop the economic rot that has set in. This is an imperative task demanding our careful attention, as without improvement in the present paralysing economic condition of the country, political progress will come to naught.

"This economic crisis is scarcely less grave than that occasioned by the Great War. If India is economically ruined, what kind of Swaraj can we build on the economic ruin of the country? It is suicidal to add to our great troubles. Why can't we live, work, progress and prosper together as we have done for centuries, sharing the joys and sorrows of each other.

"I am glad that Bombay is fortunate in having in the new Governor, Lord Brabourne, who has not only Parliamentary knowledge and experience, but has become quite familiar with the aspirations and demands of young India at the Round Table Conferences. He has been able to study at close quarters the mainspring of Indian aspirations and has come to sympathise with them, and I have no doubt that he will succeed in firmly planting autonomy broad-based on people's will in our Presidency. I am sure that in the new Governor, you will find a true friend of the people of the Presidency actuated by highest motives to promote their political and economic welfare."

In conclusion, the Aga Khan said that the time for agitation and academic discussion had passed. The stage for education of the people and for preparation for fitting Indians for larger responsibilities which will be shortly theirs had arrived.

"As we show the use we make of those responsibilities, so shall we be judged and our next advance must depend upon ourselves. I ask how India will benefit by holding up or putting back the clock of progress? Do not throw away what we have already achieved, but work hard for further achievement. The task is endless and formidable. Lost opportunities do not recur. We have now at the helm of administration an old and a tried friend of India. Sieze the olive branch held out by the great Viceroy, Lord Willingdon, and work for the common good of India, when there is yet time."

Asked about his racing programme, the Aga Khan said: "What concerns me most at the present moment is to run in the political race for India, so as to help a little bit our motherland. Take my advice. Let us put our feet firmly in the stirrup of this political opportunity and go boldly in the race and win it. . .

Source: *The Times of India*, Bombay, 15 December 1933.

A shorter account appeared in *The Civil and Military Gazette* of the same date, and a brief report was carried by *The Times* of 16 December.

The Aga Khan gave this interview on his arrival in Bombay from England by the *S. S. Rajputana*. Among other passengers alighting from the same boat were Sir Edward Benthall, Sirdar Buta Singh and Sir Arthur Worley.

The arrival of the Aga Khan was described by *The Times of India* in these words:

"His Highness the Aga Khan, who is accompanied by Begum Aga Khan and Prince Ali Khan, was accorded a most enthusiastic welcome on his arrival in Bombay on Thursday afternoon. Tumultuous scenes were witnessed at Ballard Pier where thousands of his followers had assembled to catch a glimpse of their spiritual head, many of them with children in their arms. An open space in front of the Pier was gaily decorated with flags, bunting and welcome arches where the Aga Khan's followers congregated to offer their reverent greetings to him.

"A number of Muslim volunteer corps with a band were in attendance to regulate the crowd, in addition to the extra police force which was present to cope with the rush of traffic. Many influential persons both from Bombay and outside boarded the steamer and offered their respectful welcome. The Aga Khan and his party were literally mobbed by his followers both on board and after they landed. After acknowledging the greetings and blessing his people, His Highness motored to his bungalow to meet his mother, Lady Ali Shah."

On the White Paper see Robert Gillan, *Why this White Paper?*, London, n.d.; John Hewett, *Some Reflections on the White Paper*, Southend-on-Sea, n.d. (?1933); James Johnston, *The Political Future of India*, London, 1933; *Proposals for Indian Constitutional Reform*, 1933, Cmd. 4268; Abdullah Yusuf Ali, "Indian Reactions to the White Paper", *Asiatic Review,* July 1933; and Muhammad Zafrullah Khan, "Indian Public Opinion on the White Paper", *International Affairs,* September 933.

129

THE COMMUNAL ELECTORATES

Interview with the Press

New Delhi: 7 February 1934

For the moment communal electorates will have to be retained – practical experience of working the democratic institutions by Hindus and Muslims might remove the need for them.

Discussing the general political situation with a press representative the Aga Khan said that for the present communal electorates would have to be accepted by all the parties concerned. But he was definitely of the opinion that practical experience of the working of democratic institutions, which were going to be introduced in the country by the forthcoming reforms, would teach both Muslims and Hindus to realize that neither of them stood to gain anything by the perpetuation of communalism in the political sphere in any form whatsoever.

The dawning of this realization would spontaneously sound the death-knell of communal electorates, which were a necessary evil under the present circumstances.

Similarly it would be a sheer waste of time and energy to strive to get the Communal Award altered, so long as an equally good if not better alternative scheme, which would satisfy all sections of political opinion, was not put forward before the country.

As one having vast experience of representative institutions in almost all parts of the world, His Highness felt sure that the lessons of democracy would demonstrate to all that communalism was nothing short of an anachronism in a democratic country, its existence being wholly outrageous to the spirit of democracy.

Source: *The Times of India*, Bombay, 8 February 1934.

The paper published the interview under the headlines: "Aga Khan defends Communal Award: Necessary Evil: Abolition Hope under Democratic Regime."

On 12 February 1934 the same newspaper published the following correction: "In the course of an interview to the Associated Press on Wednesday which appeared in the issue of *The Times of India* of February 9, the Rt. Hon. H. H. the Aga Khan was reported to have said 'as one having a vast experience of representative institutions in all parts of the world His Highness felt sure that communalism was nothing short of anachronism in a democratic country, its existence being wholly outrageous to the very spirit of democracy'. His Highness says he did not use these words. What he said was: 'experience and practice of a parliamentary government will show that a communal government was an impossibility and that the working of the Reforms would lead to political parties being formed and adjustment of communal claims by mutual consent and compromise'."

On the Communal Award see Philip Cox, *Beyond the White Paper*, London, 1934; N. Gangulee, *The Making of Federal India*, London, n.d. (?1937); J. P. Eddy and F. H. Lawton, *India's New Constitution*, London, 1935; Shafaat Ahmad Khan, *The Indian Federation: An Exposition and Critical Review*, London, 1937; and *Communal Decision*, London, 1932, Cmd. 4147.

130

ADVICE TO THE INDIAN MUSLIM LEGISLATORS

Speech at a Dinner

New Delhi: 12 February 1934

Role of the elected members – a realistic view of politics – immediate and future political goals – the Federation – practical wisdom and immediate goals – signatories to the Joint Memorandum.

He thanked his hosts and said that elected members represented the voice of the country better than any other set of men. It would be one of their tasks to prepare the country more to realise the importance of elected members and organise parties throughout the country for the coming reforms. They must develop independence of judgment and have discipline to follow their leader. (Cheers). Only on that principle could democracy work.

The Aga Khan commended the work of the Indian delegates who elected him as their Chairman. He did his duty to serve the community, the country and the Empire. These were not a contradiction in terms. They in India must take a practical view of politics.

"Lord Morley always used to say that politics is an art of the possible. Let us realise what is immediately possible, what is immediately in front of us, but take good care that the immediate does not jeopardise the future. (Cheers). I am a confirmed optimist and I like my friends to be the same."

He added that only by Federation in which Rulers would be included could they solve the problem of India. "Like our communal problem there will be very little logic in it, but there will be a very great deal of practical wisdom and workability in it. In that spirit we worked at the Round Table Conference and presented our joint memorandum. We were not looking farther ahead than ten years because further distance none can foresee. Who could say in 1910 that Herr Hitler will rule where the Kaiser has ruled or Lenin in place of the Czar? (Applause). Our objective was to have something immediately based on justice and fairplay, meaning real progress for all concerned. (Applause).

"Whether we have succeeded or not will not depend on the twelve humble men who put their signature to the memorandum. We who come from different sections of society and different communities with a different past, presented a united front. (Applause). I can truly say that we were one heart, one head and one mind. It is in your hands whether that spirit will go forward in achieving a new constitution and working it".

Concluding, the Aga Khan said that he and his wife would remember the evening's function with pride.

Source: *Star of India*, Calcutta, 14 February 1934.

The dinner was held at the Gymkhana Club in honour of the Aga Khan and his Begum. Sir Abdur Rahim presided, and a large number of guests were present.

In proposing the toast of the Aga Khan, Sir Abdur Rahim recalled the various stages in which the Aga Khan was associated with constitutional reforms in India, and said that his latest achievement was the Joint Memorandum of the Indian Delegation submitted to the Joint Select Committee on Indian Constitutional Reform, which was a landmark in the political history of India. The Aga Khan, he continued, had throughout his career worked for the uplift of the people of the country, not of any one section or community or class. He was a sincere Indian nationalist and a strong friend of Great Britain. "We, Mahomedans and Hindus, have a unique opportunity in the presence of His Highness to utilize all the great influence which he can exercise not only in India but [also] in England. The Aga Khan is a great advocate of [a] Federation and Hindus and Muslims would do well to unite together and give him a mandate and support in the great task he is engaged in, namely, helping India."

The Times of India, Bombay, 16 February, 1934 also reported the dinner.

131

THE MUSLIM LEAGUE AND THE NEW REFORMS

Speech at a Luncheon

New Delhi: 14 February 1934

The Muslim League and its history – organization essential for forthcoming reforms – unity before the Joint Select Committee – emphasis on the fundamentals – autonomy and the cultural progress of India.

His Highness the Aga Khan replying, thanked the Muslims for the kind welcome extended to himself and his wife and expressed his gratefulness for the generous appreciation by his co-religionists of his humble services rendered to India. He said that the Muslim League, which was the first and oldest Muslim political institution in India, had a stormy history. Its foundation was laid when quarrels had to be composed and many troubles had to be tied over. He had no doubt that the present troubles also would be surmounted.

In 1916–17 the All-India Muslim [League] and the Indian National Congress were working together in close co-operation. The matter of representation in legislatures and also the mode thereof were settled by agreement and the co-operation between the two institutions was so strong that no forces were successful in separating them. This led to the Reforms Act of 1919 . . .

. . . In early years the League was a vigorous body. It had important provincial organisations. Leading men joined them, and under the leadership of men like the late Maharaja of Mahmudabad, Sir Mohammad Shafi and Mr. Jinnah, the Chamberlain of India and the author of the "14 points" – under the guidance of these combined talents the Muslim League made a great headway. He hoped all the present Muslim organisations would work together for the common good of the country and co-operate with bodies who had the same object in view.

For the coming Reforms the Muslim organisations should organise themselves. They should illuminate and educate public opinion among the Muslims and espouse their political demands, which did not mean that they should demand more than their legitimate share.

Continuing His Highness said that they had lost two years at the Round Table Conferences and the fault was entirely their own. In the third Conference, however, the Indian delegates came closer together and at the Joint Committee they were one strong and consolidated team. That was a good example of what united action could achieve.

Was it not possible, His Highness asked, to let bygones be bygones, bury the past and only consider the fundamentals, which he was afraid they were losing?

Concluding His Highness said that a great opportunity for peaceful progress of the whole country had come, and they must do everything to make autonomy a reality. The joint memorandum was something tangible, something practical, something real, and any quarrel at the moment would undo the result of the united front, which had been achieved in London. They must all realise the great responsibility that rested on them, and that that responsibility would be exercised to attain the cultural progress of India.

Source: *Star of India*, Calcutta, 15 February 1934.

Nearly one hundred guests attended this luncheon at which the Begum Aga Khan was also present.

Hafiz Hidayat Husain, the President of the All India Muslim League, specially welcomed the Begum and thanked her for the interest she took in India and hoped that she would retain the most pleasant memories of the visit. On the Aga Khan he said that his unique personality commanded trust and confidence of everyone in India. None had worked with greater zeal in advancing India's claims, and none guided their counsels with more sagely advice. His tremendous influence had paved the way to the attainment of India's constitutional freedom.

Sir Muhammad Yakub recalled events of as far back as 1906 when the Aga Khan had led a Muslim deputation to Lord Minto, the Viceroy, which had marked the awakening of political consciousness among the Muslims of India. The foundation of the All India Muslim League had proved a turning point in the political destiny of the Muslims, and their interests were considerably advanced by the campaign started by the Aga Khan for educating the Muslim community. The fact that he was the leader of the British Indian Delegation at the Round Table Conference demonstrated the extent of the confidence and trust reposed in him by everybody. During heated communal and sectional controversies in London the Aga Khan had never forfeited the faith placed in him as leader of the Delegation before the Joint Select Committee on Indian Constitutional Reform. His visit to India on the eve of constitutional changes would prove of immense benefit to the whole country.

The Times of India, Bombay, 16 February, 1934 also carried a report of the luncheon.

POLITICAL ADVANCE BY EVOLUTION

Speech at a Dinner

New Delhi: 14 February 1934

Speed of constitutional progress in India – its peaceful nature – path of evolution – responsibility of the rising generation – blending of the past with the present and the future.

Responding the Aga Khan recalled that Sir Maneckji Dadabhoy's ancestors belonged to the same racial stock. Though Parsis stuck to their own habits and religion and produced distinguished families like the Jehangirs, the Petits, and the Jeejeebhoys, who were merchant princes in India, Sir Maneckji Dadabhoy was indeed a true successor of great men of the past, noted for their philanthropy.

Addressing Sir Maneckji Dadabhoy, [the] Aga Khan said: "Men of your age and my age are not expected to be Prime Ministers. We are too old to be of any good in that line, and I, for one, have no intention of taking any short cuts to heaven." (Laughter).

"But we must prepare the ground and make it possible for the Indian Prime Ministers in the Provinces and the Centre to function for the benefit of India. The responsibility must be accepted by the rising generation of statesmen of India and, realising the great evolution that had to come in India since the days of Lord Cross' constitution, I can boldly say India would do well not to break with the past or be impatient, and unswervingly work for evolutionary progress so that the past and present will blend into a better and greater future."

Source: *The Civil and Military Gazette*, Lahore, 16 February 1934.
The dinner was given in honour of the Aga Khan and the Begum at the Maiden's Hotel, New Delhi, and was attended by over 160 guests. Proposing the toast, Sir Maneckji Dadabhoy described the Aga Khan as "the greatest son

of India, a spiritual chief of an important community, a trusted statesman and the greatest politician", and hoped that he would be the first Prime Minister of the Federal Government of India.

The Times of India, Bombay, 16 February, 1934 also published a brief report.

COUNSEL TO THE ALL INDIA MUSLIM CONFERENCE

Address to the Executive Board

New Delhi: 15 February 1934

Grassroots and political organization – past success – future ideals
– public services – delay in implementing constitutional reforms –
relationship between the Muslim Conference and the Muslim
League – Muslims and new India – Islam and the world – Dr
Shafa'at Ahmad Khan's work – Maulana Shafi Daoodi – tribute to
Sir Muhammad Iqbal – other office-bearers.

His Highness thanked the members of the Muslim Conference
for the great confidence they reposed in his person by unanimously electing him as their sole arbitrator in reshuffling the
Conference Cabinet. He emphasized the absolute necessity of
making the people and the Electorate the real base and true
foundation of all political power and organization.

His Highness, therefore, laid great emphasis on the need of
making the Executive of the Muslim Conference responsive to
public opinion and responsible to a representative Assembly of
the people. There must be a living, real and vital link between
the Muslim Conference at the top and the Muslim people at the
foundation, otherwise it was bound to degenerate into a mere
debating Society.

Reviewing the work and the resolutions of the Conference
His Highness said: "Muslim Delegation in England worked in
pursuance of the policy of the Muslim Conference. The Conference has achieved a certain measure of success but still it has its
mission to fulfil and its ideal to achieve. To the best of my ability
I worked for the common weal and in future I will be glad to
make further efforts as desired by the Muslim Conference.

"The Conference is fully justified in attaching a great deal of importance to the subject of the Public Services. The carrying on of the administration of a country is not only a privilege but also an obligation, and suitable opportunities should be afforded to all communities to discharge this obligation.

"As to the delay in the inauguration of the Reforms the anxiety of the Conference is fully appreciated. The delay is due to manifold causes but all are agreed that there should be no further delay. Every effort will be made to promote the object in view.

"The Programme of the work before the Conference is excellent and is the only method which has not yet been tried by the Communities to secure united action. May the Conference achieve great success in this venture.

"I was very keen on amalgamating the Muslim Conference and the Muslim League two years ago and had asked several of my friends to do their best to achieve this object. I am however now convinced that the All-India Muslim Conference is all right, and that amalgamation, if it is to come, must wait. This can only come some time after the inauguration of the reform.

"I very much feel gratified at the appreciation you have expressed. I want to serve the best interest of India and feel that the best interest of India demands that India should have the benefit of the Muslims and their culture contributing to the culture of "New India" – the India of the dreams of all true patriots wherein there is neither Hindu Raj nor Muslim Raj but a Raj of Independence, Tolerance, and goodwill.

"As to Muslims abroad I will continue to strive to carry out the wishes of the Conference. I have unshaking faith in Islam which is the greatest unifying, civilizing and fraternizing influence in the world! Itteehadi – Islami – unity of Islam has been misnamed as Pan-Islamism and mis-represented as a political bogey by interested politicians but real Islam is a great cultural and spiritual force for the unity of the world and the fraternity of the Nations.

"My interest in the welfare of the Muslim Conference continues unabated. I may be far from you, but in spirit I am quite near and you can always count upon any service I may render to the Conference.

"Two of our workers have tendered their resignations. And others have followed their examples.

"Dr. Shafaat Ahmad Khan has put in excellent work for India and, in particular, for Muslim India during the last few years.

Long before the Simon Commission he went to England and did uphill work for the cause of his country and community. He was the Secretary of the Muslim Delegation and its devotion and loyalty to the ideal of the Muslim Conference are unsurpassed. His contribution to the evolution of the Reform Schemes is monumental, a contribution of which any great scholar, worker, and patriot may well be proud. While devoting himself at the Headquarters in the All-India Work, he had to neglect his province and must now make good the deficiency.

"It means that only his services for his country and community are transferred from the centre to the Province. The Conference will join me, I have no doubt, in recording our high appreciation of his services, and accept his resignation with great regret.

"I propose Dr. Shafaat Ahmad Khan to be a permanent Vice-President of the All-India Muslim Conference.

"Our second worker is Maulvi Shafi Daoodi, our zealous and untiring working Secretary. He devoted himself to the cause of Muslim Conference body and soul. His work was monumental, his devotion un-paralleled, his zeal unsurpassed. He has been in office for many years, and he wants to set the example of not remaining in office permanently, as appears to be the tendency in certain institutions. I persuaded him to change his mind but he was adamantine, and as he took his stand on the principle involved in it, I had to give way. His resignation will be accepted with great regret by the Conference and by me.

"In recognition of his great services I propose Maulana Shafi Daoodi to be a permanent Vice-President of the All-India Muslim Conference.

"Dr. Sir Md. Iqbal, an eminent thinker, philosopher, poet and statesman of international repute, one whose name is well-known throughout the Islamic world, has been your Chairman during the most important part of the political activities of the Muslim Conference, and the great determination he has shown in the discharge of his duties, the most excellent lead he gave Muslim India during this period, demand their due praise from us all. It would be difficult to have a more inspiring personality than his to occupy the Chair of the Conference, and strenuous efforts were made to persuade him to continue to give his time to the discharge of his great office. He has however done his share and more than his share, and it is but right that we place on record our high appreciation of the great services rendered by him to the Muslim Conference.

"I propose Dr. Sir Md. Iqbal to be a permanent Vice-President of the All-India Muslim Conference."

His Highness then proposed that there should be one Vice-President from Bengal. Mr. A. H. Ghuznavi was nominated for the same and accepted by the house.

His Highness then proposed that in future no office of the Conference should be held by one person for more than two successive terms. "And office bearers must not stand for re-election after holding office for two terms in succession. They, of course, may stand for election after a gap of one term; the object of this rule is to make room for new workers who want to come to the forefront by doing service and undertaking responsibility. The Conference must be prepared to welcome new workers on its platform.

"A wish was expressed by the members at large that steps be taken to make the Conference a strong and effective body, and to give it a cabinet which will work with great will. I have done my best to carry out the wishes of the members, and I place the proposals for the approval of the Board:–

"Nawab Sir Md. Ahmed Sayeed Khan of Chhatail, one who is intimately known to you all and whose excellent work during the last 14 years has won him admiration in all quarters. At my request he has been pleased to take up the onerous duties devolving upon the Chairman of a great Organization like ours.

"The selfless devotion to the work of the Conference has, I understand, been the mission of Khan Bahadur Haji Rahim Bakhsh of the Punjab, who has during the last three years made it a point to take keen interest in the affairs of the Conference and distinguished himself by his independence of judgment and action, and by helping all who have held the various offices. After very careful consideration, in view of the representation necessary from the various Provinces and the advantages of the presence of the Working Secretary at Simla and Delhi when the Central Legislature is in Session, he has at my request agreed to serve as Working Secretary. (The house resounded with long and loud cheers and Haji Rahim Bakhsh was acclaimed as a worthy successor of Maulana Shafi Daoodi, the retiring Working Secretary. All the members congratulated Haji Rahim Bakhsh and Maulana Shafi Daoodi specially assured him of his full and hearty cooperation in his work for the Muslim Conference.)

"Seth Haji Abdulah Haroon, M.L.A. from Sind, will contribute business capacity combined with the knowledge of worldly affairs and a keen political insight as the Treasurer of the Conference.

"The Hon. Syed Hussain Imam from Bihar and Orissa, a rising public man, is expected to give his best to promote the cause of the Muslim Conference.

"Mr. Zahoor Ahmad, M.L.C. from U.P., continues to fill the office of Joint-Secretary and the Hon. Syed Abdul Hafeez of Dacca will be representing Bengal in the same office.

"Mr. Md. Moazzam, M.L.A. from Madras, will act as Financial Secretary of the Muslim Conference.

"I wish the Conference, gentlemen, now good luck and pray to Almighty Allah for its success". (Thundering cheers and loud applause).

His Highness the Aga Khan then again thanked the members of the Muslim Conference and reassured them of his whole-hearted support to the Muslim Conference and its great ideal.

Source: *Star of India*, Calcutta, 21 February 1934.

The meeting of the Executive Board of the All India Muslim Conference was held in Western Hotel at 6.30 p.m. under the presidentship of the Aga Khan.

Mawlana Muhammad Shafee Daoodi, Working Secretary of the Conference, read out his letter of resignation which he had submitted to the Aga Khan on 13 February. Then he paid his tribute of gratitude to the Aga Khan for the sincerity and devotion with which he had worked in organizing Muslim opinion and unifying the Muslims from the very beginning of Muslim political life in modern India. He had always come to the rescue of the community when it sorely needed his guidance and leadership.

Among those present at the meeting were: Sir Abdur Rahim, Sir Abdullah Suhrawardy, Sahibzada Sir Abdul Qaiyum, Abdullah Yusuf Ali, Sir Muhammad Yakub, Sayyid Raza Ali, A. H. Ghuznavi, Mawlana Muhammad Shafee Daoodi, Sayyid Murtaza, the Nawab of Dacca, Sayyid Husain Imam, Nawab Muhammad Ibrahim Ali Khan, Mawlana Mazheruddin, Mawlana Abdus Samad Muqtadari, Muhammad Yamin Khan, Sayyid Abdul Hafeez, Dr. Ziauddin Ahmad, Chaudhri Muhammad Ismail, Khan Bahadur Rahim Bakhsh, Raghib Ahsan, Khalilur-Rahman, Sahibzada Fakhruddin, Nawab Rashid-ud-Din, Hafiz Hidayat Husain, Dr. Mufti Muhammad Sadiq, Captain Sher Muhammad Khan, Nawabzada Khurshid Ali Khan, Fazlul Haq Piracha, Captain Nur Ahmad, M. S. Habib, Mawlana Husain Mian of Phulwari Sharif, Mahmood Padshah and Haji Rasheed Ahmad.

134

A WORD TO THE MUSLIM LEGISLATORS

Speech at a Dinner

Bombay: 22 February 1934

Muslims and the Communal Award – fundamental rights – memorandum of the British India Delegation – separation of Sind from the Bombay Presidency – status of a full-fledged province – salvation in unity.

The Aga Khan, replying, said that the communal award was an award, not a Muslim victory. He had no doubt that Muslims in the Presidency would suffer in weightage owing to the separation of Sind but advance was possible only along the lines of the communal award and the joint memorandum. One could not expect to get more than that.

In regard to the fundamental rights, a resolution on them had been passed by the Muslim League and he was going to urge their incorporation in the Constitution, but after all they were mere legal phrases.

As regards the demand for Muslim representation in the legislature and Services, he said that such a demand had not been made in Upper India.

The Aga Khan proceeded to refer to the memorandum of the British India delegation which, he said, was a considerable improvement on the White Paper. "Within the general framework of the work of the three Round Table Conferences we could not go much further than the joint memorandum. Behind that memorandum you find the signature of every Indian representative at the Joint Select Committee. We appeal to our countrymen to give it careful attention and thought and, if they find it satisfactory, to give it that measure of support without which it will never succeed.

"On the one hand there is the organized opposition of die-hards who make capital out of our difficulties. On the other there is the joint memorandum which cannot succeed without your fullest support. I for one throughout carefully avoided advancing my personal views.

"I assure my friends from Sind that I will leave no stone unturned till I find that separation becomes an accomplished fact. I feel a special interest in Sind. I was born in Sind but, more than that, I am convinced that its people have not had a government of their own for generations past. It would be a terrible blow if the province was made a Chief Commissioner's department. One of the main grievances was that the North-West Frontier Province was under a Chief Commissioner. We did not rest till we got it changed into a full-fledged Governor's province. We cannot take anything less as the status of Sind.

"You may rest assured that I will represent your views and your case to the British government and the British public to the best of my ability. I repeat what I have emphasised on numerous occasions: The salvation of India lies in uniting in common interests. It is unnecessary to remind you that we lose by fissiparous activities."

Source: *The Civil and Military Gazette*, Lahore, 23 February 1934.
The dinner was given at the Willingdon Sports Club. Sir Sulaiman Cassum Mitha proposed the toast of the Aga Khan. A. M. K. Dehlavi, president of the Bombay Legislative Council, supporting the toast, stressed the difficulties under which the Bombay Presidency would find itself after the separation of Sind, the most serious of which would be the inadequate representation of the Muslims in the Bombay Legislative Council. He demanded statutory safeguards regarding Muslim representation in the legislatures, religious liberty and Muslim education, and objected to their omission from the instrument of instructions to be issued to the Governors.
Also see *The Times of India*, Bombay, 22 February, 1934.

135

THE MUSLIM PRESS IN BENGAL

Message to the Star of India

Calcutta: 26 February 1934

Lead the Muslims to their proper goal – keep Muslim voice strong and effective – need for a Bengali edition of the newspaper.

A great future lies in front of your paper, the "Star of India". It is the great task of your paper to lead the Muslims to their proper goal, and for that every Muslim should be proud of possessing such a well-conducted and sane paper. The "Star" has had a short history, but is now that its greatest effort are to be [*sic*]. It is the duty, and it should be the pride, of the Muslims not only in Bengal but all over India to keep the Muslim voice strong and effective.

The time has come when the "Star" should embark on a Bengali edition as well. I particularly want to emphasise the need of a paper in Bengali as well. The newspapers of the future will mould the destinies of the country, and there must be a paper which can reach the widest possible public.

Source: *Star of India*, Calcutta, 26 February 1934.

The *Star of India* began publication on 19 January 1933, and was published by the Muslim Press and Publications Ltd, 9 Dharamtala Street, Calcutta. The first editor was George Franks; the news editor, L. P. Atkinson; and the manager Nur-ul-Haq. Khwaja Nazimuddin was primarily responsible for the idea and also for most of the finances required for running the paper. In late 1935 the financial control and much of other authority were given to M. A. H. Ispahani. Pothan Joseph was one of its editors.

It was a finely edited and impeccably produced paper, with a better news coverage than any other Indian Muslim newspaper before it or since. Being an "eveninger", it was in the happy position of bringing to its readers the news of the day on the same day. It reproduced in its columns most of the significant articles, editorials and letters to the editor appearing in other papers throughout India. It played a crucial role in moulding the Muslim mind throughout the sub-continent in favour of a partition of India during the period between Rahmat Ali's Pakistan National Movement and the Muslim League's Lahore Resolution.

136

THE TASK BEFORE THE MUSLIM
LEGISLATORS OF BENGAL

Speech at a Luncheon

Calcutta: 28 February 1934

Question of jute duty and Bengal revenues – importance of Bengal
for India and Islam – Muslim representatives at the Round Table
Conferences – Muslim respect for other cultures – the Bengali
language – importance of a Bengali-English press – consensus on
crucial issues of development – problems facing the Muslims –
education – understand religion, culture and philosophy – rural
uplift.

First of all I think to-day is a day for mutual congratulation
because we have heard good news that a part of your deficit –
that a part of the need of money in this Province – is going to
be met by the Jute Duty at least half returned. The group with
which I was associated throughout the Round Table Conference
and the Select Committee all along unanimously and on every
occasion supported the return of the entire jute duty to Bengal.
True to my principle that half a loaf is better than none at all, I
welcome to-day's event. I hope that it is only a pleasure postponed
and we will have the other half as well.

I have never had in my mind the least doubt as to the importance of Bengal. Having started my political career here some 33
years ago, on Lord Curzon's Legislative Council, I learnt very
early what it means really, this wonderful and premier province
of India with its gifted population and its great capital. Just as
for India as a whole, Bengal is and will always, I think, remain,
not only on account of its historical facts but on account of the
varied gifts of its population, the premier province.

Bengal is equally, I am sure, the premier country of Islam in the world. I say advisedly, "of Islam in the world", because there is no other country in the world where you have such a large Muslim population concentrated in such a small area as in Eastern Bengal . . .

Speaking about the Round Table Conferences His Highness said, "I am glad to say that from no quarter did I get better support and to no one am I more indebted for the success of the team work of the Muslim delegation than from my friends, the Muslim representatives of the province. My friend here (Mr. Fazlul Huq), with whom I had the privilege of working during the first two Conferences and my good friend, Mr. A. H. Ghuznavi, with whom I had the privilege of working at the Round Table Conference and at the Joint Select Committee, were both towers of strength.

I am proud and happy to have been associated with them and I am sure that the association led, in a great measure, to the general success, to which you kindly referred, of the team work.

Making a few suggestions, His Highness said, "I am sure of one thing that no responsible Muslim wishes in any way to push forward his own culture at the expense of any other community. We respect the vast culture of our fellow Bengali citizens of other faiths, origins and communities, irrespective of whatever that community may be, but I feel strongly and strongly advise you, my Muslim brethren of Bengal, to take up this question very seriously, namely, that Bengali is one of the most magnificent languages in which the highest and noblest ideas and aspirations of man can be represented and interpreted.

"We want very badly suitable Islamic books to be translated into Bengali, a regular society established for the distribution of pamphlets on thought, philosophy, religious and political ideas".

Referring to the need of a Press, he said, "Without a Press a community, a country, a people, are lost. One fundamental fact is that unless you have a press, your views, your thoughts, not only will not get a hearing but will never find that full self-expression without which a hearing is not worth having. I beg of my fellow Muslim brethren of Bengal to realise the importance of a truly Bengali-English Press at your service. Without such a Press you will continue to remain dumb, and you know after all, as, [*sic*] the Holy Quran says, "One of the greatest blessings was to have given us the 'Kalam, and the national 'Kalam' in the modern language consists of a Press. Put out your Press and

SELECTED SPEECHES AND WRITINGS

you have put out your 'Kalam'. It is absolutely essential that you should awake to this."

Referring to the necessity for a general consensus of Muslim political opinion in this province organising itself for the coming constitutional changes, he remarked, "It will be a fatal mistake if these long-announced reforms still find you unprepared, unready and disorganized. There is, I should think, a general consensus of opinion, on many subjects, the need of primary education, rural welfare, and agricultural indebtedness, questions that are matters of life and death to the overwhelming majority of the Mohammedans of this province".

He added, "Let us work in hand with other communities and more than any body else I believe it is in the interest of Muslims themselves that these big questions should be taken up, not by one section of the people of this province but by that over-whelming majority who are humble and poor and find difficulty in meeting these great problems that are theirs. We have these immense difficulties before our own people, the Muslims of this province, namely, the work of education, rural welfare, indebted-ness, agricultural depression, the bread-winners not finding the bread to eat."

"As Muslims", said His Highness, "we can have in this province but three immediate objects: education, primarily education, the better understanding of our culture, of our religion, of our philo-sophy, through Bengali as a medium. We can have the vast question of primary education taken up. We must also apply ourselves, intensively through Local Boards, inspired by the Government of the Province, to the work of rural uplift, and through the legislature and other means to the immense prob-lems of indebtedness and agricultural depression".

Concluding, His Highness the Aga Khan said, "I beg of you to convey my message of thanks to the Muslims of the province. Had my health allowed, it was my intention to see larger numbers and vaster assemblies of the Muslims of this great city instead of paying this necessarily hurried visit. That has not been my privi-lege. I meant to visit many Muslim institutions and see my fellow workers in their various fields of activity. All this I have been denied, but through you and everyone of you I beg to convey my message of gratitude and recognition of the generous way in which you have throughout given me your confidence and atten-tion to my humble advice on every occasion.

"You have rightly said I do not want to be a dictator.

Gentlemen, I do not believe in dictators till after a country has tried parliamentary government for many, many decades. Then and only then is it time for a declaration in any country – successful dictatorship. We are not even trained in representative making of policy. The stage at which we Muslims are in this province is there such a general consensus of opinion among Muslims?"

Source: *Star of India*, Calcutta, 1 March 1934.

The Times of India, Bombay, 1 March, 1934 reported that the Aga Khan made the speech at a luncheon given in his honour by the Muslim members of the Bengal Legislative Council.

137

MUSLIM UNANIMITY ON INDIAN REFORMS

A Statement

Calcutta: 28 February 1934

The Communal Award must be upheld – no rivalry of opinion among Bengali and Punjabi Muslims – reforms should not be delayed.

The Aga Khan was emphatic that there was unanimity among Moslems up to 99 per cent., and even more in the two key provinces of Bengal and the Punjab, that the Prime Minister's Communal Award must be upheld. There was no appreciable difference about this anywhere. The impression of differences arose from some confusion in organization: there were rival organizations, but no rivalry of opinion or sentiment.

He appealed to Great Britain with all the earnestness at his command not to delay in pressing on with the constitutional reforms. There would, he said, be an ugly upheaval of Moslem opinion in Bengal if no progress were visible. The whole object of the Joint Select Committee was to expedite the reforms, and Moslems were as anxious for this as anyone. He recognized that the working out of responsibility at the Centre might take time, but that should not delay immediate consideration of Provincial Autonomy.

Source: *The Times*, London, 1 March 1934.

The Aga Khan, accompanied by the Begum, arrived in Calcutta on 27 February on the invitation of Bengali Muslim leaders who wanted to discuss with him the prevailing political situation and seek his guidance. "The Bengalis are excited about his visit, and a crowd of several thousand met him at the railway station", wrote *The Times* correspondent. A recent attack of fever had compelled the Aga Khan to cancel some of his engagements, yet he went through a busy programme. He stayed at Government House where, after the luncheon hosted by Muslim legislators, he "made a statement" to *The Times* correspondent.

The Aga Khan's plan was to proceed from Calcutta to Burma to study the question of its separation from India. He hoped to be back in London at the end of April.

138

THE IMPORTANCE OF INSURANCE

Reply to the Address of Welcome by the Directors of the Eastern Federal Union Insurance Company

Calcutta: 1 March 1934

Importance and benefits of insurance – Muslims and insurance – scope for indigenous enterprise – tribute to the Nawab of Bhopal.

His Highness expressed his pleasure at being able to visit the office of the Company which he said was doing a real service to the country.

He emphasised the importance of insurance and the benefits it conferred upon the people. Insurance, he said, was not a form of gambling as many people were, perhaps, inclined to think. Indeed, it was no more gambling than locking up an iron safe at night in order to protect its contents.

Mahomedans, perhaps, did not fully realise the various benefits that this particular kind of business conferred upon the people and for this reason it was necessary that greater efforts should be made to popularise insurance among them. The principles of insurance, he declared, were in no way in conflict with the teachings of Islam and Mahomedans should have no hesitation in going in for insurance – life, marine, fire, accident, etc. He pointed out that he had himself insured his life through the Agents of the Eastern Federal Union and this might be taken as a proof of his faith in insurance and his confidence in the Company, the undertakings of which were national rather than communal.

Referring to the European and American companies operating in India, His Highness said that growth of indigenous enterprise could in no way clash with their interests as the field was wide and only a very small beginning had been made. National enter-

SELECTED SPEECHES AND WRITINGS

prise alone, he said, could develop its full possibilities and in this non-Indian companies stood to gain more by co-operating with Indian enterprise than by attempting to regard insurance as their monopoly.

In conclusion, His Highness expressed his appreciation of the services of H. H. the Nawab of Bhopal to the country in general and to the Company in particular. His Highness the Nawab, he said, had been associated with the Company as a patron since its inception, and it was no exaggeration to say that but for the interest he had taken in its activities the Company would not have attained the position it had done.

Source: *Star of India*, Calcutta, 1 March 1934.

The Aga Khan, in his capacity as a patron of the Eastern Federal Union Insurance Company, paid a visit to the Calcutta office of the firm at 9 Clive Street in the morning. He presented to the board of directors an autographed portrait of himself.

Among those present on the occasion were: Khan Bahadur A. Momin, Muhammad Amin, A. R. Siddiqui, Menhirick, J. W. J. Levien, A. Ispahani, H. A. Ispahani, M. K. Khaleeli, Eric Ellis, Vali Muhammad Dada, Kamdia Cassamally Hussainally, Hussainally Cassamally, Khan Bahadur Alibhoy Muhammad, Captain Majid Khan and A. S. Bawa.

139

COMMERCIAL RELATIONS BETWEEN INDIA AND BURMA

Reply to the Address of Welcome Presented by the Burma Indian Chamber of Commerce

Rangoon: 6 March 1934

Indian pioneers in Burma and their contribution to the country – tribute to the chamber – benefits of trade for both parties and the people – example of Egypt – identification of members with Burma – loyalty to Burma – prosperity of Burma associated with India – Indians should discuss problems with their Burmese friends.

His Highness the Aga Khan, replying to the address, said that he wished, first of all to thank the members of the Indian Chamber of Commerce for so very kindly having done him the great honour of inviting him there that afternoon and for their very kind words. He could assure them that it had been a great pleasure as well as an honour to come there as their guest and to see in this great city, the capital of Burma, their representatives who had so long been associated with this Province.

As the President had just said it was now over a century when Indians first came here [*sic*], and they had contributed by their enterprise and by their commercial and economic acumen to the development of this country. (Applause.) He was very glad and happy to hear that they had organised their efforts in the Chamber, and thus they were meeting the new conditions in the world affairs and the economic conditions of the present day with the methods of this utility, organisation, co-operation and united efforts [*sic*].

This was a fine example of Indian commercial enterprise, and he hoped this example would be followed by all loyal chambers in other and more important centres and ports to be found throughout the East. They had very rightly said that Indians had helped and at that moment had vast interests in this country, and he was sure these interests were for the welfare of all concerned because he was one of those who were convinced that the essence of good trade and commerce should not be of benefit to one party but to both sides that take part in it, as well as the general public, wherever commercial and economic activities take place. (Applause.) He was convinced that whatever advantages the Indians had gained out of their commercial activities would be ultimately found of benefit by the people of Burma as a whole.

It seemed but yesterday – and he was old enough to remember it – that practically the whole of Egypt was a European economic possession. It was European capital that started agriculture, but during the last forty or fifty years the labourers had gradually bought them out, till to-day Egypt was essentially for the Egyptians. There was the inevitable law that, slowly but surely, the monies for capital brought from abroad would ultimately benefit, and would eventually come to, the people of Burma as a whole. (Applause.) He also wished to congratulate other members of the Indian Chamber for the brave and wise words they had just said, that they were prepared to work for the welfare of the country as a whole, and they were fully identifying themselves with this country (Burma) and its prosperity.

It was right and proper that those Indians who had come here and made Burma their home should accept it with all their heart, and he was glad to say from the private conversation he had had for the past twenty hours with Indian leaders that those families who had come and established themselves here had loyally accepted this country as a whole. It would be detrimental to the people of this country to upset anything which had been done in their own interest and, if they took the long view, he thought that they would come to the same conclusion he had come to. He for one had not the slightest doubt about the advice he should give, if he were asked for it, but it was for them and they were masters of the situation, and he did not believe in giving advice when it was not asked for.

However, he had not the slightest doubt as to the fact that, come what may, the prosperity of this country was, and must be, very generally ever associated with that vast Indian Empire next door. He asked them all to realise – whether they were Burmese or children of migrants – that prosperity could never come of "Beggaring-my-neighbour." His advice to his Indian friends was to meet their Burmese friends and openly discuss with them day after day and show them their troubles and their tribulations, and to do everything for the benefit of the Province as a whole.

He thanked them very much and said that, if his few words helped to bring those who had made this country their home nearer to those whose home it was, alike for civic, economic and political co-operation, he could say he had spent a very useful and happy afternoon. He also took this opportunity of thanking his fellow-guests for having done him the honour of coming there that afternoon. (Applause.)

Source: *Ismaili*, Bombay, 22 April 1934.

An At Home was given to His Highness the Aga Khan by the President and members of the Committee of the Burma Indian Chamber of Commerce on the 6th March, when the President read the following address of welcome at the gathering.

"It is my proud and pleasant privilege to extend to Your Highness on behalf of the Burma Indian Chamber of Commerce, a most cordial welcome in our midst this afternoon. I need hardly assure you, sir, how grateful our Chamber feels to you for accepting its invitation and sparing time to attend this function in spite of your multifarious affairs and varied engagements during your sojourn in Rangoon.

"As Your Highness is aware, Indians have got very old connections with Burma. Even prior to her annexation to India, Indian Co-operation had begun to contribute to its material prosperity and to-day Indians rightly claim an important share in the industrial and commercial development of the province. In view of the magnitude of the interests of the Indian community in Burma, the need for an organised body was long felt and it was with a view to supply this want that our Chamber was established in 1925. I am glad to say that, in spite of the comparatively short period of its existence, it is recognised to-day as the most influential and authoritative exponent of Indian public opinion in the province on all important questions. It has not only been able to enlist full sympathy and support of all sections of the Indian mercantile community but it has also received recognition from the Government and other public bodies. Our Chamber is at present on the Burma Legislative Council, Rangoon Port Trust, and other bodies on which commercial interests are generally represented. (Applause.)

"I hope it will now be clear to Your Highness that the whole Indian commercial community of Burma joins in welcoming you to this capital city and rejoices in having got the unique opportunity of meeting you. Although Your Highness has long been well known to each and all of us through your long record of public service, it was not given to many of us till now to meet you personally, and we are glad that such a long-looked-for opportunity has offered itself to us to-day, thanks to your courtesy in having responded to our invitation.

"Your Highness, it seems hardly necessary for me to dwell at any great length on your countless and conspicuous services in the cause of our country and countrymen both at home and abroad during your long political career. Your Highness led the Indian Delegation at the Indian Round Table Conference. By your labours at these Conferences in bringing the communalists on the one hand and the nationalists on the other, closer and closer, you have proved yourself an essential link between the two groups of Indian political thought, and your labours in this direction have been generally appreciated. I feel that the spirit which actuated and guided your deliberations and actions at the Conference is worthy of emulation. (Applause.)

"This is neither the time nor the place to discuss political matters, but I may take this opportunity of making a passing reference to a matter which during the last two years and more has been agitating the public mind in Burma. I refer to the future constitutional status of Burma which is now engaging the attention of the Joint Select Committee and His Majesty's Government. As Your Highness is doubtless aware, many financial and economic considerations are involved in the question and the Indian community, in view of their large stake in the land, are deeply concerned in the decision that may ultimately be taken on this momentous issue. We as business-men feel that the decision must be such as would ensure the economic prosperity of Burma and the welfare of her people. It is obvious that under the present day world conditions, the existing position in relation to matters pertaining to Burma's economic life or her financial equilibrium cannot be disturbed without great detriment to her interests. I hope, therefore, that these primary considerations, viz., economic and financial, will weigh with the authorities in arriving at a final decision with regard to the future constitutional status of Burma.

"Whatever the ultimate decision may be, I hope nothing will be done which would adversely affect the rights of Indians which they have so long enjoyed, such as, the freedom of entry and the right of carrying on their business and professions undisturbed. In view of the important part played by the Indian community in the commercial and economic life of Burma, it would be most unfair to put them at any disadvantage in relation to any other community residing in the province. I have no doubt, however, that Indian commerce in Burma with its usual elasticity will adjust itself to the altered circumstances – whatever they are – and while striving to protect its legitimate interests, will not fail to keep in view the best interests of Burma as a whole.

"Your Highness, it is unfortunate that in a far off place like Rangoon it is very rarely that we get the benefit of the presence of leading Indian politicians like you, and our Chamber, therefore, feels it a great honour to receive you this afternoon. We are glad that the visit of Your Highness has been well-timed, as I feel that, whatever advice you may be good enough to give us at this momentous time in the political history of Burma, will prove of immense value to us. I once more welcome Your Highness and wish you, on behalf of our Chamber a long and prosperous life in the service of our motherland. (Applause.)

"Before I resume my seat, gentlemen, I thank you all on behalf of the Chamber for responding to its invitation and for contributing to the success of this function by your presence". (Loud Applause.)

140

A CALL TO THE ISLAMIC WORLD

A Message

London: 14 March 1934

The world of Islam at a turning point – example of the Prophet –
raise the position of Muslims – learn secrets of social and intellectual power – the Japanese example – conquest of nature – spiritual
debt to the Holy Prophet.

The world of Islam to-day is at a turning point of its history. The
middle-ages are over and either Islam must now go forward or
be added to the other might-have-beens of History.

The Moslems must now awake, and taking their example from
the glorious life and the marvellous teachings of the Holy
Prophet build their spiritual and religious faith on Muhammad
and work for the development in science, knowledge, and
political, and social advance along the lines of the most progressive races of mankind.

Formalism and verbal interpretation of the teaching of the
great Arabian are in absolute contradiction with the whole history
of the Prophet. We must accept his Divine Message as the
channel of our union with the Absolute and the Infinite, and
once our spiritual faith is firmly established, fearlessly go forward
by self-sacrifice, by courage, and by application to raise the scientific, the economic, the political, and social position of the
Moslems to a place of equality with Christian Europe and
America.

Our social customs, our daily work, our constant efforts must
be tuned up, must be brought into line with the highest form of
possible civilisation. At its greatest period Islam was at the head
of science, was at the head of knowledge, was in the advanced
line of political, philosophic, and literary thought.

To-day we are in our middle-ages. We must get out of it, and begin our new era with strength and will power for the coming development of our people.

The Moslem world can to-day be divided into two general parts. (1) One consists of the vast Moslem population living under European and other non-Moslem rulers. (2) The second part consists of the independent Moslem states of Arabia, of Persia, of Afghanistan, of Egypt, of Turkey.

Now where we are under foreign rule we can, immediately by imitating as the Japanese have done, but also by keeping our own spiritual and our highest intellectual character intact, just as the Japanese have done, learn directly from the races that rule us those secrets of social and intellectual power which have made Europe so strong and so progressive.

Where we are in an independent position we can promote intensive culture, intensive education of the youth, intensive imitation if you like, but always, as in the case of Japan, keeping our highest moral and emotional and spiritual self in our own historical development [*sic*]. With that we can go forward and carry out reforms, carry out political and economic development, carry out, above all, scientific culture which will place us on the same level as the European races.

In cases like India, in countries like Java, like Morocco, and like North Africa, we can immediately learn from our European fellow-subjects, or rulers if you prefer so to call them, those secrets of power over nature, of scientific and economic, and industrial development, which has made Europe so powerful.

Along these lines, my fellow Moslems, I implore you, I beg of you, to work for the advancement of the whole world of Islam, but never forget our spiritual debt to our Holy Prophet.

With these words I hope that progress will become from now onwards thorough and regular.

Source: *Star of India*, Calcutta, 15 March 1934.

On 15 August 1934, the *Star of India* again published this message, but with minor differences. I have not been able to discover why the message was reprinted after an interval of five months. I reproduce here (for the record) the second text:

"The world of Islam to-day is at a turning point of its history. The Middle-Ages are over and either Islam must now go forward or be added to the other might-have-beens of history.

"The Muslims must now awake and taking their example from the glorious life and the marvellous teachings of the Holy Prophet, build their spiritual and religious faith on Mohammed and work for the development in Science,

Knowledge and Politics, and social advancement along the lines of the most progressive races of mankind.

"We must accept his Divine Message as the channel of our union with the Absolute and the Infinite, and once our spiritual faith is firmly established fearlessly go forward by self-sacrifice, by courage, and by application to raise the scientific, economic, the political, and social position of the Muslims to a place of equality with Christian Europe and America.

"Our social customs, our daily work, our constant efforts must be tuned up, must be brought into line with the highest form of possible civilisation. At its greatest period Islam was at the head of science, was at the head of knowledge, was in the advance line of political, philosophical and literary thought.

"To-day we are in our Middle-Ages. We must get out of it, and begin our new era with strength and with will-power for the coming development of our people.

"The Muslim world can to-day be divided into two general parts: One consists of the vast Muslim population living under European, and other non-Muslim rulers and the other consists of independent Muslim states of Arabia, Afghanistan, Egypt, and Turkey.

"Now where we are under foreign rule we can immediately, by imitating as the Japanese have done, as also by keeping our own spiritual and our highest intellectual character intact, just as the Japanese have done, learn directly from the races that rule us those secrets of social and intellectual powers which have made Europe so strong and so progressive.

"Where we are in an independent position, intensive culture, intensive education of the youth, intensive imitation if you like, should be our programme, but always, as in the case of Japan, keeping the highest moral, emotional and spiritual development in view. With that we can go forward and carry out reforms, carry out political and economic development, carry out, above all, a scientific culture which will place us on the same level as the European race.

"In cases like India, in countries like Java, Morocco and North Africa we can immediately learn from our European fellow-subjects, or rulers, if you prefer so to call them, those secrets of power over nature, of scientific and economic and industrial development, which has made Europe so powerful.

"Along these lines, my fellow Muslims, I implore you, I beg of you, to work for the advancement of the whole world of Islam, but never forget our spiritual debt to our Holy Prophet."

141

PERSIAN POETS

An Article

London: 22 September 1934

Inadequate knowledge in the West of Eastern literature and philosophy – Eastern art better appreciated than literature – limitations of Umar Khayyam's poetry – supreme example of the genius of Hafiz – his universal appeal in the Muslim East – his thoughts, ideas and expressions – difficulties of translation – other Persian poets – Mawlana Rumi – Qa'ani's portrayal of Nature – appeal to the Orientalists.

The arrangements now being made to celebrate in Europe the millennium of the birth of Firdausi, author of the immortal "Shahnama," are to be heartily welcomed. One of the world's greatest cultural losses is due to inadequate knowledge in the West of many of the best treasures of Eastern literature and philosophy.

The masterpieces of Eastern art have had an advantage over those of poetry, literature, and philosophy. Vision is the same the world over, while language and, above all, the implications of words are far apart. The trained Western eye can immediately see and appreciate the carpets of the Safavis, the buildings of Cairo, Ispahan and Agra, the exquisite paintings, porcelains and fabrics of China and Japan, the miniatures and the illuminated books of Persia and Arabia, the magnificent lamps of Egypt. These are at once understood if the observer has either natural taste or a trained intelligence. Most educated people who visited the Exhibition of Persian Art at Burlington House early in 1931 carried away feelings similar to those of an equal number of cultured Persians. But when we turn to literature the gap is indeed immeasurable, and to-day this is a serious question.

The East has begun to know the literature and thought of the West, but the West has not returned the compliment. To men like my lamented friend Edward G. Browne and Sir Denison Ross we are deeply grateful for encouraging the study of the literature of the East. One of my happiest memories is the result of giving Browne's "Literary History of Persia" to Arnold Bennett. After some weeks I had several visits from Bennett and I shall never forget the joy the book had given him. Professor R. A. Nicholson's similar, but smaller, work for Arabian literature should be known to every Englishman. Sir Mahomed Iqbal also has helped to a better understanding of Moslem culture. The recent correspondence in *The Times* on the subject of Persian poetry shows that at least some interest is being taken in that vast and almost limitless treasure.

Of the poets of Persia Omar Khayyam is best known here, and yet to no Persian can he ever be more than a moderate poet. The reason for his lacking higher consideration among his own countrymen is simple: his poetry gives only one aspect of human experience and emotion. The feelings so beautifully expressed by him (and admirably translated by Edward FitzGerald) can never be more than the passing sentiments of a hopeless waster. Most men have such passing moods. But Persians expect from a great poet a far wider and fuller, a universal series of inspirations. Just as anyone who in life practised the ideas of Khayyam would soon get bored to death or develop into a contemptible creature, so would regular reading and study of Khayyam lead to either boredom or mental atrophy. Since Persia is full of great poets, it cannot be expected that anyone who so limits his expression can enjoy higher esteem there than Khayyam has gained. A great poet should be able to inspire a man in any circumstances of his life. Can it be seriously maintained that an explorer attempting the conquest of Mount Everest could possibly get his inspiration from Omar?

We have a striking contrast when we turn to the greatest of Persian poets, the supreme example of the genius of Moslem Persia, the immortal Hafiz. We go from one extreme to the other. Provided one knows the Persian language and the implications of its words, whatever a human being's mood, emotions, and thoughts may be, he can turn to Hafiz for the highest pleasure and inspiration. Take the riddle of the universe. From the highest theism to the most realistic materialism, every point of view has been more beautifully expressed in Hafiz than anywhere else.

Every mood, every human thought, is given in language of supreme lyrical beauty.

Tolstoi said that the greatest work of art should be such as a Russian peasant could understand and appreciate. Hafiz is understood and appreciated by the humblest as well as the highest and the most intellectual in the Moslem East. We have internal evidence as well as external historical reasons for believing that even during his lifetime, when space meant so much, when there was little printing, his poetry was generally known from the Bay of Bengal to Kashmir and from the deserts of Central Asia to Egypt and the confines of Europe. To-day his empire in those regions is still supreme. In the highest religious messages we hope to find such vision as will clarify the latest speculations of scientific philosophy, without for one moment supposing that the teachers of the past knew or could have known the later developments of human thought. So in Hafiz one could easily find thoughts, ideas, expressions that would illuminate the fundamental conceptions of even such abstract hypotheses and speculations as those of, say, Einstein, Jeans, or Whitehead. Hafiz could not know the marvellous discoveries of the disciplined application of human intelligence to-day; but his supreme genius enabled him to lay such splendid foundations that place can be found within his universal temple for almost any later development.

The same is true of his vision of human thought, emotions, and action. Unfortunately this very magnificence has rendered adequate translation nearly impossible. When attempts are made to reproduce in any form or shape in a foreign language the beauty of his lyrical and imaginative expression, the variety and diversity of his thought are obscured. On the other hand, if a detailed analysis is written paraphrasing every conceivable interpretation of each word, it becomes an encyclopaedia rather than a rendering of poetry.

Between the two extremes of Hafiz and Khayyam there are any number of other poets, all worthy of diligent study. It is almost beyond our conception that one man could have produced the work of Firdausi. Were he not a historical figure and were we not sure of the "Shahnama," who could have believed it? Saadi, Jami, Nizami, Anwari, Khaqani, and many others deserve careful presentation to the West. Maulana Rumi is fairly well known to some European mystics. His "Mathnavi" is not only a fine presentation of a case, but is also narrative poetry of great beauty and force. Unlike Hafiz, however, he has only put forward the argument for mystical pantheism, while in Hafiz in a few verses all the essentials of Rumi's, and indeed of every other philosophy, are given us. From the purely lyrical point of view Rumi's "Diwan-i-Shams" is more beautiful and more splendid than his "Mathnavi."

One of the greatest poets Persia has produced was Qaani. Indeed it is difficult not to place him next to Hafiz and Firdausi, and his appeal to us is all the greater because he was almost a contemporary of our day. Even so ardent an admirer as E. G. Browne has not done full justice to this mid-nineteenth-century genius. His personal character had many blots. Like some recent European writers (such as D. H. Lawrence and André Gide), he has written on questions of sex in language of supreme lyrical beauty, but from an entirely physical and materialistic angle. The Persians, used as they were to the spiritual and sentimental interpretations of even physical love by Jami, Nizami, and others, were liable to forget the wealth of beauty and depth of thought that there is in Qaani's "Qasidas" (Odes). The very fact also that he chose Qasidas in praise of the kings, nobles, and princes who were his contemporaries, as the vehicle for pouring out his perceptions of Nature, has prevented the general public from going to him for the real gems in his book. Englishmen who are proud of their Wordsworth can well understand what joy Qaani gives to the Persian when he portrays Nature in all her aspects – the wonderful lights and shades of Iran, its landscape, its rain, thunder, lightning, drought, trees, birds, and flowers. Many varieties of "Tintern Abbey" can easily be found in those Qasidas. I only wish that European Orientalists would turn to serious study of this man of genius.

I have a suggestion to make to those Orientalists who know the Persian language well and have the gift of literary expression. It is that one of them should follow the example of FitzGerald – in a far better cause – and translate into one of the better known European languages as fully and as beautifully as he can the famous Qasida about the person of God which begins with the words: "*Nehani az nazar ay by nazir az bas aayanasty.*" ["Thou art concealed from sight, O, Matchless One, and yet manifest."] This Qasida is indeed worthy of Hafiz himself. No praise could be higher.

Source: *The Times*, London, 22 September 1934.

The journal introduced the article, which carried the full title of "Persian Poets: The Supremacy of Hafiz: A Word to Western Students", with the following words:

"Sir Denison Ross, Director of the London School of Oriental Studies, left London for Teheran yesterday to represent British Islamic scholarship in the earlier celebrations of the millenary of the birth of the great Persian poet Firdausi. Beginning at the Persian capital in the first week of October, the celebrations will be continued at Meshed, and completed towards the end of the month at Tūs, the birthplace of the poet, where a monument is to be unveiled. The British celebrations will extend over four days at the end of October."

The Times of 27 September carried a correction of the text of the article:

" 'The feelings so beautifully expressed by him (and admirably translated by Edward FitzGerald) can never be more than the passing sentiments *except* of a hopeless waster.' The word 'except' was inadvertently dropped."

On Persian poetry see Alessandro Bausani, "Notizie su poeti Persiani contemporanei", *Oriente Moderno*, 1945, pp. 28–41; Edward G. Browne, "Biographies of Persian Poets . . .", *Journal of the Royal Asiatic Society*, Vol. 32 (1900), pp. 21–762, *A History of Persian Literature: Tartar Dominion* (A.D. *1265–1502*), Cambridge, 1920, *A Literary History of Persia*, London, 4 vols, 1902–24, and *The Tadhkiratu'sh-Shu'ara (Memoirs of the Poets) by Daulatshah . . .* , London, 1901; Paul Horn, *Geschichte der persischen Litteratur*, Leipzig, 1910; G. Ouseley, *Biographical Notices of Persian Poets . . .* , London, 1846; A. Pagiliaro and A. Bausani, *Storia della letteraturá Persiana*, Milan, 1960; Shibli Nu'mani, *Shi'r-ul-Ajam*, Lahore, 1924; and C. A. Storey, *Persian Literature: A Bio-Bibliographical Survey*, London, 2 vols, 1953, 1958.

On Anwari: Henri Ferté, *Notice sur le poète Persan, Enveri*, Paris, 1895; Uto Melzer, "Uber einen Verses Anwaris", *Wiener Zeitschrift für die Kunde des Morgenlandes*, Vol. 43 (1936), pp. 19–20; and V. A. Zhukovski, *Ali Auhad ad-Din Anvari*, St Petersburg, 1883.

On Jami: F. H. Davis, *Persian Mystics: Jami*, London, 1908; T. N. Foulis, *Jami: The Persian Mystic*, Edinburgh, 1907; W. Nassau Lees, *A Biographical Sketch of the Mystic Philosopher and Poet Jami*, Calcutta, 1859; V. E. von Rosenzweig, *Biographische notizen über Mewlana Abdurahman Dsehami*, Vienna, 1840; and M. Wickerhauser, *Jami: Liebe, Wein und Mancherlei*, Liepzig, 1856.

On Khaqani: Hadi Hasan, "Khaqani's Poetry", *Visva-Bharati Quarterly*, Vol. 6 (1940–41), pp. 248–59; M. Rifaqat-ullah Khan, "Life of Khaqani", *Indo-Iranica*, Vol. 12 (1959), pp. 24–44; Nicolas de Khanikoff, "Mémoires sur Khakani, poète Persan", *Journal Asiatique*, 1864 and 1865, 2 parts; and K. B. Nasim. "Khaqani Shirwani", *Journal of the University of Peshawar*, Vol. 10 (1965), pp. 67–75.

On Qa'ani: Sidney T. A. Churchill, "Hakim Qa'ani", *Indian Antiquary*, Vol. 17 (1888), pp. 241–2; J. von Hammer-Purgstall, *Das Fruhlingsgedicht des persischen Dichters Mirsa Habib Kaani nebersetzt*, Zeitschrift der Deutschen Morgenländischen Gesellschaft, Vol. 9, Leipzig, 1855; and Vera Kubickova, "Qa'anis", *Archiv Orientalni*, supplementa III, 1954.

142

AFGHANISTAN AND THE LEAGUE OF NATIONS

Speech in the General Assembly of the League of Nations

Geneva: 27 September 1934

Impact of internal and external events on Afghanistan – her entry into the League of Nations – the danger of the League's failure to become universal – the glorious brotherhood of Islam.

They are no conventional feelings that have prompted me to address you, and it is no conventional speech that I wish to deliver. No representative of India, no Muslim, no Asiatic could play his part on this historic occasion unmoved. Times have been when the rulers of Afghanistan were content – were determined – to keep their nation aloof from the hurly-burly of the world; when even her historic and picturesque capital of Kabul was one of the world's forbidden cities. To-day, Afghanistan has set her seal on a momentous change. Times indeed have changed in all parts of the globe. There have been developments everywhere which none could have foreseen thirty, twenty years back. Nor has Afghanistan remained unaffected by the evolution of things within, or by the march of events outside. To-day, she formally and finally enters into the great comity of nations – no stranger indeed, for she has been playing her part in session after session of the Disarmament Conference. Nor does she enter into a strange Assembly, for not only can she claim the goodwill of all, she can claim that all her next-door neighbours are to-day – and we could not say this when the session began – Members like her of the League.

It is not without emotion that I play my part on this memorable occasion. Throughout all my associations with the League I have felt – you will pardon the frankness of a man who is perhaps all the more a true representative of India because he is also a citizen of the world – I have long felt that the League was in danger of becoming too occidental and too representative of one creed to be truly catholic and universal. To a Muslim like myself, it is no small thing that another Islamic nation is to-day entering the League. For I am convinced that her entry will strengthen the League in far greater measure than the number of her subjects or even the extent of her realm might suggest, and will invigorate it in the pursuit of our common ideals with fresh ideas and a fresh outlook.

No Indian will read unmoved the proceedings of to-day. For India, however much she may seek from the West her political institutions, remains a true daughter of the East, proud of her Eastern blood, her Eastern languages, her Eastern cultures. These she shares with Afghanistan, and seventy millions of her peoples share, as I share, with Afghanistan in the glorious brotherhood of Islam.

Source: *Verbatim Record of the Fifteenth Ordinary Session of the Assembly of the League of Nations, Twelfth Plenary Meeting, Thursday, September 27th, 1934, at 10. a.m.,* Geneva, 1934, p. 2.

I reproduce below the relevant proceedings from the official record:

President: M. R. J. SANDLER.
48. – APPLICATION OF THE KINGDOM OF AFGHANISTAN TO BE ADMITTED INTO THE LEAGUE OF NATIONS: REPORT OF THE SIXTH COMMITTEE.

The President:

Translation: The first item on the agenda is the examination of the Sixth Committee's report on the request of Afghanistan to be admitted to membership of the League of Nations.

The Assembly will remember that, at its meeting on the afternoon of September 25th, it took note of a telegram containing a request from the Kingdom of Afghanistan to be admitted to membership of the League of Nations. It decided to place this question on the agenda of the present session and referred the matter to the Sixth Committee for examination.

The Sixth Committee met forthwith and examined the request of Afghanistan to be admitted to membership of the League; the report of the Sixth Committee is before the Assembly this morning.

While acknowledging that the Assembly has full discretion to decide this point, I thought that, as the Sixth Committee's report was communicated to the delegations yesterday, I ought to give the Assembly an opportunity to state its opinion on this report without delay, in view of the advanced stage of the work of the session.

I therefore think I should first ask the Assembly if it is willing to take action forthwith on the Sixth Committee's report.

If no one wishes to speak, I shall interpret the silence of the Assembly as a sign of assent, and consequently shall consider that the Assembly has decided, in accordance with the conditions laid down in its Rules of Procedure, to take action in the matter forthwith.

Agreed.

The President:

Translation: I will therefore ask His Excellency Tevfik Rüstü Bey, first delegate of Turkey, Rapporteur of the Sixth Committee, and His Excellency M. de Madariaga, first delegate of Spain, Chairman of the Sixth Committee, to take their places on the platform.

(*Tevfik Rüstü Bey and M. de Madariaga took their places on the platform.*)

The President:

Translation: Tevfik Rüstü Bey, Rapporteur, will address the Assembly.

Tevfik Rüstü Bey (Turkey) Rapporteur:

Translation: The Sixth Committee has done me the signal honour of entrusting to me the pleasant task of submitting to the Assembly on its behalf the report on the admission of the Kingdom of Afghanistan to membership of the League of Nations.

I feel particular satisfaction in acquitting myself of this task since Turkey entertains relations of close friendship with Afghanistan, as with all other countries of Asia.

There is no need for me to emphasise the great importance of admitting into this body of international concord and co-operation a State which not only fulfils all the conditions required under the Covenant, but whose sincere efforts in favour of peace and progress call for the sympathy of all the nations belonging to our institution.

This country entertains good relations with all States in general and with its neighbours in particular, as was clearly evinced in the speeches made in the Sixth Committee concerning Afghanistan.

The dispute existing between Afghanistan and Persia has been referred to arbitration, as I explained yesterday in the Sixth Committee.

I therefore trust that I may be permitted to repeat my sincere hope that Afghanistan may take the place in this institution which she merits and thus give us her valuable assistance in our common task.

I am convinced, further, that this decision of the Assembly will be for this country a guarantee of the strong moral support of the League in the path of peace and progress which it is resolved to follow.

The Sixth Committee, having taken note of the report of the Sub-Committee appointed to examine the request of the Kingdom of Afghanistan to enter the League of Nations, approves that report and unanimously submits to the Assembly a proposal for the admission of the Kingdom of Afghanistan to membership of the League.

The President:

Translation: M. Sepahbodi, first delegate of Persia, will address the Assembly.

M. Sepahbodi (Persia):

Translation: As I had the honour of declaring before the Sixth Committee, I have great pleasure in giving my cordial support, on behalf of Persia, to the request of the Kingdom of Afghanistan to be admitted to membership of the League of Nations.

The President:
Translation: His Excellency Ja'far el Askari Pasha, delegate of Iraq, will address the Assembly.

Ja'far el Askari Pasha (Iraq). – There can, I think, be no two opinions as to the genuineness and the spontaneity of the welcome that is being extended to Afghanistan to-day. All the Members of our League, old and new, great and small, greet her entry as marking one more milestone towards the goal of universality.

But just as the States of Europe feel that there is an especial bond uniting them, a feeling that takes concrete shape, for instance, in the Commission of Enquiry for European Union; just as in any discussion affecting one or the other of the Republics of Latin America, the outsider is at once conscious of a strong solidarity between them all, based on their common origin, language and traditions, a solidarity that must quickly overcome any passing exhibition of temper between brothers; so we of Asia may be excused if we too feel that we are united by particularly intimate ties – for some geographical propinquity, for others historical contacts, for others a common religion, a common alphabet, a common literary and cultural tradition – within the larger framework that embraces all.

The religion on which the moral and social code of Europe is largely based came from Asia. When the dark night of the middle ages descended on Europe, it was we, the Arabs in particular, who took into our charge the smouldering torch of learning, first lit by Greece and Rome, blew it into flame again and handed it back to burn more brightly than ever before.

And now, in more recent times, Europe has repaid the debt by endowing Asia with those material wonders which the genius of her men of learning has brought into the world.

To-day we are all striving towards an ideal. I believe that co-operation between Europe and Asia is no less essential for the future than it has been fruitful in the past. The stronger and more vigorous the Asiatic element, the more successful that co-operation will be.

For these reasons, Iraq offers a hearty and brotherly greeting to the new Member which has come to reinforce us. I venture to express the hope that the day is not far distant when we shall be welcoming Egypt, Syria and other States into the League of Nations.

The President:
Translation: As no other delegate has asked to speak, I call upon the Assembly to take note of the Sixth Committee's report recommending the Assembly to decide in favour of the admission of the Kingdom of Afghanistan to membership of the League of Nations.

If there are no observations we shall, without further delay, proceed to take the vote required for the admission of a new State to membership of the League.

According to Article 1, paragraph 2, of the Covenant, a majority of two-thirds of the Assembly is required for the admission of a new State.

A vote will be taken by roll-call. The procedure prescribed in Rule 20, paragraph 1, of the Rules of Procedure will be followed. The name of each delegation will be called and one of its members will answer "Yes" or "No" or "Not voting".

The result of the vote will be recorded and announced to the Assembly.
The vote was taken by roll-call.

The President:

Translation: The result of the voting is as follows:

Number of votes cast 47
Number of votes valid for calculating the majority 47
Number of votes in favour of the application for admission 47

Consequently, I proclaim that the Kingdom of Afghanistan has been admitted to membership of the League of Nations by a unanimous vote of the Assembly.

I should like at once to congratulate this new Member of the League, and I shall welcome it as soon as its delegation has taken its place among us.

The Aga Khan spoke between the Persian and Iraqi delegates.

143

THE PROPHET OF ISLAM

A Foreword to Qassim Ali Jairazbhoy's Biography of Muhammad

Geneva: September 1934

The Holy Prophet – last and greatest messenger from the Creator – his recognition of all predecessors – Islam is universal – Allah's greatness – man's direct communion with the all-embracing Power – the Prophet's teachings – concept of Ibnu'l Waqt.

Al-Hajj Qassim Ali Jairazbhoy, the author of this volume, who is to be congratulated on the pains he has taken in giving a faithful portrait of the simple and noble life of the Prophet of Islam, is a well-known figure in Islam and requires no introduction from me. His anxiety to render service to Islam is commendable; and I am glad that he devotes his leisure to the study of the principles for which Islam stands and explaining the true message of the Prophet of Islam to the world. The author has done well in showing the great principles of Islam and the mission of its Prophet as a true messenger of the Most High.

He has made considerable sacrifices for Islam, and his donation of one lakh and twenty-five thousand rupees for founding a chair for Science and Philosophy in the Aligarh University bears witness to his catholic charities and his love for science and philosophy. His various other charities for his co-religionists as well as his contributions to the progress of Islam show his earnest desire to be of service to humanity.

As he has pointed out, the holy Prophet of Islam is to us Muslims the last and greatest messenger from the Creator, and through him man is to find salvation in both this world and the next . . . The great religious teachers before and since [Prophet] Muhammad have all limited the area of truth by excluding either some or all of their predecessors. [Prophet] Muhammad, on the

SELECTED SPEECHES AND WRITINGS

other hand, by a full recognition of all his predecessors and by admitting that no people, race, or nation had been left without some kind of divine illumination, gave his Faith universality in the past, and in fact made it co-existent with human history.

If, now, we turn from its historic background to its doctrine and to its possibility of development in the future, we will find the same potential universality. Take the central principle of "Allāh O Akbar." Here we find on one side divinity, on the other side infinity. For what is the greater – time, space, the starry heavens, intelligence, knowledge? – wherever existence goes there His greatness extends. Greaterness here, to anyone who understands the implications of the Arabic language, does not mean "greaterness" as literally translated into English. It means that everything else is within the womb of the greater – everything else is maintained and sustained by Divine Power, including the furthest spaces of imagination.

[Prophet] Muhammad told mankind *first* that the infinite sustainer and container of all existence had justice, mercy, and love as well; *secondly*, that man through these qualities and through gentleness and kindness, prayer, awe or wonder could get – howsoever infinitesimal proportion – direct communion with the all-embracing power in which he lived and moved and had his being.

I submit that this doctrine will have a universality that can be accepted as long as man is man and as long as intelligence as we understand it survives on earth . . .

We maintain that the Prophet only ordered prayer, fasting, and gentleness in all human relations, kindliness and consideration for all beasts and animals from the smallest worm to the largest mammal . . .

It is the same Prophet who advises his followers ever to remain Ibnu 'l-Waqt (i.e. children of the time and period in which they were on earth), and it must be the natural ambition of every Muslim to practise and represent his Faith according to the standard of the Waqt or space-time.

Source: Al-Haji Qassim Ali Jairazbhoy, *Muhammad: "A Mercy to All the Nations"*, Luzac, London, 1937, pp. 11–15.

The Foreword is autographed by the Aga Khan. The author of the book was a Muslim of Bombay. The frontispiece of the book is a nice photograph of the author.

The Foreword is reproduced in Sultan Nazerali El-Africi (ed.), *A Collection of Some Recent Speeches and Writings of H. H. the Aga Khan*, Mombasa, 1955, pp. 81–5, and also in *Platinum*, pp. 10–15.

Well-known works in the Western languages on the Prophet include M. Hamidullah, *Le prophète de l'Islam*, Paris, 1959; L. Caetani, *Annalis dell'Islam*, Milan, 1905, Vols. 1 and 2; Rudi Paret, *Mohammed und der Koran*, Stuttgart, 1957; M. Rodinson, *Mahomet*, Paris, 2nd edn 1968; K. Ahrens, *Muhammed als Religionsstifter*, Leipzig, 1935; T. J. E. Andrae, *Mohamed: The Man and His Faith*, London, 1936 (trans. from the Swedish original of 1918); and Montgomery Watt, *Muhammad in Mecca*, Oxford 1953, and his *Muhammad at Medina*, Oxford, 1956.

144

THOUGHTS ON IMPERIAL DEFENCE

Speech at the Navy League Dinner

London: 23 October 1934

The formation of the Royal Indian Navy – past services of India's
naval forces – Indianization of the naval services – his presence at
the Navy League dinner – adequate financial provisions – the
Committee of Imperial Defence – communications between different
parts of the Empire – suggestions for a broad-based
committee for rationalization of existing armaments.

Proposing "The glorious and immortal memory of Nelson and
his Comrades," the Aga Khan said that they were all delighted
that at the beginning of this month, with the approval of the
King-Emperor, the Royal Indian Navy came into existence. But if
in name India was last among the great oversea [*sic*] Possessions
of the Crown to have a navy, her priority in the matter of the
foundation of such a service was very great. Since the earliest
days of the British connexion in one form or another she had
had a Governmental sea service with a continuous history. Its
origin went as far back as 1612, when the East India Company's
agents at Surat found it necessary to provide themselves with
armed vessels to protect their commerce and factories not only
from the Dutch and Portuguese but also from pirates. During
these three and a quarter centuries India's naval forces had been
actively employed in peace and war in every sea of the Eastern
Empire. Indeed, these forces had made no inconsiderable contribution to the command of the sea built up in the past by the
British people.

The time was more than ripe for India to have a larger and
more responsible share in the protection of her own coasts. The
change in designation from the Royal Indian Marine to the Royal

Indian Navy marked the completion of a scheme drawn up soon after the War for the reorganization of the Service as a combatant force, a status it had not possessed since 1863. For the time being the Royal Indian Navy was mainly a training force. He looked forward eagerly to the day when the intention to Indianize the Service could be carried so much further than at present that it would evoke a "sea sense" among the educated classes in India.

Referring to his representation of India at the Disarmament Conference at Geneva, the Aga Khan said that he made no apology to any outside critic who might regard his presence at the Navy League dinner as inappropriate. He addressed them as an out-and-out supporter of the cause of peace, anxious to promote the prosperity which went therewith. But as practical men they must face realities, and look with steady gaze upon the world as it was to-day. That adequate financial provision should be made for naval security was unanimously affirmed by the Conservative Conference at Bristol early this month under the lead of Lord Lloyd. If there was one lesson more deeply written in the annals of modern strategy than another it was that the efficient cooperation of various arms was a most important factor of victory.

The Committee of Imperial Defence continued to function, and in supporting a suggestion recently made by Lord Lloyd for further inquiry he would not for one moment seem to minimize its usefulness. They had to bear in mind, however, that since the Committee was constituted early in the century the methods of defence strategy had been changed by developments in aviation, navigation, transport, and mechanization. When they also took account of the extraordinary political convulsions of the post-War period they were bound to see that the whole question of defence and security called for investigation. It was necessary to think out the means of protecting communications between all parts of the Empire in time of war, and to plan such distribution of their land forces as would prevent any large portion of them being isolated or interned within a single theatre of operations. Fresh and vigorous investigation should be brought to this task.

What might be needed was the appointment of a small but powerful committee of British statesmen, with a member for each Dominion and for India. They needed a tribunal of statesmen trained to weigh evidence and not susceptible to the anxieties of possible changes in the votes of the electorate. The committee would hear both politicians and the experts of the sea, air, and land forces, and those of the Dominions and India. It would not confine itself to any one "school" of expert thought – whatever that school might be. It would not boycott the opinions of naval, military, or air officers regarded for the time being as unorthodox. Save in technical matters, such as construction, the experts were not necessarily the best final authority, especially when they differed – as they did so often.

The committee would report to the Cabinet (who alone could have the final decision) after the fullest survey of facts and opinions, and, in his judgment, would be certain to make proposals of the utmost value and importance. It went without saying that the proposed inquiry need not be interpreted abroad as in any way inconsistent with naval agreements which might be reached, or with the continued pursuit of disarmament by international compact. The underlying intention would be not to go back upon decisions taken by international arrangements, but to consider the most effective use and dispositions of – and the prevention of waste in – the defensive forces of the whole Empire. The design would not be the increase of their armaments (unless, indeed, the evidence made such increase necessary), but the rationalization of those in existence. For these reasons he gave his unqualified support to the suggestion made by Lord Lloyd at the Bristol Conference.

Source: *The Times*, London, 24 October 1934.
 The Aga Khan spoke as the chief guest at the annual dinner of the Navy League at Grosvenor House.
 "Lord and Lady Lloyd received the guests.
 "The King sent the following message, which was read by Lord Lloyd:–
 "The King sincerely thanks you for the loyal terms of your message on behalf of the members of the Navy League assembled together at their annual dinner in commemoration of Lord Nelson. He trusts all those with you to-night will have a very happy evening together."
 "At the end of the Aga Khan's speech Air Marshall Sir Robert Brooke-Popham responded."
 "Mr. Amery, proposing 'The Imperial Forces of the Crown,' said that they included the Air Forces of an Empire which had now been flown almost from end to end in three days: forces destined, he believed, to revolutionize the whole problem of our defence and above all to enhance immeasurably the importance of sea power by arming the Navy with a weapon that could strike far inland. Who could tell what instrument of power would yet emerge from the wedding of the Blue Water and Blue Sky Schools?
 "There were, he continued, innumerable technical objections to the creation of an international force under the orders of the League of Nations. There were two fundamental difficulties. One was that the League itself included too many wolves in sheep's clothing and too many watchdogs with an occasional hankering after a bit of mutton for themselves to be likely ever to show an effective unanimity in suppressing the meat-eating habit. The other difficulty

was that no mechanical scheme, even if constructed for so desirable an object as the maintenance of world peace, could command those deep-rooted instinctive loyalties for which alone nations were prepared to take great risks or individuals to sacrifice their lives. For them those loyalties were centred, not in Geneva, but in the British Crown. Looking at the state of the world to-day could anyone suggest that the forces of the Crown were adequate?

"Lord Macmillan proposed 'The Merchant Navy.' He said they were all glad to know that during the last two years the number of laid-up ships had begun to diminish and that the number of new ships under construction had largely increased within the last 12 months.

"Captain Sir Burton Chadwick, who replied, read the following message from the Prince of Wales:– 'I am glad to learn that the toast of The Merchant Navy is to be proposed at the Navy League dinner to-night and responded to by my Deputy Master of the Honourable Company of Master Mariners. The wise cooperation of the Navy League with every one concerned in our Merchant Service will, I feel sure, help to emphasize the vital importance of the Merchant Navy to our country and our Empire, and I wish the League success in its efforts in this direction.' "

"Those present included:–

Lord Lymington, the High Commissioner for Canada and Mrs. Ferguson, Mrs. Amery, Admiral of the Fleet Sir Roger and Lady Keyes, Lady Macmillan, Vice-Admiral Sir Dudley and Lady Pound, Lieutenant-General Sir Hugh and Lady Elles, Admiral Sir Sydney and Lady Fremantle, Admiral Sir Howard Kelly, Mr. and Mrs. W. L. Hichens, Sir Christopher and Lady Bullock, Mr. T. O. M. Sopwith, Rear-Admiral and Mrs. G. Blake, Vice-Admiral and Mrs. C. C. Little, Vice-Admiral and Mrs. G. K. Chetwode, and Vice-Admiral R. G. H. Henderson."

145

ON FIRDAUSI

Speech to the Royal Central Asian Society

London: 31 October 1934

The utility of such meetings – appreciation of great works of the past – bringing together cultures of East and West – moral and spiritual expansion of man.

The Aga Khan, replying to the toast of "Our Guests," proposed by Sir Horace Rumbold, said that these occasions had a double utility. They brought realization of the great work of the past and admiration of the teachers, poets, and artists who had laid the foundations of civilization on which we thrived; and he hoped and believed they also helped to give an impetus to work for further attachment with countries which were far away from here. How necessary this was between East and West now that science had reduced space almost to nothing was more than ever evident. A conscious effort was needed to bring the cultures of the East and West together, so that with the shrinkage that had taken place over the physical part of the earth cultural and moral and spiritual expansion might take place to meet it.

Source: *The Times*, London, 1 November 1934.
The Royal Central Asian Society had a luncheon at the House of Lords to mark the millenary of the Persian poet Firdausi. Lord Lamington presided. The menu card had on its front page a fine colour reproduction of "The Meeting of Rustrum and Tamineh" (Rustam and Tahminah) from the *Shahn-amah*. The company present included Lady Lamington, Lady Diana Worthington, the Saudi Arabian Minister, Sir Aurel Stein, A. Upham Pope, Sir Ronald Storrs, Ali Asghar Zarrinkafsh, Sir Hugh Barnes, the Maharajadhiraja Bahadur of Burdwan, Mr. and Mrs. E. M. Gull, E. H. Keeling, Sir Telford Waugh, Lady Rumbold, Sir John Thompson, Sir Malcolm Seton, Lt.-Col. Sir Francis Fremantle, Mrs. Patrick Ness, Lord Carnock, Sir Henry Sharp, Nuber Gulbenkian, and Thabit Bey Abd-un-Nur.
"Lord Lamington said the celebrations of the millenary had excited wide

1051

attention. The world now knew that Firdausi was not only great in his greatness but one of a score of other poets. There had been a controversy in *The Times* as to their rival merits. One notable letter was that of the Aga Khan in which he dethroned Omar Khayyam from the high place he had hitherto occupied in Western literary estimation. It had been revealed how most educated Persians could compose poetry, and this, as the late Professor Browne stated, in the language, metre, and style of some 1,000 years ago. In short Persia was the home of poetry.

"Mr Anthony Eden, M.P., Lord Privy Seal, proposed the toast of 'Firdausi and the Poets of Persia.' He said that Firdausi's fame rested on his 'Shahnama' or Book of Kings – the great epic poem which told the history of Persia from the beginning of time to the Arab conquest in the seventh century of our era – a truly stupendous poetic achievement which had won for Firdausi a comparison with Homer. He was not sure that Dante was not a truer comparison, for Firdausi, like Dante, revived national consciousness, and was the precursor of national unity; both remained to this day emblems of such consciousness and such unity.

"The tribute now being paid to Firdausi would, he trusted, open up not only to students but to all lovers of good literature a wider understanding of the scope and power of Persian poetry. Perhaps the most popular misconception of Persia's poetry today was the belief that its range was limited. On the contrary, its range was very wide. Moreover, with no people did poetry play a more integral or more vivid part in their national life and consciousness than with the Persians. Nothing was more remarkable than the extent to which, despite the rise and fall of successive Persian dynasties, despite successive waves of foreign invasion, the spirit of Persian poetry had always risen again undaunted, and, often indeed, strengthened by the ordeal it had undergone. Firdausi made this possible. There was always the 'Shahnama' to come back to. In its 60,000 couplets the poets of a later generation could refresh their national pride and from the glory of an imperishable past draw renewed inspiration for the future.

"The Persian Minster, who responded, said that Persia during her 3,000 years of history and 1,300 years of literature had given many famous men to the world and among them Firdausi held a high place.

"A short extract from the 'Shahnama' was read by Seyyid F. Shademan, and Dr. Denison Ross explained this and read Matthew Arnold's translation of the passage."

On Firdausi see: H. T. Anklesaria et. al., *Firdausi: A Monograph in English and Persian*, Bombay, 1934; G. Marcais, "Firdousi, poète nationale de l'Iran", *Journal des Savants*, 1935, pp. 214–23; H. Massé, *Les épopées persanes: Firdousi et l'épopées nationale*, Paris, 1935; B. Nikitine, "L'oeuvre de Ferdowsi", *Asie Francaise*, 1935, pp. 55–69; E. H. Palmer, *Firdausi, Persian Poet*, London, 1866; C. J. Pickering, "Lyrical Poetry of Firdausi", *National Review* (London), Vol. 14; S. Robinson, *Sketch of the Life and Writings of Firdusi*, London and Manchester, 1823; I. Sadiq, *Firdousi: His Life, his Personality and his Work*, Tehran, n.d. (? 1945); P. Volgin and B. V. Legran, *Firdousi, 934–1934*, Leningrad, 1934; Gaston Wiet, "Firdousi", *Journal Asiatsque*, July–September 1935, pp. 101–22; and W. Von Witzleben, *Geschichten aus dem Schahnamch*, Düsseldorf, 1960.

His *Shahnamah* has had several translations in the West. Only seven persons attempted the entire work: A. G. and E. Warner (London, 1902–29), Alexander Rogers (London, 1907) and Reuben Levy (London, 1967) in English, J. Mohl and Barbier de Meynard (Paris, 1838–78) in French, and F. Rückert (Berlin, 1890–95) in German. James Atkinson translated an abridged version into

English (London, 1832) and A. F. von Schack into German (Berlin, 1851). The others have been content to present selections, passages and chosen stories in their own languages: J. Champion (Calcutta, 1785; London, 1788), Stephen Weston (London, 1815), W. T. Robertson (Calcutta, 1829), L. S. Costello (London, 1845), H. Zimmern (London, 1882), A. V. W. Jackson (New York, 1896, 1902, 1917), William Stigand (London, 1907) and H. A. Guerber (Philadelphia and London, 1913) in English; H. Kazemzadeh (Berlin, 1924), Auguste Bricteux (Brussels, 1934–5), and A. Djalali and M. Broukhim (Tehran, 1941) in French; J. R. von Wallenburg (Vienna, 1810), E. Amthor (Leipzig, 1841), Th. Nöldeke (Berlin, 1922) and H. von Witzleben (Düsseldorf, 1960) in German; Italo Pizzi (Turin, 1888) in Italian; and J. Borecky (Prague, 1910) in Czech.

Some of these translations were published in sumptuous editions illustrated with resplendent ancient and medieval paintings. Firdausi shares with Umar Khayyam the honour of having his poetry illuminated and illustrated by a variety of artists.

146

INDIA AND THE REFORMS

Interview with The Times of India

Bombay: 4 January 1935

Unity for the common good of India – practical wisdom and states-manship – disappointment at the Joint Select Committee's Report – amendments to obtain dominion status – the proposed federation of Indian princes and people – preamble to the Reforms Bill – Britain's responsibility – atmosphere of understanding needed – handicaps in presenting India's case.

His Highness shared the disappointment of his countrymen at the Joint Parliamentary Committee's report, but he thought that they should not allow the disappointment to get the better of their judgement. He added that it was essential both for the sake of Great Britain and India to restore the atmosphere that happily prevailed during the deliberations of the first Round Table Conference.

"As I have already pointed out," said the Aga Khan, "it is to be regretted that the case for India so strongly and unanimously placed before the Parliamentary Committee in the joint memorandum of the British Indian delegation has not been more generously met. Though there is cause for disappointment, it must not unduly depress us or prevent us from seeking desired amendments or working the reforms in such a way as to bring us to our declared goal, namely, Dominion Status.

"Though the reforms fall short of our expectations, in the proposed Federation of Indian Princes and the people there are essentials which must eventually lead India to a status similar to that enjoyed by other dominions. It is necessary, however, to allay distrust; reference to Dominion Status should be included in the preamble to the Reforms Bill. Great Britain should do everything to allay the charge of breach of faith.

"I am for unity, not for the purpose of destruction, for that will not help India; but unity for forwarding a constructive programme beneficial to our country. We must separate imaginary from real grievances and present a united front for their removal. All I can say, at present, is that this subject of the greatest magnitude and importance to India should be viewed not from one side but from the view of all sides. We should try to create an atmosphere of understanding and refrain from statements which may create mistrust and suspicion to which most of our troubles are due.

"I would, therefore, earnestly beg of my countrymen to realise the significance of His Majesty's declaration of his constant care for us and his desire that the Indian peoples may ever more fully realise and value their own place in the unity of one family of which he rightly claims to be the head. His Majesty's Christmas message bears testimony to his deep and abiding interest in his Indian subjects, which must bring them hope and encouragement.

"If we submit our grievances with a united voice, I have no hesitation in saying that they will receive support from Lord Willingdon and Sir Samuel Hoare, both of whom have proved to be very staunch friends of India.

"I may add that I am confident that they will be supported by all the Provincial Governors as well, including Lord Brabourne.

"I wish to say one word about the Joint Memorandum submitted by me on behalf of the British Indian delegation. Whenever I brought India's case to the attention of the authorities and the British public, I was terribly handicapped by the fact that sufficient support for it had not been canvassed in India where attention ought to have been concentrated upon it."

In conclusion His Highness declared "I shall, during my stay in India, study the situation carefully and place the Indian view before the authorities both in England and India as well as before the British public."

Source: *The Times of India*, Bombay, 5 January 1935.

The interview, as circulated by the Associated Press of India, was published by *The Civil and Military Gazette* of 5 January.

The Times of London of 5 January carried a dispatch from its own correspondent in Bombay which ran as follows:

"The Aga Khan, who arrived here early this morning, in a message of good will to his countrymen said he shared their disappointment at the Select Committee's report, but he thought they should not allow disappointment to get the better of judgment.

"It was essential for the sake of both Great Britain and India to restore the atmosphere which happily prevailed during the Round-Table Conference (he said). He regretted that the case for India strongly and unanimously placed before the Select Committee in the joint memorandum of the British India delegation had not been more generously met. 'If there is cause for disappointment it must not unduly depress us, or prevent us from seeking desired amendments, or working the reforms in such a way as to bring us to our declared goal – namely, Dominion status. It is necessary, however, to ally distrust. A reference to Dominion status should be included in the preamble to the reforms Bill. Great Britain should do everything to allay the charge of breach of trust.' The Aga Khan added that he was for unity and a constructive programme beneficial to the country. They must separate imaginary from real grievances and present a united front for their approval. They should create an atmosphere of understanding and refrain from statements which might create mistrust and suspicion, to which most of India's troubles were due. If Indians submitted their grievances with a united voice he had no hesitation in saying that they would receive support from Lord Willingdon and Sir Samuel Hoare, both of whom were staunch friends of India."

The Times of India of 4 January reported the Aga Khan's arrival in Bombay:

"His Highness the Aga Khan arrived on Friday morning at one o'clock by the s.s. COMMORIN. Soon after the boat had anchored, his son Prince Alv Khan went on board and greeted his father. By special arrangement he was able to land immediately and by his express desire the usual arrangements for his reception were cancelled.

"After greeting his son and one or two friends His Highness motored to his bungalow at Malabar Hill where his mother, Lady Aly Shah, was awaiting his arrival."

147

THE IMPORTANCE OF RURAL DEVELOPMENT FOR MUSLIM INDIA

A Statement to the Press

New Delhi: 5 February 1935

British-Indian Muslim Delegation and constitutional negotiations – concessions gained – status of the North-West Frontier Province – separation of Sind from the Bombay Presidency – local legislatures reconstituted – mode of elections – matter of services – friendly relations with other communities and the government – rural development – politics for economic ends – provincial and district centres – scope of the work – response of Indian Muslims.

The British India Muslim delegation, which I had the honour and privilege of leading, did its best to promote the cause of India's advance and secure for it certain essentials which were for the good of the country, no less than for the good of Indian Muslims. The Muslim delegation believed in cooperating with all groups. Under my responsibility as chairman of the British India delegation the joint memorandum was signed by all, and we believed that its acceptance in the report would have gone far to make the bill acceptable to Indian opinion. Our readiness thus to support all groups, as the interests of India demanded, was fully vindicated.

Firstly, certain essentials, to which we attached considerable importance and which were only just and fair, have been conceded. The Northwest Frontier Province is now, like other Indian provinces, under the Montagu-Chelmsford reforms, and when provincial autonomy comes, will, along with other provinces, advance.

Secondly, the unnatural policy of tying Sind to Bombay has been brought to an end, and a just and reasonable constitution of a separate Sind has been carried out with a little help from us. It is hoped that a free and independent Sind will become an important province of India, though small in size, strongly agricultural and with a port like Karachi which has great possibilities before it.

Thirdly, local legislatures have been reconstituted, and though the existing weightage in the case of most minority provinces remains the same, the position has not therein deteriorated. In the case of Bengal and the Punjab the position is fairer and more just than it was. The mode of election remains, for the future as in the past, separate, and this decision is liable to modification by an agreement between all parties.

Fourthly, in the matter of services, the Government of India resolution has gone some way to meet the Muslim claim, and it is believed that the principle underlying it will not fail to be reflected in the policies of the Muslim majority provinces. There were several things to which we attached a great deal of importance, and our efforts to secure those points met with little or no success. There is no finality in the affairs of this world, and we should be prepared to renew our efforts as suitable opportunity occurs.

Now I come to the crux of the whole problem. What is to be done? The programme of the all-India [Muslim] Conference for the time being has been concluded. A very important part of it remains, the development of friendly relations with other communities and with Government. Efforts in that direction should continue. The main work of the future now lies in the countryside in promoting or undertaking schemes of economic amelioration by supplementing the efforts of the cultivator and urban labourer by making it possible for him to develop cottage industries and thereby increase his income.

It is no use thinking of politics unless it be to observe economic ends. The surest way to command the vote is to serve the voter, and unless our organisations are ready to serve the voter, they cannot hope to claim to have a bright political future before them. This work is humanitarian no less than political but when dealing with the masses, all things tend to merge into one another.

To sum up, we should establish strong provincial centres so that these provincial centres may in their turn establish district centres, and it should be the duty of these district centres to take the message of help and service to the countryside, and help the cultivator and the ignorant labourer with information, advice, the organisation of co-operative enterprise and development of cottage industries.

The work is so gigantic that it can absorb the energies of all, and the scope of the work is so great that there need be no fear of any one not finding suitable opportunities to work. Whether Indian Muslims will in the future contribute to the development and the culture of India, as they aspire to do, depends upon the response they make to the call the present condition of the masses makes to them, and the extent of their effort will be the measure of their success.

Source: *The Times of India*, Bombay, 6 February 1935, and *The Civil and Military Gazette*, Lahore, 6 February 1935. The statement was also published, with different paragraphing, in the *Star of India*, Calcutta, 6 February 1935.

The Aga Khan was staying with the Viceroy, Lord Willingdon, at this time. The special correspondent of *The Times of India*, to whom this statement was given, opened his dispatch from New Delhi with the following interesting sentences:

"One of the most interesting figures lately seen on the cinema screen in Delhi has been His Highness the Aga Khan. There you saw His Highness seated at a table before a microphone in a room in London and his voice came out from the screen to you as clearly and distinctly as though he were present. The subject of this talkie was the report of the Joint Parliamentary Committee, and His Highness quietly and gravely, and with reasons, commended it to acceptance and the constitution it proposed to approval and co-operation."

148

A SOCIALIST PATH TO BETTERMENT

Speech at a Luncheon

New Delhi: 8 February 1935

Tendency to look to the past – look to and work for the future
– economic freedom of the masses – failure of private effort –
contribution of autonomous legislatures – social betterment
through socialism – guidance and advice for the voter.

The Aga Khan, in reply, thanked the members of the Delhi
Muslim Association for their warm and hearty welcome. He was
glad, he said, of the opportunity of meeting so many leading
Muslims, who, with the generosity characteristic of Imperial
Delhi, had spoken in high terms of his work and his
achievements.

The Aga Khan asked members of his community not merely
to look to the past. It had been the bane of Muslim culture
during the last two or three centuries always to look back upon
the past. The late Maulana Mahomed Ali, he said, once writing
in the "Comrade," had quoted instances of virile nations – Japan,
Germany and Italy. Everyone belonging to these nations was
thinking of the future of his race. In the same article, he continued, Maulana Mahomed Ali had referred to Muslims as being
happy in thinking of being once great. His Highness asked his
audience to leave the past alone. They had now to look to the
future. That future, he said, had to be worked for. Whatever
happened at the centre there was enough scope for work in the
provincial scheme. They would have to re-adjust themselves and
face the future.

He was sure that Muslims would be able to face the grave
problems ahead of them, which were principally one of the
economic freedom of the masses. He quoted instances of what

was happening in Soviet Russia and in America and, said that they fully testified to the failure of private effort. The betterment of the masses was impossible without provincial autonomous legislatures taking this as the main plank. The intelligence of the individual must be guided to the path of advance on lines which would lead to the goal of the economic uplift of humanity. This was the work before everyone in the country. The social betterment of the masses could only happen by Socialism when every component part worked for the entire social fabric, and it was only through the political field that the nation could achieve its aim.

Finally, the Aga Khan exhorted members of his community to work for the voter and to give him proper guidance and advice. They must get power, and use it for the betterment of the people whose representatives they would be and whose happiness and comfort in life would be their sole consideration. There was no room for jealousy in this, but there was a vast field for mutual co-operation, mutual guidance and mutual trust.

Source: *The Times of India*, Bombay, 11 February 1935, and *The Civil and Military Gazette*, Lahore, 12 February 1935.

The Delhi Muslim Association entertained the Aga Khan at an open air luncheon at the Roshanara Club. About one hundred persons were present, including Mian Sir Fazl-i-Hussain, Sir Abdur Rahim, Sir Maneckji Dadabhoy, prominent Muslim members of the Indian Legislative Assembly and the Council of State, and leading Muslim citizens of Delhi.

Khan Bahadur S. M. Abdullah, who presided in the absence of Sir Rahim Baksh (who was ill), warmly welcomed the Aga Khan on behalf of the Delhi Muslim Association which, he said, had existed for over ten years to safeguard the "political and economic interests of Muslims in Delhi". The Aga Khan, he continued, had achieved the rare feat of standing astride the gulf between East and West and of establishing a high position in both. India was proud of him, not only because he had made a name for himself and raised high the name of India, but also because he had always stood up for India's rights and had demanded for the Indians their share in the administration of the country. He had succeeded to a very large extent in bringing about the concession of certain cardinal points in the coming reforms which, undoubtedly, were a great advance on the present constitution. The country needed his valuable services to secure for the Indians their rightful position in the Commonwealth of Nations. "We assure Your Highness", he concluded, "that we have every confidence in you and we know that our future is quite safe in your hands."

149

AN APPEAL TO THE MUSLIM LEGISLATORS OF INDIA

Speech at a Dinner

New Delhi: 9 February 1935

Unity in cultural diversity – secret of the greatness of the British Empire – co-operation among different communities – disappointment at the treatment accorded to the joint memorandum of the British-Indian Delegation.

Referring to Sir Mahomed Yakub's remarks he said:– "I don't really think any country other than India has claimed me as her son. One is born to one mother. I was born here and I hope to be buried here. (Cheers). Mr. Ghuznavi has referred to the Trojan horse. Any picture of a horse is always a pleasure for me to see. (Cheers). I spent my early years in Maharashtra and I remember a divinity very popular in that part. Its image is before my eyes. It has one big body with many hands of differing lengths and proportions. I honestly believe that not only for India's sake but for her culture, for her civilisation and for her contribution to mankind India should live the life of that divinity with one centre to which all belong, having different forms of culture and civilisation but all belonging to and united by one mother. (Cheers).

"Even if historically Muslims had never entered this country, her people would have had many different varieties in historical development. This is because of the vastness of the country, its resources and of difference in climate. That should never make them warring elements but each should contribute its culture and civilisation bringing it into the centre of motherhood which is India as a whole. I believe firmly that this will come and that every Indian – Christian, Muslim, Parsee, Hindu – will be prouder of his or her motherland, because there is variety.

"Gentlemen, we belong, whether you like it or not, to the British Empire. What is the real secret of the greatness of that Empire? I spent a great deal of my early life in Russia, where they had orthodoxy, autocracy and one nationality. It crashed. That forcing of authority in the form of autocracy could not last. Look how England has treated South Africa, Canada and the Dutch and French population there and their own kith and kin. I believe if we in India treat our own people in the same way as England has treated the Dominion people, England will treat India in the same way she treated other races namely the French and the Dutch. (Applause). It is my firm conviction that variety means wealth of culture. Variety does not mean disunion. It ought never to mean disunion. It will mean greater splendour in the realm of spirit, more toleration, more recognition of each other's contribution to India's historic role in the world. I believe in more than Hindu-Muslim co-operation. I believe in co-operation among Hindus, Muslims, Parsees, Indian Christians and Anglo-Indians. If we remember the statue of divinity I have described, then we will bring ourselves together far more rapidly than anything else. In that spirit I have tried to do my best. Sometimes it is necessary to help those who have handicaps caused by historical reasons and arrange equitable understanding of social conditions."

The Aga Khan said he felt great disappointment at the treatment accorded to the Joint Memorandum of the British Indian delegation but tonight he would eschew politics and rather keep before them the image of divinity of Mother India and ask them to be proud of variety of her culture. (Cheers).

Source: *Star of India*, Calcutta, 15 February 1935; *The Times of India*, Bombay, 11 February 1935; and *Ismaili*, Bombay, 17 February 1935.
The *Star of India* reported:
"Sir Muhammad Yakub, in proposing the toast, said that many patrons claimed the Aga Khan as their son, namely, India, Persia, Egypt, and England. Being a great sportsman he was in the true sense of the word non-communalist; he was unanimously chosen the leader of the British Indian Delegation to the Joint Select Committee on Indian Constitutional Reform at a time when India was seething with communalism. The memorandum produced by the Delegation revealed the Aga Khan's great political sagacity.
"A. H. Ghuznavi, in his speech, laid stress on the fact that the Aga Khan was a true believer in Hindu-Muslim unity. As a representative of the Muslims of Bengal, he thanked the Aga Khan on their behalf for the efforts he had made in order to ensure that justice was done to them. He also referred to the efforts of the Aga Khan for bringing about Indo-British co-operation.

"All the leading representatives of the Indian Legislative Assembly and of the press were present. It was the first function of the session in which the Congress members of the Assembly participated."

The *Times of India* correspondent wrote:

"The Aga Khan was also the guest of honour at a largely attended dinner given by Muslim members of the Central Legislature. Covers were laid for over 130 guests. This was the first function which the Congress Party members attended since the beginning of the Assembly session. The dinner was held in the dining hall of the Council House. Sir Abdur Rahim presided.

"Sir Mahomed Yakub described the Aga Khan as a world personality claimed by India, England, France, Persia and Egypt. In sincerity and simplicity he was an Indian, as a statesman and politician he was an Englishman, in courtesy and polished manners he was a Frenchman and as a poet he was a Persian and Egyptian. He attracted the attention of those who came in contact with him.

"Speaking of the Aga Khan 28 years ago at Aligarh, the late Sir Muzamulullah Khan had related a story of Khalif Haroon-al-Rashid who gave a dinner at the conclusion of which he announced that the servants might pick up for themselves whatever precious gold plates or precious articles they could lay their hands on. One maid, however, took the Khalif in her arms and declared that there was nothing more precious than the Khalif himself.

"Sir Muzamulullah Khan had compared Indian Mussalmans to that maid in the story and the Aga Khan to Haroon-al-Rashid. That simile, said Sir Mahomed Yakub, was as true today as it was 28 years ago.

"The Aga Khan was a great sportsman and his outlook on life was entirely non-communal. A just recognition of that was evidenced when he was chosen the leader of the British-Indian delegation at a time when India herself was seething with communalism. That historic document, the British Indian memorandum, was a masterpiece of His Highness' political wisdom and sagacity.

"Mr. A. H. Ghuznavi, who was most closely associated with the Aga Khan during the last four years in connection with the R. T. C and the J. P. C., said: 'They tell a lie who describe you as a communalist. You are a firm believer in Hindu-Muslim unity, and it is a matter of faith with you that is the cornerstone of Indian swaraj [sic].' He thanked him on behalf of the Muslims of Bengal for his work on their behalf. He said he had unfurled the banner of Hindu-Muslim unity again on his return to India and had pleaded also for Indo-British co-operation and for the improvement of the economic condition of the masses."

Naturally, the event was reported most fully by the *Ismaili*:

"His Highness the Aga Khan was the guest of honour at a largely attended dinner given by the Muslim Members of the Central Legislature. Covers were laid for over 130 guests. This was the first function which the Congress Party Members attended since the commencement of the session. It was held in the Dining Hall of the Council House. Sir Abdul Rahim (President of the Assembly) presided.

"Sir Mahomed Yakub described the Aga Khan as a world personality claimed by India, England, France, Persia and Egypt. In sincerity and simplicity, he was Indian, as a statesman and politician he was an Englishman, in courtesy and polish he was a Frenchman, as poet he was Persian and as Egyptian he attracted attention of those who came in contact with him.

"Speaking of the Aga Khan 28 years ago at Aligarh the late Sir Muzamilullah Khan related a story of Khalifa Haroon-al-Raschid who gave a dinner at the conclusion of which the Khalifa announced that the servants might pick up for themselves whatever precious gold plates or precious articles they could lay their hands on. One maid, however, took the Khalifa in arms and declared there was nothing more precious than the Khalifa himself. Sir Muzamilullah Khan had compared Indian Mussalmans to that maid in the story and the Aga Khan to Haroon-al-Raschid. That simile, said Sir Yakub was as true as it was 28 years ago.

"The Aga Khan was a great sportsman and entirely non-communal. (applause). Just recognition of this was evidenced when he was chosen as the leader of the British Indian Delegation at a time when India herself was seething with communalism. And that historic document, the British Indian Memorandum, was the masterpiece of His Highness' political wisdom and sagacity.

"Mr. A. H. Ghaznavi who was most closely associated with His Highness during the last four years in connection with the Round Table Conference and the J.P.C. said:

" 'Your Highness is a connoisseur of horses and also the proud possessor of many horses. You have introduced many a winner to the Turf both in India and abroad, but you have been suspected of having introduced into political turf in India a Trojan horse. Do you claim it as your own or is it likely to win the race? The layout of the turf was yours. Most others who co-operated with you in 1906 are now enjoying eternal rest. The turf was relaid by you in this very city in 1928–29. Is anything still wanting to make it perfect? Have you come to give it finishing touches?

" 'I know you don't quite like the horse. You have tried to improve the animal. It still continues to be vicious. How can the animal and turf can [sic] be improved. Essentials of Muslim demand have been largely but not wholly met. They tell a lie who describe you as a communalist. You are a firm believer in Hindu-Muslim unity and it is a matter of faith with you that it is the corner stone of Indian Swaraj.' (cheers).

"Concluding, he thanked the Aga Khan on behalf of the Bengal Muslims for the efforts he had made so that justice be done to them. He also referred to the Aga Khan having unfurled the banner of Hindu-Muslim unity again on his return to India and also for Indo-British co-operation, and improvement of economic condition of the masses. This was how the turf was to be relaid and the Trojan horse was to be so improved as to bring that concord, co-operation, peace and prosperity which are the needs of India's millions.

"Following were present at the dinner [sic]:–

"Sir Abdur Rahim, Nawab of Chattari, Mr. R. B. Becket, the Consul-General for Persia, Sir Mohd. Yakub, Sir L. Graham, Sir Mohd. Mehershah, Sir Henry Gidney, Dr. Zia-ud-din Ahmed, Colonel A. H. Muir, Dr. L. K. Hyder, Messrs. R. E. L. Wingate, Yamin Khan, M. G. Hellet, A. H. Ghuznavi, Bhulabhai Desai, Sir Louis Kershaw, Nawab Muzaffar Khan, Maulana Shaukat Ali, Sir L. Hudson, the Consul-General for Afghanistan, Mr. M. S. Aney, Sir J. Dunnett, Major General Sprawson, Mr. Asaf Ali, Dr. A. G. Khan, Hakim Kibriya Khan, Hakim Jamil Khan, Mr. Jafri, Mohd. Shafi, Messrs. Zahid Ali, Nabibux Illahibux Bhutto, Hussain Imam, Nawab Abul Hussain Khan, Mohd, Ibrahim, Ferozeuddin, Mohd. Rafi, C. Rajagopalacharia, A. C. Datt, Bashir Ahmad, Amjad Ali, S. Jacobson, Munshi Iswar Saran, F. E. James, Mohd. Ghiasuddin, Sardar Nur Ahmad, K. M. Hassan, Durga Das, Maulvi Syed Ahmad Imam Sahib, R. A. Basak Sait, Raja Akbar Ali, Nanak Chand, Sir Abdul Hamid, Hakim Nasiruddin Ahmad, Hafiz Mohd. Siddique Mumtaj, S. G. Hasnain, Gulam Mohd., Mohd. Sulaiman, Maulvi Badruzaman, Nawab Siddique Ali Khan, Sir Jawahar Singh, U. N. Sen, J. N. Sahni, K. B. Zafar Hasan, D. K. Lahiri Chaudhry, M. V. H.

Collins, Haji Abdula Haroon, S. Satyamurti, M. J. Moloney, Maulvi Shafi Daudi, R. B. Dayaram Sahni, A. H. Byrt, Hydri, Ghulam Bhik Nairang, M. H. Kidvai, Sir Abdur Rahman, G. V. Bewoor, Arthur Moore, Ranga Iyer, Sir David Petrie, P. R. Rau, S. C. Sen, Mohd. Nauman, Khwaja Hasan Nizami, Murtaza Sahib Bahadur, S. P. Bose, N. M. Joshi, A. S. Iyengar, Mian Mohd. Rafi, Dr. Mansoor, Capt. Majeed, Mr. Ahmad Ibrahim Haroon Jafar, R. B. D. Dutt, H. Essak Sait, F. H. Piracha, H. Dow, W. H. Lewis, M. S. Mathur, Dr. S. N. A. Jafri, Mubarak Ali, Zaki-ud-din, J. R. T. Booth, Maj. Ahmed Nawaz Khan, Haji Rashid Ahmad, Nawab Aziz Ahmad Khan, M. Ikramulla, Seth Hussainali Kassamali, Yusuf Haroon, Mr. Verma, Alijah Sabzali Ramzanali and Alijah Currimbhai Varas Ibrahim."

According to the *Ismaili*, the Aga Khan was to leave Delhi on 18 February for Bombay, where he would stay till the end of March before visiting South Africa and Egypt on his way to England.

150

THE RENAISSANCE OF ISLAMIC CULTURE

Speech to the Islamic Research Association, Bombay

Bombay: 25 February 1935

A growing interest in Islamic culture in the West – the situation in Islamic countries – the need for research.

"It has been one of my life-long ambitions to see the renaissance of Islamic culture, knowledge, history and civilization throughout the world."

It was a curious fact that a revival should have first come through contact with the West. In the early stages, Western students of Islam knew nothing of the true spirit of that great culture, but in his (the speaker's) youth a reaction had taken place in Russia, Finland and other countries in the West. In Islamic countries, however, grinding economic poverty rendered such a reaction difficult.

If they could get in touch with ancient manuscripts dealing with Islamic culture, they could bring to light by means of new publications vast treasures, to the great joy of the individual. It was necessary that they should now begin on a small scale but with great determination.

There were, he said, two lines of advance, one was translation and the other interpretation, even critical interpretation. The latter must be fearless and must have only one objective, namely, truth.

Source: *The Times of India*, Bombay, 26 February 1935.
This was his presidential address given at the first annual general meeting of the Islamic Research Association held in the rooms of the Bombay branch of the Royal Asiatic Society at the Town Hall of Bombay. The meeting took place in the evening.
The Aga Khan also announced his donation of Rs. 1,000 to the Association

for the first year and promised to supplement it in subsequent years in accordance with the progress shown in its work.

"Mr. A. M. Mecklai, the president of the Association, in welcoming the Aga Khan, dwelt on the history and formation of the Association.

"Mr. Asaf A. A. Fyzee, the secretary, hoped the audience would think over the interpretation given to research work by the Aga Khan and act upon it.

"The report of the Association set forth its activities, which consisted of the publication of authoritative books on Islamic culture."

151

LORD LAMINGTON'S SERVICES

Speech at a Luncheon

London: 4 June 1935

Lord Lamington's qualities – services to Bombay – an advocate of good relations between Great Britain and India and with the Middle East.

The Aga Khan proposed the toast of "Lord Lamington." He said that an outstanding feature of Lord Lamington's career had been the quiet persistence of his efforts linked with freedom from ostentation, one consequence of which was that even those who had at heart the welfare of Eastern lands had come to take such services for granted, while from the public at large they had not received the recognition due to them on their merits. As Governor of Bombay the memory of his service was still treasured in the Presidency. The people found him accessible, sympathetic, and, as an administrator, practical and progressive. He had friends and admirers among all classes. He was not prepared to take his political views from others, and when he was asked, when Lord Curzon was Viceroy, to do things he did not approve he flatly refused and said that the Government itself must carry them out. Since his return to this country in 1907 Lord Lamington had filled a distinct and necessary place in our public life as an independent and fully informed advocate – from his place in the House of Lords and at the head of many societies – of good relations not only between Great Britain and India but also between them both and the lands of the Near and Middle East.

Lord Lamington, he added, had steadily upheld the ideal of friendship and understanding based on mutual respect. His sowing of this good seed had had a greater influence than some people well versed in public life were aware in the liberalizing of policy in this aspect which the post-War years had witnessed. In the presence of the Persian Minister they thought especially of his constant endeavours for Brito-Iranian cordiality. This found expression in his assisting to start, and his presidency of, the Persian Society, now incorporated in the Royal Central Asian Society. Again, in respect of Afghanistan, the independence of which country in foreign relationships was reflected in its membership of the League of Nations, Lord Lamington had been a staunch supporter of the mutual trust and confidence which had greatly eased anxieties in respect of the North-West Frontier. Their guest had recognized all through his long public career that a key to the Temple of Peace in Western Asia was the progress, contentment, and loyalty of India as a part of the British Dominions. As president for many years of the East India Association he had upheld its traditional policy.

Source: *The Times*, London, 5 June 1935.

The speech was made at a luncheon given by the Aga Khan at the Claridge's hotel in London "in recognition of the part played by Lord Lamington in promoting good relations between this country [Britain] and the countries of the Near and Middle East during 50 years of public service".

"Lord Lamington, in reply, said the occasion was not one for any political discussion, but when the extreme Zionists abused Great Britain for restricting their immigration into Palestine they forgot that were it not for this country their numbers in Palestine would in all probability be not very great. He attributed his entertainment that day to the fact that he had been connected with three Moslem societies – the British Red Crescent Society, the London Mosque Fund, and the Indigent Moslem Burial Fund. The third society appealed to him very strongly and he prayed that many who had not realized the true philanthropy of the fund would see fit to contribute and place it on a sound basis. He could not estimate the depths of Moslem feeling, but for a man whose life had been moulded on the strict observance of his faith the pathos was great that, he should die feeling forsaken in a foreign land where he would be put into a pauper's grave without any of the rites of his faith. The real strength of the three societies of which he was chairman, Lord Lamington said, was mainly due to the sympathy in spirit and in practice of the Aga Khan, whose financial assistance was ever princely. Of the members of the several committees he specially mentioned Mr. A. S. M. Anik, the hon. secretary of them all, and Mr. Waris Ameer Ali, the latter for coming forward to help to carry on his father's work."

152

THE 1935 CONSTITUTION AND THE MUSLIMS OF INDIA

Speech at an Official Dinner

London: 6 June 1935

Relative political backwardness of Muslims – confidence in their future – the Government of India Bill.

The Aga Khan, referring to the relative political backwardness of the Mohammedans said that to use the racing metaphor, they were 30 years behind their Hindu friends in that matter, but they had such a fine foundation in their philosophy and religious faith that he looked to the future in respect of his community with confidence. There were no people on earth with finer cultural foundation. The Government of India Bill which would soon become an Act had its progenitor in the Charter Act of 1833. The two measures were thus historically linked. He believed that the new Act would lead to a greater and better future and good understanding between the two countries.

Source: *The Times*, London, 7 June 1935.

These words were uttered at a dinner hosted by the British Government at Hyde Park Hotel in honour of the distinguished visitors from India to the celebrations of the Silver Jubilee of King George V. The Secretary of State for India, Sir Samuel Hoare (later Lord Templewood) was the chief host.

"In submitting the toast of 'Our friends from India' Sir Samuel Hoare said that political differences loomed large between public men and points of agreement between those in this country and public men in India tended to be blurred. Indeed the world at large was apt to think that after a long period of controversial discussion there was no means of reconciling the differences between England and India – no method of building a bridge between Asia and Europe. Then in a sudden moment came great occasions of joy or of sorrow which proved to the world that there was an indissoluble bond of solidarity between India and Great Britain. Such a moment came a few weeks ago, when a great emotion of joy on his Majesty's Silver Jubilee swept throughout the whole Empire and showed that in India no less than in Great Britain there was a devotion unequalled at any time in the history of the British Empire towards the Imperial Crown. (Cheers.) Then came an acute moment when we were overwhelmed with sympathy for India on the occasion of a great calamity when we saw in the twinkling of an eye a great city of 40,000 inhabitants swept off the face of the earth and a wide area devastated beyond recognition. As instancing this solidarity and the feeling of unity, he was glad to say that he heard that night that the Lord Mayor of London, true to the traditions of the City, was opening a fund for the relief of the sufferers in the earthquake. (Cheers.) He was glad to say also on behalf of his Majesty's Government that it was intended when Parliament resumed after Whitsuntide to ask the House of Commons to vote a sum of £50,000 towards the relief of the sufferers. (Renewed cheers.)

"There were [*sic*] present that night a very representative assembly of distinguished Indian public men to whom they extended the warmest welcome to London in this historic year. The Maharajah Gaekwar of Baroda was the doyen of the Princes of India. He had just celebrated his Diamond Jubilee as ruler of Baroda, and of all men seemed to him (the chairman) to have solved the problem of the art of government. (Cheers.) He congratulated him upon his success. He was a most experienced ruling Prince not alone of India, but of the world, and they all wished him long life and success.

"Referring to the presence of the Aga Khan, the Chairman said they all congratulated him upon his Derby success on the previous day, a success which followed closely upon that of His Highness the Maharajah of Rajpipla last year which he understood was likely to be repeated next year. (Laughter.) Next to the Maharajah Gaekwar of Baroda he did not know anybody who understood life in every continent in both hemispheres so completely as the Aga Khan, and they looked forward to the time when he would write his autobiography, which would prove an extraordinarily interesting volume. He had played a great part in the public life of India, and they were glad to have that opportunity of paying tribute to the distinguished services he had given to the Empire.

"Referring to British India, Sir Samuel said that that morning he had the greatest pleasure since he had been Secretary of State in attending a meeting of the Privy Council at which Sir Tej Bahadur Sapru had been sworn in as a member of the Privy Council.

"The Maharajah Gaekwar of Baroda, in reply, said that he had memories of the Vice-royalty of Lord Lytton, the father of the present peer. During his long rule he had endeavoured to promote friendly relations between the Hindus and Mohammedans, and there had been some encouraging instances of cordiality between them. With the coming of the new reforms he expressed the belief that there would be an increasing unity between Hindus and Moslems which was indeed essential to India taking her due place in the comity of nations.

"Sir Tej Bahadur Sapru paid a warm tribute to Sir Samuel Hoare's close observation of Indian affairs during the last four years. He would not deny that the proposals of the Government had been coldly received in India, but the manner in which he would like the matter to be approached in India was that the Bill had been carried through by a Conservative Secretary of State in a predominantly Conservative House of Parliament. In his judgment this Bill laid the foundation of Indian freedom truly and well, and it was for India herself to build upon it in a way worthy of the British Parliament and of India's aspirations. (Cheers.)"

The Aga Khan spoke after the Maharajah Gaekwar of Baroda.

153

THE SUFFERING IN QUETTA

Speech at the Quetta Earthquake Relief Fund Meeting

London: 24 June 1935

Sympathy from Britain and Australia – a disaster for 40,000 people
– need for assistance – appeal for a generous response.

The Aga Khan said that, belonging to the faith of the vast majority
of the sufferers in the disaster, he desired to express his thanks
to the British Government and to the Commonwealth of Australia
for the immediate way in which they had shown their sympathy
by coming to the aid of India. It had been suggested that since
the horrors of the War the public were less sensitive to terrible
catastrophes that came to mankind, but here they had a case in
which nature had outdone all that man had done in terror and
aggressiveness.

Quetta was one of the greatest disasters of modern times.
Forty thousand people woke from sleep either to be hurled
into eternity or to suffer death under conditions making rescue
impossible. Others escaped as by a miracle to suffer through life
disablement, incapacity, and poverty. They would die of starvation
unless there was help. He asked that it should be remembered
that his country had unfortunately not yet arrived at that stage
of political and social development where people could fall back
on such services as insurance, old-age pensions, and other allevi-
ations which existed in Western countries.

Many perplexing questions presented themselves to authority,
and the answer to them could not be given yet, though they
might be assured that Lord Zetland and Lord Willingdon would
handle them with courage and vision. Meanwhile there was one
individual question which every one at the meeting could answer.
It was not, "Should I give?" but "What and when shall I give?"

He appealed for an immediate and generous response, which would go further to unite the various nationalities of the subjects of the King.

Source: *The Times*, London, 25 June 1935.

The complete report of the proceedings of the meeting in *The Times* reads as follows:

A meeting called by the Lord Mayor in support of his appeal for the Quetta Earthquake Relief Fund was held yesterday afternoon at the Mansion House. Lord Zetland and other speakers made it clear that the need for help arising out of the disaster is urgent, and it was stated that 20,000 people are faced with destitution unless the aid granted by the State can be supplemented by private charity.

Lord Willingdon, the Viceroy of India, sent a message to the meeting in which he expressed thanks to the Lord Mayor for so generously and promptly starting the Mansion House Fund to assist them in India in repairing the very heavy personal loss and damage which had been caused by the earthquake.

"The response to my appeal in this country (India) from Indians and British alike," the message continued, "has been already splendidly generous, for since the fund opened a fortnight ago I have received over £150,000. The survivors from the earthquake have suffered very heavily indeed. The majority of them have lost everything they possessed. There are many widows and many orphans among them. I am sure that my fellow countrymen will hold out the hand of friendship and sympathy to them and will help them in their hour of need."

The Lord Mayor, who presided, said that the disastrous consequences of the earthquake were still scarcely appreciated. Seventy years ago the British assumed administrative control of this mountainous frontier tract containing Quetta. Quetta guarded the route to Kandahar. It was the headquarters of one of our largest European garrisons and the headquarters of a division of the railway. Apart from the British, the inhabitants of the city were largely Hindus, shopkeepers of a friendly type who had unbounded faith in the British soldier. British energy and organization had erected many important buildings, but the homes of the people were in the main built of unshaped stone, mud-bricks, and plaster. Thus when the terrible two minutes of trembling took place during the night the town collapsed, burying all those inhabitants beneath its debris.

Never in the past had a disaster made such a clean and terrible sweep in so limited an area. The inhabitants had lost their all. They had sunk everything in a town of our making. They were the people who followed the flag and chose to settle around a British outpost of Empire. As was known, the ruins of the city, with its thousands of dead, would be sealed for a year.

The Lord Mayor added that he had approached the Lord Mayors of the important cities in the provinces with the hope that, in spite of the many appeals that had been made this year, they might be able to help, and he had not had one refusal.

Lord Zetland, Secretary of State for India, said he supposed the Quetta earthquake was the greatest calamity which any country of our Empire had suffered. The impression created on his mind of Quetta was of a city built firmly on a rock, but in the twinkling of an eye not only Quetta, but other cities and a hundred villages within the zone of the railway, which extended over 2,500 square miles, had been blotted off the face of the earth.

He went on to express admiration of the orderly manner and the rapidity with which the situation was dealt with by the authorities on the spot: and the foresight and wisdom by which the risk of epidemic disease had been avoided. He also read a letter from an Englishwoman who was in the earthquake and took an active part in the work of relief, in which the writer said they were all wakened at three minutes past three by the unspeakable noise of the shock. She did not know how she got there, but she found herself in the garden, and while there Major-General Karslake came by in a car and said that all the town had gone. She described in the letter work at the British hospital, and also at the native hospital, to which 2,500 people were taken in one day.

The letter, said Lord Zetland, bore striking proof of the belief he had always entertained that when faced with a real emergency human nature rose to its full stature and displayed the highest qualities with which humanity was endowed. The need in the stricken area was great. The Government of India had provided 10 lakhs of rupees and the generous gifts of the Government of this country and the Commonwealth of Australia had been welcomed gratefully in India, but some 20,000 people were faced with destitution unless the aid granted by the State could be supplemented by private charity.

The Viceroy had received an immediate response, but much more was still required. In calamities of this kind all questions of race or of creed fell into abeyance. There was a common tie of sympathy which combined the nations of the earth in face of human suffering. The International Relief Union, realizing this, was appealing for funds in other countries. He felt sure that the appeal the Lord Mayor had issued would meet with a response which would come up to the greatest traditions of the humanitarian feelings of the British people.

Addresses in support of the appeal were also given by Sir B. N. Mitra, High Commissioner for India, Sir Denys de S. Bray, member of the Council of India, and General Sir Tornquhil Matheson, who had left Quetta on leave before the earthquake.

The Lord Mayor received on Saturday the following subscriptions to the Quetta Relief Fund:

Goldsmiths Company and Lever Brothers, Limited, £500 each; Merchant Taylors Company, £262 10s.; Drapers Company, £250; Howards and Sons, Limited, Imperial Tobacco Company, Limited, National Discount Company, Limited, and Union Discount Company of London, Limited, £105 each; Bass, Ratcliff and Gretton, Limited, and Glyn Mills and Co., £100 each; David Sassoon and Co. Limited, and Stansted (Essex), £52 10s. each; Octavius Steel and Co., Williams Deacon's Bank, Limited, and Sir Denys and Lady Bray, £50 each; Sir Alexander Gibb and Partners and Price and Pierce, Limited, £26 5s. each; H. Simpson, £25.

The details of the Quetta disaster are so scarce that I reprint below the dispatches from *The Times* of 1, 3, 5 and 8 June (the only authoritative and eye-witness account available to me).

From *The Times* of 1 June:

Simla, May 31

A serious earthquake occurred about 2.45 this morning 40 miles along the upland valley of Baluchistan, of which Quetta is the principal centre. Until full communication is restored it is not possible to know the extent of the disaster, but the latest figures for the casualties are:–

Europeans (civil and military):– 72 killed; 20 to 30 missing; 92 injured.

Indians:– 3,000 killed (presumably in old Quetta city); 1,500 injured and in hospital.

One officer and 43 airmen of the Royal Air Force were killed, and the missing are also mainly airmen. No casualties are reported here among military or Air Force officers and families, except that Pilot Officer Charles R. Paylor was killed and the eldest child of Flight Lieutenant F. D. Biggs is missing.

The following civil officers and their relatives are reported killed:– Mr. Meredith H. Jones (Political Department) with his wife and mother-in-law, Mrs. Bradford; Mr. H. L. Francis (Irrigation Engineer) and his wife.

Sir Norman Cater, Agent to the Governor-General and Chief Commissioner, Baluchistan, is reported safe, and other civil officers have presumably escaped. But Lieutenant-Colonel Severn Williams (Political Department), Mr. William Ruper Hay (Political, on a visit from Kabul), Mr. E. B. Wakefield (Political) and Mr. Francis are each reported to have lost a child.

The severe loss of life in the Air Force suggests that the low line of the valley suffered most. It is on this level that Quetta city lies.

LINE OF SHOCK

So far as can be gauged here the earthquake followed the line between Mastung, which was destroyed, and Quetta, which was seriously damaged. The line of the earthquakes followed the low level of Dasht-i-Bedaulat (Plain of No Riches). The shock appears to have been less severe on the cantonments which are a veritable Aldershot.

The police force at Quetta is said to have been almost wiped out, and many casualties are feared among subordinate civil and police officers. The Staff College officers are reported safe. No railway officers were killed, but heavy casualties are indicated among subordinates. Mastung and the surrounding villages are described as laid flat, while four-fifths of the population were killed. The troops' accommodation lies on the higher level on the mountain side. The R.A.F. casualties appear to be due to the fall of buildings, and machines are reported to have been damaged by a hangar which crashed. Many officers' bungalows were wrecked.

It is fortunate that only slight damage has been done to the railways, and so medical relief can be sent to the area. A relief train has already left Karachi and other units are preparing to enter the devastated district. Many must inevitably have perished in Quetta city, but late tonight there was still no authentic news to this effect. Meanwhile a cause of thankfulness is seen in the fact that Quetta, as a jumping-off ground for military operations on the frontier, has lavish supplies of food and is equipped with excellent hospital facilities. Quetta is a mobilization dump and has enough food to supply an army for some weeks. Conjectures are rife in Simla and elsewhere in India tonight, but until telegraphic communication is fully resumed the only definite information reaching Simla is *via* the Army wireless.

Karachi, May 31

Sir Norman Cater, the Agent to the Governor-General in Baluchistan, narrowly escaped death. All the bungalows in the civil station and all buildings in the native city collapsed. He has broadcast a wireless appeal to other provincial headquarters for the urgent dispatch of relief to Quetta, where British and Indian troops are engaged in succouring the injured and accommodating the destitute in camps which have been formed on the racecourse and in the grounds of the Residency. Food supplies at Quetta are fairly adequate, and as the railways and roads are passable there is little fear of starvation.

Quetta serves as a hill station for Karachi, and crowds besieged the telegraph office and newspaper offices today, seeking news of relatives and friends. No details have been available owing to a breakdown of the ordinary means of communication. Most of the news so far received comes from intercepted wireless messages sent out from the Government wireless station at Quetta.

NURSES TO FLY TO QUETTA

Lahore, May 31

Medical relief was sent from Lahore to Quetta this evening by train. Military nursing sisters have been summoned from Kasauli, in the Ambala district of the Punjab, to Lahore and will arrive tomorrow morning. They will be joined by a detachment from Lahore. As soon as they arrive they will be flown to Quetta by the R.A.F. By aeroplane Quetta is 500 miles from Lahore.

Quetta is an important military station in the Indian frontier scheme and the seat of a Staff College. The Army garrison consists of two battalions of infantry, an artillery brigade, and a tank company, in addition to Indian regiments. The headquarters of No. 3 Wing, R.A.F., are situated there, and two Army cooperation squadrons occupy the R.A.F. station.

The station is among the hills, and its climate, gratefully cool in the hot weather, may be unpleasantly cool in the "cold" weather.

From *The Times* of 3 June:

Delhi, June 2

The Government of India have issued the following statement about the earthquake:–

The whole of Quetta City has been destroyed and is being sealed under military guard from today on medical advice. It is estimated that 20,000 corpses remain buried under the debris. There is no hope of rescuing any more living. The corpses extracted and buried number several thousand, but exact figures are unobtainable. There are about 10,000 Indian survivors, including 4,000 injured.

All houses in the civil area have been razed to the ground except Government House, which is partially standing in ruins, and also the Murree Brewery.

In the cantonment area one quarter of the buildings have been destroyed; the remaining three-quarters are slightly damaged and inhabitable. Most of the damage was done in the Royal Air Force area, where the barracks have been destroyed, and only six machines out of 27 are serviceable. The railway area has been destroyed, but Hanna Road and the Staff College area are undamaged.

The surrounding villages have been destroyed, with, it is feared, heavy casualties. Military parties are being sent out to investigate and render help.

Kalat and Mastung have been razed to the ground with very heavy casualties. All villages between Quetta and Kalat are reported destroyed. Loralai and Chaman are known to be safe, and no information has been received of damage to Fort Sandeman, which appears to have been outside the orbit of the earthquake. Messages received from Kandahar show that that area escaped entirely.

Control of supplies has been assumed by the Western Command, who are rationing the civil population. Arrangements have been made to send food and collect casualties in village districts. The Indian Military Hospital has treated 3,500 patients in the last 24 hours. The Cantonment Hospital has treated over 2,000 and detained 200 for further treatment. Refugee camps have been established on the racecourse, and 14 medical officers and six nurses, with a large collection of medical stores, have been dispatched by aeroplane from various stations in India. The Viceroy's aeroplane has been sent by his Excellency for this purpose, and special trains containing medical personnel and stores have been sent from Karachi and Lahore.

Railway and road communication with Quetta is still intact. The Chief Commissioner of Railways has gone there to investigate the position. Telegraphic communication is still by military wireless, but the civil land line has now been restored with the assistance of the Army Signals. Large accumulations of private telegrams were dispatched from Quetta today; the remainder are being sent by aeroplane.

The situation is reported well in hand, but owing to the fact that nearly all subordinate civil officers and police were killed, the Agent to the Governor-General has asked the military authority for assistance in carrying on the administration. Such powers as are necessary will be provided by emergency legislation. The Punjab North-west Frontier Governments are sending, at the request of the Agent to the Governor-General, special police to assist, pending the reorganization of the Baluchistan Police Force. Refugees are being evacuated to-day, six trains leaving. This evacuation will continue as long as no epidemic disease breaks out. The Punjab and Sind authorities have been requested, in consultation with the railway authorities, to arrange food for destitute refugees at Jacobabad.

To prevent the influx of persons for whom no accommodation or supplies are available tickets are not being issued for Quetta. Travellers will not be permitted to proceed beyond Rohri, without special permission.

It is hoped that the particulars already published regarding British casualties are inclusive.

The Viceroy and Lady Willingdon have opened an earthquake relief fund with a donation of 5,000 rupees (£375). Further donations should be sent to the Private Secretary to the Viceroy, Viceregal Lodge, Simla. In an appeal to the Princes and people of India, Lord Willingdon, after recalling India's response to the Bihar fund and the magnificent contribution to the Silver Jubilee Fund, says a new and overwhelming catastrophe impels him to appeal again to the generous sympathy of the Indian public.

Messages of condolence have been received by the Viceroy from the Governor-General of South Africa, the Governor of British Guiana, the Lord Mayor of London, and the officer administering the Government of Hong-kong [sic].

While the official statement mentioned 20,000 Indian dead, the figure must necessarily be speculative; another estimate in Simla is that 70 per cent. of the Indian population of old Quetta lost their lives, which would mean

24,000. Trainloads of survivors now reaching Lahore and Karachi tell a harrowing tale of the city being laid flat at the first shock about 3 a.m.

The troops quickly began extricating victims. "The English looked like angels who had come to minister to the wounded," said an Indian refugee at Lahore. Pathans who appeared in the devastated area bent on loot were promptly arrested by the troops. Another survivor said that the bodies were being cleared out of the debris by lorry and the city looked like a vast burial ground. The earthquake was preceded by a terrific roar, and then buildings fell on the sleeping people: in attempting to escape they were buried alive and whole families were wiped out.

Multan, June 2

The calamitous nature of the Quetta earthquake is now fully realized throughout India, which is only just recovering from the disastrous catastrophe in Bihar last year. So far as relief work is concerned all roads lead to Quetta, but no unofficial person is permitted to enter the stricken area, which is now under the complete control of the military authorities.

Slight earthquake shocks continue to disturb the ruins into which Quetta has fallen, and searchers unearthing the bodies of victims find their work handicapped in consequence. But the Government of India and those provincial Governments in the neighbourhood of Baluchistan are exerting every effort to assist the harassed populace. Relief workers are being hurried into the area from all parts of Northern India, particularly from Lahore and Karachi.

The officials of the North-Western Railway are cooperating with the military authorities at Quetta in evacuating the civil population. Thousands of refugees are now leaving Quetta by rail. The problem facing the authorities has been greatly simplified by the fact that the railways are virtually intact throughout the damaged region. Four trains, including two refugee trains, left Quetta on Saturday, and six trains, bearing about 5,000 refugees pulled out of the ruins of Quetta Station today; they are bound for Rohri and other parts of Sind, from which localities most of the Sindhi traders and merchants of Quetta City originally hailed. Sir Guthrie Russell, the Chief Commissioner for Railways of the Government of India, is proceeding to the earthquake zone to superintend arrangements affecting the railways.

Meanwhile trains from Lahore and Karachi are crowded with relief workers, first-aid detachments, Boy Scouts, doctors, and nurses to work the temporary hospitals which have been created at Quetta. Special measures have been taken to bring relief to the outlying districts, particularly along the branch railway line between Nushki and Nokkundi, near the Persian border. Water rations are being borne by train to the railway staff and others placed in serious circumstances along this line.

While the seriousness of the catastrophe cannot be minimized, unofficial reports of casualties should be accepted with some reserve. Indians tend in such disasters to leave the devastated areas of their own volition, and many who are reported missing may be found to have deserted a region on which, in their eyes, the gods have looked with such disfavour.

Simla, June 2

Messages received here from Quetta on Saturday indicate that British casualties in the earthquake may be about 200. It is admittedly not easy to make any definite statement about Indian or British casualties, though naturally the British element is most easily checked. There is every evidence that the military authorities have arrangements well in hand.

The King's message to the Viceroy expressing sympathy with the Indian and British relatives of the victims is greatly appreciated here. The message from the Secretary of State to the Viceroy asking him to convey condolences to the Agent to the Governor-General in Baluchistan has also been received with gratitude. The Viceroy to-day sent a telegram to the Agent indicating the sympathy of India.

The authorities of the Punjab and the North-West Frontier Province have offered the services of police detachments and they have been sent to Quetta.

Twenty Europeans on the railway staff, including families, and 100 Indian members of the railway staff, including families, have been killed and many injured. Communications are gradually being opened. The railway water supply is not affected. The extent of the area affected is not clear here, but Kalat town and Miri Palace have been laid flat and many killed.

From *The Times* of 5 June:

Quetta, June 4

I have entered a city wrecked by earthquake before; soon after the California community of Santa Barbara had been destroyed I was among its ruins. But that Californian tragedy had no parallel with this in Baluchistan. There the line of disturbance made a clear demarcation which followed the principal street, and even after the shock the modern lines on which the town had been planned could readily be distinguished.

But here in Quetta City there is nothing to pick out. Landmarks have gone as everything has gone. No mosque rises from the ruins to show where men foregathered; the market place where men met to barter cannot be distinguished today. There is nothing but a widespread mass of grey and tawny deкbris, tapering off into the dun landscape, beyond which in turn is a rim of forlorn and sad hills where no trees grow. It is today a place of utter desolation, made poignant with the misery of a suffering people.

The first broad glimpse of this place shocks the imagination, as it emphasizes the appalling nature of the catastrophe which came in the night. In this the Baluchistan tragedy differs from that in Bihar last year. Bihar was stricken in the afternoon, when many were out and about. In Quetta it was a valley of sleeping people who went silently to their deaths. This accounts for the immense death-roll.

War conditions prevail at Quetta and in the vicinity, but it is an army moving under humanitarian orders. British and Indian troops have risen to the emergency, and everything that is being done here is being done by soldiers. They control traffic, issue rations to the civil population, and convey refugees from rest camps to the trains, and the general services which normally are supplied by private enterprise have been taken over.

As I write this on the railway platform at Quetta another trainload of refugees is about to depart. Indian and Anglo-Indian nurses and doctors make final hurried visits to each carriage. Tea and water have been dished out and food has been arranged for the refugees at stations between here and Lahore. In this the railway authorities are cooperating closely with the military. Meanwhile troops of The Queen's and The West Yorkshire Regiments superintend the final embarcation.

Indian survivors of the catastrophe are grateful to the British authorities for all that has been done since the fateful night when their city was obliterated. The work of the Army authorities is bound to rank among the most amazing emergency feats of organization in the history of India. A new community has been established on the Quetta racecourse, which Major-General Karslake, the Officer Commanding, now facetiously calls "Epsom Downs." In all conscience the racecourse is now not unlike that haunt of English sportsmen, for amid all the things the military have had to consider they have not forgotten entertainment. Gurkha pipe bands cheer up the Indian survivors and Boy Scouts have organized sports for their entertainment. All this is done as first aid workers, doctors, and nurses move among them dressing wounds.

Today the authorities spread their net wider to succour the stricken inhabitants of this region. Medical relief is being disseminated under military direction to outlying villages. This follows a tour of *reconnaissance* on the first day which resulted in food and water being taken to needy areas; medical help is now being added to this service. These efforts of the military fully justify the compliments sent them today from Simla by Field Marshal Sir Philip Chetwode, the Commander-in-Chief.

The appalling nature of the disaster so far as it involves Quetta City was aptly summarized by a British soldier who was at Ypres: "If the artillery at Quetta had turned their guns on the city they could not have demolished it more thoroughly," he said in an interval of supplying rations to the hungry Indians. This is the real fact of the situation. No stone stands upon another. In the cantonments virtually every house is damaged, and everybody, from the G.O.C. to the privates, is living in the open. But curiously there is little gloom apparent here. Even the Indians with their fatalistic spirit, are showing wonderful fortitude under the calamity, which deprived many of them of their families and everything else. The British Tommies, despite the gravity of the situation are tackling their unwonted duties with zest, and the Indian soldiers highly praised their British officers for their fine work in peculiarly trying circumstances.

Next to the military the authorities of the North-Western Railway have borne the burden of the evacuation. Sir Guthrie Russell and Mr. J. C. Highet, the Agent of the North-Western Railway, have personally superintended the evacuation in the past two days, and believe that the remainder of the inhabitants will be completely transported in two days more. Extraordinary acts of heroism are recorded among the British and Indian servants of the railway. Notable is the exploit of Mr. B. C. L. Dean, the Divisional Superintendent at Quetta, who set off in a trolly-car [*sic*] on Friday morning to see if the track was damaged. He made his way alone from Quetta to Spezand, examining the track, and was the first to inform the Government of India of the tragedy. He returned with an incoming train and acted as pilot to see if the track would stand the strain of the load. He ran the pilot engine over one culvert considered weak before entrusting the loaded train to the track. Major-General Karslake himself has been a marvellous example to the troops. Throughout the day he had been seen perambulating the district, making personal inquiries into all sorts of problems and even stopping during his tour to bury the dead. No one is now permitted in Quetta City, where the danger from decaying corpses is apparent, but the General himself daily enters the deserted place and visits the British soldiers who maintain their solitary watches among the ruins.

Salvage work has been proceeding in one part of the city where it is known

1081

no bodies lie. Precious stores have been saved to add to the supplies of the locality. It is now fairly clear that the authorities have evacuated the city before disease manifested itself, and in hurrying off survivors it was to prevent a worse disaster befalling them.

Whether Quetta city will ever be rebuilt is a moot question. To work upon the present site is impossible for some weeks. It is possible that some other part of this upland plain will be chosen for the future city, for it is clear that the obligation still rests upon the British authorities to maintain a garrison in this locality.

These have been indeed feverish days for British soldiers. Not only have they excavated thousands of Indian dead and buried or cremated them, but they have attended the funerals of many of their comrades in the Royal Air Force, as well as those of other Europeans who were killed. For two days six padres have continuously conducted burial services in the cemetery, where more than 200 Europeans and Anglo-Indians are now buried. They were placed in four long graves after the committal services of their respective religions. There have been four burial centres; British and Anglo-Indians at one, Moslems at another, and Hindus at two others. No Moslem was cremated; all the Hindus were. The Sikh community, which is small, looked after its own dead. No British soldiers were killed. Three Gurkhas on guard at the residence of Sir Norman Cater, Agent to the Governor-General, were killed, which shows how narrow was the escape of the Agent himself.

Thanks to the combined work of the Army and military authorities the whole area has been evacuated within 72 hours. All day long for two days special trains have been run from Quetta to the Punjab and Sind, carrying thousands of refugees who had been given free tickets. Many bandaged people fill the trains, and hundreds of children, sad-eyed and worn-out, tell the story of their recent tribulation. Baluchis, men of amazing physique, walk about the platforms dazed and unhappy. Whole families have been wiped out, but what is worse are those cases in which a child has survived while the parents were killed in the ruins.

All the way in to this immense valley the toll of the earthquake was disclosed. Villages lie in ruins, with only an occasional inhabitant pottering among the debris. Most of the villages near Quetta have been completely obliterated. The same applies to Kalat State. From Mastung to Kalat, a distance of about 80 miles, there is a scene of desolation. Every village had been demolished, with many dead under the ruins.

On the lawn in front of the shattered Quetta Club last night Major-General Karslake, officiating as G.O. Commanding-in-Chief, the Western Command, held a conference of the officers of his company to hear their reports on the latest situation in this derelict city. It was announced that at noon yesterday not one living soul remained in Quetta City, which was guarded by British soldiers wearing respirators.

With the completion of the evacuation the authorities are now turning their attention to salvage work and the prevention of any outbreak of disease. Elaborate precautions have been taken to prevent unauthorized persons from entering the stricken area. Cavalry picquets form an outer circle within which infantry form an impassable cordon. Trains entering Quetta are carefully searched as they approach the city to prevent any incursions by curious sightseers.

The India Office announced yesterday that, although there may be some

1082

chance of further shocks at Quetta, this need not cause undue alarm, as all precautions have been taken to minimize danger to the survivors. They, both civil and military, are being accommodated in the open. Arrangements are being made for the evacuation of British families and for embarcation of those desiring passages.

FROM OUR CORRESPONDENT

Delhi, June 4

The Government Departments in Simla are concerning themselves exclusively with earthquake relief. Twenty-one R.A.F. aircraft carried doctors and nurses to Quetta yesterday.

In spite of the recent Jubilee appeal there has been a magnificent response to the Viceroy's Relief Fund. The Governor of the Punjab in an appeal for support for the fund announces that the Punjab Government have contributed a lakh of rupees (£7,500), which the Viceroy has replaced at the Punjab's disposal for immediate relief. A large allotment has already been made. Arrangements have been made for first-aid and hospital accommodations for the injured. Leading Indians have endorsed the Viceroy's appeal.

The Viceroy and the Commander-in-Chief have cancelled the balls they were to have given in Simla.

From *The Times* of 8 June:

Quetta, June 7

The abandonment of Quetta is now virtually complete. Soldiers today were putting barbed-wire entanglements around the city to protect both the dead and the property of survivors from marauding tribesmen. The voluntary evacuation of the populace is also nearing an end, and only a few survivors remain on "Epsom Downs" – a place-name which is likely to supersede that of Quetta racecourse in the annals of this community. The evacuation of villagers will presently be undertaken.

Earthquake shocks continue, and several strong tremors yesterday and today have brought down some more of what is left among the ruins.

Lieutenant-General Sir Edmund Ironside has surveyed the scene and made his report on the situation. Doubtless his findings will have a far-reaching effect on the future of this famous military station. So far as the existing forces are concerned, the position is considered satisfactory, both for supplies and cover for the troops. While work remains for the troops to do here the garrison will not be depleted. The civil authorities are expected to resume control soon. But in view of the lack of accommodation the number of troops will probably be reduced by the winter. Western Command headquarters are being transferred to Karachi forthwith.

Relatives of the British soldiers here may feel assured that the authorities are taking every precaution in the interests of the troops. The quarters formerly occupied by the soldiers are badly damaged, and none will be asked to re-occupy them. It is clear that the nature of the subsoil is responsible for the concentration of the disaster in Quetta civil lines and cantonments. The subsoil is of mud, whereas the Staff College area, where no damage was done, is based on rock.

Martial law has disclosed none of the evils frequently associated with military control. Not one shot has been fired, except to destroy suffering animals, not one civilian has been Court-martialled, and no soldier has been guilty of any serious misdemeanour. The Indian troops, like the British, show amazing fortitude. The whole force responded with enthusiasm to the sudden call. Gratitude is being expressed by survivors, who claim that had the British soldiers not taken control their city would have been looted and themselves murdered by roving hordes from the neighbouring mountains.

Standing out in this dire tragedy is the figure of Major-General Karslake, General Officer Commanding. He has become the hero of the simple folk of this upland valley. When he visits the temporary camp on "Epsom Downs" women show their gratitude by falling at his feet, and men make low obeisances. His command of the situation is so remarkable that he even knows the names of the cows giving the largest quantities of milk at the Government dairy.

The achievements in the hospitals and relief centres have been made possible through the extraordinary work done by British women. Many without previous hospital experience entered the crude hospitals and stood beside the operating tables when cases of the most appalling kind were undertaken.

On the political side the chief burden fell on Sir Norman Cater, agent to the Governor-General, who has been unremitting in his efforts to bring every possible comfort to those people under his administration. On the medical side Colonel S. G. S. Haughton, I.M.S., has been mainly responsible both for the actual work of the hospitals and broader medical policy affecting evacuation.

I made a final visit to the city of the dead last night. A crescent moon was suspended in the clear sky and the familiar Plough lay low on the horizon. Under this spectral light the city offered an eerie scene. A slight tremor disturbed the masonry, which settled with a murmur into deep silence again. The odour of a battlefield hovered over all – completely justifying the decision of the authorities to evacuate the population at once.

I turned my back on this desolate place and tried to forget one of the saddest sights I have ever seen – an animated Oriental bazaar transformed in a few seconds into a graveyard. I never want to see the Chal Valley again, although countless soldiers from all parts of the Empire cherish happy recollections of this military station. But all I shall ever be able to picture of Quetta City will be a city whose dead out-numbered its living and with most of its living escaping in terror from their dead.

An official report telegraphed to the India Office yesterday says:–

"The range of the earthquake is estimated as having been 130 miles long and 20 miles broad. In addition to the towns of Kalat and Mastung, at least 100 villages in the Quetta sub-division and in Kalat State have been totally destroyed. The survey of villages is not yet complete, but the present estimate of the number of killed is between 12,000 and 15,000. The total death roll, including Quetta, is therefore probably in excess of 40,000. The number of destitute refugees is estimated at not less than 15,000.

"Supplies of food and medical comforts at Quetta are now adequate. Evacuation of British and Indian survivors continues with all possible speed. A Vickers-Victoria troop carrier leaves Lahore for Quetta today to assist in the transport of survivors to Karachi."

Some information on Quetta is to be found in the *Proceedings and Transactions of the Bombay Geographical Society*, Vols 5 and 17; C. Davidson, "Note on the Quetta Earthquake of December 20th, 1892", *Geological Magazine*, Vol. 10 (1893), December, pp. 356–60; and "Quetta: The Capital of Baluchistan", *The Illustrated Weekly of Pakistan*, Vol. 2 (1950), No. 44.

154

THE MUSLIM LANDS AND THE WEST

Speech to the Council of Peers

London: 15 July 1935

Progress in Muslim states – Islamic countries and Britain/USA –
the need for mutual co-operation – Muslim countries free from
debt – communications – potential for trade – Muslims in India
familiar with Western culture – the significance of Eastern culture
– tourism – a centre to promote better relations.

The Aga Khan, in replying to the toast, commended the work of
the National League under Miss Farquharson in promoting
British and Islamic friendship. He passed in review the progress
made not only by the Muslims in India, but also by all the Muslim
States, and referred briefly to present-day conditions in Turkey,
Iran, Afghanistan, Iraq, Saudi Arabia and Egypt. In regard to
Arabia he held that the changed scheme of things would promote
the development of culture and that the school of Islam established there would lead to freedom and progress. The desert,
by availing itself of science, would become a garden. With this
strengthened position the Islamic world was qualified to make a
great contribution to the service of humanity in promotion of
peace, the need for which was painfully evident. There could be
no doubt that the greatest single instrument for saving mankind
from another world war was the British Empire. And its power
was greatly reinforced by the affinity of its outlook and civilization
with those of the United States of America. Let the Islamic world
link itself with this Anglo-Saxon power to promote peace, not by
political instruments, but by the use of opportunities ready to
hand for friendship and the furtherance of mutual interests.

The need for such better understanding is all the more necessary since in so many other quarters, alas, we see, discredit,

misunderstanding, jealousy and all the possibilities of trouble. In a troubled world, if we can even improve one small corner, if we can develop it further, we have done some service to the great cause of the whole. Let us then work for a better understanding and for a mutual co-operation which has nothing to do with any kind of political instrument – but something far better – the spirit of man. Let the Islamic world show its true face to the Anglo-Saxon world. Such co-operation and understanding needs cultivation. It will not come of itself; it will not become permanently useful unless we constantly bear it in mind and work for it. I have some suggestions to make so that between the Anglo-Saxon world and Islam the great bonds of national, spiritual and economic interest can be more closely knitted than at present. Economically we are told that these countries are not ready for it, but please remember that these are the only countries in the world that are free from debt. Even in Egypt, where there is a public debt, it is so small that it is almost negligible. Hence with that essential fact before us it is only a question of time and reproductive capital outlay that much can be done for the economic development of these countries. Again, aviation and good roads have rendered the question of communications, which was so difficult thirty years ago, and seemed an impossible barrier, much more easily solved. Communications have been made easy and cheap – especially cheap. I for one am convinced that not only in British India but in the Near East there are great possibilities for potential trade of the best kind, that is trade which is beneficial to both sides. For that alone is, I believe, the foundation of prosperity for buyer and seller.

Now a very curious thing has happened during the last 35 years. Our Hindu brothers were able in India to go in for the study of Western thought and culture and civilization earlier than the Muslims. Thirty-five years ago there was little general desire amongst the Muslims in India for acquaintance or comprehension of the philosophy and culture of the West. To-day that is a thing of the past. The problem of the women has been faced and I think in India and in most other Muslim countries it is being sensibly solved. European philosophy, standard works in both literature and art are being studied and understood, but is there any mutual move forward on your side? Do you know anything about our civilization really? Do you know the culture of the East? One famous poet – a minor poet of Persia has become almost a major poet of the West – I mean Omar Khayyam. When I go through a library of books in Arabic, in Persian, in

Turkish, and in Urdu, I say to myself; "Here are vast fields of pleasure, of enjoyment, of joy closed to my European friends."

Then there is wide scope now for tourist traffic. With the return of prosperity now that the War is getting farther and farther away, the Anglo-Saxon will once more think of going far from his own country in search of sun, peace and enjoyment. We all know that in countries like Switzerland, France and Italy tourist traffic is a great source of wealth. Is it not possible in these days of aviation and motor traffic to open up the Near East to travellers? The winter sun of Iran surely must have an attraction and one day Arabia may become a winter resort. By travel there is a great possibility of better understanding and appreciating the civilization of the East. Of course we ourselves of the East have a great part to play in this. We must open our country to tourist traffic; we must have inns and reasonable accommodation; we must show that our waters are as good as those of other countries; we must open our arms and welcome visitors. Happily peace reigns. There is no danger. A traveller or trader can go from one part of Iran to another with the same security as in most of the countries of the West. That is the position to-day.

Well, are we merely going to have pious intentions? Is it not possible to begin working in a more active way by establishing first an appeal in which all these oriental nations can take an interest and under which those in this country who would like to know more about the East and who would like to have a further knowledge of its culture can also take action? May I appeal at the same time to my Muslim friends, whatever their country may be, to my English, Dominion and American friends, whether in this great city of London, in this centre between the Atlantic and the Pacific, we cannot start a Centre from which co-operation, understanding, intellectual and cultural suggestions, as well as trade and commerce may not be further strengthened?

Source: *The Muslim Times*, London, 1 August 1935, p. 4.
The Aga Khan was the guest of honour at a luncheon hosted by the Council of Peers and some Muslim leaders at the Claridge's Hotel, London, on 15 July 1935. In proposing the health of the Aga Khan, Sir Robert Horne spoke of the good work that could be done by any society or organization which aimed at promoting mutual understanding between Islam and Great Britain. It was essential, he said, that friendly contact between the two should become closer and their mutual regard aroused. To this end, he continued, the influence of the Aga Khan had been a dominating factor as a result of the powerful and beneficent part that he had played in the politics of the British Empire.

155

PROSPECTS FOR THE LEAGUE OF NATIONS

Speech in the General Assembly of the League of Nations

Geneva: 13 September 1935

Criticism of the League of Nations in India is directed to its short-comings, not ideals – the idea of collective security appeals to the Indians – the world must make a wise choice.

On the one subject that is dominating the mind of this Assembly there is much that I could say, but I am a man of few words and I shall be very brief.

In India, criticism of the League of Nations is growing. India is troubled by the League's lack of universality, the incomplete-ness of its composition and the tiny representation of Indians in its organisation. She is troubled by the great preponderance, as India sees it, of the energies the League devotes to Europe and European interests. She is troubled by the magnitude of her own contributions to the League budget, large in itself, for it is larger than the contribution of any non-permanent Member of the Council, disturbingly large when placed side by side with the poverty of so many of her many, many millions. She is troubled by the League's failures, troubled by the Disarmament Confer-ence, long drawn out and infructuous – and here I can speak feelingly as a member of the Disarmament Conference from the beginning – whereas the rearmament of States is in full swing. She is troubled above all by the wars, declared or undeclared, that have been waged between Members of the League.

Now a fresh trouble greater than any is on the horizon. Should the worst come to the worst – which Heaven forbid – who dare foretell the crisis world-spread, age-lasting, that might follow? India's criticism of the League is directed to its shortcomings, not to the ideals of which the League was the outcome and which inspired her being and the best thought of the world. On the contrary. Those ideals spring from the same source as India's own philosophy and idealism, and the conception of collective security is appealing with ever growing force to my countrymen as the only alternative to international anarchy. The world is to-day at the parting of the ways. Let wisdom guide her choice.

Source: *Verbatim Record of the Sixteenth Ordinary Session of the Assembly of the League of Nations: Sixth Plenary Meeting, Friday, September 13th, 1935, at 10.30 a.m.,* Geneva, 1935, p. 2.

The Assembly was discussing the report on the work of the League of Nations since the Fifteenth Session of the Assembly. M. Beneš was in the chair. The speaker preceding the Aga Khan was M. Laval, the first delegate of France.

156

THE SITUATION IN INDIA

Interview with the Associated Press of India

Bombay: 10 January 1936

Communal unity in India – Gandhi – the new Constitution – taxation – social services – international situation – horse racing.

The Aga Khan recalled his efforts to bring about communal unity during the second Round Table Conference and said that he had always tried for communal unity and would continue to do so. It was his firm conviction that leaders of both communities should meet and settle the communal question once and for all. He hoped to meet his Hindu friends when he went to Delhi.

He expressed grave concern at Mr. Gandhi's illness and hoped that he would soon recover as his services were needed more than anybody else's in the cause of communal unity.

The Aga Khan was on very good terms with Mr. Gandhi and hoped that fresh efforts to bring about the much desired unity would be successful.

Asked about the New Constitution, he said, "Let us get what we can out of the new Constitution and make the best use of it. It is the law of the land now and we must all play our part and try to improve the condition of the masses by trying to put the burden of taxation on the shoulders of the rich, thus reducing indirect taxation which now falls heavily on the poorer classes.

We should make an effort to spend more money on education, health, sanitation and other national services. This work may take ten or fifteen years, but it does not matter."

As regards the international situation, His Highness said that he did not believe that there would be a world war. He asked the merchants and businessmen in India to take note of this and adjust their business accordingly so that they might reap advantages therefrom.

Discussing race problems, the Aga Khan said that he had always been fortune's favourite and very lucky. He added that he did not participate in the races for the sake of mere pleasure, but that he was running his stable more or less as an industry.

Questioned if he was likely to bring more horses to India, he said, "I shall send more horses here if it is advantageous."

Source: *Star of India*, Calcutta, 11 January 1936.
The interview was given by the Aga Khan on his arrival in Bombay from Europe in the morning by the *Cathay*. He was accorded an enthusiastic reception by his followers and others.

157

THE CHANGE IN THE BRITISH MONARCHY

Interview with The Times of India

Bombay: January 1936

Tribute to the late British King George V – good wishes for King Edward VIII.

"Nowhere in the world will the death of His Majesty," said the Aga Khan, "be mourned more deeply than in India. His Majesty's message of sympathy delivered at the Guildhall Banquet on his return to London after his visit to India as Prince of Wales and his subsequent message of hope after his Coronation at Delhi, are still ringing in our ears. They were the harbingers of political progress and economic and industrial progress in India, which owes a heavy debt of gratitude to His Majesty's personal interest in its welfare.

"I can recall the scene that occurred during his Majesty's visit to Calcutta as Prince of Wales. It was a scene which I shall never forget, and I have not forgotten it. I wrote what I saw then:– 'Tears of joy ran down the faces of old men and young Bengali lads who were probably students who had been agitating several weeks before. Amongst one large group I went up to an old man, a Muslim, who seemed deeply affected. His grey beard was wet with the tears of joy he had shed, and his moist eyes shone with that happy satisfaction which one so rarely sees on the faces of very old men. I went up to him and asked why he shed tears and why he looked so happy. He turned round and told me with an expression I can never forget:– "I went to see them arrive the other day. His first glance – and his whole bearing all these days has confirmed it – has shown that he is a man, and that he looks on us as men. Oh, how good it is to have a man who does feel that we are human beings ... I cry for joy that the heir to the

Indian Empire and his Consort do consider us as human." The hundreds who surrounded the old man with one voice said "Shabash! Shabash!" and looked as if they instinctively agreed.'

"I can truly say," continued the Aga Khan, "that His Majesty was every inch a man – a man amongst rulers, and a ruler amongst men." Our beloved King George was a world figure and his sudden death is a world-wide loss. We all feel it as a grievous and personal bereavement owing to his intense love for all of us and his anxiety to share in our joys and sorrows. A deep note of sympathy for the sufferings of humanity rang in and rang out of his noble heart and he was a personification of kindness towards all. His love for India was genuine and unbounded.

"To me personally," added the Aga Khan, "his death has been a source of poignant grief and sorrow. I have experienced his gracious favours and I had enjoyed his confidence for thirty-seven years. I have the pleasantest reminiscences of his kindness towards me. The world has lost in him a safe and true guide, the Empire the greatest pillar, and India its greatest friend and wellwisher.

"We all mourn today one of the best kings of world history. I had the honour and privilege of knowing him intimately. Besides his passionate desire for the well-being of his subjects, his great qualities were justice, mercy and forgiveness. I had very many occasions of meeting the King under all sorts of circumstances, and it is no exaggeration to say that one thought only dominated his life and his work, namely, peace and the peaceful interests of his vast Empire.

"India had ever been very near and dear to his thought. From his first visit in 1905 till his last day that interest had grown with personal knowledge, and a passionate desire that the pace of India's true and peaceful development, neither too hasty nor too slow, but healthy and natural, should continue. The King set no limit to India's political progress as a dominion within the Empire and yet he fully realised the force of his famous advice to Gokhale in 1905 at Calcutta to deal urgently with the problem of raising the condition of women as an essential to national progress, which proves that he was conscious of all the complex problems of this vast Empire and eager for their right solution.

"Nothing caused the King more grief than the war, which came as a terrible shock to him and his one anxiety was to secure a lasting but just peace, with charity towards all and malice towards none.

"During the war what prompted Indian Princes and Indian people to sacrifice their all was due to the personality of His Majesty, who struck a true note of duty and patriotism to the nation, and his inspiring messages and speeches and his work amongst the soldiers were a source of great encouragement to the nation to do their duty by the Empire. His Majesty visited hospitals, shipyards, factories, ammunition works, convalescence homes, and everywhere where war work and activities were carried on, and his presence never failed to give encouragement to the workers. His visit to the fleet and the army at the front showed that his heart was with them in the hour of the Empire's trial, and his presence proved a source of inspiration to all concerned. Though he was the revered and renowned ruler of the mightiest Empire the world has ever seen, His Majesty possessed a serene dignity and was altogether a selfless person of charming habits and deep courtesy.

"No reigning king or queen of Great Britain had ever visited India, and it is an open secret that when strong pressure was brought to bear upon Their Majesties to abandon their proposed visit to India, the King would not hear of it, so great was his love for the people of India. India will ever remember that memorable visit, and His Majesty's memorable proclamation transferring the capital from Calcutta to Delhi and undoing the partition of Bengal. The King's visit to India for his Coronation showed that he regarded India as an important and integral part of the Empire. His address at the opening of the First Round Table Conference will be regarded as a great landmark in the political history of India. It was a sure guarantee of India's autonomous position within the Empire. His Majesty's historic services to India will always be cherished with affection by her children."

In conclusion, His Highness said:

"Let us hope and pray that the peace which his father longed for but was not destined to have should be the dominant feature of the reign of King Edward VIII, our new Emperor, and that reconciliation on which the welfare not only of Europe but of the whole world ultimately depends may come to pass and promote the work of civilisation and happiness of humanity. May God help our new King."

Source: Naoroji M. Dumasia, *The Aga Khan and His Ancestors*, The Times of India Press, Bombay, 1939, pp. 289–92.

158

A MEMORIAL FOR KING GEORGE V

Speech at a Public Condolence Meeting

Bombay: 11 February 1936

Tribute to the late King George V – suitable memorial to commemorate his work.

We meet today under a deep gloom cast by the death of King George V, Emperor of India. The suddenness of the blow has so dazed us and the occurrence is so recent that it is difficult to realise how great is the loss sustained by the world in general and the Empire in particular. Words fail adequately to describe our grief. The Royal family has suffered irreparable loss, the Empire and particularly India has lost a genuine well-wisher, and humanity at large has lost a true friend.

The universal mourning witnessed since King George passed away testify to the great hold His late Majesty had upon the people of the world at large. No monarch was ever called upon to rule over Great Britain and the British Commonwealth of Nations in such times of stress and storm as have been witnessed during the last 25 years.

The World War destroyed many renowned monarchies in Europe and it is the highest tribute to the late King George V that in spite of these events, the British monarchy today stands more firmly established than ever. After the war, the late King strove not only for lasting peace but for fairness to and friendship with our erstwhile enemies. His success in this direction is a striking testimony to his unrivalled influence even in former enemy countries. The latter mourn the loss as sincerely as the peoples of his own dominions.

The late King was loved and honoured not only by his own subjects, but by people of all foreign countries as well. His intimate knowledge of the component parts of the Empire, his sympathies not only with the aspirations but in the sufferings and hardships of his people and his readiness to respond to every appeal to his sense of justice or to his spirit of charity and compassion won for him the love, esteem and confidence of his people. He possessed all the kingly virtues, was jealous of the traditions and was the faithful guardian of the constitutional liberties of the people.

He performed the most arduous and manifold activities which are the inheritance of monarch with remarkable dignity and grace and succeeded in winning the love and confidence of his people by his deep solicitude for the common interests of all. His sincerity and simplicity and his strong and dominating sense of public duty and patriotism made him a model monarch.

I had the honour of knowing His late Majesty personally for nearly 40 years, and what struck me most was his ideal of service and duty to the State and his living and abiding interest in the welfare of the people of India. These two things were always present in his mind. His late Majesty was indeed a great statesman and a great sportsman in the best sense of both terms. A singular judge of men, his rare gifts of commonsense and unrivalled tact were his great possession. His Majesty was the centre and symbol of Empire unity. We cherish with affectionate memory his magnificent services to this country.

It is our loyal and agreeable duty to pay homage to King Edward VIII on his accession to the throne.

His late Majesty's deeds form a great memorial to his magnificent services but our sense of loyalty demands that we should commemorate these services by a fitting memorial and I hope rich and poor alike will rise to the occasion and supply funds for a suitable memorial for the relief of the sick and the suffering, in which he was deeply concerned, and which was nearest to his heart. I may add that His Majesty King Edward VIII has been graciously pleased to accord permission for the memorial.

I am glad to say that we shall begin the great work to which we are about to put our hands today under the most favourable auspices, as you will all agree when I tell you that the Governor of Bombay and Lady Brabourne have consented to be the President and Vice-President respectively of the Committee of the citizens of Bombay. We all know how keenly and incessantly both His Excellency and Lady Brabourne strove only last year in connection with the Jubilee Fund. We also know how keen and

1097

constant has been their lively desire to ameliorate the lot of the poor and the sick.

Source: Naoroji M. Dumasia, *The Aga Khan and His Ancestors*, The Times of India Press, Bombay, 1939, pp. 292–4.
These views were expressed by the Aga Khan in his presidential speech delivered at a public meeting convened by the Sheriff of Bombay, C. B. Mehta, on 11 February 1936 at the Bombay Town Hall to pay tributes to the dead King-Emperor. The Aga Khan was chosen to preside over the function on the motion of Sir Jamsetjee Jeejeebhoy, seconded by Sir Currimbhoy Ibrahim.

159

THE FUTURE OF THE ALIGARH UNIVERSITY

Reply to the Address of Welcome Presented by the Members of the Court of the University

Aligarh: 15 February 1936

Origins of the idea of a Muslim university – the office of Pro-Chancellor – failure to collect enough funds – the road ahead for the university – technology and agriculture – importance of the university for the whole of India.

It is not without emotion that I came here to-day after so many years. It is now thirty-three years ago that the idea of a University was definitely placed at Delhi before the Muslim public of India in 1903. I experience, for the first time to-day, the honour of coming here, not as a visitor or as one of the honorary associates, but as the Pro-Chancellor of this University. It had not been my wish to occupy this office, however, not because I was in anyway lukewarm or desirous of resting after labours of the past, but simply because I believe that these honours should go to some young ruling Princes who will take greater interest and feel more responsibilities in our central institution. No one would have welcomed it more if His Highness of Rampur, Janjira, Jaora, Junagadh, Bahawalpur, etc., had held this office and I earnestly hope that it will be soon that one of these young princes will take it up.

Since we were in the midst of very trying times, it was perhaps felt that those who had already experience of the past must be called upon to share further responsibilities for the time being. It was in this spirit that I accepted the office for a short time.

The troubles of the University are entirely due to our failure in our original schemes with which we started. It has been said and rightly said that the failure of Germany in the Great War was due to the refusal of the German Government to the demand of the Chairman. When the German Chairman asked for three more Army Corps and when they were refused by the German Government, the fate of Germany was sealed. I myself as an amateur student of history have put down the whole failure of Germany to this act of parsimony on the part of a nation faced with war. Our troubles here can similarly be put down to our failure to collect one crore. Had we started with one crore instead of thirty lakhs you would have spared an old man like myself and we should have enjoyed the pleasure of seeing young men taking work with higher motive. But unfortunately we have not been able to make up the original handicap ever since the inception of this University. We started under the fallacy that let us start with what we have, and we will get the rest later on. To make matters worse we lost that early enthusiasm. But in this matter I must be taken to task more than any one in the world for accepting and going forward with the idea of a University with the small amount of thirty lakhs, but no one could foresee such a calamity as the Great War. The financial misery that was brought about by the results of the war fell not only on the Muslims but on the whole world. Indirectly we are paying for that by the failure of the business of the merchant princes. Towns like Bombay, Karachi, etc., were very much touched by the financial crisis. These difficulties could not have been foreseen in 1910 and 1911.

But to-day the problem before us is that either we must get this additional thirty or forty lakhs to make the crore complete or we must reduce our ambition that the University should be a centre of light and leading in India. But I am certain that no Muslim will accept the latter alternative. This latter alternative is one that we have not even right to consider. Under the high patronage of His Exalted Highness, our Chancellor, and with the guidance of our late Chancellor, His Highness of Bhopal, and with the help and assistance of ruling Princes, nobles, gentry, merchants, princes and other classes of India, we should complete the work we began with the visit of His late Imperial Majesty the King-Emperor George V in 1911, with the coming visit of His Imperial Majesty the King Emperor Edward VIII, his son and successor. There are immense possibilities before us. There is the work of Technology, and improvement in special branches. There must also come in existence the Department of Agriculture, as many of our boys come from the land owning classes. In this agricultural country, the future welfare of the people is necessarily bound up with the land. For these reasons these branches must be strengthened and brought up to full strength, just as it is necessary in the outside world to work up the full resources in the field of economic regeneration. There the study of these resources must become an integral part of the education in future, but here in this country agricultural study must become a necessary part of education. I will not lay much stress on Islamic studies and culture, because I feel that they must be the very air we breathe from the atmosphere of the University, and it will influence alike those who come in for arts as well as those who come for technology, the study of which must in future be the main object of our education.

It was interesting to hear our Vice-Chancellor referring to the memorable words in which the objects and ideals of this University were put forward some sixty years ago. The net result of the seeds which were sown at that time is to be seen in the full tree that now stands out in this world for future generations. These are the problems that can be best thought of in one great centre where the seeds of the future grow, and where people co-operate and understand each other.

One of the difficulties with which you will be faced will be the growing idea that Islam in India will need provincial organisation rather than centralisation. With the development of education, the idea centered at one place fifty years ago is now spread to the Punjab, Bombay, Madras and Bengal. But, gentlemen, the two ideas are complementary and not contradictory. This University must be cherished by the whole of India as their common trust, their jewel and their child. From Madras to Peshawar we must remember that this University occupies the same position in matters of culture and educational ideals as Delhi does in matters of politics. We have in our University at Aligarh the centre from which radiate throughout India Islamic ideals and principles which had been dormant for long in the middle ages of India. It is now a period of renaissance and awakening. What the thirteenth century of the Christian era was to Europe the thirteenth century of Hijra has been for Islam. Gentlemen, we are now backward by five hundred years, and with one giant stride we should come forward to overcome this deficiency. It is this giant stride that this University needs. Let us now all rise to the occasion and make up the deficiency of five hundred years. This is not an impossible task; Japan and Russia have already done it. As to the methods, let us fully realise that it is never haste, never waste. Hurried movements which lead to immediate failure must at all events, be avoided. We must not take one step further till we have fully realised that we are in a position to achieve success within a short time. We should start the work with thoroughness and with the ideals of 1910 and 1911. I hope and believe that within the next few hours we shall be able to find ways and means by which great efforts may be made for the collection of necessary funds.

Source: Naoroji M. Dumasia, *The Aga Khan and His Ancestors*, The Times of India Press, Bombay, 1939, pp. 192–7.

The Aga Khan arrived in Aligarh by train on the same morning and was received at the railway station by Nawab Bahadur Sir Muzammillullah Khan (Rector of the Aligarh University), Nawab Ahmad Said Khan of Chchattari, Sir Muhammad Yamin Khan, Sir Muhammad Yakub, Professor Halim (Pro-Vice-Chancellor of Aligarh University), S.N.A. Jafri, Mawlawi Obaid-ur-Rahman Khan (Treasurer to the University) and other members of the University Court.   In the university ceremony, Dr. Ziauddin Ahmad welcomed the distinguished visitor by paying a glowing tribute to his unique services to the Muslims of India, particularly to the cause of the Muslim university which owed its very existence to his pioneer efforts and munificence. He drew the Aga Khan's attention to the financial position and requirements of the university. The above account of the visit is based on a report published by the *Star of India*, Calcutta, on 18 February 1936.

The address of welcome, written in Persian, was read out by Nawab Sir Ahmad Said Khan of Chchattari. Extracts from it printed by Dumasia in English translation are given below:

"So long as this University continues to function, Your Highness' name will be remembered with reverence and affection by the Mussalmans of India. We earnestly hope that under the fostering care and guidance of Your Highness this institution will soon develop into a Cordova [*sic*] of the East.

"The ideals of this institution were defined in the address presented to Lord Lytton at the time he laid the foundation stone in the following words:–

" 'To educate our countrymen to appreciate the blessings of British rule; to dispel those illusory traditions of the past which have hindered our progress; to remove those prejudices which have hitherto exercised a baneful influence on our race; to reconcile oriental learning with Western literature and science; to inspire in the dreamy minds of the people of the East the practical energy which belongs to those of the West; to make the Muslims of India worthy and useful subjects of the British Crown; to inspire in them that loyalty which springs not from servile submission to a foreign rule but from genuine appreciation of the blessings of good government,' and these are the ideals to which we have always adhered.

"We have, from the very beginning, made residential life a primary feature of our institution, and developed it so far as circumstances have permitted on lines similar to Cambridge and Oxford; we have always insisted on the development of sound judgment, good manners, common sense and self-sacrifice as essential elements of a well-balanced education. The students are taught under the supervision of their teachers, to look after their own affairs and to develop the *spirit de corps* for which Aligarh has been noted. While making religious instruction an essential part in the training of our Muslim students, we have never been inspired by any narrow communalism. We have always received ample help and assistance from our non-Muslim friends and our doors have always been open to persons of all religions, classes and creeds.

"The University, which we owe very much to Your Highness' efforts, has been functioning now for over sixteen years and it would be in the fitness of things if we submit for Your Highness' consideration some of the problems which confront us to-day. The financial position of the University has been a matter of anxiety to us all these years. Our institution, like many others, has gone through a period of acute financial stringency. In spite of economies effected by the recommendations of the Retrenchment Committee of 1933 including cut in salaries and in spite of keeping the appointment of professors in abeyance in several departments, the budget of 1935–36 left us with a deficit of Rs. 32,381. This we have for the present met by a drastic reduction of overhead expenditure; the Vice-Chancellor, the Pro-Vice-Chancellor and the Treasurer are all honorary officers, without any honorarium, and the Registrar is only getting an officiating allowance. The graded cut in the salary of the staff effecting a saving of about Rs. 40,000 per annum was imposed for a fixed period, which comes to an end on March 31, 1936, and, in accordance with the resolutions of the Court and the Executive Committee, the cut will be restored in the next budget. We hope that the Government of India will come to our rescue by restoring the cut of 10 per cent. amounting to Rs. 30,000 in their grant.

"During the last twenty years, the social and economic condition of the country has greatly changed; unemployment has grown owing to the increase in the number of graduates, and it is desired, on all hands, that our University should do its duty to the community, by giving to its students that training in technical subjects which may enable them to contribute their share to the industrial renaissance of the country. We urgently need a fully equipped Polytechnic providing instruction in various branches of engineering and industrial chemistry up to the degree stage. Next comes the necessity of providing proper training in Agriculture and Commerce. According to the estimates we have prepared, a sum of twenty-two lakhs of rupees will be required for the Colleges of Technology, Commerce and Agriculture. Besides this we require about ten lakhs of rupees for the construction of the Senate Hall, Library, University Offices, and a recurring expenditure of Rs. 75,000 per annum for the consolidation and improvement of the present Departments.

"The Prince of Wales College of Science, the foundation stone of which was laid by our late lamented King-Emperor, has grown into a first rate and well-equipped institution. Its natural development points to the establishment of an equally well-equipped College of Technology and Applied Sciences, and it is our fervent hope and ambition that under Your Highness' guidance our community shall have the privilege of petitioning to His Imperial Majesty the King-Emperor that he may be pleased to lay the foundation of our proposed new Polytechnic when His Imperial Majesty visits this country.

"The self-sacrifice and enthusiasm with which the community responded to Your Highness' appeal for converting the M.A.O. College into a Muslim University will be always remembered by those who had the privilege of working under Your Highness' command. And it is the duty of us all to see that the hopes held out to our community are fulfilled and that Aligarh by developing Departments of Islamic Studies, side by side with technical, professional and cultural departments, justifies its existence by becoming a centre of Muslim philosophy, culture and religion. In addressing the Pro-Chancellor of our own University it

1103

is not necessary to be formal. Your Highness led the movement for the Muslim University, and you alone can complete the task you have begun."

160

RESPONSIBILITIES OF MUSLIM LEADERSHIP IN INDIA

Speech at a Meeting

New Delhi: 17 February 1936

Muslim political attitudes since the Mutiny – Muslim agreement with Hindus in 1916 – Muslims are natives of India – Muslims and Indian self-government – Hindu attitude – Muslim adherence to the goal of self-government – Muslim representation – political goal of dominion status – economic and other depression in India – immediate relief called for – Islam and tolerance – uplift at home – an honourable position abroad.

The first half of the nineteenth century saw the sovereignty of India pass out of Muslim hands into British hands. The responsibility for the events in 1857 was laid at the door of Muslims and this made the thoughtful section among them think of their future position in India.

It took Indian Muslims a quarter of a century to make up their minds and the result was the great Sir Syed Ahmad Khan of Aligarh's policy concentrating on education and avoiding political agitation of an acute kind. A few Muslims joined the Indian National Congress, but the community as a whole stood apart.

As a reaction to twenty years' inactivity the All-India Muslim League came into being in 1906 and co-operation between the Congress and the League culminated in their agreement in 1916, which was to form the basis of the Montford reforms.

Thus in the first decade of the 20th century Muslim India reconsidered its policy and in the second decade formulated a new one. Had it not been for the world war things may have been different, but the problem of political advance was pressing and

Indian Muslims decided that, despite being a minority in India, they would not stand in the way of their motherland placing before itself the goal of self-government.

The Indian Muslims realised that most of them were of the same blood as their Hindu brethren, and that many of them were of mixed blood, and those who had come to India with the Muslim invaders had settled down in India for many centuries and had made India their home and had no home outside India and that they were natives just as their Hindu brethren were natives of India.

The mere fact that they professed a religion which was professed by inhabitants of other countries also made no difference.

Just as an Afghan would not like Arabian domination and the Arabs did not like Turkish domination, there is no occasion for anyone to doubt the genuine feeling of Indian Muslims for Indian nationalism.

Our cultural and spiritual links with Muslims of other countries do not and cannot prevent us from following a considerably pure national programme for self-government. Having made their choice, they were ready for political advance, and in 1916 an agreement between the League and the Congress was the result.

The Hindu leaders assured the Muslim leaders their religious and cultural integrity, and readily agreed to separate electorates and assured the Muslim leaders of adequate representation in future as the Muslim community took to politics. Unfortunately that co-operation did not last long.

What would the Muslims do in the matter of further reforms? Muslim leaders gave this matter their most careful consideration and came to the conclusion that they were in a minority, and that a weak minority. Though the attitude of their powerful sister community had been cold and distant, their patriotism and their sense of self-respect and honour did not permit their going back on their ideal of self-government for their country.

They decided to ask for the maximum reforms, and to this object they adhered all along. They knew that provincial autonomy in the Central Provinces, United Provinces, Bihar, Orissa, Madras, Bombay and Assam would spell ruin for them if worked in a communal spirit, but they hoped better sense would prevail and all communities would work for the betterment of their motherland, instead of against each other, and in return they only wanted to have the satisfaction of being a majority community in the Frontier Province, the Punjab, Sind and

Bengal, knowing full well that their majority in the Punjab and Bengal was only nominal, while the Frontier Province, on account of its geographical position and economic condition, was not likely to have much of real provincial autonomy.

Thus the Muslims were not improving their communal position in any way, but still they were for political advance. Why? For them this political advance was solely from a national motive.

Their objective, therefore, in the matter of representation was to secure such a position as would enable them to have a majority in the legislature of four provinces. They succeeded in the case of three provinces, but failed in the case of Bengal.

In the case of the Central Legislature they retained their proportion to a certain extent, but with the extinction of the official block from the communal point of view they were not going to be as strong in the future as in the past. But here again their motives for political advance were national, not communal. They failed to secure a clear enunciation of their undoubted right to adequate representation in the services in the provinces, but have been feeling that their case is so strong that no Government claiming to be civilised would be in a position to refuse their just demand. They are not elated by the success achieved, nor are they too depressed by the failures suffered. Success and failure in life and particularly in political life were inevitable and regardless of them we should go on.

India is now entering a new phase of political life. Indian Muslims are ready to take their due share in developing political life in the best interests of the country. Their political goal is dominion status. They feel that India's most pressing needs are of externally securing recognition in other countries.

Indians are not fairly treated whether in the dominions or colonies. At home the Indians must have economic reorganisation – there is a wide gulf between the different sections of Indians – extreme poverty, hunger and nakedness, emaciated and enfeebled bodies and ignorance, they are allowed to be considered as human beings by courtesy only [sic]. To add to this economically depressed status they are intellectually depressed.

With this denial of divinity in mankind, there is the denial of human brotherhood and we have developed intolerance in matters religious and sectarian. The whole economic, social and religious fabric calls for immediate relief – up-lift of the weak – economically, intellectually and culturally, so that there may be left no one to be called down-trodden.

Faith is a matter of individual convictions and should not be allowed to create ill-will between the various communities of India. Islam teaches tolerance and the smallest and the humblest should feel that in a self-governing India his faith in religion would be secure and also his culture.

I have so far referred to the past. What is the immediate future, which is to be the object of political changes that are coming? What are we to strive for and pledge as a programme to our countrymen? What is the real work to be accomplished? The future programme is for "uplift," personal, spiritual, moral, intellectual and economical [sic], not only personal, not only of families, but also of the poor masses, needy and backward.

It is this noble work of uplift with which we should concern ourselves, irrespective of the considerations of caste, colour and creed. Thus the prescription which the thoughtful Indians should prescribe for the betterment of India is 'uplift' at home, securing for her people an honourable position abroad.

Source: *Star of India*, Calcutta, 18 February 1936. The speech was also reported in *The Times of India*, Bombay, of 17 and 18 February, 1936.

This meeting of a large number of Muslim leaders was held under the presidentship of the Aga Khan to define the attitude which Indian Muslims should adopt regarding the future political situation in the country.

Among those present were: Mian Sir Fazl-i-Husain, Nawab Sir Ahmad Said Khan of Chhattari, Sir A. H. Ghuznavi, Sir Firoz Khan Noon, Nawab Sir Mehr Shah, Sir Ghulam Husain Hidayatullah, Sir Muhammad Yakub, Dr Sir Shafa'at Ahmad Khan, Abdul Qadir Badayuni, Haji Rahim Bakhsh, S. M. Habib, Mushir Husain Kidwai, Mawlana Muhammad Shafee Daoodi, Abdul Hafeez, Mahmud Suhrawardy, Sher Muhammad Khan, Muhammad Noman, Sir Muhammad Yamin Khan, Nawab Jamshed Ali, Padshah Sahib, Haji Seth Abdullah Haroon, Nawab Muhammad Hayat Khan, Raja of Salimpur, Dr Ziauddin Ahmad, Allah Bakhsh Tiwana, Asghar Ali, Raja Ghazanfar Ali Khan, Mir Maqbul Mahmud, Haji Rashid Ahmad, S. M. Abdullah, Mawlana Shaukat Ali, Abdul Matin Chaudhri, Haji Sattar Seth, Badrul Hasan, Khurshid Ali and Mazheruddin.

After the Aga Khan had read out his written speech, the meeting was converted into a session of the Executive Board of the All India Muslim Conference, and a number of resolutions were discussed and adopted.

The Times of India of 18 February 1936 reported:

"Sir Shafa'at Ahmed Khan moved a resolution that 'this meeting of the Executive Board of the All-India Muslim Conference places on record its grateful thanks to the Aga Khan for the constructive lead he has given to the community at this juncture in his statement made at this meeting, and adopts the policy enunciated therein as an integral part of its programme. The meeting appeals to Indian Muslims of all schools of thought to give effect to it.' ...

"The resolution was passed after a large number of speeches had been made, paying tributes to the services of the Aga Khan. The question of amalgamating the Muslim League and the Muslim Conference was not put forward in view of the Aga Khan's opinion that it might be left over for Muslims elected to the new provincial legislatures to decide.

"Sir Shafa'at Ahmed Khan moving his resolution, said 'but for the Aga Khan's personality, the Muslim community would not have achieved what it did and would have been exposed to danger.' (Applause). He assured all Nationalists that his friends would ally themselves with them for the development of the country and home rule.

"The Aga Khan was the leader of the delegation to the Round Table Conference and the fact that the Muslims worked in accord with the rest of the delegates was borne out by the Hindu Mahasabha delegate to the Conference.

"Mr. Syed Mahammed Padshah supported the resolution and paid tribute to the Aga Khan's services.

"Raja Ghazanfar Ali said the success achieved by the Indian delegation in London was entirely due to the Aga Khan's personal influence. He felt, however, that it was difficult to maintain two parallel Muslim organisations. The Aga Khan and Sir Fazl-i-Husain were both present, as well as Mr. M. A. Jinnah, whose services to the community were unparalleled and unique. (Cheers). Let the three meet and bring about a merger.

"The Aga Khan, replying, said both he and Sir Fazl-i-Husain had carefully considered the matter and felt, as the Democrats, that the question should not be decided just now. When the Muslim Conference was organized in 1929 the main idea was that it should be a conference of elected Muslim legislators. Shortly, provincial councils would be elected by a very wide franchise. Let those Muslim legislators who will be elected under provincial autonomy decide the question.

"Had those elections not been imminent he and Sir Fazl-i-Husain would have faced the responsibility of deciding the question. He reminded them that non-Muslims also had more than one body . . .

"Sir Muhammad Yakub deprecated any speech would give the impression outside that the Conference and the League were hostile organisations, when, in fact, they had the same objective.

"The resolution was declared carried unanimously.

"Sir A. H. Ghaznavi mentioned what the Aga Khan had done for Bengal Muslims and how a Hindu-Muslim settlement in Bengal had been almost reached through the good offices of the Aga Khan. It was a lie to say that the Aga Khan was a communalist . . ."

161

THE BROTHERHOOD OF ISLAM

Speech at a Dinner

New Delhi: 17 February 1936

Islamic brotherhood and social equality – tribute to Sir Muhammad Zafrullah Khan – spirit of cheer for Muslims.

The Aga Khan, responding, thanked the hosts and Sir. M. Zafrullah for his kind remarks. They were united by Islamic brotherhood to whose social equality, kindliness and forbearance even critics like Mr. H. G. Wells had paid tributes. "Indeed, without Islamic culture, the world would have been the poorer (cheers). The fact that King and Darwesh (beggar) were both called Shah showed the true brotherhood of Islam." Through many years of Islamic public life, His Highness had found the spirit of brotherhood still alive.

"Believe me, when in London we stood united, it was not mere selfish interest of the political situation, but that finer spirit of Brotherhood that prevented us from allowing any differences to come in our way (cheers), and you, Sir Muhammad, were so worthy an example of that spirit. For the first two years, you were almost a silent member of the Delegation. Even your guest to-night did not realise that amidst rocks diamonds are found of the purest water of brilliance. Circumstances forced you to take the lead, and your spokesmanship won the admiration of every one, not only of your countrymen, but also of British statesmen. I have known statesmen in Europe and can honestly say that among any gathering of statesmen, you would have taken the very front rank and position. (Cheers). There are few instances of men in this land, where youth is so handicapped, having risen at the age of 44 to the highest position open to your countrymen and every one of us feels that in the Federal Government, you will be a light to follow and that you may be the Prime Minister some day. (Cheers).

As for me, I have no other ambition except to be of service to you all. (Applause). We have no use for defeat. No battle is ever lost unless those who fight think it is lost. Let there be the spirit of cheer, so that Muslims may carry the light of brotherhood and service to their countrymen and to mankind generally."

Recalling the difficulties of thirty years ago, when things were almost impossible and even the idea of University was pooh-poohed, because Lord Curzon was opposed to it, the Aga Khan said that now things were easier and in this new battle of youth, he expected Sir Muhammad to be the General of India. (Applause).

Concluding, the Aga Khan said that the dinner had been like the mess of a regiment and he had enjoyed the intimate talk with friends.

Source: *Star of India*, Calcutta, 22 February 1936. Also *The Times of India*, Bombay, 19 February, 1936.

In proposing the toast of the Aga Khan, Sir Muhammad Zafrullah Khan recalled how twenty-five years ago, as a student of the Government College, Lahore, he had joined the other students in pulling the carriage of the Aga Khan. "At present", he continued, "it would be hard to discover anybody who occupies the position you occupy. Prince in Islam, both on the secular and religious sides, Prince among men, associate of Princes in Europe and Asia, Ambassador of East and West – you occupy a unique position and have worthily discharged your responsibility. As inhabitants of this great country, we are proud of you. In the modern world there is no place that you would not worthily adorn, and there is no position by occupying which you would not so honour it that it would be the pride of others to occupy it."

The dinner in honour of the Aga Khan was given by Muslim members of the Central Legislature.

162

THE EDUCATIONAL NEEDS OF MUSLIM INDIA

Presidential Address to the All India Muhammadan Educational Conference

Rampur: 21 February 1936

Primary education the foremost requirement – Sir Tej Bahadur Sapru's report on education – contemporary Muslim conditions – need for theoretical and practical commercial education – agricultural education – standards of Muslim schools – co-ordination – careers guidance – Aligarh University and the College of Technology – the likely impact – religious education – Muslims and scientific education – the task of re-interpreting Islam – primary education and the State.

Primary education which was indeed the first charge on a modern State and which I had humbly advocated in the old Viceroy's Council and for which, in my humble opinion, I had not only made an advocacy but found ways and means whereby primary and compulsory education for boys and girls could improve, is the foremost requirement of the Muslim community, leave alone the whole country and the rural population. This work is one which affects us as Indians and which is on the border line between politics and socio-educational reforms. It is right and proper to admit that in lines known as the Arts section of education, in Government service, in Law, in Medicine, there has been great progress in the last 34 years. Recently, as you are aware, the Rt. Hon'ble Sir Tej Bahadur Sapru has written a masterly report on the needs of developing our educational methods. He advocates education which can make us fit for different avenues of functional service, namely Government service, legal service and Medicine. These principles can be kept up. But, surely, there are other essential services for upkeep of the wealth, life, and, in fact, the spirit of the people requiring work that will have to be done in normal life of every nation, backward or forward.

We cannot help feeling that India is backward and that the Muslims have remained far behind in the real, economic, work of life. We are carrying it on a standard which must be called mediaeval. The number of our commercial classes is limited, specially amongst Muslims. Even the classes who carry on trade on the sea-coast, do it with the principle, learnt hereditarily which prevailed when the Arabs were the great commercial nation of the world. On the old coasts of India, here and there, we find sections of our Muslim community carrying trade on principles learnt in the cradle. And in provinces far from the sea, we are almost commercially nil. The English are a self-sacrificing people and naturally they are most advanced in commerce. Our sea-coast sections of Islamic Society are almost truly the most advanced in India. But in countries surrounded by land, such as Bavaria, Czekoslovakia [sic], people are much advanced in commerce. Similarly the peoples of Germany and France. The whole of the western continent of North America and great tracts of South America are commercially advanced. We have remained in the position which Geography has given us. Here on this line pure and practical commercial education must come, and then India will become a great commercial country. This has nothing to do with what I call the methods of applied science. It is the science of Exchange and Business organization that we should learn. This science of Exchange and Business organization must be taken up seriously by the people of the land coasts of Islamic India. For this we should have special commercial schools and classes, to which our children must be sent. People in the heart of the continent of Europe have risen on this account. Commercial education opens out ways of livelihood. Service must be given to people educated in this line as is done in Europe. Our Hindu brethren even in this have vast advantages. They have knowledge and experience in banking. There are reasons in which we need not enter, nor we need refer to, for their rise in this line. Their indigenous system is however not socially good. The less we have of it the better for the nation. The exchange side must be systematically taught.

Now, let us turn to agriculture. Here again the present state of affairs is disappointing. The present divorce between practical agriculture and theoretical education on one hand and between

1113

scientific agriculture and primitive cultivation on the other is worthy of our serious attention. An immense bridge must be found to cross this wide gulf. Here again, gentlemen, there is work to be done. Forgive me for suggesting that every landlord should be a graduate of the Imperial College of Agriculture of Delhi. What I do want to see is that the Muslim tenant and the Muslim landlord should be graduates of the Imperial College of Agriculture, or at least they should be able to understand what the graduate of agriculture says. It is a pity that the question of a technical authority does not get an answer from agriculturists.

There are again other vocations where applied sciences are of essential importance. These are Engineering, Electricity, Mechanics. They supply us with the lines along which we can advance.

We turn now from agriculture to the improvement of the position of the urban population of the present and of the future. In Aligarh we have a centre from which not only education but enlightenment, in the most generous sense of the term, can be brought to the Muslim community throughout this country. This work of enlightenment should not be misunderstood. Gentlemen, what I mean is this, that this Muslim Educational Conference, which is hand in hand now with the University, can, with the help of the University, give new and fresh ideas to all sections of Muslim education. There are Islamia schools, colleges, etc, throughout India. In some places these institutions are actually behind the similar ones maintained either by Government or by other voluntary bodies such as Missions, etc. Through co-ordination of efforts, members of this Muslim Educational Conference throughout India should bring about a unity of ideal and work amongst Islamia schools, colleges and Madrasahs which are found from one end of India to the other, that the standard should be raised to one of equality with that of the best institutions of this country. This is indeed a matter which will require immediate handling, and unless this is done our boys and girls will more and more be out of the Islamia colleges as they will find that their standard is lower than that which can be found in their rival institutions. This business of co-ordination of effort and ideal is most important, and this Muslim Conference should take it up immediately in hand.

Now, as you know, in Europe there has been a great tendency, during the last 20 or 30 years, to try and find out, as early as possible, the natural inclinations of boys and growing up students for various walks of life. There are actually what are known as career masters. There are processes to keep in touch, on one side, with the student, on the other, with his teacher, and last, but by no means the least, with the parent. Those who are naturally inclined to some particular work or who are of practical type of mentality, should be brought in touch, as early as possible, with such intellectuals as will develop their particular qualities. Here, again, we have so far left everything haphazard. There has been, along these lines, no thought out plan of action. This, to my mind, is one that can no longer be left hanging to mere accident. The Muslim Educational Conference is essentially a body from which this kind of work can be best thought out, planned, and, with the help of the Aligarh University, brought into full activity.

The idea of the Muslim University was already prevalent in Sir Syed Ahmad's time. Then it was suggested, as a memorial to his life's work after his death, by the various Presidents of this Conference at various times and ultimately realized, some 25 years ago. That great work is only half finished. The crore I asked for never came. The idea of the University was thought out in connection with the visit of our Sovereign to this country. I think it is appropriate that now, 25 or 26 years later, under similar circumstances, we should carry that work through.

What we want is that side by side with the present Muslim University with the present College of Science, and other institutions as they are, a great institution like the College of Technology should be established where engineering, electricity and all the sciences applied to life and actual work, can be taught. To this those who wish to get in, either by natural inclination, or through the advice of their career-masters we have been thinking of, or by the recommendation from the schools, may be admitted. This work, gentlemen, we should not leave, any more, in the stage of discussion and thought and idea. As soon as possible, under the patronage of His Exhalted [sic] Highness the Nizam, the Chancellor of the University, with the guidance and experience of our Life-Chancellor, His Highness the Nawab of Bhopal, with the full support and help and encouragement from our great ruling princes of Muslim India, and from a few in the urban population, as well as with mass contribution carried out systematically, and last, but by no means the least, with the help and gracious support of the Central and Provincial Governments, we should now set to work to finish the incomplete process started 25 years ago.

This school will need just the amount to complete the gulf of 40 lakhs. The money is overdue, and should be collected very soon; otherwise these 40 lakhs might in another 25 years grow to a crore. This work, gentlemen, is the immediate task before the Conference and the authorities of the University as well as the public of this country. Ultimately this money will come back to India hundred-fold. The work found will pay for it. The work will influence the idea and the imagination of Muslim parents throughout the length and breadth of India and will help the advancement of thought on modern methods of earning bread. I should like to see a resolution moved by some great person to carry this scheme through as the immediate work before the Muslim University and the Muslim Educational Conference. As early as in 1902 the idea of realizing the need of a Muslim University was the main object of our meeting at Delhi. Thirty-five years later I should like to see that work carried to completion.

Now there are two more items to which I wish to refer. First of all I come to a subject which may not appear, after the many words with which I have dealt with your wordly methods of living, out of time. This is the question of Religious Education. It would have been indeed easy for me to avoid touching this subject, placing it as one that was not of immediate practical importance, but I honestly believe that we are going on – as we have done so far – in a direction where we may find some day – and not very long ahead – a situation arisen, as has arisen in other Muslim countries . . .

Is religion different from Science or Philosophy? Is the former so interpreted and understood? No, there is possibility of bringing about the greatest intellectual reconciliation not only with modern philosophy and science but even with other subjects. Gentlemen, only a few months ago, or a couple of years ago, a well-known English paper, "Spectator," asked some leading persons to give a short and brief expression of their idea of Religion. My friend here, Mr. Abdulla Yusuf Ali, F.R.S.L., gave a short "tafsir" of the "Aetal-Kursi". I was then at Geneva, but Mr. Yusuf's "tafsir" was so beautiful, rational and soul-inspiring that for weeks all kinds of people, even some of the most distinguished figures of Europe, came up to me and said "Is it real Islam?" Once upon a time I said somewhere that other religions have taken in formalities, but Muslims have outformalized the formal. Both Christians and Hindus have made progress in Scientific education but Muslims have lagged far behind. What has happened in a country that is looked upon as the capital of Islam has inevitably happened in every Muslim country. This does not mean that the faith of Islam is not true. Nay Islam is the most rational, most social, of all faiths.

It only means that our substitution and interpretation of Islam totally fails us. To this work gentlemen, however unpleasant and offensive it may be to the conservatives, thought is necessary if we are to keep alive the name of Muslim University and Muslim Educational Conference. I should have been guilty of neglecting my duty to the faith of Islam in the truth of which I have implicit and firm faith, if I had preferred to avoid a plain and clear reference to this subject. Howsoever unpleasant it may be, this task of reinterpreting Islam will have to be done. The work which Christianity has done, we must do for Islam. In fact without serious effort on these lines, we should not be able to hold up our own in face of the stress and strife of modern life.

A faith that can be believed in sincerely by philosophers, of whom any country can be proud, can never be in contradiction with the best thought of the present. As I have once said before, whatever its objective truth, it will not maintain subjective truth if it is interpreted in this old way.

Gentlemen, there is the vast problem of primary education and education of girls. This work should be taken up by the Muslim Educational Conference through its influence at Aligarh, but how is it to be done? The present method of voluntary education is absolutely adequate, but when we think of the New Constitution of this country, none will look at this with satisfaction. But it can continue, and, at least in the Provinces, there are possibilities to make education both for girls and boys compulsory. The need for girl's education is even greater because she has to be the mother of future generation [sic]. Loud speakers, Broadcasting, Films, can be brought only to the vast masses through the State. Primary education can only be imparted by the State. To the whole country, even financially, this will be a good business. The money will come to you. Expenditure on education will ultimately reduce the military and naval expenditure. Just fancy what India would be if primary education had been adopted in its full. It is very well known to-day that, in the richest countries like America, it is the State that has taken up either as State or as Municipal Board, primary education. In Europe, Germany, France and England it is the function of the State. There is a vast educational budget in all these countries. Every Government, even a Conservative Government, is anxious for the education of all classes of boys and girls. By compulsory

primary education our children will wind back their way to prosperity.

Gentlemen, as I have explained this morning, I have not had
time of [*sic*] preparing myself for this address, and I am guilty
for not having done so. As a human being I was not able to do
so. I have given you a rough sketch of what our community wants.
I may add, that, even from the widest point of view, from the
point of view of 350 millions, the going down of 80 million
Musalmans of the Indian society, generation by generation,
decade by decade, and year by year, will be a great handicap for
the whole of India.

Source: *Star of India*, Calcutta, 14 March 1936.

It has not been possible to determine the exact date of this session of
the All India Muslim Educational Conference. As the newspaper published the
speech on 14 March, and the dateline carried the words "by mail," the most
that can be safely said is that the session would have been held in the first week
of March.

The Conference, earlier known as the Congress, was established by Sir Sayyid
Ahmad Khan, and it had its first session in Aligarh in 1886 under the presidentship of Mawlawi Haji Muhammad Salimullah Khan of Delhi. The Aga Khan
had already presided over the conference once before in 1902 at the Delhi
session (see Document 2 in this book).

163

COMMUNAL UNITY AND REFORMS IN INDIA

A Message

Bombay: 9 March 1936

Reforms – Hindu-Muslim unity.

You must work for the reforms intensively in order to get the utmost out of them. While there were no immediate prospects of a solution of the communal problem, contact between the leaders of the two communities was unbroken, and he was not going to give up his efforts for the unity which would finally be achieved.

Source: *The Times*, London, 10 March 1936.
  The message was issued by him just before leaving Bombay for Europe.

164

MIGRATION AND PEACE

Letter to The Times

France: 3(?) May 1936

H. G. Wells's views on building a world authority – a liberal approach to immigration needed.

I have read the important letter of Mr. Wells in your issue of April 28, and I entirely agree with every word that he has written as to the need of building up a practical and possible liberal world authority. I fear, however, that Mr. Wells does not go far enough, and what he proposes – even if carried out – will be only a palliative and not a cure.

There are vast spaces in the world – in Australia, South America, Canada, parts of Africa, and in Asiatic and European Russia – that can absorb the growing populations of such countries as Germany, Japan, Italy, and India which are to-day hampered in comparatively small territories.

It is very necessary that free emigration should be allowed by some central authority, and possibilities given to emigrants so that they may keep their individuality in language, habits, religion, customs, &c., within definite areas in these vast and empty lands.

Such a solution, added to the proposals of Mr. Wells would save the world from many more disasters – each worse than the last – following that of 1914. This should be as practicable as any of the other suggestions made, and should crown the work of a real liberal world federal society in the lifetime of the present generation.

Source: *The Times*, London, 6 May 1936.
    The letter, written from Villa Jane-Andrée, Le Cap d'Antibes, A.M., France,

bears no date. I assume that it was written about three days prior to its publication.

H. G. Wells's letter, appearing in the issue of 28 April, was entitled "Keeping the Peace: A World Consortium", and read as follows:

"In the discussion of foreign affairs at the present time there seems to be a constantly recurring confusion between two quite opposed sets of principles, which it is worth while attempting to distinguish more clearly than is usually done. Fundamentally these sets are quite irreconcilable, they determine entirely different lines of political conduct, and our political ideas would be infinitely more effective if we kept their essential antagonism clear. At present nearly all of us seem to slip quite easily from one to the other, we mix them both in debate and practice, and our general public is incalculably fluctuating and indecisive on that account.

"One of these groups of principles might, I suppose, be best called universalist or liberal or left, and it rests primarily on the idea that humanity is to be regarded as one community. The opposite group, for which the words nationalist and patriotic seem most appropriate, is built on the tacit assumption that humanity is an assemblage of combatant communities. Logically these ideas are flatly incompatible, but human behaviour is rarely logical, and a vast proportion of the world's distresses and dangers at the present time are due to the general lack of lucidity in this respect.

"The one-community idea is the professed idea of Christianity, Islam, Buddhism, and all the world religions. It is implicit in the catholicity of science and art. It points to a world with a common commercial and economic system, free trade, free movement, and perpetual peace. It is a product of human reason and human aspirations. It runs counter to the normal instincts of mankind. These normal instincts certainly incline towards the combatant community – defensive and isolationist when it is frightened, and arrogant when it is not. The combatant community is a far more ancient conception of collective life. If liberalism is in our heads, nationalism is in our bones. Most of us, unless we take ourselves to task about it, are in a perpetual see-saw between these two groups of ideas. Most of us in our political lives are capable of the most glaring inconsistencies, because few of us have ever taken the trouble to decide to which side we give ourselves. We are sentimentally for world peace, but nationalism is in our tradition, our habits, and our blood, and when we are confronted with the most evident imperatives if world peace is to be attained, we recoil.

"An enormous majority of people in the present world would vote for perpetual peace and an absolute end of war for ever, if they were given the chance. But they would do little more than vote. If they were asked to accept the broad things that world peace certainly entails, that majority would collapse into confusion forthwith. They do not seem to have the faintest idea what world peace really implies. May I point out the most obvious aspects of a world peace, that seem to be disregarded at the present time?

"First, world peace, like social peace, is incompatible with monopolization. Within the limits of the contemporary state that is now recognized everywhere. We are all to that extent socialists. We may have the most varied ideas about the need and benefit of private enterprise, but we insist there must be enterprise and competition, we are all against the lock-up. But it is less generally recognized that this principle can be and should be applied to international affairs also. Nations have no more right to monopolize or under-develop than have individual owners. From the liberal free-trading point of view no community, no national or imperial system, has the right to lock up its territorial advantages and resources against mankind.

"In recent years existing Governments have shown a tendency to direct economic processes, a task for which their militarist traditions and Constitution unfit them. They have invaded the freedom of private enterprise by financial and economic controls from the militant national angle. The present intense tension in international affairs between the "haves" and "have nots" among nations is the political expression of this chronic militancy. The only substitute for these combative economic controls which lead inevitably to war and which are in themselves a sort of war is a world-wide control. This does not mean a world super-Government, which thing is only conceivable after a cycle of catastrophic wars, but it does mean a world consortium, a permanent federal board, with powers to direct production, distribute natural and manufactured products, watch the seasons and harvests and the fluctuations of demand, in the common interests of mankind. Such a consortium would necessarily control the broad movements of credit and sustain a world-wide monetary system.

"A federal board for the direction of world production and trade is a quite possible thing at the present time. It may be improbable but it is fully within the compass of human ability. It requires no supermen for its organization or staffing. It is only impracticable because people's minds are unprepared for it – that is to say, because their social mentality is still fundamentally warlike.

"But a world consortium for production and exchange is not the only *sine qua non* for world peace. Equally necessary is some international organization for the primary biological interests of mankind. Without a collective control of germs and birth-rates, all the balances of human life are bound in the end to be deranged to the fighting pitch. Neither world sanitation nor that maintenance of standards of physical well-being which would involve population control is beyond the practical capacity of men today. Finally in a world of continually more facile movement, a world control of main-line transport, posts, telegraphy and radio, and also a world Scotland Yard are becoming not merely possible but eminently desirable.

"Behind these possibilities looms the need for one general level of education throughout the world. The achievement of as much federation of existing Governments as this is surely the essential foreign policy of the modern liberal and it is irreconcilably opposed to the conception of the combatant sovereign state. The liberal conception of life involves the taming of the combatant state to the level of a constituent state in a union which has delegated the wider aspects of its sovereignty, its financial and economic and indeed its world relations generally, to a treaty-made world federal authority or system of authorities. Only in this fashion can we conceive a practicable non-catastrophic world *pax*. Opposed to this idea of federation through world-boards is militant political economic and social nationalism. There is no possible reconciliation between the synthesizing and the recalcitrant isolationist idea of policy. A clear-headed man who really faces the situation of affairs must be quite definitely black or white, on one side or the other. But events have caught us piebald in a phase of transition, saying both yea and nay to peace.

"Complications of this open contrast arise in practice from the fact that no one lives legally or mentally in a world community. That is the clue to our confusedness. Every one is under some national sovereignty and must work, politically at least, through the established forms of the combatant state. There are no cosmopolitan legal forms. But these complications are in themselves a reason why we should do our utmost to keep this primary opposition of liberal and nationalist before our minds. The former is modern, rational, adult, hopeful, intellectual, experimental, and unfortunately "sketchy"; the latter is traditional, puerile, richly emotional, instinctive, organic, and intimate. Which is it to be?

"The quintessence of a modern liberal policy seems to be a bold repudiation of that return towards economic nationalism of which the late Mr. Joseph Chamberlain made himself the prophet. But mere resistance to increased tariffs and armaments is no policy at all. It is ineffective peevishness. A positive liberalism will work incessantly for the development of super-national agreements and organizations making for economic unification and general world development, for persistent world education and universal intellectual freedom. It will consider the purely negative policy of "collective security" as a provisional and quite questionable set of expedients. Support of a League of Nations which seems to embody the suggestion that "Nothing more is going to happen" is a mockery of creative liberalism. Something has to be done about backward and barbaric regions and about monopolized natural resources, and that is a business which what I may perhaps call "League of Nations Liberalism" has tacitly obstructed for the last 18 years.

"I submit that the underlying spirit of the British peoples is and has been liberal in the sense given it here and that it is high time it found clearer expression and more explicit leadership."

165

THE FORTUNES OF THE LEAGUE OF NATIONS

Speech in the General Assembly of the League of Nations

Geneva: 29 September 1936

Changes in the League's fortunes – ideals which inspired the League – foolish to condemn these ideals – necessity of learning from the past – causes of the League's failures – necessity of change and realizing what is practical – concrete problems which require attention – economic nationalism and its barriers – accord between Britain, France and the USA.

It is now four years since I first attended an Assembly of the League of Nations. In four short years I have seen the League elated – over-elated – by success; I have seen it downcast – cast down almost into despair – by failure. Within one short year, I have seen it pass through the whole gamut of emotions.

The ideals that inspire the League were conceived at a time of moral elevation, when men and nations thought that their passions had been purged by war, and were resolved that the world should never again pass through that awful experience. Those ideals appealed to the whole of India, irrespective of class or creed; to India, that land of historic and persistent idealism which I have the honour to represent. To condemn the League after these sixteen years of its short life, to abandon its ideals now that we have learnt that men and nations are imperfect still, would be as foolish as to condemn all philosophies, all religions, and all the idealism of the past, because of the state of the world to-day.

It is not in moments of depression that wisdom comes into its own, or that a wise man repudiates his ideals – those great principles which are dearer than life itself – or seeks to recast the whole scheme of his life. Nor can this be the time for us to recast the whole scheme of the League, or to abandon its ideals just because we ourselves have fallen short of them. A wise man learns from the past: he does not let the past master him. Let us not shrink from recognising the realities in us and around us: let us adjust ourselves to the needs of the moment; but let us still set our ideals before us and grope our way through fair weather and foul towards them.

I have often thought that the causes of the League's failures and rebuffs are, in the main, two-fold; and both militate against that universality which inspired the conception of the League and on which its success ultimately depends. We have stressed far too much those elements in the Covenant which make for, or seemed to make for, the crystallisation of the world as it stood sixteen years ago. But change is the very essence of life. If the League is to be a living organism, it, too, must change, or, like all living organisms, perish. But the seeds of life are present in the Covenant itself. Let them at long last fructify.

And we have at times failed because we have all too often let the better be the enemy of the good. It is an amiable weakness that besets us the more readily, the more idealistic our outlook. But the realisation of ideals in this imperfect world can only come by way of a clear appreciation of what is practical. If we aim at too high a standard, we shall not make it easier for those who have left us to return, or for those who have stood out from the beginning to come in.

So I, for one, cannot believe that wisdom lies in attempting any heroic changes of our Constitution in this hour of depression. Our Constitution, after all, is elastic and can be adjusted to our changing needs. Our present task is rather to tackle the many concrete problems that cry out for solution. There are problems of regional pacts, of peace, and of disarmament, and to my mind no problem is more immediately pressing, or more hopeful of possible immediate success, than that of breaking through the chains of economic nationalism which are impeding the natural course of trade between nations, and are crippling their economic life. For years we addressed ourselves directly to the problem of disarmament, and failed. If the world is to be saved from disaster, it must be tackled anew. If the time is not ripe for us to tackle military disarmament directly, it is at least ripe for us to tackle it indirectly. Let us now set ourselves in earnest to those monetary and economic questions which form the background to much of the present world discontent. Let us promote the suggested enquiry into the accessibility of raw materials and see whether certain misgivings on this subject can be removed. And let us see whether we cannot break down the barriers of economic nationalism before they become veritable barrages of war.

In this connection, I most heartily welcome the accord between those three great Powers – the United Kingdom, France and America – that has just been concluded, and sincerely hope that it is the first step towards world economic and monetary settlement.

Source: *Verbatim Record of the Seventeenth Ordinary Session of the Assembly of the League of Nations: Tenth Plenary Meeting, Tuesday, September 29th, 1936, at 3.30 p.m.*, Geneva, 1936, p. 5.

The Aga Khan, the First Delegate of India, was the second speaker, after M. Undén of Sweden. The Assembly was discussing the Secretary General's report on the work of the League of Nations in 1935–36. The others who spoke on that day were Bruce of Australia, Jordan of New Zealand and Krofta of Czechoslovakia.

166

HAFIZ AND THE PLACE OF IRANIAN CULTURE IN THE WORLD

Inaugural Lecture Before the Iran Society

London: 9 November 1936

Definition of spiritual forces – modern Iran and the satisfaction of man's highest aspirations – impact of major faiths on Western Asia – flowering of poetry in Islamic Iran – the essence of all poetry – Hafiz and his significance – difficulties of translating him – his universal appeal – his message – Qa'ani of the nineteenth century – Iran's rich culture in the service of the culture of the West – economic development and spiritual awakening – relevance of Hafiz today – appeal to Western intellectuals to study the East – Asiatic culture and man's common heritage.

I must thank His Excellency the Iranian Minister, Lord Lamington and the members of the Society for having done me the honour of inviting me tonight to bring before you the importance to the whole world of those spiritual forces that the ancient land of Iran has cherished in her modern history. Before I go further I want to define clearly what I mean by "spiritual forces" – I do not use this term in any question-begging sense. I do not wish to limit it merely to religious or such ideas, or to give it any other-worldly interpretation, but I do mean anything that deals with man's life of the spirit here and now on this earth and in this life. Whatever may or may not be the soul's future, there is one impregnable central fact in existence: that here and now, in this world, we have a soul which has a life of its own in its appreciation of truth, beauty, harmony and good against evil. Has modern Iran greatly contributed to the perfectioning of the soul of man thus understood? Modern Iran I define as the ancient race of that high plateau, influenced by the faith of Islam and the imaginative poetry and declamation of Arabia, welded into one by a process of slow intermarriage and movement of many races from north, west, east and south. What has this Iran done for the satisfaction of man's highest aspirations?

Just as in ancient Egypt, so in ancient and pre-Islamic Persia, philosophical, spiritual, poetical thought and effort (or such parts as still remain) are singularly arid and (at least to us modern men) rather repetitions of vainglorious titles or somewhat unconvincing and worldly-wise prayers. It may be that man at that stage had all the great powers of execution and enterprise, the fruits of which we see in the vast monuments of ancient Egypt, and the remains of similar monuments in Western Asia and Iran. But till the impact with Judaism, Christianity and Islam, man in Western Asia had not yet learned the full value of the greatest treasure in his possession – his own entity and being.

Whatever the cause, after Islam had for three or four centuries taken deep root in Iran the genius of the race blossomed out, and for all the centuries right down to our own times that garden, in spite of the terrible visitations that so often submerged it, has never ceased to bring forth roses of rare fragrance.

Anwari, Nizami, Maulana Roumi, Saadi, Qa'ani and a host of others – names that will be well known to Oriental scholars, but which will perhaps convey little to the general public here – each in his own way gave a message to mankind. But the fundamental point of each message if carefully studied is that man's greatest of all treasures, the greatest of all his possessions, was the inherent, ineffaceable, everlasting nobility of his own soul. In it there was for ever a spark of true divinity which could conquer all the antagonistic and debasing elements in nature. And let me once more stress that this faith in the soul of man expressed in a great variety of ways – in prose and verse, in art and architecture – was not simply a religious or mystic faith but an all-embracing and immediate contact with a fact which, in every human being, is the central fact of existence.

Then came Hafiz – by far the greatest singer of the soul of man. In him we can find all the strivings, all the sorrow, all the victories and joys, all the hopes and disappointments of each and every one of us. In him we find contact, direct and immediate, with the outer universe interpreted as an infinite reality of matter, as a mirror of an eternal spirit, or indeed (as Spinoza later said) an absolute existence of which matter and spirit alike are but two of infinite modes and facets. It is not for nothing that his "Divan" has become, throughout the East, the supreme *fal nama* (book of divination) of millions and millions far beyond the confines of Iran. In perplexity and sorrow, whatever the cause, whatever the standard of intellect or emotion, men throughout the Near East and India turn to Hafiz – from the Ganges to the Nile, from the Caspian to the Bay of Bengal – for comfort and solace. Incredible as it may seem to us, even in his lifetime his influence had reached Bengal, Central Asia, Kashmir, Arabia and Egypt.

Any attempt at translation of Hafiz has always led to immense disappointment. The explanation is simple; he was not merely the Hafiz of the Koran, but well acquainted with the whole field of philosophy, history, poetry and literature, with the highest thought then known to his countrymen. In each verse, with the intense concentration of thought and wisdom so singularly his own, he has produced in amazing variety facets of truth and beauty, of meaning and wisdom. I have myself tried my hand at seeing in how many ways, and with how many totally different meanings, verses of his could be translated into either English or French. I think it is no figure of speech to say that far too many versions and explanations of each word could be given, and that each verse could be interpreted according to the intelligence that one wished to reach.

This, perhaps, will explain why Hafiz has always been (as no other great poet can claim to be) the national poet, the national hero, of Iran. Pushkin, Goethe and Shakespeare in the West; Al Mutannabi, Abu Nawas and Firdausi in the East – all of them great, indeed supreme, kings in the realm of poetry – could never reach their humblest subjects. The uncultured peasants of the West, or the equally humble intelligences of the East, could never absorb their full meaning or beauty. Hafiz is different. Not only in his own Persia but in India, in Afghanistan, in Central Asia and even amongst Turkish and Arabic-speaking peoples, the moment his verses are understood you will always find an interpretation of most of them that could appeal to the humblest as well as the highest of intelligences. No wonder the muleteers call him their friend and companion! No wonder the cobbler and the water-carrier find in him – as do the keenest intellects of Asia – solace and satisfaction!

One of the greatest living Hindu statesmen, Sir Tej Bahadur Sapru, once told me that in all difficult moments of his life he turns to Hafiz. I think there is no one of Iranian race alive today who has not at some time or other – in difficulty, sorrow and misery, or in joy and triumph – turned to his national hero for comfort or further elation. Incredible as it may sound to English ears, it is a fact that there is hardly a Muslim bourgeois family in the whole of India in whose home a copy of Hafiz's "Divan" is not found. I think, too, that we can be fairly certain that the book is as popular in Afghanistan and Central Asia and over a great part of what I may call Western Muslim countries as it is in India.

Soon after the death of Hafiz the worst periods of political and social anarchy, of invasion and disruption, broke up the high civilization already reached in Iran. Bismarck and other statesmen and historians have said that Germany as the battle-ground of Europe could never bring about – except at a terrible sacrifice – the peace, civilization and unity characteristic of England and France. Persia was the battle-ground of Asia. But the genius of Hafiz was never submerged. Whenever peace came, in howsoever limited a form, the eternal tree bore fruit. Hafiz taught the appreciation of beauty, love, gentleness and kindliness; the value of all human beings; the constant glory and splendour and joy of the universe in which we live; the wonder of communion with nature. These undying, eternal truths were so immortally impressed by him on his countrymen that whenever opportunity arose in any period of peace the striving after them and the expression of those eternal values became, in Iran at least, a motive force and power.

Critics of Iranian civilization and culture have said that after Hafiz the light was not only dimmed but burned out. Nothing could be more false and unjust. No doubt Hafiz was the supreme genius of his race, and in that sense if we try to measure his successors by his standard we will find an immediate and sudden decline. But that surely is not the right way to search for his influence. Did the Persian race after him strive for expression in art and literature, in poetry and prose – for the wealth and splendour inherent in the human soul? I have no hesitation in saying "yes." Take the art of the Safavi period – poor in literature, but so rich in architecture and in textiles, in beautiful metal and glass work, in its lovely brocades and carpets. Can we deny that there is here immense search for expression of the highest aspirations of man's soul?

Whenever Iran had any breathing space from war and invasion and misery, in one form or another a national character has formed and, by the spiritual influences of its poetry, immediately turned towards the expression of appreciation and enjoyment of the eternal light within us. And during the nineteenth century one of the very greatest poets that the Iranian race has ever produced, Qa'ani, interpreted nature with a wealth of variety, a strength and beauty, which I doubt can ever be surpassed. Let the admirers of Wordsworth and the French nature poets compare in beauty, simplicity or grandeur the finest verses of the Western masters with Qa'ani's constant descriptions and references to rain, thunder, the sky and earth, the flowers and mountains, night and day, the sun, moon and stars. If the odes had mercenary motives, if the human praise and blame which he bestowed as he went along were nearly always insincere – let us not forget the fundamental honesty of his outlook on life and the universe, the sincerity of his belief in the beauty of goodness of nature.

Modern Persian critics, unconsciously influenced, perhaps, by the puritanical standards of European literature during the last century, have taken Qa'ani to task for his praise of sexual perversities. But when all is said these are but drops in the ocean of his work and, compared with similar extravagancies of many great writers of the West, they are neither prominent nor obtrusive. No one need, unless he searches in the "Divan," come across these particular passages. The music and joy of his verses, the sincerity of his conviction that life is a great, noble and splendid experience – every minute of which is to be treasured as the greatest of God's gifts – these surely are the qualities we will find in page after page and verse after verse of his work.

But is this immense wealth of Iran to remain only a treasure of the Islamic East and its fringe in India? Is Europe, is America, is the West so rich in the joys of the spirit, in its immediate satisfaction with life, that it can afford to close its doors to what Iran has to offer in the highest spiritual satisfaction to mankind? In these days of intensive nationalism – nationalism of a kind that wishes to turn even art, beauty and goodness into national possessions – is this immense lesson of Iran to be forgotten? Iran in its language, in its culture, in its highest soul expression, has taken to its bosom and freely accepted the contributions of Greece and India, the immense stream from Islam, Arabia and the Turkish race. It has assimilated the best of each in order better to express its yearning after truth and beauty. Is this fundamental influence not to be brought into the service of the highest culture of the West?

In the economic field we find today the ideal of one great source of wealth, the earth, to be enjoyed by humanity as a whole through free trade and competition, looked upon almost as an expression worthy only of a lunatic asylum. Peace, and the League of Nations co-operating to conquer disease, malnutrition and the vast waste areas of the world; to raise the poor and humble irrespective of race and religion to the standard of the highest; to feed the famine-stricken and the starving; a competition for construction between various races and countries – all this would today, as a practical suggestion, be considered only worthy of idiots and half-wits. The work of destruction has a totally different standard of appreciation applied to it. Yet, truly understood, and from the lowest material point of view, what good could come from efforts to conquer the waste areas of the world by co-operation, to bring about a standard of living in China and India that would enable people there to buy some of the luxuries of life from Europe and America, to apply the tropical lands that are impossible for European and American settlement for the benefit of the millions of the brown and yellow races and thus open up new and vast markets for the white races for healthy exchange and welcome competition. All these things would lead through prosperity to spiritual awakening and artistic creation. Such work today is not in the realm of practical politics.

Surely now there is room for us to turn to the spirit of Hafiz's teaching. For if ever there was a time when we needed the universality of Hafiz as a guiding light it is today when there are forces that threaten the roots of humanity. Class and race competition threaten to submerge the highest joy of life and living – namely, the search for, and conquest of, true beauty and goodness which, could we but know it, are ever within our grasp.

In that spirit I appeal to the intellectual classes in this country to come and join up with the Iran Society, to help forward similar associations, to study and understand Islamic, Hindu and Far Eastern philosophy, culture, literature and art. Thus the spiritual and emotional inheritance of Great Britain, Europe and America (North and South) should not be merely derived from Greece and Judaism, but from the world as a whole, for I am certain that Asiatic culture in its widest sense can bring as much to man's common heritage as either Greece or Palestine.

Source: *The Iran Society: Inaugural Lecture: Hafiz and the Place of Iranian Culture in the World by His Highness the Aga Khan*, The Iran Society, London, November 1936, pp. 1–7.

The printed lecture carries no date (only the month), but a report in *The Times* of London fixes it as 9 November. Forty years later *Ismaili* (of 13 December

1976) and *Hikmat* (of July 1976) reproduced it. I have taken the text from the original pamphlet issued by the Iran Society.

Complete information about the Iran Society at this time is given below:

OFFICERS AND COUNCIL

PRESIDENT:
The Right Hon. Lord Lamington, G.C.M.G., G.C.I.E.

HONORARY PRESIDENT:
H.E. the Iranian Minister to the Court of St. James.

VICE-PRESIDENTS:
Hussein Ala, C.M.G.
Laurence Binyon, C.H.

COUNCIL:
Leigh Ashton.
Alfred Bossom, M.P.
N. S. Gulbenkian.
E. H. Keeling, M.P.
Laurence Lockhart, PH.D.
Professor R. A. Nicholson, LL.D., F.B.A.
Professor D. Talbot-Rice.
Sir E. Denison Ross, C.I.E.

HONORARY TREASURER:
E. Wilkinson, Hazelbury, Ascot.

HONORARY SECRETARIES:
Basil Gray.
S. F. Shadman.

LIST OF MEMBERS

Afshar, H.
Alai, H. D.
Alavi, M.R.C.S., L.R.C.P., S. H.
Aminoff, D. A.
Aminoff, M. A.
Aminoff, R. A.
Andrews, O.B.E., F. H.
Ansley, G.
Asgharzadeh, Z.
Athanassoglou, Mr. and Mrs. E. H.
Azizolahoff, A. R.
Azizolahoff, Y. A.

Balyusi, M.SC.(ECON.), H. M.
Barrow, Miss V. F. M.
Beheshti, A.
Bowen, D.SC., PH.D., etc., Prof. A. R.
Brown, Mrs. Percy.

Burney, Miss P.
Burney, C.B.E., S.

Cadman, G.C.M.G., D.SC., Sir John.
Cassidy, Major and Mrs. Colin.
Cazalet, D.S.O., Major C. H. L.
Churchill, Lord Ivor.
Cox, G.C.M.G., etc., Major-General Sir Percy and Lady.
Craig, The Hon. Dennis.
Craig-McKerrow, Mrs. M.

Danesh-Poor, A. H.
Dekerckheer, E. G. G.
Djemshidoff, Mr. and Mrs. I.
Dorabjee, Mrs. J. S.
Drinkwater, Mr. and Mrs. John.
Drummond, Miss.

Earle, G.C.V.O., etc., Sir Lionel.
Ebrahimoff, Mr. and Mrs.
Edgar, S. A.
Edwards, Mr. and Mrs. Cecil.
Elgood, M.D., M.R.C.P., C.
Eliaszade, N.
Ellert, Mrs. Arnold.
Ershdi, S. S.
Ettehadieh, A.
Eumorfopoulos, G.

Fateh, M.
Fraser, Mr. and Mrs. W.

Gazvini, M. G.
Ghashghaie, M. M. S.
Ghavami, M. R.
Godson, Miss A. C.
Greenwood, C. A.

Hacobian, A. P.
Haeri, H. Y.
Haeri, M. D.
Hafezi, H.
Haldane, Miss Elizabeth.
Hancock, C. G.
Hart, Mr. and Mrs. J. G.
Hashemian, H.
Hawkins, Mr. and Mrs. C.
Hearn, A. C.
Holding, Miss C. M.
Holmes, Mrs. Margot.
Homayoun, A.
Hoormozdi, M.

Horschitz-Horst, Mr. and Mrs. W.
Hosain, M. and Dr. Maud.
Hotson, K.C.S.I., Sir Ernest.
Howkins, F.
Huffner, R.
Humphreys, F. Y.
Hunter, Lieut.-Colonel and the Hon. Mrs. J. B. Dalzell.

Idelson, V. R.
Ismailoff, A. K.
Izmidlian, Mr. and Mrs. P.

James, H. O.
Javid, A.

Kamgar, M.
Kamkar, A.
Kapurthala, G.C.S.I., etc., His Highness the Maharaja of.
Kasmaii, P.

Leather, A.F.C., Wing-Commander R. T.
Lefroy, Mr. and Mrs. L.
Lindley, M.A., Dr. L. H.
Lockhart, Mrs. L.
Loraine, BT., K.C.M.G., The Right Hon. Sir Percy.

Malik, Dr. K.
Mann, Dr. H. H.
Medlicott, Lieut.-Colonel and Mrs. H.
Minorsky, Professor V.
Mohtadi, M.
Mond, Mr. and Mrs. Emile.
Montague, D.S.O., Captain the Hon. Lionel.
Morrison, Mr. and Mrs. R. M. S.
Mulleneux-Grayson, Sir Henry and Lady.
Mylles, Mr. and Mrs. C. C.

Nabil, F.
Nagioff, A. K.
Nagioff, L.
Nasirbecoff, A. B.
Nayer-Nouri, A. H.
Ness, Mrs. Patrick.
New, G. E.
Noohi, K.

Parikhal, R.
Pazargadi, A.
Pessyan, H. A.
Pezeshgi, H.

Raffaty, H.

Rahnema, M.
Ravensdale, The Baroness.
Richter, F.

Saadet, A.
Scott, Dr. J.
Shah, S. F.
Shahinian, Mr. and Mrs.
Shahinian, A.
Shahinian, Miss H.
Shahinian, Miss S.
Shamsi, E.
Sohrab, B.
Stark, Miss Freya.
Stein, K.C.I.E., Sir Aurel.
Summerhayes, C. H.
Sykes, K.C.I.E., etc., Brig.-General Sir Percy.

Trott, A. C.

Wilkinson, Mrs. E.
Wilkinson, I.C.S. (RET.), J. V. S.
Williams, A. K.
Wood, Mr. and Mrs. J.

Yahouda, PH.D., Dr.
Yazdanian, M.

Zareh, K.

OBJECTS

1. To bring together those who are interested in Iran, her culture and art, past and present, and thereby to help the peoples of Great Britain and Iran to understand each other.

2. To foster intercourse between the two countries and to establish and maintain close relations with institutions in Iran and elsewhere working in the same fields, such as Andjomane Athare Melli, Andjomane Adabi, Société des Etudes Iraniennes, American Institute of Persian Art and Archaeology.

3. To help Iranian students in England to study Iranian culture, according to European methods.

4. To give members of the Iranian colony in England opportunities to meet one another and their English friends at social and intellectual gatherings.

5. Political problems will not fall within the province of the Iran Society.

ACTIVITIES

6. To carry out its purpose the Iran Society will organize lectures and visits to public and private collections, and, in general, take any opportunity of making better known the art and culture of Iran to the English public.

7. It is hoped that means will be found of publishing, from time to time, some of the lectures delivered before the Society, for distribution among members of that Society and for sale.

1136

8. The society will do all in its power to facilitate travel in Iran by its members.

9. The Society will arrange social gatherings for its members.

CONSTITUTION

10. Membership of the Society shall be by election at meetings of the Council. The annual subscription shall be £1. Life membership may be obtained by payment of £10. Joint membership of husbands and wives may be obtained by annual payment of £1 10s.

11. The officers of the Society shall consist of (*a*) a President, (*b*) an Honorary President, (*c*) three Vice-Presidents, (*d*) an Honorary Treasurer, (*e*) two Honorary Secretaries.

12. There shall be a Council consisting of the officers and nine other members.

13. The Representative of Iran shall be *ex officio* Honorary President.

14. The Chairman shall be elected annually by the Council.

15. The Treasurer and Secretaries shall be elected at a General Meeting, on the nomination of the Council.

16. Of the nine members of the Council, three shall retire annually, but shall be eligible for re-election.

17. Nominations to the vacancies thus caused shall be made by the Council, and the names submitted to the Annual General Meeting.

18. Four regular Meetings of the Council shall be held each year for the purpose of arranging programmes.

19. Special Meetings of the Council may be summoned at the discretion of the Chairman.

20. Three members of the Council shall constitute a quorum.

21. The accounts shall be audited annually by an Auditor nominated by the Council.

22. The address of the Society will be, until further notice, 50 Kensington Court, London, W.8.

On Hafiz see S. Abid Ali Abid, "Hafiz of Shiraz", *Iqbal*, Vol. 4 (1955), pp. 53–85; Ahmad Mian Akhtar, "The Arabic Poetry of Hafiz", *Islamic Culture*, Vol. 13 (1939), pp. 222–33; J. Arberry, "Hafiz and his English Translators", *ibid.*, Vol. 20 (1946), pp. 111–28, 229–49; M. Boyce, "A Novel Interpretation of Hafiz", *Bulletin of the School of Oriental and African Studies*, Vol. 15 (1953), pp. 279–88; Cowell, "Hafiz, the Persian Poet", *Macmillan's Magazine*, Vol. 30 (1860); G. F. Dazzmer, *Hafis*, Hamburg, 1856, Jena, 1912; C. H. Defrémery, "Coup d'oeil sur la vie et les écrits de Hafiz", *Journal Asiatique*, Ser. 5, Vol. 11 (1858), pp. 406–25; H. Abdullah Faruqi, "Religion of Hafiz of Shiraz", *Iqbal*, Vol. 7 (1959), pp. 11–18; M. Farzaad, *Haafez and his Poems*, Hertford, 1949; G. Jacob, *Unio Mystica Hafisische Lieder*, Hanover, 1922; Ann K. S. Lambton, "An Introduction to Hafiz", *Horizon*, March 1948, pp. 214–24; R. Lescot, "Essai d'une chronologie de l'oeuvre de Hafiz", *Bulletin d'Etudes Orientales*, Vol. 10 (1944), pp. 59–100; J. Mew, "Life and Writings of Hafiz", *The Nineteenth Century and After*, September 1902, pp. 492–511; E. H. Palmer, *Hafiz, the Persian Poet*, London, 1866; O. H. Roberts, "Life and Writing of Hafiz", *Overland Monthly*, new series, n.d.; A. K. Sarfraz, "Divination by Diwan of Hafiz", *Khareghat Memorial Volume 1*, Bombay, 1953, pp. 276–94; and Munir Shah Alam, "Hafiz and Sufism", *East and West* (Bombay), Vol. 13 (1914), pp. 107–25.

A large number of British, European and American translators have rendered portions of Hafiz's poetry into English and French; though the whole of his *Divan* has never been attempted. The more widely known English versions are by J. Natt (London, 1787), J. M. Hindley (Manchester, 1800), Baron Reviski (London, 1802), A. Richardson (London, 1802), E. H. Palmer (London, 1866), Herman Bicknell (London, 1875), W. H. Lowe (Cambridge, 1877), S. Robinson (Glasgow, 1883), H. Wilberforce Clarke (Calcutta, 1891), J. H. McCarthy (London, 1893), Gertrude Bell (London, 1897), Walter Leaf (London, 1898), J. Payne (London, 1901), Richard le Gallienne (Boston and London, 1903), L. Cranmer-Byng (London, 1912), Edna W. Underwood (Boston, 1917), Elizabeth Bridges (London and New York, 1921), F. M. Rundall (London, 1928), Clarence K. Streit (New York, 1928), M. P. Hanley (London, 1931), J. Arberry (Cambridge, 1947), and Peter Avery and J. Heath-Stubbs (London, 1952); those in French are by Edouard Servan de Sugny (Paris, 1852), A. L. M. Nicolas (Paris, 1898), Charles Devillers (Paris, 1922), H. Piazza (Paris, 1922), Guy (Paris, 1927), Henri Massé (Alger, 1932), V. Monteil (Paris, 1954), and Roger Lescot (Paris, 1955). Thomas Hyde's Latin translation had appeared in 1767 in Oxford. A Spanish translation by Conde de Norona was published in 1871 in Madrid.

167

THE ENTRY OF EGYPT INTO THE LEAGUE OF NATIONS

Speech in the General Assembly of the League of Nations

Geneva: 26 May 1937

Egypt's entry into the League – entry of other Eastern nations –
Egypt a connecting link between the East and the West – bonds
between Egyptian and Indian Muslims.

I account it no mean privilege to represent India at this special
session of the Assembly, for the business we have in hand is the
shaping of history itself. It is not merely that Egypt's entry into
the League of Nations marks yet another stage on the laborious
road towards that universality which is our goal. India is too
conscious of her own many millions, to find satisfaction in the
addition of numbers alone. Whatever its numerical strength,
the League has long seemed to India too representative of one
civilisation and of one creed, to be able to claim universality in
a truly catholic sense.

Additions to our great comity of nations in the last few years
have, however, wrought a vivifying change. Turkey, Iraq, Afghanistan, and now – last, but not least – Egypt, have gone far to make
up the balance between East and West. And, in Indian eyes, no
addition will be more significant than Egypt's entry into the
League to-day. For Egypt is the meeting ground of both; a connecting link between the two. Like India, with an age-long
civilisation that goes far beyond the thousands of years of known
history, Egypt has an understanding of both Eastern and Western
civilisation and will assuredly assist us in our deliberations and
our activities to convert what all too often appears to be a gulf
that divides, into a bridge that unites.

But to an Indian, the scene we are now enacting means even

more than this. To-day the crowning seal is set on Egypt's re-assumption of her ancient and glorious sovereignty. That she re-assumes her full sovereignty, sponsored by Great Britain and with Great Britain's powerful support is something that no Indian with any foresight could witness wholly unmoved, wholly untouched by imaginative vision. Least of all could a Muslim like myself, one of the 80 million Muslims of India, witness it unmoved; for, to us, Egyptians are not aliens or strangers, but brothers with the same culture, the same religion, the same outlook on the world. How intimate that union of culture between Egyptian and Indian Muslims is can best be shown if I quote the fact that an Indian Muslim or an Egyptian, whatever their social or economic position, if found in the other's country, will be immediately at home. Even if the language is not understood, the similarity of custom and habit of brotherly feeling and of religious faith, will make him feel that he has not left his own country. Thus, all the more heartily, sincerely and with pride and pleasure, in the name of India, I bid Egypt welcome to the League and God speed.

Source: *League of Nations Official Journal, Special Supplement No. 166: Records of the Special Session of the Assembly Convened for the Purpose of Considering the Request of the Kingdom of Egypt for Admission to the League of Nations (May 26th–27th, 1937),* Geneva, 1937, p. 29.

Full proceedings of the assembly are reproduced here:

President: M. RŪSTŪ ARAS.
REQUEST OF THE KINGDOM OF EGYPT FOR ADMISSION TO THE LEAGUE OF NATIONS: RESOLUTION OF THE GENERAL MAIN COMMITTEE.
The President:
Translation: The General Main Committee appointed by the Assembly this morning met this afternoon[1] under my chairmanship to consider Egypt's request for admission into the League of Nations.
The Committee unanimously agreed to recommend Egypt's admission, and has asked me to lay the following resolution before the Assembly on its behalf:[2]

"I.

"The General Committee,
"In view of the invitation addressed by numerous Members of the League to the Egyptian Government to the effect that Egypt should become a Member of the League of Nations;
"In view of the request for admission presented on March 4th[3] and 16th, 1937,[3] by the Egyptian Government;
"Noting that in its communication of March 16th the Egyptian Govern-

[1] See page 23.
[2] Document A.(Extr.).5.1937.VII.
[3] Document A.(Extr.).2.1937.

ment declares that Egypt 'has the sincere intention to observe its international obligations, and will accept such regulations as may be prescribed by the League in regard to its military, naval and air forces and armaments':

"Recommends the Assembly to admit Egypt as a Member of the League of Nations."

"II.

"The General Committee recommends the Assembly to fix the rate of contribution of Egypt to the expenses of the League for the years 1937, 1938 and 1939, subject to any decision which may be taken at the next ordinary session of the assembly, at twelve units."

The Assembly will note that the General Main Committee's resolution is divided into two parts: one recommends the Assembly to admit Egypt into the League of Nations and, in consequence, a vote by roll-call will be taken on that question, as prescribed by the Rules of Procedure. The purpose of the other part of the resolution is that the Assembly should fix Egypt's contribution to the expenses of the League for the period until the end of 1939. I shall therefore ask the Assembly to take a decision on this part of the draft resolution, which it will be asked to adopt after the vote on the admission of Egypt into the League.

The Assembly will now proceed to vote on Egypt's request for admission into the League. Under Article 1 of the Covenant, any State which asks to enter the League of Nations may become a Member if its admission is agreed to by two-thirds of the Assembly.

The procedure followed will be that provided in Rule 20, first paragraph, of the Rules of Procedure. The name of each delegation will be called, and one of its members will reply "Yes", or "No", or "Not voting".

The result of the vote will be recorded and announced to the Assembly.

(The vote was taken by roll-call.)

The President:
Translation: The result of the voting is as follows:
Number of States present: 46.
Number of States voting in favour of the resolution: 46.

I therefore announce that the Assembly has unanimously decided to admit Egypt into the League of Nations.

The delegations of Australia, the Dominican Republic, the United States of Mexico and Spain, who were absent when the vote was taken, have informed me that they associate themselves with the unanimous vote.

I should like to congratulate the new Member of the League of Nations now, and I shall offer it a welcome as soon as its delegation has taken its place among us.

CREDENTIALS OF THE DELEGATES OF THE KINGDOM OF EGYPT: REPORT OF THE COMMITTEE ON CREDENTIALS.

The President:
Translation: Before inviting the representatives of Egypt to take their places among us I had requested the Committee on Credentials to examine the credentials of the members of the Egyptian delegation.

I therefore call upon His Excellency M. Guani, Chairman of the Committee on Credentials, to submit the Committee's report.

M. Guani (Uruguay), Chairman and Rapporteur of the Committee on Credentials:
Translation: The Committee appointed by the Assembly to examine the full powers of the delegates under Rule 5, paragraph 3, of the Rules of Procedure of the Assembly met again on May 26th, 1937, to examine whether the representatives of the Kingdom of Egypt were duly accredited to take part in the work of the special session of the Assembly of the League which has opened this morning.

The Secretary-General of the League forwarded to the Committee the full powers by which, in accordance with Rule 5, paragraph 2, of the Rules of Procedure, His Excellency the Minister for Foreign Affairs of the Kingdom of Egypt accredited the delegates of the Kingdom of Egypt to the present special session of the Assembly.

The Committee, after having examined these full powers, considers that the representatives of the Kingdom of Egypt are duly accredited to take part in the work of this session.

The President:
Translation: I thank the Chairman of the Committee on Credentials for his report.

The Assembly has heard the report of the Credentials Committee on the credentials of the Egyptian delegation. If there are no observations, I shall declare the conclusions of the report adopted.

The conclusions of the report were adopted.

ENTRY OF THE KINGDOM OF EGYPT INTO THE LEAGUE OF NATIONS.

The President:
Translation: I now invite the delegates of the Kingdom of Egypt to do us the honour of taking their places among us.

(*The delegates of the Kingdom of Egypt took their seats in the Assembly.*)

The President:
Translation: In my two-fold quality as President of the Assembly and first delegate of Turkey, I have particular satisfaction in addressing you at this moment, on the solemn occasion of the entry of Egypt into the League of Nations.

This very important Mediterranean country, to which Turkey is closely bound by so many memories of a common history and by the cordial bonds of deep friendship, has in a very short space of time completed the successive stages of a process of evolution that is as peaceful as it is glorious. The young Mediterranean State, with a great future before it, has definitely attained complete independence, and has just recently secured, on the hospitable soil of Switzerland, the abolition – which it rightly had so much at heart – of the regime of capitulations.

With the disappearance of this heritage of the past, and with the entry that is so sincerely welcomed into this assemblage of States of all continents, a new era opens for this brave and vigorous people, whose high qualities the Turkish nation has always appreciated.

In speaking of Egypt's accession to the great Geneva institution, the greatest international body the world has ever yet known, I should like to recall one historic fact concerning the relations of ancient Egypt with an old people of Asia Minor.

It has been proved by archaeological documents carefully preserved in the museums of Turkey and Egypt that the most ancient international act, the oldest political treaty in the world, is that concluded and signed between the ancient Egyptians and the Hittites, those Hittites whom the Turks of the West rightly consider to be their ancestors.

A comparison inevitably suggests itself between the embryonic political life which gave birth to this first instrument of diplomacy and the great international life which to-day is developing and evolving within our League of Nations.

Egypt, which has behind her a glorious history and which unites the possession of material and spiritual resources, in every sphere, with the benefits of a most favourable geographical situation, will undoubtedly constitute a new and beneficent force working for that ideal of peace that is so dear to us all.

My country is particularly glad to see Egypt take her place among us as a Member of the League, because this young independent and sovereign State will become a new factor making for equilibrium in the Mediterranean, where the basis of Turkish policy is the maintenance of the *status quo*, which can be effectively assured only by a firm resolve that there shall be sincere collaboration among all the States bordering upon that sea.

The universality of the League is regarded as a fundamental principle that will do much to promote the organisation of peace, and Republican Turkey, which is zealously striving to achieve this end, warmly welcomes the entry of the new Egypt into the great institution of Geneva.

His Excellency Mustapha El-Nahas Pasha, first delegate of Egypt, will address the Assembly.

Mustapha El-Nahas Pasha (Egypt):

Translation: Egypt's entry into the League of Nations constitutes, for my country, an act of faith. This day has long been awaited by the Egyptian nation, for it enables that nation at last to take part in the organisation of world peace.

A number of States sent us cordial invitations, thereby paving the way for this reception, the friendliness of which will go straight to the heart of the Egyptian people. I owe sincere thanks to those States, and to the entire Assembly for its unanimous vote, and to you, too, Mr. President, for having welcomed our admission to the League in words that were as cordial as they were eloquent.

It is with a firm determination to afford her effective co-operation that Egypt, in taking her place among you, regards the high responsibility that devolves upon her; for she is here to serve, not only the ideal of peace, but also the reality of peace.

Before joining the League of Nations, Egypt was already applying the League's principles. Her sons, who down the ages have been able to preserve the characteristics of the race, its gentleness of character and its spirit of tolerance, have ensured internal peace by a regime of order and justice, by a constant endeavour to foster development and progress, by the farsightedness and moderation of the administration, by the application of the soundest principles of democracy, and by a profoundly liberal Constitution.

Following age-long traditions of hospitality, Egypt has just spontaneously

1143

opened up, at the Montreux Conference for the abolition of capitulations, a vast field of activity for loyal collaboration and sincere initiative of every kind. On her soil, foreigners as well as Egyptians will receive to-morrow, as yesterday, friendly protection under the liberal laws applied by an authority imbued with sincere understanding.

Moreover, Egypt, firmly established within her frontiers, has no need to cast envious eyes beyond her horizons. While she is happy on her own soil, she knows that to-day a nation's happiness is never assured unless there is general tranquillity. That was the primary ideal followed by those who set up the League of Nations; and it is to the triumph of this ideal, to which you have devoted yourselves, that we come here to give our sincere collaboration, in the belief that this association of peoples, the hope of the world, will surmount the obstacles that still remain . . .

The President:
Translation: His Excellency M. Yvon Delbos, first delegate of France, will address the Assembly.

M. Delbos (France):
Translation: In welcoming Egypt within its midst, the League of Nations has performed an act of happy augury. It thus completes and crowns the attainment of the legitimate aspirations of a people who now, in this consecration of their full sovereignty, obtain the recognition of their most cherished ideal. Egypt is justly proud and joyful on attaining her freedom; and France, whose history and whose institutions are imbued with the spirit of democracy, would be false to the most abiding and the highest of her traditions did she not sincerely share in that joy. She knows that independence is the strongest guarantee both of the probity and of the permanence of international relationships; and in that spirit she has unreservedly consented to the liberation of Egypt from her bonds. Together with the other Powers she gave her preference not to the surety afforded by time-honoured privileges but to the word of a nation henceforward to possess autonomy and responsibility. We are convinced that we shall never regret our response to the appeal from the Government of His Excellency Mustapha El-Nahas Pasha, when invoking the generous hospitality of his country no less than the services rendered to it by foreign collaboration, we were asked to trust it to safeguard the continuity of that collaboration.

At Montreux, we explained quite simply and frankly the anxiety we were bound to feel for the defence of our moral and material interests – interests, moreover, that Egypt herself readily recognises to be honourable, genuine and active. France, which has had her part in the evolution of a country whose past is lost in the night of time, knows that she is overlooking nothing of what she owes both to Egypt and to herself in consenting to place under the guarantee of a vigilant friendship the future of a co-operation which neither country can safely allow to be compromised.

For us, who regard liberty as the most precious of possessions, the accession of Egypt to full independence brings to the concert of modern countries the contribution of a nation, itself modern too, whose strength is redoubled by its rejuvenation. The Egyptian people will bring to Geneva the experience of the East, of an East which, far from fixing itself in static forms, strives not only to benefit the West by its wisdom but also to fertilise its own civilisation by contact with Europe. The League of Nations, by its enthusiastic unanimity, shows how greatly it values that assistance. It will gain thereby, for its equilibrium will be more broadly based and its authority will be more firmly established and better respected.

But France, whose rôle here is so closely allied to her political traditions, has particular reason to open her arms to Egypt, the most ancient of Mediterranean nations. She is happy also to extend that welcome as being herself a Mohammedan Power. For centuries closely concerned with the life of the peoples of Islam and a friend of Arab thought, the nobility and value of which she is well able to know and appreciate, France associates herself with the joy of the Egyptian people in the name of all the Mohammedans counted among her children, just as, last year, Egypt rejoiced when we emancipated Syria and Lebanon. From Aleppo, Damascus and Beirut to Tunis, Constantine, Algiers, Tlemcen, Fez and Marrakesh, one single voice congratulates Egypt at this hour. Franco-Egyptian understanding cannot but emerge strengthened by those spiritual exchanges through which neighbouring peoples bring new life to their civilisations.

Egypt's past history stands surety to us for the balanced spirit and the sense of continuity which will guide her in her international relations. Independence favours the conception and the achievement of generous designs; but independence also entails weighty obligations and even certain dangers. Egypt, we are convinced, will not fail to carry out those obligations or to avoid those dangers. To that country, whose soil owes its fertility not only to the alluvium of the Nile but equally to the toil of a frugal and courageous people, we proffer with all our heart our wishes for a brilliant and prosperous future.

To the Government of His Excellency El-Nahas Pasha, its beloved and respected leader, who after so many years of effort has had the happiness of seeing the ideals of his compatriots realised, to his collaborators, whose greatness of mind and realism of spirit we know, and, finally, to the Egyptian people, so wise, so proud and so industrious, we offer the sincerest and the heartiest good wishes.

The President:
Translation: His Excellency M. Nicolas Politis, first delegate of Greece, will address the Assembly.

M. Politis (Greece):
Translation: On behalf of Greece, which has always been the friend of Egypt, and also on behalf of the Balkan *Entente*, for whom respect for national independence – for all national independence – is an article of faith, I desire to associate myself in all sincerity with the congratulations and the good wishes which have been addressed to the Egyptian delegation. We understand and we share the joy which must at this moment fill the hearts of our Egyptian colleagues; for this day must, I think, stand as a very great date in the history of modern Egypt. It is the day on which Egypt has taken out her letters of naturalisation in the family of free nations.

It is by a stern struggle that Egypt has now won her freedom. Thanks to the noteworthy and untiring efforts of her leaders, she has accomplished the three final stages in less than a year. Scarcely nine months ago she secured the recognition of her independence by the protecting Power, which has thus once again given the world striking evidence of its lofty spirit of generous liberalism and of its rare political and administrative qualities. This recognition of independence was obtained through an agreement, the elasticity and political wisdom of which cannot be too highly admired, for it not merely granted liberty to Egypt, but raised that country to the enviable rank of ally of the greatest Power in the world.

That first stage, once achieved, made the second stage easier. It was attained scarcely three weeks ago at Montreux, where Egypt was emancipated from another form of guardianship which appeared incompatible with her political liberty. There too, this result was reached by the consent of all parties through an agreement which did the greatest honour to the Egyptian negotiators; it bore the mark of their lofty and yet practical spirit, which revealed to those associated with them, of whom I had the honour to be one, the qualities of true statesmanship.

To-day, the last stage is achieved. Egypt becomes finally free. She takes rank as an equal among free and independent nations. She witnesses the fulfilment of the great dream conceived a century ago by the great founder of her dynasty, Mehemet Ali, whose desire it was that the valley of the Nile should become a free and prosperous country. That dream is now fulfilled; and I would recall that, among the means which that great Egyptian employed for the initiation of this great work, was an appeal for European support, a support that has brought to Egypt much of her present prosperity.

Greece too has done much to help. The Greek community was, indeed, particularly favoured by Mehemet Ali, and it was happy to work hand in hand and in a community of spirit with the Egyptians for the creation of modern Egypt. That was a further bond added to the close and age-long relations between Egypt and Greece – relations, I may say, of trust, collaboration and friendship.

Twenty-five years ago, when Kavala once more became Greek, a new link was added to so many former ones. Kavala is the birthplace of Mehemet Ali. In a few months' time, that solidarity, that peculiar friendship, that new link added to so many others, will be manifested in a doubly symbolic fashion. An equestrian statue of Mehemet Ali is to be erected in a square in Kavala, which lies before the house in which Mehemet Ali was born, facing the sea and looking towards the venerable land of the Pharaohs. It will be symbolic, too, in that Mehemet Ali will be represented, his task as a soldier done, as sheathing his sword, henceforth to consecrate himself to his great work of peace, the work of making Egypt, as I have said, a free and prosperous country.

Such is the achievement, my friends, which you have the happiness to witness to-day. You may well be proud of the results obtained, and you may face the future confident of placing the economic and cultural development of your country upon a still surer basis and of seeing your country collaborate closely, in the eastern area of the Mediterranean, with the countries of the Balkan *Entente*, and becoming an element of order, progress, stability and peace.

Such, my dear Egyptian colleagues and friends, are the wishes which I, voicing the feelings of Greece and of the Balkan *Entente*, address to you on this solemn occasion for the prosperity and good fortune of your country. (pp. 24–29)

168

FAILURES AND SUCCESSES OF THE LEAGUE OF NATIONS

Presidential Address to the League of Nations

Geneva: 13 September 1937

Indian philosophy of life in tune with the League's principles – importance of goodwill and co-operation – crises in Western Europe and the Far East – failures and successes – adjustment of things in economic and social life – removal of all causes of war.

With more warmth of feeling at heart than I can bring to my lips, I thank you. You have done India, my country, a great honour, and my delight is undisguised.

It is an honour done to a country whose whole philosophy of life is attuned to the fundamental principles on which the League of Nations is grounded, and whose greatest thinkers, from time immemorial, of whatever culture of creed, have sought in the supremacy of law the sole escape from the anarchy of force.

I am very conscious of the weight of responsibility now laid upon me. In the spirit of devoted service to the League of Nations, I take it up, fortified by your goodwill, and in the assurance of your co-operation I shall bear it willingly. May your goodwill be undiminished when I lay it down.

Never, in very truth, were goodwill, co-operation and service more incumbent on all States Members of the League than to-day. We must face reality unflinchingly. The world is sorely troubled; a storm has long been raging in the extreme corner of Western Europe, another has broken out yonder in the Far East. Grievous wrong has been done to the peace of the world and to the principles for which we stand, but though it is very meet and proper that we should take stock of our failures, we must not allow failures to blind us to the reality of our successes, or to rob us of their inspiriting influence.

Without the League, would the Dardanelles or the Sanjak of Alexandretta have found their peaceful adjustment? And if there have been unforgettable defections from the ranks of the League, is it a small thing, a matter void of significance, that nations still knock at our doors for admittance? In the five years in which I have been privileged to lead the Indian delegation, no fewer than six nations, among them one of the Great Powers – the Union of Soviet Socialist Republics – have been admitted to the League. Indeed, to a Moslem like myself, the League is now more universal, more truly Catholic, than when I first knew it, and I rejoice, with great rejoicing, that I have been privileged to join in welcoming first Turkey, then Iraq, then Afghanistan, and, this very year, Egypt into the League.

These are surely portents of good omen, for light comes from the East, and if it is true that the League, like the world itself, is passing through troubled times, and that its ideals have been sorely wounded, it is no less true that the League's ideals live and shall live, and, please God, shall prevail.

And now let us turn to the business we have in hand. There is plenty of it. To the onlooker, much of it may seem undramatic, but much of what affects human life most nearly is undramatic, and if we can do something to bring about a more equitable adjustment of things in economics and in social life no less than in politics, the world will be the better for our labours and we shall have helped the League on the long road to the goal that lies and will ever lie before it – the peaceful removal of all causes of war and the establishment of the unchallengeable empire of peace throughout the world.

Source: *Verbatim Record of the Eighteenth Ordinary Session of the Assembly of the League of Nations, Second Plenary Meeting, Monday, September 13th, 1937, at 5.00 p.m.,* Geneva, 1937, p. 2.
This was the Aga Khan's first speech delivered immediately after his election to the Presidentship of the League of Nations. The election was held on 13th September under the presidentship of M. Negrín of Spain under the following procedure:

6. – ELECTION OF THE PRESIDENT OF THE EIGHTEENTH ORDINARY SESSION OF THE ASSEMBLY: PROPOSAL OF THE NOMINATION COMMITTEE.

The Chairman:

Translation: The first duty of the Assembly at the present meeting is to elect its President, after hearing the report of the Nomination Committee.

I call upon the Chairman of the Committee, M. Hambro, delegate of Norway, who has been asked by the Nomination Committee to lay its conclusions and proposals before the Assembly.

M. Hambro (Norway):
Translation: The Nomination Committee has met and has reached unanimity upon all its proposals.

On behalf of the Nomination Committee, I propose His Highness the Aga Khan as President of the Assembly.

The Chairman:
Translation: The Assembly has heard the proposal of the Nomination Committee with regard to the Presidency of the Assembly. In conformity with the Rules of Procedure, the voting will be by secret ballot by roll-call.

May I call upon His Excellency M. Guani, delegate of Uruguay, and His Excellency M. Sandler, delegate of Sweden, as former Presidents of the Assembly, to be good enough to act as tellers?

(*The votes of the delegations were taken in turn by secret ballot.*)

The Chairman:
Translation: In the first place, I wish to thank the tellers for their kind assistance.

The result of the voting is as follows:

Number of States voting	50
Blank and spoilt voting-papers	1
Valid voting-papers	49
Absolute majority	25

His Highness the Aga Khan, delegate of India, has obtained 49 votes. I have therefore the honour to declare that His Highness the Aga Khan is elected President of the Assembly.

I am particularly happy to congratulate His Highness the Aga Khan on his election as President of the eighteenth session of the Assembly of the League of Nations. It is an honour for the latter to be presided over by so distinguished a personality as His Highness the Aga Khan, representing as he does a country whose culture has influenced numerous civilisations, including that of Europe.

I call upon His Highness the Aga Khan to take the Presidential Chair, and I wish him every success in the proceedings over which he will preside.

(*His Highness the Aga Khan took the Presidential Chair.*)

On 20 September, during the debate on the Report of the work of the League in 1936–37, Anthony Eden opened his speech with the following tribute to the Aga Khan:

The Rt. Hon. Anthony Eden (United Kingdom):
I should first wish to say that we of the United Kingdom take special pleasure in the choice of the President of this year's Assembly, and in finding that the character and ability of His Highness the Aga Khan, which are so well known

to us, have been recognised in the signal honour done to him by the Assembly. But it must be of interest to the League of Nations as a whole that a representative of India has been chosen in the year in which India has embarked upon so great an enterprise in representative government. Any change in the government of three hundred million people is of interest to all the world, and this change, undertaken in full tranquillity, is a good omen in the midst of the turmoil and fury in which so much of the world finds itself to-day.

(*Verbatim Record of the Eighteenth Ordinary Session of the Assembly of the League of Nations, Sixth Plenary Meeting, Monday, September 20th, 1937, at 10.30 a.m.*, Geneva, 1937, p. 2)

169

A TRIBUTE TO DR MASARYK OF CZECHOSLOVAKIA

Speech in the General Assembly of the League of Nations

Geneva: 14 September 1937

A tribute to Dr. Masaryk – his role in the national affairs of the Czechoslovak Republic and in the international field.

It is with deep sorrow that I have to call upon the Assembly to pay a tribute of admiration and respect to a great statesman of whose death we have just learned – Dr. Masaryk, formerly President of the Czechoslovak Republic, one of the founders of his country.

I need hardly remind you of the rôle which President Masaryk played both in the international field and also in the national affairs of his country. I will merely stress his faithfulness to and confidence in the League of Nations, which inspired his whole policy.

The Assembly will wish to acclaim him as one of the best servants of the League ideal and one of the greatest intellects which influenced the destiny of the modern world. It will also wish to express its deepest sympathy with the Government of the Czechoslovak Republic and with the whole Czechoslovak nation in its mourning.

Source: *Verbatim Record of the Eighteenth Ordinary Session of the Assembly of the League of Nations, Third Plenary Meeting, Tuesday, September 14th, 1937, at 10.30 a.m.,* Geneva, 1937, p. 6.
After this short speech by the Aga Khan, who was then President of the League of Nations, the Assembly stood in silence as a tribute to the memory of the late Dr Masaryk. Then the Czechoslovak delegate, M. Krofta, thanked the President and paid his own tribute to the deceased in these words:
"*Interpretation*: Mr. President, – It is with the deepest emotion that I have

1151

listened to the words you have just spoken evoking the memory of the President and liberator of the Czechoslovak Republic, who has just passed away. I wish to thank you for the spontaneity of those words, which I feel sure will be heard with appreciation by the whole Czechoslovak nation. That nation has lost its liberator, its great inspirer, its spiritual leader. Imbued with his high ideals, my nation will remain unshaken in its faith in the League and the League's work."

Dr Masaryk was a former president of the Czechoslovak Republic.

170

THE PALACE OF THE LEAGUE OF NATIONS

Speech in the General Assembly of the League of Nations Inaugurating
the New Headquarters

Geneva: 28 September 1937

The significance of the assembly's meeting in the Palace of the
League – the Palace as a symbol of continuity and friendship.

Ladies and Gentlemen: for the first time, the Assembly is meeting
in the Palace of the League of Nations. This is a memorable
event, for it is both a token of the normal continuity of the work
of the Assembly and marks a new stage in the history of the
League.

This transfer of the Assembly, and its housing in the building
constructed for it, are worthy of more than passing attention.
When an institution such as ours erects such an edifice as its
workshop, it gives testimony of its confidence and faith in
its future. When an Assembly such as ours, after temporary residence in various places, enters into possession of a permanent
home, it gives a sign of continuity in its aims. When your delegations, in the midst of a session of the Assembly, come to occupy
the places reserved for them within these walls, each of them will
have the feeling of finding its place and of being quite at home
– I venture to say, for always – in this new Palace.

You have desired this Palace to remain open to everyone. Thus,
in these noble halls, where others will succeed me as President,
there will be perpetuated from year to year this will to continue,
this feeling of friendship between all nations, of which the Palace
itself is and will remain for ever the emblem.

Source: *Verbatim Record of the Eighteenth Ordinary Session of the Assembly of the League of Nations, Ninth Plenary Meeting, Tuesday, September 28th, 1937, at 10.30 a.m.,* Geneva, 1937, p. 1.

The Aga Khan was, at this time, President of the League of Nations.

171

THE TASK BEFORE THE LEAGUE OF NATIONS

Adjournment of the Session Speech at the League of Nations

Geneva: 6 October 1937

League's work in the humanitarian fields – a survey of the world's economic and financial problems – ventilation of views and confirmation of principles – tackling of political problems – adaptation to changing conditions – the significance of the very existence of the League – the League's mission – basic problem: the dignity of man – tribulations of one are the tribulations of all – the good of the whole world.

Ladies and Gentlemen, – Your work for the time being is at an end. But I have still a duty to perform.

As President it falls to me – and neither I nor you will look upon it as a mere formality – to voice the deep gratitude of the delegations here assembled, and my own, to the distinguished Secretary-General, M. Avenol, and his staff for their arduous labours. To the officials who have been attached to the Presidential office I am under great personal obligation. Their help has been invaluable to me, and I take this opportunity of thanking them warmly. Thanks to them and thanks to you, Ladies and Gentlemen, my task has indeed been light and pleasant.

And now let me pass in review the much heavier task that has been yours.

Your task this year was of a three-fold character. In the humanitarian fields, the Assembly has striven, however unpropitious the circumstances, to stimulate the work of the League organisations. That work is ceaseless and of almost infinite variety. Almost everything that administers to man's well-being – the great problems of health and transit, of intellectual co-operation, of penal and penitentiary reform, and of the suppression of the traffic in dangerous drugs – all these and many others come within the League's purview. But despite the variety of its activity it is all inspired by a single principle – the service of humanity. Everywhere, the League gives proof of its anxiety to serve. It places its resources for investigation and execution and all the great experience it has gained in seventeen years of toil and research, at the service of every Government, whether a Member of the League or not, and at the service of the world as a whole.

To many, the crushing difficulties of our times seem to put any solution, indeed any alleviation, of the world's malaise beyond our present reach. I for one set my face steadfastly against such an attitude of despair and pessimism. The League has done mankind true service in embarking on its difficult and realistic survey of the world's problems in economics and finance. Some may argue that such exchanges of opinion cannot be called results. I differ. In the present state of the world, when the ball of responsibility is cast backwards and forwards between politics and economics, the frank ventilation of views by the representatives of so many nations is of living importance. In our discussions, general permanent principles have gradually emerged and been confirmed. Here are being well and truly laid the foundations for future negotiations, which will give those principles concrete form.

The division of responsibility between economics and politics is indeed one of the most difficult dilemmas with which we are confronted. "Give me a sound economic position, and I will pursue a sound policy", says the Statesman. "How can I pursue a sound policy", says the Economist, "if you do not give me a sound political position?" The Assembly has declined to impale itself on the horns of this pessimistic dilemma. And rightly. What the present conditions allow it to do in the economic sphere, it has done. What those conditions allow it to do in the political sphere it has done likewise. Grasping its opportunities, facing its responsibilities, it has set itself unflinchingly to those grave problems which to-day beset the international community. And of this, our debates on the Spanish problem, on mandates and the grave situation in China are eloquent proof.

That is the second aspect of your work this session. Let me turn to the third. Your enquiry into the application of the principles of the Covenant reveals the Assembly's awareness of the need of the League to adapt itself to the ever-changing conditions involved by its own growth. Adversaries of the League who find in every new difficulty fresh reason for doubting it, and impatient friends who look upon those difficulties as reasons for asking of it too much, alike ignore the significance of one all-significant fact – the very existence of the League.

Remember how the League came into being just after the war, when everything was in disorder. How it passed through the vicissitudes of crisis after crisis – political, economic and other – crises not of the League's own making but the inevitable inescapable aftermath of pre-war, pre-League conditions. Remember all it has done in seventeen short years for the gradual rebuilding of a devastated world, and how, never losing sight of its objectives, it has yet displayed enough flexibility to preserve its ideal intact through all opposition. Think of all this, and then say whether we are not verily right in paying homage and service to the League.

Were I asked how I myself conceive the League's mission in the world I should answer in the words of the great Saadi: "The children of Adam, created of the self-same clay, are members of one body. When one member suffers, all members suffer likewise. O thou who art indifferent to the sufferings of thy fellow, thou art unworthy to be called man." Or I might borrow the words of a wise Hindu poet philosopher: "All peoples in the world are to me even as my nearest kin and kith". Or the final blessing at a Hindu service: "Let there be peace! Let there be prosperity!" The agelong experience of India had, indeed, taught its children that prosperity without peace was an impossibility; that war meant want, peace meant plenty. Even so may it be with the League of Nations.

Indeed, all the problems that fall to the League may ultimately be reduced to one – that of man, and the dignity of man. It is in that sense that the work of the League assumes its true significance and acquires its permanent value. The tribulations of one people are the tribulations of all. That which weakens one weakens all. That which is a gain to one is surely a gain to all. This is no empty ideal. It is a veritable compass to guide aright the efforts of statesmen in every country and of all men of good will who, desiring the good of their own people, desire the good of the whole world.

And now for the present, my task is over. In the circumstances in which we separate, I may not wish you farewell, but with all my heart I wish you – God-speed.

I declare the session adjourned.

Source: *Verbatim Record of the Eighteenth Ordinary Session of the Assembly of the League of Nations, Fourteenth Plenary Meeting, Wednesday, October 6th, 1937, at 5 p.m.,* Geneva, 1937, p. 2.

At this time the Aga Khan was the President of the League of Nations.

172

ORIENTAL LITERATURE

Preface to Sirdar Ikbal Ali Shah's Collection of Oriental Literature

London: 1937

The troubled state of the world – the path of calm contemplation through literature – the value of Sirdar Ikbal Ali Shah's collection.

At a time like the present, when the nations of the world are struggling for some thing to drive away the evil thoughts of human strife and yet know not its name; when the hand of a brother may be raised against his father's son; when humanity is making a habit of measuring happiness and success in terms of wealth and material gain; when, as a result of a confused modern outlook on life, the average man seems to be straying as if lost in a mental fog: surely a turning point has been reached!

In this troubled temper of the world, therefore, there is only one way for mankind to rescue itself. It is on the road of that calm contemplation, which only the sublimity of highest form of prose and poetry can give. By that channel alone can peace be attained.

The gems in the treasure-house of Oriental literature, which Sirdar Ikbal Ali Shah has collected in this volume, are not intended to dazzle and fascinate the imagination. Their value is greater. Their recitation in no small measure will contribute to the ushering in of that frame of mind which alone could save mankind from a disaster greater than anything of the past.

It is as an antidote to that venom that I recommend this collection. Read the passages in this volume and contemplate upon their inner meaning. They will fill your heart with liquid sunshine, and the enchantment of their soulful beauty will linger as a rhythmic melody amongst mankind bringing into life "The

Great Purpose Of Peace" – that Peace that rests on the earth, but like a rainbow lifts its head to heaven.

Source: *The Coronation Book of Oriental Literature* edited by Sirdar Ikbal Ali Shah, Sampson Low, Marston and Co., London, n.d., p.v. It was reprinted, probably simultaneously, in the United States by the Garden City Publishing Co., Inc., New York. Both editions are undated, but the editor's introduction is dated "London: 1937", and reads thus:

"The task of making this anthology has been a labour of love to me, for since my early days I have striven to interpret the East to the West, and Europe to Asia. Through this, I believe, lies the way of mutual sympathy between the nations; and such can only be accomplished by means of reading the effusions of one another's Great Minds; because if we but endeavour to understand about our fellow men, goodwill can come as the gentle dawn of peace. Years of study devoted to this work are as noble friends to me, whose memory, like precious odours, will abide with me to the last.

"I make grateful acknowledgements to the following for inclusion of passages in this work: Messrs. William & Norgate; Colonial Press; British Academy; R. A. Society; Sir R. Burton (H. J. Cook, Esq.); James Madden, Esq.; The Commercial Press; The French Bookstore (Henry H. Hart, Esq.); J. F. Davis, Esq.; Ralph T. H. Griffith, Esq. (Lazarus & Co.); M. N. Dutt, Esq.; Sir William Jones; E. J. Robinson, Esq. (Wesleyan Conference Office); P. E. More, Esq.; Sir Mohamed Iqbal; Professor Macdonald; Francis H. Skrine, Esq.; Sir Rabindranath Tagore; T. D. Broughton, Esq.; Dr. Adams; Messrs. Arthur Probsthain & Co. (Professor C. E. Wilson); S. Robinson, Esq.; Edward FitzGerald, Esq.; Miss G. Bell; San Kaka Sha (F. Victor Dickins, Esq.); Messrs. Fisher Unwin; Messrs. Wright & Brown; to which must be added my unqualified indebtedness to Professor Sir Denison Ross, Dr. Randell and his staff at the India Office Library, to Mr. Probsthain and Bibliotheque Sino-Internationale of Geneva for great encouragement and guidance during the progress of the work; and no mere words can adequately thank that great patron of Asia's 'Noble Things' – The Aga Khan.

"*London*: 1937. IKBAL ALI SHAH"

In 1975, the Octagon Press of London reprinted the book under the changed title of *The Book of Oriental Literature*, with the original dedication and introduction intact but omitting the Aga Khan's Preface, without any explanation for or reference to the omission.

Sirdar Ikbal Ali Shah was a prolific writer, compiler and editor. Among others he published the following books:

Afghanistan of the Afghans
Westward to Mecca
Arabia
Turkey
Eastward to Persia
The Golden East
The Oriental Caravan
The Golden Pilgrimage
Lights of Asia
Quotations from the Koran
Mohamed: the Prophet
Islamic Sufism
Kamal: the Maker of Modern Turkey

The Prince Aga Khan
Fuad: King of Egypt
Nepal: the Home of the Gods
Tragedy of Amanullah
The Controlling Minds of Asia

173

THE RELEVANCE OF THE LEAGUE OF NATIONS

Speech at the Empire Exhibition

Glasgow: 8 July 1938

The conceptions and ideals behind the League of Nations – reasons which led to its creation – handicaps – the negative image – disavowal of its authority – secondary purposes – preservation of the instrument is necessary – ideal of a Parliament of Nations – ideas of Briand and Stresemann to form a United States of Europe – alteration in the League's Constitution – mastery of destructive forces and their use for development – value of the life of the spirit – a single super-state.

An earnest appeal for the preservation of the primary political functions of the League of Nations was made by the Aga Khan, speaking in the Peace Pavilion at the Empire Exhibition in Glasgow yesterday. It was a law of life, he said, that men should labour and endure to uphold ideals and institutions and that other men should enter into their labours.

He suggested reviving the ideas of Briand and Stresemann to form a United States of Europe, when nine-tenths of the dangers to civilization would disappear.

The ideals and conceptions of which the League was the expression, said the Aga Khan, were imperishable. They were as ancient as the search of man for God. All the great religions of the world had taught the brotherhood of man and peace and good will to all men.

The War threw a lurid light, not yet quenched, on the insecurity from which the most civilized nations of the world had suffered in their relations to each other. Without reorganization there was the prospect of recurring wars, each more devastating than the last.

Thus the provision of a League of Nations became a necessity. From the beginning there were certain factors which were a heavy handicap to success. Though President Wilson had done so much to shape the Covenant, the United States refused its cooperation. Further, the attachment of the Covenant to the Peace Treaty led to the German feeling, so fully exploited later, that the new institution was in essence a victor's League against the vanquished. Before the League succeeded in changing the mentality of the generations brought up under the old power politics or to educate sufficiently the rising generation (which had little or no personal recollection of 1914–18) other voices and ideologies clamoured for hearing and demanded acceptance. There were disavowals of the authority of the League, and three great Powers forsook its ranks.

It was suggested that, having failed in the main objectives, the League might limit its activities to the many secondary purposes it had so well served for two decades – those relating to labour, health, social and economic advance, and the suppression of the drug and white-slave traffics.

To such suggestions of abandonment of the primary purpose of the League an emphatic negative must be returned by all believers in human progress. Whatever might be the weaknesses the years had revealed in the structure of the League, whatever desertions there might have been from its ranks, their task was to preserve this instrument, saving the world with loving and pious care. There were chapters in human history which showed that later generations had derived enormous benefits from the maintenance of great movements and institutions during phases in which they had been incapable of effecting the good for which they were designed. It was a law of life that men should labour and endure to uphold ideals and institutions, and that other men should enter into their labours.

The League must not be allowed to renounce the great ideal of being the Parliament of Nations, the supreme authority to ordain peace instead of war throughout the world. They might go back to the ideas of Briand and Stresemann to form a United States of Europe, if she could be grouped into an economic power unit. Then indeed it would be possible for the nations of Europe to promote the use of the undeveloped parts of the world.

A necessary alteration in the fundamental constitution of the League would be to allow the inhabitants of a portion of a country – if sufficiently numerous – to have a referendum under League direction. By this they could, through a substantial majority, be able to leave that State and either remain independent members or join some other country.

If once more the principles of Briand and Stresemann were to triumph, if the Continent of Europe outside Russia became a real "United States" with economic union, and if the great World Powers cooperated on a basis of no privilege for the development of the backward areas, then indeed nine-tenths of the dangers to civilization would disappear, and what would be left could easily be handled by the central governing body of mankind.

Science had placed at the disposal of man in this generation many forces of destruction and death dealing. But man, by spiritual progress, could be civilized enough to become the master of such forces and to use them not for destructive but for economic, physical, and cultural development.

They had to learn afresh the value of the life of the spirit and that it could flourish among the peoples only to the extent to which it overcame by collective action hatred, ill-will, and other fruits of selfish ambition in men and nations, building up that single super-State where all races, civilizations, and States could feel that they were equal parts of a Holy Whole.

Source: *The Times*, London, 9 July 1938.
    The *Glasgow Herald* of 9 July published a slightly different version:
" 'The war,' said the Aga Khan to the gathering in the Concert Hall, 'threw a lurid light, not yet quenched on the insecurity from which the more civilised nations of the world have suffered in their relations to each other. Nothing was writ larger on the history of the struggle than the fact that the immense havoc it wrought would be utterly vain unless international life was re-organised on a basis of justice, equality, and public law in replacement of the law of brute force.

" 'Without such reorganisation there was the prospect of recurring wars, each more devastating than the last, on account of the resources of science being increasingly available for both offensive and defensive conflict. The end of such recurrent wars must be the collapse not only of our modern civilisation but perhaps even of organised society.

" 'Thus the provision of a League of Nations became a necessity.'

"Whatever might be the weaknesses the years had revealed in the structure of the League, whatever desertions there might have been from its ranks, their task was to preserve this instrument. There were chapters in human history which showed that later generations had derived enormous benefits from the maintenance of great movements and institutions during phases in which they had been incapable of effecting the good for which they were designed.

"The League must be not only a security and defence against war but a recognised fount of justice which would bring about a new spirit among nations by reducing trade barriers, and by bringing to the needs of all mankind the resources of vast untapped areas in South America, Africa, and elsewhere.

"In that way the temptations to international dispute would be greatly narrowed and aggressive nations would find themselves unable to reap the fruits of their aggression.

" 'We might go back to the ideas of Briand and Stresemann to work for a United States of Europe, if she can be grouped into an economic power unit.

" 'Then, indeed, it would be possible for the nations of Europe to promote the use of the undeveloped parts of the world, bringing in America and such Asiatic countries as were advanced enough to take a hand in the work of making the world a garden for the enjoyment by all races and all nations.

" 'If once more the principles of Briand and Stresemann triumph, if the Continent of Europe becomes a real 'United States' with economic union, and if the great world Powers co-operate on a basis of no privilege for the development of the backward areas, then, indeed, nine-tenths of the dangers to civilisation would disappear, and what would be left could easily be handled by the central governing body of mankind.' "

The *Glasgow Herald* also furnished some details about the Aga Khan's activities and movements on this occasion:

"A plea for a return to the ideas of Briand and Stresemann in an effort to work for the formation of a United States of Europe was made at the Empire Exhibition yesterday by the Aga Khan, President of the League of Nations Assembly, at a meeting promoted by the Peace Pavilion Committee.

"The League of Nations, the Aga Khan declared, must not be allowed to renounce the great ideal of being the parliament of the nations, the supreme authority to ordain peace instead of war throughout the world.

"The visit of the distinguished Indian brought a large crowd to the Concert Hall. Every seat in the building was occupied, and hundreds who had queued up outside were unable to gain admission. Those who had to turn away stood about in the rain until the meeting was over to see His Highness leave.

"Earlier in the forenoon the Aga Khan, on behalf of the Indian people, placed a stone on the cairn in the Garden of the Good Neighbours at the Peace Pavilion.

"Others on the platform included the Lord Provost of Glasgow (Sir John Stewart); Sir James Lithgow, Bt.; Lady Henschel; Sir Daniel M. Stevenson, Bt.; Sir Robert Wilson; Sir Firozkhan Noon, High Commissioner for India, and Mr H. R. Cummings, of the Secretariat of the League of Nations.

"The architect of the Peace Pavilion, Mr Alister MacDonald, son of the late Mr Ramsay MacDonald, was one of the company present at the ceremony performed by the Aga Khan in the forenoon. His Highness was conducted round the building by Mrs J. M. Crosthwaite. Before leaving the pavilion, the Aga Khan talked to Mrs Aaron, wife of the warden of the Students' International Club in Glasgow, and a number of Egyptian and Indian students.

"At the royal apartments His Highness was received by Sir Cecil M. Weir, and thereafter, accompanied by Sir James Lithgow, he visited a number of the pavilions.

"Sir Alfred Pickford, chairman of the Empire Tea Market Expansion Bureau, received him at the Empire Tea Pavilion, where he drank a cup of most expensive tea.

"The blend, described as 'a gold tip flowery broken orange pekoe,' costs 600 shillings per pound. The cup of tea served to the Aga Khan was infused in a large Tibetan teapot which was formerly the property of a Dalai Lama.

"It was appropriate that His Highness, who is the owner of many famous racehorses, should make a call at the Irish Pavilion. There he saw many photographs of Irish thoroughbreds, and the gold cup which he presented for international jumping, won outright by the Irish Army team.

"Along with Mr J. R. Richmond he visited the Palace of Art before motoring to the city to have lunch with the Lord Provost. Following the meeting in the Concert Hall the Aga Khan had tea in the royal apartments, after which he left for Eastwood, where he will be the guest until this evening of Viscount and Viscountess Weir. His Highness returned to the Exhibition to have dinner in the Atlantic Restaurant. To-day he will have no public engagements. He will probably play golf on one of the courses in the West of Scotland."

174

MAJOR PROBLEMS OF TODAY

Interview with the Associated Press of India

Karachi: 7 December 1938

Hindu-Muslim unity – the Palestine issue – League of Nations – the colonial question.

The bringing about of Hindu-Muslim unity has always been near my heart and I will strive my best in this direction before I leave India.

Referring to Palestine, His Highness envisaged the possibility of a settlement of the question at a big conference to be held shortly. He said that the whole Islamic world felt about it and a settlement was bound to come.

Regarding the European situation, His Highness said that there was no possibility of war at present.

"I feel," he added, "the League [of Nations] has received a very great blow by the recent happenings, but a new League will come up sooner or later, which will be joined even by Germany, though I am not sure of America. People have come to realise that peace is the only hope for man.

"The Colonial question is a very difficult one and India is very much interested on account of the Indian population in Tanganyika."

Source: *Star of India*, Calcutta, 8 December 1938.
The interview was given at the Aga Khan's arrival from Europe by the flying boat in the evening. The following morning he left Karachi for Gwalior.

175

THE ISSUES BEFORE THE BRITISH EMPIRE

Interview with the Star of India

Bombay: 11 December 1938

Prospects for federation between Indian provinces and Princely States poor – possible solution – proposal for transfer of Tanganyika to the Germans – disabilities on Indians in Kenya and South Africa – Palestine – the League of Nations.

His Highness the Aga Khan, who arrived in Bombay on Friday, is of the opinion that the prospects of the Federation of Indian Provinces with Indian States are now darker than ever.

He thinks from what he has learnt of the attitude of the Princes that the general opinion among them is not favourable to Federation.

Moreover the Congress is determined to fight Federation as envisaged in the Government of India Act, because in the Federal Legislature, the States will have representatives of the Rulers, and not elected representatives of the subjects.

The Princes, on the other hand, will not have any such representation, and are at present concerned over the recent agitation in several States.

A deadlock has thus been reached which makes the prospects of Federation extremely doubtful. If some representation were given to States' subjects in the Lower House in the Federal Legislature there would be, the Aga Khan believes, some prospect of acceptance of the Federal plan.

In a Press interview, His Highness said that he believed that if the rulers of Indian States introduced a system of election so that their representatives, at least in the Lower House of the Federal legislature, might to a great extent voice the wishes of the respective States, it would be one solution of the problem.

The alternative was for the provinces in British India to federate; then Federation with Indian States would come about in the course of time.

The Aga Khan was one of the first few who envisaged the scheme of an All-Indian Federation, and elaborated his plans in his book *India in Transition.* He also expressed his views 10 years ago in "The Times" in a series of articles.

The Aga Khan referred to the question of colonies and expressed himself against the transfer of Tanganyika to Germany.

He suggested that Indians in Tanganyika should send a strong delegation to India. On the question of Tanganyika His Highness has very strong views. He has numerous followers in that Colony and he has intimate knowledge of the conditions of Indians and others living there.

His Highness was firmly of the opinion that India must identify herself absolutely with the opinion of Indians in Tanganyika on the question of transfer of that colony to Germany.

"It is a question of life and death," he added. In the neighbouring British colony of Kenya, the Aga Khan said, Indians had experienced every kind of restriction, some of which were most humiliating. South Africa was closed to Indians. Other British colonies and Crown colonies had been according unfair treatment to Indians. Tanganyika was the only territory in the world where, thanks to the League, there was a mandatory system which admitted of fair chances to Indians in trade and commerce. In fact such a position of equality with the Europeans had not been enjoyed by Indians in their own country.

He asked whether one territory in the whole world where Indians could maintain their honour and their self-respect should also be allowed to cease to be so. The ideal solution would be the formation of smaller territories in Africa into mandated territories and to allow Germany to have equal opportunities there. That might not be possible until the democratic people in Europe became fully democratic and not merely rendered lip service to democracy.

Asked about the Round Table Conference convened by the British Government to consider the position of Arabs and Jews in Palestine, he said that the acceptance by Egypt of the invitation to attend the conference was a good augury. He knew that Egypt would not have agreed if she had known that the dice was loaded one way or the other. He thought that the representatives of the Grand Mufti of Palestine must attend the Conference, otherwise the talks were doomed to failure. Indian Muslims had shown a keen interest in the problem and one certainly thought that Indian Muslims should be represented at the conference, but there was no prospect of this.

His Highness did not see any immediate prospects of the rehabilitation of the League of Nations but he was convinced that within the next few years there would be a movement for a new League.

Source: *Star of India*, Calcutta, 12 December 1938.
The interview was given in Bombay to "our correspondent" on 11 December.

176

WAR OR PEACE

A Broadcast Talk

Bombay: 17 January 1939

Important historical events of the past – a world war would be a
catastrophe – the need to harness positive forces – the pooling of
the earth's resources for the welfare of mankind – the need for
mutual respect.

Let good assert itself. Let good come forward and insist on justice
and fair play. Let the civilised portions of the earth be ruled by
the principles of self-determination and nationality.

We are living in a period of exceptional interest and importance to humanity. The rise and fall of Alexander, of Rome, of
Persia and of other Empires, the conversion of Rome to Christianity, the rise of Islam, the Renaissance, the Mogul invasion, and
the ruin of Persia and Baghdad, the discovery of America, the
French revolution and its war and the recent Great War have all
been periods when the world's history changed its course as a
great river changes its bed. But a world war today such as is an
inevitable alternative to peace will be a far more terrible catastrophe than anything that could have happened in the past.

How easy it is to imagine a world war in which all the British
Dominions, including Great Britain herself, the United States of
America, France and Russia against Japan, Germany, Italy and
Spain – each and every one doing its utmost to destroy all the
others – a vision of hell on earth, the negation and defeat of
good by evil.

But there is no need, no reason, for such a world disaster. Let
good assert itself. Let good free itself from the whisperings of its
evil companions and the spirit of evil. Let good come forward
and insist on moral justice and fair play. Let the settled and

1171

civilised portion of the earth be ruled by the principles of self-determination and nationality. Let there be an end to the possession and direction of one race, one culture and one civilisation by another.

Doubtful areas could be adjusted by plebiscites and by exchanges of population . . .

Trade, travel, and communications should be as unrestricted as possible and all artificial and unnatural obstacles removed. The world failed because it failed to rectify the terrible and horrible injustices of the Versailles and Sevres treaties.

The so-called law of nations has been used to strengthen the title deeds of the "haves" against the "have-nots". One country has begun to rule over races that today are in revolt against the spirit of another race. But the triumph of the spirit of good and justice is to help forward today nationality and self-determination and the pooling of the earth's resources for the welfare of mankind without racial favour and partiality. Work on that must be the object of those who wish to save this world of ours from the terrible alternative of a world war which is the only thing that can come unless we respect every culture, every nationality, every desire even of the individual to be itself, even if it were but a small portion within any State.

Source: *The Times of India*, Bombay, 18 January 1939.
The address was broadcast in the evening from the Bombay station of the All India Radio. It was published by *The Times of India* under the double headline: "Saving World From Catastrophe: Aga Khan's Appeal."

177

THE IMPERATIVES OF ISLAMIC RESEARCH

Speech to the Islamic Research Association

Bombay: 18 January 1939

Need for a centre for Islamic research in Bombay – patronage of a few not sufficient – not a sectarian institution – research on Ummayad rule in Syria and Spain – art for art's sake – appeal for membership – open Islamic Book of the past to the world.

After the excellent speech of the Hon. Secretary, Mr. Fyzee, there is really very little for me to say. I agree with every word that he has said. He has put forward before you the very important reason why the Moslem population, first of this City, then of India generally and indeed of the world should concentrate on this great work. And in this great port from which the pilgrimage to Mecca from India and beyond India starts, from Bombay this great city half way between east and west, half way between Java and Algeria, in this great city, a great centre for Islamic Research work should be started.

I am so pleased with the work that you have done in the last few years that I double my subscription for the next year. (Cheers) But ladies and gentlemen, as your Hon. Secretary has just now said, for this work to succeed, the patronage of a few alone is not sufficient. We want a full and complete control of such an institution to belong to those who subscribe in it and they ought to be those Moslems who are interested in Islamic Civilization and the work of Islam, in the purity of its thought and deed and the greatness of its past, and we certainly believe in the greatness of its future.

Your Hon. Secretary has very rightly said that this is not a sectarian institution. I hope and believe that just as you were doing work in Islamic laws in the past, attention will now be turned on the work done by one of the greatest supports, one of the greatest foundation-stones of Islam, the work done by the Ommayiads both in Syria and Spain. It is right and proper that we should now recognise the greatness of that house and it is right and proper that their work for Islamic Civilization should come from this body in which Moslems of all sects are united. Let us also realise that the Islamic Civilization for the first time, almost even for the first time, appreciated art for art's sake, beauty for beauty's sake and literature for literature's sake, which did not receive full attention either in Greece or in Rome. In Islamic Culture and Islamic literature in its very best, it is art for art's sake, beauty for beauty's sake and culture for culture's sake, irrespective of its being religious, political or economic. Let that be understood.

It will be said that in these times of poverty and war, in this country where an overwhelming majority are hungry from birth till death, there is no time to give to art for art's sake. But gentlemen, it is this very fact of impoverishment which is necessary for the appreciation of art and to make the spirit of man well prepared for satisfaction and joy. In that spirit, ladies and gentlemen, I ask all of you to become, whether you are Muslims or Non-Muslims, interested in this institution. I appeal to you who come from outside of India, that in Europe, in Paris, in Berlin and I believe in Russia, the work of this institution is realized and fully appreciated. Well, let that be the case in India and Asia.

The leading Orientalists of Paris, Berlin, Rome and Vienna have told me how much they appreciate the work you are doing here. (Cheers). That little work must become great work. I thank Mr. Ivanow, Dr. Bazlur-Rehman and others who all have aided in this work; please try and become champions and propagandists in this cause.

Perhaps, it will be worth [the] President, if more occasions were to be given not so costly as this, but meetings held on Fridays and so on, where speeches may be given by gentlemen of learning, so that attention might be drawn to this work. But we cannot now let the matter once more slide back to the position in which it was started formerly but we must go on further and further to open the Islamic Book of the past to China and Europe, to east and to west.

Source: *Ismaili*, Bombay, 22 January 1939.
Full details of the background of this speech and some information about

the Islamic Research Association are contained in the *Ismaili* of 22 January and *The Times of India*, Bombay, of 19 January.

The account given by the *Ismaili* runs as follows:

"An 'at home' was held in honour of His Highness and Begum Aga Khan by Mr. Ali Mahomed Mecklai, President, Islamic Research Association at his residence, Mecklai Mansion at Warden Road on Wednesday afternoon.

"The 'at home' was attended by the elite of Bombay, the consuls for Muslim countries, Sir Hormazdiar and Lady Dastur, Mr. D. N. D. Khandalawalla, Chief Presidency Magistrate and Mrs. Khandalawalla, Mr. and Mrs. I. S. Hajee, Dr. and Mrs. Bazlur Rehman, Dr. Daudpotta, Mr. Sultan Chinoy, Mayor of Bombay and Mrs. Chinoy, several prominent European residents of Bombay, Mukhi Hasanbhai Laljee Dewraj, Mr. Ramzanali Ibrahim, Khan Bahadur, Kamdia Kassamali Hassanali, Mr. and Mrs. Alarakhia Sonawalla, Rai Gulamhusein Bundally Somjee, Varas Ahmedbhoy Mohamed of Nairobi, Mr. Gulamali G. Merchant, Alijah Abdulla Hasan Samji of Zanzibar, Mr. and Mrs. Faiz B. Tyebji and others.

"Covers were laid for about 140 guests. His Highness and Begum Aga Khan on arrival, were received by Major Mecklai who in the course of a welcome speech said:

" 'It gives us great pleasure to welcome Your Highness and Her Highness the Begum Saheba among us today. It is a great honour which Your Highnesses have done to us and which we deeply appreciate and will try to be worthy of it. Also, we are most grateful for the keen interest Your Highness has shown in the activities and progress of our Association and are greatly indebted for the princely annual grant of Rs. 1,000 which, I am glad to say, is conditional on our deserving its continuance on the merits of our work and I do venture to hope that we have not disappointed you.

" 'I do not wish to take more time of Your Highnesses and the guests but would say that we have been fortunate enough to have published seven works during the last five years. These works have been well received and applauded by the international world scholarship. I will now, with your Highnesses' permission request our Hon. Secretary, Mr. Fyzee, to state briefly what he has to say. He has worked selflessly for our Association and before I take my seat, let me publicly acknowledge the invaluable services of my learned colleagues, Dr. Rehman, Dr. Daudpota, Messrs. Ivanow, Saif Tyebji and Asaf Fyzee to the cause of Islamic research.'

Mr. Asaf A. Fyzee then spoke as follows:

" 'We must remember that this is an "At Home" and not a meeting of the Islamic Research Association, and I shall therefore try to be as brief as is possible under the present circumstances.

" 'I join with your president in extending a most cordial welcome to our patron, His Highness The Aga Khan and Her Highness The Begum Aga Khan on behalf of the members of the Association. His Highness has not only been a patron in name, but a helper and a friend which is of very great importance to the work of the Association.

" 'On the 25th February 1935, His Highness as one of our patrons, in presiding over a special general meeting of the Islamic Research Association, offered us an annual donation of Rs. 1000 – telling us at the same time that if we deserved it, he would continue it, but if we were undeserving of it, he would altogether decrease it or stop it. And today, I have the privilege on behalf of this Association to request Your Highness to say that the confidence which Your

Highness placed in us was well placed, and the work which we have done merits the powerful patronage of Your Highness.

" 'This Association was started in 1933 and on completion of its five years' existence, our president, Mr. Mecklai, summed up the ideals for which the Association stands, in a speech which was widely circulated at the time. It will bear repetition to say that the aims and objects of this Association are to further the cause of Islamic Research by all possible means and that this Association has nothing to do with politics or with religious propaganda. We do not put forward the religion of Islam for the acceptance of non Muslims; neither do we interest ourselves in any religious controversy. We say that Islam has produced a great civilization, that this civilization should be studied critically and its study fostered in a scientific way.

" 'I wish to clear two misunderstandings that have grown up during these years. On account of the great interest and patronage of His Highness, it is suggested that this is an Ismaili organization. I need only state that it is for you to see how absurd this notion is. This Association stands for the study of all branches of Islamic learning. It has nothing to do with any sect or nationality.

" 'The other great misunderstanding which has been created is that the Association is a purely literary and scholarly organization meant only for scholars, and for this reason several people have in modesty refused to join it.

" 'I wish to say publicly that this Association is not restricted to scholars but any educated person, whatever his religion and nationality, who wishes to further its cause is welcome to join it.

" 'During the course of the last years, we have published seven works, four in Persian dealing with religious subjects, two in Arabic – one dealing with Sufism and the other with history, and one in Urdu dealing with Arab Navigation. It is, therefore, quite clear that we have published a good number of research works, and we have not restricted ourselves to one subject, one language or one particular group of sects. Our works have been reviewed and re-reviewed in the most eulogistic terms in all the foremost orientalistic journals and I must particularly mention the reviews of Prof. Nicholson in the Journal of the Royal Asiatic Society of London, praising the first four publications of our Association. They have also been reviewed very favourably by many other journals.

" 'This is the work we have done. What about the future? I know it is only a dream, but on occasions like these, you must permit me to dream about the future.

" 'We must not remain satisfied with the fostering of critical research, but we must try to build up an institute of Islamic studies on a wider basis and make Bombay a centre of Islamic Research. We must promote a library and we must have a journal. All this will come, I hope, by the patronage of His Highness The Aga Khan but much more by the work of our own members.

" 'Today efforts to preserve what is best in any particular civilization should merit the support of all those who desire that the forces of humanity should prevail over the brute in man. This ugly force is again rising rapidly in the rearmament question, and the greed for power which is displayed all over the world. It is better to read books than forge gigantic machines to destroy human life and culture; and for the protection and preservation of Islamic civilization, which is only one phase of human civilization in general, I ask you to give your support to our modest efforts.' "

The *Times of India* report is shorter but furnishes some new information:

"A fervent appeal to support the cause of Islamic research was made by His

Highness the Aga Khan at an "at home" given in his honour by Mr. Ali Mahomed Mecklai, President of the Islamic Research Association, at Mecklai Mansion, Warden Road, Bombay, on Wednesday evening. His Highness announced that he had decided to contribute to the Association Rs. 2,000, annually instead of Rs. 1000.

"Mr. Mecklai, in welcoming His Highness and Begum Aga Khan, expressed gratitude for the interest they had shown in the activities of the association. The association, which had now completed five years of its existence, had so far published seven works, which had been well received by international scholars.

"Mr. A. A. A. Fyzee, Honorary Secretary of the association, welcomed the Aga Khan not only as a patron but also as a friend whose valuable annual grant had helped the institution a great deal. He was glad that the confidence placed in them was justified by the work.

"Mr. Fyzee narrated the history of the association during the last five years. Its aim was the furtherance of scientific research in all aspects of Islamic civilization. They wanted to develop critical research and not merely pile up one work after another. It did not want to carry on any religious or political propaganda or controversy.

"Mr. Fyzee wanted to remove the impression entertained in certain quarters that the association was an Ismaili organisation.

"Referring to the future work of the association, Mr. Fyzee said it wanted to foster research, build up an institute, have a library and also a journal of their own. He hoped that it would be possible for them to realise in the not very distant future what looked like a dream today, and they would have in Bombay a centre for understanding Islam in all its phases."

178

MUSLIMS AND THE SECOND WORLD WAR

Message to the Muslims of the British Empire

Simla and London: 28 September 1939

Muslims urged to co-operate with the British in the War.

To all my brothers in India and other British Dominions: To-day a cruel war has been imposed and it is our duty to co-operate with heart and soul for the success of His Majesty the King-Emperor. Such sincere and complete co-operation will also be the best service to Islam.

I beg my brothers in Islam to realise that alike our secular duty and the best way to serve Muslim interests is by completely loyal co-operation with His Majesty's Government. Both my only grown-up son and myself have placed all our personal services at the Viceroy's disposal.

Source: *The Civil and Military Gazette*, Lahore, 30 September 1939.
    Datelined "Simla, Sept. 28", the Associated Press of India's dispatch merely said that "the following message has today been released by H. H. the Aga Khan here and in Europe".
    For the Second World War and the Muslims of India see Muhammad Zafrullah Khan, *India and the War: An Address*, n.p., n.d. (?1940); Indian National Congress, *Congress and War Crisis*, Allahabad, 1940; *India and the War*, London, May 1941 (Union of Democratic Control); P. R. Lele (ed.), *War and India's Freedom*, Bombay, 1940; White Papers bearing command numbers Cmd. 6121 (1939), 6129 (1939), 6196 (1940), 6219 (1940), 6235 (1940), 6293 (1941); Abdullah Anwar Beg, "Muslim League and the War", *The Civil and Military Gazette*, 27 September 1939; Mirza Abdul Aziz Beg, "India and War", *The Civil and Military Gazette*, 13 June 1939; Wedgwood Benn, "The War and India's Freedom", *Contemporary Review*, December 1939; "India and the War Aims", *The Times*, 18 October 1939; J. C. French, "India and the War", *National Review*, December 1939; "India and the War", *Round Table*, December 1939; "India and the War", *The Times*, 5 December 1939; Muhammad Zafrullah Khan, "India and the War", *Listener*, 23 November 1939; Iqbal Ali Shah, "Indian Muslims and

the War", *Great Britain and the East,* 21 December 1939; Abdullah Yusuf Ali, "The Muslims of India, the War and the Political Field", *Asiatic Review,* April 1940; J. C. French, "India's War Effort", *National Review,* May 1941; "India and the War", *Round Table,* December 1941; "The War and Indian Politics", *Round Table,* September 1941; "India: War and Politics", *Round Table,* September 1942; Mumtaz Daultana, "Muslim League and War Effort", *The Civil and Military Gazette,* 24 May and 10 June 1944; and L. S. Amery, "Indian Constitutional Development: The War Years", *Asian Review,* October 1953.

179

A CONSTITUENT ASSEMBLY FOR INDIA

Interview with the Press

Bombay: 8 February 1940

Constituent assembly as a possible solution of the constitutional deadlock.

The Aga Khan said that the majority of Englishmen would welcome a settlement with India but there was still a diehard minority in England. He declined to express any opinion with regard to the Congress attitude which had culminated in the resignation of the Congress Ministries but reiterated the view that in his opinion Sardar Patel's suggestion of a constituent assembly composed of members of Central and provincial Legislatures had at last opened the door to a possible understanding between Hindus and Muslims, between British India and the Indian States and finally with the British Government.

Asked whether he would meet Mr. Gandhi and other leaders in the country with a view to solving the dead-lock he said: "I am not a member of the Congress or the Muslim League nor of any legislature. But as a life-long student of politics, as one who has had some practical experience, if any responsible body calls for my opinion or advice, I shall be ready to place my services at their disposal."

Source: *The Civil and Military Gazette*, Lahore, 10 February 1940.
The suggestion referred to by the Aga Khan had been made by Sardar Vallabhbhai Patel on 3 February at a public meeting in Surat. Patel had explained the Congress demand and had added that the Congress wanted the undiluted right for Indians to frame their own constitution through a constituent assembly. If a constituent assembly elected by an electorate based on adult franchise was considered impracticable, a substitute, such as a constituent assembly elected on the basis of the current provincial franchise, would do, provided that the assembly was given the sole right of framing India's consti-

tution without outside interference and further provided that in case of a difference arising out of any communal issue resort would be to arbitration.

On the very controversial issue of the creation of a constituent assembly as a step towards the complete independence of India see D. R. Gadgil, *The Federal Problem in India*, Poona, 1947; J. G. Narang, *Constituent Assembly and Our Demand*, Lahore, 1940; K. P. Mallikarjunudu, *Constituent Assembly and its Work*, Bombay, n.d. (?1946); G. N. Singh, *The Constituent Assembly*, Lahore, n.d. (?1946); J. B. Durkal, *Conservative India*, Ahmedabad, 1941; K. M. Munshi, *A New Outlook*, Lahore, 1947; A. K. Azad, *India Wins Freedom: An Autobiographical Narrative*, Bombay, 1959; Iftikharul Huq, *Pakistan and Constituent Assembly*, Lahore, n.d.; *Proceedings of the Indian Legislative Assembly*, New Delhi, 17 September 1937; A Muslim Correspondent, "What Muslim India Thinks", *The Civil and Military Gazette*, 18 December 1933, and 8 July and 7 August 1934; "Opposition in India", *The Times*, 15 January 1937; "What is a Constituent Assembly? Empty Nature of Congress Demand", *The Civil and Military Gazette*, 11 April 1937; Shafaat Ahmad Khan, "The Constituent Assembly", *20th Century*, December 1939; Gulshan Rai, "A Constituent Assembly", *The Civil and Military Gazette*, 5 December 1939; Muhammad Azam, "A Constituent Assembly", *The Civil and Military Gazette*, 8 March 1940; "The Political Dilemma in India", *Round Table*, March 1940; and Kerr Fraser-Tytler, "The Great Betrayal", *National Review*, December 1946.

His Highness Aga Khan III presiding at the League of Nations. He was elected the League's President in 1937.

Aga Khan III at the League of Nations.

Aga Khan III: A Portrait.

Aga Khan III with Mahatma Gandhi and Mrs Sarojini Naidu in London during the
Round Table Conference of 1931.

The Aga Khan offering prayers at a Muslim League function in Johannesburg, 1945.

Aga Khan III laying a wreath at the mausoleum of Quaid-i-Azam, Muhammad Ali Jinnah in Karachi.

His Highness the Aga Khan and the Governor General of Pakistan, Mr Ghulam Mohammed. Mr M. Ikramullah, Ambassador of Pakistan in France, is in the centre.

His Highness the Right Honourable Sir Sultan Muhammad Shah Aga Khan.

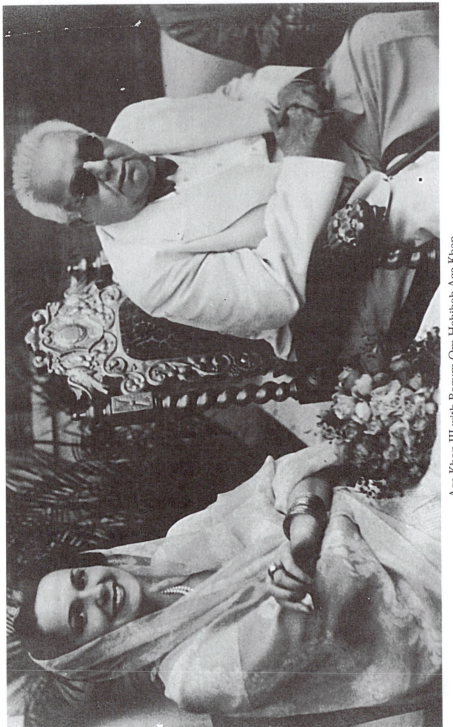

Aga Khan III with Begum Om Habibeh Aga Khan.

Aga Khan III: A Portrait c. 1956.

CONCERN FOR HUMAN VALUES

Message on the Occasion of the Opening of a New Mosque in London

Zurich: 1 August 1941

Good wishes for the Muslims – hopes for a better world.

The Aga Khan telegraphed from Zurich expressing his happiness on the opening of the Mosque and added, "My prayers join yours for victory and justice and human values, also that Moslems may enjoy their rights in the new world of equity."

Source: *The Times*, London, 8 August 1941.

The mosque in East London was opened on 1 August (reported by *The Times* of 2 August). Sir Hasan Suhrawardy was the chairman of the Committee of the Mosque. He also received a telegram from the Chief of the Royal Cabinet in Cairo conveying the best wishes of the King of Egypt and his prayers for the welfare and glory of Islam (*The Times*, 8 August).

THE RELIGIOUS REVIVAL OF ISLAM

An Article (with Dr Zaki Ali)

Lahore: 1944

Islam at a turning point in its history – reasons for Islam's supremacy as a universal religion – the problem of religious revival – a liberal interpretation of Muslim law required – flexibility of Muslim law – inspiration from the Quran – Traditions of the Prophet – religious and moral education – religious unity of all believers – technical and economic progress of Muslims – the Quran and nature – genuine Islam in agreement with reason – use of technical and mechanical genius of the West – co-operative Muslim enterprise for economic development of Muslim lands – social progress, political freedom and world peace – spread of Islamic culture in India, Africa and the Dutch Indies – Pan-Islamism – unfounded fear of Islam among Christians – Muslim centres of culture – Islam has no aggressive intentions against other religions and peoples – aspirations of modern Islam.

Nowadays, Islam must be looked upon as being at a turning point in its history. Islam, whose faith is extremely powerful and unshakable [*sic*], owes its supremacy as a universal religion to its spiritual forces. Endowed with a remarkable power of adaptability to the conditions and necessities of different ages and spaces, its spirit exceeds the narrow framework of a purely literal interpretation of its laws and codes.

Among the vital and very serious problems, with which Muslims are faced today, is that of religious revival. There is a growing recognition among Muslims that they must show themselves to be alive to the present, facing forward and feeling responsibility for the future. In accordance with the Muslim principle of *Ijma'* (i.e. the majority of opinion of the learned doctors of the Islamic religion), Muslim jurists (*Fuqaha*), savants (*Ulama*), and doctors of Muslim Law can gather together to discuss the religious problems affecting the welfare of Muslim peoples around the world. . .

. . . It must not be forgotten that, according to the principle of *Ijma'* already mentioned, the interpretation of the precepts and laws which regulate the lives of the Faithful, as laid down in the Quran and in the Traditions of the Prophet, can be done at any time and for any generation. Such an interpretation, by means of the *Ijtihad* which is a personal and living research, can be made, within the general limits of the Quran and Traditions. The suppleness of Muslim Law enhances its value, and its broad lines leave room for vigorous growth and adaptation to the changing and unforeseeable circumstances of international life. Muslim Law must, therefore, be freed of the rigid character, given to it by ancient codifications. It would be erroneous to assume that the door to interpretation has been shut, because the four leading juridical schools of Muslim orthodoxy had already decided, for all time, as to the prescriptions of Muslim Law. Even with regard to these four schools (Hanafite, Shafi'ite, Malikite and Hanbalite), an individual Muslim is free to choose among them the rules to follow on different points; and to do that, he may not be obliged to strictly adhere to a single school. The practical result of this universally admitted freedom is quite obvious; it simplifies the carrying on of law and more easily meets modern conditions of life. As regards the Quran, we stress the fact, that to be better understood – without being blindly attached to the exegesis of ancient authorities – it would inspire Muslims to a revival of religious thought and action. The Traditions and Sayings of the Prophet are to be seriously and critically studied with a view to freeing them from posterior deviations and infiltrations. As regards the four juridical schools, we may point out that their divergences are of little importance, and there are no antagonisms between them.

It is, therefore, necessary to seek, again, a direct contact with the Quran and with the authentic Traditions, and thus secure a doctrinal and moral purification. It is also necessary to eliminate from the beliefs all popular superstitions. Educational reform is one of the fundamentals of Renaissance, we mean religious and moral education. And as it is essential to re-establish the religious unity of the *Ummat* (the nation of Believers) a real *rapprochement* and consequent union between Sunnites and Shi'ites should be aimed at and worked for. Even a unification of the four juridical schools, which exist within the orthodoxy itself, may be realised.

A tremendously powerful and unshakable [*sic*] religious unity may thus be achieved . . .

Any neglect in this supreme task would entail a serious problem for Islam. Muslim youth might be led astray and would risk, in modern times of materialistic Western civilisation, clashing doctrines and spiritual confusion, becoming agnostic, sceptic or influenced through atheist writings. The older members of the community would have neither the energy nor the necessary power to bring about, alone, the desired religious revival by means of a general and collective movement. This is an issue too vital and too serious to permit of neglect.

As far as technical and economic progress is concerned, we admit that Muslim countries are, in fact, one or even two centuries behind Western Christendom in this material domain. Muslims are much to blame in this respect, because they have neglected the injunctions of the Quran to discover all the secrets of nature and fully utilise its immense resources. In fact, Islam encourages its followers to study and dominate it economically. Says the Quran: "Behold! In the creation of the Heavens and Earth, and the alternation of the Night and the Day, there are indeed signs for men of understanding." – S. iii, 190. "Seest thou not that God has made subject to you (men) all that is on the Earth . . ." – S. xxii, 65. "It is God Who has subjected the sea to you, that ships may sail through by His command, that ye may seek of His bounty, and that ye may be grateful. And He has subjected to you, as from Him, all that is in the Heavens and on the Earth: behold, in that are signs indeed for those who reflect." – S. xlv, 12–13 . . .

Awakened Islam strongly aspires to religious revival, a revival worthy of the great periods of its glorious history. Religion, then, would have found its primitive vigour, liberated, as it should be, from a fixed static juridism and theology. Without danger, Islam would become able to occupy itself with modern sciences and material inventions, which today make the power of the West and cause its material superiority over the Muslim world. Genuine Islam is in perfect agreement with reason, and none of the real acquisitions of reason can be contrary to it. It is able to assimilate modern sciences and methods, without allowing them to interfere with the Faith and Muslim tradition. It would be able to catch up with the obstacles which separate it from the Western world and to undertake a fertile and efficient reorganisation in all domains. This reorganisation will not only be spiritual, but also material, in order to assure to the Muslim peoples a complete

economic and industrial equipment and a technical independence, without which no permanent national satisfaction may be
attained . . .

[We must] . . . emphasise the necessity of mastering the economic resources of nature, as the Western nations have already
accomplished. Awakened Islam will learn to make use of the
mechanical and technical genius of the West.

The little developed but vast tracts of land in various Muslim
countries in Asia and Africa, if their resources were exploited by
means of co-operative Muslim enterprise along modern scientific
lines, could certainly help to remove the destitution, hunger and
economic distress existing in a terrible state among many Muslim
peoples. The ensuing social progress will particularly help to
relieve the rural masses of their deep state of misery, for their
material conditions of existence will be greatly improved. In this
connection, modern and efficient sanitation and hygiene should
be widely applied. Physical fitness and mental ability are necessary
conditions of progress. This economic and social progress would
constitute an important factor towards permanent political
freedom of the Muslim people. It is our belief that a free and
progressive Muslim world, a land which commands the very
centre of the world's inter-continental traffic, and which possesses
an important wealth in raw materials will constitute an important
stabilising factor in the world peace of tomorrow. Its freedom
will constitute the best guarantee against conflicts and rivalries
between the Great World Powers of tomorrow . . .

[There is a need to] . . . encourage and work out the best
measures of Muslim activity for spreading Islamic culture both
in India and in Africa. As for India, the Indian Muslim community might be able to carry out this task among the non-
Muslims. But, unfortunately, in Africa, the local Muslim populations are very weak and backward, culturally, economically and
socially. They cannot stand alone against the onslaught of the
numerous Christian Churches, let alone the question of the conversion of other African races to Islam. Unless we look seriously
and quickly to the African Muslims, the same tragedy which had
happened in the past in Muslim Spain, during the Islamic period,
would repeat itself in Muslim Africa. A supreme duty claims us
to avert such a disaster. We should organise efficient help and
proper religious education by means of well selected and able
missions to those regions. The spread of Islamic education among
them is fundamental. Again, similar missions ought to be sent to
the vast Muslim regions of the Dutch Indies . . .

Pan-Islamism is a real heritage of every Muslim. Every true Muslim must be a Pan-Islamist. But by Pan-Islamism we do not mean political Pan-Islamism such as was practised by Sultan Abdul Hamid of Turkey. We mean a spiritual union of Muslims, a religious and moral unity of the Muslim peoples all over the world, and a consolidation of Muslim solidarity and an up-to-date social and economic outlook.

It has always been the foolish, unfortunate and unfounded political fear of Islam more than that of Hinduism or Buddhism that caused the Christian nations to continuously attack Islam and to belittle the life of the Prophet, exposing it to false and libellous interpretation. Churches were deliberately garbling and maliciously raising prejudices against Islam. We cannot allow this false propaganda to go unchallenged. As an antidote to this flood against Islam, staunch efforts should be made to set up Muslim centres of culture in an increasing number all over the lands of Islam. This is a vast field in which the intervention and activity on the part of Muslim States is essential . . .

There is nothing menacing or antagonistic in Muslim revival to the happy evolution of other communities. Islam has no aggressive intention or plan of violence against other world religions or peoples, either socially or materially. For we Muslims believe that mankind should live as one great family. We respect other communities. But we wish to raise ourselves to the standard of modern and advanced nations, and to protect ourselves from the disintegrating forces that threaten to keep us behind and constitute a serious obstacle to our full development. Only thus will it be possible for Muslim countries to take their worthy place in the rebuilding of the post-war world and to render the highest services to mankind.

Source: Prince Aga Khan and Dr. Zaki Ali, *Glimpses of Islam*, Shaikh Muhammad Ashraf, Lahore, first published 1944, 2nd enlarged edn 1954, repr. 1961, 1965, 1973, pp. 72–83.

The book has four chapters: "The Fundamentals of Islam" by the Aga Khan (pp. 1–10), "Islam and Medieval Sciences" by Dr Zaki Ali (pp. 11–58), "Islam and Mental Health" by Dr Zaki Ali (pp. 59–71), and "Religious Revival of Islam" by the Aga Khan and Dr. Zaki Ali (pp. 72–83). It carries a two-page Foreword in which the authors say: "The post-war period affords an excellent opportunty for international co-operation and progress.

"In the organisation of peace, the Islamic world is likely to be a strong stabilising factor. Mutual understanding between the nations is essential to the desired co-operation and our purpose in writing this small book is to promote this understanding. . .

"We believe that Islam has a brilliant future, and we wish to see the future of Muslims shaped to the spirit of Islam. A free and progressive Muslim world is essential, not only for the mutual advantage of the Muslim peoples, but for the maintenance of the peace of tomorrow and for the common good of humanity."

182

LOOKING TOWARDS THE POST-WAR WORLD

Interview with The East African Standard

Nairobi: 26 March 1945

Impressive developments in Kenya – advance in education –
training to adapt to new conditions – avoid mistakes of India –
need for practical education – local Indians and agriculture –
possibilities of agriculture in the Lake area – future of the world
with Britain, America and the Soviet Union – British should not
adhere to the old idea of a "White Commonwealth" – ideal of a
triple Commonwealth – oil in Arab countries – hopes from the
Arab League – all the three parties in India can find a common
denominator.

Dealing first with the changes he had observed in East Africa
since his last visit, he said that he had been strongly impressed
with the nature of the development which indicated great hopefulness in the future of the Colony. "My recent impression of
Nairobi," he said, "is that everything has been tidied up to a
great extent; large and permanent buildings and other developments all indicate optimism in future prospects and already you
have the basis of a capital of a great and thriving country.

"It is, also, noticeable that both the Indian and indigenous
communities are better dressed, look to be better fed and generally more prosperous than they were seven years ago. The chief
impression seems to be a note of optimism in the future."

His Highness has always taken a keen interest in education
problems and when last in East Africa laid down general lines of
policy and development for his own followers, the members
of the Ismailia community.

"I have already noticed a great advance in this direction," he
said, "and I hope that much more will be done during the next

eight years. This advance should not, in my view, be so much along the lines of what is termed 'book learning' as in training which will enable those receiving such training to adapt themselves to new conditions. We do not want here a repetition of what I regard as the curse of India – graduates who earn less than a syce; men who cannot make use of the education they have received and who are unable to adapt themselves to other work.

"The emphasis should be upon agricultural, technical and vocational training; turning out useful citizens with a sound, practical training behind them, as well as the more academic aspects of an education. There are many avenues that could be profitably followed, rather than adding to the numbers of commercial and clerical workers with which the community is overburdened.

"I consider there is ample scope in agriculture. The country needs and could easily support a larger agrarian population. There is still much land undeveloped; in the Lake area, for instance, there is much rich land still untouched and it is possible that on demobilisation many more Indian husbandmen could be accommodated. In this connexion, I have Tanganyika particularly in mind. There is far more scope for further agricultural development there than in Kenya and the indigenous population is comparatively small in relation to areas awaiting development once they can be opened up, provided with water and cleared of fly, and so on.

"While advocating that the Indian community should go in much more widely for agriculture, I am not advocating opening the door to agriculturalists from India, but that more local Indians should take the opportunities which offer for settling on the land. In my view there are as many Indians here as these countries can, at the present moment and in the present circumstances, accommodate economically at this stage of their development. But given a proper start in good conditions I think Indians on the land could be a great asset to these territories."

It is understood that His Highness will remain in East Africa for several months, during which he intends to visit the four territories (Kenya, Uganda, Tanganyika and Zanzibar). He stated, however, that no cut and dried programme had been arranged. "My movements and my programme," he said, "depend more on the wishes and needs of my local spiritual children than upon myself. They will, naturally, think first of my comfort and health,

1190

but as they make the arrangements I shall carry them out to the best of my ability."

His Highness had some particularly interesting things to say on the broader international issues facing the world at the present time. He was, in 1937–39, President of the Assembly of the League of Nations, but did not feel that he could express any view on the possible revival of the League in a new or revised form. He did not, however, visualise a return to the League yet.

"I think the immediate future of the world lies with the 'Big Three' – Britain, America and the Soviet Union. If they work together in their true self-interest – and I think their own interests will make them work together – then there will be peace and, possibly, prosperity. If they work together for selfish reasons, only, I think there will be peace and some prosperity as well, but much unhappiness, also.

"I visualise that France, too, will be invited to share in this partnership and if the partners honestly believe in and work towards the welfare of the small and weak nations, as well as for themselves, and give to these other nations the same opportunities as they would wish for themselves, I foresee a far brighter future. I should be able to say that a good world was coming after a bad one and could die a happy man.

"I emphasise working in their true and real self-interest, for this implies the best interests of the world as a whole. It must be evident, with all the millions involved in China and India, for example, that any economic set up which did not take cognisance of these people and which left them too poor to buy on the world markets would again lead to collapse.

"As a life-long friend of Britain and a loyal subject of the King-Emperor I am convinced that in this partnership of the 'Big Three' there are only two possible places for her – she can be first, or third, according to the policy adopted by her leaders. If, in their conception of a world order, they adhere to the old idea of a 'White Commonwealth' – that is Britain, Canada, Australia, New Zealand and South Africa – then I do not think they will have either the population or the wealth to be as important a factor in the partnership as America or Russia.

"America is a creditor nation with a highly developed industry and a big population. Russia is another great entity and her sphere of influence is likely to include Turkey, Hungary, Czechoslovakia and the Balkans, also. Both, in wealth and indigenous populations, would be more powerful than what is termed the 'White Commonwealth.'

"What I hope for, and would like to see, would be a triple commonwealth. One would be the White Commonwealth (Britain, Canada, Australia, New Zealand and South Africa); the second would be a commonwealth of Britain and the Muslim world (Cyrenaica, Egypto-Sudan, Saudi Arabia, the Yemen, Iraq, Syria, the Lebanon, Trans-Jordan, Muscat and Bahrein); the third would consist of Britain and India, Ceylon, Burma, and possibly Malaya. You can call them what you will, commonwealths, confederations, or what name seems most suitable, but they would have this in common, complete equality and freedom within the commonwealth, or confederation. Nominally they would be equal; in practice Britain would necessarily take a leading part.

"I do not believe it is possible to get a homogenous and harmonious mixture of all peoples of whatever colour, caste or creed in one, single commonwealth, but each of them, with Dominion status or its equivalent, could work together in their own and in their common interest; they could have a common foreign policy, for instance, in the same way as they have agreed upon a common war policy. There are other and innumerable ways in which they could work for their own, and at the same time, each others' interests.

"I regard this as a practical and sound solution of the problems of the future for it would have the benefit of bringing in willing partners who would work together by virtue of the fact that their own interests would, also, be the interests of the whole. It is, I am convinced, the only real solution as there can be no workable political compromise unless the partners are willing partners and free to choose for themselves. Anything on the lines of the old Imperialism will, I am convinced, break down sooner or later."

His Highness had some interesting things to say on two other important issues. The first concerned the recent Conference in Cairo of the Arab countries, in which Egypt, too took a prominent part. "I take an especial interest in this matter," said His Highness, "and I think it provides a great opportunity for Britain, who is on cordial terms with the Arabian countries, to bring peace and a settled prosperity to the Middle East.

"There has been a complete revolution in the economy of many Arabian countries in the last 30 years which – due to the discovery of oil and the likely presence of still larger, undiscovered deposits – have risen from being among the poorest to some of the potentially richest countries, relative to their size and population, in the world; Saudi Arabia, Iran and Bahrein all have tremendous possibilities. The Sheikh of Bahrein, for example, draws something like a million sterling a year in oil royalties alone. Saudi Arabia is, potentially, even richer.

"I have the greatest optimism in and hope of [sic] the Arab League. It was bound to come sooner or later, and it is better that it should come now. For the present Kings of the Arabian countries, and for the King and statesmen of Egypt, I have the greatest admiration and, as a power for stable and prosperous conditions, I shall give the Arab League all the encouragement that is in my humble power."

On the subject of India, His Highness was not quite so optimistic. "I have not been in India for some time and am, therefore, not so conversant with current affairs as otherwise I might be. But I am convinced that, ultimately, the people of India alone are the only ones who can solve their political difficulties, which cannot be resolved by any outside source whatever.

"It has been suggested that Britain should make an immediate announcement to the effect that a year after the end of hostilities, power in India should be handed over to the Indian political parties provided that they reach agreement between themselves. Failing this agreement, Britain, it has been suggested, should make an award to India of Dominion status by Act of Parliament and draw up a constitution, according to British ideas.

"I cannot deprecate the latter suggestion too strongly; it would be the ultimate humiliation. You cannot force ideals on a people from without and it would be far preferable for Britain herself to insist upon retaining governing power and responsibility, as at present, than to try and force her essentially foreign ideals permanently on India's growth. This must come from the people of India themselves, and among these I include those English people who have made their permanent homes in India. If India showed, in the event, that it was incapable of governing itself, it would be a different matter altogether. But to impose a constitution from without would violate the self-respect of all parties.

"Personally, I feel most strongly that with goodwill and ordinary commonsense, all parties – the Congress, the Muslim League, and the Indian Princes – could find a common denominator to the satisfaction of all three main exponents. Each party would, undoubtedly, have to make some concessions in order to ensure the general good, but I think that is quite possible and, in fact, essential if the political problems of India are to be solved."

Source: *The East African Standard*, Nairobi, 27 March 1945.

The newspaper does not mention the date on which the interview took place; I presume that it did a day before its publication. The Aga Khan was on his first visit to East Africa after eight years. The paper carried the report of the interview under a three-column headline: "Aga Khan's views on world affairs", with a secondary two-column headline: "Foresees big future for East Africa."

It added:

"It is almost exactly eight years since His Highness was last in East Africa and in that time the whole world structure had undergone a greater or lesser degree of transformation everywhere. His Highness has been in close touch with the West and the Middle East during those years and his observations are founded not alone on wide experience, but, also, upon a more than unusually informed knowledge of the trend of events."

183

THE FUTURE OF ISLAM IN
EAST AFRICA – I

*Reply to the Address of Welcome from the East African Muslim
Conference*

Mombasa: 16 June 1945

No political ambition – no ill-will towards any other faith or religion
– tribute to Christian missionaries – local Muslims will have to
answer one question: "What did you do to save Islam in Central
Africa?" – past glory of Islam – help the Africans, Arabs, Swahilis
and Somalis – the practical solution – a permanent organization –
cultivate the African Muslim allies – help them to become leaders
– send African Muslims abroad for education – mosques with
schools – general education – propagate Islam – financial pledge
– gratitude to Prince Badru.

Dr. Rana, Ladies and Gentlemen:

First of all I must thank you and thank Hon'ble Shams-ud-
Deen for his speech of welcome. It is a great honour and also a
great pleasure for me to meet you here to-day and preside at this
meeting. Before I proceed further I may say that I am not going
to make a speech: I am going to stick to the job for which we
have met here. Before I proceed I want to make it perfectly clear
as my friend Mr Shams-ud-Deen has said here that we have no
political ambition. No doubt, we all in other walks of life touch
politics but in connection with this conference and in this
assembly and for the purposes of the organization we have in
mind to form, politics are barred. Also I must make it clear that
we have not met here in any spirit of ill-will towards any other
faith or religion. Certainly, I have been greatly influenced and, I
am sure most of you may have been influenced, by the vast efforts
that the honourable members of the Christian Faith have made

in their propagation. They have made great sacrifices mentally, physically and financially during the last 150 years. That offers an object lesson for us and I hope it is nothing more than paying flattery to them by imitating them. With these words, gentlemen! I shall proceed with the objects for which we have met.

Well! It is going to be a very simple one. I am going to put to every one of you here, without exception, one simple question – a question which I have very often put to myself. This question, which I had put to myself, I am as convinced as I am sitting here and facing you, I am sure, will be put to you as it will be put to me on the Day of Judgment. To those of you who doubt it, and there may be some, I do not put this question; they can go ahead in their own old way; but to those who are convinced as I am convinced that there is such a day, I will ask them to prepare for the answer properly; otherwise they will be sorry for having allowed one good question go unanswered . . . You will have no mistakes; but to this question everyone of you shall have to answer. This will be the final and decisive question and on this you will fall or you will be saved. This is what will be the question: "What did you do to save Islam in Central Africa?" Mr. Shams-ud-Deen, when he referred to the greater glory of Islam has forgotten Islamic history of Spain in the past 1,400 years. Islam was once in ascendent glory there and reigned supreme for more than 600 years. He forgot what befell to Islam there and in Andulas and in Sicily from where it has now disappeared alto-gether. And if you do not wake up now – this is the last opportunity – history may repeat itself here also. I am sure that Islam will not end in Central Africa. In Juba, Sudan, a Hindu gentleman begged me: "This is your country and you make no effort." Well! If you have to save Islam in this part of the world, you should help and raise the Africans, Arabs, Swahilis, and Somalis. The reason why I insist on this is not because they are Africans but because they need it more. We must give help to those who are most exposed to danger. If worse comes to worse, Indians can go back to their own country, but the bulk of Africans will have to face it here and it is to place them on a basis which will remove future danger and give them the possibility of becoming so numerous as to save Islam. The Muslim Africans here are not in a microscopic minority, but they are a large people. You must take steps to stop the repetition of Spanish tragedy happening here. For many years I have been thinking of ways and means. It is all very well to see the disease, but it is a totally different thing

SELECTED SPEECHES AND WRITINGS

to see what is going to be the best remedy. You must think it over.

Well! If any of you here really believes in that Day of Judgment and having had to answer the question I have put to you, anyone of you who feels like that, I shall put a practical solution or a course of action.

Firstly, create a permanent organization. Well! This permanent organization will later have to set on a four or five years' plan and again for another four or five years' course, which, I hope, will be permanent for all future times. This is most important of all, because without a permanent organization nothing can be done.

Secondly, you must have an African Muslim ally. An ally is more important than anything else. It is because the [Muslim] Indians can give Islam a lead here until it is possible to see the day that in a meeting like this, this chair is occupied by an African Muslim. The main leader here should be an African Muslim by his knowledge, upbringing and ability. We are here as friends. We Asiatics will be mere on-lookers. As brothers in faith you are here to help and assist them to become leaders.

Well! Again, in the building of an ally, an active ally, send 400, 500 or 1,000 persons from amongst the Arabs, Somalis, Swahilis or Africans in East or Central Africa – or as large a number of them as possible – to England, India, America or Egypt for Law, Medicine and Dentistry or what are known as liberal professions. Even send them to Makerere College in great numbers; and to Al-Azhar in Egypt and India for theology and study of religious propaganda. From this you should build up an African Islamic ally. Whatever Government may be in power at the time the Africans are responsible people of their country; they are the sons of the soil; they can build up and fight for the interest of Islam.

Then, if you want to advance, you have got to advance in all walks of life. Your advance should be all along. It must be a general advancement. You should not advance on one point and leave and forget other lines. You cannot do this piece-meal, as on these lines no good can come out.

Thirdly, in order of importance, you must have mosques where they are necessary. To the mosques you must attach schools which should give religious and secular education. I must say that if you Muslims want to keep a general standard of well-being, and you want to move with the times, you must teach them [Africans] English.

1197

Then comes the question of general education outside mosques. You must try to get them to go to the Government Schools. Where there are no Government Schools, you must ask for them. It is no politics to claim that. It is natural. Remember, if a large number of Africans of another Faith know English and are capable of going into Post Offices, Telegraph Offices and similar Government institutions or offices, while Muslim Africans are incapable of doing so, then the Muslim Africans are doomed, because they are bound to have an inferiority complex. They will fail to exercise their rightful influence. Muslim Africans must therefore be well educated as Christian Africans are. Muslim Africans should not belong to the lower class. They must belong to a raised strata of society where they can hold their own. That is number two.

Number three is, of course, the duty to propagate Islam. Attracting or bringing more and more people in the fold of Islam. Great efforts shall be required by those who want to answer the question I have put to you to-day – a question which is put to you in this world and that will be put to you in the world hereafter before Heaven. You must do your best. I have been in Egypt a great deal . . . I am sure, if an Arab, Somali and African delegation can come to Egypt when I am there I will be able to make all of them take an interest in them. I will see that they get proper help there. I doubt the position in India due to political uncertainty obtaining there at present. When the position is clear in India, however, it will then be possible to do something for them in India as well.

These are the problems I have put before you. I give you the help that should satisfy everybody here. In the first four years whatever total collection is made by the Non-Ismaili Muslims, I will double it. It is for you to come forward and show what mettle you are worth and also show us that Islam is alive.

Now I am going to leave you. I have always said that if a leader is there all the time like father, then you will do nothing. I must leave you here and ask you to organize by tomorrow what I call a skeleton scheme. That is to make a permanent organization. It is no use having one organization which will do all the four things; one body should be for one thing. One should look after the organization, one should look after the education and for sending students to Makerere, India, England and America and the third should build up mosques and so on.

Well! By tomorrow I hope to hear that this skeleton scheme is framed. You form your Committees and go into the questions. I will come back tomorrow and every day thereafter at 3 o'clock until you had [*sic*] made the progress desired by me.

Before I leave you I am sure you will all join with me in thanking Prince Badru for coming down to Mombasa to participate in this Conference. As you may all be knowing, Prince Badru has very generously donated a valuable piece of land for building thereon a mosque and school which very valuable piece of land I have myself seen whilst I was in Kampala recently. I sincerely hope that Muslims will build a grand and beautiful mosque there. I hope to come here again for another Jubilee and find it in this place [*sic*] a gentleman like Prince Badru [Kakungulu] or the Liwali or any other son of the soil occupying this chair. (Cheers).

Source: *Proceedings of the East African Muslim Conference,* Mombasa, 1945.

The East African Muslim Welfare Society was established in 1937 under the patronage of the Aga Khan. It was re-organized in 1945 at the Conference and its head-quarters was transferred from Kampala, Uganda, to Mombasa, Kenya. For more details, see Document 223.

Honourable Shams-Ud-Deen delivered the following address of welcome:

"Your Highness: I consider myself to be singularly fortunate for having been chosen for the unique privilege of extending a hearty welcome to Your Highness on behalf of the Moslems from all parts of East Africa.

"Ordinarily I think it should have been the right and the rightful privilege of the esteemed leader of Muslims of Mombasa, Dr. Mohamed Ali Rana, for the indefatiguable and strenuous work he has put in for convening this conference to perform this pleasant duty but since he himself has been a party for this duty being entrusted to me I have great pleasure in welcoming Your Highness to preside over this conference. Your Highness will recollect that about forty years ago when I waited upon Your Highness on behalf of the Muslim Association on your first visit to Nairobi, you instilled the sense of duty which the Muslims of Asia generally owed to the sons of the soil of Africa in showing them the path to Islam and sharing with them the blessings of the faith enjoyed by themselves.

"Ever since that time the Asians in this country have made a sort of half-hearted and unorganized effort to perform their duty in showing the path of Islam to Africans as a result of which quite an appreciable number of Africans have adopted the faith of God as preached by Abraham and all the prophets who followed him and in its final stage by our prophet Mohamed (Peace of God be upon him). But the results thus achieved in this irregular manner are by no means commensurate with the traditions of Islam when it is introduced into a new country. It is for this reason that the Muslims of East Africa including the African converts have invoked the help and guidance of Your Highness in laying the foundations of a proper and systematic society for a really serious propagation of Islam amongst the indigenous Africans which may ultimately not only be confined to East Africa but quite feasibly extend to the South and West Coast of Africa not excluding Central Africa. This programme may sound to some as too ambitious and even fantastic but those acquainted with the true traditions of Islam know perfectly well how it originated and commenced in a small sphere and how it assumed universal dimensions, until the decade set in from which incidentally even the Arab Rulers of East Africa could not escape. In any case while undue and unjustifiable optimism is not encouraged by Islam, pessimism does not form part of the precepts of Islam and it should not deter us from doing our duty in the right direction and leaving the results of achievement to God Almighty.

"Your Highness, this is no occasion for indulging in oratorical demonstrations but I cannot help referring to one historical matter of fact which the world has witnessed during the last 1,400 years. During this period nations have sprung up and have vanished, Empires have come into existence and have disappeared. Vast areas of this Earth have been conquered by Nations and have been lost but Islam has reigned supreme in all lands into which it has been once introduced. Islam has won lands and countries not by War but by the simple message of peace and goodwill to all human beings and showing to the humanity the path to salvation and an eternal life after this very brief span of life of this world which is no more than a dream.

"Your Highness, I am sure, I am voicing the sincere feelings of all Muslims in Eastern Africa when I express their heart-felt gratitude to Your Highness for having consented to preside over this conference which we all hope will prove to be an historic event calculated to awaken the interests of all the Muslims of Asia in Africa in the welfare of the Natives of Africa and which will prove to be the beginning of the advent of Islam in this vast continent.

"In conclusion, I wish to make it quite clear to all concerned that it is not the intention of this conference to be involved into any political activities or controversies or in any programme calculated to be inimical to the interests of any other community or communities residing in East Africa or indeed the inhabitants of the whole world or any sections thereof."

184

THE FUTURE OF ISLAM IN
EAST AFRICA – II

Speech at the East African Muslim Conference

Mombasa: 17 June 1945

Selection of students for further studies – the task before the Muslim Welfare Society – become good Muslim citizens of the country – help co-religionists to attain a place in society – specialists for preaching Islam – simultaneous material progress necessary – re-orientation of education.

Gentlemen!

"I heartily approve of all those resolutions adopted by you in this morning's session. You have deliberated in a business-like way. You have thus shown the purpose for which you met here.

"As I told you before opening the proceedings, we had really met here to work and not to make speeches. I have seen all these Resolutions and I entirely agree with the spirit and letter of every one of them. There is one point that I should like to make clear and that is about the Arab, Swahili and other African Muslim students. In order not to lose time and not to start late, you should try and find out from Government, Muslim and all other schools in Dar-es-Salaam, Zanzibar, Uganda, Kenya and from Somaliland the names of the likely boys who would agree to proceed to Makerere, India and Europe as soon as possible so that at least we can start that part of our work right away. We have now to make a lot of preparations. If the boys are ready and their names ready, we can put this work in our hand. If there are any objections to this procedure, please tell me now so that I shall try to remedy them. Don't be influenced by the fact that I have said so. [Nobody expressed any objection]. Well! So there is no practical objection. I think that is the first start. That means you know business. I hope to leave before August and I hope before that time, you will give me the names of Muslim boys intending to go for higher studies."

His Highness asked: "How is admission to the Makerere College governed? Is it open for any one to join or do they admit only a limited number of students?"

Mr. A. K. Ismail (Kampala) informed His Highness that every year a limited number of students are taken on passing an Entrance Examination.

Continuing his speech, His Highness the Aga Khan said: "If you experience difficulty in getting students admitted into the Makerere College, you can then send them to India, Egypt or elsewhere. Gentlemen! Your Welfare Society will have to do that. If in India there is no vacancy, we can send the boys to England. Something of that kind must be done . . .

"All possible avenues should be explored, calculated to produce best and quickest results. If you find courses in India long, you should then send them to England. Every Government College in Cairo would be open for your boys."

Concluding, His Highness referring to the Resolutions adopted in the morning's session expressed again his satisfaction and asked whether anybody wanted to make any suggestion or ask anything. There was no suggestion and His Highness before leaving the Hall impressed on his hearers the necessity of their becoming good propagandists of Islam by becoming good Muslim citizens of the country.

His Highness said: "Unless you reach the same social and economic standard as others have done, you will pose yourselves as second class people and others who steal an advance on you will look down upon you and you will have to look up to them. For that reason, you have got to help your African and Arab and Somali and Swahili co-religionists to attain a place of honour and respect in the society. This is number one.

Number two is that those who are going to be doctors or men of profession, they must also learn the elements of Islam which they can easily do so [*sic*] and then they should disseminate them in their own way. But at the same time, we must try to get specialists for preaching Islam amongst the Africans. You can bring them from India or by sending your students to receive further religious studies in Aligarh or Beirut or Al-Azhar."

Replying to a question asked by Mowlana Mohamed Hussain Aloomi of Kisumu, His Highness affirmed the necessity of giving specialized training to such students among the Muslim Africans, Arabs or Somalis as showed special aptitude or particular leaning towards it for preparing them to undertake Tabligh work; but His Highness at the same time emphasised that efforts must be concentrated on the material or worldly progress so as to keep the standard of life up. The first thing for which the conference had been called was to make Islam a nation of masters instead of slaves and this was to be done by re-orientation of education.

Arising out of the queries made by His Highness the Aga Khan, the Hon'ble Shams-ud-Deen undertook to do his level best to persuade the Kenya Government to send to the Makerere College as large a number of the African Muslims students as possible.

Source: *Proceedings of the East African Muslim Conference,* Mombasa, 1945.

185

THE FUTURE OF ISLAM IN
EAST AFRICA – III

Speech at the East African Muslim Conference

Mombasa: 18 June 1945

A small deputation to go to Cairo – the need for funds – remember
what happened to Islam in Spain and the South of France.

The announcement of the appointment of the first Supreme
Council [of the East African Muslim Welfare Society] by His
Highness the Aga Khan met with the approbation of all.

His Highness then observed that he wanted a small deputation
of Africans and Arabs to come to Cairo and see him in the
beginning of October next by which time he would be there
when he would do all in his power to get them necessary support
and assistance for furthering the aims and objects of the
Society . . .

His Highness addressed the delegates and among other things
said: "Gentlemen! Without money we might not have as well met.
It is no good talking tall things. Again, like my opening speech,
I am not going to make a speech [*sic*]. With words only we can't
go on. I think the minimum amount that from all sources we
should have found to do any good should be Shs. 700,000/- or
800,000/- or 1,000,000/-. Without this, I think, we had better not
met. . . .

"The cost of sending boys to India and England etc., for the
courses that I want them to do cannot be less than £300 per
annum, if that is a minimum; the Governments there do not
encourage extravagance. We want at least 20 to 25 students from
amongst the Arabs, Somalis and Swahilis and Africans who show
signs of intelligence. Well! This shall require some Shs. 150,000/-
to 200,000/-. I suppose that at least Shs. 200,000/- to 250,000/-

should go to Kampala for building a befitting mosque as a 'Nishan of Islam'. You have got a wonderful and dominant situation for a mosque in Kampala through the generosity of Prince Badru . . .

"Then there are other mosques to be built and schools to be opened . . . [periods of suspension in original – Ed.] All this means money. If the money is not coming in the way you should have, it is not business like. I have some experience of the community of which I have the honour of being the Head. The only proper way is to have an annual budget with everything earmarked. You should set to yourself that so much shall be collected [sic]. As I told you before, whatever you collect I will double it. This is the procedure of business. Well! If you are not prepared to contribute money, it is no use – Gentlemen! . . . The minimum number of Arab, Swahili, Somali or African – the latter comprising from all tribes – Muslim students that you should arrange to send overseas every year for prosecuting higher studies should be 20 or 25. This is the minimum number that you have got to do this [sic]. Then you should give scholarships for enabling them to join Government schools. Last but not least is Tabligh. You should send some missionaries for training in the Al-Azar or in the Beirut University or in India, whichever may be found more convenient or economical. Unless money comes forward you can't do all this . . .

"You must remember what happened to Islam in Spain and in South of France. You must have read the 'Mersiya' written by the renowned poet Iqbal about the beautiful land of Sicily. If you haven't read it, better read it [sic]. This is the Spain of East Africa and what my friend the Mowlana and other gentlemen have said I admire the thing [sic]; but let them realize that if you go to another modern civilization with other matters except this, it will crush you [sic]. Nothing can stop it. Its own arms must therefore be used as defence, that is knowledge, science and knowledge of history. I think I can serve other better and more useful purposes without giving you lecture [sic] on history, and on the way civilization should be made. The question is that which my old friend Nawab Mohsin-ul-Mulk used to say: 'Chanda. Chanda. Chanda.' I have said what I had to say and I hope you will make great efforts each in your own conscience and be prepared to answer the question on the Day of Judgment or Qiyamat."

Source: *Proceedings of the East African Muslim Conference*, Mombasa, 1945.

186

THE MUSLIMS OF TANGANYIKA

Reply to the Address Presented by the Tanganyika Muslim Association

Dar-es-Salaam: 22 July 1945

Appeal to Indian Muslims – Welfare Society not political – Muslims first pioneers in the area – education for Swahilis and others – uplift of women.

The Aga Khan, replying, urged all Indian Muslims "to work for the uplift of all Muslims of indigenous origin". The Welfare scheme planned was in no way political, he said, and should be supported by them all, its main objects being general welfare, education, social uplift and religious training.

Pointing out that Muslims were the first pioneers "in this land", he said that events had shown that the Swahilis were not only quite capable of attaining the standard of education given at Makerere College but also of higher technical studies, and should be given the facilities and opportunities for such studies in Britain, America or in India. To that end, the Indian Muslims must help them, though it must not be forgotten by the Arabs, Somalis and Swahilis in East Africa that they must also take full advantage of the facilities for education offered to them "by their paternal Government".

The Aga Khan also referred to the uplift of women of those communities and spoke of the great work and intelligence of some of them in the past.

Source: *The Tanganyika Standard*, Dar-es-Salaam, 28 July 1945.

The Tanganyika Muslim Association represented the Arab, Somali and Swahili communities of Dar-es-Salaam. It hosted a tea party for the Aga Khan and the Begum. The Liwali (the representative of the Sultan of Zanzibar) presided and presented an address to the Aga Khan in Arabic, which was translated into English and Kiswahili. In the address, the Liwali expressed the gratitude of these communities for having established the East African Muslim Welfare Society on the lines suggested by the Aga Khan, and added that all of them would take full advantage of the scheme as, apart from the benefits to be derived from it, it would lead to "concord and harmony among all sections of Muslims in East Africa".

The *Tanganyika Standard* published the news under the headline: "Aga Khan and Indigenous Muslims."

187

INTER-RACIAL COOPERATION IN TANGANYIKA

Interview with The Tanganyika Standard

Dar-es-Salaam: 2 August 1945

Planning for the advancement of the African – future of Tanganyika
lies with the African – his prosperity from within – opportunities
for the non-Africans – co-operation between the races.

"I am not a Communist," said His Highness the Aga Khan,
but I think that the Russians have done amazing things for their
backward peoples."

His Highness was discussing, in an interview given to the Tanganyika Standard, the future of Tanganyika and he emphasised
the need of comprehensive and energetic planning for the
advancement of the African. "Of course," he said, "the Africans
have further to go than the Russians, but the Russian way shows
the sort of thing that is possible."

Asked to enlarge upon his reference, in a speech shortly after
he arrived in Dar es Salaam to the "clear horizon ahead", His
Highness said:

"The future of Tanganyika does not lie with the settler or the
Indian, but with the African. The advancement of the African is
the foundation of progress."

The present way was good, but far too slow. The surface of
Tanganyika had just been scratched. The Territory was only in
its babyhood.

What would happen, His Highness asked, if every one of the
millions of Africans in Tanganyika were able to buy a pair of
shoes – one of his greatest needs for health reasons – or two suits

of clothes, or a mackintosh? The benefits would be enormous and all would share in them.

Asked about the sort of steps that should be taken, His Highness emphasised that there should be close and personal interest in [*sic*] the part of the rulers in the advancement of their people. Careful planning on a large scale and over many years should be undertaken. It should not be confined to one corner of the economic field but should be general. Above all, the Aga Khan emphasized, the future prosperity of Tanganyika, which had great possibilities, must be built up from within, on the foundation of African prosperity, with Africans their own proprietors. Uganda was a good example.

"You will get nowhere if you regard Tanganyika as a sort of plantation from which the crop is to be exported and for which Africans provide the labour," he said.

What would be the scope for non-Africans in Tanganyika, he was asked.

Indian and European, he thought, could cooperate in catering for a planned increase in African prosperity. There was no need for undesirable competition. He preferred the word "cooperation". There was a place for all. Europeans, for example, could not possibly carry out the duka [retail] trade which was so suited to many Indians. Such work as banking, at the higher levels, was specially suited to Europeans.

So far as social relations between the races was concerned, His Highness expressed his delight at the sort of parties that he had witnessed last week, with Indians, Europeans and Arabs mingling happily on the dance floor. Such occasions were, of course, exceptional and could occur when a rich man or firm gave a party. He expressed interest in the efforts to promote racial understanding of such organisations as the Dar es Salaam Cultural Society and said that he would be glad to deliver a lecture to the Society on the next occasion on which he visited Dar es Salaam. He thought, however, that the best way in which members of the different races could get to know each other better was on the sports field, and looked forward to regular matches of cricket, tennis and hockey.

Source: *The Tanganyika Standard,* Dar-es-Salaam, 3 August 1945.
The report was published under two-column headlines: "The Future of Tanganyika Lies With the African: The Aga Khan Looks Ahead."

188

GUIDELINES FOR THE MUSLIMS OF TRANSVAAL

Reply to the Address of Welcome from the Transvaal Muslim League

Johannesburg: 12 August 1945

The folly of racialism – need for political unity – risks of a division between the rich and the poor – friendship on an intellectual basis – dangers of alcohol and tobacco – instruction through night classes – education for women – Muslims and science – Muslim welfare – rise of the Arab League – Hindu-Muslim unity in India.

"Of all things that separate man, racialism is the most dangerous. We have seen something of the kind in Europe and we have seen its fruits."

Replying to an address presented by the Transvaal Muslim League in the Johannesburg City Hall on August 12th, 1945, His Highness had sounded a true note of warning.

His Highness asked the meeting to forgive him for lecturing them, but being very nearly seventy years of age and having had well over fifty years of experience in various activities, he would be failing in his duty if he did not proffer them the advice which his years and experience permitted.

First of all he urged them to be politically united.

"Do not allow Mohammedan or any other sectarian differences to divide your united front in South Africa. Believe me, there are great temptations, but whatever happens, do not disunite."

In South Africa they had managed to unite as friends, but there was a second danger – a division between the rich and the poor.

It was vital to the Indians in South Africa that such a division should not occur. It had no place in their national political movement. They were nationally exposed in the Union, they were 250,000 people in a vast country surrounded by people of many races and it was of the greatest importance that they should not be divided on an economic issue. Rather they should make friends on an intellectual basis. Truth and wisdom were unanswerable, because truth was always established by time in the long run.

"The greatest danger to every Moslem citizen – I have not the least hesitation in saying it – is alcohol. Time has shown that it is an injury to you; an injury to your person; an injury to your health. It is forbidden because it carries greater evil than good. Believe me, in a community like yours, alcohol is a very grave danger. Once you got into the alcohol habit, I do not know where it would lead you. A handful, here and there, of the weak, or of the unhappy, find their way to this terrible poison. Avoid it at all costs. Avoid it, I say, for in this country you cannot afford to lose one man."

Although the habit was not forbidden, His Highness warned them of tobacco. "It is not a religious question" he said, "but it is a question of economy. What would you think of a man who went about the streets burning up ten shilling notes? You would call him a madman, wouldn't you? But people go around buying cigarettes and burning them."

"Also, many doctors will tell you that tobacco smoking is bad for you. So although smoking is not forbidden, it is from my long experience of life that I strongly urge the young not to acquire the habit and the more mature to reduce it to the minimum. I assure you that the economic position will greatly improve."

His Highness speaking on the question of education said there were many causes which hampered educational effort in South Africa, but it was his opinion that night classes, as they had done in other countries, might perform a great service in the Union.

"Night classes where there are a number of Moslems together using books on Muslim history and Muslim literature would bring you in through the Western door into the palaces of Eastern culture."

Education for women was a thing which His Highness stressed. Without it there would inevitably result other great drawbacks for the Moslem community.

"Personally, if I had two children, and one was a boy and the other a girl, and if I could afford to educate only one, I would have no hesitation in giving the higher education to the girl.

The male could bend his energies to manual effort for reward, but the girl's function was the maintenance of home life and the bringing up of the children. Her influence in the family circle was enormous and the future of the generation depended upon her ability to lead the young along the right paths and instruct them in the rudiments of culture and civilisation."

The League should bear this in mind and arrange for the proper night classes for boys and men and lectures for girls and women.

His Highness undertook to supply to every Moslem community with [sic] the necessary books which would further their cultural advance. His Highness said that, unfortunately since the fall of Spain and Baghdad, Moslems had forgotten science. In this respect the leaders of the Moslems had taken a back place.

"Even the Chinese have long since passed us. The Hindus have long since passed us. It is not only by books but also by night classes that you will go far in preparing the way in which you should be brought up."

His Highness the Aga Khan then spoke of the duties of Moslems. In East Africa a society had been formed at last. Rich and poor alike were doing all in their power to help Islam. It involved, he said, a science in which every Moslem should participate for the welfare of the people.

It required the observance and furtherance of hygiene, dietetics and social welfare. The rich had to help the poor in this important matter and the poor had to co-operate with their benefactors.

"The high standard upon which you insist for yourselves, will win for you the respect of all the other communities in South Africa."

This was all that he wished to say to them now. If they could not accomplish that which he had proposed and which was in their power to accomplish, then they could not hope to cope with that which at present was outside their ability.

"Once more, forgive me for lecturing you and for showing – to the best of my ability – where there is light and where there is darkness. I know that if it has some influence in your life in the future, then my time and your time has not been wasted."

The rise of the Arab League and its consequent influence

upon the Syrian and Lebanese nations, beginning with Yemen and going as far as Somaliland, and the Atlantic, may lead to a great revival which might make Islam once more as glorious and as splendid a religion as it was once upon a time.

"In India, also, I believe firmly that a strong united League will come to brotherly fraternal terms with our Hindu brethren in the long run; and the long run may now be a very short run indeed.

So, there are on the horizon two helpful signs. One of a united brotherhood of our Mohammedan-speaking world and one in Southern Asia of a united brotherhood of the Indian people who will grow in strength and respect.

"I do not wish to dwell in intellectual argument. It is your daily life which interests me."

Source: A. J. Chunara, *Platinum Jubilee Review*, Karachi, 1954. It is also reproduced in Habib V. Kheshavjee, *The Aga Khan and Africa*, Pretoria 1946.

The meeting took place in the Johannesburg City Hall. The Vice-President of the Transvaal Muslim League, M. A. Dinath, in his address of welcome said:

" 'It is too well-known to need a statement from me, that Muslims all the world over hold Your Highness in high respect and esteem, and are conscious and highly appreciative of the many services that you have rendered to the cause of Islam and Muslims from time to time.

" 'The several addresses of Your Highness to Muslims to acquire high education in all branches of knowledge have borne their fruits. And mainly through Your Highness' efforts Aligarh College was raised to the status of a University, to give realistic feature to those desiderata which Your Highness so impressively advocated at the Muslim Educational Conference.'

The Aga Khan's solicitude for the welfare of his countrymen, continued Mr. Dinath, had never given him a pause in his long and arduous life.

" 'Its manifestation was only too visible when Your Highness pleaded only yesterday in this country for the opening of the gate of knowledge and the extension of human rights and tolerance to Indians here.

" 'In all the great events of the first World War and post-war period, which had their centre in the East, Your Highness was there ready to throw your weight upon the scale of reason and order.'

"Mr. Dinath recalled the Aga Khan's great work in the cause of international peace as a delegate to and President of the League of Nations, and his forceful declaration at the Disarmament Conference that "with Muslims, the ideal of peace is no mere economic expedient; it is an element deep-rooted in its very name.'

"The Aga Khan's speech was followed by a great outburst of applause which lasted until Mr. M. A. Haye, Secretary of the Transvaal Muslim League, rose to thank His Highness for his presence and express gratitude 'to this most distinguished living man of our time for the golden pieces of advice he has given us here.'

"He referred to the Aga Khan's past achievements. 'Even before Nawab Mohsin-ul-Mulk, the successor of Sir Sayed Ahmed, requested His Highness to preside at that memorable gathering of the elite and intelligentsia at Delhi, His Highness had already created a mark on time when he displayed the qualities of statesmanship while at the head of a Muslim delegation to Lord Curzon, the then Viceroy of India.

" 'The unique honour of the establishment of the London League for the propagation of the Muslim cause, in the heart of the Empire, goes to His Highness. The crowning success of the negotiations of the famous Lucknow Pact in 1916 was due to the untiring efforts of this towering personality whom we are fortunate to have amid us this afternoon.

" 'The Muslim world eagerly looks forward to sound and constructive counsels and guidance by this magnetic and experienced genius – the greatest living authority on internationalism, the most fervent advocate of peace and equality even when the horizon of the Muslim world is so much overcast with ominous clouds and while the Moslems are passing through a momentous period of their political, religious and social history.'

"After inspecting a Guard of Honour provided by the 3rd Muslim Division of the St. John Ambulance Brigade the Aga Khan left for Pretoria, where he met his followers at the Ismaili Mosque.

"In the evening the management of the Langham Hotel had arranged a private dinner and a musical concert in his honour at which a colourful gathering assembled and many distinguished guests paid tribute to His Highness and the Begum."

189

INDIANS IN SOUTH AFRICA

Speech Before the Natal Indian Congress

Durban: 16 August 1945

Indians should owe their allegiance to South Africa – an honourable position in spite of difficulties – avoid divisions on the basis of religion or wealth – what Indians can contribute to South Africa – educational progress – women's education – Gandhi's teachings – sympathy from European fellow citizens – increase in the moral strength – faith in the higher destiny of mankind – judgement of conscience will solve the problems of South Africa.

"While you Indians in South Africa may rightly be proud of your heritage as descendants of the great cultural leaders of India, yet once you have come here your allegiance to South Africa no matter what South Africa does to you must be, I assure you, wholly and in toto to South Africa.

"Any son of India coming abroad to this country is proud to see how in spite of artificial difficulties placed in your way, you have been able, while not doing so much as you might had circumstances been otherwise, to maintain an honourable position for yourselves.

"But enough of the past. Let us think of the present and the future. Forgive me if, after spending only a short time in your midst, I venture to give you a few words of advice. The onlooker often sees most of the game, and I have known and studied the case of the Indians in South Africa for a very long time.

"First of all, and by far the most important, let there never be any question of Hindu and Moslem in South Africa. The Hindu and Moslem difficulties and squabbles and differences in India, are not articles for export. Here, once and for all, you are all in the same boat. You will sink or swim together and, for goodness sake, do not allow questions of religion or geography ever to disunite the Natal Indian Congress." His Highness implored his audience to avoid a division of the rich and the poor.

"I appreciate that the struggle of the underdog is a world-wide one. But when peace has come you will unite with the others for a better material position, a better return for the good things of life, for security and for having the amount of leisure given to you which your labours demand."

His Highness reminded them that they owed an allegiance to the country in which they lived, from which they got their sustenance, in which most of them had been born and in which most of them would die and be buried.

"To it as such, you can bring your contribution, the thoughts of the East; your profound faith in peace and goodwill; of charity of thought and good action. While you bring all these to South Africa's future you must look upon it and yourselves as humble servants of this land. The glory of this land must always be before you as a guiding thought. Only then will you have the right to say that, in spite of the difficulties of the past, you want fair play in the future . . ."

"I implore you, with all my strength, to go in more for education," His Highness said. "No one can stop you if you sincerely and honestly try to raise the standard of every Indian boy to that of the level of the European. Fortunately, there are men of wealth among you, and bursaries could be provided so that the poor may achieve a standard of education which their own resources make difficult, if not impossible.

"If certain avenues are closed, there are many that are open. Boys could be sent to the highest educational centres in Britain or the United States, and even in South Africa there are opportunities at the Universities. In the long run this education will go further than any amount of other action in bringing about a better understanding of your qualities as citizens of South Africa. These doors are open. They must always be kept open, for the standard of material life will depend upon the standard of moral and cultural life."

His Highness insisted that in the standard of education, essentially there should be equality between both sexes. He pointed out that it was only when a nation could bring into its service both the men and the women to carry on the social and home life as well as its secular and economic activities and when both the men and the women contributed to the utmost that the greatest success and advantage could be gained.

"Could Great Britain have won the war without the contributions of the women?" asked the Aga Khan. "Could the United States have reached her international status without her womenfolk? And we all know the tremendous contribution of the women in Russia since the Revolution in 1917.

"By constant effort if all these advantages are brought to our mothers and sisters and daughters, a great advance will have been made in achieving those principle [sic] of right and dealings of fair play.

"A higher standard of moral force, of sobriety, of honour and of integrity which must break down even the greatest of prejudices, was Gandhi's teaching.

Brethren, let that standard of integrity, which the greatest of Indian sons preached here to the world at large, be your guiding star.

"Already there is no doubt that there are hopeful signs that a great many of your European fellow citizens of South Africa realise and sympathise with your just ambitions. But their number can only grow greater when, in the cities and in the places where you are well known, it is felt that side by side with your national confidence, with that natural political awakening, there is an individual effort towards betterment of not only yourselves but of your neighbours.

"Isolated here – far from the roots of your history – it would be a good and advantageous system if everyone of my countrymen said to himself: 'How can I better my knowledge, my integrity and my ability to help my brother more to-day?' Such a self-searching question will lead to a great increase in that moral strength to which Mahatma Gandhi attached such great importance.

"You may have fights politically here, but at least be of such a character that those, however reluctantly they may be your opponents, will ever and ever respect you and say: 'Our Indian citizens are as good as citizens as we are.'

"Here there is bravery, happily not on the battle-field but in the faith in the higher destiny of mankind, no matter what be his colour or creed – that quality which makes man; that judgment of conscience. I am sure that judgment of conscience, if firmly believed in and acted upon, will go far to solving the problems of South Africa."

Source: Habib V. Keshavjee, *The Aga Khan and Africa*, Pretoria, 1946.
It is also reproduced in A. J. Chunara, *Platinum Jubilee Review*, Karachi, 1954.

190

THE INDIAN SITUATION

Interview with the United Press of India

Karachi: 9 November 1945

Hindu-Muslim relations – the Diamond Jubilee.

"Time has come when Hindus and Muslims should realise their responsibility to their country. By their differences they are in fact holding back the progress of the entire continent of Asia," said His Highness the Aga Khan to-day.

Replying to a question if he would act as "an ambassador of peace" and work for Hindu-Muslim unity, the Aga Khan said that this was a difficult task and he had not come to India for this purpose. He might, however, meet Mr. Gandhi and Mr. Jinnah if he came across them.

He added that he would be busy with his jubilee celebrations, when he would be weighed against diamonds in Bombay on March 20 and for which 200 pounds of diamonds have already been procured by his followers, that being his approximate weight.

He declined to comment on the Muslim League's demand for partition of India.

Source: *The Civil and Military Gazette,* Lahore, 11 November 1945.
The interview was given on his arrival in India for the purpose of attending the ceremonies in celebration of his Diamond Jubilee. Soon after this very short interview, the Aga Khan, seated on a silver chair, performed mass marriage of fifty couples belonging to the Ismaili Khoja community.

191

THE IMPORTANCE OF SCIENCE

Reply to the Address from the Court of the Aligarh Muslim University

Bombay: 9 March 1946

Plea for the establishment of a research institute – 10 million rupees needed – importance of science – location of the institute.

His Royal Highness said that it would require a crore of rupees. They could collect Rs. 90,00,000 while he would contribute Rs. 10,00,000.

The world of the future, stated His Royal Highness, depended upon science. There were no limits to the possibilities of sciences. He remembered having been told in London years ago that with atomic energy there was no reason why the other planets should not be new Americas. Muslims who were once forward in science were now backward. What they needed, therefore, was a great Research Institute.

He would prefer the institute to be located in Karachi, which had always maintained contact with Muslim countries on Western border of India. It would be advantageous to the people of South Iran, East Africa, Afghanistan and Baluchistan. The natural resources of these areas would also be an asset to the Institute.

It would not be difficult, His Royal Highness thought, to collect Rs. 90,00,000 in a year. India was to have Home Rule in 1946. The institute should also be completed in that year. If he were young he would have made the collection himself. This was the opportunity and if they failed he did not know what the future would be for them. Certainly it would not be one in which the Muslims could hold their own.

Source: *The Times of India*, Bombay, 10 March 1946.

The meeting at which the address was presented and the reply given was held at the Sir Cowasjee Jehangir Hall.

ADVICE TO THE EAST AFRICAN MUSLIMS

Interview with the Observer (Nairobi)

Nairobi: June 1946

Distressing condition of African Muslims – full educational facilities
for progress – mutual love and sacrifice according to the teachings
of the Holy Prophet – call for a Muslim conference.

... His Highness the Aga Khan, expressed grave concern at the
distressing condition of African Moslems. His Highness said that
everywhere – in Arabia, Syria, Egypt, Iraq, India and Indonesia –
the Moslems were on the march, but over here in Africa things
were different. "Our African brothers-in-faith were living in the
most appalling condition. There was no adequate provision for
the education of their children, no institution to look after their
welfare and no organization to safeguard their rights and
privileges."

His Highness emphasized that if the African Moslems were to
progress side by side with their Christian brothers, it was imperative that full educational facilities should be made available for
them. His Highness the Aga Khan stressed that it was the sacred
duty of every Moslem to make all possible sacrifices to ameliorate
the terrible state of their less fortunate brothers-in-faith. His
Highness called upon all Moslems to remember that geographical and racial affiliation did not form the basis of Islam
brotherhood, but the spirit of mutual love and sacrifice infused
into the Moslem minds by the teaching of the Prophet
Muhammed. His Highness advocated that a conference of
Moslem leaders should be held at Mombasa on 23rd July, 1946,
to discuss this unique problem.

Source: *The Sunday Post*, Nairobi, 2 June 1946.
    The *Observer*, a Muslim weekly of Nairobi, started publication in May 1946.

EDUCATION AND PROGRESS OF MUSLIMS IN EAST AFRICA

Reply to the Address of Welcome from the (Second) East African Muslim Conference

Mombasa: 27 July 1946

Collect funds first – the strides made by Christian Africans – the condition of African Muslims – a pan-Islamic university needed – its location.

First of all allow me to thank you for your good wishes and welcome to myself and for referring to my Diamond Jubilee and [I] am most grateful for the good wishes of the gentlemen here. I also take this opportunity of welcoming the various delegates who have come here to attend this meeting.

Last year, we had laid down and I would again repeat it to-day that this is in no way a political meeting. We have nothing to do with politics, because political opinions differ, but one thing does not differ with the Muslims and that is Muslims upliftment [*sic*]. Hence politics are barred which as we saw last year, and see to-day also, allows officials of the Government like my friend Liwali Mbarak [Hinawy] and others to participate in it.

Now gentlemen! Last year I told you that we had great lessons to learn from what happened in Spain. I have got another example of this type to put before you. If we go on as we have been going on and if we do as we have done during the last 75 to 100 years, what happened in India will be repeated here. There will be two kinds of citizens in Africa. There would be Brahmin Christians and Shudra Muslims and the inevitable result will be that the African Muslims will be left outside of the sphere of education and knowledge, of science and modern outlook, and he would be chained down in the economic sphere and generally he would be going down and down like the Aborigines of India did 400 or 500 years ago. On the other hand, the Christian Africans have made immense strides. They have improved in every respect because of the work of the Christian Missions. That is practically what I told you last year. The result of this one section of the population getting education, higher standard of life, knowledge, activity and health, while the other remaining [sic] in the old groove carrying on work more and more of a servile nature will naturally be to bring about two sorts of citizens, Christian Brahmins and Shudra Muslims. Are we going to accept this? Are we going to do nothing to remove this terrible inevitable menace? Believe me, Gentlemen, I am not telling you things just to frighten you. It may be in the hands of a few Muslims to escape. But what about the bulk of the African Muslim population who remains behind? What would be their future?

We have also seen from the examples which are being quoted by my friends here how unsatisfactory products the Makerere College is producing. While the young Christian boys who have come out from that College have become sources of strength to Christianity in this part of the world, the Muslim boys have become acute Communists, anti-God and anti-religious propagandists. I have no personal knowledge of this and I am only repeating to you what I have heard from my friends. Believe me, it is in no spirit of hostility to Christian Missionaries that I am telling you this. I have got best and grandest admiration for their work, but my only regret is that their spirit is not seen in Muslims. They (Christian Missionaries) have made great sacrifices. I am paying them the biggest of all compliments in asking you to imitate their activities.

Now comes the practical advanced position. On what lines can we solve the problem of African Muslims irrespective of whether their origin was Arab or Indian? How are we to raise the standard of Somalis, Swahilis and other Muslims as well as of the Arabs of the Coast so that they can be brought up to the standard of proper competition with the Europeans and other advanced sections of the African races?

Last year we had laid down a programme of work the results of which our friends present here have read. From the results of these last 12 months, I have thought it over and have come to the conclusion that on those lines alone success of a permanent nature is not possible. If you know anything about history, you will know very well how the Bulgarian Nation was built up by

Robert. . . . [periods of suspension in the original – Ed.] If you know anything about history, you know the immense influence of the Beyrout College and University on Near East thought. Also what the Muslim League in India has been able to do would not have been possible without a Muslim University at Aligarh. It would never have otherwise come into power. Pakistan, the League and the Grouping system in India will lead very soon to the construction of a great Muslim body in both East and West India. These are both results of the intellectual work done by the M.O.A. [The Muhammadan Anglo-Oriental] College and later by the Aligarh University. Here you have got to have an intellectual aristocracy of Arabs, Africans and Indian Muslims and until they build up this aristocracy, it should itself become a source of light for the whole of the community.

For this reason, while we should continue the work on the same lines as laid down last year, which I believe, have given some satisfaction, time has come for us to consider whether it is not possible to build a University on the lines of the Aligarh and/or Beyrout Universities for all races and sections in the Muslim community. Well, first of all, I have seen a rough scheme and I hope and insist too that in any event it should not be connected with any individual names or life so that you must not mention anything about my Diamond Jubilee. It should have no connection except building of a house [sic]. Only that had been done in Aligarh's case. I also insist that this should be a purely Muslim University. Where it should be? Most would like to have it at Zanzibar or Mombasa. I do not think, much as I like to see it at Zanzibar or Mombasa . . . [periods of suspension are in the original – Ed.] which are the ancient seats of Islam . . . [periods of suspension in the original – Ed.] that this is possible. You very well know that Tanganyika is a Mandated Territory and will have some kind of influence and relation by UNO. Now you will not be able to run the University except with the help of Egypt and India without which it is impossible. Now do you think India and Egypt will give money like £1,000,000 or £2,000,000 or may be £3,000,000 to put up a University on the charity work where they have no influence [sic]; where their own citizens . . . this may not be actually true in the case of Egypt . . . [periods of suspension in the original – Ed.] are discriminated against or subject to disabilities, etc., except in a place like Tanganyika. Now what will this University [be] like? It should begin from boys of seven years of age. It should be on the same lines as the Beyrout one which make them Doctors, Engineers, high class professional mathematicians, commercials and all kinds of other activities. The more I think the more I come to the conclusion that young boys can start and can go up as they have done in Beyrout University. Some must have been in Beyrout and you know what it is like. This, of course, must be a purely Muslim University open to all sections, and races of the Muslims, Indian, South African, Arabs, Africans or from anywhere else.

Nothing can be done except when a substantial part of £1,000,000 as minimum is raised. It will go very short these days, but nothing can be done except substantial part of it had been raised. These are my views. You have met here not with preconceived ideas but to work by finding out each other's opinions and ideas and can have a free and open conference where you can place suggestions freely. And think of the question of raising the standard of African Muslims, their standard of intelligence and life and wealth. Of course, I know that the Missionary activities or Tabligh are an essential part of Muslim religion. Believe me, Gentlemen, if we are losing ground that is the reason all the more that the home policy should be built up first so that we gain and not lose ground. With these words, I will ask the President to read his report of the work done so for and then ask for a free and open discussion.

Source: *Combined Report of the 2nd. East African Muslim Conference and the Annual General Meeting of the East African Muslim Welfare Society*, Mombasa, 1946.

The Liwali was the official representative of the Sultan of Zanzibar in Kenya.

The Aga Khan's speech was preceded by two addresses of welcome. The first one was by Dr. Najmudean, Chairman of the Reception Committee, who said: "Your Highness, Ladies & Gentlemen:

"It is my proud privilege as the Chairman of the Reception Committee of the Muslim Conference to extend a most warm and hearty welcome to all who have come, in the case of outside delegates at considerable expense and inconvenience, to participate in this 2nd Muslim Conference of the East African Muslims. We have received messages from Muslim brethren all over the country regretting their inability to come due to want of travelling facility these days.

"As you all know, the first Muslim Conference was held in June last year under the same distinguished Chairmanship as this Conference. That Conference was the first of its kind and as a result of its momentous deliberations the East African Muslim Welfare Society came out invigorated and re-organized on sound and solid basis. I am sure you will all rejoice to hear of what it has so far done or achieved when its worthy President, Sheth A. H. Kaderbhoy, and its able Honorary Secretary, Mr. A. C. Satchu, at the end of this Conference will give you their account of work. That first conference was as unique in its conception as it was adjudged unique in its fruitful results. That was all primarily due to His Highness The Aga Khan whose presence in Kenya inspired the holding of the said Conference and whose able direction and guidance saw it through. This second Conference is likewise being held at his irresistible inspiration and sagacious guidance [and] will undoubtedly help us in our no less momentous deliberations to achieve still more fruitful results.

"This Conference I have no doubt in my mind will go to prove another turning point for Islam in East Africa. Ladies & Gentlemen: a grave responsibility devolves upon us all. Here to-day are gathered a galaxy of intellects indeed some of the best brains in the Muslim Community drawn from all walks of life where in one way or other they have distinguished themselves in their respective spheres, vocations or avocations. Let us therefore apply our minds seriously and earnestly to the tasks and responsibilities that lie ahead of us. Momentous decisions of far-reaching import await us. Let our deliberations prove us worthy of the genius of our great heritage by bringing into play policies, schemes and influences that will ensure the opening in true sense, of a new era of awakening, enlightenment, unity, solidarity and happiness in our Community. Let us combine and bend our energies and pool our experiences and wisdom to solve in a manly manner, I mean in a courageous and firm manner, various knotty and vexed problems confronting us.

"Our hearts to-day are justly overflowing with joy and pride to find amidst us the most brilliant star of the present day world of Islam in the person of His Highness The Aga Khan from whom flows an unending stream of wit, window and benefaction. Let us take full advantage of his ripe experience, sagacious advice and unbounded wisdom.

"On behalf of my Committee and myself I once more welcome you Your Highness & Brother and Sister Delegates and offer you our warmest thanks for participating in this Conference and thus practically helping us to make this a success. Let us all pray from the core of our hearts for the unqualified success of this Conference."

Sheth A. H. Kaderbhoy, M. B. E., the President of the Society then read the following address of welcome:

"Your Highness,
"On behalf of my Society as well as on my own, and also on behalf of the entire Muslim population of Mombasa, irrespective of any section or race, I am sure I am voicing their inmost feelings, it is both a great privilege and honour to extend to Your Highness a very warm and sincere welcome. In fact, our gratitude and felicitation over the fact that Mombasa had once again been honoured to receive another august visit from Your Highness and behold second Conference of the East African Muslims under the able and distinguished Chairmanship of Your Highness make us to offer our humble thankfulness to the Almighty God Whose infinite Grace and Mercy had made this possible. Every praise therefore be to God. It goes without saying that your auspicious visits have invariably done, and are bound to do always in future as well, wonders in bringing about a new consciousness and a new spirit amongst the Muslims culminating in the re-vitalisation of Islam.

"Within comparatively a short space of time Your Highness would be officially celebrating your Diamond Jubilee at Dar-es-Salaam. It is but befitting therefore for me to take this opportunity to offer, on behalf of the entire Muslim Community of Mombasa, nay Kenya, Uganda, Tanganyika and Zanzibar whose delegates are assembled here to-day, our humble but warmest felicitations on the forthcoming happy, auspicious event which will be followed with undiminished interest by the entire Muslim world.

"When the history of the Muslim inhabitants of this Dark Continent comes to be written, the solid noble, constructive and decisive part played by Your Highness in raising them up and putting them on their onward march towards progress, prosperity and happiness, is bound to be written in gold letters; and posterity shall always take just pride in your wonderful achievements with a sense of deep gratitude. This is compatible with your distinguished record of sterling services to the Muslims elsewhere in general and to Islam in particular. In point of fact, no words can do full justice in giving expression to our deep feelings of gratitude and appreciation which are presently running riot in our hearts.

"Once again I beg to thank Your Highness from the core of our hearts for condescending to visit Mombasa and to preside over this momentous Conference which is the second of its kind: the deliberations of which I do hope and trust will result in elevating the East African Muslim Welfare Society to new heights of prestige, power and influence and produce an edifice which will prove of permanent and lasting growing benefit to all the Muslims of East Africa in general and the downtrodden and backward sections in particular."

194

A UNIVERSITY FOR EAST AFRICA

Speech at the (Second) East African Muslim Conference

Mombasa: 28 July 1946

Finances for the proposed university – the role of local Muslims – the vision of a world Islamic centre of learning – Islamic Culture Society.

... First of all you should collect the funds; say at least 30%, 40% or 50%. Once we have got 50% of the capital, then it will be very easy for two or three gentlemen from here to go out to Beyrout and make a thorough study of the Dodge University there and then report to the local people here. In this way we shall get more quickly to the work. The only difference is in the local work. Local Muslims can do better work than Egyptian people or experts from India who do not know local conditions and local needs. There is a point to be raised about the second part of the resolution: although I realize that it will be an Islamic University to serve Muslims of East and Central and South Africa of all nationalities and also Somalis. It must be a world Islamic University from China to Morocco. First of all we must have funds on hand; for this each and every Muslim should be approached and funds collected and then I will double it as promised last year. But to count on India and Egypt alone is not fair. It must be a Pan Islamic University. What is the use of these Committees unless their members do not go house to house to collect funds? You should get money from local people by annual round ups. There is no need of useless Committees without their collecting funds. Let poor Africans should also be approached [*sic*]; even poor Somalis and Swahilis be asked to contribute. I should like this resolution to be reconsidered.

[Liwali Mbarak (Ali Hinawy) explained the background as well

as what the members had at the back [*sic*] when they adopted
the resolution to which His Highness made a reference. His
Highness appeared satisfied.]

His Highness then referred to the establishment of the Islamic
Culture Society in Mombasa whose Patron he said he had gladly
agreed to become. He said that in his opinion this body could
play a very useful and important part for the intellectual or
mental advancement of the East African Muslims and create a
new consciousness among them. Continuing His Highness said
the Society's inception was necessary and it should work separ-
ately for Muslims of all nationalities or races. It should be given
liberal support by the Muslims. His Highness then called upon
Liwali Mbarak to explain to the meeting the aims and objects of
the Islamic Culture Society of which he is the President.

Source: *Combined Report of the Second East African Muslim Conference and the Annual
General Meeting of the East African Muslim Welfare Society,* Mombasa, 1946.
During the meeting of the East African Muslim Welfare Society, the Aga
Khan promised to use his influence in India and Egypt and other Islamic
countries for augmenting the funds for the proposed Muslim University.

195

WORLD PEACE AND ITS PROBLEMS

A Lecture at the Dar-es-Salaam Cultural Society

Dar-es-Salaam: 3 August 1946

Question of peace an all-absorbing one – messages of Buddha and Christ – Islam means peace – history has been full of wars – terrible wars of the twentieth century – the work of the League of Nations – its serious weaknesses and defects – its collapse – what the future organization should be – the union of Great Britain and daughter dominions with the United States – other countries will join in – forms of government in colonies to satisfy indigenous populations – free trade – hopes for India, Indo-China and Indonesia – if Britain, the USA and daughter nations unite for peace, the Soviet Union will feel safe – a world organization will succeed.

I must first of all thank you for having invited me here and for having left me to choose the subject that I would like to speak upon. After some consideration I come to the conclusion that if there was not going to be any peace it was worthless and useless to talk about anything else, because we would not know what would happen to any of the schemes that we might have in these days. Now there is one point without which no other scheme for betterment is worth seriously considering, namely, are we or are we not going to have some kind of breathing space, if not permanent peace? This has been a problem in one form or another in the past in a very small way, now it is an all-absorbing question before men.

The desires, dreams and hope, the ideal of all that is best in the spirit of man is peace. What is the practical apart from the theoretical and philosophical teachings of Buddha? Peace to living beings. In a largely Christian gathering, such as I am addressing today, it is not necessary for me to refer to the teaching of the great founder of Christianity and its application to international, inter-racial, inter-continental relations, but I am sure you will agree that the final result of that great Teacher's work would be, if carried out, peace.

And now about the faith to which I belong. Islam means peace, Muslim means Pacifist. Our salution [*sic* salutation] "Salaam alikum", "Peace be with you", and the reply "Alikumsa-laam", "And upon you be Peace". The Holy Prophet of Islam laid down as the rule of life, peace between man and man, peace in thought and in action, and he always insisted on kindliness and gentleness towards all animals and all human beings. Islam frankly accepts the right of other living beings apart from human beings to treatment worthy of not only man's soul but the spirit which is manifested in all life.

Such were the dreams, the teachings of the outstanding figures of the past. Such have been the yearnings of most ordinary mortals from time immemorial, and yet what is history except on rare occasions one long, long story of war and warfare? In Islam during the greater part of the golden age of Omiyyas in Syria and Spain, my own ancestors in Egypt, periods of peace, in all the odds and ends, made up together some hundred years of peace, but not in one extension. With those rare occasions, 30 to 40 years here and 30 to 40 years there, there has never been peace. In Rome there was a glorious period of some 60 years' peace. But that is about all. The middle ages and the age there-after consisted of minor and constant struggles. The horrors of the Mogul [Mongol] invasion of Western Asia of Changizkhan and Tamerlain are well-known facts, which leave us with some-thing like the impression of a nightmare. The bloody battles of the crusades which in the name of the noblest led to untold miseries for East and West are glaring facts.

But all these horrors of the past have been put into [in the] shade in the twentieth century and our own times. In the seven-teenth and eighteenth century and perhaps in the early years of nineteenth century warfare in Europe and Asia had a picturesque and chivalrous appearance, and so limited an extension that perhaps it could mislead men and their imagination to something resembling national [or] international competition for bravery and courage.

These wars were limited in numbers. The civil population practically escaped except on rare occasions, and the rules and regulations of war were so laid down that they might be compared to international duels rather than battles. Curiously this phenomenon was true both in Europe and Asia and North Africa, as well as the inter-colonial struggles in America. But there was a rude awakening in this century. The first world war was already something so terrible that it had put into [in the] shade with its consequence, namely, the terrible epidemic of 1918, 1919 and 1920, killing more than all the world war No. 1 itself [*sic*]. Millions and millions died of influenza and its consequences in India alone in one year. In India alone it wiped out no end of young children and young men, and the same was true of America and Africa. That first world war opened the eyes of men of goodwill throughout the world to the dangers of living in an unorganized society.

Then we had the nightmare through which we lived when for the first time we had the organized murder of civilians and the concentration camps which went with warfare. These then are the glaring facts.

After 1918, a serious and honest effort was made by the victors to give the world an organization that would prevent a repetition of such horrors and would save mankind from new experiences of a similar kind and make both impossible and unnecessary a repetition of war with its horrors. That led to the League of Nations.

To serve the cause of international peace was then my own main occupation and object in life, and from 1931 to 1938 I was with with [the] Disarmament Conference and representing India not only at its main sessions but on nearly all special occasions. I was intimately connected with the Geneva Institute.

I was a regular member of the then League of Nations. Of course I believed in it, like so many other millions. Of course, it had all my hopes in it. Of course, up to the end and even in 1938, like so many others, I believed that we would escape the immediate danger, and once that was over we could re-organize and enlarge the then existing organization and give it strength and power and extensions. But all this did not blind us, I must admit we, who were, so to speak, the permanent representatives of our countries at headquarters, from realising the serious weaknesses and defects of the institution.

America, after [President Woodrow] Wilson, one of its sponsors, in fact, the chief sponsor, was the first to quit, attracted by isolation and its idealism, dismayed and disgusted by the selfishness of the Continental politics. The idealism of Wilson's character and confidence was dropped by his countrymen for a mistaken realism of pure Americanism. We did get Russia in and [Maksim Maksimovich] Litvinov, its distinguished representative who was my colleague for many years, made speeches which were unexceptional from the point of view of peace and International Law and Order. I must say in those days Russia stood for world peace in the Geneva institution, with a regularity and firmness that was [sic won] our admiration. But what else took place? Germany, Japan and Italy were in fact leaving and the League had shrunk, in fact, to Britain, Russia and France, the smaller states of the Continent, the Dominions, India, Egypt, Iraq, Iran and some but by no means the most important of the South American States.

It had lost such moral influence as it might have had with the non-League powers. These, however, were not its greatest shortcomings. The worst was nominal responsibility for Peace – Yes! of power it had none: it not only had no air force, army or navy of its own, but no power of inspection and of acquiring knowledge of hostile intentions through organised agencies; no power to really help or be of assistance to the victims of aggression. It could be taken by surprise. No doubt there were some people here and there who gave warnings, but it was difficult to suspect without taking part in an active hostility towards the suspected ones.

Its final collapse in 1939 and 1940 was the inevitable result of its constitutional weaknesses and short-comings. To me, who had hoped against hope, continued against obvious signs, to the country [sic contrary] like so many others, like the majority of people in Britain, to believe in the possibility of its development into a really world peace league, it came as a shock, all the same, when World War No. 2 proved the inefficiency of the first organisation [sic].

All this is of the past. What about the future? There [is] one fact beyond which we cannot look for any lesson in history, in fact, I may almost say in [the language of] material science, similar causes lead to similar results. The absence of proper provisions for regional alliances organised under the League itself for the maintenance of peace was another and perhaps the most serious of the causes of its break-down when it came up against the realities of power politics.

What are the lessons for future? I feel that the ideological constitution for a world parliament, however, well made, will not have that basis of national inspiration and interest for which great people are ready to lay down their lives.

Let us look at the facts of international and inter-racial institutions on this beautiful but perhaps unfortunate planet. No amount of constitution which has not behind it the vital living, constant interest of great nations to sacrifice all in its higher national interest – without that backing – no amount of paper guarantees will give us peace. Can anyone doubt that if we really wish to have a permanent central power for good to lead mankind not front to back but hand in hand we must look forward for a time and hope for an absolute permanent, loyal and comprehensive central unit that will be, by its ideological as well as material and economic interest, the centre, the guardian, the champion of peace for its centre.

And that central unit can only be the union of Great Britain and the daughter dominions on one side with the United States.

I go further – it seems to me the only hope for permanent peace and it is essential that the people of the United States and Great Britain and daughter dominions should not look upon each other as foreign countries but as sister associates. I hope and believe that whatever the difference in form, in nomenclature and in variety of interest, that union will become a reality.

I look forward that the reign of George VI will undo the disaster for mankind that took place under George III. However excellent the paper guarantees of U.N.O., its written constitution, its aspirations, but [sic] without a common peace policy of these two central world powers, namely, Great Britain and the daughter nations and the United States, we will be building on the sands of the seashore. Once this central world-wide confederation of the United States, Great Britain, Ireland, Canada, New Zealand, and South Africa has in fact taken a permanent common policy of peace and guardianship of world peace and is ever ready to stop aggression at its very first signs of a revival of that aggressive spirit in international relations then naturally peaceful countries of the world will be inevitably drawn and attracted into being junior partners in this greatest and most powerful of all the central societies.

The world of Islam – peaceful, wishing only to live and let live, true to the principles of the Prophet; Egypt, the Arab States and Arab League, Turkey and Iran and Afghanistan can have no other foreign policy or desire or ambition than attachment alike for ideal and practical reasons to the Anglo-American central peace power.

On the Continent, leaving Russia and the East out, France will be the leading – in fact by far the leading – individual nation, and can anyone doubt that if England and America are united in a peace policy, that the overwhelming majority of the French people will not heartily join in with it!

Holland and Belgium, the Scandinavian States will be fast drawn towards that centre and sooner or later the fast growing and essentially healthy daughter nations of Spain and Portugal in the new world, which are certainly not going to be the creators of adventure and aggression, but will play an ever more important part in world economy and advancement.

Now what about the great Chinese, the immense Chinese, world, for it is a world of its own, the peaceful – there has been internal strife in China but it has been from time immemorial essentially peaceful, still essentially Confucian, and has for thousands of years never shown any spirit of aggression and has been one of the bastions of moral peace and live and let live in the world. Is it now going to look out for adventure! Has it any interest to risk the little amount of goodwill and leisure and happiness that nature gives to its vast and overcrowded populace in gambles of the kind that brought disaster to Germany and Japan! No, China's natural place will be a position of equal and honoured association with America, Britain, Dominions and the Muslim world.

I, for one, am convinced that Italy, Germany and Japan have now learnt their lesson provided always that Anglo-American guardianship of peace is awake and constant, provided they realise that the solidity of Anglo-American guardianship of peace will not be a matter of passing fashion, but the permanent unity of these two essential centres of world power. There and then only they will try to win back respect and self-respect by supporting the world peace ring.

Now we come to one of the last possibilities of warfare by that dangerous but comprehensive [sic comprehensible] cupidity of the "have-nots".

What about India, the British Crown colonies, the Colonies of France and Holland, Portugal and Belgium? These vast, rich, varied areas, and let us call "a spade a spade," foreign owned areas – what is the part they are going to play? What of the future? If in fact, whatever the nominal relationship with the owing [sic. owning?] countries they are to be the plantations of the so called protecting powers then sooner or later they will become inevitably the apples of discord, perhaps they will lead to misunderstanding even between Britain and America.

About one quarter of the human race, about one third of the richest lands on earth however you may sugarcoat the pill, cannot remain plantations and plantation workers for long without raising those very sentiments which are the opposite of pacificism among non-plantation owners.

No! No! these areas, even populations, must be, whatever the name, whatever the form, must in fact, be open to all that is best in modern political idealism if they are to become the pillars of peace instead of breeding ground for future world warfare. They must first of all be, as soon as possible, as soon as conditions will permit, brought into a form of Government that will satisfy their indigenous population and the sentiments of self-respect and honour.

Secondly the present beneficiary plantation owners must give in trade and commerce to worldwide and equal economic activity on which alone real world prosperity and peace of the world can be built. That good old Free Trade doctrine, now out of fashion, must at least for these and not self-governing areas be looked upon as the best antidote to dangerous ambitions that lead to warfare.

It is a hopeful sign that India at last has now a chance, if only its nations rise to the occasion, to become a powerful confederation of states within the World States organisation to free itself from even suspicion of being the greatest plantation property of all. India has at last the chance of taking its place among the great nations of the world, and it depends on its sons whether it takes the message. There are signs that Indo-China and let us hope Indonesia will also move forward along a similar line, the only line that could give security and prosperity on a permanent basis to such areas.

Near, where we are now, these other areas will take time but some form or other of trusteeship, whether guaranteed by written or unwritten laws, whether of one country or of the world, something of that nature must be attempted, not only for its own immediate objective and advantages but to prevent those rich and yet semi-virgin lands from being objects of international jealousy, suspicion and ambition and cupidity.

In such a world, as I have now tried to adumbrate, on howsoever vague and general a basis in a world in which England and America and the daughter nations are united as one for peace, standing with their ever-readiness to sacrifice all, and realising that peace is indivisible, the first true doctrine which, alas, we let go in Geneva, if England and America make it their permanent first principle of life and policy, this indivisibility of peace, then I am certain that, in such a world Russia will have every reason to be satisfied and proud of her immense, in fact unique position, and she will join in as one of the greatest and most important of the world powers.

She will be impregnable, not only by her own strength but by the fact of being surrounded everywhere by peace-loving nations, united in a union on the solid facts of each country's self-respect and vital needs being satisfied by world commerce and trade. Only then and then [sic] will the new world peace league, whatever its written constitution, be free from the danger of fears and from the internal and external weaknesses of our first world attempt at world organisation. Only then will men also be free to give time to that peace of God on earth for which alone we ought to labour and strive and to bring up our families.

Source: *Special Golden Platinum Jubilee Day Number,* Ismailia Association for Tanganyika, Dar-es-Salaam, n.d. (?1956), pp. 1–14. The pamphlet was edited by Ismail H. Ebrahim and issued by the Literature Section, Dar-es-Salaam Committee, Shia Imami Ismailia Association for Tanganyika.

196

THE FOLLY OF HATE AND FEAR

Speech at the Diamond Jubilee Celebrations

Dar-es-Salaam: 10 August 1946

Failure of the League of Nations due to hate and fear – Africans, Europeans and Indians should not fear each other – human relations in the future – white, black and brown complement one another.

Now one word, if I may be allowed to say it, of general advice to inhabitants here, whatever their race, colour or creed.

I have had some experience of the causes of strife and I was a very active member of the League of Nations and of the Disarmament Conference for some seven years. Why did it fail? Ultimately because of hate. And yet why did people hate each other? Fear. Where there is fear there is no love, but hate easily enters through the windows even if the door is shut.

I appeal to all of you, Africans, Europeans and Indians – do not fear each other. Work together. The country is big enough. There is virgin soil which has hardly been scratched. Unlike China, India and Europe, the population is still very small. We have no need to struggle for existence here for a century at least, so why foresee trouble for your great-grandchildren. There may be none. Thanks to atom bomb and the progress of knowledge and science. And if things take a turn for good instead of evil, then the new forces of nature, we are certain, will make human relations easier and give each and all security.

To-day, strife here on racial lines is imaginary. The onlooker sees most of the game, and I have been here an onlooker. There is no getting away from it – if you will throw fear out of your minds and you will soon realise that white, black and brown are complementary members of a common body politic.

Source: *The East African Standard*, Nairobi, 12 August 1946.

It also appeared in *The Tanganyika Standard*, Dar-es-Salaam, 11 August 1946. It has been reproduced in Habib V. Keshavjee, *The Aga Khan and Africa*, Pretoria, 1946, p. 194.

197

THE FUTURE DEFENCE PROBLEM OF SOUTH ASIA

Letter to The Times

Lausanne: 19 July 1947

Anxiety over the division of the Indian Army between India and Pakistan – what the United Nations could do – indivisibility of peace – responsibility of India and Pakistan.

Much anxiety prevails as to Indian defence and the effects of the division of the army between India and Pakistan. I hold that the term "Indian defence" is no more a problem of practical politics – it is peace or nothing. Either the United Nations organization will be strong enough to prevent aggression or to suppress the aggressor with overwhelming force, or it is good-bye to the future of mankind, including, of course, India. The one fundamental lesson of the last war is that for all future time Mr. Litvinov's dictum "Peace is indivisible" alone stands.

We in Geneva realized, when heart-broken Mr. Eden was forced to accept Italy's violation of Abyssinia, that World War II became a probability. Now, however, it is the indivisibility of peace or nothing. The future defence of India will not be along the Hindu Kush or the plains of Chamman but in Massachusetts, Moscow, Nanking, or Rio. The only practical service the new Governments of India and Pakistan could render to Indian defence would be to place their resources at the disposal of the U.N. and world peace, and use all their influence with fellow members of the Commonwealth – and all other peace-loving nations – to make war and aggression as much an impossibility in future as organized banditry is today in Switzerland.

Source: *The Times*, London, 23 July 1947.

It was written from Lausanne Palace Hotel, Lausanne on 19 July. The journal published it under the title of "Indian Defence", though in fact the Aga Khan is concerned with the defence problems of the future Indian Union and Pakistan after the withdrawal of British rule from the subcontinent.

For the issues of the defence of the subcontinent and the division of the British Indian Army see Chaudhri Muhammad Ali, *The Emergence of Pakistan*, New York, 1967; Fazal Muqeem Khan, *The Story of the Pakistan Army*, Karachi, 1963; Penderel Moon, *Divide and Quit*, London, 1962; Khalid bin Sayeed, *Pakistan: The Formative Phase*, Karachi, 1960; L. F. Rushbrook Williams, *The State of Pakistan*, London, rev. edn 1966; Richard Symonds, *The Making of Pakistan*, London, 1950; Alan Campbell-Johnson, *Mission with Mountbatten*, London, 1951; Lord Ismay, *The Memoirs of General the Lord Ismay*, London, 1960; E. W. R., *The Transfer of Power in India, 1945–1947*, London, 1954; V. P. Menon, *The Transfer of Power in India*, Calcutta, 1957; Leonard Mosley, *The Last Days of the British Raj*, London, 1961; and K. K. Aziz, *Britain and Muslim India*, London, 1963.

198

THE CREATION OF PAKISTAN AND THE MUSLIM WORLD

Message to the People of Pakistan on the Eve of the Creation of Pakistan

Switzerland: 17 August 1947

Tribute to Muhammad Ali Jinnah – advice to work for Pakistan – need for helping the Muslims still under foreign dominion.

Thanks to the immense and almost miraculous efforts of Governor-General Jinnah, who alone brought about the greatest Muslim State in the world, Pakistan is now an accomplished fact. But our work now begins.

If the Muslims were depressed by the misfortunes of the last 200 years throughout the world, now, at last, the wheel of fortune has turned and we are no longer justified in being either half-hearted or pessimistic.

We must, with all our energy, heart and soul, with faith in Islam and trust in God, work for the present and future glory of Pakistan and give help to the unfortunate Muslims who still suffer under foreign dominion.

We must work for a better world, and be no more hypnotised by the dead glories of the distant past, or by the misfortunes of the near past.

Source: *Message to the World of Islam by Aga Khan III*, Karachi, 1977, p. 1.

The message, as reproduced in the above work, carries the words "Switzerland, August 17, 1947", without specifying the town or city from where it was sent.

On the making of Pakistan see Chaudhri Muhammad Ali, *The Emergence of Pakistan*, London and New York, 1967; K. K. Aziz, *The Making of Pakistan: A Study in Nationalism*, London, 1967; Hafeez Malik, *Moslem Nationalism in India and Pakistan*, Washington, D.C., 1963; Ian Stephens, *Pakistan: Old Country, New Nation*, Harmondsworth, 1964; Richard Symonds, *The Making of Pakistan,*

London, 1949; L. F. Rushbrook Williams, *The State of Pakistan*, London, 1962; Khalid bin Sayeed, *Pakistan: The Formative Phase*, Karachi, 1960; Ian Stephens, *Pakistan*, London, 1963; Choudhary Rahmat Ali, *Pakistan: The Fatherland of the Pak Nation*, Cambridge, 3rd edn 1947; and K. K. Aziz, *A History of the Idea of Pakistan*, Lahore, 1987, 4 vols.

199

CAN WE STOP THE NEXT WAR?

An Article

October–November 1947

Fear of a third world war – the First and Second World Wars – no
mad men in power today – conditions which lead to war – danger
signs of today – dream of world peace through history – birth of
the League of Nations – its Covenant not suitable for human beings
– failures of the League – Charter of the United Nations – its
limited powers – forces in favour of international consolidation –
let peace-loving nations assert their will – respect for the United
Nations' Constitution – Great Britain's prestige – decolonization –
frontier adjustments through honest plebiscites – security – no
dreams of nineteenth-century imperialism.

Many people in Western Europe, North America, and outside
that zone, live with the conscious or subconscious fear of another
world war.

With the sense of approaching calamity goes the legitimate
deduction, from given data, that this third war will be a thousand
times more destructive than the last one, that vast areas, cities,
whole countries and States may be reduced to wilderness, and
that sooner or later not only the chief antagonists but the whole
world will be drawn into it on one side or the other, with possible
revolutions and fifth columns destroying what little is left by the
military.

Is this fear justified? Is it only a vast wide-world [*sic*] illusion?

Of course, reasoning dispassionately, there should be no such
disaster. But what reason did the world have in 1914 to set the
ball rolling downward, to put an end to prosperity and peace,
and to begin a series of upheavals which, far from settling any

problem for the better, have complicated and actually worsened the situation of all human beings?

The case of 1939 is perhaps not on all fours with that of pre-1914 or with the situation today. At that time one demented person – who had the extraordinary power of making men like the late Earl Lloyd George, and many others, including myself, believe that on no account would he draw the sword – got such a hold on his own people by his successes that he could lead them to disaster in a totally unnecessary world conflict brought about by himself.

At that time any sane man could have foreseen the inevitable ruin of the German race and unfortunately, of much besides.

Luckily we have no madmen in supreme power anywhere in the world today. On the other hand, we have now a danger that the inevitable clash of power politics may bring about a calamity which no one man can create or prevent.

We must look back to history. When two more or less equally strong Powers are face to face, across land or water, and especially when there are religious or economic differences, and ideals totally opposed to each other, Time works like an explosive.

Notwithstanding the good sense of the majority of the people, the governing classes on both sides, weary of undecisive conflict, worn out by responsibilities too heavy to bear, finally drift to that trial by force which has led to wars innumerable.

Something of that situation is arising today. It would be wishful thinking to imagine that the bickerings of Flushing Meadows, the oppositions of the partisans of East and West in every country, the Iron Curtain, and the inevitable support given by the powerful to the weak neighbours of the Iron Curtain – it would be wishful thinking to imagine that all this can go on permanently and that the world can live on fear and escape disaster.

If a fundamental change is not brought about, you will find that some day the atom bombs will go off on their own. You cannot sow distrust and not reap the reward of disaster.

From time immemorial men have dreamt of world peace, of super-States, of central authorities that might enforce universal peace.

The Roman Empire had this dream and, up to a point, realised it in the West. The Moslem Caliphate Empire, and Islam, which means peace, hoped and tried for it over its vast dominions successfully for at most two generations only, and strove for it unsuccessfully for the rest of its history.

In the Middle Ages the Papacy tried to impose universal peace under Christendom. The Spanish monarchy, at the height of its power, dreamt of being so strong as to suppress all opposition for all time.

Later, Castlereagh's and Canning's theory of brokerage politics, and Salisbury's Concert of Europe system were attempts by different methods to prevent warfare among the Great Powers.

In spite of the Crimean War and the Franco-German War, the methods of Canning, Bismarck, and Salisbury gave the world peace and prosperity for a hundred years. Unfortunately for mankind, the disaster of 1914 broke once and for all the system that had prevailed from 1815 onward.

As the first World War drew to its close and Allied victory seemed inevitable, leading thinkers and the governing classes among the victorious Powers, led by Wilson, saw that only a world government, overshadowing all States and guarding peace, could prevent future risks of wholesale destruction.

For this, many eminent men, headed by Wilson, Smuts, and others, set to work. The chief outcome of their deliberations was the League of Nations, the Constitution of which they thought more important than the Treaty between the Allies and Germany.

I was intimately associated with this League for seven years and saw its day-to-day working, its many serious failures, and its rare successes.

The League Covenant was a perfect instrument – for angels. Human beings, with their passions and weaknesses, with their loves and hatreds, with the long traditions of autonomy, national sovereignties, of former wars and jealousies, could never have worked the Covenant successfully over long periods.

The League could not settle the German question. It failed in the Far East, and ended by withdrawing even its pinpricks from aggressive Italy. It was very strong in dealing with third-rate questions and still more so in removing the least cause of dissatisfaction for France, Britain and Russia.

But with America absent, with Japan, Germany, and Italy walking out, by the time I left it in 1938 it had become, for all practical purpose, impotent. Powerless from its very beginning, it had lost even its prestige. It died with the last war.

Now we have the present Charter. And once more there is

disappointment, for in all real activity it seems to be as powerless as its defunct predecessor. Excellent on paper, ideally perfect in its fine adjustment of regulations, it is impotent the moment it touches the fundamental rights of any State that has the power and energy to challenge its decisions.

Gradually it is leading to open opposition among the Great Powers and their friends and clients, or to make-believe, face-saving resolutions that lead nowhere. Neither atomic energy nor military, naval and air force budgets are within its grasp.

It has shown itself to be a wonderful platform for airing opposite views. If it is left as at present, sooner or later we will find the Great Powers settling things among themselves, either at the cost of the small fry, or with such bitterness after each so-called pacific settlement of a thorny question as to make future warfare a probability first, a certainty later. So drift will replace the grandiose objectives of the founders of the United Nations, and the disillusions of the League be repeated.

What are we to do? Is there a remedy? What does history teach? What is our own reading of the human heart, its desires and passions?

The world is getting smaller. Even these half-hearted attempts at Customs unions, the Marshall Plan, the 16 Nations' economic requests to America – these are all indications that, despite almost chauvinistic nationalisms, some forces are working for international consolidation.

But these methods will be far slower in the long run than the opposite currents of violent criticism, of military and atomic preparations, of alliance safeguards, of looking out for friends to face the enemy.

Once more I ask: What is the remedy? There is only one that can be called effective and just. Let all the peace-loving nations, all the nations who are ready to fight future aggression as they fought Hitler's Germany, all who believe differences should be settled not by warfare but by arbitration and jurisdiction – let all these show their will.

They must not wait for this, or look behind, but here and now begin the making of an overwhelming peace league, with the Charter in its hands and the veto thrown to the winds, ever ready to use all its force to crush an aggressor, great or small, and to compel respect for the U.N.'s just constitution.

For this, an association of nations, with the pooling of all resources is necessary, whether that association starts in Europe,

America, or Asia. Political geography must change over generations, just as the geological characteristics of the Earth vary with the passing of the ages.

Great Britain has won the esteem and friendship of all Asia by her magnificent acts towards India, Pakistan, Burma, and Ceylon.

Just as Britain is infinitely stronger in prestige and power in Asia than she was when the King was Emperor of India, so possessors of colonies must learn that a vast stream of peace-loving nations cannot exist with suppressed nationalities struggling for freedom under various member States.

The position will be all the stronger if former dependent areas that have reached a certain standard of modernisation can be brought in as willing associates. Frontier adjustments over decades and generations are inevitable, but they must come from honest plebiscites organised by a supreme court of nations.

Security – yes. But only those who are responsible for security must have the force, and not continue behind a façade of supernational organisations the covetous and aggressive dreams of 19th-century imperialism.

Source: *The Sunday Post*, Nairobi, 16 November 1947.

It was originally published in the *Egyptian Mail* of Cairo, and this fact is confirmed by *The Sunday Post*, but the date of original appearance is not given. The date on which the Aga Khan wrote it or sent it to the Cairo newspaper is not available. Later it was also reproduced by *The Tanganyika Tribune*, Dar-es-Salaam of 27 December 1947.

The Sunday Post prefaced the article with a box which read: "Spiritual leader of 100,000,000 Moslems and reputedly one of the richest men in the world, reviews the failures of the past, the difficulties of the present and the possibilities of the future."

200

GANDHI'S POLITICAL PHILOSOPHY

Letter to The Times

France: 2 (?) February 1948

Interview with Gandhi in 1946 – Gandhi's ideals and Marx's philosophy – civilisation – theories of Kroptokin – man and the
commands of the conscience.

Some opinions expressed by the late Mahatma Gandhi on matters
of general importance may interest the public, so I venture to
report them.

The Nawab of Bhopal and I had interviews with him in the
spring of 1946 at Poona to find a formula that might satisfy both
Congress and League, and after we had failed I had another
interview with him on the question of Indians in South Africa.
When it was over I asked him his opinion of Marx's philosophy.
Gandhiji at once said that his own ideal was the same as Marx's,
i.e., "that the State should wither away," but that he did not
believe the desired end, the collapse of all Governments, could
ever come by Marx's Dialectic. On the contrary, the principles of
non-violence and obedience to conscience once practised would
inevitably make "the State wither away."

Then he said that a society's civilization should not be judged
by its powers over the forces of nature, nor by the power of
its literature and art, but by the gentleness and kindness of its
members towards all living beings. He reminded me of Kropotkin's theories that primitive man hated bloodshed and cruelty
and that if this were proved exact then there had been a growth
of the power of evil. He also remarked that the ancient South
American custom of human sacrifice, with the proud consent of
the victim, was less degrading than mass murder by conscript
armies maddened by a scientific propaganda of hate and lies.

There was never any suggestion of "other-worldliness" as the motive force to bring about a truly civilized society built on love and forbearance but that man's proud place in the universe was justified only if he obeyed the highest commands of conscience.

Source: *The Times*, London, 5 February 1948.

The Aga Khan signed the letter from "France", and did not date it.

On Gandhi and his ideas see his own *An Autobiography or The Story of My Experiments with Truth*, Ahmedabad, 1945, and *Satyagraha*, Ahmedabad, 1951; D. G. Tendulkar, *Mahatma: Life of Mohandas Karamchand Gandhi*, New Delhi, 1951, rev. edn 1960, 8 vols.; Pyarelal, *Mahatma Gandhi: The Last Phase*, Ahmedabad, Vol. 1, 1956, Vol. 2, 1958; Robert Payne, *The Life and Death of Mahatma Gandhi*, London, 1969; Edmond Privat, *Vie de Gandhi*, Geneva and Valence, 2nd edn 1949; Geoffrey Ashe, *Gandhi: A Study in Revolution*, London, 1968; Glorney Bolton, *The Tragedy of Gandhi*, London, 1934; G. Dhawan, *The Political Philosophy of Mahatma Gandhi*, Delhi, 1962; Louis Fischer, *The Life of Mahatma Gandhi*, New York, 1951; Sankaran Nair, *Gandhi and Anarchy*, London, 1958; Romain Rolland, *Mahatma Gandhi*, London, 1924; and Taya Zinkin, *Gandhi*, London, 1965.

201

SPELLING REFORM

Letter to The Times

Paris: 19 March 1949

Suggestion for English spelling reform.

After reading Mr. Bernard Shaw's letter I feel it is strange that nobody has proposed a very simple change in spelling and phonetics that will save not one letter but the useless repetition of a half letter in many words. Make "c" into a "ch" pronounced, and let all the "s" sounds in "c" words be transferred to "s". Thus thousands of people, including our future Sovereign, will be saved from writing the ancient name of Charles at its present length, not to mention the useless "h" in Chichester. This is only half a loaf, but it is better than none.

Source: *The Times*, London, 23 March 1949.
  G. B. Shaw's letter to which the Aga Khan refers was published in *The Times* of 19 March and ran as follows:
  "Mr. Follick and Mr. Pitman have been lucky enough to break virtually even with a pitiably recalcitrant Cabinet over spelling reform.
  "In the debate Sir Alan Herbert took the field as the representative of Oxford University, the university of Henry Sweet, greatest of British phoneticians. After debiting the stale tomfooleries customary when spelling reform is discussed by novices and amateurs he finally extinguished himself by pointing out that a sample of Mr. Follick's spelling saves only one letter from the conventional Johnsonese orthography. This was the champion howler of the debate. I invite Sir Alan to write down that one letter, and measure how long it takes him to get it on paper, and how much paper it covers: say a fraction of a second and of a square inch. "Not worth saving" is his present *reductio ad absurdum*. But surely a University Member must be mathematician enough to go deeper. In the English-speaking world, on which the sun never sets, there are at every fraction of a moment millions of scribes, from bookkeepers to poets, writing that letter or some other single letter. If it is superfluous, thousands of acres of paper, months of time, and the labor of armies of men and women are being

wasted on it. Dare Sir Alan now repeat that a difference of one letter does not matter?

"The rest is poppycock. Simplified spelling, Rational spelling, Symphonic spelling are swept away, economically because phonetic spelling with the present alphabet is impossible without the enormous expense of using two letters for one sound, and psychologically because without some new letters simplified spelling looks illiterate or childish. The notion that the value of the Bible and the plays of Shakespeare lies in their spelling, and will vanish if it be changed, need not trouble anyone primitive enough to entertain it, seeing that both have survived the outrageous transmogrification of changing their spelling to Johnsonese. The fact that no two people have the same vowels any more than the same fingerprints does not matter provided they understand one another's speech. Oxford graduates, inhabitants of the Isle of Dogs, and most coster-mongers, will still call my native country Awlint, and speak, not as I do of sun and luggage but of san and laggij. No matter: we understand.

"In short, what we immediately need is not an international language, nor an official persecution of Johnsonese, nor a New Spelling Bible of Old Spelling Shakespear [sic], nor an alphabet of more than 40 letters, nor a revival of Bell's Visible Speech, nor any of the scores of phonetic fads that now confuse the issue and defeat reform, but a statistical enquiry into the waste of labor by Johnsonese spelling. The rest may be left to the Minister of Education, be he Labor, Conservative, Liberal, Communist, or what not. The roughest estimate will be irresistible; and until it is made public the promotion of Spelling Reform Bills by private members will be waste of time."

202

THE FUTURE OF MUSLIM STATES IN THE BACKGROUND OF HISTORY

An Address to the Pakistan Institute of International Affairs

Karachi: 8 February 1950

Central position of Pakistan – relations among Muslim states – emergence of independent Pakistan in its historical perspective – Turkey, Iran, North Africa and Afghanistan – efforts of Jinnah and the support of the Muslims of India – advantages enjoyed by Pakistan – causes of decline of Muslim states in the past – dynamic nature of Islam – the Umayyad period – comparison with the first 100 years of Islam – the late Sayyid Ameer Ali's contribution to Islam – clash between conservative and progressive elements – Pakistan's destiny – neutrality – Muslim unity.

I thank you most sincerely for inviting me today to address this distinguished assembly. I am happy that in Pakistan there exists a body for the study of its relations with other countries and the world generally. My subject this afternoon may not immediately be of such importance in international studies as some others. Nevertheless, what is to be the future of the Muslim states, and what is to be the example that we must set for them is as important from the international point of view as anything else. For Pakistan holds in one way or another a very central position in the world, from the Pacific to the Atlantic, from the Philippines to Morocco. You will find, from Indonesia right up to Zanzibar, vast Muslim populations. The inter-relation of these must be ultimately intellectual and cultural and spiritual, rather than political and legal. But all the more important is the fact that these relations should be on those lines and not binding.

The importance of the position of Pakistan as an independent Muslim state cannot be fully understood nor the fundamental issues before her in the future, unless certain historical facts are realised and their consequences courageously faced. Incredible as it may seem, there has not been before Pakistan a really independent Muslim state since 1750, i.e., the last 200 years. No doubt, the Moghul Empire nominally existed and its autonomous *subas* that had become, in fact, states, had a certain form of national independence. But one and all were in a precarious position *vis-à-vis* the expanding colonial forces of Europe, as represented by England and France. Nor had the Muslim states such prestige and popularity amongst their subjects as to give them that self-assurance and self-reliance, without which outside dangers cannot be faced.

Turkey then had a vast and potentially powerful empire, which had gradually become so weak in relation to Russia, Austria, England and France, that already at that period, and much more so as time went on, her very existence depended on the mutual jealousies of Christendom. In the 19th century, she was known as the Sick Man of Europe and Asia. Province after province, including Muslim Egypt, was lost. Her Government's policy both external and internal, was one long struggle against total collapse and to save what she could from day to day.

Iran, after Nadir Shah, had been so weakened by internal divisions and intellectual decay and other disorders, that it had also fallen, like Turkey, to dependence on European jealousy for her survival.

The same was true of Morocco and North Africa generally. The vast African and Asiatic dominions of Sultans of Muscat were just British protectorates. Though since the time of Ahmad Shah Abdali, an Afghan national state existed, it, too, owed its independence ultimately to the policies of her neighbours, rather than to her own strength. None of these Muslim states had a national population sufficiently important to stand up against European encroachment. On paper Turkey, indeed, did possess a powerful empire. But its internal, racial and religious divisions and sub-divisions rendered her a comparatively easy prey to the ambitions of her avowed and secret enemies. I think this is a fair picture of the world of Islam from the middle of the 18th century till our own times. But there are natural forces greater than the wisdom of the West. Pride and folly are often fellow travellers. The enmity of England and Germany brought about in the 20th century a new world, in which the birth of a truly independent Muslim state, with all the advantages that can give a nation trust in her own destiny, was made possible by the efforts of the Quaid-i-Azam and the support of the Muslim population of India. That mighty infant is the Pakistan of today.

As a member of the Commonwealth, which, I for one, hope in her own interests, she will remain, she belongs to a confederation that is not limited to what was once known as the British Empire, but includes inevitably that most powerful nation in the world, the United States of America, and behind her, sooner or later, the rest of the new world. The days of foreign intervention and interference are gone. Her numbers, her resources, her geographical position, the fundamental unity of her population in sentimental aspirations, give Pakistan all the advantages which the Muslim world lost some 200 years ago. The prospect is indeed attractive and we should have every confidence in the future. But destiny, as presented in history, must be understood and its dangers avoided. There were other Muslim independent states in the past, with even far greater might than Pakistan can ever have and they gradually degenerated to utter helplessness in the 19th century. What was the cause?

Our critics of the West and the East alike maintain that Islamic society carried within it, by its static character, the germs of decay and death. According to them, the disease is congenital and not acquired. Easy optimism, and just ostrich-like disregarding the lesson of the past is to play into the hands of our enemies, secret and open.

The soul of our nation is ultimately more important than its other resources. I have long pondered over the causes of the downfall of Muslim empires and I am convinced that the disease was acquired and was not congenital. Just as in the life of the individual, the difference between youth, health and vigour, and old age and illness is ultimately adaptability to the changes brought about by environment, so no society that allows its spirit to be limited by conventions and customs can have that dynamic quality without which the society, and later the state, will decay.

Believe me, Islam was and is dynamic and not static. It was dynamic, simple and clear during the glorious Omayyad period, when the foundations of Islam were laid wide and deep, so wide and deep that in spite of all its relative weaknesses, it survived the terrible Mongolian invasions and the far more terrible enmity of Europe in later centuries. Ask your historians, ask your calm thinkers to concentrate on that glorious 100 years of Omayyad rule and take that for example, with its simple faith and open mind, with its dynamic qualities without scholasticism and its legal servitudes.

Muslim histories were mostly written by our enemies under the Abbasides and yet with all their bitter prejudices, they cannot help glorifying, not in words but by facts, that period of simple faith and activity. Some of the very greatest saints of Islam, like the Khalifa Umar Ibne Abdul Aziz, the great Hasan Basri, the Spanish ruler Hisham bin Abdur Rahman, were the children of that period. Unfortunately, it ended and with it the certainty of the Islamisation of Europe and with it of the world.

While Damascus looked to the open world through the Mediterranean and the Atlantic, Baghdad was land bound. History's lesson, the supremacy of water over land, was lost to the Muslim world. It is now a well known fact that the small isolated Muslims of Spain did actually sail to the new world and the Cape of Good Hope, but when they returned home, the then weak and isolated Muslim Spain, without help from Asia and North Africa, had not the resources behind it to complete the work of the sailors as Christian Spain and Portugal did a century later.

With the fall of Damascus, Baghdad became the centre of Islam. The very people and the very system whose Mobeds and Dasturs, by narrowness and verbal and legal quibbles, had weakened and destroyed, first the faith of Zoroaster, and then the empire of Iran, took the helm of Islam and played the same disastrous part over again.

Two simple examples may be quoted. The free, social and intellectual part played in the life of Arabia during the first century by Imam Husain's daughter, Sakina, and by the daughter of Talha, and the great grand daughters of Khalifa Abu Bekr, can be contrasted with the position of women in the 19th century. Again, we know what high standard of music and art had been attained in Mecca and Medina as early as the Khilafat by the early Omayyads and compare it with the disdain with which art is looked upon by some misguided Muslims today.

When the mind and spirit of the people are bound down and limited by subtleties and reservations, by turning every custom into law, as was done by the Mobeds and Dasturs in Magian Persia, downfall was only a question of time. The Muslim world was so handicapped in Baghdad that, in spite of its advance in science and philosophy, from its very nature, it could not go forward, as Europe did two or three centuries later, from the same science and philosophy which it first acquired from the Muslims.

You have many problems in this country, economic, military, scientific. I am sure with God's blessings, you will overcome your period of difficulty, but be careful of the soul and the spirit of the people. Do not look to the third century of Islamic history, but to the first.

The late Syed Ameer Ali rendered many great services to Islam. His book: *The Spirit of Islam,* is a great monument. But, as I often told him, his greatest service was a small concise explanation of Islam, which he published and which has now been forgotten. I wish the people of Pakistan could find it again and make its study compulsory for religious training in all Muslim schools, whatever the sect or sub-sect. Take care of all your resources, but the greatest of all resources is the mind and spirit of man.

And finally, the fact must be faced that there is either an open or a hidden clash between the conservative and the progressive elements in Muslim countries. In Turkey this clash has led to a secular state. In Egypt, it is there between the Ikhwan and the governing classes. It threatens itself in the opposition between the so-called Dar-ul-Islam and the responsible Government of Indonesia. These dangers are very grave for the future of the Muslim state. Thank God it is not so in Pakistan, but unless a healthy middle way, such as existed in the first century is found, the ship may be on the rocks again. The pious Muslim thinkers who face realities in Egypt, in North Africa and Iran know all about it. I hope and pray that it may be the destiny of Pakistan, where there is no clash, whose creator, the Quaid-i-Azam, was essentially a modern man, to bring about this spiritual and intellectual unity throughout the other Muslim states. Here and now, and by not only its example, but by its influence and mediation and courtesy, prevent it ever again from leading to final break, as it did in Turkey, in any other Muslim state and society. It is not influenced by such an effort on the part of Pakistan. The consequences may be a form of secularism in conflict with the thought and spirit of the people. With this prayer I wish you every success in the material, intellectual and spiritual world.

Summary of Discussion

Question: The distinguished speaker has said that Muslim peoples should be clear about certain contingent dangers. I should like to know the learned speaker's opinion with respect to the attitude that they should adopt about dollar diplomacy on the one hand and communism on the other; whether they should remain neutral or take sides with the one or the other party. In case the reply is that they should remain neutral, whether neutrality is feasible under the existing circumstances.

His Royal Highness The Prince Aga Khan: My answer is that neutrality is obviously to everybody's interest. No country has ever prospered by going to war. But the problem today is whether such an attitude is possible or impossible. You see the world is shrinking. Tibet, Sinkiang and the heart of China may be within twelve hours of New York or London. Before the atomic or hydrogen bomb comes, the world will have reached probably that stage through jet planes. The question is: Is it possible to be neutral? I doubt it. But what should be our policy then? It is impossible in politics to look too far ahead. You cannot say now what you should do then. You must have certain principles. When the time comes, I hope our statesmen will act according to their principles. Look, what has happened in the short space of time. At the time of the Round Table Conferences, even the Quaid-i-Azam did not ask for Pakistan. We would have been satisfied with much less. I have been through the fight myself. I know what we asked for and see what we have got. See what we were and what we are today. When the time comes, our leaders will decide what is their interest then. One great quality of Bismark [*sic*] was that he never made up his mind for anything for more than three months ahead.

Question: Do you think the idea of Islamistan would materialize?

His Royal Highness The Prince Aga Khan: What do you mean by Islamistan? Do you mean by it intellectual, religious and cultural unity or political unity? If you mean political unity, how can that be? All the Muslim countries want their independence. Some day, perhaps, there might be a sort of federal arrangements [*sic*]. But that is far away in the future. Now we have a national state and the spirit, which is more important than material strength. I am sure our statesmen of the time will choose the right policy.

Source: *Pakistan Horizon*, Karachi, Vol. 3, pp. 3–8.

This was an address delivered at a meeting of the Pakistan Institute of International Affairs, Karachi, and was published in the institute's journal.

203

WHAT PAKISTANIS SHOULD DO

A Broadcast Message

Karachi: 19 February 1950

Change over the spirit of Karachi – realization among women of
their role – a clash between the conservative and modernist
elements must be avoided – build up a "free Islamic state mentality"
– Islam essentially a natural religion – control of the forces of
nature for survival – Pakistan a virgin country – use hope and faith
for the immense work before you.

Thank God, what a change over the spirit of Karachi. Sleepy
Karachi of four years ago is today not only the capital of a great
State but of a nation which obviously is almost unique, in these
days of pessimism and depression, for its obvious hope and trust
to make by its efforts and by its work a better world and its
faith in God that this new world of Pakistan will be Islamic and
righteous.

Under the leadership of Begum Liaquat Ali Khan, the women
too have realised to a great extent, especially amongst the
younger generation, the part they have to play in nation building.
The feeling of responsibility towards the future of the nation and
the State will become general amongst the women even of the
older generation and their eyes will be opened to see that they
too must put their weight and energy into the cause of Islamic
revival.

There is still time to prevent the repetition here of that clash
between the conservative and modernist elements in Muslim
society. I know that the educated classes hope that with the
general spread of instruction and learning amongst the people,
there will be no need to work for a better understanding of
dynamic Islam as it prevailed in the first century. But if a middle

1260

way is not found now while there is time, there is almost a certainty that the day will come when the progressive elements faced with the dangers of being left far behind amongst the nations of the world, will clamour and demand a secular state, or decay. But now is the time to build up that free Islamic state mentality of toleration, mental and spiritual charity, forgiveness towards each other, on one side, and, what Quran and the Tradition both insisted on, namely, that nature is the great daily book of God whose secrets must be found and used for the well-being of humanity. Islam is essentially a natural religion, the miracles quoted in the Quran are the great phenomena surrounding us and we are often told that all these manifestations can be used and should be, with intelligence, for the service of man. Let us never forget that in the struggle for existence of the future only those will survive who control the forces of nature to the greatest extent.

You have in Pakistan the great advantage of practically a virgin country, with all its resources not only untouched but to a vast extent unknown. Now is the time to use that hope and faith for this immense work under the leadership of our Government that is fully aware and wide awake – a Government, the leading members of which can one and all be taken as an example for the nation.

Source: *Message to the World of Islam by Aga Khan III*, Karachi, 1977, pp. 18–20.

It was broadcast from the Karachi station of Radio Pakistan. The *Zanzibar Times* of 11 April published a shorter version with the title "The Aga Khan's Farewell Message to Pakistan."

204

A TRIBUTE TO MUHAMMAD ALI JINNAH

Message to the Quaid-i-Azam Memorial Fund

Karachi: (?) February 1950

Creator of Pakistan – his iron will and "lion courage" – a memorial to pay homage to him.

The Quaid-e-Azam was the creator of Pakistan and the Father of the Pakistani Nation. It is inconceivable how this could have ever come about without his iron will and lion courage.

While his memory will remain, I am sure, in the hearts of the people of this country as well as the general body of Muslims throughout the world, yet a useful memorial of the kind that will help Pakistan to become what he and Muslims generally dream, is an humble way of our paying homage to his creative work. A simple dignified marble mausoleum, taking inspiration from the Moti Masjid of Delhi Fort, should be our first objective.

Next to that, a large mosque with plenty of open space, taking inspiration from the Badshahi Mosque in Lahore and worthy of Karachi by its size and proportion.

There will also be a Darul Ulum, Islamic Historical and Religious Research Institute based on an Arabic conception. And last, but by no means least, is the Institute of Technology.

These four institutions would, in my opinion, form a fitting memorial to Quaid-e-Azam Mohammad Ali Jinnah.

Source: *The Zanzibar Times*, Zanzibar, 11 April 1950. Also *Message to the World of Islam by Aga Khan III*, Karachi, 1977, pp. 2–3.

Jinnah still lacks a national biographer and a competent editor of his works. Useful information is available in Hector Bolitho, *Jinnah: Creator of Pakistan*, London, 1954; Stanley Wolpert, *Jinnah of Pakistan*, New York, 1984 (the best account in existence and an excellent work in its own right); Ilahi Bakhsh, *With the Quaid-i-Azam During his Last Days*, Lahore, 1949 (repr. 1976); Kanji

Dwrarkadas, *Ruttie Jinnah*, Bombay, 1963; S. Shamsul Hasan, *Plain Mr Jinnah*, Karachi, 1976; M. H. Saiyid, *Muhammad Ali Jinnah*, Lahore, 1945; G. Allana, *Quaid-i-Azam Jinnah: The Story of a Nation*, Lahore, 1967; S. A. Lateef, *The Great Leader*, Lahore, 1947; A. A. Ravoof, *Meet Mr. Jinnah*, Madras, 1944; Z. A. Suleri, *My Leader*, Lahore, 1946; M. S. Toosy, *My Reminiscences of Quaid-i-Azam*, Islamabad, 1976; M. A. H. Ispahani, *Quaid-i-Azam as I Knew Him*, Karachi, 2nd rev. edn 1967; Waheeduzzaman, *Quaid-i-Azam Muhammad Ali Jinnah: Myth and Reality*, Islamabad, 1976; Jamiluddin Ahmad (ed.), *Quaid-i-Azam as Seen by his Contemporaries*, Lahore, 1966; Malik Muhammad Jafar, et al., *Jinnah as a Parliamentarian*, Lahore, 1977; Sharifal Mujahid, *Quaid-i-Azam Jinnah: Studies in Interpretation*, Karachi, 1978; and C. M. Naim (ed.), *Iqbal, Jinnah and Pakistan: The Vision and the Reality*, Syracuse, 1979.

205

A SCHOOL OF TECHNOLOGY FOR EAST PAKISTAN

Speech at the University of Dacca

Dacca: 28 January 1951

The LL.D. degree a source of pride – the university's future role in the country – the development potential of East Pakistan – suggestion for a technological institute – Pakistan is the home of every Muslim.

Prince Aga Sultan Sir Mohammed Shah, P.C., G.C.S.I., G.C.I.E., G.C.V.O., thanking the University authorities for the honour they had shown by conferring the degree of LL.D., said that "there is nothing in the world of which I am more proud of than this LL.D. from this Muslim University".

He added: "The Vice-Chancellor said that one who had received so many other honours might not find this a very great addition, but I can assure you Mr. Vice-Chancellor, Your Excellency [Governor of East Bengal, who was by virtue of his office the Chancellor of the university] and Members of the Court [of the university] that there is nothing in the world of which I am more proud of than this LL.D. from this Muslim University. This means to me more than you can imagine. This University is today probably one of the greatest hopes for the future, not only for the people of Pakistan, but for Islam. Here is a country which is in all essentials a new country. What America was to England and Spain, we can almost certainly say that East Pakistan is for the Muslims of this subcontinent. The natural riches are in abundance and there is a still virgin soil. It is, of course, certain that this University, once its technology is started on firm foundation, will be [the] main element for the development of her soil and richness. My followers will certainly play in future though a humble but useful part. The first essential is that here we should start with the object of an institute like the famous Zurich Technological School as our ideal. This will be a huge work which I am sure that the Government and people of Pakistan will take in hand in the fullness of time. If I am spared a few more months [of life] I may be able with God's grace to do a little in that line myself, but the work is enormous and time is short.

"Once more I thank you Mr. Vice-Chancellor for your generous references to my humble services in the past. I am one of those who cannot live in the past. I am one of those who live in future [sic], but my thoughts are not turned to what I may have done in the past. There is the huge globe, one must try even a little bit to push forward and forward. The rock of Ceciphilous [sic Sisyphean] must not be allowed to come back and hit us in the chest.

"Let me thank you for all the kindness we have received – my wife and myself – in Dacca and Pakistan. There is always kindness for us. Pakistan is the home of every Muslim."

Source: *The Pakistan Observer*, Dacca, 29 January 1951.

The newspaper's report of the function at the University of Dacca, at which the Aga Khan was awarded the honorary degree of LL.D., ran:

"His Royal Highness the Aga Khan received the degree of Doctor of Laws honoris causa at a special convocation of the Dacca University early afternoon yesterday at a solemn function which lasted for about twenty minutes and [was] witnessed by a record audience.

"Malik Feroz Khan Noon [the Governor of East Bengal], Chancellor of the university, presented the degree to His Highness.

"Earlier the Vice-Chancellor, in the course of his address of welcome, referred to the 'great services and sacrifices that you have so relentlessly made all through your life for the welfare of the people in general and for the cause of learning and culture in particular'.

"The Chancellor, in his address, said: 'Your political services in the Indian subcontinent gave you a place of eminence among our [*or* other] leaders and your special efforts and support in the cause of Mussalmans of this subcontinent have during the past been instrumental in creating a public opinion in support of the Muslim claims. Your position in the international, political and social sphere is an asset to the Muslim world.'

"Besides the Members of the Executive Council and the Senate of the University, who were in their academic robes, guests included the Chief Minister, Mr. Nurul Amin, and other Ministers of the Cabinet, the Chief Justice and other Judges of the High Court, members of the diplomatic corps, leaders of the minority [Hindu] community, and leading officials and non-officials, Begum Aga Khan and Begum Noon, and a large number of ladies witnessed the ceremony. His Highness inspected a guard of honour drawn up on the grounds of Curzon Hall before entering the Convocation [hall] in a procession."

Dawn's (Karachi, 29 January 1951) report of the ceremony was as follows:

"The Vice-Chancellor, Mr. Mahmud Husain, in his speech said: 'Your Royal

1265

Highness is widely known in every nook and corner of Pakistan as the oldest of those political thinkers in this subcontinent who had prepared the ground for the establishment of Pakistan by taking the initiative along with the illustrious son of this historic city, the late lamented Nawab Sir Salimullah Bahadur of Dacca, for bringing into existence the Muslim League in 1906.

" 'Your services to the Muslim nation of the Indo-Pak[istan] subcontinent have been too great to be forgotten – as the President of the All-India Muslim League during its first formative years and as leader in 1906 of the Muslim delegation [deputation] to the then Viceroy, Lord Minto, which presented a strong case for encouraging [the] abandonment of the studied aloofness of the Muslims from Indian political life. It was this deputation which, for the first time, brought into prominence, under your able leadership and guidance, the rights of the Muslims as a separate political entity.'

"The Vice-Chancellor continued that [the] Dacca University was 'proud to have on its rolls a great and world famous personality – a scion of the great Royal family of Egypt and Iran and the spiritual head of a great community spread almost all over the world.'

"After recounting 'the wide scope of [the] interests and activities' of His Highness, the Vice-Chancellor recalled the position held by the Aga Khan as member of the Viceroy's [Legislative] Council in 1902, his 'influence in the political sphere' as leader of the British Indian delegation to the Round Table Conferences of 1930–31 'in which fateful decisions were taken regarding the rights of the Muslims of India as a nation'."

Dawn of the following day (30 January) carried an editorial on the Aga Khan's speech, and a report that, prior to his departure for Agra in India, the Aga Khan, in an interview with the Associated Press of Pakistan, said that although he was not present at the historic meeting in Dacca in December 1906 when the All India Muslim League was founded, the ground had been prepared for that meeting 'by the principles enumerated and accepted at the Simla Conference [*sic* Simla Deputation's meeting with the Viceroy] earlier' to which he was a party. 'The long struggle of the Muslims of the subcontinent launched in 1906 had ended with the achievement of Pakistan,' he added."

206

PAKISTAN AS A MUSLIM STATE

Speech at a Public Meeting

Dacca: 28 January 1951

Proud to be in East Pakistan – the achievement of Pakistan "a miracle" – the Simla Deputation and the foundation of the Muslim League – the need for communal peace in the new country – Pakistan not hostile to non-Muslims – the state religion in England and other European countries – the true meaning of Islam – the example of Caliph Umar – the first century of Islam as a model for Pakistan – the need for unity and solidarity in Pakistan.

The achievement of Pakistan by the Quaid-i-Azam had been a "miracle", declared His Highness the Aga Khan, addressing one of the largest public meetings held in Dacca, on Sunday afternoon. His Highness emphasized the imperative need for unity and solidarity of the people of what he described as "this infant State" which was also the largest Muslim State in the world. Communal harmony, said His Highness, was a precondition for progress.

His Highness advocated that the first century after the Holy Prophet should be taken as the model on which Pakistan should make its creative efforts. This period of Islamic history represented the rise of Islam and was also the best period when the noble principles of Islam were put into practice most.

The Aga Khan said that the term Islamic State as applied to Pakistan has been much misunderstood and even misconstrued by the enemies of Islam and those "who do not want to face facts". He said he was not only addressing the people of East Pakistan, who had gathered at the meeting, but he was addressing the nations and countries of the world.

Raising his voice, the Aga Khan said: "I want to tell them that a Muslim State does not mean hostility against anyone." A truly Islamic country, continued the Aga Khan, implied the pursuance of the ideology of equality and kindly treatment to all.

His Highness also urged that, in accordance with this principle, there should be good fellowship and friendliness among all peoples of Pakistan and there should be no communal feelings. He commended the "Communal Harmony Week" inaugurated in East Pakistan on Sunday.

At the outset the Aga Khan said: "It is a proud moment for me to be here and to address such a large number of the citizens of East Pakistan, which is the most important part of the greatest Muslim State in the world."

The Aga Khan continued that for centuries there had been no independent Muslim country in the world with the area, population and resources that Pakistan had. The people of Pakistan should be confident of their future and proud of their past.

The achievement of Pakistan by the Quaid-i-Azam, said the Aga Khan, had been a "miracle", and he hoped that the people of Pakistan would make their State grow and develop as it should.

The Aga Khan recalled that in 1906, when the foundation of the Muslim League was laid in Dacca, the late Nawab Sir Salimullah and leading Muslims carried out the "principles laid down by the Simla Conference" [sic].

Since then it had been one long struggle for the Muslims.

Now, the Aga Khan continued, they would have to decide what "this new State" was going to be like. Firstly, there must be perfect communal peace and concord in the country as a precondition to progress.

In a Muslim country there should be no hostility towards anybody. Today a "Communal Harmony Week" had been inaugurated and he hoped that this would not be a week of merely passing goodwill but that it would be the beginning of the creation of lasting goodwill and fellowship between the communities.

Referring to the term "Islamic or Muslim" as applied to Pakistan as a country, the Aga Khan said that much had been made by the enemies of Islam to give out that Pakistan was hostile towards non-Muslims. "Nothing could be farther from the truth," the Aga Khan continued.

Under a truly Islamic State there could be no loading of the dice against any section of the people. The term Muslim or

Islamic State was much misunderstood and was "misquoted by those who did not want facts".

The Aga Khan said that most of the Western countries had a state religion. In England, for example, the Church of England was the state religion. It did not therefore mean that in England there was no room for people who did not belong to the Church of England. Similarly in the European countries there was state religion but people of other faiths also enjoyed rights of citizenship.

The Aga Khan continued that the word Islam meant peace and according to Bokhari [the classical Traditionalist or *muhaddith*] this peace extended even to the animal kingdom. In other words, to be a true Muslim connotated [*sic*] that he bore no ill will against anyone and treated everyone with kindness or generosity. This was the philosophy of Islam and the outlook of the true Muslim.

His Highness said that he was not only addressing the people of East Pakistan, who [had] gathered at the meeting, but also the people of other countries and nations of the world. Raising his voice he said: "I want to tell them that a Muslim State does not mean hostility against the non-Muslim."

There was no compulsion in Islam, said the Aga Khan, quoting from the Holy Quran and the Hadis [Prophetic Tradition], and everyone should be treated with kindness and generosity. There should be no ill will or malice against anyone. When Hazrat Umar, the Caliph, went to Jerusalem he was asked by the head of the Christians to enter the Holy of Holies.

But Hazrat Umar declined to enter the "Holy of Holies" because he felt that if he did so then other Muslims would also enter the Church and this would hurt the feelings of the Christians.

That was the noble example of which there were many others set by the early Muslims in the first century of Islam, said the Aga Khan.

He hoped that Pakistan, "this greatest child of Islam", would take for its model the first century of Islam which represented not only the rise of Islam but was also its best period.

He did not favour the idea of adopting the subsequent centuries of Islam as a guide, the Aga Khan added. The first century of Islam also demonstrated the greatest unity among Muslims and there was need for unity and solidarity in this "infant State" which required to be nurtured carefully for its growth and progress.

Source: *Dawn*, Karachi, 29 January 1951.

The *Pakistan Observer* of Dacca of the same date carried a slightly different report of the speech, which is reproduced below:

"His Royal Highness the Aga Khan, addressing a very big gathering of Dacca citizens yesterday afternoon in the Paltan Maidan, passionately appealed to all Pakistanis, particularly the members of the majority community, to maintain communal peace and harmony and establish most cordial relationship with the members of the minority communities who are inhabitants of this great land of ours. There must not exist any ill will, he said, between Muslims, Hindus, Christians or Jews.

"Nawab Bahadur of Dacca, who presided over the meeting, in his address welcoming the respected guest on behalf of the citizens, narrated the contribution of the Aga Khan towards the emancipation of the Muslims of the Indian subcontinent in particular and of the Muslim world in general.

"Replying to the address of welcome, His Royal Highness the Aga Khan expressed his pleasure for [*sic*] being able to come over to East Pakistan, the richest and most popular [*sic* – populous?] wing of Pakistan. Paying his tribute to the memory to [*sic*] the Quaid-e-Azam, he stressed the need for furthering the cause of Pakistan and to lead the country and nation to its goal of prosperity and progress. Since 1906, when the first stride in the emancipation of the Muslims began, the achievement of Pakistan was the greatest success, he added, and underlined the urgent need of unity and amity within the state as a prerequisite for the all round development of the new state. 'Goodwill between the communities must be supplemented by active fellow-feeling and warm friendship'.

"Keeping mainly the outside world in his view, His Royal Highness said that a section of interested persons and parties were carrying out anti-Pakistani propaganda in foreign countries by saying that as Pakistan was an Islamic state so the minorities would not be given their legitimate rights there. They also added that Pakistan was an anti-Hindu state which, according to His Royal Highness, was the greatest travesty of truth. In a truly Islamic state there could not be any oppression on any minorities because that was against the fundamental teachings of Islam was being misquoted and misrepresented [*sic*].

"In England, His Highness added, the Church of England was recognised as the state Church but all communities there were living in complete harmony and peace. So was also the case in many of the other European states. So if Islam was the state religion of Pakistan there could not be any cause of oppression on minorities. Islam means peace.

"Concluding his 10-minutes [*sic*] short speech he hoped that the new revival which was showing itself amongst the Muslim nations after a decade of downfall would be continued and 'our future shall be as bright as our past'.

"The meeting came to an end after thanksgiving on behalf of the City Muslim League and Provincial Muslim League was over [*sic*]."

Dawn of 29 January reported:

"Nawab Habibullah Bahadur of Dacca, who presided, recalled the Aga Khan's services and the distinctions he had obtained. 'It was in this city that the first political conference of the Muslim leaders was held, which has [*sic* – had] resulted in the formation of the Muslim League of which later His Royal Highness became the President', said the Nawab.

" 'Your movement for a separate electorate that you started in 1906 brought about the national awakening in the Muslims.'

"The Nawab said: 'The dream of Pakistan would have been shattered and would never have been realised had you not fought for a separate electorate for the Muslims.'

"After acknowledging the services of the Aga Khan to the cause of Islam, the Nawab said that the Aga Khan was taking keen interest in the growth of Pakistan and Pakistani people looked to him for guidance and advice.

"The Nawab also assured His Highness that the members of the Ismaili community in East Pakistan would enjoy the same rights and privileges as those enjoyed by other Muslim citizens. 'We regard your great community as an integral part of the great Muslim nation,' he concluded.

"The *Pakistan Observer* of 28 January had reported that 'Radio Pakistan Dacca will broadcast at 8.25 p.m. today January 28, 1951, the speech of His Highness the Aga Khan delivered at the public meeting at Purana Paltan Maidan.

" 'His Highness arrived on 26 January, 1951 in Dacca from Rangoon on a three day visit.' "

ARABIC AS THE NATIONAL LANGUAGE OF PAKISTAN

Speech Before the Motamar-al-Alam-al-Islami

Karachi: 9 February 1951

His views could be controversial – significance of the language of
a nation – Pakistan should choose Arabic rather than Urdu –
arguments against Urdu – it was not the language of Muslims in
India during their rule – it became their language after the downfall – reasons for adopting Arabic as the national language – links
with Muslims of other lands – discuss the language question.

I can assure you that it is not with a light heart that I address
you this evening. I fully realise that what I am going to say
will make me most unpopular with important sections of the
population. However, I would be a traitor to Islam if I let this
opportunity pass without placing before the people of this
powerful and populous Islamic nation the views which I consider
my duty to place before the Muslims with as many of the arguments as I am capable of using in a short address. I fear some of
my arguments will mortally offend those who under totally different conditions gave so much of their life for the support of
the cause which I think today has been passed by, by events far
more important than any dreamt of in those days.

I feel the responsibility greater than any I can think of to
place my views and arguments before the Muslim population of
Pakistan as a whole – each and every province – while what I
consider a tragic and deadly step is not yet taken and not added
to the constitution of this realm.

The language of a nation is not only the expression of its
own voice but the mode of interpretation with all other human
societies. Before it is too late, I, an old man, implore my brothers

in Islam here not to finally decide for Urdu as the national language of Pakistan but to choose Arabic. Please hear my arguments.

First my argument against Urdu. If what was the other part of the former British Empire of India had made Urdu its national language, there would have been a great argument for Pakistan doing ditto. It could have been a linguistic and important point of contact with the vast Republic of the South. I am the last man on earth to desire to break any bridge of contact and understanding between Pakistan and its immense neighbour. Friends, not only Urdu but even Hindustani has been replaced by Hindi throughout Bharat as the national language. The people of Bharat were perfectly justified to choose any language which the majority considered most appropriate and historically justified to be their national language. The majority there had the right to choose what was most suitable for them as the official language of the country. Your choice in Pakistan of Urdu will in no way ameliorate or help your relations with your southern neighbour nor will it help the Muslim minorities there in any conceivable way. Howsoever you may add Arabic and Persian words to Urdu, there is no denying the fact that the syntax, the form, the fundamentals of the language is [sic] derived from Hindi and not from Arabic.

Was Urdu the language of the Muslims of India at the time of their glory? During the long Pathan period, Urdu was never considered the language of the rulers. Now we come to the Moghul Empire in the period of its glory. It was not the language of the educated. I defy anybody to produce a letter or any other form of writing by Emperors Aurengzeb, Shah Jehan, Jehangir, Akbar, Humayun or Babar in Urdu language. All that was spoken at the Court was Persian or occasional Turkish. I have read many of the writings of Aurengzeb and they are in beautiful Persian. Same is true if you go to the Taj Mahal and read what is written on the tombs of the Emperor and his famous consort. Persian was the Court language and the language of the educated and even till the early 19th century in far Bengal the Hindi intelligentsia wrote and used Persian and not Urdu. Up to the time of Macaulay, Persian was the language of Bengali upper classes irrespective of faith and of official documents and various Sadar Adalat.

We must look historical facts in the face. Urdu became the language of Muslim India after the downfall. It is a language associated with the downfall. Its great poets are of the downfall

1273

period. The last and the greatest of them was Iqbal who with the inspiration of revival gave up Urdu poetry for Persian poetry. There was a meeting in Iqbal's honour in London organized by men such as Prof. Nicholson. I was present at that meeting. Iqbal said that he went in for Persian poetry because it was associated with the greatness of the Islamic epoch and not with its misfortunes. Is it right that the language of the downfall period should become the national language of what we hope now is a phoenix like national rising? All the great masters of Urdu belong to the period of greatest depression and defeat. It was then a legitimate attempt by the use of a language of Hindi derivation with Arabic and Persian words to find ways and means of better understanding with the then majority fellow countrymen. Today that vast British dependency is partitioned and succeeded by two independent and great nations and the whole world hopes that both sides now accept partition as final.

Is it a natural and national language of the present population of Pakistan? Is it the language of Bengal where the majority of the Muslims live? Is it what you hear in the streets of Dacca or Chittagong? Is it the language of the North-West Frontier? Is it the language of Sind? Is it the language of the Punjab? Certainly after the fall of the Moghul Empire, the Muslims and Hindus of certain areas found in it a common bond, but now today other forms of bridges must be found for mutual understanding.

Who were the creators of Urdu? What are the origins of Urdu? Where did it come from? The camp followers, the vast Hindi-speaking population attached to the Imperial Court who adapted, as they went along, more Arabic and Persian words into the syntax of their own language just as in later days the English words such as 'glass' and 'cup' became part of a new form of Urdu called Hindustani.

Are you going to make the language of the Camp or of the Court your national language of your new born realm? Every Muslim child of a certain economic standard learns the Quran in Arabic whether he is from Dacca or Quetta. He learns his 'Alif-Be' to read his Quran. Arabic is the language of Islam. The Quran is in Arabic. The Prophet's Hadiths are in Arabic. The highest form of Islamic culture in Spain was in Arabic. Your children must learn Arabic to a certain extent always. The same is true of your West whether Sind, Baluchistan or the North. From the practical and worldly point of view, Arabic will give you, as a national language, immediate contact not only with the 40 million Arabic speaking people of independent nations on your

SELECTED SPEECHES AND WRITINGS

West but the other 60 million more or less Arabic speaking people who are not independent but who exist in Africa. Right up to the Atlantic, not only in North but as far South as Nigeria and the Gold Coast, Arabic is known to the upper classes of the population. In all the Sudans, on the Nile or under French rule, Arabic is the language right up to the borders of Portuguese West Africa. In East Africa, not only in Zanzibar but amongst the Muslim population of even countries as far apart as Madagascar and Portuguese East Africa, Arabic is known. If we turn to the East on Arabic [sic], Islam has been founded and prospered throughout the 80 million Muslims of Indonesia and Malaya – the 80 million Muslims right up to the Philippines. In Ceylon Muslim children of the well-to-do classes get some knowledge of Arabic. Is it not right and proper that this powerful Muslim State of Pakistan with its central geographical position, its bridges between the nearly 100 million of Muslims of the East and 100 million Muslims of the West – its position of the East from Philippines and the Great States of Indonesia and Malaya and Burma and then westward with the hundred millions in Africa, right up to the Atlantic, should make Arabic its national language and not isolate itself from all its neighbours and from the world of Islam with a language that was associated with the period of downfall of Muslim State? And finally while Arabic as a universal language of the Muslim world will unite, Urdu will divide and isolate.

Gentlemen, brothers in Islam, people of Pakistan, people of every Province, I appeal to you, before you take the final and what I unfortunately must say, I consider the fatal jump down the precipice, please discuss and let all and everyone contribute their views. Take time and think over it.

Once more I appeal to those whom I have offended, for Islamic charity in the discussions that inevitably will take place and all others to look facts in the face historically and the present world of today [sic].

I pray that the people of this country may be guided by the Divine wisdom before they decide.

Source: *Message to the World of Islam by Aga Khan III*, Karachi, 1977, pp. 21–6.
The speech was reported in full by *Dawn* in its issue of 11 February 1951. On 14 February the newspaper reproduced the resolution on Arabic passed by the Motamar-al-Alam-al-Islami.

208

CHANGING FACE OF ASIA

Interview with the Ittla'at of Tehran

Tehran: February 1951

Awareness about the dangers of another world war – increase in armaments – independence of India and Pakistan – emergence of China.

What are the views of Your Highness on the state of affairs in the world today?

Prince Aga Khan replied: "The world today is passing through a dangerous phase indeed, and there can be no doubt about it. But there is a source of satisfaction and hopefulness in the thought that the Governments of the various countries know fully well that another world war will cause such destruction and havoc as is beyond our mental calculation. I, therefore, think that another world conflagration will not come. All Governments will try to find out a way to peace before they welcome war. There is no fear of a war taking place out of an accident this time: but if war does come accidentally, the reason will be that 'practical peace' has become rare and difficult under the present circumstances. The number and quality of destructive weapons, the armed forces and unnecessary ammunitions of war have been increased to such an extent that one day either this side or that side will go to war because they will think that war is better than 'forced peace'. If, God forbid, a day is reached when mental conflict increases and becomes intolerable, that day world war will become inevitable and will overtake the world" . . .

What has been the most exciting thing in the life of Your Highness?

"The incidents which have occurred during the seventy years of my life are numerous, but the events which came into existence during the last three years are very important in my opinion.

These events are the independence of India and Pakistan, the migration of the English people from the seat of their old empire and the creation of two powerful states – India and Pakistan. These events are to be regarded as occurrences of a revolutionary nature. They have changed not only the face of Asia but also of the whole world. As we are discussing this subject I may also say that the emergence of New China, the powerful China of today, is also a major phenomenon in the history of the world. There can be no doubt that during the next fifty years, South-East Asia, that is Pakistan, India and China, will rise to that height of power which America and Russia have attained these days. These two events are of the greatest importance to the world. I do not know what shape Asia will take after the emergence of these new powers."

Source: *H.R.H. Aga Khan's Visit to Iran*, Karachi, 1951, pp. 46–8.
   Ittla'at was an important journal issued from Tehran, Iran.

209

THE ISMAILIS AND NATIONAL LOYALTY

Speech at a Dinner of the Aga Khan Students' Union

London: June 1951

Loyalty to countries where Ismailis live – dangers of extreme nationalism – win the esteem of the indigenous people – example of Burma – keep religion in its proper place.

The Aga Khan . . . told Ismailis from all over Asia and Africa that it was to the countries in which they chose to make their homes that they owed their loyalty and affection. They must, he said, identify themselves with those countries if they wished to prosper in years to come.

Speaking of the dangers of extreme nationalism and religious fervour, he said they could not hope to continue in Africa unless they succeeded in winning the esteem of the African people.

"Take as an example for your patriotism your brothers in Burma," the Aga Khan declared. "They have identified themselves 100 per cent with Burma. They don't look across the border. Whatever country you choose to live in, work for it, mix with its people, achieve its outlook and keep religion in its proper place – in your soul. If you do this, you will find many of your problems solved.

"In Africa the day will come when the people of that vast continent will want to know who foreigners are and it is the people who have made the country their home who are going to have the best opportunities in that country. For that day, prepare yourselves.

"I don't like the idea of calling yourselves Asians in Africa any more than I like the idea of the African living in India, Pakistan or Burma continuing to call himself an African. When you live permanently in a country you become a member of that country." . . .

Source: *The East African Standard*, Nairobi, 8 June 1951.

The dinner was held at the Savoy Hotel, London, and was attended by two hundred guests. Among them were the Kabaka of Buganda and the Nabagereka; Britain's Home Secretary, Mr Chuter Ede; Lord Thomas MacPherson; the blind M.P., Sir Ian Fraser and Lady Fraser; the Ambassodors of Burma, Iran, Indonesia and the East African High Commissioner, Mr Roger Norton.

210

INDIA–PAKISTAN RELATIONS

Letter to The Times

London: 1 August 1951

Strained relations between India and Pakistan – their highest
interest demands friendship and alliance – consequences of fear –
great statesmanship needed – twenty-year bilateral treaties suggested.

Lovers of peace throughout the world must be distressed to
read again this year of the strained relations between India and
Pakistan.

We all know the disastrous results in Europe of fear and suspicion between neighbouring nations, and every one must have
hoped that these two Asian States with their newly gained independence would realize that their highest interest is in friendship
and, much better still, in alliance. Unfortunately there is fear.
Fear begets suspicion and suspicion leads to strained relations
which result in disaster and war – occasionally against the deliberate will of the responsible rulers. From all accounts fear now
prevails in that part of Asia.

I think it is now within the power of Great Britain, all the other
Commonwealth nations, and the United States, in their own
interest as well as that of the two Asian States concerned and the
rest of the world, by bold and decisive action to remove that fear.
Perhaps wrongly, but none the less surely, collective guarantees,
security pacts, the United Nations and the late League of Nations
conventions have lost real safety value. Only great statesmanship
such as Gladstone and Granville displayed in their treaties with
France and Prussia in 1870, can now bring peace and confidence
to the general and innocent public in India and Pakistan.

If these countries entered into bilateral treaties, binding themselves for about 20 years to defend the established and recognized frontiers of either of the two States against the aggressor, the sense of fear would be removed for as long as we can foresee. Of course in this case there is no buffer Belgium to defend, but the principle is the same. The frontiers as established at the time the British left when the two new States were born, would then be defended by all the signatories of the treaties between India and Pakistan and there would be no favouritism, just as there was none in 1870 between Prussia and France.

Source: *The Times*, London, 2 August 1951.

It was written from the Ritz Hotel, London. The journal published it with the headlines: "India–Pakistan Dispute: Treaties to Remove Fear."

The Aga Khan's hopes of good relations between India and Pakistan were dented their fulfilment by the forces of history, the injustice of the boundaries drawn by the British in 1947, the hostility of India, the problem of Kashmir, the dubious roles played by the United States and the Soviet Union, and the ignorance and ineptitude of the rulers of Pakistan. These unfortunate developments and factors are described in S. M. Burke, *Mainsprings of Indian and Pakistani, Foreign Policies*, Minneapolis, Minn., 1974, and *Pakistan's Foreign Policy: An Historical Analysis*; B. R. Nanda (ed.). *Indian Foreign Policy: The Nehru Years*, Delhi, 1976; Bimal Prasad, *India's Foreign Policy: Studies in Continuity and Change*, Delhi, 1979; S. Gupta, *India and Regional Integration in Asia*, Bombay, 1964; Robert Jackson, *South Asian Crisis: India, Pakistan, Bangladesh*, London, 1975; A. W. Wilcox, *India, Pakistan and the Rise of China*, New York, 1964; P. K. Mishra, *South Asia in International Politics: A Book of Readings*, Delhi, 2nd edn 1986; Chaudhri Muhammed Ali, *The Emergence of Pakistan*, New York, 1967; William J. Barnds, *India, Pakistan and the Great Powers*, New York, 1972; Z. A. Bhutto, *The Myth of Independence*, London, 1969; Liaquat Ali Khan, *Pakistan: The Heart of Asia*, Cambridge, Mass., 1950; Josef Korbed, *Danger in Kashmir*, Princeton, N.J., 1966; Alastair Lamb, *The Kashmir Problem*, New York, 1966; Khalid bin Sayeed, *Pakistan: The Formative Phase*, Karachi, 1960; Latif Ahmed Sherwani, *Foreign Policy of Pakistan*, Karachi, 1964; Aslam Siddiqui, *Pakistan Seeks Security*, Lahore, 1965; and G. W. Choudhury, *Pakistan's Relations with India, 1947–1966*, London, 1968.

211

THE TOLERANCE OF ISLAM

Letter to The Times

Cannes: 3 November 1951

Negative references to Islam in *The Times* of 22 October 1951 – ignorance among Western writers – Islam tolerant – respect for other faiths – Christian and Jewish minorities survived under Muslim rule – in the first century of Islam the best in Roman and Greek cultures was preserved – Muslim search for knowledge encouraged by the Quran – negative attitude to the West due to the behaviour of the Westerners – the West should change its mental attitude.

In your leading article of October 22 under the heading "The Middle East" you have stated that "in the Muslim countries the second tendency (a violent reaction against the west) is exaggerated by an intolerant religion which teaches the duty of shunning foreign influences." This sweeping generalization, not only against Muslims but against their faith and Islam itself, is both untrue and unfair, and, indeed, shows a lamentable dearth of knowledge regarding Islam and its legal and religious principles, even among leading writers of the leading journal of the west.

Even a little knowledge of Islam will show that its religion is not only tolerant of other faiths, but most respectful, and, indeed, fully accepts the divine inspiration of all theistic faiths that came before Islam. It does not only teach tolerance to its followers, but goes a step farther and enjoins on them all to create the godly quality of "Hilm," that is, tolerance, forbearance, patience, calmness, and forgiveness. It is due to the spirit of tolerance of Islam that even the smallest Christian and Jewish minorities survived and kept all their doctrines during the thousand years of Muslim rule. Nothing like what happened to Muslims in Spain after the Christian conquest has ever happened to a non-Muslim faith in any Islamic dominion.

How can Europeans be so ignorant as to have forgotten that in the first century of Islam the Kalifs ordered that all that was best in Greek and Roman cultures should be assimilated; that not only the philosophy, medicine, and science of Greece, but its poetry and drama, were carefully translated into Arabic and were generally sought not only by the learned but also by the pious?

The Muslim attitude towards the absorption of ideas was based on the principle of Islam which enjoins to acquire knowledge wherever available, and there is a well-known and authentic saying of the Prophet that "his followers should seek learning even if they have to go to China." Islam, by its geographical position, suffered the terrible Mongol invasions one after the other, just at the time when it was weakened by the long and immense efforts with which it had mastered the many successive crusades. It should not be forgotten that the Tartar invasions came one generation after the other. In fact, in the interest of the universal unification of mankind the Quran ignores the minor differences and says: "Come, let us unite to what is common to us all," which obviously encourages Muslims to assimilate ideas and even customs from others.

It is, of course, true that Muslim countries, like modern European races, have acquired in this century a strong sense of nationalism which has no connexion with their religion. As such, if there has been violent reaction against the west in some of the Muslim countries, the reason is to be found in the attitude and behaviour of the westerners, their ignorance, and want of respect for the faith and culture of Islam, of which the reference to that faith in your leading article is a typical and usual example. Only recently I was in all the Muslim States where there is a so-called anti-western agitation, and I have no hesitation in saying that if the Atlantic nations and the west generally want better relationship with the Muslims, the solution lies in their own hands, and this can be done only if they change their mental attitude and cultivate better understanding of the Muslims' material needs and the loyal recognition of the high quality of their national culture and the purity of their faith.

Source: *The Times*, London, 6 November 1951.

The letter bore no date and was written from Cannes, Alpes-Maritimes, France. It was published under the headline: "Tolerance of Islam."

The leading article of 22 October 1951 to which the Aga Khan refers was entitled "The Middle East" and ran as follows:

"Events since the war have forced the western Powers to concentrate on the struggle against Russian Communism in Europe and the Far East. As a result they have been inclined to neglect other parts of the world which did not seem to be so urgently threatened and assume too readily that nations who were not already on the side of Moscow could be counted as loyal allies of the west. This is a dangerous error. Even if the 'Communist world' can be lumped together for the purpose of strategy and propaganda, the 'western world' is a phrase without any precise meaning. There are still many nations, inhabited by many millions of people, who refuse to accept this choice, who have their own wishes and desires, and who, if they fear the Soviet Union and dislike Communism, often feel more 'oppressed' by the western nations who claim to be their allies and protectors.

"The most striking example of this is provided by the countries of the Middle East and North Africa whose violent passions and social insecurity have just been so frighteningly revealed. Nothing is to be gained by blaming the people of this area for their actions. What is happening there is essentially no different from what is happening in other parts of Asia and Africa and is the inevitable result of the impact of western industrial civilization upon primitive communities. This causes a desire to imitate the west, especially in such matters as national independence and military technique, but also a violent reaction against the west, which has upset their traditional way of life. In the Muslim countries this second tendency is exaggerated by an intolerant religion, which teaches the duty of shunning foreign influences. Its natural political expression is a resentment of Britain, which was for so long the chief Power in the region and which still reminds them of their own inferiority.

"Neither the Soviet State nor the Communist faith has yet played a great part in this, though both have had an indirect effect. The Russian revolution, especially as it appeared in the Asiatic Republics, first taught the peasant masses in their fearful poverty to think that the traditional order of society might not be immutable. The present leaders in these countries, who are rarely poor themselves and are often extremely rich, are well aware of the discontent stirring beneath them and are clever enough to distract attention from their own privileged position by protesting against the 'exploitation' of the 'foreign imperialist.' The very existence of the Soviet Union is an advantage to them by providing an alternative to the western Powers. Dr. Moussadek has already found how potent this threat can be when skilfully used, and some of the Egyptian newspapers this week-end have been toying with the idea of a Soviet alliance.

"As yet, indeed, the Arabs do not really believe that they are in any danger from Russia, and therefore feel no need of protection against her. They regard the presence of Britain as an obstacle to their neutrality. On the other hand they felt that they were threatened by the Jews who poured into Palestine after the war. So long as Britain stayed in Palestine and restricted Jewish immigration, they had at least one reason for welcoming British support; when Britain left, they had none. What is more, they felt they had been betrayed. In the eyes of the Arabs and Egyptians the creation of Israel was an act of aggression condoned and even supported by the western Powers. The failure of the United States Government to appreciate this is not the least cause of the present trouble. The United States, which has had a strong and constructive policy in Europe and a strong policy in the Far East, has until recently had no policy in the Middle East at all. It is hardly sufficient excuse that the British Government often gave the impression that they had no need of help or advice.

"A proper understanding of the feelings and wishes of the Arab peoples is essential before any sound policy can be formed, but it should not lead to sentimentality. Little reliance can be placed on these nations until, like Turkey and Pakistan, they have reached a more advanced stage in their social and industrial revolution. (Even Pakistan is still threatened by the religious fanaticism that is so potent throughout the Middle East and which threatens the lives of all moderate and realistic statesmen.) In the meantime the world cannot wait. No matter what the Arabs may feel, they are as yet unable to defend this vital area or even to carry out the reforms necessary to improve their own standard of living. The western Powers cannot possibly allow the precarious system of States in the Middle East to become weaker than it is already. This would be true even if the Soviet Union had no far-reaching plans for spreading Communism, for history shows that any great Power will overflow into the territories next to it unless some barrier is placed in the way.

"The first need is for the western Powers, acting together, to make it plain that they will not be dislodged from the Middle East and North Africa and that they are determined to hold the bases they need to defend this area. If this is not done appeals neither to reason nor to the Security Council will prevent their remaining strongholds from being undermined and washed away by the flood-waters of Arab nationalism. To stand fast, however, is not itself a policy and the western Powers must still try to persuade the Arab peoples that cooperation with the west is also in their interests. The difficulties of this are immense and no quick or easy solution is likely, but recent events have at least taught certain lessons about what to avoid.

"The Persian dispute may not have been in vain if these lessons have been learned. The divorce of economic matters from diplomacy, even if disguised as strict attention to business, leaves the way open to charges of exploitation. If that feeling is allowed to grow unchecked it quickly reaches a point of unreason when it can no longer be satisfied by the most generous offer. This situation can be avoided only by a constant effort to share the wealth that is created and to see that it is properly used. On the other hand it would seem a mistaken principle to help countries that will not help themselves. Countries fortunate enough to have large resources in oil can hardly expect economic aid from the west if they refuse to accept reasonable commercial arrangements to exploit them.

"Some of the sting can be taken out of such arrangements if they are made international. A small nation, for instance, may think it less humiliating to make an agreement with the World Bank or the United Nations or even the North Atlantic Powers than to make one with a single Power. It would be still better if the Arab nations themselves could be persuaded to form some kind of organization for Middle Eastern economic cooperation which could act for all of them. In this way individual nations might be more prepared to accept expert advice and technical assistance. The four-Power proposal to Egypt was an admirable example of the right approach but it would be foolish to imagine that it will be acceptable to any Arab Government at this moment. The western Powers can afford to be patient so long as they show themselves determined."

ECONOMIC DEVELOPMENT IN PAKISTAN AND OTHER MUSLIM STATES

An Address to the Pakistan Institute of International Affairs

Karachi: 1 February 1952

Spiritual and religious ideals which made Islam great – importance of material development – world events and Pakistan and other Muslim nations – capital investment in USA and Russia – American lead – in both lands the forces of nature are put to use – possibility of colonialism or communism in developing countries – present generations must reduce consumerism and "welfarism" – development through investment – science in industry and agriculture – general national awakening about investment – machinery and investment.

When two years ago I had the honour and pleasure of being amongst you, the whole of my address was taken up with, what I may call in short, the soul of Pakistan. Though your objective is political, economic and of worldly affairs and not religious and spiritual, yet I felt that it was necessary to place before you the spiritual and religious ideals and principles of conduct, which made Islam great in the first century of the Hijri era and departure from which has brought about the general decline and fall of Muslim nations and peoples. Without a proper spiritual motive power, a great nation is never built. For that reason I was entirely absorbed with what should be the spirit of Islam in Pakistan.

According to Muslim ideas, perfection is only reached when body and soul alike have reached their zenith. So a nation like Pakistan must also think of its material body. Today therefore I shall place before you some considerations relative to material development in Pakistan particularly and other Muslim countries generally.

The earth is getting smaller and smaller and its countries and people are becoming more and more dependent on each other. Some hundred years ago, economic conditions and processes in Northern America or China, though ultimately of influence over the life of the people here and in the Middle East, could at least be considered of no immediate importance. Today scientific discoveries, leading to improvements in methods of production, and the use of such primary materials as iron and oil, in one country, can, very seriously and very soon, affect even the life of the individual in another part of the world. Pakistan and other Muslim nations cannot ignore or pass by world events, without fatal consequences to their own independence and well-being. So, let us look at the world outside. What is the fundamental fact and what is only a passing phase of the present political and economic situation. The fundamental fact is that the only two really independent and master nations of the world – the United States and Russia – have both one and the same objective, though the methods they follow are totally different. The national effort of the one, as well as the national effort of the other, has for its objective constantly increasing capital investment, with its inevitable consequence, proportionate increase in production. The end of the two is the same. Their methods are incredibly different. In the United States and to a lesser extent in Canada, this vast and ever-growing capital investment has been brought about by free competition, ever taking advantage of mechanisation in an effort to increase production. Having been the first to realise that human effort directly applied cannot, by any stretch of imagination, increase the fruit of labour to the extent needed, the Americans were the first to try and replace manpower, wherever possible, by machine and to reduce to a minimum human physical effort in production. America leads in the race for capital investment on a constantly increasing scale, which is the essential foundation of modern productivity, and for improving standards and techniques. After the Revolution of 1917, Lenin and his immediate associates, brought up in the production theories of Marx and Engels, having seen for themselves the consequences in industry and agriculture of what I may briefly call manpowerism, realised that the new idealistic Republic could never survive, unless all its efforts were concentrated on capital investment. I believe it was Lenin who said: "Socialism is electricity". In a nutshell, this saying puts the case for the concentration of effort on capital investment.

Without the extensive background of the American competitive effort, the rulers of Russia had, and have, no alternative but to follow a system, which necessitates that, for a generation or two, consumer production and consumer needs should be reduced to a minimum and all effort concentrated on capital investment as the great objective of national activity. Capital investment in Russia is going ahead, though at present it is still behind investment in America. But neither the one nor the other is a happy go as-you-please welfare state, with the minimum of effort and with natural manpowerism. By different methods, the race is being run to attain the highest replacement of paltry human creative capacity by the use of the forces of nature, harnessed and controlled by man's intelligence. For those who are not prepared to follow this course, whether in Europe or Asia, there are only two alternatives, colonialism or communism. Colonialism is not a political process. It is the absence of production in proportion to population, resulting from an absence of capital investment in relation to the past, present or future. Nobody dreams of changing the political conditions of certain European countries. But if their present methods are continued, they will be – in fact, they already are – on the brink of colonialism, although not in name.

What about us here? What about the Muslim world generally? If real independence is desired for Pakistan or, for that matter, for any Muslim country, the present generation must be ready to reduce welfarism and consumerism to the very limit and replace it by capital investment. If the whole effort of the nation is conscientiously, as in Russia, devoted to the reducing of consumption and the increasing of capital investment, you may, say in 20 years, build up the elements of a free system, independent alike of communism and colonialism. Imperialism and colonialism are not brought about by the desire for dominance by one party and for servience by the other. When the so-called imperialist country, with its dominating productive power, produces so much more that the colonial power, producing little, is ready to receive from the abundance of the former what it cannot produce itself, that day colonialism has come to stay, whether it be in Europe or Asia. Every year, during peacetime, there is, in each country, a profitable balance somewhere. If that balance is used for the purpose of capital investment and no other, and the amount of it is constantly increased by sacrifices made by the people, it will be possible for this country and for the countries of the Middle East to turn a new leaf of life.

We know that vast plans are being made by your Government

for development. But unless every man realises the importance of investment, howsoever small, and there is, at the same time, guidance from the authorities for the investments to be diverted to the production of capital goods, either directly or indirectly, by the production of such essentials as power and food, you cannot build a healthy independent national state. Science must come into industry, in which, of course, I include the biggest of all industries, agriculture. It must have behind it the conscientious and willing effort of the people. If such effort is not made, and the nation is left to go-as-you-please methods, a time may come when, for its very survival, it may be compelled to try some form of compulsory investment such as in Russia. The alternative to that would be total economic dependence on either one or the other of the two capital investing countries, viz. America or Russia. It is for this reason that our statesmen and religious leaders, who, as true Muslims, must realise that the soul and the body are interdependent and indeed are one in life, use their influence with the masses to bring about a general awakening to the necessity of constant investment. With the standard of life already low and precarious, it is difficult to forego the immediate advantage. But not to forego it will mean future loss. Nevertheless the choice must be made now. The people should be taught, not merely to read and write, but also to realise the value of power produced by machinery; and machinery can only be had by investment.

Source: *Pakistan Horizon*, Karachi, Vol. 5, pp. 3–6.

It was an address delivered at the Pakistan Institute of International Affairs, Karachi, and published in the official journal of the Institute, *Pakistan Horizon*.

It was reproduced in the *Ismaili* of 10 February 1952 (p. 4) under the misleadingly amended title of "Future Economic and Political Development of Pakistan and Other Muslim States", and with changed paragraphing, and in the *Message to the World of Islam by Aga Khan III*, Karachi, 1977, pp. 27–32, under a still different title of "Future Development of Muslim States" and with the text following that in the *Ismaili* and not the original one. It also appeared in *Dawn* of 2 February 1952.

On the economic development of Pakistan in her early years see M. A. Pithawalla, *An Introduction to Pakistan*, Karachi, 1948; Government of West Pakistan, *Report of the Land Reforms Commission for West Pakistan*, Lahore, 1961; J. Russell Andrus and Azizali F. Muhammad, *The Economy of Pakistan*, Stanford, 1958; S. M. Akhtar, *Economics of Pakistan*, Lahore, 2nd edn 1955, 2 vols; A. F. A. Husain, *Human and Social Impact of Technological Change in Pakistan*, Dacca, 1956, 2 vols; Nazmul Karim, *Changing Society in India and Pakistan: A Study in Social Change and Social Stratification*, Dacca, 1956; and Akhtar H. Siddiqui, *The Economy of Pakistan: A Select Bibliography, 1947–1962*, Karachi, 1963.

ISLAM AND THE MODERN AGE

Letter to the President of the Arabiyyah Jamiyyat, Karachi

Marseilles: 4 April 1952

The principle of "Islam as a natural religion" enabled the
Umayyads and Turks to achieve supremacy – Europeans advanced
in knowledge of nature – Christianity adapted itself to science –
Islam is drifting away from science – agenda for universities in
Pakistan – make spirit of the Quran spirit of Pakistan – Aligarh
and the creation of Pakistan – we want many more Aligarhs.

... Islam is fundamentally in its very nature a natural religion.
Throughout the Quran God's signs (Ayats) are referred to as
the natural phenomenon, the law and order of the universe, the
exactitudes and consequences of the relations between natural
phenomenon in cause and effect. Over and over, the stars, sun,
moon, earthquakes, fruits of the earth and trees are mentioned
as the signs of divine power, divine law and divine order. Even in
the Ayeh of Noor, divine is referred to as the natural phenomenon of light and even references are made to the fruit of the
earth. During the great period of Islam, Muslims did not forget
these principles of their religion.

Under the Khalif Muavia and the great Omaiyyad Khalifs of
Damascus, the Islamic navy was supreme in Mediterranean; better
ships, better knowledge of wind and tide were placed at the
disposal of the Muslim navy and thus the land conquests of half
Western Europe rendered possible and easy.

Even the historian Gibbon says that when the Turks conquered
Constantinople, the Muslim artillery was far superior to any other
in Europe, and far greater knowledge was known [*sic*] of the
consequences of powder and fire than anything that the Greeks
had at their disposal. This alone led to the rapid Turkish conquest

of the Balkan Peninsula and Constantinople and coming up to Vienna. Just as under the great Omaiyyads they had almost reached Paris.

But at the end of the 17th century and beginning of the 18th, the European Renaissance rapidly advanced in knowledge of nature, namely all those very Ayats of God to which the Quran refers, when Muslims forgot the Ayats, namely, natural phenomenon, its law and order which are the proofs of divine guidance used in the Quran, but we stuck to our rites and ceremonies, to our prayers and fast alone, forgetting the other half of our faith. Thus during those 200/300 years, Europe and the West got an advance out of all proportion to the Muslim world and we found everywhere in Islam (in spite of our humble prayers, our moral standard, our kindliness and gentleness towards the poor) constant deterioration of one form or another and the Muslim world went down. Why? Because we forgot the law and order of nature to which the Quran refers as proof of God's existence and we went against God's natural laws. This and this alone has led to the disastrous consequences we have seen.

Today public opinion in Pakistan is standing at a critical moment. If again we look upon Islamic principles as only rites and ceremonies and forget the real Ayats of God's natural phenomenon, then not only Europe but China and India will go so far ahead of us that either we will become like North Africa, humble protectorates or we may have like Turkey to throw over much that is most valuable and precious in our mental outlook. To avoid this, what are we to do? Any fool can tell you of the disease but what is the remedy, how are we to save both teaching of Islam, knowledge of nature and our daily Islamic life of kindliness, gentleness and prayers? If the present method by which the Ulema being brought up on one line of studies and the scientific youth on a different one continues, the disaster will come because there will be a fundamental misunderstanding in the outlook of intellect and faith in the soul of the nation. We must learn from our enemies what saved Christianity for Europe. It was the fact that as the Universities at the time of the Renaissance and centuries that followed went forward with natural studies, at the same time the same universities had faculties of divinity in which the priesthood was trained. The atmosphere of science permeated the atmosphere of Christian divinity studies and the atmosphere of the Christian divinity students permeated the atmosphere of the scientific studies, thus both grew and developed together. Christianity adapted itself to science, though it is any thing but a natural religion being based on fundamental irrational principles which are the break up of natural law and order, while science accepted these extraordinary miracles as temporary breaks of the natural law of the universe.

Alas, Islam which is a natural religion in which God's miracles are the very law and order of nature drifted away and is still drifting away, even in Pakistan, from science which is the study of those very laws and orders of nature.

You, gentlemen, have a great responsibility. The only practical hope I see is that all your universities in Pakistan should have a faculty of Islamic religious and philosophical studies attached to ordinary curriculum for post-graduate students, who alone could be recognized as Ulemas. Something of the kind I know is being prepared in Egypt. A great Muslim divine, alas dead far too soon, the late Sheikh al-Maraghi, insisted in Azhar that natural laws should be taught according to the latest discoveries; but if we turn to Iran, Pakistan, North Africa, outside Egypt, we find that the Ulemas are being still brought up on the same old lines and the modern students on a totally different line. There is no unity of soul without which there can be no greatness.

My voice alone is the voice of an old sick man in the wilderness, but you members of the Jamiyyat are not old members and sick men. Insist, you who have taken up the study of the language of the Quran, to make the spirit of the Quran also the spirit of Pakistan. Remember that in the great first century they knew more about sea and wind than Europe ever did for hundreds of years to come. Today where are you? Unless our universities have the best graduated Ulema school for men brought up in the same atmosphere as the science students, realizing the fundamental truth that Islam is a natural religion of which the Ayats are the universe in which we live and move and have our being, the same causes will lead to the same disastrous results.

You, members of the Jamiyyat should bravely request the enlargement of our universities and the increase of their numbers on Aligarh lines, and insist on post graduate degrees for Ulema, just as there is [sic] for scientists brought up in the same way. I influenced my friend Mohsenul Mulk to do something of the kind in Aligarh. Alas, he died and after his death my direct influence on the powers of Aligarh got less and less, though something of the kind to which I here refer did come in Aligarh. It did not go the whole way as it would have gone, still if Mohsenul Mulk had lived and I had been able to continue my influence, but it was an improvement and it has given you Pakistan. Without

Aligarh no Pakistan would have come, but to live we want many Aligarhs with science and religious philosophy and education blended in one atmosphere realizing that God of the Quran is the one whose Ayats are the universe.

This is my most important message to you, brothers of Jamiyyat. If your prayers have given me life enough to write this letter, your prayers have done some good.

Source: *Message to the World of Islam by Aga Khan III*, Karachi, 1977, pp. 36–40.
The letter was sent to H. E. Dr. Zahid Husain, President of the Arabiyyah Jamiyyat of Karachi, from Marseilles, France.

214

INDUSTRIAL INVESTMENT IN PAKISTAN

Communication to the Dawn of Karachi

Cannes: 16 May 1952

His family investment in Pakistani industries – new projects – modernization of the cotton industry.

My family investment in industry is not limited to what we have already done, but while I am here I am trying to get associates for further and newer forms of industry to be started by specialists in partnership with ourselves and to study what can be done to make the cotton industry further modernised by newer methods. In spite of my illness I am in contact with various industrialists in Europe.

Source: *Dawn*, Karachi, 17 May 1952.

215

THE STATUS OF WOMEN

Message to the Ismaili Women's Association of Karachi

March 1953

The Holy Prophet's view on the status of women – importance of women in society – social advancement where women are least debarred – women and national regeneration.

The Prophet of Islam (who has been so cruelly libelled in the Western world, by ignorance or malice) was wont to say that men can but follow in the footsteps of their mothers towards Paradise. And it was not for nothing, according to Muslim belief, that his first convert was a woman.

Biologically the female is more important to the race than the male. While average women are capable of earning their own livelihood like men, they are the guardians of the life of the race, and only through their natural constitution are they able to bear the double burden. Experience shows the strong probability that the active influence of women on society, under free and equal conditions, is calculated not only to bring about practical improvements in the domestic realm, but also a higher and nobler idealism into the life of the state. Those who know Moslem society from within readily admit that its higher spiritual life owes a great debt to the example and influence of women. Today, as in the lifetime of the Prophet, probably the majority of devout and reverent followers of his teaching are women.

No progressive thinker of to-day will challenge the claim that the social advancement and general well-being of communities are greatest where women are least debarred, by artificial barriers and narrow prejudice, from taking their full position as citizens.

The progressive modernization which depends on co-operation and understanding will be impossible unless women are permitted to play their legitimate part in the great work of national regeneration on a basis of political equality.

Source: *Message to the World of Islam by Aga Khan III*, Karachi, 1977, pp. 43–4.
The place from where the message was sent is not mentioned in the source.
On the women of Pakistan see I. H. Qureshi, *The Pakistani Way of Life*, New York, 1956; Muhammad Mazheruddin Siddiqui, *Women in Islam*, Lahore, 1952; Stanley Maron (ed.), *Pakistan: Society and Culture*, New Haven, 1957.

216

THIS I HAVE LEARNT FROM LIFE

An Article

Karachi: 3 February 1954

Causes of disease in an individual must be analysed – similar diagnosis of social ills – only 250 years ago Islamic world was superior to the West – today things are different – causes of reversal of positions – intellectual and spiritual revolution in the West after Renaissance – power over the forces of nature – strength of Europe and America – Islam fundamentally a natural religion – Sayyid Ahmad Khan and Muhsin-ul-Mulk were misunderstood – conquer the forces of nature through science.

Is the Muslim world at last going to turn its thought and culture to what is fundamental teaching of the Holy Quran? It is for the public of Pakistan and indeed for the Muslim world to adjust its cultural foundations of knowledge to the study and ultimate victory over the forces of nature ever at our disposal through science.

When an individual's health deteriorates, when a strong healthy body begins to lose its various powers, all physicians worthy of their salt search for its cause by careful diagnosis. Only then when this process of analysis has brought to light the underlying causes and not the symptoms can real cure be found and when the diagnosis has been successful the cure is facile and usually rapid.

Society consists of individuals and when we find civil societies that were once upon a time vigorously their own and indeed with obvious superiority amongst other organized social bodies, and are then left behind while others progress far beyond even the imagination, leave alone the knowledge of their former supervisors, then indeed, unless we want to commit suicide, it is necessary to look deeper and to ask questions and find answers.

All the greater is the necessity for our search because the societies that have remained stationary have had one thing in common namely, what we call Islamic culture and those that have gone forward have drawn their force from other intellectual sources. Yet this world phenomenon is of comparatively recent date. Only 250 years ago towards the end of the 17th century, all European travellers and indeed general opinion as well as the remains of architecture prove beyond question that the Islamic world was superior to the Western in civilization and the amenities of life.

European travellers' records leave no doubt that cities such as Isfahan, Istanbul, Cairo and Delhi were healthier with far better sanitary arrangements, cleaner with better quality water, light, law and order than their contemporary rivals in Europe. If we can judge a nation by its personal cleanliness, then the Muslim world was far ahead according to all contemporary evidence specially from European sources.

In medicine and armaments, two totally different but necessary indications of national power and vigour, the Muslim world had nothing to learn from either the non-Muslim East or West. Yet today, 250 years later, how different! Can we really compare the atomic power of America and Russia with our few survived Muslim free countries? Even, in spite of the birth of Pakistan, independent Indonesia, when we turn to the Muslim world we find either colonialism as in Africa or vast industrial economic and military weakness compared even with Europe or Japan, leave alone America.

What has brought about between say the year 1650 and 1950, this immense reversal of positions? When I had the honour of presiding at the Muslim Educational Conference early in 1903 at Delhi, I referred to some of what I then described as the causes of the downfall. But the greatest and by far the most important, indeed the mother of all the other causes direct or indirect, is the intellectual and spiritual revolution that took place in the West soon after the Renaissance but which unfortunately for us we misunderstood at the time and have suffered from it ever since. This revolution led to immense power over the force of nature. The control of nuclear energy today is the latest example of that which the West gained and which we failed to realise. Until soon after the Renaissance both East and West looked for their philosophy of nature, for their explanation of phenomena to what I may call the classic [*sic*] interpretation of the facts of the Universe.

This classical interpretation had various minor sources, some of them from China and India; but the principal [*sic*] and indeed its foundation was mainly Greek modified by Arab thought. This natural philosophy was the foundation of both Eastern and Western nations and technology plus their means of production were based on the same until some 400 years ago, then the West under the influence of certain men of genius such as Leonardo de [*sic*] Vinci and Bacon, and a good many others, began to question the truth of the Greco-Arabian [*sic*] explanations and finally broke away with classical traditions and turned directly to nature. Observation of natural phenomena and questionings by experiment became the foundations and the guiding stars of the mind and thought of the West.

Alas, at the critical time in the Muslim East more and more thought and concentration was given to further study of the classical discoveries of the past. The "Allama" theory of knowledge in which the past was given complete wisdom and the future was to follow rather than go forward, put a stop to what was most important for political, economic and indeed cultural life.

Both East and West are agreed that the Greeco–Arab [*sic*] period produced some of the greatest intellectual giants of the human race. But while we were satisfied to look at the world through the eyes of our giants, the West insisted on more and more pigmies sitting one over the other on the top of the giants' shoulders till their accumulated height was infinitely greater than that of the original giant on which they had built their foundations.

What has been the result? All through the 13th and 19th centuries right up to the middle of the 20th century, we find Europe and America constantly getting greater and greater power over nature and thus their ability to conquer and indeed, when necessary, to crush those who had turned their back on the possibility of progress; and it is all the more extraordinary that this should have happened to the Muslim world. Islam is fundamentally a natural religion. All its dogmas and doctrines of whatever sect or school, are ultimately based on the regularity and order of natural phenomena, on the natural inclination of human beings for survival and reproduction, while the religion of the West, Christianity, is based on a miraculous event and faith in miracles, that is to say, a break in that very regularity to which the Holy Koran refers on a thousand occasions.

Today perhaps we are farthest away from control over nature while the West from America to Russia increases its great and overwhelming power of natural forces. Towards the end of the 19th century two men of genius among Indian Muslims, with one of whom I had just the honour of being acquainted, but the other was my intimate friend and collaborator during the early years of the century, Sir Syed Ahmed and Mohsin-ul-Mulk, were the first to realize that it was this command over nature and its forces that gave power and strength to human beings and that if we searched for power and strength, for uplift, it could only come if we also acquired by the same methods those very powers that led to more and more improved means of production and its obvious result – greater and greater mastery over the forces at our disposal.

Our Holy Koran so often refers to the fact that we are surrounded by so many God-given gifts which we should understand and profit from. Alas, we Muslims, who should have been the first to realize it, have become the last. Sir Syed and Mohsin-ul-Mulk were abused for they were misunderstood. Today the Muslim world is almost at the last stage, almost at the last hour between a final collapse and revival. The birth of Pakistan is undoubtedly the result of that very revolt of Sir Syed and Mohsin-ul-Mulk. The birth of Indonesia, the phoenix-like revival of Turkey, can all give us hope. But the essential weakness is everywhere in the Muslim world. Production per head of population is still far behind not only the West but even parts of the East.

Is the Muslim world at last going to turn its thought and culture to what is the fundamental teaching of the Holy Koran and the meaning of all Muslim sectarian interpretations of our Holy Book namely, knowledge gained by the observation and questionings of the world which Allah Almighty has given to us and in which we live and move and have our being? Is that blessing to remain in the hands of others to be further developed? Incredible new powers are attained while we remain humble followers and in truth condemned even to lose our individuality. It is for the public of Pakistan and indeed of the Muslim world, to adjust its cultural foundation of knowledge to the study and ultimate victory over the forces of nature ever at our disposal through science and thus once more as in the first thousand years of Muslim history, we will be in the vanguard of mankind.

Source: *Dawn*, Karachi, 4 February 1954, "Special Supplement to Commemorate the Platinum Jubilee of H.H. the Aga Khan."

It was also reproduced in *Message to the World of Islam by Aga Khan III*, Karachi, 1977, pp. 52–7.

The Times of London published a summary of this article on 6 February (strangely date-lined "Delhi, Feb. 5"):

"On the occasion of his platinum jubilee, celebrated in Karachi, the Aga Khan said the Muslim world was at the last stage, almost the last hour, between collapse and revival, and it was necessary to find the causes if suicide was to be avoided.

"In an article published in *Dawn*, he said all the stationary societies had what was called an Islamic culture, and those that had gone forward had drawn their force from other intellectual sources. Even newly independent countries like Pakistan and Indonesia had vast industrial, economic, and military weaknesses. Yet this was only a recent world phenomenon; 250 years ago the Islamic world was superior to the west in civilization and the amenities of life.

"The direct cause of this reversal of positions was the intellectual and spiritual revolution which took place in the west after the Renaissance, but which Islam misunderstood. This revolution led to immense power over the forces of nature, but at the critical time Islamic thought was concentrated on further study of the classical discoveries of the past. A full stop was put to fresh inquiry; the Allamah theory, in which the past was credited with complete wisdom and the mission of the future was to follow rather than to go forward, put a stop to what was most important for political, economic, and cultural life.

"Fundamentally, Islam was a natural religion; its dogma and doctrine were based on the regularity and order of natural phenomena, while Christianity, the religion of the west, was based on a miraculous event and faith in miracles. It was a break in that very law and order, that very regularity, to which the Koran referred.

"Nevertheless an essential weakness could be found everywhere in the Muslim world, and while incredible new powers were being developed in the west Muslims remained humble followers, condemned even to lose their individuality. If they were to regain their place in the vanguard of mankind, Muslims must adjust their cultural foundations of knowledge to study and gain ultimate victory over the forces of nature placed by science at their disposal."

217

PATRIOTISM AND LOYALTY

Speech at Platinum Jubilee Ceremony

Karachi: 3 February 1954

Tribute to the Quaid-i-Azam – Ismailis owe entire loyalty and devotion to their countries of domicile – patriotism and loyalty must be active and productive – voting and the rights of citizenship – unity and sacrifice – examples of Turkey, Germany and Japan – prayer for all Muslims.

I am proud and happy that I was born in Karachi, the city which had the honour of being the birth place of the Father of the Nation, the late Quaid-e-Azam, whose untimely and early death we all so deplore and whose loss I particularly feel with personal grief, for shortly before his death, he had asked me to take up the general direction and supervision of Pakistan representation in Europe and America, which alas, then my health was so bad that not only myself but all my doctors and family expected my death before his.

You Ismailis know perfectly well that it is a fundamental point in your religion that wherever you be, whatever the state where life and honour are protected, you must give your entire loyalty and devotion to the welfare and service of that country. You who have the honour of being citizens of Pakistan, to you, I give this advice: do not interpret your citizenship purely in a passive form but patriotism and loyalty must be active and productive. I realise fully that the overwhelming majority of the population have to look after their means of livelihood and the up-bringing of your children, but work if carried out intensively, is service to God and Fatherland. Make your daily labour, labour of love howsoever difficult and hard it may be. Do remember that in a democracy, voting and the rights of citizenship should be used with care and attention with serious thought howsoever humble with the full realisation to the best of your ability that not personal, parochial or provincial interests are to be served but the greater good and the welfare of the population as a whole and the security of the state as such. If the people of a nation are united and self-sacrificing, any amount of difficulties and overwhelming misfortunes can be overcome. We have seen how Turkey has come out stronger than ever after a hundred years of misfortunes and disasters. There are two other cases which should be an example and should not discourage anyone in the face of difficulties. Germany and Japan after the greatest defeats known to history have by hard work and devotion raised themselves to be honoured, respected and powerful members of the comity of nations. If every Ismaili living in Pakistan remembers and interprets his citizenship, howsoever humble his contributions may be, with the spirit of courage and devotion, then indeed I am happy to think that after many years of surgical operations and illness, I am still alive to give you this fatherly advice.

From the religious point of view, though you must firmly stick to the tenets of your Faith, yet you should not forget what I have always considered the most beautiful of all Muslim prayers namely, that Allah Almighty in His infinite mercy may forgive the sins of all Muslims.

Source: *Dawn*, Karachi, 4 February 1954; Sultanali Nazerali El-Africi (ed.), *H.R.H. Prince Aga Khan III*, Mombasa, 1955, pp. 43–5; and *Message to the World of Islam by Aga Khan III*, Karachi, 1977, pp. 47–8.
The jubilee celebrations marked the seventieth year of the Aga Khan's spiritual headship of the Ismaili community.

218

IN SUPPORT OF THE PAKISTAN MUSLIM LEAGUE

A Message

Dacca: 3 February 1954

The coming elections in Pakistan – Islam, Pakistan and the Muslim League – vote for the League and propagate for it.

As you are well aware, the elections are now coming and in service of Islam it is absolutely necessary that the Government Party, Muslim League, should win completely in both East and West Pakistan. Otherwise, Islam's power will be weakened in this early stage when still it is a young Government and a young country.

For this reason all of you must sincerely help to the best of your ability and carry on strong propaganda with your other Ismailites and Muslims and help for the great hope of the Government Party, the Muslim League, and work with all sections for success.

This is a great service you will be rendering to Islam and Ismailies.

Source: *Dawn*, Karachi, 5 February 1954.
This message was sent to the President and members of the Ismaili Councils and members of the Ismaili Jamiats in Pakistan. A copy of it was released to the press by Ghyasuddin Pathan, Joint Secretary of the Pakistan Muslim League. It was circulated by the Associated Press of Pakistan. It must be recalled that the Aga Khan was the founder and for several years the president of the All India Muslim League, the predecessor of the Pakistan Muslim League.
On the fortunes and activities of the Pakistan Muslim League (the successor of the All India Muslim League) see Richard D. Weekes, *Pakistan: Birth and Growth of a Muslim Nation*, Princeton, N.J., 1964; W. S. Metz, *Pakistan: Government and Politics*, New Haven, 1956; Herbert Feldman, *A Constitution for Pakistan*, Karachi, 1955; Robert D. Campbell, *Pakistan: Emerging Democracy*, Princeton,

N.J., 1963; Rafique Afzal, *Political Parties in Pakistan, 1947–1958,* Islamabad, 1976; Keith Callard, *Pakistan: A Political Study,* London, 1957; Khalid bin Sayeed, *The Political System of Pakistan,* Boston, 1967; Leonard Binder, *Religion and Politics in Pakistan,* Berkeley and Los Angeles, 1963; Karl von Vorys, *Political Development in Pakistan,* Princeton, N.J., 1965; Mushtaq Ahmad, *Government and Politics in Pakistan,* Karachi, 1959, 2nd edn 1963; and K. K. Aziz, *Party Politics in Pakistan, 1947–1958,* Islamabad, 1976.

219

THE REFUGEE PROBLEM IN PAKISTAN

Interview with the Dawn of Karachi

Karachi: 4 February 1954

Effort by the public and the government – Germany's experience in the past – a commission to study experiences elsewhere – recovery in Turkey and Japan – solution in industrialization, as in Germany.

"I have read with great sympathy the editorial of *Dawn* in which a reference has been made to the plight of the refugees, but I feel that this problem can be effectively solved only by a determined effort of the country's population as a whole and the Government.

"Sporadic private charity can at best only tinker at it. Either a nationwide charity drive or the Government takes it over. I am sure under the guidance of our present Prime Minister ways and means will be found for meeting the refugee problem.

"... You are not the first country to deal with a problem of this nature. Germany had a very big problem of the same kind with far less possibilities of meeting it successfully. The area of West Germany and the whole population of West Germany would be about half that of Pakistan, yet it has been dealt with very successfully. I suggest that a commission should study how the refugee problem has been settled in other countries and then adjust ours to our special conditions by following the same successful methods in principle. Perhaps a commission of selected official experts should visit Germany and other countries and learn how to handle the problem in Pakistan."

He also referred to Japan and Turkey and said that these were the examples that Pakistan should follow. His Highness pointed out that all these countries had been very badly defeated in wars and suffered great economic and physical destruction and yet they had made tremendous recoveries.

"Let us go and see what Turkey is today. Any Government can, when faced with such a problem, either carry on a charitable drive by all means, both giving pleasure and going around from house to house, or by a special loan meet the refugee problem. But ultimately the refugee problem is the same as the unemployment problem of each and every country. It depends for its healthy solution on new industries and extension of existing industries. After all the German problem of refugee [sic] was solved by the union of capital and labour directly for production but indirectly for the solution of the refugee problem over a long period of time."

Source: *Dawn*, Karachi, 5 February 1954. *Dawn* reported that on the same day:
"The 150-hut Omme Habiba Aga Khan Colony at Drigh Village was declared open by Begum Aga Khan.... The single-room huts were built from Begum Aga Khan's Rs one lakh (100,000) donation to the Prime Minister's Hut Building Fund.

"Prime Minister Mohammad Ali, in a speech at the opening ceremony, appealed to the 'generous minded men and women' to come forward with donations.

"The number of huts built from the Prime Minister's Hut Building Fund in the Colony had now gone up to 250. The Prime Minister hoped: 'This is only a beginning'.

"Begum Aga Khan made a brief speech. She spoke feelingly of the refugees. They deserved all help and assistance, she said.

"She was full of praise for the 'dynamic young' Prime Minister. She said she was confident that under the leadership of Prime Minister Mohammad Ali, Pakistan will make rapid progress.

"The ceremony held in the far away Drigh Village Colony was largely attended.

"The guests included the Sind Governor, Cabinet Ministers, heads of diplomatic missions, and Viscount Astor.

"The Prime Minister and Begum Mohammad Ali showed one of the huts to Begum Aga Khan. The huts have cost Rs 600 each, and stand on 80 square yards plots. The refugees living in the huts are expected to build, on their own, another room, bath and kitchen.

"The Prime Minister explained to Begum Aga Khan the lay-out of the 150-hut colony built over 27.5 acres. APP [Associated Press of Pakistan] adds: Performing the opening ceremony, Begum Aga Khan announced that besides Rs one lakh (100,000) already donated by her, she was giving another Rs 50,000 so that the Colony, which bears her name, may further be extended.

"She suggested: 'Apart from donations, I do feel that attempts should be made to organise concerts, bazaars or similar projects to raise funds for financing this very urgent work. I am told that there have been hockey, cricket and polo matches organised for the purpose. This is very good; but more and still more must be done, knowing how the women and men of Pakistan are devoted to working selflessly for their people. I am sure that this suggestion of mine will receive serious consideration.

" 'It is a terrible thought that there are still homeless refugees in this great and growing capital of Pakistan, but I hope that with energy, determination and enthusiasm, under the leadership of your brilliant young Prime Minister there will one day be not a single refugee without a home.

" 'I am very impressed with what I have seen in the recent progress in building huts and I should like to express my thanks to the Prime Minister and to all who helped in creating this little colony.' "

On the gigantic migration of Muslims from India into Pakistan in 1947 see Richard Symonds, *The Making of Pakistan*, London, 1950; Z. Islam, *East Punjab's Blood Bath*, Karachi, 1948; D. M. Malik, *Tragedy of Delhi*, Lahore, 1948; and S. K. Shaida and Z. K. Shahid, *Blood Bath*, Lahore, 1948.

220

GOOD WISHES FOR THE PAKISTAN INSTITUTE OF INTERNATIONAL AFFAIRS

A Message to the Institute

Karachi: 5 February 1954

First address on the study of the first century of Islam – and the second on the material aspects and science – progress made by the institute.

Man proposes and God disposes. I am sorry to inform you that after a bad cold I have now a slight temperature and you can well understand that at my age I cannot go out with the temperature.

I am very sorry not to be with you as on two previous occasions. I had the honour of addressing you on what I believe to be the most important subjects of a man, a community, a state or a super state like the Muslim world, for the spiritual and material health and vigour.

As I consider the spiritual and mental being superior to the material body, my first address to you was a call to the Muslim world to study and take example from the first century of the great Ommayads period, before Islam was swaddled by a number of customs and inhibitions borrowed from Sassanian Iran by the Abbasides.

My second address to you dealt not only with your material well being but even with conditions without which in the modern world, survival is impossible, namely a serious attempt to increase production to its utmost by means based on modern and progressive discoveries of science.

Today I feel I cannot do better than to draw your attention to the two addresses which I have had the honour of delivering. I am glad to hear that this institution is to be put on a healthy financial basis with a building of its own, a library, a reading room, with all kinds of journals, magazines, reference books, etc. Allow me to contribute my little help to this excellent cause and subscribe Rs. 20,000. Wishing you every success and hoping that you will soon be in a position to tell the world that in Karachi we have a body established for the serious and continuous study of international affairs.

Source: *Dawn*, Karachi, 6 February 1954.

The Pakistan Institute of International Affairs is a semi-official institution created to study the country's place in the world community. It issues a quarterly journal called *Pakistan Horizon*. Its headquarters continue to be located in Karachi though the federal capital was shifted to Rawalpindi and later to Islamabad in the 1960s.

The text was also reproduced in *Message to the World of Islam by Aga Khan III*, Karachi, 1977, pp. 50–1.

221

THE SPIRIT OF THE ALIGARH UNIVERSITY

Speech to the Aligarh Old Boys' Association

Karachi: 12 February 1954

Revival of Islam in India through the Aligarh Movement – Aligarh and separate Muslim electorates – recognition of Muslims as a nation – importance of the spirit of Aligarh for Pakistan – new Aligarhs wanted – duty of the Aligarh old boys.

Aligarh has always meant to me so much because I was convinced that the revival of Islam in India at least could only come through the Aligarh movement. It was a dream for me in those days. Thank God, today it is a reality. How many in life live to see a dream realise[d] is far beyond their expectations. We only hoped that Aligarh would raise the status of the Muslims in India to the same level as other communities. What do we find today? An Empire built by Aligarh boys. (No Aligarhs, no separate electors, recognition that the Muslims were a nation, an idea fundamentally that of Sir Syed.) My dear boys, I would always like to consider you as Aligarh boys, however, old, your work is not over. It has only really just begun. The spirit alone can give this unique double horned country its proper strength power and influence in the world of today. Boys, you must agitate. You must not sit quiet. We want new Aligarhs. When I was at Dacca, the first thing I said: "We wanted an Aligarh in East Pakistan."

If you have that ambition bring it out to the new generation in this independent country. Do not let independence be an excuse for just saying: well we will go on, we will get education, we will learn science, we will learn technology, we will learn law in a free country. You must have at least till the end of this century the spirit of Aligarh in many of your institutions.

If my talk with you will make every Aligarh boy realise that he is still a boy, that age is the beginning of youth and to fight it on those lines to make this responsibility to become once more a champion of a cause victorious to-day but we wanted to be victorious throughout the world by its moral standard, by its integrity, by the respect which I hope and believe and I am convinced the spirit of Aligarh will win for Pakistan and Pakistanis.

Source: *Dawn*, Karachi, 13 February 1954.

It was also reproduced in Sultanali Nazerali El-Africi (ed.), *Message of H.R.H. Prince Aga Khan III*, Mombasa, 1955, pp. 59–60.

The speech was delivered before a gathering of the Aligarh Old Boys' Association (former students of the MAO College and Aligarh Muslim University). Before the Aga Khan's speech, the President of the Association, Justice Z. H. Lari, said in his address presented to the guest:

"You sounded the clarion call 'Now or Never' which electrified Muslim India from one end to the other. You were not content with propagating the idea of the Muslim University but as man of action you took practical steps to put the scheme into practice. In 1911 you led a deputation all over the country and collected the sum of Rs. 35 lakhs (3.5 million) for the establishment of the University. Your Royal Highness's deep solicitude for the educational progress of the Muslim youth was also manifested in your grants for scholarships for higher studies in foreign countries.

"On the political side also for the advancement of Muslims in the subcontinent, Your Royal Highness was already ready and willing to help and guide them with your wise counsel and powerful support."

On the Aligarh Movement see M. S. Jain, *The Aligarh Movement: Its Origin and Development, 1858–1906*, Agra, 1965; Theodore Morison, "An Indian Renaissance", *Quarterly Review*, April 1906; Aziz Ahmad, *Islamic Modernism in India and Pakistan, 1857–1964*, London, 1967; and Muhammad Sadiq, *A History of Urdu Literature*, Karachi, 1965.

222

RACIAL COOPERATION IN KENYA

Letter to The Times

Le Cannet: 24 March 1954

Tribute to Oliver Lyttleton on his constitution for Kenya – other countries will also derive benefits – racial co-operation in Kenya – similar results for other multi-racial states in Africa.

Mr. [Oliver] Lyttleton has sown the seeds of a multi-racial democratic State in Kenya and all such countries in Africa as have the multi-racial problem will sooner or later reap the full benefits of this great act of constructive statesmanship.

As one who has watched the possible development of Kenya on these lines for the last 50 years, I most heartily congratulate him on having achieved, by his visit and by the energy and strength, as well as the wisdom, of his decisions of what seemed to be almost a hopeless problem.

It is for the Africans, Europeans, and Asians (I consider the Arabs a part of the Asians) now so to cooperate that in the fullness of time all these races will be proud and patriotic Kenyans and that similar results will be achieved, by Kenya's example, in other multi-racial States of Africa.

Source: *The Times*, London, 24 March 1954.
    The letter, written from Yakymour, Le Cannet, Cannes, is not dated. It was published under the headlines "Development in Kenya: Time for Racial Cooperation."

223

A WARNING AGAINST SECTARIANISM

A Special Message to the East African Muslim Welfare Society

Evian les Bains: 10 July 1954

Difficulties facing Muslims in Africa – understanding between different sects – what Pan-Islamism means.

Moslems in Africa to-day are exposed to so many difficulties – internal weakness and external, if not hostility, at least unfriendly competition – that the first and the foremost principle to remember is comprehension of each and every sect and sub-sect by the others under the general brotherhood of those who say LA ILAHA ILLA-LLAH MOHAMED RASUL ALLAH.

Pan Islamism does not mean that one gives up one's own historical interpretation of Islam but that one accepts that of the other brother Moslems as an equally earnest endeavour to put to practice the Faith in God and the Prophet (S.A.W.) which illuminates and which, we hope, will save all Moslem Souls.

Source: *Souvenir of the East African Muslim Welfare Society*, n.p.p., 1954, p. 3.
The Society was founded by the Aga Khan on 16 June 1945. It played a leading role in promoting the education and general welfare of the Muslims of East Africa. As little is known about it outside East Africa I reproduce below an account of its history and activities between 1945 and 1954 as given in the pamphlet from which I have taken the text of the Aga Khan's message:

Our Founder and Patron in Chief

"World historians will record, in glittering letters of gold, the unique services rendered by this mighty prince of Islam to the Cause of Islam in East and Central Africa. His Highness' services are termed unique because there is not a single instance in the history of East Africa where one individual Muslim has made such a great personal sacrifice for Islam – for the revival of the religious, cultural, educational aspects of the life of indigenous Muslims, Arabs, Somalis and Sudanese.

" 'I will give you the help that should satisfy everybody here: I shall double whatever you will collect for the Cause of Islam, that is if you will contribute £1 for the erection of mosques and schools and for Tabligh I will give you a personal donation of £1 from myself and make the sum £2. If you want to come forward to show your mettle you are worth [sic] and also show us that Islam is alive. . . .' These words will ever remain historic, for they were uttered by His Highness [the] Aga Khan when he laid down the foundation of the East African Muslim Welfare Society in 1945.

"But the interest H. H. The Aga Khan takes in the welfare of Islam is as old as 1899 when he first came to visit East Africa. At this time he was greatly alarmed at the condition of Muslims. He saw a double danger hanging on the religion of Islam in East Africa: One by the fall of King Kalema in Uganda and the other by the weakness of Muslim Government in the Eastern Coastline. With mixed feelings of gloom and optimism His Highness left the shores of East Africa in 1899. Gloom for the downward trend in Muslims and optimism for the conviction that one day he will play his part to ameliorate the condition of Muslims.

"1905 saw His Highness again on the shores of East Africa. Full of life and young as he was he called the Muslims of Uganda in Kampala and heard from them their difficulties, grievances, hopes and sorrows. It was at this opportune meeting that two illustrious princes of Islam met each other – Prince Nuhu Mbogo and Prince Aga Khan. This meeting left lasting effects on the heart of His Highness but no progress was practicable in absence of the support of Asiatic Muslims. After that His Highness visited East Africa in 1914 and in 1926 but the conditions had not been propitious to start anything concrete. At last in 1937, the year which also witnessed his Golden Jubilee His Highness called a Round Table Conference of all prominent Muslims to discuss the uplift of Muslims in East Africa. The East African Muslim Welfare Society was formed in that year. His Highness set the ball rolling by a personal donation of Shs. 20,000/-. Sheth Abdullah Karimjee, O.B.E., was nominated the President of the Society. But soon the grim years of the Second World War encircled the horizon and whatever progress was materialized was retarded at the outset.

"His Highness visited East Africa in 1945 and once again called Muslims to organise themselves for a great era of progress in the postwar Africa. A conference was called at the Muslim Hall, Mombasa, under the Presidentship of His Highness [the] Aga Khan. It was participated by Muslims from every nook and corner of Africa: Muslims of all sects and sub-sects and races participated in the deliberations of the historic conference. At this conference the historic offer of "POUND TO POUND" was declared by His Highness The Aga Khan and the East African Muslim Welfare Society was re-organised, the steering of the "ship of Islam" was given to Sheth A. H. Kaderbhoy, M.B.E. – a benevolent and public spirited Muslim.

"Ever since that illustrious day in 1945 His Highness has contributed enormous sum [sic] of money for various welfare projects. No progress would have been possible had His Highness not contributed the sum of shillings three million for the welfare of African, Arab and Somali Muslims. In almost all prominent places in East Africa and in many villages the hope and aspiration of His Highness is seen today symbolised in the form of Mosques and Schools and Technical Centres. All these Mosques and schools have received "POUND TO POUND SUPPORT" from His Highness [the] Aga Khan. Apart from giving monetary help His Highness has always been in keenest touch with the affairs of Muslims in East and West Africa and from time to time issues guidance and direction.

"There are so many other examples of His Highness' charity and benevolence in East Africa but this short article does not permit us to go into details. His Highness is loved and venerated, as he is honoured and respected in the whole of Islamic World, by millions of African Muslims for what he has done for them in religious, educational and cultural spheres, leaving aside his immense political services."

A Short History of the East African Muslim Welfare Society

By: A. H. Kaderhoy, M.B.E.
President, Supreme Council E. A. Muslim Welfare Society.

"It was in 1937, the momentous year which witnessed the celebration of his Golden Jubilee, that H. H. the Aga Khan was the inspiring force behind the inception of the East African Muslim Welfare Society. It was he who first realised the growing necessity and importance of founding an institution of this type.

"It is, solely for altruistic and selfless objects since it is meant for the uplift, advancement and welfare of indigenous populations of East Africa – Africans, Arabs, etc. Not only is the manpower for managing and directing it drawn from among the immigrant races who have made the East African territories their adopted home, but these people are also called on to supply generously its life blood – funds. His Highness set the ball rolling by a personal donation of £1,000.

"In 1945, at the first East African Muslim Conference, it was obvious that His Highness was not content with the progress made by the East African Muslim Welfare Society. Through his inspiration, it was again reorganised and revitalised.

"He threw a sort of challenge to the entire Muslim community to contribute to the funds of this society, and he undertook to double the total collections from non-Ismailis. To my knowledge, never was such a magnanimous offer made by anyone. At this juncture, in response to the call of His Highness the Aga Khan, I agreed to serve this society as its president.

"During the unbroken period of the ten years of my presidency, the E. A. Muslim Welfare Society has collected, as at the end of June 1954, Shs. 6,332,912/07, which includes the princely contributions amounting to Shs. 2,765,462/20 from H. H. the Aga Khan. To date we have built 88 new mosques, including the magnificent ones at Tanga, Kibuli (Kampala) and Soroti. Also 82 new schools including many Secondary Schools and one Muslim Teachers' Training College, the first of its kind in East Africa, has just been completed at Kibuli. Many technical schools, dispensaries etc., have also been built.

"Apart from these, the society has to build 17 more schools and 5 more mosques, for which a sum of £3,250 has been reserved by the society from the above funds. Therefore, the society has issued grants for erecting a total of 99 schools and 93 mosques in East Africa.

"The society employs scores of Muslim Missionaries all over East Africa and due to the combined efforts of these missionaries and teachers the society runs and maintains many religious schools also.

"Apart from these figures, huge sums were added for educational purposes by the respective Governments of Kenya, Uganda, Tanganyika and Zanzibar, which are beyond our capacity to mention.

"The society has published thousands of books in African languages on Islam.

"This society is the first of its kind in East Africa and for that matter in the whole of Africa which champions the cause of Islam and humanity at large. It is the only society in the whole of East Africa which does immense welfare work among the backward indigenous population of Africa, at the same time it encourages the Arab and Somali Muslims. The Society has 5 patrons each having subscribed £1,000 and 19 vice patrons each having subscribed £250 and 170 life members each having subscribed £50. All these generous Muslims belong to all denominations of Islam from all over East Africa and in some cases even belonging to countries overseas. Apart from these the society has an ordinary membership of scores of Muslims all over East Africa each paying 6/- per year in the case of Africans and 60/- in the case of non-Africans.

"The Society radiates its activities throughout East Africa by the provincial councils and district councils mentioned below which cater for needs of all the 3,000,000 Muslims:

Kenya: Mombasa (Headquarters of Supreme Council and provincial council), Nairobi and Kisumu.

Uganda: Kampala, Jinja, Masaka, Mbale, Fort Portal and Soroti.

Tanganyika: Dar es Salaam, Moshi, Tanga, Dodoma, Lindi, Singida and Kigoma.

"The Society has sent 13 students from Uganda to the world renowned centre of Islamic learning – Al Azhar University at Cairo for religious education. Within another few years these young people will help the religious aspect of Muslims.

"Our activities, limited though they have been for reasons which I need not dwell upon here, have undoubtedly kept the banner of Islam flying, and have, to some extent, given an impetus to Islam.

"This is mainly due to the foresight, inspiration and help of His Highness who is the man of the age. He is among the very few men whom destiny made to wield world-wide influence and power, and who is universally held in veneration and affection because of the wise and scrupulous use of that power and influence for the good and betterment of others, recognising no limitations or boundaries of countries or continents. Long may he live to continue his good undying work to the glory of Islam."

SUMMARY

Summary of the activities of the Society since its formation in June 1945 by H. H. the Right Honourable the Aga Khan, P.C., G.C.V.O., G.C.S.I., G.C.I.E., LL.D., to June, 1954.

Country	Schools	Mosques	Teachers Training College	Boardings	Technical Schools	Water Reservoirs	Pauper Clamps
Kenya	21	16	–		–	1	–
Uganda	48	30	1	1	3	–	–
Tanganyika	29	38	–	–	–	–	1
Zanzibar and Pemba Island	1	9	–	–	–	–	–
Total Institutions for which Grants approved	99	93	1	1	3	1	1
Institutions yet to be built	17	5	–	–	–	–	–
Total Institutions completed	82	88	1	1	3	1	1

SUMMARY OF FUNDS
JUNE, 1945 TO JUNE, 1954

Total funds of the Society (donations, patronship fees, life and ordinary membership fees, rents, etc.,) from June 1945 to June, 1954	Shs.	3,567,499. 87
Total donations made by our Patron in Chief, H. H. the Aga Khan from June 1945, to June 1954	Shs.	2,765,462. 20
	Shs.	6,332,912. 07

From the above Fund, a sum exceeding to Shs. 650,000/- is held by the Society for 17 mosques and 5 schools which are yet to be built in various places

Report of the Hon. Gen. Secretary
"Dear Readers,

"It has been our earnest desire to publish a small souvenir to show what little work the Society has been able to do for our Arab and African Muslim brothers during the last 9 years. We have now been able to achieve our desire by presenting this souvenir to you. The Society's thanks for this publication are due to our sub-committee consisting of Hon'ble Sheikh Mbarak Ali Hinawy, Dr. Najmudeen and Mr. A. H. Nur-mohamed who had the able assistance in its compilation of Mr. Sultanali Nazerali el-Africi.

"The East African Muslim Welfare Society was established in June 1945, at the Muslim Conference held under the Presidentship of His Highness the Agakhan at Mombasa. Its objects are social, religious, educational and cultural welfare and advancement of the Arab and African Muslims. The Society is a non-political body. It has been registered in Kenya, Tanganyika and Uganda. The Executive Committee of the Society known as the Supreme Council consists of influential members of all races throughout East Africa. Our present Trustees are Sheth A. H. Kaderbhoy, M.B.E., of Mombasa, Hon'ble Sheikh Mbarak Ali Hinawy, O.B.E., of Mombasa, Hon'ble Mr. Abdulla Karimjee, O.B.E., of Tanga and Count Hassan Kassim Lakha of Kampala.

"Our Society has up-to-date [*sic*] built 82 schools including many secondary schools, 88 mosques, half a dozen staff quarters, two large water reservoirs in East Africa. The Society has further approved the sum of Shs. 650,000/- to build further 5 schools and 17 mosques. We have over 10,000 students in the said schools and most of these schools are recognised and aided by the Government.

"The Society has published and distributed a large number of religious books in Kiswahili. We hope to publish and distribute more and more literature for tabligh work.

"The Society is grateful to our goodwill mission which went to West Africa at great expense.

"The Society's thanks are due to the Governments of Kenya, Uganda, Tanganyika and Zanzibar specially their Departments of Land and African Affairs. Mr. Ch. Gallanos, Mr. Hitchcock, Mr. J. T. Gleeve, the Mombasa Times press and many other friends for their kind co-operation and assistance.

"The Society's thanks are also due to our grand old man Sheth A. H. Kaderbhoy, M.B.E., Sheth Yusufali A. Karimjee Jivanjee, Sheth Tayabali H. A. Karimjee, Hon'ble Sheikh Mbarak Ali Hinawy, Mr. Abdulla M. A. Karimjee, Hon'ble Dr. S. G. Hassan, Dr. Najmudeen, Dr. M. A. Rana, Count Kassamali R. Paroo, late Mr. M. S. Kalyan, Mr. A. A. Khandwalla, Mr. A. H. Nurmohamed, Prince Badru [Kakungulu], Mr. Osman Macci, Count Hassan Kassim Lakha, Mr. Adamali E. Kaderbhoy, Hon'ble Mr. Abdulkarim Y. A. Karimjee, Mr. Mohamedali Sheriff, Count Fatehali Dhalla, Count A. H. Ganghji, Hon'ble Count V. M. Nazerali, Mr. A. G. Sheikh, and all other members of the Supreme and Provincial Councils and also to the Standard Bank of South Africa Ltd., Messrs. D. S. Trivedi & Co., Mr. H. B. Esmail, Mr. Karimbhai Abdulhusein and many other friends for their kind cooperation and assistance.

"I do trust that this small souvenir will interest you and that you will do your best to assist our noble work.
Yours faithfully,
A. C. SATCHU, Hon. Secretary."

THE EAST AFRICAN MUSLIM WELFARE SOCIETY

TANGANYIKA:– SCHOOLS BUILT, AIDED OR ISSUED WITH GRANTS BY THE SOCIETY

The following is the list of the schools built, aided or issued with grants by the Society for African Muslim brethren in the Tanganyika Territory ever since its formation in 1945. In all 29 schools were either built, aided or issued with grants by the Society in the Territory the details of which are as follows:–

Name of the School or Town	Amount spent in Shillings
1945–1946	
1. Dar es Salaam African Muslim School	146,884/85
2–6 Various Schools in Moshi Dist. and Mt. Kilimanjaro	51,356/12
1947	
7. African Muslim School Mwanza	2,000/00
8. Iringa Muslim School	12,000/00
9. Bukoba Muslim School	30,000/00
1948	
10. Upare Muslim School	10,700/00
11. Moshi Muslim School	6,000/00
12. Ujiji Muslim School	17,000/00
13. Arusha Muslim School	12,600/00
1949	
14. Machame Muslim School and Mosque	1,000/00
15. Tanga Muslim School	193,000/00
16. Singida Muslim School	9,100/00
17. Korogwe Muslim School	24,000/00
18. Msimbazi Muslim School	200/00
19. Mbulu Muslim School	88,900/00
1950	
20. Songea Muslim School	1,600/00
21. Dar es Salaam Muslim Girls' School	100,000/00
22. Dodoma Muslim School	4,000/00
1951	
23. Mudio Moshi Muslim School	3,000/00
24. Usangi Muslim School	4,100/00
25. Shinyanga Muslim School	6,000/00
1952	
26. Kigoma Muslim Mosque and School	57,834/00
27. Ugweno Pare Muslim School	2,100/00
1953	
28. Makuyunia Muslim School	9,000/00
1954 (June)	
29. Uchira Moshi Muslim School	1,500/00
	793,874/97

THE EAST AFRICAN MUSLIM WELFARE SOCIETY

TANGANYIKA:– MOSQUES BUILT, AIDED OR ISSUED WITH GRANTS BY THE SOCIETY

The following is the list of Mosques built, aided or issued with grants by the Society ever since its formation in 1945. In all, more than 38 Mosques were either aided, issued with grants or built in Tanganyika Territory details of which are mentioned below.

Name of the Mosques	Amount spent in Shillings
1945–1946	
1. Jamiyya Mosque, Tanga	188,500/00
2. Soni Mosque, Lushoto	15,000/00
1947	
3–7 Various five Mosques on the Kilimanjaro mountain Moshi district	51,356/12
8. Bukoba Mosque	72,500/00
1948	
9. Kange Mosque (Sisal Estate Tanga)	40,000/00
10. Dar es Salaam Comorian Mosque	20,000/00
11. Mahako (Tanga) Mosque	24,000/00
12. Machame (Moshi) Mosque and School	1,000/00
13. Machame (West) Moshi Dist. Mosque	6,200/00
14. Monduli (T.T.) Mosque	8,000/00
15. Korogwe Mosque	14,000/00
16. Darwesh Mosque Dares Salaam	429/50
1950	
17. Mwarongo Mosque (Tanga)	300/00
18. Nkumbhi (Muhesa Tanga) Mosque	41,500/00
19. Ngomeni Mosque Tanga	41,500/00
20. Manyonjoni Mosque Tanga	11,000/00
21. Ilala Mosque, Dar es Salaam	86,000/00
22. Byiti Mosque Tanga	2,000/00
23. Jamiyya Mosque (Mwanza)	2,000/00
1951	
24. Tambarani & Mwarongo Joint A/C Mosque Tanga Dist.	6,700/00
25. Manyoni Mosque (Dar es Salaam)	15,450/00
26. Machame (Mkuu) Mosque	3,000/00
27. Ponde Moa Mosque	450/00
28. Matembe Mosque (Bukoba)	2,550/00
1952	
29. Kilimanjaro Bwani Machame Mosque	12,000/00
30. Kilimanjaro Kindi Juu Mosque	9,000/00
31. Kilimanjaro Kibo Hay Mosque	9,000/00
32. Kilimanjaro Kibonghoto Mosque	9,000/00

33.	Kilimanjaro Kindi Njoro	6,000/00
34.	Ngerengere Mosque	60,000/00
35.	Dar es Salaam Jamiyya Mosque	150,000/00
36.	Ugwengo (Upare) Moshi Mosque 1954	4,500/00
	1954 (June)	
37.	Bagamoyo Jamiyya Mosque	15,500/00
		926,435/62

NOTE:– All figures mentioned here are approximate as various donations were added during construction, etc.

THE EAST AFRICAN MUSLIM WELFARE SOCIETY

UGANDA:– SCHOOLS ETC., BUILT, AIDED OR ISSUED WITH GRANTS BY THE SOCIETY

The following is the list of the Schools, Teachers' Training College, Technical Schools and Boarding Houses built, aided or issued with grants by the Society in Uganda ever since its formation in 1945.

Totally thirty-one Primary and Secondary Schools: one Boarding House: one grand Teachers' Training College; three Technical Schools have been either built, aided or issued with grants by the Society for African Muslims of Uganda. The following are the details.

Name		*Amount in Shillings*
1.	Kibuli. Kampala Jun. or – Secondary School and Boarding House	110,470/00
2.	The African Muslim School Jinja	12,579/85
3.	Wadengeya African Muslim School Kampala	101,060/00
	1947	
4.	Kakira Muslim School and Mosque	8,000/00
5.	Kawempe Muslim School	17,840/00
6.	Kumi Muslim School	4,000/00
7.	Namalambe Muslim School Jinja	28,360/00
8.	Kamuli Muslim School	1,000/00
9.	Bulange African Muslim School	1,200/00
10.	Bwala African Muslim School	48,350/00
11.	Bugembe African Muslim School	12,000/00
12.	Busia African Muslim School	10,000/00
13.	Bukoyo African Muslim School	52,000/00
	1948	
14.	Kibigi Muslim School	7,350/00
15.	Katoro Muslim School	11,400/00
16.	Wakatayari Muslim School	4,200/00
17.	Arua Muslim School	22,000/00
18.	Buniantole African Muslim School	20,900/00
19.	Lukalu Muslim School	25,100/00

1949

20.	Soroti Muslim School Mosque and School	322,700/00
21.	Kumi Muslim School	1,480/00
22.	Kibigi Muslim School	3,400/00
23.	Kavoko Muslim School	2,000/00
24.	Kasavo Muslim School	1,985/00
25.	Kabu Kunge Muslim School	4,000/00
26.	Kigoowa Muslim School	1,400/00

1945–1946

27.	Lira Muslim School	37,000/00
28.	Kampala Arab Muslim School	10,000/00
29.	Bukedi Muslim School	80,000/00
30.	Hoima Muslim School	2,000/00
31.	Bugembe Muslim School	53,150/00
32.	Kabasanda Muslim School	1,000/00
33.	King Kalema School	2,000/00
34.	Kyaba Goma Muslim School	800/00
35.	Kidugala Muslim School	3,600/00
36.	Kibuli African Muslim Tech. School	22,500/00
37.	Kibuli African Muslim Teachers' Training College	51,076/00
38.	Mbarara Noor – el – Islam Madrasa	1,300/00

1951

39.	Bukoyo Muslim Teachers' School	34,650/00
40.	Kabukye Muslim School	37,510/00
41.	Ngora Soroti Muslim School	23,250/00
42.	Katakwi Muslim School	6,150/00
43.	Amuria Muslim School	12,900/00
44.	Kyera Muslim School	4,200/00

1952

45.	Bombo Sudanese Muslim School	14,050/00
46.	Majengo School Jinja	6,700/00
47.	Namtumba School, Jinja	3,000/00

1954 (June)

48.	Mbale Muslim Mosque and School	11,750/00
		1,253,410/85

THE EAST AFRICAN MUSLIM WELFARE SOCIETY

UGANDA:– MOSQUES BUILT, AIDED OR ISSUED WITH GRANTS BY THE SOCIETY

The following is the list of Mosques either built, aided or issued with grants by the Society ever since its formation in 1945. In all more than 30 mosques were either built, aided or issued with grant by the Society in Uganda, the details of which are given below:

Name	Amount in Shillings
1945–1946	
1. Kibuli Mosque Kampala	313,239/56
2. Wadengeya Mosque, Kampala	26,000/00
3 Bugemba Mosque Jinja	15,000/00
1947	
4. Bugembe Mosque Jinja	8,000/00
5. Mbarara Mosque	9,500/00
6. Kakira Muslim Mosque and School	8,000/00
1948	
7. Busia Mosque	10,000/00
8. Kayaka Mosque	6,000/00
9. Entebbe Mosque	1,200/00
1949	
10. Bukoto Mosque Jinja	24,700/00
11. Karungu Mosque Masaka	2,000/00
12. Nambhi Mosque Kampala	3,675/00
13. Soroti Mosque and School	322,750/00
14. Bale Butambala Mosque	4,000/00
15. Bukima Mosque	1,400/00
16. Bujuta Mosque	8,700/00
17. Nyakato Mosque	7,700/00
18. Masaka Mosque	6,000/00
1950	
19. Ngambhi Mosque Kampala	3,300/00
1951	
20. Bunianotole Mosque	8,000/00
21. Kabukunge Mosque	5,100/00
22. Bulange Mosque	2,150/00
23. Ibwere Mosque	900/00
24. Majengo Jinja Mosque	63,850/00
1952	
25. Masaka Mosque	84,900/00
1953	
26. Bunia Mosque	4,300/00
27. Kaliro Mosque	13,600/00
28. Kyaba Goma Mosque	1,800/00
29. Kikoto Mosque	6,000/00
1954 (June)	
30. Mbale Mosque and School	11,750/00
	983,714/56

NOTE: All figures mentioned here are approximate as various donation were added during construction. etc.

THE EAST AFRICAN MUSLIM WELFARE SOCIETY

KENYA:– SCHOOLS EITHER BUILT, AIDED OR ISSUED WITH GRANTS BY THE SOCIETY

The following is the list of the Schools which were either built, aided or issued with capital grants by the society for African, Arab, Somali Muslims since 1945. In all 21 Schools were either built, aided or issued with grants, details of which are as follows:–

Name	Amount spent in Shillings
1945–1946	
1. Mumias School and Mosque	107,600/00
2. Primary Arab School Kisumu	65,000/00
3. Maragoli School Kisumu	31,600/00
4. Kindu Bay School Kisumu	800/00
1947	
5. Nyeri Muslim School	26,750/00
6. Kisi Muslim School	4,000/00
7. Wah Muslim School (Funds reserved for the project.)	100,000/00
1948	
8. Malindi Muslim School (Funds reserved for the project)	28,900/00
9. Voi Muslim School	10,000/00
10. Fallah Muslim School (For Extension.)	11,000/00
11. Sio Muslim School	5,000/00
12. Eldoret Muslim School	39,800/00
13. Maria – Kani Muslim School	4,500/00
14. Gyambogi Muslim School	37,700/00
15. Nairobi Muslim School	12,500/00
1949	
16. Taveta Muslim School	400/00
1950	
17. Kilifi Mosque and School	9,475/00
18–19. Two Nairobi District Schools	12,000/00
1951	
20. Digo District School	4,170/00
1953	
21. Rabai Muslim School	300/00
	502,495/00

THE EAST AFRICAN MUSLIM WELFARE SOCIETY MOMBASA

KENYA:– MOSQUES BUILT, AIDED OR ISSUED WITH GRANTS BY THE SOCIETY

The following is the list of the Mosques either built, aided or issued with grants by the Society for African Muslims since 1945. In all 16 mosques were either built, aided or issued with grants by the Society in Kenya, the details of which are as follows:–

Name	Amount spent in Shillings
1945–1946	
1. Mumias Mosque and School	107,600/00
2. Malindi Mosque and School (Funds reserved for project.)	28,900/00
3. Ukunda Digo District Mosque	5,700/00
4. Jomvu Mosque	4,000/00
5. Jomvu Kwa Shehe	2,000/00
1947	
6. Sakina Mosques, Mombasa	40,800/00
1948	
7. Maragoli Mosque	14,700/00
1949	
8. Kisumu Kaloleni Mosque	1,000/00
1950	
9. Kilifi Mosque	9,475/00
10. Thivi Mosque	29,200/00
11. New Jamia Mosque	39,900/00
1951	
12. Moyale Jamiyya Mosque	15,000/00
1952	
13. Takwa Mosque Mombasa	500/00
1953	
14. Kisumu Arab Mosque	3,750/00
15. Shibo Shimba Mosque Mombasa	7,500/00
16. Makunumbi (Lamu) Mosque	7,500/00
	317,525/00

THE EAST AFRICAN MUSLIM WELFARE SOCIETY

ZANZIBAR & PEMBA:– MOSQUES BUILT, AIDED OR ISSUED WITH GRANTS BY THE SOCIETY

The following is the list of Mosques either built, aided or issued with grants by the Society in Pemba and Zanzibar ever since 1945. Totally nine mosques were either built, aided or issued with grants by the society in Pemba and Zanzibar, details of which are as under:

Name	Amount spent in Shillings
1948	
1. Zanzibar Kisiwa Ndui Mosque	2,500/00
1949	
2. Zanzibar Jamiyya Mosque	60,000/00
3. Wete Pemba Jamiyya Mosque	114,500/00
1951	
4. Makawani Pemba Mosque	15,000/00
5. Chale Chambani Mosque	5,500/00
6. Ngwachani Pemba Mosque	12,600/00
1953	
7. Vikokotoni Mosque	2,000/00
8. Mzingani Mosque Zanzibar	32,500/00
1954 (June)	
9. Tumbatu Island Muslim School	22,700/00
	267,500/00

THE EAST AFRICAN MUSLIM WELFARE SOCIETY
PEMBA SCHOOL BUILT BY THE SOCIETY
The following is the detail of a school built by the Society in Pemba:
PEMBA SCHOOL
1951
1. Sayyid Bin Said Muslim School   192,600/00

NOTE:– All figures mentioned here are approximate as various donations were added during construction, etc.

The Muslim Teachers' Training College

"**Background**: In order that masses of the African Muslims be educated a dire need was felt for the African Muslim Teachers. The idea of Muslim Teachers' Training College originated around 1935 and in 1949 a European Principal by name Mr. J. T. Gleeve, M.A., M.Ed., was appointed as its first principal. The College was originally situated at Kasawo, some 40 miles north of Kampala, in rather camped [[*sic.* cramped?]]buildings. It was felt that the College should be in Kampala and the question as to where exactly it should be placed was solved when the illustrious Prince of Islam, Badru Mbogo, the leader of the

African Muslims, gave 80 acres of the most valuable piece of land around prominent Kibuli Mosque for the development of the Islamic religion and education – both secular and religious. The fact that a large Muslim primary school (now Kibuli Demonstration School . . .) already existed at Kibuli Hill was an additional advantage."

"In 1952 and 1953 generous Government grants were given for the new College and by the beginning of 1954 enough buildings had been completed to allow a start to be made in pleasant new and modern surroundings. A European Principal had arrived and the whole College was moved from Kassawo to Kibuli Hill, Kampala on 12th February, 1954.

"**Staff**: The Training College has a European Principal and a staff of six. One of these is at present at Kyabogo Government Teachers' Training College, Kampala. A European specialist in Arts and Crafts has been appointed. A third European is expected later."

"The Demonstration School has a Head Master and a staff of ten-Class [*sic*] Masters and Mistresses. There are Ten Classes – 1a, 1b, 2a, 2b, 3, 4, 5a, 5b, 6a, 6b.

"**Buildings and General Development**: At present the building situation is as follows: Completed – Assembly/Dining Hall, Art and Crafts Wing, Large Dormitories (2), Class Rooms, Library, Office and Staff Room.

"**Programme begun on 1st July, 1954**: Four Staff Houses – College, one Dormitory – College, Servants' Quarters, three Staff Houses – Demonstration School. In addition, the Uganda Muslim Educational Association, Kampala and the East African Muslim Welfare Society are taking steps to provide a mosque for the College and they also contemplate the building of a small hospital/dispensary, which will be a material advantage to the College.

"Further developments completed in 1954 include a preparation of three large football pitches, one of which is to be surrounded by a running track, and two volley ball pitches. In addition a number of internal roads have been cut as well as two roads connecting the College main buildings with the main road to Kampala. Water supply has also been adjusted to meet the water supplies of the College. In all these undertakings a good deal of thought has been given to the eventual "look" of the layout from an aesthetic point of view, and also the possibility of future expansion.

"**Students**: There are 61 students in residence –

(a) 1st. year pre-professional	17
(b) 2nd year pre-professional	17
(c) Vernacular Trainees	17
(d) 1st and 2nd Year Primary Trainees	10
	61

"Shortly the College will have about 100 students. The College requires as students very best type of Muslim boys. However, it cannot be too much stressed that the College is not just interested in numbers: it is essential for future healthy growth of Muslim Schools that those responsible for recommending students to the College should pay particular attention to their "quality" not only academically but, perhaps more important, religiously. The College can do much with a boy who has a steady character and lives his religion, even if he is not academically brilliant. This is specially important since it is becoming clear that the move from Kasawo and the swiftness of the development the last few years, has awakened a tremendous amount of interest and keenness with the Muslim Community, resulting a [*sic*] marked increase in the number of applications reaching the College from would be entrants.

"Candidates who have passed the Junior Secondary Leaving Examination are eligible to apply for the two-year professional course. Candidates who have passed Primary Leaving Certificate or who have not completed junior secondary course are eligible to apply for pre-Professional Course. In pre-Professional years, the aim of the curriculum is to raise the standard of the students academically particularly in English, so that all instruction in Professional Courses can be in English. It also helps to weld together quickly students who come from all parts of the Protectorate.

"The College has an up-to-date curriculum for indoor and outdoor methods of teaching. The internal organisation of the College is of a very high standard on famous European College standard [*sic*]. There are proper lodging and boarding facilities with ample recreation for the students and the diet provided to the students is also hygienic and nutritive. Proper medical treatment is also given to the students. Real attention is given for character and religious practices by the College authorities.

"Later an agricultural specialist is to join the staff; the tentative plans are being made for the students to develop plots on the North Side of the great Kibuli Hill. This will take the form of a co-operative project under the Agricultural Instructor.

"A College Board of Governors is to be appointed on which representatives of the Uganda Muslim Educational Association and the East African Muslim Welfare Society will sit so that there is complete liaison between Government and informed Muslim opinion.

"All correspondence should be addressed to Principal, P.O. Box 263, Kampala, Uganda."

224

MEMOIRS:
WORLD ENOUGH AND TIME

Extracts from a Book

London: 10 September 1954

EARLY YEARS

Seasonal movements of the family – daily routine – short-sighted-
ness personal tutors – his mother's religious outlook – her interest
in poetry – atmosphere in the home – study of languages, history
and science – a solution for poor eyesight – relationship with his
mother – her practical outlook – his wide reading – journey to
northern India – beginning of interest in Muslim education –
enthusiasm for the Muhammadan Anglo-Oriental College –
endeavours to raise it to the status of a university – the emergence
of Aligarh University.

My education for the responsibilities and tasks which I had
inherited was serious and strenuous and it had to be fitted into
a regular system of seasonal family migration. From November
to April during the cold weather of each year we were in Bombay;
in April and May we were at Mahabaleshwar; from June to
October we were in Poona and in October we went for a short
spell to one of the smaller hill stations, and thence back to
Bombay. For ten years – from 1885–1895 – this system continued
unchanged; and in it there was no room for a holiday for me, a
month, a fortnight, even a week off the chain; at the most a rare
day. And relentlessly was I held on the chain.

This was the typical and unchanging pattern of my days: I was called between six and half-past, and had my breakfast – a weak tea, bread, butter, jam, and a Persian sweet. At seven, whether I wanted to or not, I had an hour's riding – a canter or sometimes a gallop on one of the Poona rides or on the racecourse, or at Bombay along the sands. From eight to half-past eleven I had lessons with my English and French teachers. Then I had luncheon and I was free until two o'clock. Thereafter I had three hours' instruction in Arabic. A drive or some tennis in the garden, or some sort of relaxation, was then permitted until dinner at seven o'clock . . . no one had realized that I was from birth so short-sighted that to read or write I had to hold a book or paper an inch or two from my nose, and in my vision of the world farther than those few inches from my nose there was no definition and no delight, for everything I saw – garden, hills, sea, or jungle – was a haze . . .

I had three British tutors – a Mr. Gallagher, who was Irish, a Mr. Lawrence, and another Irishman, Mr. Kenny. All three were found for me by the Jesuits in Bombay. It may seem strange that my family turned to the Jesuits for my education in Western matters, but both in Bombay and in Poona there are big and important Jesuit schools, and both quite near where we lived – St. Mary's in Bombay and St. Vincent's in Poona. All the children of our considerable household – the ever-multiplying descendants of my grandfather's hangers-on, pensioners, relatives, and old soldiers – went to these Jesuit schools. The whole household knew the Jesuit fathers well, and nothing was easier than to get their advice and help.

There was never a hint, by the by, of their attempting to convert any of our Muslim children to their own creed. They respected Islam and never by open argument, by suggestion, or insinuation did they seek to weaken a Muslim's faith . . .

So far as I was concerned, the three teachers the Jesuits found for me were all excellent men. The schooling which they gave me was not in the least narrow or restricted. They lifted my mind to wide horizons, they opened my eyes to the outside world. They were wise, broadminded men, with a stimulating zest for knowledge and the ability to impart it – whether in science, history, or politics. Most important of all perhaps, they encouraged me to read for myself, and from the time I was ten or thereabouts, I burrowed freely into our vast library of books in English, French, Persian, and Arabic. My three tutors gave me the key to knowledge, and for that I have always been profoundly grateful to Mr. Gallagher, Mr. Lawrence, and Mr. Kenny . . .

In addition, my mother was herself a genuine mystic in the Muslim tradition (as were most of her closest companions); and she habitually spent a great deal of time in prayer for spiritual enlightenment and for union with God. In such a spirit there was no room for bigotry. Like many other mystics my mother had a profound poetic understanding. I have in something near ecstasy heard her read perhaps some verses by Roumi or Hafiz, with their exquisite analogies between man's beatific vision of the Divine and the temporal beauty and colours of flowers, the music and the magic of the night, and the transient splendours of the Persian dawn . . .

The home in which I was brought up was, as you can see, a literary one. I have referred to my mother's poetic sense. She was deeply versed in Persian and Arabic literature, as were several of her ladies-in-waiting and closest women friends. My mother knew a great deal of poetry by heart and she had a flair for the appropriate classical quotation – a flair which, I may say, she never lost throughout her long life. Even when she was nearly ninety she was never at a loss for the right and apt quotation, not merely from one of the great poets such as Hafiz and Firdausi or Roumi, but from many a minor or little-known writer.

One little anecdote may illustrate this. Shortly before she died a cousin of mine quoted one night at dinner a verse of Persian poetry which is rarely heard. In order not to bother my mother or worry her, I attributed it to Hafiz. Not at all, said my mother, that is not by Hafiz, and she gave the name of the line and the name of the rather obscure poet who wrote it.

A consequence of this characteristic was that at mealtimes at my mother's table there were no occasions of idle gossip or tittle-tattle. Our conversation was of literature, of poetry; or perhaps one of the elderly ladies, who travelled to and from Tehran a great deal, would talk about her experiences at the Court of the Shah.

A clear light shines on this phase of my boyhood. Was I happy or unhappy? I was solitary, in the sense that I had no companions of my own age, except my beloved cousin Aga Shamsuddin and his brother Abbas who were of the same age and the same outlook and were the closest and dearest friends of my youth, but I had so few holidays and so little free time, what could I have done with a host of friends? One fact stands out extremely clearly – I worked hard, a great deal harder than most young schoolboys. By the time I was thirteen I could read and write English, tolerable French, perfect Persian, and fair Arabic; I had a sound knowledge of Roman history as well as of Islamic history. I was well grounded in at least the elements of science – chemistry and physics, botany, biology, and zoology. Nor was my scientific education merely theoretical; in each of our houses I had a small laboratory and I had a set period of practical, experimental laboratory work every day . . .

And a year or two later my reading and indeed my whole outlook on life, were profoundly and permanently transformed by a small, wise decision; much that had hitherto been pain and hardship became pleasure and delight; my health was immediately improved, and I am sure I was saved much trouble and misfortune in later life. Mr. Kenny, the third and last of my European tutors, had at one time been employed by a firm of opticians. As soon as he saw me settle down to work he realized how terrible – and how dangerous – was the torture to which, through my congenital shortsight and the ignorance on these matters of those by whom I was surrounded, I was being daily and hourly submitted.

It is strange and sad to recall that already, more than once before Mr. Kenny's arrival, I had in fun picked up and put on a pair of glasses left lying about by one of our family or friends. The moment I put them on I discovered the joy of a new and exciting world; a world of human beings of definite and different shapes, a world of green trees and brightly coloured flowers, and of sharp, strong light, instead of the perpetual haze and fog, the world blurred at the edges, which was all that an extremely myopic little boy could see. But those minutes of joy were of short duration, and were indeed forbidden, for the servants had orders to take the glasses away from me, since my family could not believe that a child could be shortsighted and thought I was being self-indulgent and silly. Mr. Kenny immediately recognized my present plight and its implications for my future. He insisted on taking me to the firm of opticians whose employee he had been; he had my eyes tested and had me fitted with proper glasses both for reading and for distance. My uncles strove to interfere, but Mr. Kenny was adamant, he carried with him the prestige of the West, and he won the day. This sensible and kindly action saved me infinite pain and worry, and gave me a new world in which to live . . .

With approaching manhood my life shaped itself into new channels of its own. More and more the duties and decisions implicit in my inherited position devolved on me. I was never indeed subject to any Regency, in the accepted sense, and as my capacity to take decisions increased, so my mother and my uncles encouraged me to accept responsibility. My mother, who had insisted on the educational discipline of my early boyhood, was as shrewd and watchful as she was loving. She and I remained – as we did throughout her long life – in the closest, most affectionate intimacy. Every night in those years I would go to her apartments and join with her in prayer – that prayer for unity, for companionship on high, which is the core of Muslim faith. This shared experience gave us both, I think, the strength to bear our load of fatigue and anxiety, mental and spiritual, which was by no means light during these difficult years. But my mother's religion was resolutely practical as well; she saw no virtue in faith without works, and from the outset of my public career I accepted and sought to practise the same standards . . .

My mind was opening rapidly to new horizons; in my reading I began to range widely, in English and French as well as in Persian and Arabic; I discovered the intellectual delight – the precision and clarity – of Mill's system of logic. I read voraciously in history and biography, and with my cousin Shamsuddin I became an insatiable reader of novels – a diversion, I may say, whose pleasures have never faded . . .

In October [?1895], when the great heat of the summer was over and the monsoon rains had passed, I made my first journey to Northern India. Hitherto my travelling outside Western and Southern India, except for visits to Baghdad and to Bushire and Muscat, had been extremely restricted, I now however acquired a taste for travel which I have certainly never abandoned. On this first trip I visited the great shrines and centres of Muslim India at Agra, Delhi, and Lahore: that magnificent group of monuments to Islamic civilization and culture – the Taj Mahal, the Red Fort in Delhi, and the Friday Mosque, and those exquisite gems, the Pearl Mosques at Delhi and Agra. My way led me, too, to the Anglo-Muslim College (as it then was) at Aligarh, where I met Sir Syed Ahmed and Nawab Mohsen-ul-Mulk. This was the origin of what was for many years one of the crucial concerns of my life – my interest in the extension and improvement of Muslim higher education, and especially the College and University at Aligarh.

I took up its cause then with a youthful fervour which I have never regretted. Aligarh in the 1890s was an admirable institution, but it was hampered and restricted by lack of funds and lack of facilities. Did I realize then, young as I was, that it had in it to become a great power house of Muslim thought and culture and learning, in full accord with Islamic tradition and teaching, yet adapted to the outlook and the techniques of our present age? No one could have foretold all that did in fact happen; but I do know that I was on fire to see Aligarh's scope widened and its usefulness extended, and to find the money for it, by any short-cut means if necessary. Why not, said I in my youthful rashness, go to some great American philanthropist – Mr. Rockefeller or Mr. Carnegie – and ask for a substantial grant?

My new friends were older and sager. It was our responsibility, they said, within our own sixty or seventy million-strong Muslim community in India; if we sought for outside help, even from the richest and most philanthropically inclined of American multi-millionaires, we should be dishonoured for all time. They were right, of course. For this was an age which had not experienced two World Wars, and had never heard of Point Four. But that decision, and my own zeal in the cause which I had taken up, led (as such decisions are apt to lead) to years of arduous and all-demanding toil, the journeyings, the speech-making, the sitting on committees, the fight against apathy and the long, long discussions with those in high places, which are the lot of those who commit themselves to such an endeavour.

Often in civilized history a University has supplied the springboard for a nation's intellectual and spiritual renascence. In our time it has been said that the American Robert Missionary College in Constantinople led to the re-emergence of Bulgaria as an independent, sovereign nation. Who can assess the effect on Arab nationalism of the existence of the American University of Beirut? Aligarh is no exception to this rule. But we may claim with pride that Aligarh was the product of our own efforts and of no outside benevolence; and surely it may also be claimed that the independent, sovereign nation of Pakistan was born in the Muslim University of Aligarh.

[Extracts from pp. 11–36]

IN THE LEGISLATIVE COUNCIL

Appointment to the Viceroy's Legislative Council – friendship with G. K. Gokhale and journalists – the gulf between the Government of India and the people – faith in educational advancement –

Indian National Congress and the aspirations of the Muslims – the realization that Muslims needed recognition as "a nation within a nation" – acquaintance with Sayyid Ameer Ali – processes which led to the partition of the Indian subcontinent.

I returned to India in November of that year, 1902. I was surprised to find waiting for me a letter from the Viceroy, Lord Curzon, asking me to become a member of his Legislative Council. This was a considerable honour to a young man still in his twenties (I was by far the youngest member), for the Viceroy's Legislative Council in those days was a small, select body of influential people, wielding real authority. My acceptance necessitated my moving for the time being to Calcutta, which was then the seat of British power in India.

The two years in which I was a member of the Legislative Council (I was asked if I would accept nomination a second time, but I refused) had a profound and permanent effect on my life and character, in their private and personal as well as their public aspects. For the first time in my life I had a real, normal home of my own, with the ordinary complement of servants and the ordinary social and domestic life of a man in my station, free of the extraordinary accretion of hangers-on and ne'er-do-wells (remnants of whom never entirely disappeared from Bombay and Poona) ...

The effect on my public and political life was hardly less marked. I found myself working alongside men of the calibre and quality of Lord Curzon himself, and of the Commander-in-Chief, the redoubtable Field-Marshal Lord Kitchener of Khartoum. Among my Indian colleagues there was the brilliant Mr. G. K. Gokhale, the outstanding Indian nationalist statesman until the rise of Mahatma Gandhi and the Nehrus, father and son. Gokhale and I struck up a friendship which only ended with his death. He was a caste Hindu and I was a Muslim, but our friendship crossed the barriers of creed and race. He was a man of vision, courageous and generous. His influence on my thought and outlook was probably considerable. Not of course that he was the first political thinker of a different background from my own with whom I had come in contact, or with whom I found the exchange of ideas stimulating. Some years previously in Bombay I had come to know and like Mr. Navroji Dumasia, a talented Parsee in the service of the *Times of India* and Mr. (later Sir) Frank Brown, a British journalist and publicist who was on the staff of the *Bombay Gazette* and subsequently of *The Times*; to both these friends I owe a great deal, both in what I have done and what I have tried to do in my political work.

In Gokhale I encountered a powerful as well as lovable personality. I realized how deep and strong were the forces in India of which he was the spokesman. I also saw how remote the Government had become from the people of India, not the masses only, but the increasing and ever more articulate and active intelligentsia. I saw at close quarters how foreign the Government was in spirit and in atmosphere. On the other side, I saw that India's political leaders, dissatisfied at not having succeeded in obtaining their earlier moderate demands, began to seek not merely administrative reforms but the full control of their own political destiny.

For myself, I continued to pin a great deal of faith on educational advancement. Illiteracy I saw as a menace to people and Government alike. Poverty and disease were its sinister consequences and accompaniments. More than once my speeches in the Legislative Council turned into strong pleas for generous and judicious expenditure on education. I urged the adoption of a system of universal primary education such as almost every civilized country possessed, and pointed out as often as I could that in my view the fundamental cause of India's extreme poverty was India's extreme ignorance.

At the same time I began to realize, during these two crucial years, that the Congress Party, the only active and responsible political organization in the country, would prove itself incapable – was already proving itself incapable – of representing India's Muslims, or of dealing adequately or justly with the needs and aspirations of the Muslim community. The pressure of Hindu extremism was too strong. Already that artificial unity which the British Raj had imposed from without was cracking. Deep-seated and ineradicable differences expressed themselves once political activity and aspirations had advanced beyond the most elementary stage. The breach was there – in Hindu intransigence and lack of perception of basic Muslim ideals and hopes. I did all I could to prevent the breach being widened. I maintained a campaign of remonstrance with Sir Pherozeshah Mehta, who was high in the counsels of the Congress Party, who was a friend of my family and who had known me since childhood. I begged him to use his influence and make Congress realize how important it was to win Muslim confidence; but all to no avail.

Whatever the reason for their attitude, the Congress leaders persisted in ignoring the realities of the communal situation.

There were provinces in which the Muslims were in a clear majority, in Bengal for example, and in the Punjab, out of which the N.W. Frontier Province had not then been carved. And about Delhi, Agra, and Aligarh there had been built up a spiritual home, sanctified by some of the most valuable of Muslim traditions and adorned with imperishable treasures of Islamic art and culture. Some comprehension of what this meant in Muslim minds was all we asked. And the time was propitious – as never again – for an understanding; earlier grave differences of opinion with Congress had dwindled into comparative insignificance and even the memory of them that remained could have been wiped out – as I argued as forcibly as I could – if certain proposals which we made for equitable representation and a fair ratio of Government employment for Muslims had been accepted and acted upon.

The primary step was that Congress should choose as its representative on the Viceroy's Legislative Council a Muslim from Bengal or the Punjab. We drew a blank there. For Congress obstinately continued to send third-rate Muslims from preponderantly Hindu provinces like Madras and Bombay. Gokhale, I am convinced, was sincerely anxious to do all he could to change his Party's attitude. He could never publicly admit it, but privately he was deeply distressed to watch his political friends and associates thus deliberately sowing the seeds of permanent disunity between Hindu and Muslim. I made frequent, urgent representations of practical, feasible steps by which we could have integrated Muslim political feeling into the Congress Party and presented a united front to the British Government. Yet even the private support which Gokhale gave to my representations brought no change of mind or heart.

I turned to my friends at Aligarh, and in particular to Nawab Mohsen-ul-Molk, who had succeeded Sir Syed Ahmed as Muslim leader. Mohsen-ul-Molk was not hidebound, he was moderate and realistic, and was not at all antagonistic either to Congress or to Hindus in general. If there had been give-and-take in what were then quite minor matters he was willing to join forces with Congress. In such an atmosphere – assisted by the fact that there was a joint electorate and joint representation – a political alliance between the two communities was possible. Our hopes were dashed again and again. Conditions deteriorated at the next elections; and by 1906 Mohsen-ul-Molk and I, in common with other Muslim leaders, had come to the conclusion that our only hope lay along the lines of independent organization and action, and that we must secure independent political recognition from the British Government as a nation within a nation.

While I lived in Calcutta, I came to know the Right Honourable Syed Amir Ali, later a Privy Councillor, then a Judge of the High Court in Calcutta. I had of course read his famous books on Islam; my admiration for his learning, and for his capacity to expound and interpret our Muslim religion, was unstinted. Although of course he was excluded from any participation in politics, I had no hesitation in going to him for advice and help in my own political endeavours – above all, to secure equitable representations of Muslims, and to open the eyes of the then Congress High Command to the perils of the course on which they seemed set. But when our hopes were frustrated, it was a great encouragement that Syed Amir Ali, with all his personal prestige, and his great knowledge of Hindu-Muslim political relations (especially in Bengal) urged us on in our efforts for the establishment of a separate Muslim organization, and gave us quiet, constant support when Nawab Mohsen-ul-Molk and I argued that our only hope of getting a fair deal from the British was to convince them of the width of the gulf – historical, cultural, and religious – that yawned between us and our neighbours.

The Congress Party by its blindness to legitimate claims and aspirations, and by its persistence in its ridiculous habit of choosing Muslim yes-men from Madras and Bombay as its representatives on the Viceroy's Legislative Council, lost a great opportunity which was not to recur. These then were critical years, not merely in my own political development, but in that vast and complex process which brought about, in little more than forty years, the partition of the Indian subcontinent into the separate states of Bharat and Pakistan.

[Extracts from pp. 73–7]

MORLEY-MINTO REFORMS

Realization in England that there was a Muslim problem in India – the status of Muslims in India in the post-Mughal period – the limited nature of the Morley-Minto reforms – the Muslim deputation to Simla – its demands – the consequences of the principle established – the attitude of Muhammad Ali Jinnah – the founding of the All India Muslim League – John Morley's attitude – separate electoral representation for Muslims – Muslim political consciousness.

The electoral change in England in that crucial year 1906 had its effect on India. While I was in England that summer my friends in India wrote and told me that at last the Government were beginning to realize that there was something called a Muslim problem in India, and that they could no longer dismiss it as an idle fabrication.

Since 1857 and the transference of authority in India from the East India Company to the Crown, the Muslims had, in a political sense, been more or less ignored by the British. Perhaps not unnaturally the new rulers of India turned away from those who, by religion and by language, were connected with the rulers who had been ousted. Muslims were not brought into the administration or into politics; few studied or read English. If the end of the Moghul Emperors was pitiable, its effects lingered on for two generations in the sense of isolation and powerlessness which enveloped the Muslims of India in their own land. The Hindu majority were in an advantageous position under their new rulers; and they made full use of it. The Muslims had been for long what the French call "quantité négligeable", but at long last we were going to be heard. The Viceroy, Lord Minto, had agreed to receive a deputation from us and I was to lead that deputation.

We were acutely aware that we had long been neglected, that to the Hindu majority – as represented by its leaders in the Congress Party – we seemed a tiresome splinter in the flesh of the body politic, and that though there was great talk of nationalism we were not ever considered in the aspirations that were being fostered, the plans that were being laid. They continued to send to the Viceroy's Legislative Council third-rate yes-men instead of truly representative Muslims, with the result that our separate identity as a community and the status that would have appertained to it had been forgotten by the British.

Now we decided that the time had come to make a stand for a change in attitude. If constitutional advancements were to be mooted, we must have our say in their disposition. Reform was in the air, but it must be understood – in the utterly different political atmosphere of more than forty years later – that it was reform within extremely limited terms of reference. British supremacy in India, administrative and legislative, was to remain uninfringed, unaltered. In the Morley-Minto reforms, as they came to be known, and in the Indian Councils Act of 1907 in which they were embodied, there was no hint of a process of evolution towards ultimate Indian self-government, no hint of transference of power from British to Indian hands. John Morley himself said, "A fur coat may be all very well in Canada, but no use at all in India" – the political and constitutional evolution which had been Canada's experience was thus by implication rejected for India (though not, of course, *by* India). All that the Morley-Minto proposals were intended to achieve, and did achieve, was a modest devolution in communal and local matters and the admittance of Indians, on a rigidly restricted basis, to consultation – though not to decision – about their own affairs.

Within these limits, however, they were an advance; and from the Muslim point of view they were especially significant. Our experience from the time of the Cross-Lansdowne reforms in 1892 onwards had pointed the way; there was no hope of a fair deal for us within the fold of the Congress Party or in alliance with it. Now in 1906 we boldly asked the Viceroy to look facts in the face; we asked that the Muslims of India should not be regarded as a mere minority, but as a nation within a nation whose rights and obligations should be guaranteed by statute. History has amply demonstrated since then, after the First World War and again and again later, that the existence of minorities – of one nationally conscious community within another, numerically weaker perhaps but not less firmly aware of itself as a nation than the majority – is one of the major issues of our time. Ireland, Poland, Czechoslovakia, Jugoslavia – the world's maps are plentifully dotted with these minority problems, with all their complexity and difficulty.

For ourselves in 1906 we asked for the establishment of a principle, a principle which would have to be embodied in any legislation as a consequence of these proposals for reform. We asked for adequate and separate representation for Muslims both on local bodies and on the legislative councils, we asked that this representation be secured by a separate communal franchise and electoral roll. In short, we Muslims should have the right of electing our own representatives on it. We conceded that in areas where we were in the majority, like the Punjab and what was then the Province of Eastern Bengal, we would give a certain number of extra seats to the Hindus, in order to safeguard their interests, and in return we asked that in areas in which there was a big Hindu majority we likewise should be conceded a certain number of extra seats.

Lord Minto listened with sympathy to our statement of our case. He assured us that the political rights and interests of the Muslim community would be safeguarded in any change in administration that might occur. Our principle was accepted. Most of our demands in detail were conceded, though not all. It would in my view have been better had there been provision for two Indian members of the Viceroy's Executive Council – one Muslim and one Hindu – instead of the one finally provided for. But after all it was John Morley himself who said to me when I raised this point, "You mustn't get too much power, you know."

It is perhaps unnecessary to stress the irony of history's comment on that observation. But within their own time, the Morley-Minto reforms were a genuine step forward. We had had established a major political principle; its application in practice was to be a permanent feature of all constitutional developments in India henceforward. It was not, however, conceded without opposition. And if in retrospect there is an element of irony about Lord Morley's remark which I have just quoted, there is a much more freakishly ironic flavour about the name and personality of the chief Muslim opponent of the stand which we took. For Lord Minto's acceptance of our demands was the foundation of all future constitutional proposals made for India by successive British Governments, and its final, inevitable consequence was the partition of India and the emergence of Pakistan.

Who then was our doughtiest opponent in 1906? A distinguished Muslim barrister in Bombay, with a large and prosperous practice, Mr. Mohammed Ali Jinnah. He and I first became acquainted when he, having been called to the English Bar, settled in Bombay and – entirely without private fortune and without influence – rapidly built up his successful practice there. We had always been on friendly terms, but at this juncture he came out in bitter hostility towards all that I and my friends had done and were trying to do. He was the only well-known Muslim to take up this attitude, but his opposition had nothing mealy-mouthed about it; he said that our principle of separate electorates was dividing the nation against itself, and for nearly a quarter of a century he remained our most inflexible critic and opponent. In a later chapter I shall discuss more fully the circumstances – most of all the stubborn folly and intransigence of the Hindu majority in Congress – which converted this stoutest champion of Indian unity into its most determined opponent; and I shall trace in detail the paths of destiny which brought him, as the unchallenged leader of eighty million Muslims, that victory – the creation of the separate and independent State of Pakistan – for which we at the beginning were working unconsciously and indirectly, and he at the end consciously and directly and with all the force of his will and intellect. For the moment I merely reflect upon the irony implicit in it all.

Our achievement in 1906 seemed important enough; and it was obvious to those of us most closely associated with it – especially Nawab Mohsen-ul-Molk and myself – that, since we had obtained separate electoral recognition, we must have the political organization to make that separate representation effective. The All-India Muslim League was therefore founded at a meeting at Dacca later that year at which, as it happened, I was unable to be present. I was however elected its first President, and as such I remained until 1912 . . .

1907 saw the Morley-Minto constitutional reforms in India turned from tentative proposals, whose shape and pattern we had been able effectively to influence, into law. John Morley, with his liberal background and outlook, of the purest theoretical and academic kind, was extremely reluctant to accept the principle of separate electoral representation for the Muslims. It went against the grain of his character. However, the Viceroy, Lord Minto, had given his undertaking and Morley – however scrupulous his theoretical objections – could not be permitted to go back on it. For Syed Amir Ali and myself, 1907 was a period of what I can best describe as guerrilla warfare, whose aim was to keep Morley up to the mark. We won in the end, but it was hard going . . .

These were the years in which the Morley-Minto reforms were being put into practice. It was proved that the principle of separate electoral representation for Muslims, which we had fought so hard to have established, was sound and workable as well as theoretically just. Muslim political consciousness, under the leadership of men like Nawab Ali Chowdry and the Nawab of Dacca in Bengal, and of Sir Muhammad Shafi and Sir Sulfiqar Ali Khan in the Punjab, matured and strengthened steadily.

[Extracts from pp. 91–114]

ALIGARH

The Aligarh Movement – Lord Hardinge's and Sir Harcourt Butler's support – his own vision of Aligarh – fund raising – the Muslim Educational Conference at Nagpur – the significance of the Aligarh University.

I myself was devoting a good deal of time, energy, and interest to the affairs of Aligarh. I suppose that I was a sort of one-man "ginger group" on behalf of the project of converting Aligarh into a great Muslim university. Steadily during these years we aroused interest in and extended support for our project. Of course it provoked opposition too from that powerful British element whose argument was that a Muslim university would be undesirable and that its tendencies and teachings would be narrowly sectarian and particularist. I strove hard to counter these criticisms, making it a cardinal point of all my appeals for help, all my speeches and articles, that the sons of Aligarh University would go forth "through the length and breadth of the land to preach the gospel of free inquiry, of large-hearted toleration, and of pure morality".

I was not without support in high places. To Lord Minto there succeeded as Viceroy Lord Hardinge of Penshurst, a statesman and diplomat with a wide and long experience of life with and among Muslim people in Iran and throughout the near East. As the member of the Viceroy's Executive Council responsible for education there was a brilliant and devoted administrator, Sir Harcourt Butler, uncle of Mr. R. A. Butler, Chancellor of the Exchequer in Sir Winston Churchill's Government of 1951 onwards, and the minister responsible for Britain's great Education Act of 1944. Interest in education is a tradition in the Butler family. Both Lord Hardinge and Sir Harcourt understood our Muslim position and were aware of the fundamental differences in the social, cultural, and spiritual background of Muslim and Hindu. For myself, I tried again and again to make it clear that I regarded Muslim educational advancement not as an end in itself, but as a means to an end. If we were to advance down the road towards independence and self-government – however distant that goal might seem – we must, as a community, possess the knowledge and the intellectual equipment to cope with the political responsibilities to which we were beginning to aspire. I had no narrow sectarian purpose in view. I urged from the outset that Sanskrit should be taught, and with it the history and evolution of Hindu civilization, religion, and philosophy, in order that our people should be able better to understand their neighbours. A university of our own was essential because it was the best and most enduring means of developing the spiritual unity of Islam.

The work of converting others to this belief which I held so ardently, of building up support for it, and of raising funds, was extremely strenuous. I travelled all over India, I went to great Muslim leaders, to the poor and to the rich, to princes and to peasants. My own monetary contribution was 100,000 rupees, which was quite a sum in those days; in all I collected more than three million rupees. These were years of unremitting hard work. For days and weeks at a time, it seemed, I lived in railway trains. In every town the train stopped at I would address Muslim gatherings on the platform of the railway station. At every opportunity I preached the cause of Aligarh. My honorary private secretary, and my right-hand man throughout the campaign, was the late Maulana Shaukat Ali; without his steadfast, unwearying help I doubt if I should ever have been able to make a success of it.

We reached a climax in the long campaign with the Muslim Educational Conference at Nagpur in 1910 at which the Aligarh project was the principal item on the agenda, and indeed dominated the proceedings. Our aims were well expressed by the Chairman of the Conference, Mr. Yusuf Ali, who defined the scope of the university which we hoped to establish in these words: "It will have no tests, freedom and originality of thought will be encouraged. It will be a Muslim university in the sense that it will promote the ideals which the Muslims of India have evolved out of the educational experience of two generations."

Now when all is said and done, when I look back on all that the Muslim University of Aligarh has stood for and achieved in the past forty years, this is without doubt one of the facts of my life which I can record and contemplate with real and abiding satisfaction. I do not want only to stress its political consequences, momentous as these have been. Where else than in a Muslim university would it have been possible to establish and maintain, alongside and fully integrated with the libraries, the laboratories and all the facilities essential for a full understanding of our world and our time, a true centre of Islamic faith and culture, in which can be expounded and practised the principles of our

religion, its universality and its real modernity, its essential reasonableness, its profound spirit of tolerance and charity and respect
for other faiths? That I played my part in establishing such a
centre is for me one of the happiest, most consoling, and most
fortifying thoughts to take into old age.

[Extracts from pp. 114–16]

TURKEY AND THE FIRST WORLD WAR

The British request to persuade the Turks not to join the Central
Powers – negotiations with the Young Turks – the role of Taufiq
Pasha – the attitude of the Western Allies – German influence at
Constantinople – the Turkish declaration of war on Russia – his
personal position on the issue – the consequences of Turkey's
decision.

Most significant of all, it had not passed unnoticed by the British
Government that I had won and held the respect and trust of
many important Turks. Lord Kitchener requested me to use all
my influence with the Turks to persuade them not to join the
Central Powers, and to preserve their neutrality. I discovered that
Kitchener was by no means alone in his idea of the sort of
employment to which I could best be put. His opinion was shared
and supported by the Secretary of State for India, by the Foreign
Secretary, Sir Edward Grey, and by the Prime Minister, Mr.
Asquith. Indeed even the King, when I had the honour of lun-
ching with him, referred to it.

Therefore, while overtly I busied myself with rallying young
Indians in England – of whom there were considerable numbers
– to volunteer for the Indian Field Ambulance Corps, and in
raising a comforts fund for them, discreetly and urgently I got
in touch with the Turkish Ambassador, Tewfiq Pasha. At my
request he sent an invitation to the Young Turks, who had
assumed power in Turkey's revolution of 1908, to send a ministerial delegation to London to enter into direct negotiations with
His Majesty's Government. Britain was prepared, on her own
behalf and on behalf of Russia and her other allies, to give Turkey
full guarantees and assurances for the future.

We had high hopes of bringing off what would have been, from every point of view, a diplomatic victory of first-rate importance. I was quite aware that my own emotions were deeply involved. As a Muslim I was most anxious that Turkey should be spared the trials and the horrors of renewed war, not against a ramshackle alliance of small Balkan States but against the mighty combination of some of the greatest industrial and military nations in the world. The Turks had but lately emerged from their earlier ordeal; they were in desperate need of a breathing space; it seemed impossible that they could enter a new struggle and not face almost illimitable catastrophe. It had to be admitted that the Turks were justifiably suspicious of "guarantees", however specific, offered by the Western Powers; they had had too recent and too rueful experience of similar guarantees, which seemed to them promises made only to be broken. Yet even allowing for the most cynically realistic appreciation of the situation, as it existed in the last months of 1914, neutrality (which was all the Western Powers asked of Turkey) would have given the Young Turks the time they needed in which to carry out their programme of social, economic, and military reform.

Tewfiq Pasha was a key figure in our approaches. He had been for many years the Sultan Abdul Hamid's Foreign Minister. The Young Turk Revolution had displaced him from that office, nevertheless the new régime maintained their trust in a most experienced and capable statesman. In London and other Western capitals he was held in the highest esteem. Venerable, sage, and shrewd, he was a good friend of my own; he and I trusted each other implicitly. What was even more important, he was in full agreement with my attitude in this business.

He took occasion, however, immediately to warn me that our negotiations would have had a much greater chance of success if the Allies had asked Turkey to come in on their side rather than proposed mere neutrality, for which at the end of the conflict nobody would thank her. He went on to say that he was convinced also that Russia would never agree to Turkey joining the Allies, as such a step would put an end to all Russia's hopes of expansion at Turkey's expense, either in the North East, around Erzerum, or southwards from the Black Sea. In confidence I communicated these observations to Lord Kitchener. Within a few hours he told me that the Allies had no desire to bring Turkey into the war on their side. In view of this preliminary exchange, we entered negotiations under a considerable handicap. Nevertheless I was an optimist for several days, and my optimism seemed far from groundless.

Suddenly it became known that two German warships, the *Goeben* and the *Breslau*, had evaded Allied naval vigilance and were lying at anchor off Constantinople. Their presence drastically altered the whole situation. The Turks accorded them hospitality and protection. They were a visible sign of German naval vigour and capacity. Combined with the remarkable moral ascendancy which had been established in Constantinople by the German Military Mission, under its extremely able and resolute commander, General Liman von Sanders, the ships presented the gravest possible menace to our hopes – lately so high – of maintaining Turkish neutrality. By the close of 1914 the Central Powers were confident of a quick victory on their own terms; an elderly Prussian general named von Hindenberg had inflicted a crushing defeat on the immensely gallant but incompetently led Russian armies in the marshes of Tannenberg in East Prussia; in the west, the German armies, held almost within sight of Paris, had stabilized themselves along that 600-mile front which, with pitiably little variation and at appalling cost of life on both sides, was to be maintained until August 1918; a solitary cruiser, the *Emden*, at large in the Indian Ocean, had inflicted spectacular shipping losses on the Allies, and turned up impudently in Madras Roads. Tragically misled by all these signs and portents dangled before their eyes by the exultant Germans, the Turkish Government took the irrevocable step of declaring war on Russia. This automatically involved the Ottoman Empire in war with Great Britain and France.

To a strategist like Churchill this decision offered an opportunity (which was never fully seized) of ending the slaughterous deadlock on the Western Front, and of striking at Germany and Austria from the South-east. To myself at that moment it was a shattering blow. Its sharpness and severity were mortifying in the extreme; and when the Turkish Government, striving to put a respectable and popular façade on what was in fact unprovoked, inexcusable aggression, proclaimed this a *jehad*, a holy war against Christendom, my distress and disappointment crystallized into bitter resentment against the irreligious folly of Turkey's rulers. My resentment was given a razor edge by my knowledge of how near we had been to success in our negotiations. The fruit was just about to be plucked from the tree when not merely the tree but the whole garden was blown to pieces. . . .

However, I do still regard the failure of our attempt to open my negotiations with the Sublime Porte in the last months of 1914 as a tragic turning-point in modern history. Had Turkey remained neutral the history of the Near East, and of the whole Islamic world, in the past forty years, might have been profoundly different. What had been Islam's natural centre and rallying point for hundreds of years, the Sultanate in Constantinople, was destroyed. Turkey, as we shall see later, emerged from her tribulations under the inspiring leadership of Mustafa Kemal, restored and purified in spirit, but shorn of her Empire. Millions of Arabs, who had lived for centuries under the tolerant suzerainty of the Turks discovered, not only on the high plateau of central Arabia but in the lands of the fertile crescent, the joys and sorrows, the difficulties and the ardours of nationalism. And the British Empire, in the years from 1918 onwards, fell heir – by accident rather than by intention – to that Near and Middle Eastern hegemony so long exercised by the Ottoman Empire; and to *vilayet* and *pashalik* succeeded mandatory government. French involvement in Syria, the Greek adventures and disasters in Asia Minor, the clash of Zionism and Arab aspirations, Ibn Saud's carving of a new kingdom in Arabia, the emergence of the Sharifi family from a local chieftainship in Mecca to the foundation of ruling dynasties in two kingdoms – all these complex consequences and many more were to flow from the Young Turks' rejection, under German pressure, of the advances made to them at the end of 1914.

[Extracts from pp. 132–6]

TURKEY AFTER THE FIRST WORLD WAR

Discussion on the future of the Ottomon Empire – conflicting claims of various parties – anti-Turkish sentiments in British political circles – activities of the European powers – sympathy for Turkey among Indians – the campaign to place the issue before British and world public opinion – proposal for an Indian deputation to Britain – the Treaty of Sèvres – British and French hegemony over the Arabs – the emergence of Mustafa Kamal Ataturk – the British Government's mood – his mediation – the French policy – Lord Beaverbrook's role – revelations in the *Daily Express* – Lloyd George's departure from office – the British recognition of new Turkey.

One of the countless major questions which faced the victorious

Powers in the immediate post-war period was: What was to be done about the Ottoman Empire, over vast regions of which the Allies were, by the end of 1918, in military Occupation? It was true that the Turks retained control of their own homeland, Anatolia, and of the historic, ancient capital, Constantinople, but from Tripolitania in the west to Kurdistan in the east, from north of Aleppo to Wadi Halfa, in enormous territories whose populations, in a great diversity of races and culture but predominantly Muslim, had once owed allegiance to the Sultan of Turkey, the controlling authority was now an Allied Military Governor.

In the heat of war many promises of spoils in the hour of victory – spoils to be torn off the vanquished body of Turkey – had been made; few were by the beginning of 1919 capable of fulfilment, nearly all were irreconcilable one with another. The MacMahon letters, addressed by the acting High Commissioner in Egypt in 1915 to the Sharif Husain in Mecca, could not possibly be reconciled with the Balfour Declaration issued in 1917; both conflicted sharply with the Sykes-Picot agreement, by which Britain and France shared out huge areas of the Ottoman Empire as "spheres of influence". The most flagrantly impossible undertaking of all was that Constantinople (since Tsarist Russia had retained an historic interest in what had once been the Graeco-Roman city of Byzantium) should be given to Russia. This at least could be ignored, since the Bolshevik leaders had made their own peace arrangements with the Germans in the Treaty of Brest-Litovsk, and since the Soviet régime and the Western Allies were in a state of undisguised hostility. But for Turkey as a whole the hopes of a tolerable peace settlement looked slender.

Almost all the British political leaders who were to have any influence over the peace discussions were markedly anti-Turkish. Lloyd George, the Prime Minister, was a friend and admirer of Venizelos, the Greek leader; he saw certain similarities in historical experience and outlook between Greece and his own Wales; he was therefore enthusiastically pro-Greek, and though not actively anti-Turkish he was quite indifferent to the fate of the Ottoman Empire. Arthur Balfour, the signatory of the letter to Lord Rothschild announcing that it was Britain's intention to establish a National Home in Palestine for the Jews, was openly and actively pro-Zionist, and was also extremely prejudiced against the Turks historically and racially . . .

And the Zionists were only one group among many, anxious to extract all they could from the carve-up of Turkey. Arab nationalism was hardly less strongly in the ascendant, and it possessed many powerful friends and zealous advocates in and near the British Government... The British had already established a military administration in Palestine. The French advanced the remarkable claim that they had an historic right to protect the Holy Places in Jerusalem. The Greeks, encouraged by another group of romantic, philhellene Englishmen, were in a mood of dangerous expansionism. And at the very heart of real power in the Peace Conference, Clemenceau had no love for the Turks; and President Wilson, in the one interview which I had with him, frankly admitted that he really knew very little about the whole problem.

Almost the only support, therefore, on the side of the victors that Turkey could muster was Indian. The greater part of Muslim interest in India in the fate of Turkey was natural and spontaneous and there was a considerable element of sincere non-Muslim agitation, the object of which, apart from the natural revolt of any organized Asiatic body against the idea of European imperialism, was further to consolidate and strengthen Indian nationalism in its struggle against the British.

The reasons for Muslim concern were profound and historic. Turkey stood almost alone in the world of that time as the sole surviving independent Muslim nation, with all its shortcomings, the imperial régime in Constantinople was a visible and enduring reminder of the temporal greatness of Islam's achievements. In the Caliphate there was, too, for all of the Sunni sect or persuasion, a spiritual link of the utmost significance. As the war drew to its close anxiety had intensified in India in regard to the safety of the Holy Places of Islam and the future of the Caliphate. Gandhi, who had succeeded my old and dear friend, Gokhale, as leader of Congress political movement and organization, shrewdly seized what he saw to be a chance of maintaining and heightening anti-British sentiment throughout the whole subcontinent. The storm of agitation that swept India on this issue was formidable. The Indian delegates at the Peace Conference, the Maharajah of Bikaner and Lord Sinha, heartily and sincerely supported by Edwin Montagu, the Secretary of State for India, made an emphatic protest against the various proposals for the partition of Turkey and the practical dissolution of the Caliphate that were being eagerly canvassed around and about the Conference.

It had been decided to settle the fate of defeated Germany first. This thorny task was accomplished in considerable haste, and the Treaty of Versailles was signed on 28th June, 1919. Thereafter, protracted discussions continued about the treatment of the other vanquished nations. My friend Syed Amir Ali and I began an energetic campaign to put the real issues, so far as Turkey was concerned, before British, and indeed world public opinion. I had private interviews with numerous influential statesmen, together we wrote long letters to *The Times*; on every possible public and private occasion we made our views known.

We drew vigorous attention to certain specific pledges given by the Prime Minister, and in a letter to *The Times* quoted these pledges *verbatim*:

> We are not fighting [Lloyd George had said] to deprive Turkey of its capital or of the rich and renowned lands of Asia Minor and Thrace. While we do not challenge the maintenance of the Turkish Empire in the homelands of the Turkish race with its capital at Constantinople, the passage between the Mediterranean and the Black Sea being internationalized and neutralized, Arabia, Armenia, Mesopotamia, Syria and Palestine are in our judgment entitled to a recognition of their separate national condition.

We tried to sum up the outlook of those for whom we knew we had a right to speak.

> What do the Muslims want? What do we plead for? Neither they nor we ask for any new status for Turkey. We consider it, however, our duty to urge, for the fair name of England, nay of the British Empire, that the pledge the Prime Minister in the name of England gave to the world, and in particular to the world of Islam, should be maintained; and that the Turkish sovereign, as the Caliph of the vast Sunni congregation, should be left in absolute possession of Constantinople, Thrace, and Asia Minor stretching from the north of Syria proper along the Aegean coast to the Black Sea – a region predominantly Turkish in race. It would in our opinion be a cruel act of injustice to wrench any portion of this tract from Turkish sovereignty to satisfy the ambitions of any other people. Instead of bringing peace to Western Asia, such a settlement will sow the seeds of constant wars, the effect of which cannot be expected to remain confined to the country where they happen to be waged. For the defection of the adventurers who dragged their stricken people, who had already undergone great misery, into the world war, Turkey has been sufficiently punished by the

secular expropriation of some of her richest provinces. But we submit that the maintenance of the Ottoman sovereign's spiritual suzerainty in these countries, whilst maintaining his prestige and thus conciliating Muslim feeling, would be the means of making the position of the Muslim rulers or governors of those countries unimpugnable. But so far as Thrace, Constantinople, and the homelands of the Turkish race are concerned, Muslim feeling is absolutely opposed to any interference under any shape with the Sultan's sovereignty.

In India itself, as the months wore on, and as the time came near for signing a Treaty with Turkey, the agitation grew to such proportions and was of so unanimous a character as gravely to worry the Viceroy, Lord Chelmsford, and the Secretary of State, Edwin Montagu (whose personal sympathies, as I well knew, were warmly engaged on the Turkish or Asiatic side). Most of all they were disturbed at the thought that the Montagu-Chelmsford reforms, on which such high hopes had been pinned, were to be launched in practice into this atmosphere of turbulence and hostility.

In the Viceroy's Legislative Council it was proposed that I should be sent to London as the leader of a deputation to the Prime Minister, representing the views, not only of Muslims but of the whole articulate population of India.

The other members of the deputation were: the President of the Khilafat movement, Mr. Chatani; one of India's most eminent advocates, Hassan Imam; and Dr. Ansari, a leading member of Congress. Lloyd George saw us, but we realized that our mission was doomed to failure, for meanwhile the Turkish Treaty, known to history as the Treaty of Sèvres, was being prepared, with strangely little regard for the realities which, within a few years, were to shape the Near East anew. The unfortunate Sultan was under rigorous supervision, a solitary and helpless prisoner in Constantinople. Turkish, Arab, and Greek deputations were hurrying backwards and forwards between the Mediterranean and London. Sometimes their arguments were listened to; often they were not. The Treaty of Sèvres was to be an imposed, not a negotiated, treaty.

Constantinople was at first promised to the Greeks, then this promise was taken back. It was at last decided that Thrace and Adrianople in European Turkey should be Greek, and Smyrna in Asia Minor. Turkey was reduced to a sort of "rump" State in the highlands of Asia Minor, with a strip of coastline along the

Black Sea. There was even talk of an independent, sovereign State of Armenia in the far North-east – if the Russians could be persuaded to stomach it. Some sort of order was hacked out of all these conflicting claims. In August 1920 the hapless Turkish representatives appended their signatures to the document which embodied them all.

This concluded in a sense the first phase of my own campaign for a just treatment of defeated Turkey. Before I record the events of the second phase which rapidly followed, it may be proper to consider what was the effect of the decisions which the peace-making politicians took in 1919–20, in stubborn and bland disregard of the advice which we proffered to them.

Muslim opposition to the break-up of the Turkish Empire had a basis – however much misunderstood it may have been – of true statesmanship and of understanding of the absorbing political realities of the Middle East. First, we felt that the separation of the Arabs from the Turks (hailed at the time as emancipation from a tyranny, although within a few years all Arab nationalists were singing a very different tune) would not lead to the emergence of a single strong Arab nation extending from Egypt to Persia and from Alexandretta to Aden and the Indian Ocean. We foresaw in large measure what actually happened; the formation of a number of small Arab nations, for many years of little more than colonial status, under British and French overlordship. We predicted that the Arabs would in fact merely be changing masters, and where these masters had been Muslim Turks they would now be Christians, or (as ultimately happened in a large part of Palestine) Jews ...

Consider for a moment how different matters might have been had there emerged after the First World War a federal union of Turkey, the Arab States of the Middle East, and Egypt, with a single defence force and a united foreign policy. Our instinctive Muslim faith in the idea of the continuance of Turkey as a Great Power had wisdom in it, for it would have achieved practical results, in the security and the stability of the Middle East, far transcending anything that the makeshift, haphazard policies of the years since the end of the Second World War – piecemeal withdrawal of political suzerainty by Britain, piecemeal financial, economic, and military aid by the United States have been able to effect. Consider the disruption and the political *malaise* which have been the lot of the Middle East in recent years; consider all the unavailing effort that has gone into the attempt to build up a Middle East Defence Organization, in any degree paralleling

N.A.T.O., and ponder how easily, how honourably all this might have been avoided.

It is, however, no use crying over spilt milk. The victors of World War I, unlike the victors of World War II, were intoxicated with their triumph and the sense of their own victory, and believed that they could build a brave new world according to their hearts' desire. History was as tragically as categorically to give the lie to that belief.

The Treaty of Sèvres, harsh though it was, was practically still-born. Even by the following spring of 1921 events had overtaken it, and it was obvious that it must be urgently reconsidered. A new conference was called in London. At the Viceroy's request I put the Muslim point of view to this gathering. Its sittings, however, proved abortive. For what everyone in West and East alike had ignored was the emergence – from the ruin of Turkey – of a soldier and statesman of genius, Mustafa Kemal Ataturk, who in the time of their deepest tribulation had rallied his sorely stricken but indomitable people. Denied access to Constantinople, he had set up a provisional capital at Angora – now Ankara – high on the Anatolian plateau; he had rebuilt, re-equipped, and retrained the shattered Turkish Army. Having obtained a secret understanding with Russia, he could arm his troops, and he was assured of protection in his rear. He was thus prepared to defend his country's cause, not around some distant conference table, but in his homeland and on the field of battle. Few were at first aware of the magnitude of this new development.

The Greeks who, being nearest of all to the scene, should have known most, were blinded by their own lust for military victory and territorial expansion. Taking exception to the establishment of the Turkish Provisional Government in Angora, they began an ambitious, grandiose, and, as it proved, utterly disastrous series of military operations in Asia Minor.

To add to the complications, the British Government became restive over their demands for the release of certain British prisoners held in Turkey. Over this, at least, I was able by direct intervention and a direct appeal to the new Turkish authorities, to secure a certain relief in an increasingly critical situation. The Turks released the prisoners, and this crisis blew over.

By the late summer of 1922, however, the prospect looked blacker than ever. Mustafa Kemal's tattered but valiant armies had stood at bay in their own hill country, had stemmed the tide of Greek invasion, and now were in the full flush of victorious advance. They captured Smyrna, the great Graeco-Levantine port on the coast of Asia Minor, put it to the sack, and before the eyes of the crews of Allied warships lying in the harbour set whole areas of it on fire. It was the Greek army now which was a tattered, defeated remnant in flight. Mustafa Kemal's forces stood at the gates of Constantinople, and demanded the right of free, unimpeded passage to reoccupy Thrace and Adrianople.

The whole situation was both ominous and confused. A mixed Allied military force, under the command of a British general, Sir Charles Harington, held Chanak and the approaches to Constantinople, which the Turks had already renamed Istanbul. A vigilant, cautious but resolute man, Harington awaited orders from London. A single reckless or unconsidered action on his part, even a stray shot developing into a fusillade, might precipitate a general conflict a little less than four years after the cease-fire at the end of the First World War. But the character of the military commander on the spot was not the only factor in this grave and delicate crisis. The British Government were in a curiously unrealistic and bellicose mood. A long, trying period of industrial unrest, with a protracted coal strike and a huge roll of unemployed had been succeeded by the difficult and involved negotiations which ended the worst of the "troubles" in Ireland and were clinched by the signature of the Irish Treaty. But Lloyd George's second coalition Government, returned to power with a huge majority in the "coupon" Election of 1918, had run its course. The Liberals had never really forgiven Lloyd George for his brusque ousting of Asquith in December 1916, in the central political crisis of the war. The Conservatives supplied the bulk of his Parliamentary support, but they were becoming increasingly restive and suspicious of the Prime Minister's incurable political adventurism. Did he think that in the Chanak crisis, as it was called, he perceived an opportunity to end the dissension and dissolution in the ranks of his supporters, to prevent his own increasing isolation, and to rally Parliament and people behind him in a great united effort? Was it a gambler's throw or was it gross miscalculation?

I was in London when the crisis was at its worst, and I exerted every effort to prevent it culminating in what I knew would be a disastrous as well as an unjust war. This time I was not fighting a solitary battle against an overwhelming tide of contrary opinion. Now I had powerful allies and supporters. The columns of *The Times*, as so often in my public career, were open to me. The first Lord Rothermere, who had just assumed personal control of the group of newspapers built up by his brother, Viscount Northcliffe, was my staunch supporter. And Lord Beaverbrook, the man by whose influence and eager advocacy exercised at the right moment Lloyd George had come to supreme power as Prime Minister in 1916, was now as sincerely convinced that Lloyd George was set on a course that would bring nothing but suffering and hardship. However, the first concern was not to encompass Lloyd George's fall, but to prevent – of all unnecessary wars – the most unnecessary that could ever have been waged.

Early in September the British Government issued a statement on Chanak which was both pugnacious and injudicious, and ended with an appeal to the Dominions for their help in the event of another war with Turkey. The tone of this pronouncement thoroughly alarmed British public opinion, which was in no mood to contemplate all the pain and sacrifice involved in another war in support of what could only be described as Greek intransigence and stubbornness. Protests were loud from all sides. The faction that was pro-Government and philhellene had only one strong card to play, and this was that Turkish forces were already almost in contact with the Allied – predominantly British – Occupying forces in the Straits and Constantinople area. General Harington on his side was quietly determined to avoid any action which might involve his slender forces and commit them to any form of hostilities with the veteran, tough, and resolute forces which Mustafa Kemal had already deployed with skill. On the other hand I, at the earnest request of my friend, Lord Derby,[1] was able to get in touch with the Turkish leaders and point out the grave perils inherent in any attack on the Allied forces; and I assured them that, pending a provisional settlement, their troops' strategic position would not in any way be prejudiced if they abstained from any offensive action. I pressed these considerations on my Turkish friends with all the urgency I could command. I am glad to say that sanity prevailed. An important contributory factor was that France had come to a secret understanding with Kemal and his Government; and French influence exerted by Monsieur Raymond Poincaré was all for a peaceful settlement. The decision for war could only have been a rushed one; once British public opinion had time to ponder the issues it could crystallize and express itself, and it

---

[1] We met, I remember, at Newmarket, and Lord Derby asked me to use all the influence which I possessed.

was firmly for peace. The very real menace of another war in the Middle East was averted.

A vivid account of the handling of this crisis has been given by Lord Beaverbrook.[1] Throughout it Lord Beaverbrook was as active as he was staunch. Seriously worried by the drift in affairs, he often discussed this matter with me. I was happy to see that we were in full agreement, and that in all my endeavours to assist the Turks I had his moral support. He, too, had reached the eminently sound and practical conclusion that "for Britain to fight Turkey in pursuance of the exploded policy of supporting Greek imperialism was a monstrous error which must be avoided at all costs". Beaverbrook sought the support of his friend and fellow-Canadian, Bonar Law, then leader of the Conservative Party, which supplied the bulk of the Government's voting strength in the House of Commons.

Beaverbrook's words to Bonar Law were blunt. "These men mean war," he said.

Those four words spelled doom for Lloyd George's Coalition Government. A meeting of the Conservative Party was held at the Carlton Club, the Party's great socio-political stronghold; the speech that swayed the meeting and brought about its decision to withdraw support from Lloyd George was made not by Bonar Law, who was already an extremely sick man, but by a comparatively unknown back-bench M.P. named Stanley Baldwin, who less than a year later was to succeed Bonar Law as Prime Minister.

Lord Beaverbrook maintained his onslaught on the pro-Greek, anti-Turkish policy of the Coalition Government. On 16th December 1922, the day after the House of Commons had adjourned for the Christmas recess, the *Daily Express* gave a sensationally detailed account of the happenings of the previous September. It said that within ten days of the fall of Smyrna, when the Greek rout had already begun and it had been recognized by the Greek Government in Athens that their military position in Asia Minor was hopeless, Lloyd George encouraged them to continue fighting. Lloyd George (said the *Daily Express*) took this step after having had inquiries made by his principal private secretary, Sir Edward Grigg,[2] of someone attached to the Greek Legation, who had said that the Greek army could not possibly hold out longer without active British assistance in munitions and in credit. On 2nd September, the *Daily Express* went on, when

[1] In *Politicians and the Press*.
[2] Now Lord Altrincham.

the Athens Government appealed to Lloyd George to arrange an armistice, another of his private secretaries telephoned the Greek Legation advising them that "their government should be very careful to avoid the mistake made by the Germans in 1918 and not conclude an abject armistice in a moment of panic".

Lloyd George never returned to office . . .

For myself an eventful period of close association with the politics and diplomacy of the Middle East in general and Turkey in particular drew to a close. The first abortive Lausanne Conference was followed by a second, more fruitful, during which I held what may be described as a watching brief. Britain's new Conservative Government was represented by Lord Curzon, the Foreign Secretary; the Turks sent a strong and capable delegation. Britain's mood was realistic and sensible. It was decided to accept the facts, to give *de jure* as well as *de facto* recognition to the new Turkey, and to let this revived and vigorous State retain not merely its homeland in Anatolia, and the sea coast of Asia Minor, but also Thrace, Adrianople, and Istanbul. Along these lines agreement was reached, and the Treaty of Lausanne signed. Subsequently the Montreux Convention regularized arrangements for dealing with the passage of international shipping through the Dardanelles.

[Extracts from pp. 149–62]

THE ISLAMIC CONCEPT

The origins of man's religious and scientific experiences – early philosophy and thought – the flowering of thought in Arabia – the ideas of Ibn-i-Rushd, Rumi and Hafiz on "religious experience" – ordinary human beings and "the higher experience" – the significance of Sura Nur in the Quran – the fundamental principles of Islam – Prophet Muhammad's religious and secular authority – the Quran and its different interpretations – divine messengers before Prophet Muhammad – Islam's basic principle of "monorealism" – the Islamic idea of creation – the duties of man – the concepts of Divine justice and free will – Islamic doctrine on the presence of the soul and spirits.

The origins of man's religious aspirations are to be found in what we nowadays call science. Those who have studied mythology and primitive psychology know that magic in various forms started various trains of thought in primitive man by which he achieved what seemed to him to be rational accounts of the natural phenomena he saw around him. It seemed to him rational that these phenomena, these events like the rising and the setting of the sun, the passage of the seasons, the flowering of the bud and the ripening of the fruit, the wind and the rain, were caused and controlled by deities or superior beings. Primitive religious experience and primitive scientific reasoning were linked together in magic, in wizardry. Thus, at one and the same time, mankind's experiences in the realm of sensation and his strivings to explain and co-ordinate those experiences in terms of his mind led to the birth of both science and religion. The two remained linked throughout prehistoric and ancient times, and in the life of the early empires of which we have knowledge. It was difficult to separate what I may call proto-religion from proto-science; they made their journey like two streams, sometimes mingling, sometimes separating, but running side by side.

Such is the background to Greek and Roman thought and culture as well as to ancient Iranian and Hindu philosophy before the beginning of the Christian era. Aristotle, however, gave a more scientific turn to this mingling, introducing as he did categories and concepts that were purely reasonable and shedding those vestiges of religious awe and mystery that are visible even in Plato.

With the decline of the Roman Empire and the break-up of the great and elaborate system of civilization which Roman Law and administration had sustained for so many centuries, the Dark Ages enfolded Europe. In the seventh century of the Christian era there was a rapid and brilliant new flowering of humanity's capacity and desire for adventure and discovery in the realms of both spirit and intellect. That flowering began in Arabia; its origin and impetus were given to it by my Holy ancestor, the Prophet Mohammed, and we know it by the name of Islam. From Arabia the tide of its influence flowed swiftly and strongly to North Africa and thence to Spain.

Ibn-Rushd, the great Muslim philosopher, known to Europe as Averroes, established clearly the great distinction between two kinds of apprehensible human experience; on the one hand, our experience of nature as we recognize it through our senses, whence comes our capacity to measure and to count (and with that capacity all that it brought in the way of new events and new explanations), and, on the other hand, our immediate and immanent experience of something more real, less dependent on thought or on the processes of the mind, but directly given to us, which I believe to be *religious experience*. Naturally, since our brain is material, and its processes and all the consequences of its processes, are material, the moment that we put either thought or spiritual experience into words this material basis of the brain must give a material presentation to even the highest, most transcendent spiritual experience. But men can study objectively the direct and subjective experiences of those who have had spiritual enlightenment without material intervention.

It is said that we live, move, and have our being in God. We find this concept expressed often in the Koran, not in those words of course, but just as beautifully and more tersely. But when we realize the meaning of this saying, we are already preparing ourselves for the gift of the power of direct experience. Roumi and Hafiz, the great Persian poets, have told us, each in his different way, that some men are born with such natural spiritual capacities and possibilities of development, that they have direct experience of that great love, that all-embracing, all-consuming love, which direct contact with reality gives to the human soul. Hafiz, indeed, has said that men like Jesus Christ, and Muslim mystics like Mansour and Bayezid and others, have possessed that spiritual power of the greater love; that any of us, if the Holy Spirit[1] ever-present grants us that enlightenment, can, being thus blessed, have the power which Christ had, but that to the overwhelming majority of men this greater love is not a practical possibility. We can, however, make up for its absence from our lives by worldly, human love for individual human beings; and this will give us a measure of enlightenment attainable without the intervention of the Holy Spirit. Those who have had the good fortune to know and feel this worldly, human love should respond to it only with gratitude and regard it as a blessing and as, in its own way, a source of pride. I firmly believe that the higher experience can to a certain extent be prepared for, by absolute devotion in the material world to another human being. Thus from the most worldly point of view and with no comprehension of the higher life of the spirit, the lower, more terrestrial spirit makes us aware that all the treasures of this life, all that fame, wealth, and health can bring are nothing beside the happi-

---

[1] It must be realized that the Muslim concept of the Holy Spirit differs profoundly from the Christian idea of the Third Person of the Trinity.

ness which is created and sustained by the love of one human being for another. This great grace we can see in ordinary life as we look about us, among our acquaintances and friends.

But as the joys of human love surpass all that riches and power may bring a man, so does that greater spiritual love and enlightenment, the fruit of that sublime experience of the direct vision of reality which is God's gift and grace, surpass all that the finest, truest human love can offer. For that gift we must ever pray.

Now, I am convinced that through Islam, through the ideal of Allah, as presented by Muslims, man can attain this direct experience which no words can explain but which for him are absolute certainties. I have not discussed experience of this order with non-Muslims, but I have been told that Buddhists, Brahmins, Zoroastrians, and Christians – I have not often heard it of Jews, except perhaps Spinoza – have also attained this direct, mystical vision. I am certain that many Muslims, and I am convinced that I myself, have had moments of enlightenment and of knowledge of a kind which we cannot communicate because it is something given and not something acquired.

To a certain extent I have found that the following verse of the Koran, so long as it is understood in a purely non-physical sense, has given assistance and understanding to myself and other Muslims. I must, however, warn all who read it not to allow their material critical outlook to break in with literal, verbal explanations of something that is symbolic and allegorical. I appeal to every reader, whether Muslim or not, to accept the spirit of this verse in its entirety:

Allah is the light of the heavens and the earth; His light is as a niche in which is a lamp, and the lamp is in a glass, the glass is as though it were a glittering star; it is lit from a blessed tree, an Olive neither of east nor of the west, the oil of which would well-nigh give light though no fire touched it, – light upon light; – Allah guides to His light whom He pleases; and Allah strikes our parables for men; and Allah all things doth know.
(Chapter XXIV – Light – 35)

From that brief statement of my own personal beliefs, I move on to as concise and as uncontroversial an exposition as I can give of Islam as it is understood and practised today. The present condition of mankind offers surely, with all its dangers and all its challenges, a chance too [sic] – a chance of establishing not just material peace among nations but that better peace of God on earth. In that endeavour Islam can play its valuable constructive part, and the Islamic world can be a strong and stabilizing factor, provided it is really understood and its spiritual and moral power recognized and respected.

I shall try, therefore, to give in a small compass a clear survey of the fundamentals of Islam, by which I mean those principles, those articles of faith, and that way of life, all of which are universally accepted among all Muslim sects. First, therefore, I shall propound those Islamic tenets which are held in common by the larger community of Sunnis, and by Shias as well . . .

First it must be understood that, though these fundamental ideals are universally accepted by Muslims, there does not exist in Islam, and there has never existed, any source of absolute authority, we have no Papal Encyclical to propound and sanction a dogma, such as Roman Catholics possess, and no Thirty-Nine Articles like those which state the doctrinal position of the Church of England. The Prophet Mohammed had two sources of authority, one religious which was the essential one of his life, and the other secular which, by the circumstances and accidents of his career, became joined to his essential and Divinely-inspired authority in religion.

According to the Sunni school – the majority of Muslims – the Prophet's religious authority came to an end at his death, and he appointed no successor to his secular authority. According to Sunni teaching, the faithful, the companions of the Prophet, the believers, elected Abu Bakr as his successor and his Caliph; but Abu Bakr assumed only the civil and secular power. No one had the authority to succeed to the religious supremacy, which depended on direct Divine inspiration, because the Prophet Mohammed and the Koran declared definitely that he was the final messenger of God, the Absolute. Thus, say the Sunnis, it was impossible to constitute an authority similar to that of the Papacy; it remained for the Faithful to interpret the Koran, the example and the sayings of the Prophet, not only in order to understand Islam but to ensure its development throughout the centuries. Fortunately the Koran has itself made this task easy, for it contains a number of verses which declare that Allah speaks to man in allegory and parable. Thus the Koran leaves the door open for all kinds of possibilities of interpretation without any one interpreter being able to accuse another of being non-Muslim. A felicitous effect of this fundamental principle of Islam, that the Koran is constantly open to allegorical interpretation, has been that our Holy Book has been able to guide and illuminate the thought of believers, century after century, in accordance with the conditions and limitations of intellectual apperception imposed by external influences in the world. It leads also to a greater charity among Muslims, for since there can be no cut-and-dried interpretation all schools of thought can unite in the prayer that the Almighty in His infinite mercy may forgive any mistaken interpretation of the Faith whose cause is ignorance or misunderstanding.

I am trying to put before my Western readers, not the doctrine of the Ismaili sect to which I belong, not Shia doctrine, nor the teachings of the Sufi school of Islamic mysticism, of men such as Jalaleddin Roumi or Bayazid Bostami, nor even the views of certain modern Sunni interpreters who, not unlike certain Christian sects, look for literal guidance in the Koran as Christians of these sects find it in the Old and New Testaments; but the main and central Sunni stream of thought, whose source is in the ideas of the school founded by al-Ghazali, and whose influence and teaching have flowed on from century to century.

First, however, we must ask ourselves why this final and consummate appearance of the Divine will was granted to mankind, and what were its causes. All Islamic schools of thought accept it as a fundamental principle that, for centuries, for thousands of years before the advent of Mohammed, there arose from time to time messengers, illuminated by Divine grace, for and amongst those races of the earth which had sufficiently advanced intellectually to comprehend such a message. Thus Abraham, Moses, Jesus, and all the Prophets of Israel are universally accepted by Islam . . . Thus Man's soul has never been left without a specially inspired messenger from the Soul that sustains, embraces, and is the Universe. Then what need was there for a Divine revelation to Mohammed? The answer of Islam is precise and clear. In spite of its great spiritual strength, Jewish monotheism has retained two characteristics which render it essentially different from Islamic monotheism; God has remained, in spite of all, a national and racial God for the children of Israel, and his personality is entirely separate from its supreme manifestation, the Universe.

In far-distant countries such as India and China, the purity of the Faith in the one God had been so vitiated by polytheism, by idolatry and even by a pantheism which was hardly distinguishable from atheism, that these popular and folk-lore religions bore but little resemblance to that which emanated from the true and pure God-head. Christianity lost its strength and meaning for

Muslims in that it saw its great and glorious founder not as a man but as God incarnate in man, as God made Flesh. Thus there was an absolute need for the Divine Word's revelation, to Mohammed himself, a man like the others, of God's person and of his relations to the Universe which he had created. Once man has thus comprehended the essence of existence there remains for him the duty, since he knows the absolute value of his own soul, of making for himself a direct path which will constantly lead his individual soul to and bind it with the universal Soul of which the Universe, as much of it as we perceive with our limited vision, is one of the infinite manifestations. Thus Islam's basic principle can only be defined as monorealism and not as monotheism. Consider for example the opening declaration of every Islamic prayer: "Allah-o-Akbar." What does that mean? There can be no doubt that the second word of the declaration likens the character of Allah to a matrix which contains all and gives existence to the infinite, to space, to time, to the Universe, to all active and passive forces imaginable, to life and to the soul. Imam Hassan has explained the Islamic doctrine of God and the Universe by analogy with the sun and its reflection in the pool of a fountain; there is certainly a reflection or image of the sun, but with what poverty and with what little reality, how small and pale is the likeness between this impalpable image and the immense, blazing, white-hot glory of the celestial sphere itself. Allah is the sun; and the Universe as we know it in all its magnitude, and time, with its power, are nothing more than the reflection of the Absolute in the mirror of the fountain.

There is a fundamental difference between the Jewish idea of creation and that of Islam. The creation according to Islam is not a unique act in a given time, but a perpetual and constant event; and God supports and sustains all existence at every moment by His will and His thought. Outside His will, outside His thought, all is nothing, even the things which seem to us absolutely self-evident such as space and time. Allah alone wishes: the Universe exists; and all manifestations are as a witness of the Divine will. I think that I have sufficiently explained the difference between the Islamic doctrine of the unity of god and on one side the theistic ideas, founded upon the Old Testament, and on the other the pantheistic and dualistic ideas of the Indian religions and that of Zoroaster. But having known the real, the Absolute, having understood the Universe as an infinite succession of events, intended by God, we need an ethic, a code of conduct in order to be able to elevate ourselves towards the ideal demanded by God.

Let us then study the duties of man, as the great majority interpret them, according to the verses of the Koran and the Traditions of the Prophet . . .

A man who does not marry, who refuses to shoulder the responsibilities of fatherhood, of building up a home and raising a family through marriage, is severely condemned. In Islam, there are no extreme renunciations, no asceticism, no maceration, above all no flagellations to subjugate the body. The healthy human body is the temple in which the flame of the Holy Spirit burns, and thus it deserves the respect of scrupulous cleanliness and personal hygiene. Prayer is a daily necessity, a direct communication of the spark with the universal flame. Reasonable fasting for a month in every year, provided a man's health is not impaired thereby, is an essential part of the body's discipline, through which the body learns to renounce all impure desires. Adultery, alcoholism, slander, and thinking evil of one's neighbour are specifically and severely condemned. All men, rich and poor, must aid one another materially and personally. The rules vary in detail, but they all maintain the principle of universal mutual aid in the Muslim fraternity. This fraternity is absolute and comprises men of all colours and of all races: black, white, yellow, tawny; all are the sons of Adam in the flesh and all carry in them a spark of the Divine light. Everyone should strive his best to see that this spark be not extinguished but rather developed to that full "Companionship-on-High" which was the vision expressed in the last words of the Prophet on his deathbed, the vision of that blessed state which he saw clearly awaiting him. In Islam the Faithful believe in Divine justice and are convinced that the solution of the great problem of predestination and free will is to be found in the compromise that God knows what man is going to do, but that man is free to do it or not.

Wars are condemned. Peace ought to be universal. Islam means peace, God's peace with man and the peace of men one to another. Usury is condemned, but free and honest trade and agriculture – in all its forms – are encouraged, since they manifest a Divine service, and the welfare of mankind depends upon the continuation and the intensification of these legitimate labours. Politically a republican form of government seems to be the most rightful; for in Islamic countries, which have witnessed the development of absolute monarchs with a great concentration of power within them, the election of the monarch has always remained a lifeless formula which has simply legitimized the usurpation of power.

After death Divine justice will take into consideration the faith, the prayers, and the deeds of man. For the chosen, there is eternal life and the spiritual felicity of the Divine vision. For the condemned, there is hell where they will be consumed with regret for not having known how to merit the grace and the blessing of Divine mercy.

Islamic doctrine goes farther than the other great religions for it proclaims the presence of the soul, perhaps minute but nevertheless existing in an embryonic state in all existence in matter, in animals, trees, and space itself. Every individual, every molecule, every atom has its own spiritual relationship with the All-Powerful Soul of God. But men and women, being more highly developed, are immensely more advanced than the infinite number of other beings known to us. Islam acknowledges the existence of angels, of great souls who have developed themselves to the highest possible planes of the human soul and higher, and who are centres of the forces which are scattered throughout the Universe. Without going as far as Christianity, Islam recognizes the existence of evil spirits which seek by means of their secret suggestions to turn us from good, from that strait way traced by God's finger for the eternal happiness of the humblest as of the greatest – Abraham, Jesus, Mohammed.

[Extracts from pp. 169–77]

ALL INDIA MUSLIM CONFERENCE

Lord Irwin's pronouncement on Indian constitutional advance – dominion status – the appointment of the Simon Commission – the All India Muslim Conference and its significance – the principles adopted – unanimity in the conference – the coming of M. A. Jinnah to the conference point of view.

I was being drawn back into political and public life. Lord Irwin, the Viceroy, in a momentous pronouncement, had shown Indians what – in the British view – was to be their ultimate goal in their constitutional evolution, but he had omitted to indicate with any precision the steps or the road to that goal.

"In view of the doubts which have been expressed," said Lord Irwin, "both in Great Britain and India regarding the interpretation to be placed on the intentions of the British Government in enacting the statute of 1919, I am authorized to state clearly that in their judgment, it is implicit in the Declaration of 1917 that the natural issue of India's constitutional progress as there contemplated is the attainment of Dominion status."

The two words, "Dominion status", were to focus and bind Indian ambitions and aspirations for a decade and more, in an ever more forceful and dynamic drive towards independence; and in the end there emerged not one, but two independent and sovereign States – Muslim and Hindu – the latter of which was almost immediately, to throw away even the vestigial and nominal link of being called a Dominion and proclaim itself (as it had the constitutional right and ability to do) a Republic within the Commonwealth.

In 1928–9, however, all this was to be striven for. Congress met in Calcutta and prepared its own scheme for self-government and Dominion status; but it was marred by the fatal, obsessive flaw of all such Congress schemes to the end, that of underrating – indeed ignoring – Muslim claims to be considered as a nation within a nation. Muslim opinion was therefore alert. A Royal Commission – that classic British instrument for tackling a grave political or constitutional problem, at home or overseas – was by now touring India, taking evidence in impressive quantities and with vast thoroughness; its chairman was Sir John Simon,[1] the great lawyer-politician, then almost at the zenith of his dazzling career; among its members was the pertinacious but personally self-effacing Mr. Clement Attlee, on whose knowledge of India this experience was to have a profound and lasting effect. The Viceroy had announced that after the Simon Commission issued its report it was intended that a conference should be held between the Government, the representatives of British India, and the representatives of the Indian States, in order to try to reach agreement on the way in which constitutional progress should be ensured.

It was decided therefore to hold an All-India Muslim Conference in Delhi at the end of 1928, to formulate Muslim views on the way in which Indian independence should evolve. I was asked to preside over this conference. It proved to be, I am convinced,

[1]Afterwards Viscount Simon.

one of the most important in the long series of such assemblies which marked the road towards total and final independence for the whole subcontinent. It was a vast gathering representative of all shades of Muslim opinion. I can claim to be the parent of its important and lasting political decisions. After long, full, and frank discussions we were able to adopt unanimously a series of principles which we set out in a manifesto. They were as follows:

> In view of India's vast extent and its ethnological divisions, the only form of government suitable to Indian conditions is a federal system with complete autonomy and residuary powers vested in the constituent States.

> The right of Muslims to elect their representatives in the various Indian legislatures is now the law of the land, and Muslims cannot be deprived of that right without their consent.

> In the provinces in which Muslims constitute a minority they shall have a representation in no case less than that enjoyed by them under the existing law (a principle known as weightage).

> It is essential that Muslims shall have their due share in the central and provincial Cabinets.

We agreed to concede a similar kind of "weightage" to the Hindu minorities in Sind and other predominantly Muslim provinces, but we insisted that a fair proportion of Muslims should be admitted into the Civil Service and into all statutory self-governing bodies. I myself demanded appropriate safeguards for "the promotion and protection of Muslim education, languages, religion, personal law, and charitable institutions" – all causes for which, over years, I had fought as strenuously as I could. I also thought it right to warn my co-religionists and compatriots of the perils of being too easily taken in by Congress's protestations of undefined goodwill.

The principles which we had enunciated were to be our guiding lights henceforward in all our encounters with British or Hindu representatives and negotiators, with the Government of India or with the Congress Party, in every discussion of schemes of reform and new projects for the administration of the country. We now had our code-book, and we did not intend to deviate from it.

The unanimity of this conference was especially significant, for it marked the return – long delayed and for the moment private and with no public avowal of his change of mind – of Mr. M. A.

Jinnah to agreement with his fellow-Muslims. Mr. Jinnah had attended the Congress Party's meeting in Calcutta shortly before, and had come to the conclusion that for him there was no future in Congress or in any camp – allegedly on an All-India basis – which was in fact Hindu-dominated. We had at last won him over to our view.

[Extracts from pp. 208–10]

THE INDIAN ROUND TABLE CONFERENCES

The report of the Simon Commission – the civil disobedience campaign – the delegation to the First Round Table Conference – his election as leader of the Muslim delegation and chairman of the British-Indian section of the Conference – the British monarch's appeal – the Hindu preference for a strong central government – the Muslim position – attempt to bring about a consensus in the Muslim delegation – rejection of the federal idea by the Hindu delegation – its acceptance by the princes – Ramsay MacDonald's position – differences between the Hindus and the Muslims in India – the aspirations of the Indian intelligentsia – the powerlessness of the princes – the Second Round Table Conference – the political atmosphere – Gandhi's decision to participate – his impressions and recollections of Gandhi and Mrs Sarojini Naidu – deliberations during the Conference – the gulf between the Hindus and the Muslims – the separation of Sind from Bombay – the outcome of the second Conference – the appointment of the Joint Select Committee of Parliament – India's representation – the Joint Memorandum prepared by all communities – his definition of "responsible government" – the Government of India Act of 1935 – its weaknesses – the ultimate partition of the Indian subcontinent.

In the summer of 1930 the Simon Commission issued its report. Its analysis of India's political history under British rule and of her contemporary situation was as masterly as it was lucid; it was, however, on the constructive side of its task that the Commission's report fell sharply short of the high expectations and hopes that its appointment had aroused. It particularly disappointed the Congress leaders, and their resentment of it was loudly and unequivocally expressed. Lord Irwin, the Viceroy, was on leave in England in the earlier part of 1930, and when he returned to India he announced that His Majesty's Government proposed to convene a Round Table Conference in London to consider the future of the country and to reform its constitution. The announcement came at a time of considerable tension, when a civil disobedience campaign, launched by Mahatma Gandhi, was at its height. It eased the tension for the time being; and the Viceroy was able to receive, in a calmer political atmosphere than had seemed possible a few weeks before, a representative delegation[1] to discuss the date and the personnel of the Round Table Conference, and the question of an amnesty for political offenders gaoled in connection with the civil disobedience campaign. Agreement, however, was not reached at this preliminary meeting; Mahatma Gandhi withdrew, and refused to give any undertaking that Congress would attend the Round Table Conference. The Indian National Congress in session at Lahore, passed a resolution in favour of a renewed resort to civil disobedience.

The Viceroy pertinaciously maintained his hopeful, sympathetic, and wise attitude. If Congress would not, at the outset at any rate, co-operate in the attempt to find a way out of India's political perplexities, the attempt would still be made. As many eminent and representative leaders of Indian political thought and feeling as possible – outside the ranks of Congress – would be invited. Mr. Nehru, in his *Autobiography* which was published in 1936, when the whole issue of Indian independence was still unsettled, made some caustic observations about the personal qualifications of the delegates to the Conference; in the longer perspective of history, however, it can be seen as a remarkable assemblage of men and women of widely differing background and outlook, all genuinely anxious to discover a peaceful and honourable path to the independence and self-government which had explicitly been proclaimed to be the objectives of Britain's rule in India.

The British representatives included the Prime Minister, Mr. Ramsay MacDonald; the Lord Chancellor, Lord Sankey; the Secretary of State for India, Mr. Wedgwood Benn;[2] and –

---

[1] The members of the delegation were: Mahatma Gandhi, Sir Tej Bahadur Sapru, Pandit Motilal Nehru, Mr. M. A. Jinnah, and Mr. V. J. Patel, then President of the Indian National Assembly.
[2] Now Lord Stansgate.

representing the Conservative Opposition – Sir Samuel Hoare,[1] who was later, in some years that were crucial to India's destiny, to be Secretary of State for India; and Lord Reading, a Liberal leader and former Viceroy. The British-India delegation, of which I had been appointed a member, included Muslim, Hindu, and Parsee representatives drawn from many shades of political opinion and other delegates representing numerous smaller communities; among the Muslims, Mr. M. A. Jinnah, Sir Muhammad Shafi, Sir Zafrullah Khan, and Maulana Muhammad Ali; and two women delegates, the Begum Shah Nawaz and Mrs. Subbaroyan. Among the Hindus were Sir Tej Bahadur Sapru, the Rt. Hon. V. S. Srinivasa Sastri, Sir C. P. Ramaswami Aiyar, Sir Chimanlal Setalvad, Mr. M. R. Jayakar, and Dewan Bahadur Rama Mudaliar; among the Parsees were Sir Phiroze Sethna, Sir Cowasji Jehangir, and Sir H. P. Mody. Mr. Ambedkar, himself born an "untouchable", represented the Depressed Classes, and Sir Henry Gidney, the Anglo-Indian community. The representation of ruling princes was as impressive as it was stately, including as it did many of the bearers of the greatest and most famous names in Indian chivalry. The Maharajah Gaekwar of Baroda was their leader, and others with him were the Maharajahs of Bikaner, Patiala, Bhopal, Kashmir, Rewa, and Jamnagar – better known perhaps to millions of British citizens as the unforgettable "Ranji" of cricket fame. The Princes were accompanied, many of them, by their Diwans – their Prime Ministers – who included statesmen of the quality and distinction of Sir Akbar Hydari and Sir Mirza Ismail, and other eminent men.

We assembled in London in the autumn of 1930. I had the honour of being elected leader of the Muslim delegation. We established our headquarters in the Ritz Hotel, where it has long been my custom to stay whenever I am in London. It is no formality to say that it was an honour to be chosen to lead so notable a body of men – including personalities of the calibre of Mr. M. A. Jinnah, later to be the creator of Pakistan and the Quaid-i-Azam, or Sir Muhammed Zafrullah Khan, for many years India's representative at numerous international conferences and first Foreign Minister of Pakistan, or my old and tried friend, Sir Muhammad Shafi, one of the founders of the Muslim League.

The happiness of being thus chosen was for me one of the many joys of an exceptionally happy, as well as eventful, period of my life . . .

---

[1] Now Lord Templewood.

Later, then, in this – for me – memorable year the full first Round Table Conference began with a formal inaugural session in the House of Lords, presided over by His Majesty King George V. My colleagues then accorded me the further honour of electing me to be Chairman of the British-Indian section of the Conference, that is, of all the Indian representatives except the ruling princes, who had come, of course, as their own representatives and in their own capacity as the sovereigns of their various Principalities and States.

The King, not long recovered from his extremely serious illness, made of his opening speech a most moving appeal to us all to contemplate the momentous character of the task to which we had set our hands. He said:

> I shall follow the course of your proceedings with the closest and most sympathetic interest, not indeed without anxiety but with a greater confidence. The material conditions which surround the lives of my subjects in India affect me nearly, and will be ever present in my thoughts during your forthcoming deliberations. I have also in mind the just claims of majorities and minorities, of men and women, of town-dwellers and tillers of the soil, of landlords and tenants, of the strong and the weak, of the rich and poor, of the races, castes, and creeds of which the body politic is composed. For those things I care deeply. I cannot doubt that the true foundation of self-government is in the fusion of such divergent claims into mutual obligations and in their recognition and fulfilment. It is my hope that the future government of India based on its foundation will give expression to her honourable aspirations.

Other eloquent and stirring orations followed; and the Conference, moving to St. James's Palace, settled down to its complex and formidable task. We achieved a surface harmony, but underneath there were deep and difficult rifts of sentiment and of outlook whose effect was bound to be felt from the outset. In order to understand this, it is necessary to restate briefly the political situation and the state of Indo-British relations as they both stood in this autumn of 1930. The Simon Commission's Report advanced a scheme which denied central responsibility and also relegated the idea of a federation of India to a distant and undefined future. This could not really be satisfactory to anybody, for it offered not a workable compromise but an evasion of an existing – indeed a pressing – political conflict. For while the whole drive of the Hindu movement to self-government was concentrated on the idea of a strong central government and the establishment of an immediate democracy, conceived solely in terms of numbers, in which religious differences counted as such and as nothing more, Muslim opinion had crystallized steadily in favour of a distribution of powers from the centre to virtually self-governing and autonomous provincial governments. Finally, no one had as yet evolved the conception of an All-India federation in which the States would be partners. Therefore none of the major parties at the Conference arrived with any definite scheme – only with conflicting claims. The British Government, not unnaturally, were somewhat at sea when presented with what seemed to be a series of contradictory and irreconcilable claims and counter-claims.

The first essential task, as I saw it, was to find some way of bridging the gulf between the Muslim and Hindu sections of the British-Indian delegation. Only when we had achieved that bridge did it seem to me that we could offer to the British representatives our conjoint proposals for the constitutional development of India.

Pre-eminent among those whose efforts were devoted with zeal and enthusiasm to the same or closely similar ends was my friend, His Highness the Nawab of Bhopal. He was an outstanding figure among the ruling princes of his time – a devout Muslim, a man of driving energy and will-power, of great physical strength, a sportsman and athlete and a first-class polo player. He was also a convinced Indian nationalist, eager to throw off India's semi-colonial yoke, and do away with her dependent status. He agreed with me entirely that, if we of British India could not find ways and means of settling our own differences of opinion, we could not go to His Majesty's Government with any formulated set of demands; and this was leaving out of consideration altogether the protected States. From the first moment that we met at the Nawab's house, it was my deep conviction that this was what mattered most, which made me a champion of a Muslim-Hindu understanding about our ultimate view of an independent India – on the one hand a truly confederate State, or on the other a State such as Canada, in which the principal and overriding authority and power are reserved for the central government.

As a preliminary to reaching agreement with our Hindu col-leagues we had to secure agreement inside our own Muslim delegation. At first several of the Muslim delegates, in particular Mr. Jinnah, were – as they had long been before the Conference

– suspicious of the idea of federation. Its dangers were, I well knew, neither remote nor unimportant; to associate a growing democracy with a number of States in which personal rule was the established and, as it then seemed, inalienable custom, might well be a risky as well as a complex innovation; and also there was the danger that since the majority of ruling princes were Hindu, there might be a serious diminution of the political influence of the Muslim community within the federation as a whole. However, I was convinced that, whatever the temporary difficulties and risks involved in a federal scheme, it still offered the best and the most acceptable solution of India's political problems, that it offered an opportunity which might never occur again, and that if it required compromise to make it effective, that would be a small price to pay for its obvious and numerous advantages.

I am happy to think that when within the Muslim delegation we had made our decision in favour of federation, Mr. Jinnah, who had been its doughtiest opponent, was an inflexibly loyal and irreproachably helpful colleague throughout all the subsequent discussions and negotiations.

Since the ruling princes had signified their assent to some federal form of government, it remained now only to win the agreement of the Hindu representatives. I strove to convince them that if they made the concession of accepting the principle of a federated and not a united India they – and we – would reap the harvest of the benefits of immediate and large-scale political advancement for the country as a whole. The guarantees which we asked consisted of: a truly federal constitution; undertakings that the Muslim majorities in the Punjab and Bengal would not, by artificial "rigging" of the constitution, be turned into minorities; the separation of Sind from Bombay, and its establishment as a separate province; the introduction of a full-scale system of constitutional government in the North-west Frontier Province; and the assurance of the statutory reservation of a certain proportion of places in the Army and in the Civil Service for Muslims. If they gave us assurances of this character, we in our turn would offer them a united front in face of the British. I even went further and offered, as a special concession, unity of command under a chosen Indian leader whose orders we would bind the Muslim community to accept. In his memoirs, Sir Chimanlal Setalvad has referred to these offers of mine, and his evidence at least stands firmly on record that if the first Round Table Conference did not achieve all that was expected of it, and if, ultimately, not only was "Dominion status" not brought about, but India had to be partitioned, some at least of the beginnings of these momentous happenings are to be found in the Hindu delegation's refusal to accept my offer. I am certain that Sapru and Sastri, in their heart of hearts, wanted to accept our Muslim proposals, but that they were afraid of their Hindu colleagues and, above all, of the influence of the Mahasabha.

I must formally record my solemn conviction that had my views been accepted then and there, later history would have taken a profoundly different course, and that there would now have long since been in existence a Federal Government of India, in which Muslims and Hindus would have been partners in the day-to-day administration of the country, politically satisfied, and contentedly working together for the benefit of India as a whole.

In a subsequent chapter I shall have occasion to refer to the continued stubbornness and intransigence of Hindu opinion, which at a much later date rejected the constitution offered it by the British Cabinet Mission. The formulation of this constitution, in outline and in principle, should have marked the beginning of the Round Table Conference, if the Hindu representatives, when we met them in the Nawab of Bhopal's house, had accepted my offer on behalf of the Muslims with the sincerity with which I put it forward.

That acceptance denied us, the rest of the first Round Table Conference was not of much essential or practical importance, since the foundation on which its deliberations should have been built was vague and fragile, instead of strong and firm.

One successful step forward seemed then to be of great importance, but time and a train of great events have shown it to have been minor and transient. This was the princes' announcement of their acceptance of the idea of federation. The British representatives at the Conference hailed it – perhaps not unnaturally from their point of view – as a significant and constructive advance, of real assistance in the task of securing a devolution of power from the United Kingdom Parliament to a so-called Indian Federal Parliament.

It gained in impressiveness from the fact that Lord Reading, the Leader of the Liberal Party in the House of Lords, enfolded with the august aura of prestige which his status as an ex-Viceroy gave him, and strongly convinced as he was of the importance of a centralized responsibility in all major spheres of administration and executive authority, gave it his hearty if measured approval. To the Prime Minister, Mr. Ramsay MacDonald, it seemed salvation and success for the Conference, rather than the shipwreck which – so it appeared at the time – would have been disastrous. Mr. MacDonald's situation throughout the Conference was complicated and delicate, though hardly unique, for it was the kind of situation which he frequently had to face in his career. At the height of his power he faced it with aplomb and adroitness, but it was difficult to disregard the fact that, despite all his diplomatic skill and finesse, he was not unlike the driver who has eight spirited horses in his coaching team and is aware that any couple can and probably will go off on its own and seek to pull the coach in a totally different direction from that which he intends.

To the Indian representatives at the Conference Mr. MacDonald had to be – and was – our Chairman, presiding with shrewd and benevolent impartiality over our deliberations, wise and venerated, our guide, philosopher, and friend in the tricky mazes of democratic, constitutional procedure and theory in which we were having our protracted initiation. To his own party, burdened with office – in 1930, that year of dark foreboding and hints of turbulence and the sorrow that were imminent – but without that support of a solid and unthreatened majority in the House of Commons which alone could ensure effectiveness and permanence to its decisions, he had to appear as the leader in the long crusade against out-of-date imperialism and obstructive vested interests, and the emancipator, the creator of Indian freedom and independence which he sincerely desired to be. In this role he was conscious that his was an advanced and most progressive view of India's problems, and that he and his party were eager to travel swiftly the whole road to Dominion status, with few and minor reservations or restrictions. But the Conservative Opposition, whose patience he could not possibly afford to test too highly, was jealously watchful of Britain's imperial interests; and both in Parliament and in the Press the right-wing "die-hard" elements of the Conservative Party possessed powerful and authoritative citadels whence to challenge – perhaps to overthrow – him, if he too flagrantly disregarded their views.

In these circumstances it was perhaps inevitable that an especial atmosphere of hopefulness and optimism should envelop this, the Conference's one major tangible achievement. Something, it was felt, above and beyond mere provincial autonomy had been established and ensured. The lawyers among us, like Sir Tej Bahadur Sapru, let themselves become zestfully absorbed in the details of what they then believed would lead to a serious and permanent advance along the road to Indian self-government. I must say that I in my heart of hearts was always suspicious that our work might not procure any real or lasting results, because the great realities of India in 1930 were being forgotten.

It was forgotten that there were, first and foremost and all the time, fundamental differences between the Muslim and Hindu peoples that inhabited the subcontinent; and that these differences were most apparent between the Muslims of the two north-western and eastern sections of it and the Hindu majority in the rest.

It was forgotten that the intelligentsia – although only ten per cent of the total Hindu population – numbered between forty and fifty million, who could not possibly be dismissed as "a mere microscopic minority". It was forgotten that they desired the British to quit India, bag and baggage, finally and for ever; this was the aim for which they laboured and strove, and indeed it was brought to pass in 1947. All the minutiae of an elaborate paper constitution, with all its cautious safeguards, its neat balancing of power by abstract and theoretical formulae which were to be embodied in it, seemed to them a pack of cunning and pernicious nonsense, a lot of irksome tricks by which all that the British seemed with one hand to give could be – and would be – snatched back with the other.

It was forgotten that the princes, for all their wealth, ability, personal charm, prestige, and sincere loyalty to the British connection, had in fact very little power or influence. They were not, of course, the sinister stooges that hostile propaganda often dubbed them, but both their actual authority and their capacity to sway opinion by their influence had been sapped in long years during which their subjects – and the Indian people at large – had come to realize that they were powerless, and incapable of holding an independent view or making an independent decision, if that view or that decision conflicted with the policy of the all-powerful British Residents. Thus gradually their support of the federal constitution – though it took in the British ruling class – was shown to possess very little reality, and to be a shadow without the substance of power.

By the time the second Round Table Conference assembled in the autumn of 1931 the world situation had changed vastly, and so had the state of Indo-British relations. The economic crisis, in all its sharpness and severity, had hit Europe and the United Kingdom. The collapse of the famous Austrian Credit-Anstalt Bank had led to a general and hasty restriction of credit, and a long steep tumble in world trade. In Britain the number of unemployed mounted to a vast, grim total in the region of three millions; the publication of the May Report, an authoritative, officialy-ordered survey of the country's economic, financial, and fiscal condition, which contained a number of recommendations for economy measures [*sic*] which were totally inacceptable [*sic*] to the majority of Mr. Ramsay MacDonald's Cabinet colleagues, precipitated a major political crisis. In September the King interrupted his annual and cherished holiday at Balmoral and returned to London summoning to meet him the various leaders of the political parties. Thereafter a National Government was formed, charged with the task of dealing with the crisis; Mr. MacDonald was Prime Minister, supported by Conservatives and Liberals like Mr. Baldwin, Sir Austen Chamberlain, Sir John Simon, and Sir Herbert Samuel. In the General Election which followed quickly on the formation of this government, its supporters, mainly Conservatives and National Liberals, were returned to power with an overwhelming majority, and Labour representation in the Commons was reduced to "rump" proportions – almost the only ex-Ministers left in the House being Mr. George Lansbury, the veteran pacifist, and Mr. Attlee.

These changes could not but affect the second Round Table Conference; but, grave and preoccupying as were the events in which Britain and the British Government were involved, they did not cause its postponement. Meanwhile the patience and the considerable powers of persuasion of the Viceroy, Lord Irwin – "the tall Christian" as Mr. Muhammad Ali called him in an historic phrase – had prevailed and Mahatma Gandhi agreed to come to London. He went in his own personal capacity, but it was generally felt that, even if he did not come as the nominated leader and representative of Congress, his was the voice of authority and decision so far as the vast majority of Hindus were concerned.

We Muslims for our part hoped that Mahatma Gandhi, with his unique political flair allied to his vast personal prestige, would appreciate the fact (and act upon it) that to make a combined front of Hindus and Muslims would in itself be a major step forward, and all realized that it would offer an unparalleled opportunity for extracting out of the Round Table Conference a constitution which would be a genuine transference of power from British to Indian hands, and would give India the status of a world Power. Though Mahatma Gandhi could not possibly in 1930 have foreseen or hoped for anything like the final solution of 1947, he must, when he arrived, have hoped, as did most of us from the East at the Conference – that real power would be transferred, even if India and Whitehall were still linked by one or two silken strings.

Mahatma Gandhi arrived in London in November 1931 as the sole representative of Congress. He was accompanied by the eminent Indian poet, Mrs. Sarojini Naidu. Our first meeting in our capacity as delegates to the second Round Table Conference occurred at midnight in my own room at the Ritz Hotel. It may be a suitable moment therefore to pause in my narrative and sum up my impressions and recollections of two truly remarkable personalities.

One way and another I knew and was in touch with Mahatma Gandhi for more than forty-five years. I first heard of him about 1899 or 1900 when both he and I were actively concerned with the status and future of Indians in South Africa, a perennial problem which was to engage our attention across many years. At that time his philosophy was only beginning to coalesce, and he had not made the major personal decision of his life, which was the break with, and the turning away from, modern material progress. On and off we were in touch for the next ten or twelve years, usually on some facet of the Indian problem in South Africa. We were in London at the same time shortly after the outbreak of the First World War; as he had done at the beginning of the South African War he offered his assistance to the British Government for ambulance and field hospital work. Already he had, however, travelled far along his own mental and spiritual road, and I was aware that he had decided that salvation for India and for his fellow countrymen lay in renouncing contemporary, industrialized and materialistic so-called civilization. I have given an account of our contacts at the time of the Khilafat agitation in 1920–1; thereafter Mahatma Gandhi was, for the rest of his life, a major figure in world history.

I believe that both in Mahatma Gandhi's philosophical outlook and in his political work there were certain profound inconsistencies, which all his life he strove, without complete success, to reconcile. The chief, formative spiritual influences of his life were Christ, as revealed in the New Testament, Tolstoy, Thoreau, and certain exponents of various forms of Hindu asceticism; yet he was not, in the ordinarily accepted sense, a pure ascetic; he had little patience and no sympathy with the merely contemplative life of the mystic totally withdrawn from the world, or with monks, whether Buddhist or Christian, who accept the rule of an enclosed order. If I may say so, I am convinced that Gandhi's philosophy was not renunciation of this world but its reformation, with mutual and associative human love as the dynamic spark in that reformation. Yet this involved for him a certain degree of renunciation. This attitude to the products of the industrial and technical revolution of our time was characteristically ambivalent. He believed that all men ought to have the full benefits – in generally diffused well-being – of the power over nature which science has put at man's disposal. Yet he felt that, at man's present level of social and spiritual development, if some individuals accepted these benefits, then the vast majority would be deprived of them and would be both proportionally and absolutely worse off than before.

This ambivalence, rooted as it was in a profound mental and spiritual contradiction, was always evident throughout his life, in his relations with his nearest and dearest friends, and in his teaching and in his practice.

I remember that I once had a long conversation with him in Poona after he had been gravely ill, and had undergone an operation. He was in bed at the Sassoon Hospital, where I went to see him. His praise and his admiration for the hospital, for the British surgeon who had operated on him, for the consultants and the nursing staff, were unstinted. Yet he could not but feel that since such a standard of treatment and attention could not be given to every single one of the millions of India's population, it must be wrong for it to be at his disposal here in Poona. Just as much as everyone else, however, he realized that it would be a crime to abolish the Sassoon Hospital – and everything which it symbolized and represented – that its benefits must go to some, since they could not go to all, but to whom? And yet, he felt, and yet, and yet . . . his philosophy tailed off into a question mark that was also a protest.

There in his bed in that Poona hospital he faced the impossibility of complete adjustment. It was this hard fact of incomplete adjustment, in the world as it is, which made him appear at some moments "for" material progress, and at others "against" it. It gave some critics cause to doubt either the sincerity of his Christian Tolstoyan ideals or the efficacy of his activities in the world of practical politics and economics. It would perhaps be more just as well as more charitable to realize that Mahatma

Gandhi was far from alone in the contradictions and the conflicts of his inner and his outer life. Are not such contradictions the very foundation of life for all of us, in its spiritual as well as its material aspects, and if we seek to be of any use or service to ourselves and to our fellow men can we do otherwise than live, as best we may, in the light of these contradictions?

Our last talk in 1945–6 was in its way a reflection in miniature of the whole of Mahatma Gandhi's spiritual and intellectual life. Its setting and its circumstances illustrated, forcefully enough, the simple fact that in our world as it is we can never get away from contradictions. I had come to talk politics with Gandhi; since I was no longer actively a participant in Indian politics, I had to some extent come as a companion of my old and valued friend, the Nawab of Bhopal. Bhopal, Chancellor of the still existent Chamber of Princes, was a free-lance in the Muslim ranks of the time, for he had not accepted the Quaid-i-Azam's conviction that only a partition of the subcontinent could give the Muslims what they wanted. I for my part still cherished some hopes that the full and final amputation could be avoided, if something on the lines of the constitution proposed by the last British Cabinet Mission could have been acceptable. Now I see clearly that I was wrong; amputation was the only remedy. Mahatma Gandhi and I talked of these matters; we talked too of South Africa; and then I changed the subject and asked: "What really is your opinion of Marxism – of Marx himself, of Engels, of Lenin, and of Stalin?"

His answer was as characteristic as it was adroit: "I," he said, "would be a hundred per cent communist myself – if Marx's final stage were the first stage, and if Lenin's economic ideals were put immediately into practice."

If – there lay the contradiction. If, as Marx had laid it down, the State would "wither away" not as the last phase of the revolution but as the first; and if Lenin's economic axiom, "From everyone, according to his capacity; to everyone according to his needs," could be put immediately into practice, then indeed the Marxist millennium would begin. I countered him with the orthodox Stalinist argument: the world as it is today contains capitalist-imperialist States, whose productive capacity is geared not to peace and utility but as a means to the possible end of aggressive and imperialist war; in such a world the Communist State must be organized in its own defence; and how can there be a free society in which the State has indeed "withered away" without the essential preliminary phase of the world triumph of organized socialism?

"Well," said Gandhi, "let one country do it. Let one country give up its State organization, its police and its armed forces, its sanctions and its compulsions. Let one State really wither away. The happiness that would there prevail would be so great and so abiding that other countries would, for very shame, let their capitalist-imperialist societies and States wither away."

Mahatma Gandhi no more than anyone else could evade the contradiction that lies at the base of life in this epoch. We have constantly to put up with second-best and probably worse, since we cannot achieve our full ideal. Gandhi, too, realized this, despite his hope that mankind could attain Marx's final phase – a goal which, if it is ever attainable at all, will be reached by another route than an immediate short cut by way of selected portions of the lives of Christ, Mohammed, and Buddha.

Mrs. Naidu, Gandhi's companion in his midnight conference with me at the Ritz that autumn night in 1931, was in her way hardly less fascinating a personality. She was one of the most remarkable women I have ever met, in some ways as remarkable as Miss Nightingale herself. Her home after her marriage was in Hyderabad. Although her original inclinations and her upbringing were extremely democratic, she was a poet. Her sensitive and romantic imagination was impressed by the originality and strangeness as well as the glamour of the character of the then Nizam of Hyderabad – the father of his present Exalted Highness – a gentle and timorous man, of a delicate and refined sensibility and sentiment, yet endowed with great clarity of vision, independence of judgment, and generosity, and withal the possessor of a great heart in a sadly frail frame. He, too, had poetic aspirations, and some of his Urdu writings could indeed almost be dignified with the name of poetry. Mrs. Naidu sang his praises; but she herself was a real poet, who wrote strongly and tenderly of love and of life, of the world of the spirit and the passions. In that linking of tenderness and strength which was her nature there was no room for malice, hatred, or ill-will. She was a vigorous nationalist, determined that the British must leave India and her destiny in the hands of India's children, yet her admiration for Western civilization and Western science – above all for English literature – was deep and measureless. Her proud freedom from prejudice she demonstrated at the time of the death of Rudyard Kipling. Kipling's out-and-out imperialism, the rigid limitations of his view of the political capacity and potentialities of Indians – despite his recognition of their qualities of intelligence and fidelity – were inevitably at the opposite pole from Mrs. Naidu's outlook. Yet when he died Mrs. Naidu published a statement in which she paid her full and generous tribute of admiration to his genius – to the poet, the novelist, the unequalled teller of tales – making it clear beyond all argument that this recognition of the artist by the artist was utterly distinct from and unaffected by her profound and abiding dislike of his racial and political philosophy.

Such then were the notable pair who were ushered into my sitting-room at the Ritz at midnight. We posed together for the Press photographers, and then settled down to our conversation. I opened it by saying to Mahatmaji that, were he now to show himself a real father to India's Muslims, they would respond by helping him, to the utmost of their ability, in his struggle for India's independence.

Mahatmaji turned to face me. "I cannot in truth say," he observed, "that I have any feelings of paternal love for Muslims. But if you put the matter on grounds of political necessity, I am ready to discuss it in a co-operative spirit. I cannot indulge in any form of sentiment."

This was a cold douche at the outset; and the chilly effect of it pervaded the rest of our conversation. I felt that, whereas I had given prompt and ready evidence of a genuine emotional attachment and kinship, there had been no similar response from the Mahatmaji.

Years later – in 1940 – I reminded him of this. He said that he completely recollected the episode. "I am very, very sorry," he said then, "that you misunderstood that answer of mine. I didn't mean that I was aware of no emotional attachment, no feeling for the welfare of Muslims; I only meant that I was conscious of full blood *brotherhood*, yes, but not of the superiority that *fatherhood* would imply."

And I, on my side, had only meant in that word "father" to show respect for the frailty of his age – not of course, frailty in health or mental capacity – and not to hint at any superiority.

This unfortunate initial misunderstanding over words had more than a passing effect. For it left the impression, which persisted not only that night but throughout the Round Table Conference, that our attempts to reach a Muslim-Hindu *entente* were purely political and lacked the stabilizing emotional ties of long fellow-citizenship and of admiration for one another's civilization and culture. Thus there could be no cordiality about any *entente* we might achieve; we were driven back to cold politics, with none of the inspiring warmth of emotional understanding to suffuse and strengthen our discussions.

This preliminary talk did not take us far. Thereafter we had a further series of conversations – usually at midnight in my rooms at the Ritz – I myself presiding as host, and Mr. Jinnah and Sir Muhammad Shafi negotiating on one side and Mahatma Gandhi on the other. The story of these discussions is long and not, alas, particularly fruitful.

They were informal talks and no record was kept. I said little and left the bulk of the discussion to Mr. Jinnah and Sir Muhammad Shafi, and to other delegates who from time to time took part, notably Sir Zafrullah Khan, Mr. Shaukat Ali, and the late Shaffat Ali Khan. Much of the disputation vividly recalled FitzGerald's verse:

> Myself when young did eagerly frequent
> Doctor and Saint, and heard great argument
> About it and about: but evermore
> Came out by the same door as in I went.

Always the argument returned to certain basic points of difference: was India a nation or two nations? Was Islam merely a religious minority, or were Muslims in those areas in which they were in a majority to have and to hold special political rights and responsibilities? The Congress attitude seemed to us doctrinaire and unrealistic. They held stubbornly to their one-nation theory, which we knew to be historically insupportable. We maintained that before the coming of the British Raj the various regions of the Indian subcontinent had never been one country, that the Raj had created an artificial and transient unity, and that when the Raj went that unity could not be preserved and the diverse peoples, with their profound racial and religious differences, could not remain fellow-sleepers for all time, but that they would awake and go their separate ways. However close, therefore, we might come to agreement on points of detail, this ultimate disagreement on points of principle could not be bridged.

The Mahatma sought to impose a first and fundamental condition: that the Muslims should, before they asked for any guarantees for themselves, accept Congress's interpretation of Swaraj – self-government – as their goal. To which Mr. Jinnah very rightly answered that, since the Mahatma was not imposing this condition on the other Hindu members of the various delegations attending the Round Table, why should he impose it on the Muslims? Here was another heavy handicap.

Our conditions were the same throughout: very few powers at the centre, except in respect of defence and external affairs; all other powers to be transferred, and especially to those provinces in which there were Muslim majorities – the Punjab, Bengal, Sind, Baluchistan, and the North-west Frontier. We were adamant because we knew that the majority of the Muslims who lived in Bengal and the Punjab were adamant.

Mahatma Gandhi fully recognized the importance of having us in his camp. Who knows? – perhaps he might have seen his way to accept our viewpoint, but Pundit Malaviya and the Hindu Mahasabha exerted great pressure against us, deploying arguments based on abstract political doctrines and principles which – as the partition of 1947 proved – were totally unrelated to the realities of India.

As time went on the hair-splitting became finer and finer, the arguments more and more abstract: a nation could not hand over unspecified powers to its provinces; there was no constitutional way of putting a limit on the devices by which a majority could be turned into a minority – fascinating academic issues, but with little or no connection with the real facts and figures of Indian life.

In fairness I ought to mention one practical reform which did emerge from all our discussions and in the end contributed something to the settlement of 1947. This was the separation of Sind from Bombay and its establishment as a province with a Governor and administration of its own. For at least thirty years previously the continued connection of these two had been an anachronism; its existence explains much of Sind's so-called backwardness, and the rivalry and the jealousy that arose between Bombay, the older city which ruled, and Karachi, the younger city which was ruled.

In the Province of Bombay the I.C.S. officials who attained the highest ranks of the service tended to have spent years in Marathi or Gujerathi districts. Sind differed from other parts of the province in race, language, religion, and the physical shape of the land: and service in it required a quite different outlook, mentality, and training. Sind had been neglected in matters like communications, roads, and internal development, by an administrative centre from which it was far distant and with which its only connections were by sea or across the territories of princely States.

A special committee to consider the whole question of the separation of Sind was set up. The Muslim representatives on it – of whom I was one – did not argue the case on communal lines; we urged that Sind be separated from Bombay as an act of common justice to its inhabitants, and on practical and administrative grounds. Apart from one or two members who represented Bombay and were anti-separation, our other Hindu colleagues supported us, and our proposal was carried . . .

In the end, the many long sessions achieved little. Mahatmaji returned to India; the sum total of all our work was a vast array of statistics and dates, a great many speeches, and little or no positive understanding. The second Conference finished, all the delegates dispersed, and we awaited what was in fact the third Round Table Conference, but was officially known as the Joint Select Committee appointed by Parliament under the chairmanship of the Marquess of Linlithgow, to draw up the Indian Federal Constitution . . .

The third of the series of Indian Round Table Conferences was upon us. On the British side there had been changes, consequent upon the formation of the MacDonald-Baldwin National Government. Mr. Ramsay MacDonald was still Prime Minister, but his support in the House of Commons came now from the enormous Conservative majority of which Mr. Baldwin was the master. This removed Mr. MacDonald from direct and close concern in our deliberations about India; consulted in all important matters he doubtless continued to be, but the effective decisions were, one could not help feeling, being made by the man in charge of the India Office. This, of course, was Sir Samuel Hoare, a sensitive, sagacious, broadminded, and keenly intelligent statesman, who was acutely aware of the realities of our mid-twentieth-century world, and – so far as India was concerned – fully realized that the day of the diehard imperialist was ended.

The Joint Select Committee assembled in London in the spring of 1934. The Chairman, Lord Linlithgow, was later to be Viceroy of India. The composition of the Committee was as varied as it was strong. The British representation contained inevitably a heavy Conservative preponderance; the knowledge and experience of India of individual members varied in quantity and quality. Respected and influential leaders like Lord Derby and Sir Austen Chamberlain were at the outset non-committal; there were others who were frankly opposed to the whole idea of a federal solution to India's problems. India's representation was on the whole good. Mahatma Gandhi did not attend, but there was a sizeable element of advanced Indian nationalism, drawn from outside the ranks of Congress. Looking back now on what happened in the course of this Committee, I think I regret Mr. Jinnah's absence as much as that of Mahatmaji. It was, I think, extremely unfortunate that we Muslims did not insist on having Mr. Jinnah with us; had he been a member of the delegation he might have subscribed to what I consider was the most valuable result of these Round Table Conferences.

This was the Joint Memorandum, which – for the first time in the history of Indo-British relations – put before the British Government a united demand on behalf of all communities, covering practically every important political point at issue. It propounded what would have been, in effect, a major step forward – the penultimate step indeed before Dominion status. By it we sought to ensure continuity in the process of the further transfer of responsibility. It was signed by all the non-official Indian delegates; it had been drafted by the delegation's brilliant official secretary and myself. It was a claim for the transfer to Indian hands of practically every power except certain final sanctions which would be reserved to the British Government. Had a constitution been granted along these lines, later critical situations – India's declaration of war in 1939, the problems which faced the Cripps Mission in 1942, and the final and total transfer of authority – might all have been much less difficult. Had this constitution been fully established and an accepted and going concern, it would have been in due course a comparatively simple operation to lop off those reserve powers which in our draft marked the final stage of constitutional devolution.

As I said in the course of evidence which I gave before the Joint Committee on the Government of India Bill:

> I accept the term "Responsible Government" though as an ideal my preference is for self-government either on the American federal plan or on Swiss lines leaving ultimate power through the Initiative, the Referendum, and perhaps the Recall. But the facts of the situation have to be recognized . . . "Responsible Government" must be our way towards evolving in the future some plan more suited to a congeries of great States, such as India will become, and I believe the way will be found in something akin to the American Federal Plan.

Despite all (as we thought) its merits, our Joint Memorandum was disowned by Congress, and therefore the British Government felt compelled in their turn to reject it. In its stead they brought into being the constitution adumbrated by the Government of India Act of 1935, which left far too many loopholes for British interference, and indeed actual decision, on matters which every Indian patriot believed should have been solely for India to decide – for example India's entry into the Second World War. Its grossest failing was that it offered no foundation on which to build; Sir Stafford Cripps, during his mission in 1942, and Lords Alexander of Hillsborough and Pethick-Lawrence on their subsequent mission, were halted by this unpalatable fact. Neither did the act supply an impetus to any effort to bridge the rift between Hindus and Muslims; and in the testing times of 1942 and 1946–7, the emptinesses in the Act were glaringly revealed. By its reservations and by its want of clarity about the real meaning of Indian independence, the 1935 Act made a United India an impossibility. It had to be set aside and the effort made to build up Indian independence from scratch. Then it became harshly clear that Indian unity was impossible, unless it were based on extremely wide federal, or confederate, foundations.

The second Cabinet Mission of 1947 did finally propose a constitution which would have maintained the unity of India, but at the price of handing over all ultimate power to the three confederate States of a Federal India. This was the sort of constitution for which our Joint Memorandum of 1934 could have naturally and steadily prepared the ground. Congress's attitude to this last effort was, to say the least, lukewarm; and it, too, fell by the wayside. In the end, the only solution was that which occurred, and those strange Siamese twins – Muslim India and Hindu India – that had lived together so restlessly and so uncomfortably, were parted by a swift, massive surgical operation.

[Extracts from pp. 212–34]

THE LEAGUE OF NATIONS

Appointment as a delegate to the Disarmament Conference and as the chief Indian representative to the 1932 Assembly of the League of Nations – his views on disarmament – the continuation of the League's work – friendship with Arthur Henderson – the gloomy international scene – his speech at the League of Nations Assembly – Italy's invasion of Ethiopia – Mussolini's intentions – the crisis in the League – Soviet and Nazi attitudes – British policy – his suggestion to Anthony Eden to close the Suez Canal – the consequences of the appeasement of Italy.

When arrangements were in train for the Disarmament Conference and the Indian delegation to the League of Nations was in process [*sic*] of being appointed, Sir Samuel Hoare took the whole matter up with characteristic energy and thoroughness, drew the Viceroy's attention to the fact that I had deserved more useful employment, and insisted that I be given a chance to serve India in the international field. Someone had used about me the phrase "Ambassador without Portfolio". The Secretary of State urged that it was high time for me to be given official status.

I think that I may claim that I brought to my new task a mind fairly well versed in its main issues. My grounding in European as well as Eastern political and social history had been thorough. Ever since adolescence I had read widely and steadily. I was – and still am – a diligent student of the newspapers, and of those political magazines and quarterlies which, in Britain and France especially, give an authoritative and often scholarly commentary on all the main events and trends of our time. I had also for many years lived an active life in both national and international affairs . . .

The Secretary of State's wishes prevailed in the Secretariat in New Delhi. I was appointed a member of the Indian delegation to the Disarmament Conference, nominally as second-in-command to Sir Samuel Hoare, but to take charge as soon as he left. I was also appointed chief Indian representative at the 1932 Assembly of the League. Thus began a phase in my public life which was protracted, with little or no intermission, until Hitler's armies marched into Poland and the fabric of world peace which the League strove so hard to maintain was violently shattered.

The optimism that was prevalent in Geneva in 1932 was a mood which I could not fully share. A more strenuous and a more realistic effort was needed, I felt sure, to bring about the fruition of our hopes. As best I could, I sought to expound my own ideas and beliefs in this new arena to which I had been summoned. I made a speech of some length, and with all the earnestness that I could muster, at the fourteenth plenary session of the League:

We have found that armaments still hold sway and that the feeling of insecurity still persists. It is by no means certain that the war to end war has been fought and won. On the moral side we must set ourselves to remove the paralysing effects of fear, ill-will, and suspicion. On the material side it is absolutely essential that the non-productive effort devoted to warlike preparations should be reduced to the bare minimum. In distant India, no less than in Europe, the World War created a host of mourners and left a legacy of bitter tragedy. Over a million of my fellow-countrymen were called to arms, of whom more than fifty thousand laid down their lives. India's own scale of armaments allows no margin for aggressive uses. The size of her forces has to be measured with reference to the vastness of her area and the diversity of her conditions. The fact is so often forgotten that the area of India is more than half that of the whole of Europe, and her population nearly one fifth of that of the entire globe. There is a cry going up from the heart of all the peace-loving citizens of every country for the lessening of their military burdens, for a decrease of the financial load which those burdens impose, for the security of civil populations against indiscriminate methods of warfare, and above all, for security against the very idea of war.

The words of many of us who, in those years, spoke out in the effort to prevent a second World War, have gone down the wind. But that is not to say that the effort was not worth making, or that we were not right to make it. The vast palace in Geneva that housed the League of Nations is no longer put to the purpose for which it was built, but the United Nations Organization, which has arisen out of the ruin and the tragedy which we strove to avert, shows – by continuing our work in a new era and with new techniques – that we did not labour entirely in vain.

For the rest of the thirties the work of the League, and of its off-shoot the Disarmament Conference, absorbed most of my time and my interest. I found myself in Geneva for months at a time, through many harassing and disillusioning happenings – Japan's aloof snubbing of the League, Germany's dramatic exit from it, and then the direct challenge of Mussolini's aggression in Ethiopia. Early in this period I cemented a close friendship with Mr. Arthur Henderson, the President of the Disarmament Conference. Henderson was perhaps one of the most remarkable statesmen who have come out of the British Labour Movement. He had been a conspicuously successful and much-liked Foreign

Secretary in Mr. Ramsay MacDonald's second Labour Administration, but he had not found himself able to support his leader in the rapid and dramatic changeover which resulted in the formation of the National Government. He retained therefore the passionate and proud loyalty of Labour in Britain, but the immediate effect of his decision was to deprive him of power and of office. It was universally felt that it would be disastrous, for the world as for Britain, to lose his sagacity, his experience, and his flair in the spheres of international affairs in which he had made so notable a mark.

Henderson was therefore appointed permanent President of the Disarmament Conference and until his untimely death he discharged his duties in this post – in face of much disappointment and a heartbreakingly uphill struggle – with courage and distinction. Our acquaintance ripened rapidly into a sincere and mutually affectionate friendship of great warmth. His mind and his achievements were as remarkable as his character was lovable. Like most of the Labour leaders of his generation he was a genuine son of the people who from humble beginnings had made his way upward in the world to the high, onerous, and lonely position which he occupied. He was modest and forthright, shrewd, imperturbable, quiet of speech, and of rock-like integrity. A Labour leader of a younger generation, Mr. Morgan Phillips, has said that the origins of the British Labour movement are to be found in Methodism rather than Marxism; this was certainly true of Arthur Henderson, for he remained all his life a serenely devoted Methodist. His wife had been his faithful companion on his long and strenuous road; she was a woman of great sweetness and generosity of character, staunch and true and, in her own fashion, very wise.

Henderson was often my guest at my villa at Antibes; Bernhard Baron, the millionaire and philanthropist, would sometimes drive to Monte Carlo to spend an hour or two in the Casino, and Henderson would happily go along for the ride. When they reached the Casino, however, Henderson sat contentedly in the car, waiting till Baron came out again. Henderson was as steadfast as he was good, as selfless as he was courageous. We came to rely on each other for advice and support in the difficult and trying times through which we steered our way in Geneva.

But the international scene by now was gloomy and its skies were darkly overcast. The little, glimmering lights of peace and hope which had been set burning since the end of the First World War were going out, one by one. Exactly a fortnight before

Mussolini launched his attack on Ethiopia, I spoke in the Assembly of the League of Nations. The time had passed, I was convinced, for smooth glib words. On my own and my country's behalf I spoke as frankly and as gravely as I could.

India is troubled by the League's lack of universality and by the great preponderance of energy which the League devotes to Europe and European interests. India is troubled by these dramatic failures, by the long-drawn-out and fruitless Disarmament Conference and by the fact that the rearmament of States members is in full swing. India's criticism of the League is directed to its shortcomings and not its ideals. The world is at the parting of the ways. Let wisdom guard [*sic.*, guide] her choice.

... The next great crisis which faced the League was Italy's assault on Ethiopia in 1935. It presented a more serious challenge even than the Sino-Japanese dispute, for however aggressive Japan's actions were, there were explanatory, if hardly ameliorative, factors involved, which – as I have indicated – made it impossible for any of the Great Powers at least to regard that as a clean-cut case. All the various concessions, with all their legal equivocations about status, and (since the Japanese occupation of Korea) a common frontier along the Yalu River, were in themselves occasions for quarrels in which lack of diplomatic satisfaction could – and usually was – made the excuse for military action. The whole situation was morally indefensible, of course, but it had centuries of usage to sustain it and give it at least the superficial appearance of respectability.

Italy, however, possessed none of these opportunities or facilities for whitewashing her aggressive, imperialistic designs on Ethiopia. Italy's only case was one of naked need for living space for her ever-increasing population, if they were to remain Italian. Libya's possibilities of intensive and large-scale exploitation and colonization were few; fertile areas in this long stretch of the Mediterranean littoral were limited, and the desert was vast. Italy's surplus population seemed therefore faced with one of two possibilities. Either they could emigrate across the Atlantic to North or South America, or to neighbouring Mediterranean lands like Egypt, Morocco, Tunisia, and Algeria, and be lost to Italy as citizens; or they could remain in Italy, always below the margin of subsistence, millions too many for her limited soil to bear, with a standard of living far below that of any of their western European neighbours and thoroughly unworthy of the nation that had succeeded Imperial Rome.

Mussolini made no secret of his intentions. He made stirring speeches in towns and cities all over Italy, and his eloquence roused thousands to passionate enthusiasm and sympathy. At the diplomatic level he gave no more than one warning, couched in terms, however, which were ambiguous enough for him to be able to interpret the silence with which France and Britain greeted them as consent, if not as direct encouragement to him. Whatever the shadowy background of the Duce's mental processes, there could be no ignoring the blatant openness of his preparations, throughout the summer of 1935, for the military conquest and annexation of the free, independent, and sovereign State of Ethiopia, on pretexts which were flimsy in the extreme. The Ethiopians were faced with a tragic choice: either to accept an ultimatum from Mussolini; or rejecting it, to wage a hopeless war which could only end in total military defeat and subjection.

The League was thus thrust into a hopelessly difficult situation; and there developed that deep and catastrophic division of opinion in Britain and in France, and indeed throughout much of the world, which was to persist with such unfortunate results until the outbreak of the Second World War four years later. In two countries, however, there was no chance for any division of opinion to show itself: the U.S.S.R and Nazi Germany. Russian policy was simple and monolithic; Litvinov had proclaimed Russia's doctrine, "Peace is indivisible", and whatever weaknesses and drawbacks communist policy may possess, there has nearly always been about it a façade of logical unity between dogma and practice. The Nazis, of course, saw a superb opportunity to break up what remained of unity among the Powers who had been victorious over Germany in the First World War and who had sought to make their victory permanent by the guarantees written into the Versailles Treaty. They had the shrewdness not to proclaim their satisfaction too loudly; public opinion in Britain and France was therefore not alert to the hidden dangers in the German attitude, any more than it recognized the hidden dangers in Russia's expressions of shocked virtue.

In Britain confusion and irresolution were woefully apparent. There was the "realism" – grossly mistaken, as the naval history of the Second World War was to demonstrate – of old-fashioned imperialists like the late Lord Lloyd, then President of the Navy League, who argued that the Royal Navy had been so weakened by the years of disarmament and economic stringency that it could not risk being brought into the open conflict which severe and legitimate action against Italy's aggression would be bound to entail. Therefore they were opposed to any resolute policy.

Another school of thought argued that to annoy Italy would be – as the phrase went – "to drive her into the arms of Germany", and saw in this plea reason enough to submit to Mussolini's high-handedness. There were others who saw a practical political escape-ladder in what came to be known as the Hoare-Laval arrangements.

In Geneva there was a deep and widespread resentment and sense of humiliation at the easy success which apparently attended this shameless policy of aggression, on *condotteori* lines, with a twentieth-century technique in international relations and propaganda.

I saw my friend Mr. Eden and I said to him: "If you want international policies to have a foundation of justice, if you want the League really to be what it is supposed to be, if you want to give it a chance to grow into a real society of nations, deciding matters of right and wrong among themselves, then here is an outstanding case which must be tackled. Here there is no valid excuse of any kind. There is no large Italian minority in Ethiopia deprived of their independence or their civic and economic rights. Here is a case of open and inexcusable aggression. And the remedy is in our hands. *All we need do is shut the Suez Canal.* Or if we must have sanctions, let them be applied to oil as well, and thus make them a reality and put some teeth into them. But I still think the best solution is a simple, unanimous resolution by the League to close the Canal."

Instead we found ourselves passing resolutions in favour of sanctions, which I found silly and futile. Yet ineffective as we knew them to be we had to vote in support of them; for if we did not, we would seem to be condoning Italy's aggression, but the only sanction which would have achieved anything – the sanction of withholding petrol – was barred. I could foresee that it was inevitable from that moment onwards, that there would come a bitter day when those of us who had once held such high hopes for the League would have to go to the Assembly and, with misery in our hearts, ask for the removal of sanctions. I saw too – and I have no hesitation in admitting it – that, once the moment came for us to submit to the Italian conquest of Ethiopia, it would be much better for us to swallow our pride and our anger and do it with a good grace.

2

8

Here, then, was an important phase in the development of the policy and practice of appeasement. Here was an instance in which appeasement and conciliation of the aggressor were morally wrong; but once the Great Powers had appeased on this issue – a thoroughly bad and unjustified issue – there would follow the inevitable consequence that sooner or later we should have to stomach a new dose of appeasement, either in the matter of Japan in China, where there were loopholes both historical and juridical, or in the matter of some sort of German aggression, where there would be the pleas of oppressed minorities, of plebiscites demanding reunion, and a whole specious façade of legality and morality.

[Extracts from pp. 238–59]

JINNAH AND THE MAKING OF PAKISTAN

The political leaders in India – a comparison between Muhammad Ali Jinnah and other statesmen – consistency in both Jinnah's and Mussolini's careers – Jinnah in the Indian National Congress – his alienation from the Congress – his role in the Round Table Conferences – how he embodied the beliefs and sentiments of Muslims of India – Muslim League under his leadership – contrast between Jinnah and Mussolini – the political situation in India in 1946 – his meeting with Gandhi and conversations with Lord Wavell and Sir Claude Auchinleck – Muslim political determination – the British Cabinet Mission's final offer – Jinnah's unconditional acceptance of the plan – its rejection by the Congress – Clement Attlee's acceptance of the Muslim principles – partition of the subcontinent – the birth of independent India and Pakistan.

The political leaders, with whom ultimately decision and authority rested, were four in number: on the Congress-Hindu side, Mahatma Gandhi, Mr. Nehru, and Sardar Patel; on the Muslim side, Mr. Jinnah – the Quaid-i-Azam. On their agreement or disagreement, translated into economic and political facts, depended the future of the subcontinent.

The Quaid-i-Azam's brilliant and epoch-making career, so untimely ended, reached its summit in these momentous years of 1946 and 1947. Now he belongs to history; and his memory, I

1396

am certain, is imperishable. Of all the statesmen that I have known in my life – Clemenceau, Lloyd George, Churchill, Curzon, Mussolini, Mahatma Gandhi – Jinnah is the most remarkable. None of these men in my view outshone him in strength of character, and in that almost uncanny combination of prescience and resolution which is statecraft. It may be argued that he was luckier than some – far luckier for example, than Mussolini, who perished miserably in utter failure and disgrace. But was Jinnah's success all good luck, and was Mussolini's failure all bad luck? What about the factors of good and bad judgment?

I knew Jinnah for years, from the time he came back from England to Bombay to build up his legal practice there, until his death. Mussolini, I met once only . . . Yet between these two I detect one important similarity.

Each of them between his youth and his prime, travelled from one pole of political opinion to the other. Mussolini made his pilgrimage from a Socialism that was near-Communism to the creation of Fascism, from Marx to Nietzsche and Sorel. Jinnah in his earlier phases was the strongest supporter, among all Muslim political leaders, of Indian nationalism along Congress lines, with as its goal a unified Indian state; yet, he, in the final analysis, was the man primarily responsible for the partition of the Indian Empire into the separate states of Pakistan and Bharat. He who had so long championed Indian unity was the man who, in full accordance with international law, cut every possible link between India's two halves, and – in the teeth of bitter British opposition – divided the Indian Army.

Different in many superficial characteristics, different (above all) in the success which attended the one and the failure the other, these two, Mussolini and Jinnah, both apparently inconsistent in many things, shared one impressive, lifelong quality of consistency. Each had one guiding light; whatever the policy, whatever the political philosophy underlying it, it would be successful and it would be morally justified, so long as he was at the head of it and directing it. In neither of them can this be dismissed as mere ambition; each had a profound and unshakable [*sic*] conviction that he was superior to other men, and that if the conduct of affairs were in his hands, and the last word on all matters his, everything would be all right, regardless of any abstract theory (or lack of it) behind political action.

This belief was not pretentious conceit; it was not self-glorification or shallow vanity. In each man its root was an absolute certainty of his own merit, an absolute certainty that, being endowed with greater wisdom than others, he owed it to his people, indeed to all mankind, to be free to do what he thought best on others' behalf. Was this not the same sort of supremely confident faith which guided and upheld the prophets of Israel and reformers like Luther and Calvin? In our epoch we have seen at least two other men who were animated by the same dynamic faith which shakes the nations, and each – one for good and one for terrible evil – was conscious of a cause outside himself: Hitler who dreamed of a German-imposed New Order that was to last a thousand years; and Mahatma Gandhi whose vision was of an India whose society, economy, and whole life would be based on certain pacifist, moral principles, the objective existence of which meant much more to the Mahatma than anything in himself. Britain's two leaders in the two World Wars were also men sustained by an irresistible and buoyant self-confidence, but both Lloyd George and Churchill were incapable of transgressing the limitations on the exercise of executive authority which are set by British life, and by British civic, parliamentary, ethical, and religious traditions and beliefs.

In the view of both Mussolini and Jinnah, opposition was not an opinion to be conciliated by compromise or negotiation; it was a challenge to be obliterated by their superior strength and sagacity. Each seemed opportunist, because his self-confidence and his inflexible will made him believe, at every new turn he took, that he alone was right and supremely right. Neither bothered to confide in others or to be explicit.

Mussolini travelled the long road from Marxism not because of doctrinal doubts and disagreements, but because, in the world of Socialist politicians and theorists in which he spent his stormy youth as an exile in Lausanne, doctrines and theories were constant obstacles across the only path of practical achievement which mattered to him – practical achievement in which Benito Mussolini was the leader. When Fascism first emerged as a political force in Italy nobody knew what it was, nobody could define its principles or its programme, for it had none. Mussolini simply said: "Let us have a Party, let us call it Fascist" – which meant anything or nothing. The Party's only principle, its sole duty, was to do what the leader told it to do. And its leader believed implicitly – and went on so believing for a long time – that everything the Party did would be excellent, because everything was conceived and executed by Mussolini.

Jinnah throughout his career displayed a similar characteristic. He would admit no superior to himself in intellect, authority, or moral stature. He knew no limitations of theory or doctrine. The determined and able young barrister, who – against all the omens, without influence, and without inherited wealth – triumphed within a few years despite entrenched opposition, became an Indian nationalist when he turned to politics. He joined Congress because he, like the Congress politicians, wanted to liberate India from British colonial and imperialist domination, and because he believed that he himself could do it if he had a free hand.

Yet in association with Congress Jinnah was a fish out of water. He worked to be the champion of Indian liberty, but his ideas of championship differed sharply from those of Congress's other leaders. He came back and rejoined those to whom he was linked by ties of race and religion. Nominally in the Muslim League of those days he was one leader among others, but he was unable to impose his beliefs and his policy, for the general tenor of Muslim thought ran strongly contrary to the convictions which he had held when he was in the Congress camp. He had worked hard and energetically for Congress; but, from his point of view, he was dogged by failure after failure. There was too deep a gulf between his concept of the duties and responsibilities of a political leader in a free society and those of the people with whom he worked. The instruments which he took up broke every time in his hands, because it was impossible to reconcile policy as he conceived it with policy hammered out by compromise and negotiation in the committees and the councils of which he found himself a member. He met barrier after barrier and his frustration and his dissatisfaction deepened. His "point of no return" was, of course, the critical Congress meeting in Calcutta in December 1928, dominated by the Nehrus, father and son. His disillusionment and disappointment there led him to the conviction that Muslims had no chance of fair and equitable treatment in a United India.

I here reaffirm that at the Round Table Conferences Jinnah played a loyal and honourable part throughout, as a member of the Muslim delegation. His work there, however, had not shaken his faith in his own means to his own end. The Muslims' sense of their own political needs and aspirations had been fortified and developed by years of discussion and negotiation with British officials and Congress representatives, and the Muslims very rightly followed and gave their full confidence to Jinnah.

In an era in which "no compromise" was coming to be the mood of something like a hundred million Muslims, Jinnah, the man who did not know the meaning of the word "compromise", was there to seize – not only on his own behalf, but on behalf of those whom he was destined to lead – the chance of a lifetime, the chance perhaps of centuries. He embodied, as no one else could do, the beliefs and sentiments of the overwhelming majority of Muslims all over India.

Boldly, therefore, he came out and said: "We want a Muslim party. We want a unified Muslim organization, every member of which is ready to lay down his life for the survival of his race, his faith and his civilization."

But what programme this organization should have, what specific and detailed proposals it should lay before its supporters, how its campaign should be timed and what form it should take he would never say. What he intended, though he never said so publicly, was that all these matters he reserved for his own decision when the time came – or rather, when he thought the time came.

The Muslim League, as it emerged under Jinnah's leadership, was an organization whose members were pledged to instant resistance – to the point of death – if Indian independence came about without full and proper safeguards for Muslim individuality or unity, or without due regard for all the differences between Islamic culture, society, faith, and civilization and their Hindu counterparts.

Jinnah gave always the same order to his Muslim followers: "Organize yourselves on the lines I have laid down. Follow me, be ready – if need be – to die at the supreme moment. And I will tell you when the time comes."

A few intellectuals who could not sustain this unwavering faith in Jinnah fell away, and their criticisms of him were a reiteration of the cry, "What, how, where, and when?"

I myself am convinced that even as late as 1946 Jinnah had no clear and final idea of his goal, no awareness that he would, within a twelvemonth, be the founder of a new nation, a Muslim Great Power such as the world has not seen for centuries. Neither he nor anyone else could have imagined that fate was to put so magnificent, so incredible an opportunity into his hands as that which occurred in the crucial phases of the negotiations with the British Cabinet Mission, and gave [sic] him the initiative when Lord Mountbatten arrived. Pakistan was born: a new nation, with the fifth largest population in the world, of whom ninety per cent are Muslims. And it was the creation of an organization which had only one guiding principle: "Follow the leader."

1400

Jinnah, as I shall shortly relate, made the right choice at the right moment. How different might Mussolini's end have been, had he, when the supreme moment came, chosen right instead of wrong. For him there waited a criminal's end, humiliation and ignominy. Jinnah on the other hand attained immortal fame as the man who, without an army, navy, or air force, created, by a lifetime's faith in himself crystallized into a single bold decision, a great empire of upwards of a hundred million people.

When I reached India in 1946 these mighty events were in train. However, while the principle of conceding to India immediate and total independence had now won universal acceptance in Britain, there still remained the great questions: was it to be a united India, with a single army, navy, and air force, or was the subcontinent to be divided, and how complete was the division to be? There was still a faint hope, too, that some sort of understanding might yet be possible between the Muslim League and Congress, or – in terms of personalities – between the Quaid-i-Azam and the Mahatma. In such an understanding lay, of course, the answers to the questions which I have just enumerated.

The Chancellor of the Chamber of Princes, my old and dear friend, the Nawab of Bhopal, went with me to see Mahatma Gandhi, to explore the possibilities of reaching an understanding. There were also one or two other outstanding problems to discuss: for the Nawab, the future of the ruling princes and their States in a free India; for myself, the question of the Indian community in South Africa. In our two long conversations with him (the second of which terminated with the Mahatma's remarks on Communism which I have quoted elsewhere) we came to the conclusion that there was no hope of a settlement between him and Jinnah. The Mahatma still firmly believed in a uni-national India; Jinnah even more firmly held that there were two nations. I pointed out to the Mahatma that, having accepted the principle of the separation of Burma from India, he ought really to see that there was no reason why the Muslim lands of the North-west and the North-east should not be similarly separated, since they – like Burma – had only become part of a United India as a result of British conquest, and therefore the idea of their union with the rest of India was artificial and transient. However, I made no impression on the Mahatma; and I went away, leaving Bhopal to tackle the problem of the princes.

From Poona I went to New Delhi. I had conversations both

with the Viceroy, Lord Wavell, and the Commander-in-Chief, Sir Claude Auchinleck. Both were fully convinced of the justice, as well as the necessity, of conceding Indian independence at once. Both, however, held firmly to the idea of Indian unity, doubtless because the military facts meant, in the end, more to them than the political facts. And the major military fact of 1946, in the vast region extending from the Persian Gulf to Java and Sumatra, was the existence of the Indian defence forces, above all of the Indian Army. It happened that both Lord Wavell and General Auchinleck[1] had had a great part, as Commanders-in-Chief in succession to – indeed in alternation with – each other, in building up the Indian Army, the Royal Indian Navy, and the Indian Air Force, to their magnificent and powerful condition at the end of the Second World War. They were especially aware of the value to Britain and the Commonwealth, to the Western Allies, and to the United Nations, of the continued and unified existence of these superbly disciplined and well-equipped forces. They appreciated, too, the dangers that would loom if the Indian Army were divided. Not merely might the two armies of the successor-States watch each other across the frontier with jealousy and suspicion, but a perilous strategic vacuum would be created in a huge and important part of the world's surface. They endeavoured, therefore, to find some solution which would preserve unimpaired the unity of the Indian Army. That they failed, and that all who strove with the same end in view failed, is a measure of the magnitude and resolution of the Muslims' determination, against every argument however powerful, every obstacle however stubborn, to achieve their just rights and full political, religious, and cultural independence and sovereignty ...

The British Cabinet Mission made what turned out to be Britain's final offer and final proposal for a unified India. It was ingenious and – had unity on any terms been possible – it was constructive. It was a three-tiered constitution, combining the highest possible degree of sovereignty in the three great regions into which British India would have been divided – the North-west and North-eastern areas predominantly Hindu – with an extremely limited concentration of essential power at the centre, covering foreign affairs, defence, and major communications.

Now Jinnah saw his chance and took it resolutely and unerringly. He announced his unconditional acceptance of the British

[1] Now Field-Marshal.

scheme. In that one decision, combining as it did sagacity, shrewdness, and unequalled political *flair*, he justified – I am convinced – my claim that he was the most remarkable of all the great statesmen that I have known. It puts him on a level with Bismarck.

At this critical juncture when Jinnah stood rocklike, the Congress leaders wavered. With incredible folly they rejected the British proposals; or rather they put forward dubious and equivocal alternative suggestions, which so watered the scheme down that it would have lost its meaning and effectiveness.

However in Britain, as more than once at high moments in her history, there was found statesmanship of the highest quality to respond to Jinnah's statesmanship. Mr. Attlee had from the outset closely interested himself in the efforts to achieve a solution of India's problems. Now with a boldness almost equalling Jinnah's own he accepted the basic principles for which we Muslims had striven so long. The long-ignored yet fundamental difference between the two Indias was recognized, and the recognition acted upon, quickly and resolutely. It was decided that India should be partitioned. One swift stroke of the pen, and two different but great nations were born. Lord Wavell, who had borne the heat of the day with modesty and magnanimity, resigned. The brilliant, still youthful, energetic, and supremely self-confident Lord Mountbatten of Burma was appointed to succeed him, with a clear directive to accomplish, within a strictly limited period of time, the end of British rule and responsibility in India and the handing over of authority to the two successor-States of Pakistan and Bharat.

Lord Mountbatten himself shortened the period of demission and devolution. The 15th of August 1947 was set as the date for the final and total transference of power. On every senior official's desk in New Delhi and Simla the calendars stood, in those last months, with the fateful day warningly marked. And on that day power was transferred; the two new nations took over the functions of government, and stood forth as independent, sovereign members of the Commonwealth.

[Extracts from pp. 291–9]

RACE RELATIONS IN EAST AFRICA

The plural societies of East and Central Africa – mutual inter-dependence of Africans, Europeans and Asians – the positive influence of Islam – its healing and creative power.

In East and Central Africa the problem is at present complicated by the presence of a European settler population. I believe that there can be a healthy and satisfactory adjustment, provided all sections in these multi-racial communities – indigenous Africans and immigrant Europeans and Asians – face the simple, fundamental fact that they are all dependent upon each other. No one section can dismiss any other from its calculations, either about contributions to past development or about plans for the future. The immigrant, be he European or Asian, has no hope of prosperity without the African; the African cannot do without the European farmer or the Asian trader, unless he wants to see his standard of living fall steeply, and with it all hope of exploiting and enhancing the natural wealth of the land in which all three have their homes and must earn their bread.

To a Muslim there is one quietly but forcibly encouraging element in this situation. Wherever the indigenous population is Muslim there is remarkably little racial antagonism or sense of bitterness against the European, in spite of the European's obvious economic superiority. Islam after all, is a soil in which sentiments of this sort do not take root or flourish easily. This is not a shallow and fatalistic resignation; it is something much more profound in the essence of the teaching of Islam – a basic conviction that in the eyes of God all men, regardless of colour or class or economic condition, are equal. From this belief there springs an unshakable [*sic*] self-respect, whose deepest effects are in the subconscious, preventing the growth of bitterness or any sense of inferiority or jealousy by one man of another's economic advantage.

Islam in all these countries has within it, I earnestly believe, the capacity to be a moral and spiritual force of enormous significance, both stabilizing and energizing the communities among whom it is preached and practised. To ignore Islam's potential influence for good, Islam's healing and creative power for societies as for individuals, is to ignore one of the most genuinely hopeful factors that exist in the world today.

[Extracts from pp. 331–2]

THE LAST WORD

The spark of the Divine in man – illumination and union with Reality – the Universe – an enduring lesson of life.

I can only say to everyone who reads this book of mine that it is my profound conviction that man must never ignore and leave untended and undeveloped that spark of the Divine which is in him. The way to personal fulfilment, to individual reconciliation with the Universe that is about us, is comparatively easy for anyone who firmly and sincerely believes, as I do, that Divine Grace has given man in his own heart the possibilities of illumination and of union with Reality. It is, however, far more important to attempt to offer some hope of spiritual sustenance to those many who, in this age in which the capacity of faith is nonexistent in the majority, long for something beyond themselves, even if it seems second-best. For them there is the possibility of finding strength of the spirit, comfort, and happiness in contemplation of the infinite variety and beauty of the Universe.

Life in the ultimate analysis has taught me one enduring lesson. The subject should always disappear in the object. In our ordinary affections one for another, in our daily work with hand or brain, we most of us discover soon enough that any lasting satisfaction, any contentment that we can achieve, is the result of forgetting self, of merging subject with object in a harmony that is of body, mind, and spirit. And in the highest realms of consciousness all who believe in a Higher Being are liberated from all the clogging and hampering bonds of the subjective self in prayer, in rapt meditation upon and in the face of the glorious radiance of eternity, in which all temporal and earthly consciousness is swallowed up and itself becomes the eternal.

[Extract from pp. 334–5]

Source: *The Memoirs of Aga Khan: World Enough and Time,* Cassell and Co., London, 1954.

It is a 350-page volume with twenty-seven illustrations and a seven-page Foreword by W. Somerset Maugham. The Foreword carries no date, and there is no Preface by the author. *The Times* of 11 September 1954 reported the news of its publication, from which fact I deduce that it appeared on 10 September.

225

THE SPIRIT OF UNITY IN ISLAM

A Message to the Ismailis

Cairo: 20 February 1955

Ismaili respect for other interpretations of the Divine Message –
other Muslims accepted as brothers in Islam – charity and prayer
for all Muslims.

Though Ismalis [*sic*] have been always staunch and firm believers
in the truth of their own faith in the Imamat Holy Succession,
they have never, like some other sects, gone to the other extreme
of condemning brother Muslims who have other interpretations of the Divine Message of our Holy Prophet (S.A.S.).

Ismailis have always believed and have been taught in each
generation by their Imams that they hold the rightful interpretation of the succession to the Holy Prophet, but that is no
reason why other Muslims, who believe differently, should not be
accepted as brothers in Islam and dear in person and prayed for
and never publicly or privately condemned, leave alone abused.

I hope that in these days when the Muslims have to hold
together in view of all the dangers, external and internal, from
all quarters, I hope and believe and pray that Ismailis may show
their true Islamic charity in thought and prayer for the benefit
and happiness of all Muslims, men, women and children of all
sects.

Source: *Message to the World of Islam by Aga Khan III*, Karachi, 1977, p. 33.
   The Aga Khan was in Cairo in connection with the celebrations to mark the
Platinum Jubilee of his spiritual headship of the Ismaili community.

226

MATERIAL INTELLIGENCE AND SPIRITUAL ENLIGHTENMENT

An Address at the Platinum Jubilee Ceremony

Cairo: 20 February 1955

Gift to the Diamond Jubilee Investment Trust – changes during the last seventy years – worlds of material intelligence and spiritual enlightenment – attitude of Ismailis to fellow Muslims and others – mental and physical training to meet difficult conditions.

On this unique occasion when you make this wonderful offering of platinum and its equivalent as an unconditional gift, I must immediately tell you that I give it to the Diamond Jubilee Investment Trust as further addition to its capital. You have referred to my seventy years Imamat which, indeed, is unique in the history of the 48 Ismaili Imams by its long duration, but also it began in another world, the world of horse carriages and candle lights, and today we are in the world of nuclear power, physics, jet air-travel and serious discussion amongst the most learned as to how and when we can visit the stars and the moon.

But, as I have explained in my Memoirs for the whole world to understand there are two worlds – the world of material intelligence and the world of spiritual enlightenment. The world of spiritual enlightenment is fundamentally different from the world of material intellectualism and it is the pride of the Ismailis that we firmly believe that the world of spiritual enlightenment has come as a truth from the inception of Islam to this day with the Imamat and carries with it as one of its necessary consequences love, tenderness, kindliness and gentleness towards first, our brother and sister Muslims of all sects and, secondly, to those who live in righteousness, conscience and justice towards their fellow men. These religious principles of Ismailism are well known to you for you have heard them from me and through your fathers and grandfathers and from my father and grandfather until I fear that by long familiarity with these teachings some of you forget the necessity of re-examination of your heart and religious experience.

But, as I started by telling you, there is also the world of matter and intellect which go side by side with reason and deductive and inductive powers. I have never, as you say in your own address, neglected to encourage schools and universities, and by welfare societies for the health of children, maternity, and more and more up to date needs that you may have, as far as it is possible in the areas in which you live, to get both mental and physical training that will make you capable of meeting the more and more difficult conditions of life and competition. . . .

Source: *Ismaili*, Bombay, 6 March 1955.
The celebrations were being held to mark the seventieth year of the Aga Khan's headship of the Ismaili community.

227

IS RELIGION SOMETHING SPECIAL?

An Article

Undated

Concept of religion in England – concept among Muslims – formal and informal prayer – God's will – let religion permeate life.

In an interview with a correspondent of the *Daily Sketch*, His Highness the Aga Khan said: The Churches of England have taught that religion is something special and separate from ordinary life. And so the ordinary man, even the one who clings to the observance of religion, keeps it for special occasions. His everyday life goes on apart and unaffected by his religious life, and the everyday life gets the best of it.

Now Islam holds that religion should be an affair of everyday minute–like breathing. "In Him we live and move and have our being." Allah is the Sustainer. He sustains us always and everywhere. The Faithful son of Islam is ever conscious of that fact, and in the ordinary course of business will pause or go aside to get into direct touch with the Almighty, the Sustainer.

You say that this is the Christian's conception of God, and is the practice of your Church. Well I have not observed it. I have, anyhow, met many persons nominally Christian who seem to think that in the beginning God created the world and then left it to its own devices. They seem to regard Him as a Being infinitely removed from them and their affairs. Whereas my Faith is, as you say yours is, that God is ever present, ever creative, and that His Providence sustains us in the smallest detail of our daily life. And He watches while we sleep.

Whatever be the true Christian attitude – and you must pardon an outsider if he judges it from the general teaching of your Churches and the general practice of your people – whatever the true Christian attitude may be, it must be admitted, I think, that the sort of religion I speak of is dormant in England to-day, that religion does not permeate all the thoughts and acts of English men and women, and that for them God is afar off in an inaccessible heaven.

Let me give you an example. On a fine Sunday a bus-driver will take the air on a common, where he can banish from his mind the sense of petrol, or the apprehensive clutch on the steering-wheel, and the unwavering watch on the traffic, and where he can enjoy the beauty of the world in tranquillity.

Good! He could not do better. He needs the holiday. But he does not feel religious on the common and he would be embarrassed if you suggested that he should. He does not realise that he might profitably thank God for the glory of the earth and the all-surrounding heaven. His religion, if he is ever conscious of it, is a quite separate thing.

Now, if I were on a golf-course, let us say, and it was the due occasion, I should pray to God. I should not make a show of it, but I should go apart to pray, and I should turn myself towards the South-East, towards Mecca. There would be no feeling that I was passing from one mood, much less from one world to another. My delight in God's world, my delight in the free movement of my body as I swung my club would culminate naturally in a prayer of thanksgiving to God who gives and sustains.

There is value in formal observances. I think it is well that a man should make a habit of formal prayer night and morning, for protection and in thanks. But, I place emphasis on the continual direct relation between God and man. And of recent years the best of Islam has done the same.

No. I do not believe in a union of all religions. That would destroy them all. I am an anti-mixer. Let each Church give its witness and its message. I gather that theosophy is a mixture, tolerating all creeds; I know nothing about it, except that it is neither a religion nor a science . . .

You think that we have forgotten the message of Christ? That is where we disagree with you. We think that we are the true Christians, and that your Church distorted the message. We think that the Fatherhood of God and the Sonship of Man has no particular and special application to the One Son of Man . . .

Of course, we hold fast by the Koran, for it is from the Koran that we get the texts which buttress our faith in the ever-watchful eye and sustaining hand of God.

Have we become less vehemently propagandist than we were of old time? Well, we have our mission in London. But I do not know that I should like the whole of England converted to Islam. Let each message be given clearly and boldly! But I wish that some well-known Englishman might, like Lord Headlam, become a convert and found a mosque in London. I should like to see a flourishing mosque in the centre of London, so that London might see what the message of Islam really is . . .

The business of your Churches is to teach the ever-present and ever sustaining God, and the business of the religious man is to live in continual consciousness and intimate relation with the Might and Glory of God.

Associated with that is the need to accept God's will joyfully, to acclaim what happens to us as a benefit, however much it may seem to the irreligious a misfortune. "It is the will of Allah", is said by us of Islam, not with sad resignation, but with pious hope.

When I say that religion should permeate life, I am thinking not only of private life but of national and international life. As you know, I am doing my best to persuade Europe not to rush madly into another Great War. The last Great War of 1914–18 was one of the greatest catastrophes of all time. Another Great War would destroy civilization.

Source: *Message of H.R.H. Prince Aga Khan III*, Mombasa, 1955, pp. 23–5.

228

MY PHILOSOPHY OF HAPPINESS

An Article

Undated

Advice to his heirs – satisfaction within oneself – the twin problem of existence – misfortunes in life – beauties of nature – need for healthy body and fitness – happiness depends on oneself – sports – duty of the government – war is always a mistake – need for peace.

"Learn to wish for the thing that happens and not try to mould the event to your desire." In these words the Aga Khan gave his last Will and Testament in an interview to Mr. W. R. Titterton.

He thinks that war is a ghastly affair and that the last war was almost the death-blow to civilization.

"I should, first of all, advise my heirs to learn to desire the thing that happens, and not try to mould events to their desires. It was silly of the poet Omar to write:

> Ah love, could you and I with Him conspire
> To grasp this sorry scheme of things entire,
> Would we not shatter it to bits, and then
> Remould it nearer to the heart's desire?

"That way lies unhappiness, destruction. It is not a sorry scheme of things, and the business, the duty of man, is to get himself into harmony with it.

"I would counsel my heirs to seek satisfaction, not in the flux of circumstances, but within themselves; I would have them resolute, self-controlled, independent, but not rebellious. Let them seek communion with that Eternal Reality which I call Allah and you call God! For that is the twin problem of existence –

1413

to be at once entirely yourself and altogether at one with the Eternal.

"I say that you should endeavour to suit your desire to the event, and not the event to your desire. If a wall tumbles down and crushes my foot, I must say: 'That is the best thing that could happen to me.'

"An uncle of mine had a son who was killed. The father gave thanks to Allah for the event. You think that he did not love his son? You are wrong. He loved him dearly. I confess that I may not yet have risen to such a spiritual height. But I believe that I shall rise to it. I know that this is the way to happiness.

"I should have a word to say to those who deem themselves unfortunate from a worldly point of view. I should say to them: do not look up and lament that you are not as well off as those above you; look down and congratulate yourself that you are better off than those below you.

"To a man who looks with such eyes upon the world it is not a prison but a garden. A marvellous garden – the garden of the Lord. I shall invite my heirs to feast their eyes on the miraculous beauty of the earth – rivers and seas to slake the earth's eternal thirst, hills like the tents of a great encampment, forests like an army with banners; wide open spaces, dawns and sunsets, the indomitable arch of the sky.

"All these great gifts are freely given to the man with open eyes, open hands and open heart. But the eyes must be clear, the hands and heart must be strong. I would impress upon my heirs the absolute need to be healthy. If they neglect their body, they will be at odds with the universe.

"Therefore I say: Keep your bodies clean – bathe them frequently – wear clean clothes – eat clean food, drink clean water, breathe clean air. I know that society may make it difficult for some of its citizens to get these things. Instead it should make it easy.

"But we are not, as individuals, to put the onus on society. As I have said, it is our business to 'use' events, conditions, limitations. If we cannot be as fit as an Achilles champion, we may yet aim at absolute fitness, and be well content with the fitness we achieve.

"Never forget this: The society in which we live cannot give a man happiness. If we miss that, you miss my point altogether. Society can give a man space to breathe and freedom to move in it; it can afford him the means of keeping himself healthy and making himself strong. But happiness never depends on one's surroundings; it depends altogether and exclusively on oneself.

"Of course, health is not static, but dynamic. I can only judge a racehorse for example when I have seen it in motion. Therefore I shall speak to my heirs of the vital importance of exercise. And since to take joy in your activities is one of the secrets of health, I should counsel them to play games.

"Naturally my heirs will be riders of horses. That is in the blood. The 'horse and the rider' have been the sign manual of my race for a thousand years. But I speak of concerted games.

"Knowing something of tennis and a little golf, I can advise them to play those games. Knowing very little of cricket except as a spectator, I must be content to regard that great game with benevolent neutrality. But, play games! Play them joyfully, vehemently, with all your heart.

"My final word would be to civilised society at large. I have already suggested that society should give a man space and the means to make himself healthy. Now pursue the implication and tell society that it should give the individual peace. That is what a government is for, it is the final test; if a government cannot give us that it is not worth having. I am a pacifist.

"I would have the whole world unite to defend itself against aggression. Your nationalist instincts may be opposed to this. But see what those instincts have done for you! You have broken Germany. Yes! but you have broken yourselves. I don't say that you were at fault. I don't say that you could have avoided doing what you did. For the pre-war Prussian was – no, not criminal – impossible. But I do say that War is always a ghastly mistake, and that this last war was almost the death-blow to civilisation.

"And so in my testament I should say to the rulers of the earth: Prove yourselves: Prove that you are worth having; give the world peace!"

Source: *Message of H.R.H. Prince Aga Khan III*, Mombasa, 1955, pp. 26–8.

THE FINAL RECONCILIATION BETWEEN SUNNI AND SHIA DOCTRINES

A Declaration

Undated

The foundation of Imami Ismailism – the position of the *Ulu'l-amr Menkom* – public proclamation of the reconciliation between Shia and Sunni doctrines.

It is more than ever necessary that the foundation of Imami Ismailism should be understood by the new generation of Ismailis throughout the world. If those who believe that Hazrat Aly was the rightful successor of the Prophet to be the 'Ulu'l-amr Menkom must accept the principle of that succession for the same reasons they accept in the case of Hazrat Aly his rightful Imam descendants.

The Imami Ismailis maintain that the position of the 'Ulu'l-amr Menkom never dies out and this succession goes on till the day of judgement on earth. For this reason Ismailis celebrate the exceptionally long Imamat as they would celebrate every ascension to the spiritual throne of the Imamat in each century. In the present Imamat the final reconciliation between the Shiah and Sunni doctrines has been publicly proclaimed by myself on exactly the same lines as Hazrat Aly did at the death of the Prophet and during the first thirty years after that. The political and worldly Khalifat was accepted by Hazrat Aly in favour of the three first Khalifs voluntarily and with goodwill for the protection of the interests of the Muslims throughout the world.

We Ismailis now in the same spirit accept the Khalifat of the first Khalifs and such other Khalifs as during the last thirteen centuries helped the cause of Islam, politically, socially and from a worldly point of view. On the other hand the Spiritual Imamat remained with Hazrat Aly and remains with his direct descendants always alive till the day of Judgement. That a spiritual succession to the Imamat makes the Imam the 'Ulu'l-amr Menkom always according to the Koran and though he has his moral claim to the Khalifat as well, always he can, like Hazrat Aly himself owing to the conditions of the world accept and support such worldly authorities as the Imam believes help the cause of Islam. Thus a final reconciliation without upsetting either Sunni or Shiah doctrine has been proclaimed always by me as the faith of all the Ismailis.

Source: *Itehad-el-Islam, Otherwise Known as the Cultural, Religious, Economic Pan-Islamism,* Pan-Islam Series no. 5, n.p., n.p.p., n.d., pp. 1–4.

The introductory note in the pamphlet ran:

"As Imam of the Ismailis H.R.H. Prince Aga Khan made two very important declarations for the unity of Islam to the Muslim world on the final reconciliations of the Sunni and Shiah doctrines as understood by the Ismailis."

APPENDICES

British Monarchs

	date of accession
Victoria	20 June 1837
Edward VII	23 January 1901
George V	6 May 1910
Edward VIII	20 January 1936
George VI	11 December 1936
Elizabeth II	6 February 1952

British Prime Ministers

	date of taking office
Marquess of Salisbury, *Conservative*	2 July 1895
Arthur James Balfour, *Conservative*	12 July 1902
Sir Henry Campbell-Bannerman, *Liberal*	5 December 1905
Herbert Henry Asquith, *Liberal, Coalition*	8 April 1908
David Lloyd George, *Coalition*	7 December 1916
Andrew Bonar Law, *Conservative*	23 October 1922
Stanley Baldwin, *Conservative*	22 May 1923
James Ramsay MacDonald, *Labour*	22 January 1924
Stanley Baldwin, *Conservative*	4 November 1924
James Ramsay MacDonald, *Labour, Coalition*	8 June 1929
Stanley Baldwin, *Coalition*	7 June 1935
Arthur Neville Chamberlain, *Coalition*	28 May 1937
Winston Spencer Churchill, *Coalition*	11 May 1940
Clement Richard Attlee, *Labour*	26 July 1945
Winston Spencer Churchill, *Conservative*	26 October 1951
Sir Anthony Eden, *Conservative*	6 April 1955
Harold Macmillan, *Conservative*	13 January 1957

Secretaries of State for India

	date of taking office
Lord George Francis Hamilton	4 July 1895
William St. John Brodrick	9 October 1903
John Morley	11 December 1905
Earl of Crewe	7 November 1910
Joseph Austen Chamberlain	27 May 1915
Edwin Samuel Montagu	20 July 1917
Viscount Peel	21 March 1922
Lord Olivier	23 January 1924
Earl of Birkenhead	7 November 1924
Viscount Peel	1 November 1928
William Wedgwood Benn	8 June 1929
Sir Samuel Hoare	26 August 1931
Marquess of Zetland	7 June 1935
Leopold Stennett Amery	15 May 1940
Lord Pethick-Lawrence	3 August 1945
Earl of Listowel	23 April 1947

Governors General and Viceroys of India

	date of taking office
Earl of Elgin	20 January 1894
Baron Curzon of Kedleston	6 January 1899
Earl of Minto	18 November 1905
Baron Hardinge	23 November 1910
Baron Chelmsford	4 April 1916
Earl of Reading	2 April 1921
Lord Irwin	3 April 1926
Earl of Willingdon	18 April 1931
Marquess of Linlithgow	18 April 1936
Earl Wavell	20 October 1943
Viscount Mountbatten	24 March 1947

BIOGRAPHICAL NOTES

Abbas, Shah (1557–1628)
Safavi emperor of Persia. Ruled, 1585 till death. Won back lost territory from the Uzbeks, Turks and the Indian Mughals. A great patron of literature and the arts.

Abdali, Ahmad Shah (c. 1722–1773)
Real name: Ahmad Khan. Son of Malik Muhammad Zaman Khan, who lived in the vicinity of Herat. Taken prisoner by Nadir Shah when he captured Qandhar in 1738. Starting as a mace-bearer he was, by degrees, promoted to a considerable command in the army. On Nadir Shah's death, he was able to build, for the first time, an Afghan kingdom. Later he took for himself the title of *Durr-i-Durran* (Pearl of Pearls), and thus his tribe, the Abdalis, also come to be known as Duvranis. During his 26-year reign (1746–73), he invaded India eight times. In 1752 he captured the Punjab and fixed the boundary of his Indian empire at Sarhind; in the same year he occupied Kashmir. In 1756 he marched up to Delhi, but had to retreat because of an outbreak of cholera in his camp. In 1761 he routed the Marathas at the third Battle of Panipat. Later he worsted the Sikhs but could not put an end to their power because they refused to face him in pitched battles. He did not return to India after 1769. Among the results of his incursions into India were the further weakening of the Mughal Empire, the final end of Maratha presence in north India, the rise of the Sikh power, and a prolonged period of anarchy and oppression in the Punjab.

Abdul Hamid II, Sultan (1842–1918)
Sultan of Turkey. Second son of Sultan Abdul Majid. Succeeded, 1876, on the deposition of his brother, Murad. His reign was

notable for wars with Russia in 1877–78 and Greece in 1897. Deposed and exiled in 1909.

Abingdon, 7th Earl of: Montagu Arthur Bertie (1836–1928)
Educated at Eton. Succeeded father, 1884. Married, first, 1858, Caroline (died 1873), second, 1883, Gwendeline.

Abu Bakr (d. 634)
The first Khalifa of Islam. His real name was Abdullah; Abu Bakr ("father of the maiden") is a *kunyah,* a paternity name. Originally a rich merchant of Mecca, he was the second, after Bibi Khadijah, to believe in the mission of the Prophet and accompanied him on his escape from Mecca to Medina. He was known as as-Siddiq on account of his unswerving loyalty to the Prophet and an unshakeable belief in the new faith. He took the Prophet's place to lead the prayers during the latter's illness. His daughter, Aisha married the Prophet. During the early days of Islam, Abu Bakr used his wealth to help the Muslim community through its difficult times. He was elected Caliph in 632, and for two years held together the Muslim community and consolidated Islam's victories in Arabia.

Adamson, Sir Harvey (1854–1941)
Son of Rev. Alexander Adamson. Educated at the University of Aberdeen; read mathematics. Entered ICS, 1875. Joined the Burma Commission, 1877. Deputy Commissioner, 1886–93. Commissioner, 1894–99. Judicial Commissioner, 1900–05. Member Indian Legislative Council, 1903–05, 1906–10. Chief Judge of Burma, 1905–06. Lt.-Governor of Burma, 1910–15. Knighted in 1906. Created KCSI, 1910.

Ajmal Khan, Hakim Muhammad (1863–1927)
Educated traditionally in Arabic and Persian learning and in medicine. Later taught himself English. Personal physician to the Nawab of Rampur, 1892–1901. Member, Indian Muslim Deputation, Simla, 1906. Founder-Member, All India Muslim League, Dacca, 1906. Member, Board of Management, Nadwat-ul-Ulema; President of the Nadwa's annual session, 1906. Founded Unani Tibbia organization, 1906. Vice-President, All India Muslim League. Created Haziq-ul-Mulk, 1907, renounced the title, 1920. Chairman, Reception Committee, Indian National Congress, Delhi Session, 1918. President, All India Muslim League, Amritsar Session, 1919. President, Indian National Congress, 1921. First Chancellor of the Jamia Millia, 1920. Trustee, MAO College,

Aligarh, till 1920. Chairman, Reception Committee, All India Hindu Mahasabha, Delhi Session, 1921. President, All India Khilafat Conference, Ahmedabad Session, 1921. Joined the Congress Swarajya Party, 1923. Retired from politics, 1925. A close friend of the Viceroy, Lord Hardinge, after whom he named the hospital he established in Delhi.

Akbar, Jalaluddin Muhammad (1542–1605)
Mughal emperor of India. Son of Humayun. Succeeded father in 1555. Took power into his own hands, 1560. Expanded the empire to cover nearly the whole of the subcontinent. Consolidated, stabilized and administered the empire with exceptional zeal, tolerance, wisdom and vigour. Patron of literature. Attempted to promulgate a new eclectic religion.

Alexander II (1818–1881)
Emperor of Russia. Son of Nicholas I. Married the Princess Marie (1824–80), daughter of the Grand Duke of Hesse, 1841. Succeeded father, 2 March 1855. Emancipated the serfs, 1861. Established elected legislative assemblies in the provinces, 1865. Extended the Russian empire into Central Asia. Fought the Ottoman Empire, 1877–78. Married Katharina Dolgorukova, 1880. Assassinated on 13 March.

Alexander III (1845–1894)
Emperor of Russia. Son of Alexander II. Married Princess Marie Dagmar of Denmark (1847–1928), 1866. Crowned in 1883. Conquered the Turkoman states of Central Asia.

Alexander of Hillsborough, 1st Earl: Albert Victor Alexander (1885–1965)
British Labour politician. Son of an engineer. Member of Parliament (Co-operative Party), 1922. First Lord of the Admiralty, 1929–31, 1940–45, 1945–46. Minister of Defence, 1946–50. Leader of the Labour peers in the House of Lords, 1955. Created Viscount in 1950, Earl in 1963, CH in 1941, and KG in 1964.

Ali ibn Abi Talib (598–661)
A member of the house of Hashim, a cousin of the Prophet, who was to become his son-in-law, and eventually the fourth Caliph, he was one of the first converts to Islam when he was only 13 years of age. He became renowned as a warrior during Islam's struggle for survival. He married Fatimah, the Prophet's daughter, and it is from their two sons, Hasan and Husain, that

the *Sharifs*, or progeny of the Prophet, descend. A third son, Muhsin, died in infancy; there was also a daughter, Zainab. Ali was elected Caliph after Usman's assassination at a time of unrest and mounting difficulties. First, he defeated Talhah and az-Zubair at the Battle of the Camel and then faced the might of Mua- wiyah at the inconclusive Battle of Siffin. After long mediation and negotiation, in which the dice were loaded against Ali, he established himself at Kufah in Iraq. He was assassinated by a Kharijite, ibn Muljam.

Ali is highly revered by the Sufis as the fountainhead of esoteric doctrine. More generally, he is remembered for his piety, nobility, learning, generosity and magnanimity.

In the Shiah faith, Ali is the first Imam, in the special sense in which they understand the term. His tomb in Najaf, Iraq, is a place of pilgrimage.

Ali Imam, Sayyid Sir (1869–1932)
Belonged to Bihar. Elder son of Shams-ul-Ulema Sayyid Imdad Imam. Called to the bar in London, June 1890. Legal practice in Patna. President, All India Muslim League, 1908. Member, Vice- roy's Executive Council, 1910–15. Judge, Patna High Court, 1917. President, Hyderabad Executive Council, 1919–22. Trustee, MAO College, Aligarh. The only leading Muslim to oppose separate electorates for his community.

Altrincham, 1st Baron: Edward William Macleay Grigg (1879–1955)
Son of H. B. Grigg of the ICS. Educated at Winchester and New College, Oxford. On the editorial staff of *The Times*, 1903. Assistant Editor, *Outlook*, 1905–06. Again in *The Times*, 1908–13. Served in World War One. Private Secretary to Lloyd George, 1921–22. MP, 1922–25, 1933–45. Governor of Kenya, 1925–31. Financial Secretary, War Office, 1940. Joint Parliamentary Under Secretary of State for War, 1940–42. Minister Resident in the Middle East, 1944–45. Editor, *National Review*, 1948–55. CMG 1919, KCVO 1920, KCMG 1928, PC 1944. Author.

Ambedkar, Dr. Bhimrao Ramji (1893–1956)
Belonged to Bombay Presidency. Educated at Elphinstone College, Bombay, Columbia University, and London School of Economics. Called to the bar in London, 1923. Professor of Economics, Sydenhan College of Commerce and Economics, Bombay, 1917–20. Legal practice in Bombay, 1924. Founded and edited several Marathi weeklies, 1919–30. Professor, Government Law College, Bombay, 1928. Perry Professor of Jurisprudence,

University of Bombay, 1935. Member, Bombay Legislative Assembly, 1926–34. Delegate to the Round Table Conference, 1930–31. Founded the Independent Labour Party of India, 1936, and the All India Scheduled Castes Federation, 1942. Member, Viceroy's Executive Council, 1942–46. Minister of Law, India, 1947–51. Embraced Buddhism, 1956. Author of several books.

Amery, Leopold Stennett (1873–1955)
Son of Charles F. Amery of the Indian Forest Department. Educated at Harrow and Balliol College, Oxford (double first). Fellow, All Souls College, Oxford, 1897. On the editorial staff of *The Times*, 1899–1909. Called to the bar, 1902. Member of Parliament (Unionist), 1911–45. Served in the War, 1914–16. First Lord of the Admiralty, 1922–24. Secretary of State for the Colonies, 1924–29. Secretary of State for the Dominions, 1925–29. Secretary of State for India, 1940–45. PC, 1922. Created CH in 1945. Honorary doctorates from the Universities of Oxford, Durham and Cambridge. Author of many books.

Ampthill, 2nd Baron: Arthur Oliver Villiers Russell (1869–1935)
Born in Rome. Succeeded father, 1884. Educated at New College, Oxford. President of Oxford Union Society, 1891. One of the founders of the National Party, 1918. President of Council, National Party, 1919. Assistant Private Secretary to Joseph Chamberlain, 1895–97; Private Secretary, 1897–99. Governor of Madras, 1899–1906. Served in World War One. President, London Rowing Club. Chairman, Bedfordshire County Council.

Amr ibn al-Asi (d. 663)
A Quraishi who, after his conversion to Islam, went on to become one of the most successful Muslim military leaders. He took part in the campaign in Syria in 635 and conquered Egypt in 641. He was appointed the governor of Egypt and founded a camp city at Fustat on the eastern bank of the Nile, near the present-day Cairo. Dismissed by the Caliph Usman and sensing the victory of the Umayyads in the struggle following the assassination of Usman, he joined the army of Muawiyah and fought against Ali at the Battle of Siffin in 567. He is said to have devised the idea of having Muawiyah's troops attach leaves of the Quran to their lances. When Muawiyah became Caliph he reinstated Amr as governor of Egypt. He died in office at a very advanced age.

Andrews, Charles Freer (1871–1940)
British journalist and priest. Worked in South Africa, 1913–14,

where he met Gandhi, and in Fiji, 1915–17. Adviser, Indian Delegation to Kenya Negotiations, London, 1923. Correspondent of the *Manchester Guardian, Natal Advertiser, Toronto Star* and the *Hindu.* A close associate and friend of Gandhi.

Anwari, Auhaduddin Ali bin Wahiduddin Muhammad (c. 1126–1189/90)
Persian poet, the greatest in the circle of poets around Sanjar at the Saljuq court. Equally versed in poetry and the sciences of the time, mathematics, astrology and philosophy. Ended his life in retirement and scholarly pursuits. Regarded as the greatest poet of *qasida.* Also distinguished in *ghazal.* Composed *rubaiyyat* and *muqattaat* of a more personal character. Among his scientific writings is a commentary on Ibna Sina.

Arcot, Prince of: Sir Ghulam Muhammad Ali Khan (1882–1952)
Succeeded father, Sir Muhammad Munawwar Khan, 1903. Premier Muslim nobleman of Southern India, being the direct male representative of the sovereign rulers of the Carnatic. Member, Madras Legislative Council, 1904–06, 1916. Member, Imperial Legislative Council, 1910–13. President, All India Muhammadan Association, Lahore. Khan Bahadur, 1897. KCIE, 1909. GCIE, 1917. Personal distinction of His Highness, 1935. Lived in Madras.

Arnold, Sir Thomas Walker (1864–1930)
Educated at Magdalene College, Cambridge. Teacher in Philosophy, MAO College, Aligarh, 1888–98. Professor of Philosophy, Government College, Lahore, 1898–1904. Assistant Librarian, India Office, 1904–09. Educational Adviser for Indian Students in England, 1900–20. Professor of Arabic and Islamic Studies, University of London, 1921–30. Knighted, 1921. Fellow of British Academy, 1926. Orientalist. Author of several books on Islam.

al-Ashari, Abu-l-Hasan Ali ibn Ismail (873–935)
Founder of the Sunni *Kalam* or theology. Born and raised in Basrah, until the age of forty he was a Mutazilite and thenceforth a Hanbali Sunni; yet he ended up as a reformed rationalist. He believed in the doctrine of *Kasb* (lit. "acquisition") regarding action. One of the most accepted authorities in theology. Author of several works.

Ashoka (fl. 3rd century BC)
An emperor of ancient India. Ruled 264–223 BC. A convert to Buddhism, he organized it as the state religion.

Asquith, Countess of Oxford and Asquith: Emma Alice Margaret (generally known as Margot) (1864–1945)
Sixth daughter of Sir Charles Tennant (1823–1906), MP, merchant and art patron. Married H. H. Asquith as his second wife in 1894. Her magnetic personality made her a legend in her lifetime. Greatly influenced taste and fashion. Author of three volumes of reminiscences.

Auchinleck, Field Marshal Sir Claude John Eyre (1884–1981)
British soldier. Entered the Indian Army, 1904. Served in World War One in Egypt and Mesopotamia. Commander-in-Chief in India till July 1947 and 1943–46. Commander-in-Chief in the Middle East, 1941–43. Supreme Commander, India and Pakistan, 1947. Created Field Marshal in 1946, CB in 1934, and GCB in 1945.

Augustus, Gaius Julius Caesar Octavianus (63 BC–14 AD)
First Roman emperor. Son of Gaius Octavius and Atia. His sister, Octavia, married Mark Antony. Became sole ruler of the Roman world, 31 BC. Beautified Rome, and built many new cities in the empire. His age in literature produced men like Virgil, Ovid, Properitus and Livy.

Aurangzeb, Muhayyuddin Alamgir (1618–1707)
The last great Mughal emperor of India. Son of Shahjahan. Imprisoned his father and killed his brothers to ascend the throne in 1760. Pious and hardworking, but intolerant in religion and illiterate in culture. Fought the Shia Muslim states of South India for many years, thus weakening the empire.

Babur, Zahiruddin (1483–1530)
Founder of the Mughal Empire in India. Descended on his father's side from Timur (Tamerlane) and on his mother's side from Chingiz Khan. Inherited from his father the principality of Farghana, now in Chinese Turkistan. Entered the Punjab in 1524 and occupied Lahore, but was obliged to return to his base in Kabul. Returned to India in 1526, defeated Sultan Ibrahim Lodi at the Battle of Panipat on 21 April, vanquished the Rana of Mewar on 16 March 1527, and humbled the recalcitrant Afghan chiefs of Bihar and Bengal at Gogra on 6 May 1529. These strings of victories made him the master of the territories lying between Afghanistan and Bengal and extending from the foot of the Himalayas to Gwalior. His five direct male descendants ruled

the subcontinent till 1707 in unprecedented glory and (except for Aurangzeb) with undiminished power.

Bacon, Francis: Baron Verulam of Verulam, Viscount St. Albans (1561–1626)
English philosopher and statesman. Younger son of Sir Nicholas Bacon (1509–79), English statesman and Lord Keeper of the Great Seal. Educated at Trinity College, Cambridge. Called to the bar at the Gray's Inn, 1576. MP, 1584. Knighted in 1603. Commissioner for the Union of Scotland and England, 1603. Published *Advancement of Learning,* 1605. Married the daughter of a London alderman, 1606. Solicitor General, 1607. Attorney General, 1613. Privy Councillor, 1616. Lord Chancellor, 1618. Published *Novum Organum,* 1620. Created Viscount in 1621. Arraigned by the House of Lords and imprisoned; released and pardoned by the King after a few months. Author of several essays and books.

Baldwin of Bewdley, 1st Earl: Stanley Baldwin (1867–1947)
British Conservative statesman. Educated at Harrow and Trinity College, Cambridge. In the family iron and steel business. MP, 1906. President of the Board of Trade, 1921. Prime Minister, 1923–31 and 1935–37. Lord President of the Council, 1931–35. Resigned and was created an Earl, 1937.

Banerjee, Sir Surendranath (1848–1925)
Second son of Dr. Durga Charan Banerjea, a physician. Educated at Doveton College, Calcutta, and University College, London. Entered ICS, 1871; left it, 1874. Professor of English Literature, Metropolitan Institution, Calcutta, 1875. Founded Indian Association, 1876. Founded Ripon College, Calcutta, 1882. President, Indian National Congress twice. Member, Bengal Legislative Council for 8 years. Member Imperial Legislative Council, 1913–20. President Moderate Conference, 1918. Member, Franchise Committee, 1918. Minister for Local Self-Government, Bengal. Edited the *Bengalee.* Knighted in 1921. Married, 1867.

Baroda, Maharajah Gaekwar of: Sir Sayaji Rao III (1863–1939)
Educated at Maharajah's School, Baroda. Succeeded to the throne, 1875; invested with powers, 1881. Represented India at the Imperial Conference, 1937. Salute of 21 guns. Hon. LL.D., Benares Hindu University, 1924. GCSI, 1881. GCIE, 1919. Author.

Bayazid Bistami, Abuyazid Taifur bin Isa (d *c.* 777)
One of the most celebrated Islamic Sufis. Spent most of his life in Bistam and died there. In his sayings (he wrote nothing) he is very daring and implies a state of mind in which the mystic has an experience of himself as of one merged with the deity and turned into God. The numinous sense is very highly developed in him.

Beaman, Sir Frank Clement Offley (1858–1928)
Son of Surgeon-General A. H. Beaman. Educated at Oxford. Entered ICS, 1879. Served in Baroda and Kathia. Sessions Judge, 1896. Judicial Commissioner and Judge of Sadar Court, Sind, 1906–18. Knighted in 1917. Author of some philosophical writings.

Beaverbrook, 1st Baron: William Maxwell Aitken (1879–1964)
Born in Canada. Educated at the Public Board School, Newcastle, New Brunswick. MP (Unionist), 1910–16. Minister of Information, 1918. Minister for Aircraft Production, 1940–41. Minister of Supply, 1941–42. Lord Privy Seal, 1943–45. Knighted 1911. Baronet 1916. PC 1918. Baron 1917.

Benn, Sir Ernest John Pickstone (1875–1954)
British Publisher. Son of Sir John Williams Benn, 1st Baronet. Succeeded father, 1922. Married 1903. School education. Chairman, Benn Brothers, 1922–41, and Ernest Benn, 1924–25. President, Society of Individualists, 1942. CBE 1918. Author.

Bennett, (Enoch) Arnold (1867–1931)
Educated at Middle School, Newcastle under Lyme. Solicitors' clerk in London, 1888–93. Editor of *Woman*, 1896–1900. Lived in Paris, 1902–12. Powerful journalist in aid of war effort, 1914–18. Contributor to the *Evening Standard* of London. Novelist. Playwright. Man of letters.

Bhopal, Nawab of: Sir Muhammad Hamidullah Khan (1894–1960)
Succeeded mother, 1926. Married Princess Maimunah. Educated at the MAO College, Aligarh. President, Bhopal City Municipality, 1915–16. Trustee, MAO College, Aligarh, 1916. Chief Secretary, Bhopal Government, 1916–22. Minister of Law, Justice and Finance, Bhopal, 1922–26. Chancellor, Aligarh University, 1930–35. Chancellor, Chamber of Indian Princess, 1931–32 and 1944–47. GCIE 1929. GCSI 1932.

Bhopal, Nawab of: Sultan Jahan Begam (1858–1930)
Succeeded mother (Shahjahan Begam), 1901. Married Ahmed

Ali Khan, 1874. Salute of 21 guns. Abdicated in favour of her only surviving son, 1926. GCIE, 1904. GCSI, 1910. GBE, 1918.

Bhownagree, Sir Mancherjee Merwanjee (1851–1933)
A Parsi of Bombay. Educated at Elphinstone College, Bombay. Began life as a journalist. State Agent of Bombay for the territory of Bhavnagar, 1873. MP (Conservative) for Bethnal Green, 1895–1906. Order of the Lion and Sun, Persia. KCIE, 1897. Author.

Bismarck, Otto Edward Leopold Von (1815–1898)
German Chancellor. Studied law and agriculture at Göttingen, Berlin and Greifswald. Member of Prussian parliament and of the resuscitated German diet of Frankfurt. Minister to St. Petersburg, 1859, and to Paris, 1862. Foreign Minister and President of the Cabinet, 1862. Annexed the duchies of Schleswig and Holstein, 1863. Defeated Austria, 1866. Reorganized Germany under Prussian leadership. After the Franco-Prussian War, in February 1871, he dictated the terms of peace to France. Created a Count in 1866 and a Prince in 1871. Appointed Chancellor of the new German Empire, 1871. He gave Germany universal suffrage, reformed coinage, codified law, nationalized the railways, enlarged army and protective tariff. Presided over the Congress of Berlin, 1878. Resigned the Chancellorship in March 1890, and was created Duke of Lauenburg.

Botha, Louis (1862–1919)
South African statesman and soldier. Member of Transvaal Volksraad. Commander-in-Chief of the Boer forces, 1900. Prime Minister of the Transvaal Colony, 1907. First Prime Minister of the Union of South Africa, 1910. Conquered German South-West Africa, 1914–15.

Brabourne, 5th Baron: Michael Herbert Rudolph Knatchbull (1895–1939)
Son of 4th Baron. Succeeded father, 1933. Educated at Wellington and Royal Military Academy, Woolwich. Served in World War One, 1915–18. MP (Unionist), 1931–33. Parliamentary Private Secretary to the Secretary of State for India, 1932–33. Governor of Bombay, 1933–37. Governor of Bengal, 1937–39. Died in office. GCIE, 1933. GCSI, 1937.

Brassey, 1st Earl of: Thomas Brassey (1836–1918)
Son of Thomas Brassey (1805–70). Educated at Rugby and Uni-

versity College, Oxford. Called to the bar in 1866. Civil Lord of the Admiralty, 1880–84. Governor of Victoria, 1895–1900. Founded and edited (1886–90) *The Naval Annal.* Author of political and naval studies.

Bray, Sir Denys de Saumarez (1875–1951)
Educated at Stuttgart and Balliol College, Oxford. Entered ICS 1898. Served in the Punjab, Baluchistan and the North-West Frontier Province. Deputy Secretary, Foreign Department, Government of India, 1916; Joint Secretary, 1919; Foreign Secretary, 1920–30. Member Indian Council, 1930–37. Adviser to the Secretary of State for India, 1937. Member, Imperial Legislative Council, 1918; Council of State, 1921; Indian Legislative Assembly, 1922–29. Indian Delegate to the League of Nations, 1930–37. KCIE, 1925; KCSI, 1930. Author.

Briand, Aristide (1862–1932)
French socialist and statesman. Framed the law for the separation of Church and State, 1905. Foreign Minister, 1925–32. Prime Minister for eleven times. Shared (with Gustav Stresemann) the Nobel prize for peace, 1926. Advocated a United States of Europe.

Brown, Sir Frank Herbert (1868–1959)
Son of Rev. J. Brown. Leader writer and assistant editor, *Bombay Gazette,* for 5 years. Editor, *Indian Daily Telegraph,* Lucknow, for 2 years. London correspondent of *The Times of India.* On the editorial staff of *The Times,* 1902–54. Honorary Secretary, East India Association, 1927–54. Created CIE, 1921. Knighted in 1937. Coronation Medal, 1953. Author of several works.

Browne, Edward Granville (1862–1926)
Educated at Pembroke College, Cambridge. Fellow of Pembroke, 1887. Visited Persia, 1887–88. Lecturer in Persian, University of Cambridge, 1888, and Sir Thomas Adams's Professor of Arabic, 1902. Fellow, British Academy, 1903. One of the foremost British Orientalists and author of *A Literary History of Persia.*

Buddha, Gautama (*c.* 568–*c.* 488 BC)
Founder of a great religion in India. Son of the Raja of the Sakya tribe. Personal name was Siddhartha. At the age of 30 he abandoned his palace, power and family for a life of asceticism and search for truth. His religion was a revolutionary reformation of Brahmanism.

Burke, Edmund (1729–1797)
Educated at Trinity College, Dublin. Private Secretary to William Gerard Hamilton, 1759–64, and to Lord Rockingham, 1765. MP, 1766. Led the impeachment of Warren Hastings. One of the proprietors of the East India Company. Statesman, orator, democrat and philosopher.

Butler, Sir Spencer Harcourt (1869–1938)
Educated at Harrow and Balliol College, Oxford. Entered the ICS, 1889. Secretary, Foreign Department, 1907–10, and Education Department, 1910–15, Government of India. Lieutenant Governor of Burma, 1915–18, and the United Provinces, 1918–21. Governor of the United Provinces, 1921–23, and of Burma, 1923–27. Chairman, Indian States Committee, 1927–29. Created KCSI, 1911, and GCSI, 1928.

Cadell, Sir Patrick Robert (1871–1961)
Son of Col. Thomas Cadell, VC. Educated at Edinburgh Academy, Haileybury College, and Balliol College, Oxford. Played football for Oxford and England. In the ICS, 1891–1926, in Bombay and Calcutta. Chairman, Bombay Port Trust. Commissioner of Sind, 1925–26. Retired, 1927. President of the Council of Junagadh State, 1932–35. President of the Council of the Sangli State, 1937; and of Rajkot State, 1938. Created CIE, 1913; CSI, 1919. Knighted in 1935. Author of several works.

Caesar, Gaius Julius (100 or 102 BC–44 BC)
Roman emperor. Son of a Roman practor. Married Cernelia, aughter of Cinna, 83 BC. Elected pontifex, 74 BC. Became leader of the democratic party, 70 BC. Quaestor in Spain, 68. Married Pompeia, a relative of Pompey, 67 BC. Elected consul, 60 BC, and formed, with Pompey and Crassus, the First Triumvirate, 60 BC. Conquered a large part of Europe and England, 58–48 BC, and Egypt and Africa, 47–46 BC. Given the title of "Father of His Country" and *imperator*, made dictator for life, and elected consul for 10 years. His person was declared sacred, and even divine. Assassinated on 15 March. Ruler, conqueror, mathematician, philologist, jurist and architect.

Canning, 1st Earl: Charles John Canning (1812–1862)
Educated at Eton and Christ Church, Oxford. MP, 1836. Created a Peer, 1837. Under Secretary of State for Foreign Affairs. Postmaster General. Governor General of India, February 1855. Viceroy of India, 1 November 1858–11 March 1862. The first

Governor General and Viceroy to be appointed under the Indian Councils Act of 1858. Created Earl in May 1859.

Carnegie, Andrew (1835–1918)
Scottish ironmaster. Son of a weaver. Family emigrated to Pittsburgh, USA, in 1848. Factoryhand, telegraphist and railway clerk, he invested his savings in oil lands, and, after the Civil War, in business which grew into the largest steel and iron works in America. Retired in 1901. His benefactions exceeded £70 million. Author of a few works.

Carnot, Lazare Hippolyte (1801–1888)
French politician. In early life a disciple of St. Simon. Then devoted himself to a more orthodox and virtuous socialism. Minister of Public Instruction, briefly, 1848. Member of the Corps Législatif, 1863, and of the National Assembly, 1871. Elected a Senator, 1875. Author.

Carnot, Marie François Sadi (1837–1894)
French statesman. Son of Lazare Hippolyte Carnot (1801–88), French politician. Educated at the École Polytechnique and became a civil engineer. Member of the National Assembly, 1871. Finance minister, 1879 and 1887. President of the Republic, 1887. Assassinated by an anarchist on 24 June.

Carr, Sir Hubert Winch (1877–1955)
Educated at the Abbey, Beckenham. Managing Director, Balmer, Lawrie and Co., Calcutta. President, European Association of India, 1922–25. Delegate to the Round Table Conferences, 1930–33. Director of Tea and Coffee, Ministry of Food, India, 1939–44. President, India Burma Association, 1945–47. Knighted 1925. KCIE 1936.

Castlereagh, 2nd Marquess of: Robert Stewart (1769–1822)
British statesman. Son of the Marquess of Londonderry. Educated at St. John's College, Cambridge. Member, Irish parliament, 1790. Keeper of the Privy Seal, 1796. Chief Secretary for Ireland, 1797. President of the Board of Control, 1802. Minister for War, 1805–06, 1807–09. Secretary of State for Foreign Affairs, 1812–22. Succeeded to his father's marquisate, 1821. Committed suicide.

Chamberlain, Arthur Neville (1869–1940)
British statesman. Son of Joseph Chamberlain by his second marriage. Lord mayor of Birmingham, 1915–16. Chancellor of the

Exchequer, 1923–24, 1931–37. Minister for Health, 1924–29. Prime Minister, 1937–40.

Chandavarkar, Sir Narayan Ganesh (1855–1923)
Educated at Elphistone College, Bombay. Legal practice in Bombay. English editor of *Indu Prakash*. General Secretary, Indian National Social Conference. Vice-Chancellor, University of Bombay, 1909–12. Judge, Bombay High Court, 1901–13. Officiated as Chief Justice of Bombay, June 1909-June 1912. Chief Minister of Indore, 1913–14. President, Bombay Legislative Assembly, 1921–23. Knighted in 1910.

Charlemagne or Charles the Great (742–814)
King of the Franks and Roman Emperor. Eldest son of Pepin the Short, and grandson of Charles Martel. Succeeded father (jointly with his own brother), 768. Sole King, 771. Fought and subdued the Saxons. Stopped Moorish expansion in Spain. Crowned the Roman Emperor, 800. Consolidated his vast empire, 800–814. Zealously promoted education, agriculture, arts, manufactures and commerce. Built sumptuous palaces and churches.

Chaubal, Sir Mahadev Bhaskar (1857–1933)
Educated at Deccan College, Poona. Assistant master, Elphistone High School, Bombay, 1879–83. Vakil, High Court, Bombay, 1883. Government pleader, 1906. Acting Puisne Judge, Bombay High Court, June-July 1908. Member, Executive Council of the Governor of Bombay, 1910, 1915. Member, Royal Commission on the Public Services in India, 1912. CSI, 1911. KCIE, 1917.

Chchattari, Nawab Sir Ahmad Said Khan of (1887–1981)
Educated at the MAO Collegiate School, Aligarh, 1903–07. Succeeded to the family estate, 1898. Honorary Bench Magistrate, 1910. Special Magistrate, 1911. Member, United Provinces Legislative Council, 1920. Minister in the UP Government, 1923. Home Member, UP Executive Council, 1923–26. Governor of UP, June–August 1928, April–November 1933. Delegate to the Round Table Conference. Member, Viceroy's Executive Council for nine weeks, 1932. President, Nizam's Executive Council, 1941–July 1946, June–November 1947. Pro-Chancellor, Aligarh University, January 1950. Chancellor, Aligarh University, December 1965. Honorary LL.D., Aligarh, 1933. Created MBE, 1919; Nawab, 1915,

Hereditary Nawab, 1919; KCIE, 1921; KCSI, 1933; GBE, 1946; renounced all these titles in 1946.

Chelmsford, 1st Viscount: Frederic John Napier Thesiger (1868–1933)
Son of 2nd Baron Chelmsford. Succeeded father, 1905. Educated at Winchester and Magdalen College, Oxford. Fellow of All Souls, Oxford, 1892. Called to the bar at the Inner Temple Inn of Court, 1893. Governor of Queensland, 1905–09, of New South Wales, 1909–13. Viceroy of India, 1916–21. First Lord of Admiralty, 1924. Re-elected Fellow of All Souls, Oxford, 1929; Warden, 1932–33. Privy Councillor, 1916. Viscount, 1921.

Chingiz Khan (1162–1227)
Mongol conqueror. Son of a Mongol chief. Succeeded father at the age of 13. In 1206 he dropped his name Temunjin for that of Chingiz or Jingis or Genghis. Overran the North China empire, 1211. Conquered and annexed Kara-Chitai, 1217. Conquered the Khwarazam empire, 1218–25. His generals conquered Southern Russia. Other lieutenants completed the conquest of Northern China, 1217–23. Warrior, conqueror, administrator and ruler. Organized conquered territories into states.

Chirol, Sir (Ignatius) Valentine (1852–1929)
Born and educated abroad. Clerk in the Foreign Office, 1872–76. Travelled widely, especially in the Near East, 1876–92. In charge of the Foreign Department of *The Times*, 1896–1912. Visited India seventeen times. Member, Royal Commission on Indian Public Services, 1912–14. Knighted in 1912. Author of several books.

Clive, Baron: Robert Clive (1725–1774)
Eldest son of an impoverished Shropshire squire. Arrived in India in 1744 as a writer in the service of the East India Company. Took part in the military action leading to the capture of Fort St. David. In 1751 he was made a Captain in the army and distinguished himself in the taking of Trichinopoly in 1752. Returned to England in 1753 and made an unsuccessful attempt to enter Parliament. Returned to India in 1755, was commissioned as a Lieutenant-Colonel, and was appointed Governor and Commander of Fort St. David. Came to Bengal in 1756, captured Hoogly and Calcutta, and forced Siraj-ud-Daulah to sign a peace treaty at Alinagar. Later through intrigue, courage and the fortune of circumstance, he defeated the Nawab of Bengal at Plassey. Returned to England in 1760, and was raised to the Irish peerage as Lord Clive, Baron of Plassey. He won a seat in

the House of Commons but did not cut a prominent figure in politics. Returned to Bengal as its Governor in 1765, signed a treaty of friendship with the King of Oudh and forced the Mughal Emperor, Shah Alam II, to grant the Company the *diwani* rights over Bengal, Bihar and Orissa. Returned to England in January 1767. Later charged with corruption and nepotism, but acquitted in 1773 after a long and agonizing trial. Committed suicide in 1774. Generally recognized as the founder of the British Empire in India.

Connaught, Duke of: Arthur William (1850–1942)
Third son of Queen Victoria. Born in London. Educated at Woolwich Academy. Married the Princess Louise Margaret of Prussia, 1879; she died in 1917. Created Field Marshal, 1902. Inspector General of Forces, 1904–07. Commander-in-Chief, Mediterranean, 1907–09. Governor General of Canada, 1911–16.

Conrad, Joseph (1857–1924)
Of Polish parentage; original name: Teodor Josef Konrad Korzeniowski. Father died in 1869. Seaman in French merchant marine, 1874. First landed in England, 1878. Naturalized as British subject, 1886. Ship's master; 1886. Left sea merchant service, 1894. Novelist of the first rank.

Cox, Sir Percy Zachariah (1864–1937)
Educated at Harrow and Sandhurst. Entered the army, 1884. Political Agent and Consul, Muscat, 1899–1904. Acting Political Resident and Consul-General, Persian Gulf, 1904–09; Resident, 1909–14. Chief Political Officer, Indian Expeditionary Force "D" in Mesopotamia, 1914–18. Acting Minister in Tehran, 1918–20. High Commissioner in Iraq, 1920–23. Created KCSI, 1911; KCSI, 1915; GCIE, 1917; GCMG, 1922.

Crewe, 1st Marquess of: Robert Offley Ashburton Crewe-Milnes (1858–1945)
Son of Baron Houghton. Educated at Harrow and Trinity College, Cambridge. Succeeded father, 1885. Viceroy of Ireland, 1892–95. Lord President of the Council, 1905–08, 1915–16. Lord Privy Seal, 1908–11, 1912–15. Leader of the House of Lords, 1908. Secretary of State for Colonies, 1908–10. Secretary of State for India, 1910–15. President, Board of Education, 1916. Chairman, London County Council, 1917. Ambassador in Paris, 1922–28. Secretary of State for War, 1931. Leader of the Independent Liberals in the House of Lords, 1936–44. Chancellor,

University of Sheffield, 1918–44. Created Privy Councillor, 1892; Earl, 1895. Knight of the Garter, 1908.

Cripps, Sir Richard Stafford (1889–1952)
British Labour statesman. Son of 1st Baron Parmoor, Charles Alfred Cripps (1852–1941), and Theresa, sister of Beatrice Webb. Educated at Winchester and New College, Oxford (reading chemistry). Called to the bar, 1913. Became the youngest barrister in the country in 1926 and made a fortune in patent and compensation cases. Solicitor General, 1930. Associated with extreme left wing movements, 1931–39. Expelled from the Labour Party, 1939. Ambassador to Moscow, 1940. Lord Privy Seal and Leader of the House of Commons, 1942. Went to India with his "offer", summer 1942. Minister of Aircraft Production, 1942–45. Readmitted to Labour Party and made President of the Board of Trade, 1945. Member, Cabinet Mission to India, 1946. First Minister of Economic Affairs, 1947. Chancellor of the Exchequer, 1947. Resigned in October 1950 on grounds of health. Rector of Aberdeen University, 1942–45. FRS, 1948. CH, 1951.

Cromer, 1st Earl of: Evelyn Baring (1841–1917)
Entered the British Army, 1855; overseas service, 1858–67. Private Secretary to the Viceroy of India (Lord Northbrook), 1872. First British Commissioner in Egypt, 1877; resigned, 1879. British Controller in Egypt, 1879–80. Finance Member, Viceroy's Executive Council, India, 1880–83. Agent and Consul-General in Egypt, 1883–1907. Entered the House of Lords, 1908. President, Dardanelles Commission, 1916. Created KCSI, 1883; GCMG, 1888; Baron, 1892; Viscount, 1899; Earl, 1901. Reviewer of books, *Spectator*, 1912–17. Author of several books.

Cromwell, Oliver (1599–1658)
Educated at Sydney Sussex College, Cambridge. MP for Huntington, 1628, and for Cambridge, 1640. Governor of the Isle of Ely, 1643. Lieutenant General, 1644. Lord Lieutenant of Ireland, 1649. Commander-in-Chief of Britain, 1650. Dissolved the Long Parliament, 1652. Then became the virtual ruler of the country. Refused the title of King, 1657. Protector. Buried in Westminister Abbey, 23 November 1658. Disinterred and hung on the gallows at Tyburn, 30 January 1661.

Cross, 1st Viscount: Richard Assheton Cross (1823–1914)
Son of William Cross. Educated at Rugby and Trinity College,

Cambridge. MP, 1857–86. Secretary of State for Home Affairs, 1874–80, 1885–86. Secretary of State for India, 1886–92. Lord Privy Seal, 1895–1900. Created GCB, 1880; GCSI, 1892. Privy Councillor.

Curtis, Lionel George (1872–1955)
Educated at Haileybury College, and New College, Oxford. Served in South Africa for several years. Beit Lecturer in Colonial History at the University of Oxford. Secretary to the Irish Conference, 1921. Adviser on Irish Affairs, Colonial Office, 1921–24. Coined the word and evolved the concept of "dyarchy" for India, and influenced the making of the Montagu-Chelmsford reforms.

Curzon of Kedleston, Marquess: George Nathaniel Curzon (1859–1925)
Educated at Eton and Balliol College, Oxford, where he was President of the Union, BA, 1882. Fellow of All Souls College, Oxford, 1883. MP 1886. Travelled in Canada, USA, Japan, China, Singapore, Ceylon, India, 1887–88; Russia, Caucasia, Turkistan, 1888–89; Persia, 1889–90; USA, Japan, China, Siam, 1892; the Pamirs, Afghanistan, 1894. Parliamentary Under Secretary of State for India, 1891; for Foreign Affairs, 1895–98; Viceroy of India, 1898–1905. Chancellor, University of Oxford, 1907. Entered the House of Lords as an Irish representative peer, 1908. Lord Privy Seal, 1915. President, Air Board, 1916. In the inner War Cabinet, December 1916. Secretary of State for Foreign Affairs, October 1919, and November 1922. Disappointed at not being designated prime minister, 1923. Lord President of the Council, 1924. Created Baron, 1898; Earl, 1911; Marquess, 1921, Knight of the Garter, 1916

Dadabhoy, Sir Maneckji Byramji (1865–1953)
Educated at St. Xavier's College, Bombay. Called to the bar at Middle Temple, 1887. Legal practice in Bombay. J P, 1888. Shifted to the Central Provinces, 1890. Member, Nagpur Municipal Committee, 1890–1930. Government Advocate, Central Provinces, 1896. Member, Imperial Legislative Council, 1908–16. Governor of the Imperial Bank of India, 1920–32. Member, Indian Council of State, 1921–46; President, 1933–36, 1937–46. Delegate, Round Table Conference, 1931. Knighted 1921. KCIE, 1925. KCSI, 1936. Author.

Dalhousie, 1st Marquess of: James Andrew Broun Ramsay (1812–1860)
Of Scottish lineage. Educated at Harrow and Christ Church, Oxford. Spent a decade in the Parliament, and was President of

the Board of Trade in Sir Robert Peel's administration, 1845–1847. Governor General of India, 1848–56; the youngest person to be appointed to the office. Among the important events of his rule in India were the conquest of the Punjab, treaties with Afghanistan and Qallaat, conquest of Lower Burma, a profitable war in Sikkim, annexation of a large number of native States, a uniform system of centrally-controlled administration, development of modern communications and a new educational policy. Guided by the utilitarian philosophy of Jeremy Bentham and John Stuart Mill. One of the ablest pro-consuls in the long history of British imperialism.

Dante Alighieri (1265–1321)
Italian poet. Son of a lawyer. Baptized as Durante, afterwards contracted into Dante. Met and fell in love with Beatrice, May 1274, and the event determined the whole future course of his life. She died on 9 June 1290, but his Platonic love for her survived her death and his own subsequent marriage. Married Gemma Donati, 1291. Fought at Campaldino, 1289. Minor offices at home and in embassies abroad, he was elected one of the six priors of Florence, 1300. Sent on an embassy to Rome, 1301, and he never went back to Florence. An exile in several countries and states, he settled in Ravenna, where he died and was buried. Author of the *Vita Nuova*, the celebrated *Divina Commedia*, and other works.

Dehlavi, Sir Ali Muhammad Khan (1871–1952)
Barrister-at-Law, 1896. Legal practice at Bombay and Gujerat, 1896–1900; in Sind, 1900–08. Founder-Editor of the Anglo-Sindhi paper, *Al-Haq*, 1902. Chairman, Reception Committee, All India Muslim League, Karachi Session, 1907. Diwan of Mangrol State, 1908–12. Judge, Small Causes Court, 1913. Chief Justice, Palanpur State, 1914–22. Member, Bombay Legislative Council, 1923–37; President, 1927–36. Minister of Agriculture and Excise, Bombay, 1923–27; of Public Health and Local Self-Government, 1936–37. Member (Muslim League), Bombay Legislative Assembly, and Leader of the Opposition, 1937–46. Member, All India Muslim League Working Committee. Retired from public life, 1946.

Derby, 17th Earl of: Edward George Villiers (1865–1948)
Son of the 16th Earl, Frederick Arthur (1841–1900). Director of Recruiting, 1915–16. Secretary of State for War, 1916–18, 1922–24. Ambassador to France, 1918–20.

Dickens, Charles John Huffam (1812–1870)
Son of a government clerk. Started as a labourer. Reporter and journalist, 1835. Visited the United States of America, 1843, 1867, 1868. Settled at Genoa in Italy, 1844. Manager of a theatrical company, 1847. Buried in the Westminster Abbey. Novelist of the first rank.

Disraeli, Benjamin: 1st Earl of Beaconsfield (1804–1881)
Eldest son of Isaac D'Israeli. Privately educated. Member of Parliament, 1837. Leader of the Tories in the House of Commons, 1848. Prime Minister, 1867 and 1874–80. Made imperialism into a policy of state. Statesman and man of letters. Born a Jew.

Doyle, Sir Arthur Conan (1859–1930)
Studied medicine at the University of Edinburgh. Made his name by the short stories of which Sherlock Holmes was the hero, which began appearing in the *Strand Magazine*, 1891. Served as physician in the South African War, 1899–1902. In later years absorbed by the subject of spiritualism. Knighted in 1902. Novelist. Author of *The War in South Africa: Its Causes and Conduct*, 1902, which was a vindication of England's role in the conflict.

Dufferin and Ava, 1st Marquess of: Federick Temple Hamilton-Temple Blackwood (1826–1902)
Born in Florence. Son of Helen Selina Sheridan. Educated at Eton and Christ Church, Oxford, 1844–46. Created Baron Clandeboye, in English peerage, 1850; KCB, 1861. Under Secretary of State for India, 1864–66; and to War Office, 1866–68. Chancellor of the Duchy of Lancaster, 1868. Created Earl, 1871. Governor General of Canada, 1872–78. Created GCMG, 1876. Ambassador to Russia, 1879. Ambassador in Constantinople, 1881. In Cairo, 1881–84. Viceroy of India, 1884–88, where he annexed Upper Burma. Created Marquess, 1888. Freedom of the City of London, 1889. Ambassador in Rome, 1889–91. Lord Rector, St. Andrews University, 1891. Ambassador in Paris, 1891–96. Lord Rector, University of Edinburgh, 1901. Suffered loss of money and reputation as chairman of London and Globe Finance Corporation, 1901. Honorary LL.D., University of Cambridge, 1891.

Duke, Sir Frederick William (1863–1924)
Educated at Arbroath High School. Entered the Indian Civil Service, 1882. Served in Bengal, 1884–1902. Commissioner of Orissa, 1905–08. Chief Secretary, Bengal, 1908. First Lieutenant Governor of Bengal, 1911. Senior Member of the Council of

the Governor of Bengal, 1912–14. Member, Council of India, 1914–20. Accompanied E. S. Montagu to India, 1917–18. Permanent Under Secretary of State for India, 1920–24. Created KCIE, 1911.

Earle, Sir Archdale (1861–1934)
Educated at Queen's College, Oxford. Entered 1CS, 1882. Served in Bengal and Bihar. Home Secretary, Government of India, 1910–18. CIE, 1909. KCIE, 1911, KCSI, 1918. Knight of Grace, St. John of Jerusalem, 1917.

Eden, Sir Robert Anthony: 1st Earl of Avon (1897–1977)
British statesman. Only surviving son of Sir William Eden. Educated at Eton and Christ Church, Oxford. Served in World War One, winning an MC in 1917. MP, 1923–57. Under Secretary of State for Foreign Affairs, 1931. Lord Privy Seal, 1934. Foreign Secretary, 1935–38. Secretary of State for the Dominions, 1939–40. Secretary for War, 1940. Foreign Secretary, December 1940–45, 1951–55. Deputy Leader of the Opposition, 1945–51. Prime Minister, April 1955–January 1957. Created Earl, 1961. Married Beatrice Beckett, 1923; divorced, 1950. Married Clarissa Churchill, the daughter of Winston Churchill's younger brother, 1952. Author of several books.

Edward VII (1841–1910)
Eldest son and second child of Queen Victoria and Prince Albert. Taught by private tutors. Visited France, 1855, Switzerland, 1857, and Italy, 1859. Student at Christ Church, Oxford, 1859–60. Visited Canada and the United States, 1860. Student at Trinity College, Cambridge, 1860–61. Bencher of the Middle Temple, 1861. Visited Palestine and Turkey, 1862. Took his seat in the House of Lords, 5 February 1863. Married Princess Alexandra, 10 March 1863. Created Field Marshal, 10 June 1875. Toured India, October 1875–May 1876. Grand Master of the Freemasons, 1875. Ascended the throne, 22 January 1901.

Edward VIII (1894–1972)
The eldest son of George V. Educated at Osborne, Dartmouth, and Magdalen College, Oxford. In naval service as Prince of Wales and in the army during World War One. Travelled much. Succeeded father, 20 January 1936. Abdicated on 11 December of the same year on account of his proposed marriage to Mrs. Wallis Simpson. Created Duke of Windsor. Married Mrs. Simpson on 3 June 1937. Governor of Bahamas, 1940–45. Lived in France.

Edwardes, Stephen Meredyth (1873–1927)
Son of Rev. Stephen Edwardes, Fellow, Merton College, Oxford.
Educated at Eton and Christ Church, Oxford. Entered ICS, 1895.
Compiler and editor of the *Bombay City Gazetteer.* Commissioner
of Police, 1909–16. Municipal Commissioner, Bombay, 1916–18.
Retired, 1918. Joint editor, *Indian Antiquary,* 1923. Author of
several works on India. CSI, 1915. CVO, 1912.

Einstein, Albert (1879–1955)
German born mathematical physicist, who ranks with Galileo and
Newton as one of the great conceptual revisers of man's understanding of the universe. Born in Bavaria of Jewish parents.
Educated at Munich. Moved with parents to Milan, 1894, but
completed his education at Aarau and the Zürich Polytechnic.
Took up Swiss nationality in 1901. Examiner in the Swiss Patent
Office, 1902–05. Attained world fame by his special (1905) and
general (1916) theories of relativity. In 1909 a special professorship
was created for him at Zürich. Professor at Prague, 1911. Returned
to Zürich, where, from 1914 to 1933, he was Director of the Kaiser
Wilhelm Physical Institute in Berlin. After Hitler's rise to power he
renounced his German citizenship, left Germany, and lectured at
Oxford and Cambridge, and, from 1934, at Princeton. Became an
American citizen, 1940. Awarded the Nobel prize, 1921. Foreign
Member of the Royal Society, 1921. Author.

Elgin, 9th Earl of: Victor Alexander Bruce (1849–1917)
Son of James Bruce, the 8th. Earl. Born in Canada. Educated at
Eton and Balliol College, Oxford. Succeeded father, 1863. Held
office in the Liberal administration, 1886. Viceroy of India,
1893–98. Knight of the Garter, 1899. Chairman, Royal Commission to inquire into Military Preparations for the South
African War, 1902. Chairman, Commission on Free Church Care,
1905. Secretary of State for Colonies, 1905–08.

Eliot, George: Mary Ann or Marian Cross (1819–1880)
Educated at a school in Coventry, 1832. Visited Geneva, 1849.
Assistant editor, *Westminster Review,* 1851; resigned, 1853. Formed
a lifelong union without legal form with George Henry Lewes,
1854. Visited Berlin, 1854; Florence, 1860, 1861; and Spain, 1867.
After Lewes's death in 1878, married J. W. Cross, then a banker
in New York, 1880. Novelist.

Ellison, Grace Mary (died 1935)
Second daughter of Captain Ellison. Educated at Rochester Girls'

Grammar School and in Germany and France. Unmarried. Continental correspondent of *Bystander* for 6 years; later of the *Daily Telegraph* in Turkey and Germany. Author.

Elphinstone, Mountstuart (1779–1859)
Joined the East India Company as Writer, 1795. Governor of Bombay, 1819–27. Twice refused the Governor Generalship of India. Author of several books on Indian history.

Engels, Friedrich (1820–1895)
Born at Barmen. From 1842 onwards lived mostly in England. First met Marx in Brussels, 1844, and collaborated with him on the *Communist Manifesto*, 1848. Spent his later years in editing and translating Marx's works. Died in London.

Faraday, Michael (1791–1867)
English chemist and natural philosopher. Son of a blacksmith. Assistant to Sir H. Davy at the Royal Institution, 1813. Professor of chemistry (succeeding Davy), at the Royal Institution, 1827. Created DCL, 1832. Made several discoveries of the first importance: induced electricity (1831), electronic state of matter (1831), electro-chemical decomposition (1834), electro-static induction (1838), hydro-electricity (1843), diamagnetism (1846–49), and atmospheric magnetism (1851). Adviser to the Trinity House, 1862. A devout Christian.

Fazlul Haq, Abul Kasem (1873–1962)
Educated at Presidency College, Calcutta. Deputy Magistrate, 1906–12. Member, Bengal Legislative Council, 1913. Secretary, Bengal Provincial Muslim League, 1913–16. President, All India Muslim League, 1918. Education Minister, Bengal, 1924. Delegate to the Round Table Conferences, 1930–32. Mayor of Calcutta, 1935. Member, Indian Legislative Assembly, 1935. Member, Bengal Legislative Assembly, 1937–47. Chief Minister, Bengal, 1937–43. Advocate General, East Bengal, 1948–53. Member, East Bengal Legislative Assembly, 1954. Chief Minister, East Bengal, April–May 1954. Minister, Government of Pakistan, 1955–56. Governor of East Pakistan, 1956–58.

Firdausi, Abul Qasim Mansur (940–1020)
The Persian poet. Born in Tus. Author of the Persian national epic, the *Shahnamah*. Called "Firdausi" by Sultan Mahmud of Ghazna, who said that the poet's verses turned his court into an assembly of paradise (*firdaus*).

Fitzgerald, Edward (1809–1883)
Educated at Bury St. Edmunds and Trinity College, Cambridge; graduated, 1830. Lived a retired life in Suffolk. Translated Umar Khayyam's *rubaiyyat* from the Persian, first anonymous edition, 1859. Poet and translator.

Fox, Charles James (1749–1806)
Third son of Henry Fox, first Baron Holland. Educated at Eton and Hertford College, Oxford. MP, 1768. A Lord of the Admiralty, 1770. Lord of the Treasury, 1773. Foreign Secretary, 1782. Formed a coalition with Lord North, April–December 1783. Formed connection with Mrs. Armitstead, whom he married in 1795. Attacked Warren Hastings, 1786–87. His name was erased from the Privy Council for giving the toast "Our sovereign, the people", 1798. Statesman.

Fremantle, Admiral Hon. Sir Edmund Robert (1836–1929)
Fourth son of the 1st Baron Cottesole. Entered the Navy, 1849. Captain, 1867. Admiral, 1896. Commander-in-Chief, East Indies, 1881–91. Commander-in-Chief, China, 1892–95. Commander-in-Chief, Plymouth, 1896–99. Rear Admiral, 1901–27. KCB, 1889. GCB, 1899. GCVO, 1926. Justice of the Peace. Author.

Gait, Sir Edward Albert (1863–1950)
Educated at University College, London. Joined ICS, 1882. Served in Bengal and Assam. Census Commissioner for India, 1903. Member, Bengal Legislative Council, 1905. Member, Bihar and Orissa Executive Council, 1912–15. Lieutenant Governor of Bihar and Orissa, 1915–20. Member, India Council, 1922–27. Honorary Ph.D., University of Patna. CSI, 1912. KCSI, 1915. Author.

Gandhi, Mohandas Karamchand (1869–1948)
Son of Chief Minister of Porbandar. A Hindu of Vaisya sub-caste of merchants. Called to the bar at Inner Temple, 1891. Legal practice and public life in South Africa, 1893–1914. Returned to India, 1914. Indian National Congress leader. Active in non-co-operation campaigns and the Khilafat agitation. Delegate to the second session of the Round Table Conference, London, 1931. Totally opposed to but unable to prevent the creation of Pakistan. Assassinated by a Hindu in Delhi. Author, editor, politician.

George V (1865–1936)
Second son of Edward VII and Queen Alexandra. Naval cadet, 1877. Travels, 1879–82. In naval service, 1882–92. Created Duke of York, 1892. Married Princess Victoria Mary (May) of Teck, 6 July 1893. Stamp collector of some fame. Ascended the throne, 6 May 1910. Visited India, December 1911. Adopted the name of Windsor for the royal house and family, 1917.

George VI (1895–1952)
Second son of George V. Educated at Dartmouth Naval College, and at Trinity College, Cambridge. Served in the navy and the air force, 1914–18. Created Duke of York, 1920. Married Lady Elizabeth Bowes-Lyon, 1923. Succeeded to the throne in December 1936 on the abdication of his brother, Edward VIII. An outstanding tennis player.

Ghaznavi, Sir Abdul Halim Abul Husain Khan (1876–1953)
Muslim landlord, merchant and politician of Bengal. Son of Abdul Hakim Khan. Educated at St. Xavier's college, Calcutta. Joined the Indian National Congress in 1905, but left it in 1907. Member, Bengal Muhammadan Association. Member, Indian Legislative Assembly, 1926–45. President, Muslim Conference, Cawnpore, 1929. Delegate to the three sessions of the Round Table Conference, 1930–32, and to the Joint Committee on Indian Constitutional Reform, 1933–34. Adviser, Indian Delegation to the World Economic Conference, 1933. Sheriff of Calcutta, 1934–35. President, Muslim Chamber of Commerce, Calcutta, 1939–40. President, Indian Chamber of Commerce, 1945–46. President, Central National Muhammadan Association, Calcutta. Member, Court of Dacca University. Member, Court of the Aligarh Muslim University. Belonged to East Bengal, but lived in Calcutta. Migrated to East Pakistan after 1947. Knighted in 1935.

Gibbon, Edward (1737–1794)
Educated at Westminster and Magdalen College, Oxford. In Lausanne, 1753–58. Served in Hampshire Militia, 1759–70. Toured Italy, 1764–65. Settled in London, 1772. Professor of Ancient History, Royal Academy. MP for Liskeard, 1774–80, and for Lymington, 1781–83. Commissioner of Trade and Plantations, 1779–82. Issued the first volume of his *Decline and Fall of the Roman Empire*, second and third volumes, 1781. Retired to Lausanne, 1783, where he finished the work. Returned to England, 1793.

Gide, André Paul Guillaume (1869–1951)
Born in Paris. Author of fiction, poetry, plays, criticism, biography, belles-lettres and translations. Co-founder of *Nouvelle Revue Française*, 1909. Received the Nobel prize for literature, 1947. His influence on contemporary letters was great. One of the most brilliant and most widely recognized and respected writers of this century.

Gidney, Sir Henry Albert John (1873–1942)
Educated at Calcutta, Edinburgh, London and Cambridge. Entered the Indian Medical Service, 1908. President, Anglo-Indian and Domiciled European Association of all India and Burma. Leader of Anglo-Indian Deputation to England, 1925. Member, Indian Sandhurst Committee, 1931. Delegate to the Round Table Conferences, 1930–32. Delegate to the Joint Committee on Indian Constitutional Reform, 1933–34. Member, Indian Legislative Assembly, 1921–40. Knighted in 1931.

Gladstone, William Ewart (1809–1898)
Son of Sir John Gladstone. Educated at Eton and Christ Church, Oxford. President, Oxford Union Society, 1830. MP, Conservative, 1832. Junior Lord of Treasury, 1834. Under Secretary of State for War and Colonies, 1835. Master of Mint, 1841. President of the Board of Trade, 1843. Secretary of State for the Colonies, 1845–46. MP for Oxford University, 1847–65. Chancellor of the Exchequer, 1852–55, 1859–66. Lord Rector, University of Edinburgh, 1861. MP for South Lancashire, 1865–68, and for Greenwich, 1868–74 and 1874–80. Prime Minister, 1868–74. Resigned leadership of the Liberal Party, 1875. Lord Rector of Glasgow University, 1877. MP for Midlothian, 1880–95. Prime Minister, 1880–85. Declined offer of Earldom, 1885. Prime Minister, 1886, 1892–94. Buried in Westminster Abbey.

Gleichen, Major General Lord Albert Edward Wilfred (formerly Count Gleichen) (1863–1937)
Son of Admiral Prince Victor of Hohenlohe-Langenburg. Educated at Charterhouse and Sandhurst. Joined the British Army, 1881. Served in Egypt, Morocco, Sudan, South Africa and Europe. Major General, 1917. Retired, October 1919. Vice-President, Royal African Society. DSO, 1900. CMG, 1898. CB, 1906. KCVO, 1909. Author.

Gokhale, Gopal Krishna (1866–1915)
A Marhatha Brahmin. Professor of History and Economics,

Fergusson College, Poona, till 1902. Joint Secretary, Indian National Congress. Member, Bombay Legislative Council, 1902, and later, Imperial Legislative Council. Founded the Servants of India Society, 1905. President, Indian National Congress, 1905. Member, Royal Commission on Indian Public Services, 1912–15. A leading Hindu nationalist.

Gour, Sir Hari Singh (1866–1949)
Educated at Hislop College, Nagpur, and Downing College, Cambridge, and Trinity College Dublin. Called to the bar at the Inner Temple. Legal practice at Nagpur. President, Central Provinces Hindu Association. Indian Delegate to the Joint Committee on Indian Constitutional Reform, 1933. Leader of the Opposition, Legislative Assembly, 1921–34. Vice-Chancellor, University of Nagpur, 1936. First Vice-Chancellor, University of Delhi. Founder (1946) and Vice-Chancellor, University of Sangor. Honorary D. Litt, University of Delhi. Member, Indian Constituent Assembly, 1946. Knighted in 1925.

Granville, 2nd Earl: Granville George Leverson-Gower (1815–1891)
Educated at Eton and Christ Church, Oxford. Attaché at the British Embassy in Paris, 1835. MP (Whig), 1836. Under Secretary of State for Foreign Affairs, 1840–41. Succeeded to peerage, 1846. Vice-President of the Board of Trade, 1848. Secretary of State for Foreign Affairs, 1851–52, 1870–74, 1880–85. President of the Council, 1852–54, 1859. Chancellor of the Duchy of Lancaster, 1854. Leader of the House of Lords, 1855. Chancellor of the University of London, 1856–91. Secretary of State for the Colonies, 1868–70, 1886. Knight of the Garter, 1857.

Grey of Falloden, 1st Viscount: Edward Grey (1862–1933)
British statesman. Educated at Winchester and Balliol College, Oxford. Liberal MP, 1885–1916. Secretary of State for Foreign Affairs, 1905–16. Ambassador to Washington, 1919–20. Chancellor of the University of Oxford, 1928–33. Created KG, 1912. Wrote on birds and fly-fishing.

Grierson, Sir George Abraham (1851–1941)
Educated at Trinity College, Dublin. Joined ICS, 1873. Served in Bengal and Bihar. On special duty with the Government of India in charge of the Linguistic Survey of India, 1898–1902. Retired, 1903. Honorary doctorates from the Universities of alle, Dublin, Cambridge and Oxford. KCIE, 1912. OM, 1928. Author of several works.

Gwalior, Maharajah Sindhia of: Sir Madho Rao (1876–1925)
Succeeded to the throne, 1886. Honorary Colonel in the British Army, 1898. Granted a salute of 11 guns in 1911; made hereditary in 1917. Honorary LL. D., Cambridge. Honorary DCL, Oxford. Honorary ADC to the King. Honorary Lieutenant General. GCSI, 1895. GCVO, 1902.

Habibullah Khan of Afghanistan, Amir (d. 1919)
Succeeded father, Abdur Rahman Khan, 1901 as king. Secured from the British Government the right of being addressed as His Majesty. Visited Britain, 1906. During the First World War he maintained a neutrality friendly to the British. Played an important part in the modernization of his country. Assassinated. Succeeded by his son, Amanullah Khan.

Hafiz, Muhammad Shamsuddin (d. *c.* 1388)
The greatest of Persian lyrical poets. Born, lived and died in Shiraz. Many of his *ghazals* are on wine, women and other sensuous subjects, but they have an esoteric significance to the initiated and the mystic-minded.

Haldane, 1st Viscount, Richard Burdon (1856–1928)
Educated at the Edinburgh Academy, and the Universities of Göttingen and Edinburgh. Called to the bar at Lincoln's Inn, 1879. Good legal practice. MP, Liberal, 1885–1911. Queen's Counsel, 1890. Secretary of State for War, 1905–12. Lord Chancellor, 1912–15. Created Viscount, 1911. Chairman, Royal Commission on University Education in London, 1909. Lord Chancellor in the Labour administration, 1924. Fellow, Royal Society, 1906. Fellow, British Academy, 1914. Statesman and philosopher. Author of several works.

Hallaj, Abul Mughith al Husain bin Mansur al- (857–922)
Muslim mystic and theologian. His experience and death mark a turning point in the history of Islamic mysticism and protest. Born at Tur, in the north-east of Baida in Fars. Son of a wool carder (*hallaj*). Learnt Quran by heart before he was 12. Moved to Wasit, and later to Basra. Performed several pilgrimages to Mecca. His preaching in Baghdad annoyed the conservative *ulema*. Tried for having taught and expressed allegedly anti-Islamic sentiments and beliefs, and executed after much torture in March 922. In Islamic history, mysticism, literature and general lore he is the permanent symbol of courage, conviction, protest

1447

and sacrifice. His most famous works include *Akhbar-al-Hallaj* and *Kitab-al-Tawasin.*

Hammick, Sir Murray (1854–1936)
Son of Rev. Sir St. V. Hammick, 2nd. Baronet. Educated at Charterhouse, King's College, London, and Balliol College, Oxford. Entered ICS, 1875. Served in Madras. Member, Madras Legislative Council, 1902. Member, Madras Executive Council, 1906–13. Governor of Madras, 1912. Member, Royal Commission on the Public Services in India, 1912. Member, India Council, 1915–22. Fellow, King's College, London. CSI, 1907. KCSI, 1911.

Hardinge of Penhurst, 1st Baron: Charles Hardinge (1858–1944)
Grandson of the first Viscount Hardinge. Educated at Harrow and Trinity College, Cambridge. Entered Foreign Office, 1880; served successively in Constantinople, Berlin, Washington, Sofia, Bucharest, Paris, Tehran and St. Petersburg; Assistant Under Secretary of State, 1903–04. Ambassador to Russia, 1904–06. Permanent Under Secretary of State, 1906–10, 1916–20. Viceroy of India, 1910–16. Censured by the commission of inquiry into the Mesopotamia expedition, 1917. Ambassador in Paris, 1920–22. Created Baron, 1910. Knight of the Garter, 1916.

Haroon, Seth Haji Sir Abdullah (1876–1942)
Indian Muslim trader and merchant. A self-made man. Proprietor and director of several companies and establishments. Member, Indian Legislative Assembly, 1926–42. President, All India Muslim Conference, 1934. President, Sind Khilafat Committee and Sind Provincial Muslim League. Member, All India Muslim League Working Committee. Chairman, Reception Committee, Sind Provincial Muslim League Conference, Karachi, October 1938. Philanthropist. For several years the only important Muslim League leader in Sind. Supported the idea of a Pakistan long before Jinnah came round to it. Knighted in 1937.

Harrington, General Sir Charles (1872–1940)
Educated at Sandhurst. Entered British Army, 1892. Deputy Chief of Imperial General Staff, 1918–20. General Officer Commanding-in-Chief, Black Sea, 1920–21; Allied Forces of Occupation in Turkey, 1921–23; Western Command in India, 1927–31. Governor and Commander-in-Chief, Gibraltar, 1933–38. KCB, 1919. GBE, 1922. GCB, 1933.

Harris, 4th Baron: George Robert Canning Harris (1851–1932)
Born in Trinidad. Succeeded father, 1872. Played cricket for Eton, 1868–70, and Oxford, 1871–74. Captain of England, 1880–1884. Under Secretary of State for India, 1885–86, and for War, 1886–89. Governor of Bombay, 1890–95. Popularized cricket among the Indians. President, Marylebone Cricket Club, 1895. Created GCIE in 1890, GCSI in 1895, and CB in 1918.

Hasan al-Basri (642–728)
A famous Sufi. Born in Medina, son of a freed slave. Settled in Basra, Iraq, where his learning and spiritual insight attracted a wide cricle of students. In his school were treated many ideas that were to grow into Islamic law, theology and Sufism. One of the great influences on later major thinkers and men of letters.

Hasan Imam, Sayyid (1871–1933)
The second son of Shams-ul-Ulema Sayyid Imdad Imam. Younger brother of Sir Ali Imam. Belonged to Bihar. Born in Neora, district Patna. Called to the bar in London, 1892. Member, Bihar Provincial Congress Committee, October 1909. Judge, Calcutta High Court, 1912–16; resigned and resumed legal practice in Patna. President, Indian National Congress, 1918.

Hastings, Warren (1732–1818)
Came to India as a clerk in the East India Company in 1750. Member, Calcutta Council under Henry Vansittart, 1761. In England, 1764–68. Councillor in Madras, 1768–72. Governor of Bengal, April 1772. Brought about many reforms in administration, judiciary and army. With the Regulating Act of 1773, he became Governor General of Fort William in Bengal. A sound Orientalist with a good knowledge of Persian and Bengali. His interest in history and literature led to the founding of the Asiatic Society of Bengal. Encouraged the work of Sir William Jones. In May 1784 the House of Commons passed a vote of censure against his conduct, but this did not result in his removal or resignation. Left India in January 1785. In May 1786 the House of Commons decided to impeach him for "high crimes and misdemeanours." The trial opened in 1788, dragged on for seven years, and finally ended in an acquittal on all counts. Edmund Burke was his chief prosecutor. Created a Privy Councillor in 1814.

Heaton, Sir John Henniker (1848–1914)
First Baronet. Postal reformer. Went to Australia, 1864. Journalist

in Sydney. Settled in London, 1884. MP, (Conservative) 1885–1910. Opened his postal reform campaign, 1886. Created Baronet, 1911.

Henderson, Arthur (1863–1935)
British, Labour politician. Worked as an iron moulder in Newcastle. Chairman, Labour Party, 1908–10, 1914–17, 1931–32. Served in the Coalition Cabinets, 1915–17. Home Secretary, 1924. Secretary of State for Foreign Affairs, 1929–31. President, World Disarmament Conference, 1932–34; awarded the Nobel Peace Prize, 1934.

Hidayat Husain, Hafiz (1861–1935)
Educated at MAO College, Aligarh. Called to the bar at Middle Temple. Legal practice at Cawnpore. One of the founders of the All India Muslim League. Home Rule Leaguer. President, Cawnpore Khilafat Committee. President, All India Conservative Association. President (twice), United Provinces Muslim Educational Conference. Member, United Provinces Legislative Council, 1923. Chairman, Reception Committee, Tanzim Conference, Fatehpur District, 1925. Member, United Provinces Simon Committee, 1928. Delegate to the Round Table Conference. Honorary Secretary, All India Muslim League. President, All India Muslim League, Delhi Session, 1933. Created CIE, 1933.

Hill, Sir Claude Hamilton Archer (1866–1934)
Son of Captain Edward Hill. Educated at Emmanuel College, Cambridge. Entered ICS 1887. Served in Bombay. Resident in Mewar, 1906–08. Agent to the Governor in Kathiawar, 1908–12. Member, Bombay Executive Council, 1912–15. Member, Viceroy's Executive Council, 1915–20. Retired, 1920. Director General of the League of Red Cross Societies, 1921–26. Lieutenant Governor of the Isle of Man, 1926–33. KCSI, 1917.

Hisham, Abul Walid (c. 757–796)
Second Umayyad ruler of Muslim Spain. Son of Abdur Rahman I, whom he succeeded in October 788. Born in Cordova. Though he reigned for only $7^1/_2$ years, he gave stability to Muslim Spain, conquered some new areas, re-built the bridge over the Guadalquivir and extended or renovated the Cordova mosque. With his encouragement the new Maliki school began to make headway in al-Andalus. Died in April.

Hitler, Adolf (1889–1945)
Born in upper Austria. Son of a minor customs official. Educated

in schools in Linz and Steyr. After father's death attended a private art school in Münich. Lived on his wits in Vienna, 1904–13. Draughtsman in Munich, 1913. Fought in the war, 1914–18, winning the Iron Cross. Joined a minor political party and changed its name to National Socialist German Workers' Party, 1920. Chancellor of Germany, 1933. Began the rearming of the country, 1935. Invaded Austria, 1938. His march into Poland started World War Two in September 1939. Faced with defeat and with the Russians only several hundred yards away, on 30 April, he poisoned his newly-wed wife, Eva Braun, and shot himself dead.

Hogg, Sir Malcolm Nicholson (1883–1948)
Educated at Eton and Balliol College, Oxford. Joined Forbes, Forbes, Campbell and Co., 1904; went to their Bombay office, 1905. Member, Bombay Legislative Council, 1915–17. Chairman, Bombay Chamber of Commerce. Member, Imperial Legislative Council, 1917–19. Member, Southborough Franchise Committee, 1918. Member, India Council, 1920–25. Knighted in 1920.

Horne of Slamannan, 1st Viscount of Slamannan: Robert Stevenson Horne (1871–1940)
Son of Rev. R. S. Horne. Educated at the University of Glasgow, where he had a brilliant career in philosophy. Lecturer in Philosophy, University College of North Wales, 1895. Called to the Scottish bar, 1896. MP (Unionist), 1918–37. Served in World War One. Minister of Labour, 1919. President of the Board of Trade, 1920–21. Chancellor of the Exchequer, 1921–22. King's Counsel, 1910. Lord Rector, University of Aberdeen. Created PC, 1919; GBE, 1920; KBE, 1918; Viscount, 1937.

Hunter, Sir William Wilson (1840–1900)
Scottish statistician. Educated in Glasgow, Paris and Bonn. Entered ICS, 1862. Superintendent of Public Instruction, Orissa, 1866–69. Secretary to the Bengal Government and later to the Government of India. Director General of the Department of Statistics, Government of India, 1871. Retired in 1887 and returned home. Created CSI, 1878, and Knighted in 1887. Author of several historical works on India. Initiated, planned and edited the gigantic *Imperial Gazetteer of India.*

Husain, Imam (624–680)
The second son of Ali and Fatimah, and maternal grandson of the Prophet. Martyred at the Battle of Karbala. For the Sunnis,

the event is the deplorable and tragic murder of the second closest descendant of the Prophet. For the Shi'ites, it is a personal, religious and national trauma.

Hyderi, the Rt. Hon. Sir Akbar (1869–1942)
Educated at St. Xavier's College, Bombay. Entered the Indian Finance Department, 1888. Served in the United Provinces, Bombay, the Central Provinces and Delhi. Accountant General, on loan, Hyderabad State, 1905. Accountant General, Bombay, 1920. Finance and Railway Member, Nizam of Hyderabad's Executive Council, 1921–27. President, All India Muhammedan Educational Conference, Calcutta, 1917. Led the Hyderabad delegation to the Round Table Conferences, 1930–32, and to the Joint Select Committee on Indian Constitutional Reform, 1933–34. Chairman, Committee of Indian States' Ministers, 1934–41. Vice-Chancellor, Osmania University, Hyderabad, 1935. President, Hyderabad State Executive Council, 1937–41. Member for Information, Viceroy's Executive Council, 1941–42. Knighted in 1928.

Hyndman, Henry Mayers (1842–1921)
On the staff of the *Pall Mall Gazette*, 1871–80. One of the founders and leaders of the (Social) Democratic Federation, 1881. Left the British Socialist Party and formed the National Socialist Party, 1916. Published *England for All*, 1881, several books defending political Marxism, and two autobiographical works.

Iqbal, Shaikh Sir Muhammad (*c.* 1877–1938)
Born in Sialkot, Punjab, in a Kashmiri family. Educated at Scotch Mission College, Sialkot, Government College, Lahore, Trinity College, Cambridge, and the University of Münich. Called to the bar at the Lincoln's Inn of Court, London. Taught at the Oriental College and Government College, Lahore, and at the University of London. Legal practice in Lahore, 1908 onwards. Member, Punjab Legislative Council, 1926–30. President, All India Muslim League, 1930, and All India Muslim Conference, 1932. Delegate to the second and third sessions of the Round Table Conference, 1931–32. Knighted in 1923. A ranking world poet and one of the greatest philosophers of all times.

Ismet Pasha: Inönü (1884–1973)
Born in Izmir. In the Ottoman army. Chief of Staff to Kamal Atatürk in the war against the Greeks, 1919–22. Prime Minister of Turkey, 1923–37. President of Turkey on Atatürk's death,

1938–50. Leader of the Opposition. Prime Minister under General Gürsel, 1961–65.

Jahangir, Nuruddin (1569–1627)
Mughal emperor of India. Son of Akbar. Succeeded father, 1605. Husband of Nur Jahan. Patronized art, literature and architecture. Autobiographer. His memoirs have been translated into English by Rodgers and Beveridge, 1909–14.

Jami, Nuruddin Abdur Rahman (1414–1492)
Born in Jam in Khurasan. One of the greatest Persian poets of all times. Died in Herat.

Jeans, Sir James Hopwood (1877–1946)
Educated at Trinity College, Cambridge; bracketed second wrangler, 1898; Fellow, 1901. University lecturer in Mathematics, 1904–05. Stokes Lecturer, 1910–12, at Cambridge. Professor of Applied Mathematics, Princeton University, 1905–09. Fellow, Royal Society, 1906; an honorary secretary, 1919–29. President, British Association, 1934. Professor of Astronomy, Royal Institution, 1935–46. Mathematician, theoretical physicist, astronomer, and popular expositor of physical science and astronomy. Knighted in 1928. Order of Merit, 1939. Author of several works.

Jenkins, Sir Lawrence Hugh (1857–1928)
Called to the bar at the Lincoln's Inn, 1883. Judge, High Court, Calcutta, 1896. Chief Justice of the Bombay High Court, 1899–1908. Member, Council of India, 1908–09. Took large part in drafting the Government of India Bill of 1909. Chief Justice of Bengal, 1909–15. Member, Judicial Committee of the Privy Council, 1916. Knighted in 1899.

Jinnah, Muhammad Ali (1876–1948)
Called to the bar at Lincoln's Inn, 1896. Legal practice in Bombay. Member, Imperial Legislative Council, 1909–19. Member of the Indian National Congress and the All India Muslim League, leaving the former in 1920. Member, Indian Legislative Assembly, 1919–47. Delegate to the Round Table Conference, London, 1930–31. Lived in England, 1931–34. Returned to India in 1934 to lead and revitalize the Muslim League. The supreme Muslim leader of India, 1937–47. Governor General of Pakistan, 1947–48. The creator of Pakistan.

Joglekar, Rao Bahadur Ramchandra Narayan (1858–1928)
Educated at Deccan College, Poona. Held non-gazetted appoint-

ments in Nasik, Satara, Ahmednagar, Poona and Sholapur districts, 1883–99. Deputy Collector, 1899. Collector, Baroda State, 1917–20. ISO, 1913. Author.

Khalid ibn al-Walid (d. 642)
Probably the greatest warrior and general of early Islam. A Quraish by origin, Caliph Abu Bakr made him the commanding general of the Muslim armies. Called the "Sword of Islam" (*Saif-ul-Islam*).

Khaqani, Afzaluddin Badil bin Ali (1121/22–1199)
Persian poet. Son of a carpenter. His mother was converted from Christianity to Islam. Educated as a physician. His teacher and father-in-law was Abul Ala Ganjavi, the poet laureate of the court of Manuchehr, whom he succeeded after his death. Spent his years of retirement in Tabriz and died there. His work represents the culmination of the *qasida* genre. Uses scientific terminology and obscure allusions. A religious spirit and a keen awarness of the beauties of nature permeate his poems. There are several allusions to Christian concepts. Influenced by Unsuri, Sanai and Manuchehri. Wrote the first travel account in verse in *masnavi* form *Tuhfat-ul-Iraqain.*

Kitchener of Khartoum and of Broome, 1st. Earl: Horatio Herbert Kitchener (1850–1916)
Entered the British army, 1871. Governor General of Eastern Sudan, 1886. Adjutant General of Egyptian army, 1888. Created CB, 1889. Sardar of Egyptian army, 1892. Created KCMG, 1894. Major General and KCB for services in the River War, 1896. Conqueror of Khartoum, 1898. Created Baron, 1898. Governor General of the Sudan, 1898. Chief of Staff to Lord Roberts in South Africa, 1899. Commander-in-Chief in South Africa, 1900–02. Created Viscount and awarded the Order of Merit, 1902. Commander-in-Chief in India, 1902–09. Created Field Marshal, 1909. British Agent and Consul General in Egypt, 1911. Secretary of State for War, 1914. Knight of the Garter, 1915. Drowned when HMS *Hampshire* went down off Orkneys on way to Russia.

Kropotkin, Prince Peter (1842–1921)
Born in Moscow. Entered the Corps of Pages, 1857. Explored Siberia, 1862–67, and the glacial deposits of Finland and Sweden, 1871. Joined the International, 1872. In prison, 1874–76. Escaped to England. In prison in France, 1883–86. Lived in England,

1886–1917. Author of works on anarchism, Russian literature, the French Revolution, mutual aid in evolution, and Asia. Revolutionary, anarchist, geographer, nihilist, savant.

Lake, 1st Viscount: Gerard Lake (1744–1808)
British general. Served in Germany, 1760–62, in America, 1781, and the Low Countries, 1793–94. Received the surrender of the French near Cloone, 1798. Served in India, 1801–07, beating Scindia and Holkar and taking Aligarh, Delhi and Agra.

Lamington, 2nd Baron: Charles Wallace Alexander Napier Ross Cochrane (1860–1940)
Educated at Eton and Christ Church, Oxford. Assistant Private Secretary to Lord Salisbury, 1885. MP, Conservative, 1886–90. Succeeded father, 1890. Governor of Queensland, 1895–1901. Governor of Bombay, 1903–07. Created GCMG, 1900, and GCIE, 1903.

Lansdowne, 5th Marquess of: Henry Charles Keith Petty-Fitzmaurice (1845–1927)
Son of the 4th. Marquess. Educated at Eton and Balliol College, Oxford. Influenced by Benjamin Jowett. Succeeded father, 1866. Inherited liberal traditions. Junior Lord of Treasury, 1869. Under Secretary of State for War, 1872–74. Under Secretary of State for India, 1880; resigned for his lack of sympathy with Gladstone's Irish policy, 1880. Governor General of Canada, 1883–88. Viceroy of India, 1888–94. Secretary of State for War, 1895–1900. Secretary of State for Foreign Affairs, 1900–05. Leader of the Conservative Party in the House of Lords, 1903. Member, Asquith's first war coalition, 1914. In favour of a "peace of accommodation" with Germany, 1916; published his famous letter to the *Daily Telegraph* on same lines as the memorandum of 1916, 29 November 1917. Knight of the Garter, 1894.

Law, Sir Andrew Bonar (1858–1923)
Born in Canada. Brought up in Glasgow by his mother's relations from the age of eleven. Educated at Glasgow High School. In business, 1874. MP, Unionist, Glasgow, 1900. Parliamentary Secretary to the Board of Trade, 1902. Leader of the Opposition in the House of Commons, 1911. Secretary of State for Colonies, 1915. Chancellor of the Exchequer, 1917–18. Lord Privy Seal and Leader of the House of Commons, 1918; resigned, March 1921. Prime Minister, October 1922–May 1923.

Lawrence, 1st Baron: John Laird Mair (1811–1879)
British administrator in India. Born in Richmond. Trained at Haileybury College, and entered the Indian Civil Service. Early postings in Delhi. Commissioner and later Lieutenant Governor of the Punjab at its annexation in 1849. Led the Punjabi troops in the assault on Delhi during the Mutiny of 1857–58. Viceroy of India, 1863–69. Created Baron, 1869. Chairman, London Schools Board, 1870–73. Founder of what came to be known as the Punjab school of administration.

Lawrence, David Herbert (1885–1930)
Schoolmaster at Croydon until 1911. Thenceforth devoted himself to literature. Left England in 1919 largely because of hostile attitude towards himself and his writings. Lived in Italy, Sicily and Mexico, and then in Italy again. Died at Vence. Poet, novelist, essayist.

Lenin, Valdimir Ilyich (1870–1924)
Born in Simbrisk. Educated at the University of Kazan. Legal practice in Samara, 1892. Moved to St. Petersburg in 1894 and organized the illegal Union for the Liberation of the Working Class. Exiled to Siberia for three years. In exile in Switzerland, 1903, where, with Plekhanov, he founded the underground Social Democratic Party. Leader of the Bolshevik wing, 1903. In Russia, 1905–07. Again in Switzerland, 1907–17. Manipulated the Bolshevik revolution in Russia and inaugurated the dictatorship of the proletariat. Started implementing his new economic policy, 1922. Devoted Marxist and ruthless and authoritarian ruler. Author of several works.

Leonardo da Vinci (1452–1519)
The natural son of a Florentine notary. Settled in Milan, 1482. Painter of outstanding genius. Devised a system of hydraulic irrigation of the plains of Lombardy. In 1500 entered the service of Cesare Borgia in Florence as architect and engineer. Completed in about 1504 his most celebrated easel picture, *Mona Lisa*. Employed by Louis XII of France, 1506. Author, sculptor, architect, engineer and painter.

Liaquat Ali Khan (1895–1951)
Indian and Pakistani politician. Educated at Oxford. Called to the bar at the Inner Temple. General Secretary, All India Muslim League. Member, Indian Legislative Assembly. Prime Minister of Pakistan, 1947–51. Assassinated. Married twice.

Liaquat Hayat Khan, Nawab Sir (1887–1948)
Son of Nawab Muhammad Hayat Khan of the Punjab. Educated privately. Deputy Superintendent of Police, Punjab, 1909; Superintendent, 1919. Home Secretary, Patiala State, 1923; later Home Minister. Prime Minister of Patiala State, 1930–40. Patiala representative at the Round Table Conferences, 1931, 1932; and at the Joint Committee on Indian Constitutional Reform, 1933. Political Adviser, Nawab of Bhopal. Brother of Sir Sikandar Hayat Khan. Knighted in 1933. KBE, 1939.

Linlithgow, 2nd Marquess of: Victor Alexander John Hope (1887–1952)
Succeeded father, 1908. Educated at Eton. Served in World War One, 1914–18. Civil Lord of the Admiralty, 1922–24. Deputy Chairman, Unionist Party, 1924–26. President, Navy League, 1924–31. Chairman, Royal Commission on Indian Agriculture, 1926–28. Chairman, Joint Committee on Indian Constitutional Reform, 1933–34. Viceroy of India, 1936–43. Lord High Commissioner to General Assembly of the Church of Scotland, 1944 and 1945. GCIE, 1929. GCSI, 1936. PC, 1935. KT, 1928. KG 1943.

Litvinov, Maksim Maksimovich (1876–1951)
Soviet diplomat and foreign minister. Born a Polish Jew. Moved to Western Europe, 1902. Deported from France, 1908. Lived in London, where he worked for a publishing house and married, 1916, an English girl, Ivy Low. Deported in 1918 for mustering support for the Bolsheviks in London. Returned to Moscow and was given an appointment in the Commissariat of Foreign Affairs. Deputy Commissar, 1921. Commissar, 1930–39. Upheld the policy of collective security. Established diplomatic ties with the USA, 1933. Joined the League of Nations, 1934. Concluded a mutual defence pact with France, 1935. Ambassador to the USA, 1941–43. Continued to serve in the foreign affairs commissariat until his retirement in 1946. One of the few Jews to hold high office in the Soviet Union.

Lloyd, 1st Baron: George Ambrose Lloyd (1879–1941)
Educated at Eton and the University of Cambridge. Travelled widely in Asia. Honorary Attaché at Constantinople. Served in World War One. Governor of Bombay, 1918–23. MP, Conservative, 1924–25. High Commissioner for Egypt and the Sudan, 1925–29. Secretary of State for the Colonies, 1940–41. Died in office. President Navy League, 1930. President, Royal Central Asian Society. Chairman, British Council, 1936. Created GCIE, 1918, GCSI, 1924, PC, 1924. Created Baron, 1925.

Lloyd-George of Dwyfor, 1st Earl of: David Lloyd George (1863–1945)
Of very poor Welsh background. Qualified as solicitor with honours, 1884. Made a mark as an advocate and a speaker on religious, temperance and political subjects. MP, Liberal, 1890–1945. President, Board of Trade, and Privy Councillor, 1905. Chancellor of the Exchequer, 1908. Minister of Munitions, 1915–16. Secretary of State for War, July-December 1916. Prime Minister, 7 December 1916. Creator of War Cabinet and Supreme War Council. Order of the Merit, 1919. Resigned, October 1922. Chairman, Parliamentary Liberal Party, 1926–31. On grounds of health refused invitation to enter Churchill's government, 1940. Ambassador in Washington, 1940. Created Earl, 1945. Author of a few books.

Ludendorff, Erich Von (1865–1937)
Staff officer in the German army, 1904–13. Quartermaster-general in East Prussia, 1914. A leader of the Hitler *putsch* in Munich, 1923, but acquitted of treason. Defeated in election to the presidency of the Reich, 1925. Member of the Nazi party for some time. From 1925 onwards led a minority party of his own. Strongly opposed to the Jews, Jesuits and freemasons.

Lyautey, Louis Hubert Gonzalve (1854–1934)
Born in Nancy. Held administrative posts in Algeria, Tongking and Madagascar. Resident commissary-general in Morocco, 1912–16, 1917–25. Created Marshal, 1921.

Lyttleton, Oliver: 1st Viscount Chandos (1893–1972)
British politician and businessman. Educated at Eton and Cambridge. A golf blue. Served in the army in World War One, winning a DSO. Managing Director of British Metal Corporation, 1928. President of the Board of Trade, 1940, Minister of State in Cairo and Minister of Production in Churchill's War Cabinet. Secretary of State for Colonies, 1951; resigned in 1954 to return to business. Created Viscount in 1954.

Lytton, 1st Earl of: Edward Robert Bulwer (1831–1891)
Son of Edward George Earle Lytton Bulwer-Lytton, first Baron Lytton. Educated at Harrow and in Bonn. Private Secretary to his uncle, Lord Dalling, at Washington and Florence. Paid attaché at the Hague and Vienna; then served in diplomatic assignments at Copenhagen, Athens, Lisbon, Madrid, and Paris. Succeeded to his father's title, 1873. Viceroy of India, 1876–80. Ambassador to Paris, 1887–91. Statesman and poet.

Macaulay, 1st Baron: Thomas Babington Macaulay (1800–1859)
British author and politician. Son of Zachary Macaulay, a West
India merchant. Educated at Trinity College, Cambridge,
1818–22, winning the Chancellor's Medal and the Craven Prize.
Fellow of Trinity, 1824. Called to the bar, 1826. MP, 1830. Com-
missioner and then Secretary to the Board of Control. Legal
Adviser to the Supreme Council of India, 1834–38. MP, 1839–47,
1852–56. Secretary of State for War in Melbourne's cabinet. Lord
Rector of the University of Glasgow, 1849. Created Baron in 1857.
Buried in Westminster Abbey. Historian, essayist, poet, orator and
unrivalled picturesque narrator.

MacDonald, James Ramsay (1866–1937)
Educated locally at Lossiemouth, Morayshire. Pupil teacher.
Joined the Social Democratic Federation, 1885, and the Fabian
Society, 1886. Spent some years in extreme poverty and intensive
study in London. Unsuccessful attempt at entering Parliament as
an Independent Labour Party candidate from Southampton,
1895. Earned his living by journalism. Married Margaret Ethel,
1896, and the match obtained for him financial independence
and upper middle class background; she died in 1911. Secretary,
Labour Representation Committee (later the Labour Party),
1900–1912; treasurer, 1912–14. MP, 1906–18, 1922–35, 1936–37.
Chairman, Independent Labour Party, 1906–09; and of Parliamentary Labour Group, 1911. Chairman, Parliamentary Labour
Party and Leader of the Opposition, 1922. Prime Minister (and
Secretary of State for Foreign Affairs), first Labour politician to
hold the offices, January 1924 and 1929–35. Planned and pre-
sided over the London Naval Conference, 1930. President, Indian
Round Table Conference, London, 1930. Lord President of the
Council, June 1935. Author of a few books.

Mahmudabad, Maharajah of: Sir Muhammad Ali Muhammad Khan
(1877–1931)
Indian leader. One of the richest taluqdars of the United Prov-
inces. President, Aligarh Muslim University Constitution
Committee. President, All India Muslim League. Home Member,
Government of the United Provinces, and Vice-President of the
Executive Council, till 1926. Married, 1906. Created KCIE, 1921,
KCSI, 1922.

Malabari, Behramji Merwanji (1854–1912)
Indian Parsi social reformer. Founder and editor of *Indian Spectator*, which he edited for more than 20 years. Helped to start the

Voice of India. Editor and proprietor of *East and West.* Led a strong and popular movement in favour of social and religious reform. Mainly instrumental in securing the passage, of the Age of Consent Bill, 1891. Clashed with B. G. Tilak whose conservative ideas on reform he resented. Author.

Malcolm, Sir John (1769–1833)
British soldier and diplomat. Entered the Madras army, 1782. Ambassador to Persia, 1800, 1807 and 1810. Governor of Bombay, 1827–30. MP, 1831. Knighted in 1812. Author of several books on India and Persia.

Mamun, Abul Abbas Abdullah al (783–833)
An Abbasid Caliph. Son of Harun al-Rashid. A great patron of learning, science and research. Founded an academy in Baghdad called the *Bait-ul-Hikmat* ("House of Wisdom"). Encouraged the translation of Greek classics into Arabic.

Marx, Karl (1818–1883)
Son of a Jewish lawyer. Studied law at Bonn and Berlin. Editor, *Rheinische Zeitung,* 1842. Married, 1843, and moved to Paris. Expelled in 1845, and settled in Brussels. With Engels, he reorganized the Communist League, which met in London in 1847. Wrote the famous *Communist Manifesto,* 1848. Settled with his family in London, 1849. Died in London and buried there. Author of several works. One of the great influences in modern history.

Mary, Queen (1867–1953)
Consort of George V. Formerly Princess Victoria Mary Augusta Louise Olga Pauline Claudine Agnes of Teck. Born in London. Married George V, 1893. Collector of antiques and *objects d'art.*

McMahon, Sir Arthur Henry (1862–1949)
Educated at Haileyburg College, and Royal Military College, Sandhurst. Joined the British Army, 1883; transferred to Indian Service Corps, 1885. Joined Indian Political Department, 1890. Political Agent, Gilgit, 1897–98; Dir, Swat and Chitral, 1899–1901. Revenue and Judicial Commissioner, Baluchistan, 1901–02. Agent to the Governor General and Chief Commissioner, Baluchistan, 1905–11. Foreign Secretary, Government of India, 1911–14. First High Commissioner in Egypt, 1914–16. KCIE, 1906. GCVO, 1911. GCMG, 1916.

Mehta, Sir Pherozeshah (1845–1915)
Belonged to Bombay. Graduated from the University of Bombay,

1865. Called to the bar in London, 1868. Additional Member, Legislative Council of the Governor of Bombay, 1886. President, Indian National Congress, 1890; also elected for the 1909 Lahore session, but resigned a week before the meeting. Parsi by religion. Controlled the Congress from 1894 to 1904. Chairman, Reception Committee, Indian National Congress Bombay session, 1904. Member, Imperial Legislative Council, 1901. Vice-Chancellor, University of Bombay, 1915. Knighted in 1904.

Meston, 1st Baron: James Scorgie Meston (1865–1943)
Educated at the University of Aberdeen and Balliol College, Oxford. Entered the Indian Civil Service, 1885; served in the North-Western Provinces of Agra and Oudh. Financial Secretary to the Government of India, 1906–12. Lieutenant Governor, United Provinces, 1912–18. Finance Member, Viceroy's Executive Council, 1918–19. Main designer, with Lionel Curtis, of the Royal Institute of International Affairs, London; first Chairman of its Board of Governors, 1920–26. Chancellor, University of Aberdeen, 1928–43. President, British Liberal Party Organization, 1936–43. Created KCSI, 1911, and a Baron, 1919. Author.

Milner, 1st Viscount: Sir Alfred Milner (1854–1925)
Educated in Germany, King's College, London, and Balliol College, Oxford. On the staff of the *Pall Mall Gazette* and other papers, 1882–85. Private Secretary to Goschen, 1887–89. Governor of the Cape of Good Hope, 1897–1901. Governor of Transvaal and Orange River Colony, 1901–05. High Commissioner for South Africa, 1897–1905. Member, War Cabinet, 1916–18. Secretary of State for War, 1918–19. Secretary of State for Colonies, 1919–21. A pro-consul of immense influence and considerable power.

Minto, 4th Earl of: Gilbert John Murray Kynynmond Elliot (1847–1914)
Educated at Eton and Trinity College, Cambridge. In the British army, 1867–79. Military Secretary to the Governor General of Canada (Marquis of Lansdowne), 1883–85. Succeeded father, 1891. Governor General of Canada, 1898–1904. Viceroy of India, 1905–10. Lord Rector, University of Edinburgh. Created Knight of the Garter in 1910. Owned about 16,000 acres of land. Married, 1883, Mary, daughter of General the Honourable Charles Grey.

Mitra, Sir Bhupendra Nath (1875–1937)
Educated at Presidency College, Calcutta. Entered Government Service, 1896. Assistant Finance Secretary, Government of India, 1910; Deputy Secretary, 1915. Military Accountant General, 1919. Member, Viceroy's Executive Council, 1924–30. High Commissioner for India in London, 1931–36. Represented India at several international conferences. KCIE, 1924. KCSI, 1928.

Montagu, Edwin Samuel (1879–1924)
Son of 1st Baron Swaythling. Educated at Trinity College, Cambridge; president of the University Union, 1902. MP, Liberal, 1906–22. Private Secretary to H. H. Asquith, 1906–10. Parliamentary Under Secretary of State for India, 1910–14. Financial Secretary to the Treasury, 1914–16. Chancellor of the Duchy of Lancaster with seat in cabinet, 1915. Minister of Munitions, 1916; resigned in December. Secretary of State for India, June 1917–March 1922; toured India, November 1917–May 1918. Forced to resign owing to divergences with his colleagues over the Turkish policy.

Morison, Sir Theodore (1863–1936)
Educated at the University of Cambridge. Taught at the MAO College, Aligarh, 1889; Principal, 1899–1905. Member, Governor General's Legislative Council, 1903–04. President, All India Muhammedan Educational Conference, 1904. Member, Council of India, 1906–16. Member, Royal Commission on the Public Services in India, 1913–15. Served in the War, 1916–19. Principal, Armstrong College, Newcastle-upon-Tyne, 1919–29. Director, British Institute, Paris, 1933–36. Author.

Morley of Blackburn, 1st Viscount: John Morley (1838–1923)
Educated at Cheltenham College and Lincoln College, Oxford. Freelance journalist in London, 1860–63. Joined staff of the *Saturday Review*, 1863. Editor of *Fortnightly Review*, 1867, which he made a leading organ of liberal opinion. Much influenced by George Meredith and John Stuart Mill. Unsuccessful attempt at entering Parliament, 1868–69. Messenger of rationalism, progress and radicalism. Worked with Joseph Chamberlain and Sir Charles Dilke at programmes of disestablishment, secular education, land reform, and progressive taxation. Editor, *Pall Mall Gazette*, 1880, which he changed from conservatism and imperialism to radicalism and Cobdenism. Second unsuccessful attempt at entering Parliament, 1880. MP, 1883–1908. Chief Secretary for Ireland, 1886, 1892–95. Secretary of State for India, 1905–10. Created

Viscount, 1908. Resigned from cabinet, 1914. Chancellor, University of Manchester, 1908. Order of Merit, 1902. Edited "English Men of Letters" series. Statesman, man of letters, philosopher, liberal orator, and biographer. Author of many books.

Muawiyah (d. 680)
One of the sons of Abu Sufyan. Founder of the Umayyad dynasty. Compelled the leading men of the court and empire to acknowledge his son, Yazid, as successor to the Caliphate, thus establishing the first kingship in Islam.

Muhammad Ali (c. 1769–1849)
An Albanian officer of Militia who was sent to Egypt in 1798. In 1805 he had himself proclaimed Viceroy of Egypt by his Albanians and was then confirmed in this post by the Ottoman Sultan. He then massacred the Mamluks, formed a regular army, improved irrigation and modernized the land. Reduced part of Arabia, 1816, annexed Nubia and part of the Sudan, 1820, conquered parts of Syria, 1831. Became insane in 1848 and was succeeded by his son, Ibrahim.

Muhsin-ul-Mulk, Nawab Mehdi Ali Khan (1837–1909)
Belonged to the United Provinces. Born in Etawah in a Barha Sayyid family. Self-taught. Entered the East India Company's service as an *ahalmad* (clerk), 1857. Rose to be a *tahsildar*, 1861. Deputy Collector, 1867. In the service of the Nizam of Hyderabad, 1874–93, starting as Inspector General of Revenue and ending as Financial and Home Secretary. Resigned on account of intrigues in the Court. Took over the Secretaryship of the MAO College, Aligarh, in succession to Sir Sayyid Ahmad Khan. One of the pillars of the Aligarh Movement. Secretary and President (twice), All India Muhammadan Educational Conference. An ardent supporter of Urdu language, and founder of the Urdu Defence Association. Arranged the Simla Deputation of 1906 and inspired the concept of separate electorates for the Muslims. Played a leading role in the founding of the All India Muslim League, and was appointed one of its Joint Secretaries (the other being Nawab Viqar-ul-Mulk). Muhsin-ul-Mulk was a Hyderabad title, others bestowed by the Nizam were Munir Nawaz Jang and Muhsin-ud-Daulah. Orator, theologian, journalist, educationist, prose writer.

Mussolini, Benito (1883–1945)
A blacksmith's son. Edited the Socialist *Avanti*. Served in the

army during World War One. Founded the *Popolo d'Italia* and organized the Fascisti as militant nationalists to defeat socialism. Established himself as dictator, 1922. Annexed Abyssinia in 1936 and Albania in 1939. Entered World War Two on Germany's side. Defeated and caught by Italian Communists on 28 April 1945 and, after some form of trial, shot.

Mustafa Kamal Atatürk (1881–1938)
Turkish general and statesman. Born in Salonika. In the Ottoman army. A general in World War One. After the Turkish defeat, in Anatolia he led the great movement of national resistance stirred by the Greek invasion. Established a provisional government in 1920, and led the Turks to victory in the War of Independence, 1921–23. Declared Turkey a republic and was elected its President in 1923–38. Modernized and Westernized the country to the limits of its capacity.

Nadir Shah (1688–1747)
King of Persia. Born in Khurasan of a Turkish tribe. Expelled the Afghan rulers of Persia and restored Tahmasp to the throne. Defeated the Turks in 1731, imprisoned Tahmasp, and made his infant son, Abbas III, the ruler of Iran, 1732. On the boy's death in 1736, he assumed all powers himself. Conquered Afghanistan. Invaded the Mughal empire and looted Delhi and north-west India. Reduced Bukhara and Khiva. Assassinated.

Naidu, Sarojini (1879–1949)
Indian poet and politician. Educated at Madras, London and Cambridge. President, Indian National Congress, 1925. Attended the second Round Table Conference in London, 1931. Governor of the United Provinces, 1947. An active feminist. Her English verse shows her mastery of the lyric form and was translated into many Indian languages.

Nair, Sir Chettur Sankaran (1857–1934)
Legal practice in Madras. Judge, Madras High Court, 1907–15. Member, Viceroy's Executive Council, 1915–19. Member, Council of India, 1919–21. Chairman, Indian Central Committee to co-operate with the Indian Statutory (Simon) Commission. Knighted in 1912. Of liberal, independent views. Author.

Naoroji, Dadabhai (1825–1917)
Indian politician. Born in Bombay. Professor of Mathematics, Elphinstone College, Bombay. Member, Indian Legislative

Council. President, Indian National Congress. MP for Finsbury, 1892–95, the first Indian to sit in the House of Commons.

Nehru, Pandit Motilal (1861–1931)
Indian politician. Son of Gangadhar Nehru. Born posthumously in Agra. Kashmiri by origin. Educated in Cawnpore and Allahabad. Passed Vakils' examination in 1883. Legal practice in Cawnpore, later moved to Allahabad. Joined the Indian National Congress, 1888. President, Home Rule League branch, Allahabad, 1917. Founder, *Independent* daily, 1919. President, Indian National Congress, 1919. Member, United Provinces Legislative Council. Abandoned legal practice in response to Gandhi's call for non-co-operation, December 1921. Founded (with C. R. Das and others) the Swaraj Party, 1924. Leader of the opposition, Indian Legislative Assembly, 1923–29. President, Congress-appointed committee to draft a new constitution for India (whose report is known as Nehru Report), 1927–28. Chairman, Indian National Congress Working Committee, 1930. Father of Jawaharlal Nehru.

Nicholas II (1868–1918)
Emperor and Czar of Russia. Son of Alexander III. Succeeded father, 1894. Initiated the Hague Peace Conference, 1898. He made an alliance with France, an *entente* with Britain and a disastrous war on Japan. Established the Duma, 1906. Took command of Russian armies against the Central Powers, 1915. Overthrown by the Communist Revolution and shot with his family.

Nicholson, Reynold Alleyne (1868–1945)
Distinguished Orientalist. Educated at the University of Aberdeen and Trinity College, Cambridge. Fellow, 1893. University Lecturer in Persian, 1902–26. Professor of Arabic, 1926–33. Fellow, British Academy, 1922. Distinguished orientalist. Edited, translated and interpreted Jalaluddin Rumi's *Mathnawi* in eight volumes, 1925–40.

Nizami, Abu Yusuf Muhammad Iliyas ibn Yusuf Nizam al-Din (1141–1202)
A Persian poet and mystic. Born in Ganja. Author of the *Khamsah* ("the Five"), which includes the Arab love story of "Lailah and Majnun" and the "Seven Princesses."

Noon, Malik Sir Firoz Khan (1893–1970)
Educated at Aitchison Chiefs College, Lahore, and Wadham

College, Oxford. Called to the bar in London at the Inner Temple. Legal practice in Lahore, 1917–26. Member, Punjab Legislative Council, 1920–36. Minister for Local Self-Government, Punjab, 1927–30, and Education, 1931–36. High Commissioner for India in London, 1936–41. Member, Viceroy's Executive Council, 1941–45. Member, Punjab Legislative Assembly, 1946. Member, Pakistan Constituent Assembly, 1947, 1955. Governor of East Bengal, 1950–53. Chief Minister, Punjab, 1953–55. Foreign Minister of Pakistan, 1956–57. Prime Minister of Pakistan, 1957–58.

Northcliffe, 1st Viscount: Alfred Charles William Harmsworth (1865–1922)
Largely self-educated. Took up freelance journalism, 1882. Served in a publishing firm in Coventry, 1885–87. Formed, with his brother Harold (later Viscount Rothermere), a general publishing business in London, Amalgamated Press, 1887, and issued several periodicals from it. Acquired the *Evening News*, 1894. Founded the *Daily Mail*, 1896; and the *Daily Mirror*, 1903. Created a Baronet, 1903, and a Baron, 1905. Chief proprietor of *The Times*, 1908. Led the British War Mission in USA, 1917. Created Viscount, 1917. Director of Propaganda in Enemy countries. 1918. World tour, 1921–22. He changed the whole course of British journalism. Elder brother of Harold Sidney Harmsworth, 1st Viscount Rothermere (1868–1940), another newspaper proprietor.

Northcote, 1st Baron: Henry Stafford Northcote (1846–1911)
Second son of Sir Stafford Northcote (Earl of Iddesleigh). Educated at Eton and Merton College, Oxford. Clerk, Foreign Office, 1868. Private Secretary to Lord Salisbury, Constantinople Embassy, 1876–77; to the Chancellor of the Exchequer, 1877–80. Financial Secretary to the War Office, 1885–86. Surveyor General of Ordinance, 1886–87. Charity Commissioner, 1891–92. MP (Conservative), 1880–99. Governor of Bombay, 1899–1903. Governor General of Australia, 1903–08. Married 1873, Alice, adopted daughter of 1st Baron Mount Stephen. Created Baron, 1900. Privy Councillor, 1909.

Nurul Amin (1897–1974)
Educated at the University of Calcutta. Legal practice at Mymensingh, 1924–45. Member, Bengal Legislative Council, 1942. Member, Bengal Legislative Assembly, 1946. Speaker, Bengal

Legislative Assembly, 1946–57. Minister of Civil Supplies, East Bengal, 1947–48. Chief Minister, East Bengal, 1948–54.

Parmoor, 1st Baron: Charles Alfred Cripps (1852–1941)
Educated at Winchester and New College, Oxford. (4 firsts in Mathematics, History, Law and BCL). Fellow, St. John's College, Oxford. Honorary Fellow, New College, Oxford. Attorney General to the Prince of Wales, 1895, 1901, 1912. MP (Conservative), 1895–1914. British representative at the League of Nations, 1924. Lord President of the Council, 1924, 1929–31. Leader of the House of Lords, 1929–31. Member, Judicial Committee of the Privy Council, 1914. KC, 1890. KCVO, 1908. Baron, 1914. Author. Father of Sir Stafford Cripps.

Patel, Sardar Vallabhbhai Jhaverbhai (1875–1950)
Barrister-at-Law, 1913. Legal practice at Ahmedabad. Member, Ahmedabad Municipal Committee, 1917; Chairman, 1924–28. President, Indian National Congress, March 1931 Session, Delhi. Information Member, Interim Government, 1946–47. Deputy Prime Minister and Home Minister, Government of India, 1947–50. One of the strongmen of the Congress.

Paul, Saint (fl. first century AD)
The Apostle of the Gentiles. Born of Jewish parents at Tarsus in Cilicia. Executed under Nero. The ancient church recognized 13 of the New Testament Epistles as Paul's, but did not unanimously regard Hebrews as his.

Peter I (1672–1725)
Emperor of Russia. Son of the Tzar Alexei. Married Eudoxia, 1689. Joint ruler with brother, 1676–96. Effected many social and economic reforms. Reorganized the National Church. Founded the new capital, St. Petersburg in 1703. Conquered the Baltic provinces and a portion of Finland, 1710. Married his mistress, Catherine, 1712. Fought Persia, 1722. Succeeded by his wife, Catherine I.

Pethick-Lawrence, 1st Baron: Frederick William Pethick-Lawrence (1871–1961)
Educated at Eton and Trinity College, Cambridge (double first, and President of the Union, 1896). Fellow of Trinity, 1897. Editor, *Echo*, 1902–05; *Labour Record and Review*, 1905–07. Joint Editor, *Votes for Women*, 1907–14. MP (Labour), 1923–45. Delegate to the

Indian Round Table Conference, 1931. Secretary of State for India, 1945–47. Created Baron, 1945. Author of several books.

Pickthall, Marmaduke William (1875–1936)
Educated at Harrow and on the Continent. Lived for some years in the Near East. Editor, *Bombay Chronicle*, 1920–24. In the service of the Nizam of Hyderabad, 1925. Editor, *Islamic Culture*, Hyderabad Deccan. Translated the Quran into English. Converted to Islam. Novelist and author.

Pollen, John (1848–1923)
Educated at Trinity College, Dublin. Called to the bar. Entered the Indian Civil Service, 1871. Served in Bengal, Bombay and Sind, 1871–1905. Special correspondent of the *Daily Mail* in Russia, 1905. President, British Esperanto Association, 1904. On special duty with the Nawab of Radhanpur, 1906–07. President, 3rd International Congress of Esperantists, Cambridge, 1907. Honorary Secretary, East India Association, 1909–20. Honorary Fellow, University of Bombay. Additional Member, Bombay Legislative Council, 1902. CIE, 1903. Author.

Qaʾani, Habibullah Farsi (1808–1854)
Persian poet. Born in Shiraz. Died in Tehran. Last of the classical poets. Son of Gulshan, a poet of Shiraz. Studied in Shiraz and Isfahan. Interested in the exact sciences and philology. Wrote commentaries on Khagani and Anvari. A protégé of the governor of Fars. Court panegyrist in Tehran. Wielded a facile pen, and was a witty improviser. Also wrote many *ghazals* on philosophical, erotic-mystical and nature themes. His *Kitab-i-parishan* is a parallel to Sa'di's *Gulistan*. Learned French and probably some English.

Rafiuddin Ahmad, Sir (1865–1954)
Barrister-at-Law. Was one of the founders of the All India Muslim League, 1906. Minister of Education, Bombay, 1928–32. He lived in Poona.

Rampur, Nawab of: Sir Sayyid Muhammad Hamid Ali Khan (1875–1930)
Succeeded to the throne, 1889. Salute of 15 guns. ADC to the King. GCIE, 1908. GCVO, 1911. GCSI, 1921.

Ranade, Mahadev Govind (1842–1901)
Indian social reformer and judge. Educated in Poona, Bombay and Edinburgh. Entered Bombay civil service. Posted sub-judge,

Poona. Retired as Judge of the Bombay High Court. Member, Poona Sarvojanik Sabha, the Deccan Education Society, and Parathana Samaj. Social and religious reformer in the fields of child marriage, *purdah* system, and widow remarriage. Inaugurated the Indian National Social Conference. Rehabilitated the character of Shivaji and his empire. Believed, with some reservations, in the benevolent nature of British rule in India. A moderate in the Indian National Congress.

Rayleigh, 4th Baron: Robert John Strutt (1875–1947)
English physicist. Son of the 3rd Baron, John William (1842–1919). Professor of Physics, Imperial College of Science, London, 1908–19. Fellow of the Royal Society, 1905. Rumford Medallist. Notable for his work on rock radioactivity. Author of two biographies, one of his father, the other of Sir J. J. Thomson.

Reading, 1st Marquess of: Rufus Daniel Isaacs (1860–1935)
Son of a Jewish fruit merchant in Spitafields. Entered family business, 1875. Ship's boy on Blair Athole, 1876–77. Jobber on stock exchange, 1880–84. Called to the bar at the Middle Temple, 1887. Legal practice. Queen's Counsel, 1898. MP (Liberal), 1904–13. Solicitor General, March, and Attorney General, October, 1910. Privy Councillor and KCVO, 1911. Entered Cabinet, 1912. Implicated in the controversy over Marconi Company, 1912–13. Lord Chief Justice, 1913–21. Created Baron, 1914, and Viscount, 1916. High Commissioner for Finance in USA and Canada, September-November 1917. Created Earl, 1917. Ambassador and High Commissioner in USA, 1918–19. Viceroy of India, 1921–26. Supported the Government of India's request for a revision of the Treaty of Sèvres with Turkey with the result that the Treaty of Lausanne went far to relieve Indian Muslim anxiety. Created Marquess, 1926. Took a prominent part in the Indian Round Table Conferences, 1930–32. Secretary of State for Foreign Affairs, August–October 1931. Lord Warden of Cinque Ports, 1934–35. President, Imperial Chemical Industries. A remarkable example of speedy ascent to power in British politics and peerage.

Reed, Sir Herbert Stanley (1872–1969)
British editor and politician. Son of William Reed, a grocer of Fremantle Villa, Bristol. Educated privately. Joined journalism as a profession. On the staff of *The Times of India*, Bombay, 1897. Travelled extensively in India. Editor of the paper, 1907. Director of Publicity, Government of India, 1914–18. Vice-President,

Central Publicity Board of India, 1918. Retired from India, 1923, but for many years wrote for the paper from London. MP (Conservative), 1938–50. Married Lilian, 1901; she died in 1947. They had no children. Knighted in 1916; created KBE in 1919. Founder of the *Indian Year Book*, 1922. Author.

Ripon, 1st Marquess of: George Frederick Samuel Robinson (1827–1909)
Son of 1st Earl of Ripon. MP for Hull, 1852–53; for Huddersfield, 1853–57; for Yorkshire, West Riding, 1857–59. Under Secretary of State for War, 1859–61, for India, 1861–63. Secretary of State for War, 1863–66. Secretary of State for India, 1866. Lord President of the Council, 1868–73. Viceroy of India, 1880–84. First Lord of the Admiralty, 1886. Secretary of State for Colonies, 1892–95. Mayor of Ripon, 1895–96. Succeeded father, 1859. Created Marquess, 1871. Knight of the Garter, 1869. Owned about 21,800 acres of land. Married, 1851, Henrietta Anne Theodosia (died 1907), daughter of Captain Henry Vyner and grand daughter of 1st. Earl de Grey.

Rockefeller, John Davison (1839–1937)
American millionaire and philanthropist. Clerk in a commission house and then in a small oil refinery. Founded, with his brother William (1841–1922) the Standard Oil Co., 1922, which soon secured control of the oil trade of America. Founded the Rockefeller Foundation, 1913. He gave $500 million in aid of medical research, universities and Baptist churches.

Ross, Sir Edward Denison (1871–1940)
Educated at Marlborough and University College, London. Studied oriental languages on the Continent. Doctorate from the University of Strasbourg. Professor of Persian, University College, London, 1896–1901. Principal, Calcutta Madrasah, 1901–11. In charge of collections of Sir Aurel Stein at the British Museum, 1914. Director, School of Oriental Studies, and Professor of Persian, University of London, 1916–37. Counsellor, British Embassy in Istanbul, 1939–40. Knighted in 1918.

Rumbold, Sir Horace George Montagu (1869–1941)
Eldest son of the Rt. Hon. Sir Horace Rumbold, 8th Baronet. Succeeded father, 1913. Educated at Eton. In diplomatic service, 1890–20. British High Commissioner and Ambassador in Constantinople, 1920–24; in Madrid 1924–28; in Berlin, 1928–33. Second British Plenipotentiary at the Lausanne Conference, Nov-

ember 1922 – February 1923, and Chief Delegate, April – July 1923. Vice-Chairman, Royal Commission on Palestine. Created PC, 1920; GCB, 1934; GCMG 1923.

Rumi, Jalaluddin (1207–1273)
The greatest mystic poet Islam has produced. Of Persian origin of Balkh. Son of Bahauddin Walad. Leaving home with his father at an early age, he settled in Iconium, now Konia, in Turkey. Author of the celebrated 6-volume *Mathnawi*. Founder of the Mevlevi or Mawlawi Sufi order. In Persian poetry and Islamic lore of Iran, Central Asia, India and Turkey he has been since his death a powerful spiritual influence.

Rushd, ibn (Averroës) (1126–1198)
Muslim Spanish philosopher. Son of the Qazi of Cordoba. Himself a Qazi successively in Cordoba, Seville and Morocco. An acute commentator on Aristotle's writings. Offered the doctrine of a Universal Reason. Also wrote on medicine.

Sa'di, Shaikh Maslehuddin (c. 1208–1292)
Persian author and poet. Born in Shiraz, and died there. Travelled extensively in Muslim countries for 30 years, returning to Shiraz in 1256. Composed his *Bustan* in 1257, and the *Gulistan* in 1258. Also wrote *ghazals*. Considered as the perfect master of classical Persian style – flowing, graceful, harmonious and refined. He has been called the most human Persian author and the philosopher of common sense who teaches correct and elegant behaviour.

Salimullah Khan, Nawab Khwaja Sir (of Dacca) (1884–1915)
Indian politician. Son of Nawab Ahsanullah Khan of Dacca. Originally Kashmiri. A big landholder. Supported the Simla Deputation, 1906. One of the founders of the All India Muslim League, 1906. President, All India Muslim League, 1907, 1912. Vice-President Bengal Provincial Muslim League, 1912–15. KCSI, GCIE.

Samuel, 1st Viscount: Herbert Louis Samuel (1870–1963)
British Liberal statesman and philosophical writer. Born into a Jewish banking family. Educated at Balliol College, Oxford. Entered Parliament, 1902. Chancellor of the Duchy of Lancaster, 1909. Postmaster General, 1910, 1915. Home Secretary, 1916, 1931–32. High Commissioner for Palestine, 1920–25. President,

Royal Statistical Society, 1918–20. Created Viscount, 1937, and OM, 1958. Author of several books.

Sandow, Eugene (1867–1925)
Born in Königsberg of Russian parents. Exponent of physical culture and an artist's model. Founded the Institute of Health in St. James's Street, London. A household name for a strong man.

Sankey, 1st Viscount: John Sankey (1866–1948)
Educated at Jesus College, Oxford. Called to the bar at Middle Temple, 1892. Judge of the King's Bench Division, 1914–28. Lord Justice of Appeal, 1928–29. Lord Chancellor, 1929–35. Member, Permanent Court of Arbitration at the Hague, 1930–48. Chairman, Federal Structure Committee, Round Table Conference, 1930. High Steward, Oxford University, 1930. Honorary Fellow, University College, London. Honorary doctorates from Oxford, Wales, Cambridge and Bristol. Knighted in 1914, GBE, 1917. PC, 1928. Baron, 1929.

Sapru, Sir Tej Bahadur (died 1949)
Educated at Agra College, Agra. President, Indian Liberal Federation. Member, All India Congress Committee. Member, United Provinces Legislative Council, 1913–16; of Imperial Legislative Council, 1916–20. Law Member, Viceroy's Executive Council, 1920–23. Delegate, Round Table Conferences, 1930–32; and Joint Committee on Indian Constitutional Reform, 1933–34. KCSI, 1923. PC, 1934.

Sastri, the Rt. Hon. V. S. Srinivasa (1869–1946)
Educated at the Government College, Kumbakonam. Taught at and later headed a school. Resigned in 1907 and joined the Servants of India Society, Poona, of which he was President, 1915–27. Secretary, Indian National Congress, 1908. Member, Madras Legislative Council, 1913, Imperial Legislative Council, 1915–20, and Council of State, 1921. Delegate, Imperial Conference, 1921, and League of Nations, 1921. Member, Indian South Africa Conferences, 1922, 1932. President, National Liberal Federation of India, 1922. Agent General of India in South Africa, 1927–29. Delegate to the first two sessions of the Round Table Conference, 1930–31. Vice-Chancellor, Annamalai University, 1935–40. Privy Councillor, 1921. Companion of Honour, 1930. Freedom of the City of London, 1921, and of Edinburgh, 1931. Author of several books.

Sayyid Ahmad Khan, Sir (1817–1898)
Belonged to Delhi. In the East India Company's service, 1838–58. Munsif at Bijnore, Muradabad, Ghazipur, Aligarh and Benares, 1858–78. Member, Governor General's Council, 1879–86. Founded MAO College, Aligarh, 1875. Founder of the Aligarh Movement. Author, historian, editor, educationist, social reformer, religious scholar and thinker.

Sethna, Sir Phiroze (1866–1938)
Educated at the University of Bombay. In business. Delegate, Round Table Conference. British Indian Delegate to the Joint Committee on Indian Constitutional Reform. President, Bombay Municipal Corporation. President, Indian National Liberal Federation. Member, Council of State. Justice of the Peace. Knighted in 1926.

Shafā'at Ahmad Khan, Sir (1893–1947)
Born in Muradabad, United Provinces. Educated at Trinity College, Dublin, and Sydney Sussex College, Cambridge. Taught at the University of Madras, 1919–20. Professor of Modern Indian History, University of Allahabad. Member, United Provinces Legislative Council, 1924. President, Bengal Muslim Conference, 1930. Delegate to all the three sessions of the Round Table Conference, 1930–32, and to the Joint Select Committee on Indian Constitutional Reform, 1933. Honorary Secretary, Muslim Delegation to the Round Table Conference, 1930–31. President, Muslim Youth League, Calcutta, May 1931. Chairman, All India Muslim Conference, 1933–34. President, All India Modern History Congress, Poona, June 1935. High Commissioner for India in South Africa, 1941–44. Member for Health, Education and Arts, Viceroy's Executive Council ("Interim Government"), September – October 1946. Knighted in 1935. Author of several books.

Shafi, Mian Sir Muhammad (1869–1932)
Belonged to a suburb of Lahore, Punjab. Educated at the Forman Christian College and Government College, Lahore. Called to the bar at the Middle Temple Inn of Court, London, 1892. Legal practice in Hoshiarpur (briefly) and Lahore. Member, Simla Deputation, 1906. Member, Punjab Legislative Council and Imperial Legislative Council, 1909–19. President, All India Urdu Conference, 1911. Refused the offer of a judgeship of the Madras High Court in 1912 and the Punjab High Court, 1918. Founder of the Punjab Provincial Muslim League. President, All India

Muslim League, 1913 and 1927. President, All India Muham-medan Educational Conference, 1916. Member, Viceroy's Executive Council, 1919–24; Vice-President, 1923–24. Leader of the Council of State, 1922–24. Delegate, Imperial Conference, 1930, and the first two sessions of the Round Table Conference, 1930–31. Appointed Member of the Viceroy's Executive Council (temporary), but died before he could enter office. Knighted in 1922.

Shafi Daudi (b. 1879)
Belonged to Bihar. Educated at the University of Calcutta. Legal practice in Calcutta and Patna. Active in the Khilafat and non-co-operation movements. Secretary, Bihar Khilafat Committee. President, Bihar Provincial Congress Committee, 1921. Leader of the Bihar Swaraj Party. Opposed the Nehru Report. One of the founders of the All India Muslim Conference, 1928, and its able, devoted and energetic General Secretary for many years. Formed an Ahrar Party in Bihar, 1937, and on its defeat in the elections of that year retired from public life.

Shahjahan (1592–1666)
Mughal emperor of India. Son of Jahangir. Succeeded father in 1627. Vanquished Ahmadnagar, Bijapur and Golcanda in the South. Failed to recover Qandhar from Persia. Made helpless and imprisoned by his ambitious son, Aurangzeb, 1658. Died in captivity. Builder of the Taj Mahal. His age was unequalled in Indian history for its magnificence of the court and the loveli-ness of the works of art produced.

Shakespeare, William (1564–1616)
Pre-eminent English dramatist and poet. Born in Stratford-on-Avon. Son of John Shakespeare, a glover, and his wife, Mary Arden. Eldest of three sons. Came to London, *c.* 1585. Wrote plays and was associated with a few theatrical companies. Lived in Silver Street, 1602–06, and then moved to the south side near the Globe. Retired to his own house, New Place, in Stratford. Married Anne Hathaway.

Sinha, 1st Baron: Satyendra Prasanno Sinha (1864–1928)
Born in Bengal. Called to the bar at the Lincoln's Inn, 1881. Standing Counsel to the Government of Bengal, 1903. Advocate General of Bengal, 1908. Law Member, Viceroy's Executive Council, 1909 (first Indian to enter the Council). President, Indian National Congress, 1915. Member, Imperial War Cabinet

and Conference, London, 1917. Parliamentary Under Secretary of State for India, 1919. Governor of Bihar and Orissa, 1920–21. Member, Judicial Committee of the Privy Council, 1926. Knighted in 1914, created Baron, 1919, Privy Councillor, 1919.

Sly, Sir Frank George (1866–1928)
Educated at Balliol College, Oxford. Entered ICS, 1885. Inspector General of Agriculture, 1904–05. Commissioner of Berar, 1908–12. Member, Royal Commission on Public Services in India, 1912–14. Vice-Chairman, Southborough Committee on Franchise, 1918–19. Chief Commissioner, Central Provinces and Berar, 1920. Governor of Central Provinces, 1921–25. Honorary D. Litt, University of Nagpur, 1924. CSI, 1911. KCSI, 1918.

Smith, Vincent Arthur (1848–1920)
Educated at Trinity College, Dublin. In the ICS, 1871–1900. Lecturer in Indian History, Trinity College, Dublin; later at University of Oxford. Fellow, University of Allahabad. Gold Medallist, Royal Asiatic Society, 1918. Created CIE, 1919. Historian and author.

Smuts, Jan Christian (1870–1950)
Born in Cape Colony of Dutch origin. Educated at Stellenbosch and Christ's College, Cambridge. Admitted to Cape bar, 1895; shifted to Transvaal, 1896. State Attorney, 1898. Boer delegate to Pretoria, 1902. Colonial Secretary and Minister of Education in Transvaal, 1907–10. Minister of Defence, Union Government, 1910–19. Lieutenant General in the British army to command imperial forces in East Africa, 1916. In the imperial war cabinet and conference, London, 1917. Chairman, War Priorities Committee. A chief sponsor of the League of Nations. Prime Minister of South Africa, 1919–24. Deputy Prime Minister under J. B. M. Hertzhog, 1933–39. Prime Minister, 1939–48. Created Field Marshal, 1941. Rector of St. Andrews University, 1931–34. Chancellor, University of Cape Town, 1936–50, and Cambridge, 1948–50. Companion of Honour, 1917. Fellow, Royal Society, 1930. President, British Association, 1931. Order of Merit, 1947.

Southborough, 1st Baron: Francis John Stephens (1860–1947)
Educated at King Edward VI School, Louth. Admitted as solicitor, 1882. Entered the Board of Trade, 1885; Permanent Secretary, 1901–07. Permanent Under Secretary for the Colonies, 1907–10. Vice-Chairman, Development Commission, 1910–12. Civil Lord of Admiralty, 1912–17. Chairman, War Trade Committees,

1914–18. Secretary, Irish Convention, 1917–18. Chairman, Indian Franchise Committee, 1918–19. Created KCB, 1901, Privy Councillor, 1912, Baron and GCVO, 1917, and KCSI, 1920. Civil servant.

Spinoza, Baruch (1632–1677)
Dutch–Jewish philosopher. Born in Amsterdam in a Jewish émigré family from Spain and Portugal. In 1656 he was excommunicated by the synagogue on account of his deep interest in optics, new astronomy and Cartesian philosophy, and made a living grinding and polishing lenses. Became the leader of a small philosophical circle. Published his *Short Treatise on God, Man and his Well-being* and *Tractatus de Intellectus Emendatione*, 1677, and *Ethica* (1677, posthumously). Refused the Professorship of Philosophy at Heidelberg, 1673.

Stansgate, 1st Viscount: William Wedgwood Benn (1877–1960)
English politician. Liberal MP, 1906–27, Labour, 1927–41. Joined the Labour Party, 1927. Secretary of State for India, 1929–31. Secretary of State for Air, 1945–46. Served in the two World Wars, winning the DSO and DFC. Created a Viscount, 1941.

Stresemann, Gustav (1878–1929)
German statesman. Born in Berlin. Entered the Reichstag, 1907, as a National Liberal, and rose to be the leader of his party. After World War One founded and led his German People's Party. Chancellor of the new German (Weimar) Republic for a few months in 1923. Minister of Foreign Affairs, 1923–29. Secured the entry of Germany into the League of Nations, 1926. Shared with Briand the Nobel prize for peace, 1926.

Sykes, Sir Frederick Hugh (d. 1954)
Son-in-law of Prime Minister Bonar Law. Entered the British Army, 1901. Major General, 1918. First Controller General of Civil Aviation, 1919–22. MP (Unionist), 1922–28. Governor of Bombay, 1928–33. MP (Unionist), 1940–45. Lees-Knowles Lecturer, University of Cambridge, 1921. Chairman, Royal Empire Society, 1938–41. President, East India Association. Vice-President, Royal India Society. KCB, 1919. GBE, 1919. GCIE, 1928. PC, 1928. GCSI, 1934. Author.

Talhah ibn Ubaidullah (d. 683)
One of the Companions of the Prophet. He took part in the

insurrection against Caliph Ali and was killed in the Battle of the Camel.

Tamerlane: Timur (1336–1405)
Tartar conqueror. Born in Samarqand. Son of a Mongol chief. King of Samarqand, 1369. Conquered Persia, Georgia and the Tartar empire and all the states between the Indus and the lower Ganges. Won Damascus and the whole of Syria. Defeated the Turkish emperor Bayazid. Died on the march towards China. One of the great world conquerors and rulers.

Templewood, 1st Viscount: Sir Samuel John Gurney Hoare (1880–1959)
British Conservative politician. Educated at Harrow and Oxford. Entered politics in 1905 as assistant private secretary to the Colonial Secretary. MP, 1910–44. Secretary of State for Air, 1922–29, and for India, 1931–35. Piloted the Government of India bill through the House of Commons. Foreign Secretary, 1935; resigned on account of the criticism of his part in negotiating the Hoare-Laval pact. First Lord of the Admiralty, 1936. Home Secretary, 1937–39. Ambassador on special mission in Madrid, 1940–44.

Thackeray, William Makepeace (1811–1863)
English novelist. Born in Calcutta, where his father served the East India Company. Educated at Charterhouse and Trinity Hall, Cambridge, 1829; left without taking a degree. Travelled abroad. Spent one year in Paris studying art. Married, 1836. Entered journalism. Started writing novels. On the staff of *Punch* for many years. Editor, *Cornhill*, 1854. Lecture tours in Britain and America.

Thomson, Sir Joseph John (1856–1940)
British mathematical physicist. Son of a Scottish bookseller of Manchester. Educated at Owen's College, Manchester, and Trinity College, Cambridge. Cavendish Professor of Experimental Physics (succeeding Lord Rayleigh), 1884. Work concerned with electromagnetic theories and cathode rays. Discovered the isotope. Made the Cavendish Laboratories the greatest research institution in the world. Master of Trinity College, Cambridge, 1918–40. Won the Nobel Prize, 1906. Knighted in 1908. OM, 1912. President, British Association, 1909. President of the Royal Society, 1915–20. Wrote his *Recollections and Reflections* in 1936.

Tilak, Bal Gangadhar (1856–1920)
Indian politician. A Chitpavan Brahmin of Bombay. Born in Ratnagiri. Studied mathematics and law. One of the founders of the New English School in Poona, 1880. Founded Deccan Education Society, 1884. Issued his *Kesari* in Marathi, 1881, and *Maratha* in English. Gave private coaching in law. Aroused Hindu nationalism through religious festivals and historical revivalism: Ganapati festival in 1894 and Shivaji festival in 1896. Attacked Christian missionaries and Muslims in general. Opposed Hindu social reform. A bitter critic of Indian National Congress moderates, he split the Congress in 1907 at Surat by forming his own extremist wing. Hindu religious scholar.

Trotsky, Leon alias Lev Davidovich Bronstein (1879–1940)
Russian Jewish revolutionary. Born in the Ukraine. Educated in Odessa. Arrested in 1898 as a member of a Marxist group and sent to Siberia. Escaped in 1902 and joined Lenin in London. President of the first Soviet in the 1905 abortive revolution. Revolutionary journalist among Russian émigrés in the West. Returned to Russia in 1917, joined the Bolshevik party and, with Lenin, organized the November revolution. Commissar for Foreign Affairs, 1917. Commissar for War during the civil war. Driven out of the Politbureau by Stalin, 1926. Exiled to Central Asia, 1927. Expelled from Russia, 1929. Lived in several countries, and in 1937 found asylum in Mexico. Assassinated there by Ramon del Rio. Ruthless, energetic; orator, visionary, and a writer of power, wit and venom. Author of several works.

Turner, Sir Montagu Cornish (1853–1934)
Educated at Winchester College. Joined the firm of Mackinnon Mackenzie and Co., Calcutta, 1877. President, Bengal Chamber of Commerce, 1898, 1901, 1902. Additional Member Viceroy's Council, 1901–02. Knighted in 1903.

Tyabji, Badruddin (1844–1906)
Indian politician, judge and social reformer. Educated at Elphinstone Institution, Bombay, and London. During a second stay in London he was called to the bar, 1867. First Indian barrister to be enrolled as an advocate at the Bombay High Court. Member, Bombay Legislative Council, 1882. Founder (with Pherozeshah Mehta and Kashinath Telang), Bombay Association, 1885. President, Indian National Congress, 1887. Founder, Anjuman-i-Islam; its President, 1890–1906. President, All India Muhammadan Educational Conference, 1903. Fellow, University of Bombay. Judge,

Bombay High Court, 1895; officiated as Chief Justice, 1903. Died in England, where he had come for the treatment of an eye ailment.

Umar ibn al-Khattab (d. 644)
The second Caliph, succeeding Abu Bakr. The first to assume the title of *Amir-ul-Muminin,* and to promulgate the *Hijra* calendar. Assassinated by a certain Abu Lu'lu'ah Firoz, a Persian slave of the Governor of Basra. Famed for his strong will, directness and decisiveness.

Umar Khayyam (*c.* 1050–*c.* 1123)
The astronomer-poet of Iran, famous for his celebrated quatrains. Born and died in Nishapur. Reformed the Islamic calendar. Wrote treatises on mathematics. His quatrains were freely rendered into English verse by Edward Fitzgerald in 1859.

Usman ibn Affan (d. 656)
The third Caliph of Islam, succeeding Umar. Ordered the compilation of the Quran from the memories of the Companions of the Prophet and such written records as existed. His later reign was marked by troubles, insurrections and a virtual civil war. Assassinated.

Vámbéry Arminius (1832–1913)
Hungarian traveller and philologist. Assistant to a ladies' dressmaker. Teacher. Taught French in the house of a minister in Constantinople. Issued a German-Turkish dictionary, 1858. Travelled disguised as a *dervish* through the deserts of the Oxus to Khiva and Samarqand, 1862–64. Professor of Oriental Languages, Budapest University, till 1905. Author of many works.

Venizelos, Eleutherios (1864–1936)
Greek statesman. Studied law in Athens. Led the Liberal Party in the Cretan chamber of deputies. Minister of Justice, Crete. Prime Minister of Greece, 1910–15. Promoted the Balkan League against Turkey. Forced the abdication of King Constantine. Defeated in the 1920 general elections, which brought the Royalists and the King back to power. Prime Minister, 1924, 1928–32 and 1933. Fled to Paris, 1935, where he died.

Victoria, Queen Alexandrina (1819–1901)
Queen of the United Kingdom. Only child of George III's fourth son, Edward, Duke of Kent, and Victoria Maria Louisa of Saxon Coburg, sister of Leopold, King of the Belgians. Born in London.

Ascended the throne on the death of her uncle, William IV, 20 June 1837. Crowned at Westminster, 28 June 1838. Married Prince Albert of Saxon Coburg and Gotha, 10 February 1840. Strongly influenced by her husband. First Empress of India.

Voelcker, Dr. John Augustus (1854–1937)
Educated at the University College, London, and Universities of Giessen (Hesse) and Cambridge. Specialized in the study of chemistry in relation to agriculture. In India on official duty, 1889–90. Analytical and consulting chemist. CIE, 1928. Author.

Wavell, 1st Earl: Archibald Percival Wavell (1883–1950)
British soldier and administrator. Educated at Winchester and the Royal Military College, Sandhurst. Entered the British Army, 1901. Served in India and South Africa. Wounded in 1916 and lost the sight of one eye. Given the Middle East Command, 1939. Viceroy of India, 1943–47. Created Field Marshal and a Viscount, 1943, and an Earl, 1947. Constable of the Tower, 1948. Lord Lieutenant of London, 1949. Author.

Wells, Herbert George (1866–1946)
Son of an unsuccessful tradesman. Educated at a commercial school and by wide reading. Apprenticed to pharmacy and drapery, successively. Student assistant, Midhurst Grammar School, 1883–84. Studied at the Normal School of Science, South Kensington, London, under T. H. Huxley, but failed the third year examination. Graduated in science, University of London, 1890. Tutor, University Tutorial College, London, 1891. Started writing short stories, 1895; later romances, science fiction and novels. Foresaw war in air, tanks and atomic bomb. Increasingly preoccupied with the ideal of a "World State". Flounced in and out of party socialism and other movements, notably the Fabian Society. Author, novelist, historian.

Whitehead, Alfred North (1861–47)
Educated at Trinity College, Cambridge; fourth wrangler, 1883; Fellow, 1884–1947; Lecturer, 1884–1910. Fellow, Royal Society, 1903. With Bertrand Russell published *Principia Mathematica*, 3 volumes, 1910–13, the "greatest single contribution to logic since Aristotle" (*Dictionary of National Biography*). Professor of Applied Mathematics, Imperial College of Science and Technology, London, 1914–24. Professor of Philosophy, University of Harvard, 1924–37. Put forward the doctrine that ultimate components of reality are events. Defined his mature thinking as "philosophy

of organism". Fellow, British Academy, 1931. Order of Merit, 1945. Mathematician, philosopher, teacher.

William II, Kaiser (1859–1941)
Third German emperor (ruled 1888–1918) and ninth King of Prussia. Eldest son of Frederick III and of Victoria, the daughter of Britain's Queen Victoria. Born at Potsdam. Received a strict military and academic education at the Kassel gymnasium and the University of Bonn. Had a deformed left arm. After dismissing Bismarck in 1890 he ruled with untrammelled authority. Visited Arab countries of the Middle East, 1898. Led Germany into World War One, 1914. Defeated in war, he abdicated and fled the country on 9 November 1918 to settle in Holland. Married Princess Augusta Victoria, 1881, and, after her death in 1921, Princess Hermine of Reuss.

Willingdon, 1st Marquess of: Freeman Freeman-Thomas (1866–1941)
Educated at Eton and Trinity College, Cambridge; captain of cricket, 1889. MP, Liberal, 1900–10. Created Baron, 1910. Governor of Bombay, 1913–18. Governor of Madras, 1919–24. Created Viscount, 1924. Governor General of Canada, 1926–30. Viceroy of India, 1931–36. Created Earl, 1931, Privy Councillor, 1931, and Marquess, 1936. Head of trade mission to South America, 1940.

Wilson, Thomas Woodrow (1856–1924)
American statesman and 28th President of USA. Born in Virginia. Educated at the Universities of Princeton and John Hopkins. Legal practice at Atlanta. Lecturer at Bryn Mawr College and the University of Princeton. President of Princeton, 1902. Governor of New Jersey, 1911. President of the country, 1912–20. Author.

Wordsworth, William (1770–1850)
English poet. Son of an attorney. Lost both parents at an early age. Studied at Cambridge, 1787–91. Lived in France, 1791–93. Married Mary Hutchinson, 1802. Poet laureate, 1843. His works and letters were edited by De Selincourt in 1935–40.

Yakub, Sir Muhammad (1879–1942)
Born in Muradabad in the United Provinces. Educated at MAO College, Aligarh. Legal practice in Muradabad. Trustee, MAO College, Aligarh. President, United Provinces Provincial Muslim League, 1926, All India Muslim League, 1927. Member, Indian

Legislative Assembly, 1924–38; Deputy President, 1927–30; President, 1930. Member, All India Palestine Conference, Bombay, 1929. Honorary Secretary, All India Muslim League, 1930–35. Member, Indian Franchise Committee, 1932. Member, Council of State, 1938–42. Officiating Member for Commerce and Industries, Viceroy's Executive Council, 1938. Knighted in 1938.

Yusuf Ali, Abdullah (1872–1953)
Educated at Wilson College, Bombay, and St. John's College, Cambridge. Called to the bar at Lincoln's Inn. Entered the Indian Civil Service, 1895. Deputy Secretary, Government of India, 1911–12. Retired 1914. President, United Provinces Industrial Conference, 1909. President, All India Muslim Educational Conference, Nagpur, December 1910. Lecturer on Hindustani, Hindi and Indian Religions, Manners and Customs, School of Oriental Studies, University of London, 1917–19. Member, Committee on India, Imperial Institute, 1916–19. Lecture tour in Denmark, Sweden, Norway, April-May 1918; and in Holland, October-November 1920. Sarf-i-Khas Counsel, Hyderabad Deccan, 1919–20. Revenue Minister, Hyderabad Deccan, 1921–22. Legal practice in Lucknow, 1922–24. Principal, Islamia College, Lahore, 1925–27. Indian representative at the League of Nations, 1928. World tour, 1929–30. President, Sind Azad Conference, 1932. President, All India Muslim Conference, 1933. Member, Punjab University Inquiry Committee, 1932–33. Principal, Islamia College, Lahore, 1935–37. Lecture tour of Canada, 1938–39. CBE, 1917. Author. English translator and commentator of the Quran.

Zafrullah Khan, Sir Muhammad (1893–1985)
Indian and Pakistani statesman. Belonged to the Punjab. Educated at Government College, Lahore, and King's College, London. Legal practice in Sialkot, 1914–16, and in Lahore, 1916–35. Editor, *Indian Cases*, 1916–32, and *Criminal Law Journal of India*. Lecturer, Law College, Lahore, 1919–24. Member, Punjab Legislative Council, 1926–32. Member, Punjab Reform (Simon) Committee, 1928. Delegate to the three sessions of the Round Table Conference, London, 1930–32, and to the Joint Select Committee on Indian Constitutional Reform, 1933–34. Member, Indian Legislative Assembly, 1932–40. President, All India Muslim League, 1931. Member, Viceroy's Executive Council, 1932, 1935–41. Agent General of the Government of India in China, 1942. Leader, Indian Delegation to the League

of Nations, 1939. Judge, Federal Court of India, October 1941 – June 1947. Constitutional Adviser to the Nawab of Bhopal, June–December 1947. Minister of Foreign Affairs and Commonwealth Relations, Pakistan, 1947–54; forced to resign by the anti-Ahmadiyya agitation. Permanent Representative and Envoy Extraordinary of Pakistan in the United Nations, 1961–64; President, United Nations General Assembly, 1962. Member, International Court of Justice, 1954–61, and 1964 onwards; President of the Court, 1970 onwards. Knighted in 1935. Ranking leader of the Ahmadiyya community. Author of several books on world affairs, Pakistan and Islam. Translated the Quran into English.

Zetland, 2nd Marquess of: Lawrence John Lumley Dundas (1876–1961)
British politician and author. Born in London. Elder surviving son of the 3rd Earl, later 1st Marquess, Zetland, Viceroy of Ireland. Educated at Harrow and Trinity College, Cambridge. ADC to Lord Curzon, 1900. Travelled extensively in the East. Earl of Ronaldshay, 1892. MP, 1907–16. Member, Royal Commission on the Public Services in India, 1912–14. Governor of Bengal, 1917–22. Declined High Commissionership in Egypt, which went to Lord Lloyd. Expected to be offered the Viceroyalty of India, but the appointment went to Lord Reading. Delegate to the Round Table Conference, 1930–32, and to the Joint Select Committee on Indian Constitutional Reform, 1933–34. Secretary of State for India, 1935–40. Governor of the National Bank of Scotland. President, Royal Geographical Society, 1922–25, and its Trustee till 1947. Chairman, National Trust, 1931–45. Married Cicely Alice, 1907; she died in 1973. Author of several books. Created GCIE, 1917, GCSI, 1922, PC, 1922. Succeed his father in 1929.

Ziauddin Ahmad, Dr. Sir (1878–1947)
A graduate of the MAO College, Aligarh. Lecturer in Mathematics, MAO College, Aligarh. Graduated from Cambridge, 1904. Studied at the University of Göttingen, Germany, 1904. Doctorate from Bologna University. Returned to Aligarh, 1907. Member, Sadler Commission on Calcutta University, 1917–19. Principal, MAO College, Aligarh, 1919–20. Pro-Vice-Chancellor, Aligarh University, 1920–28; Vice-Chancellor, 1935–47. Member, Indian Legislative Assembly, 1930–47; first independent, then Muslim League. Created CIE, 1915, Knighted 1938. Died in London in December 1947.

Zulfiqar Ali Khan of Malerkotla, Nawab Sir Muhammad (1875–1933)
Educated at Cambridge and Paris. Member of the ruling family of
Malerkotla State. Member, Indian Legislative Assembly. Member
Indian Council of State. Knighted in 1919. Author.

BIBLIOGRAPHY

Books

Abbasi, M. Yusuf, *London Muslim League (1908–1928): An Historical Study*, National Institute of Historical and Cultural Research, Islamabad, 1988.

———, *The Political Biography of Syed Ameer Ali*, Wajidalis, Lahore, 1989.

Aga Khan, The, *India in Transition: A Study in Political Evolution*, Philip Lee Warner, London, and The Times of India Press, Bombay, 1918.

———, *The Memoirs of Aga Khan: World Enough and Time*, Cassell, London, 1954.

———, *Message to the World of Islam by the Aga Khan III*, Karachi, 1977.

———, *Itehad-el-Islam Otherwise known as the Cultural, Religious, Economic Pan-Islamism*, n.p., n.p.p., n.d.

Aga Khan, Prince, and Dr. Zaki Ali, *Glimpses of Islam*, Shaikh Muhammad Ashraf, Lahore, 1944.

Ahmad, Aziz, *Islamic Modernism in India and Pakistan, 1857–1964*, Oxford University Press, London, 1967.

Ahmad, Sayyid Nur, *Mian Fazl-i-Husain: A Review of his Life and Work*, Punjab Educational Press, Lahore, n.d. (?1936).

Ahmad, Waheed, *Road to Indian Freedom: The Formation of the Government of India Act, 1935*, The Caravan Book House, Lahore, n.d. (?1979).

——— (ed.), *Letters of Mian Fazl-i-Husain*, Research Society of Pakistan, Lahore, 1976.

Ali, Sayyid Mujtaba, *The Origin of the Khojas and their Religious Life Today*, Ludwig Rohrscheider Verlag, Bonn, 1936.

Ali, Sayyid Raza, *A'mal Nama*, Hindustani Publishers, Delhi, 1943. In Urdu.

Allana, G., *Our Freedom Fighters, 1562–1947*, Paradise Subscription Agency, Karachi, 1969.

All India Muslim Conference, *Report of the All India Muslim Conference held at Delhi on 31 December, 1928, and 1st January, 1929*, compiled and published by authority by Hafizur Rahman, Aligarh, n.d.

Ambedkar, B. R. *Thoughts on Pakistan*, Thacker, Bombay, 1941.

An Indian Mahomedan, *The Indian Muslims*, Ardenne, London, 1928. The pseudonym belongs to Nawab Sayyid Sardar Ali Shah.

Arberry, A. J. (ed.), *Religion in the Middle East: Three Religions in Concord and Conflict, Vol. 2: Islam*, Cambridge University Press, Cambridge, 1969.

Aziz, K. K., *A History of the Idea of Pakistan*, Vanguard, Lahore, 1987, 4 volumes.

———, *Britain and Muslim India: A Study of British Public Opinion vis à vis the Development of Muslim Nationalism in India, 1857–1947*, William Heinemann, London, 1963.

———, *History of Partition of India*, Atlantic, New Delhi, 1988.

———, *The All India Muslim Conference, 1928–1935: A Documentary Record*, National Publishing House, Karachi, 1972.

———, *The Indian Khilafat Movement, 1915–1933: A Documentary Record*, Pak Publishers, Karachi, 1972.

———, *Ameer Ali: His Life And Work*, Publishers United, Lahore, 1968.

Bahadur, Lal, *The Muslim League: Its History, Activities and Achievements*, Agra Book Store, Agra, 1954.

Barclay, Thomas, *The Turco-Italian War and its Problems*, Constable, London, 1912.

Barni, Z.A., 'Azmat-i-Rafta, T'alimi Makaz, Karachi, 1961.

Barrow, Andrew, *Gossip: A History of High Society from 1920–70*, Hamish Hamilton, London, 1978.

Beck, George Thompson, *The Caliphate Agitation in India, 1919–1923, and its influence on British Near Eastern Policy*, n.p., 1952.

Bhatnagar, S. K., *A History of the M.A.O. College, Aligarh*, Asia Publishing House, Bombay, 1969.

Bikaner, Maharaja of, *The Insistent Claims of Indian Reform*, Philip Lee Warner, London, n.d. (?1919).

Blunt, Wilfed S., *My Diaries: Being a Personal Narrative of Events, 1884–1914*, Martin Secker, London, 1919–20.

Bose, Mihir, *The Aga Khans*, World's Works, Kingswood, England, 1984.

Brendon, Piers, *Eminent Edwardians*, Secker and Warburg, London, 1979.

Browne, Edward G., *A Literary History of Persia*, Cambridge University Press, Cambridge, 1902–24, 4 volumes.

Buchan, John, *Lord Minto: A Memoir*, Thomas Nelson, London, 1924.

Budhwani, N. M. (ed.), *The Aga Khan and the League of Nations*, The Ismaili Office, Dhoraji, 1938.

Chiragh, M. A., *Akabaran-i-Tahrik-i-Pakistan*, Sang-i-Meel Publications, Lahore, 1990. In Urdu.

Chunara, A. J., *Platinum Jubilee Review*, Karachi, 1954.

Coatman, John, *Years of Destiny: India, 1926–32*, Jonathan Cape, London, 1932.

Cox, Philip, *Beyond the White Paper: A Discussion of the Evidence Presented before the Joint Select Committee on Indian Constitutional Reforms*, Allen and Unwin, London, 1934.

Criticos, George, *The Life Story of George of the Ritz as Told to Richard Viner*, Heinemann, London, 1959.

Cross, J. A., *Sir Samuel Hoare: A Political Biography*, Jonathan Cape, London, 1977.

Daftary, Farhad, *The Ismailis: Their History and Doctrines*, Cambridge University Press, Cambridge, 1990.

Das, M. N., *India Under Morley and Minto: Politics Behind Revolution, Repression and Reforms*, George Allen and Unwin, London, 1964.

Donaldson, Dwight M., *The Sh'ite Religion*, Luzac, London, 1933.

Dumasia, M. Naoroji, *A Brief History of the Aga Khan with an Account of His Predecessors, the Ismailian Princes or Benefatimite Caliphs of Egypt*, the Author, Bombay, 1903.

———, *The Aga Khan and His Ancestors: A Biographical and Historical Sketch*, The Times of India Press, Bombay, 1939.

Dwarkadas, Kanji, *India's Fight for Freedom, 1913–1937: An Eyewitness Account*, Popular Prakashan, Bombay, 1966.

East African Muslim Welfare Society, *Souvenir of the East African Muslim Welfare Society*, n.p.p., 1954.

Engineer, Asghar Ali, *The Bohras*, Vikas, New Delhi, 1980.

Fani, Muhsin, *Dabistan-i-Mazahib*, M. Walter Dunn, Washington and London, 1901.

Frischauer, Paul, *Der Mensch Macht Seine Welt*, Mosaik Verlag, Hamburg, 1962.

Frischauer, W., *The Aga Khans*, The Bodley Head, London, 1970.

Gangulee, N., *The Making of Federal India*, James Nisbet, London, n.d. (?1937).

Gilbert, Martin, *Servant of India: A Study of Imperial Rule from 1905–10 as told through the Correspondence and Diaries of Sir James Dunlop-Smith*, Longman, London, 1966.

Greenwall, H. J., *His Highness the Aga Khan: Imam of the Ismailis*, Cresset Press, London, 1952.

Hamer, D. H., *John Morley: Liberal Intellectual in Politics*, Clarendon Press, Oxford, 1968.

Hamid, Abdul, *Muslim Separatism in India: A Brief Survey, 1859–1947*, Oxford University Press, Lahore, 1967.

Haq, Mushir U., *Muslim Politics in Modern India, 1857–1947*, Meenakashi Prakashan, Meerut, 1970.

Hardy, Peter, *The Muslims of British India*, Cambridge University Press, Cambridge, 1972.

Hasan Mushirul, *Mohamed Ali: Ideology and Politics*, Manohar, New Delhi, 1981.

———— (ed.), *Mohamed Ali in Indian Politics: Select Writings, Volume One*, Atlantic, New Delhi, 1982.

Hollister, J. N., *The Shia of India*, Luzac, London, 1953.

Husain, Azim, *Fazl-i-Husain: A Political Biography*, Longmans Green, Bombay, 1946.

Ikbal Ali Shah, *Eastward to Persia*, Wright and Brown, London, n.d.

————, Sirdar (ed.), *The Coronation Book of Oriental Literature*, Sampson Low, Morston and Co., London, n.d.

Imad-ul-Mulk Bahadur, Nawab (Syed Hossain Bilgrami, C.S.I.), *Speeches, Addresses and Poems*, Government Central Press, Hyderabad Deccan, 1925.

Iqbal, Afzal, *Life and Times of Mohammed Ali: An Analysis of the Hopes, Fears and Aspirations of Muslim India from 1778 [sic.] to 1931*, Institute of Islamic Culture, Lahore, 1974.

Ikbal Ali Shah, *Eastward to Persia*, Wright and Brown, London, n.d.

————, Sirdar (ed.), *The Coronation Book of Oriental Literature*, Sampson Low, Morston and Co., London, n.d.

————, *The Prince Aga Khan: An Authentic Life Story*, John Long, London, 1933.

————, *The Controlling Minds of Asia*, Herbert Jenkins, London, 1937.

Iran Society, The, *Inaugural Lecture: Hafiz and the Place of Iranian Culture in the World by His Highness the Aga Khan*, The Iran Society, London, November 1936.

Ismail Khan, M., *Problems omitted from Politics*, the Author, Agra, 1907.

Jackson, Stanley, *The Aga Khan: Prince, Prophet and Statesman*, Odhams Press, London, 1952.

Jain, M. S., *The Aligarh Movement: its Origin and Development (1885–1906)*, Sri Ram Mehra and Co., Agra, 1965.

Kaura, Uma, *Muslims and Indian Nationalism: the Emergence of the Demand for India's Partition, 1928–1940*, Manohar, New Delhi, 1973.

Keshavjee, Habib V., *The Aga Khan and Africa*, Pretoria, 1946.

Khan, Muhammad Yamin, *Nama-i-A'mal*, A'ina-i-Adab, Lahore, 1970, 2 volumes. In Urdu.

Khan, Muhammad Zafrulla, *Tahdis-i-N'imat*, Dacca, 1971, rev. ed., Lahore, 1982.

————, *Servant of God: A Personal Narrative*, n.p., London, 1983.

Khan, Najmul Ghani, *Mazahib-i-Islam*, Lucknow, 1924.

Khan, Shafa'at Ahmad, *The Indian Federation: An Exposition and Critical Review*, Macmillan, London, 1937.

Lewis, Bernard, *The Assassins*, Weidenfeld and Nicolson, London, 1967.

————, *The Origins of Ismailism*, Heffer, Cambridge, 1940.

Lokhandwalla, S. T. (ed.,), *India and Contemporary Islam*, Institute of Advanced Study, Simla, 1971.

Mahmood, Safdar and Javid Zafar, *Founders of Pakistan*, Publishers United, Lahore, 1968.

Major, E., *Viscount Morley and Indian Reforms*, James Nisbet, London, 1910.

Malick, Qayyum A., *His Royal Highness Prince Agakhan IIIrd: Guide, Philosopher and Friend of the World of Islam*, Ismailia Association for Pakistan, Karachi, 2nd. ed., 1969.

Mary, Countess of Minto, *India: Minto and Morley, 1905–1910*, Macmillan, London, 1934.

Masood, Mukhtar (ed.), *Eyewitnesses of History: A Collection of Letters addressed to [the] Quaid-i-Azam [Jinnah]*, Guild Publishing House, Karachi, 1968.

Mathur, D. B., *Gokhale: A Political Biography: A Study of his Services and Political Ideas*, Manaktalas, Bombay, 1966.

Minault, Gail, *The Khilafat Movement: Religious Symbolism and Political Mobilization in India*, Columbia University Press, New York, 1982.

Mitra, N. N. (ed.), *The Indian Quaterly Register, July–December 1928*, The Annual Register Office, Calcutta, n.d. (?1929).

Mody, Homi, *Sir Pherozeshah Mehta: A Political Biography*, Asia Publishing House, London, 1963. First published in 1921.

Moin, Mumtaz, *The Aligarh Movement: Origin and Early History*, Salman Academy, Karachi, 1976.

Montgomery-Massingberd, Hugh and David Watkins, *The London Ritz: Social and Architectural History*, Aurum Press, London, 1980.

Morley, John (Viscount), *Recollections*, Macmillan, London, 1917.

Muhammad, Shan, *Successors of Sir Syed Ahmad Khan: Their Role in the Growth of Muslim Political Consciousness in India*, Idarah-i-Adabiyat-i-Dilli, Delhi, 1981.

Muslim League, All India, *The Moral Side of the Turkish Question*, n.p., Lucknow, n.d. (?1919).

Muslim League, London, *The Indian Muhammadans and the Government*, London, n.d. (?1909).

Nanda, B. R., *Gandhi: Pan-Islamism, Imperialism and Nationalism in India*, Oxford University Press, Bombay, 1989.

———, B. R., *Gokhale: The Indian Moderates and the British Raj*, Princeton University Press, Princeton, N.J., 1977.

Nasr, Seyyed Hossein (ed.), *Ismaili Contributions to Islamic Culture*, Imperial Iranian Academy of Philosophy, Tehran, 1977.

Nehru, Jawaharlal, *An Autobiography with Musings on Recent Events in India*, Allied Publishers, Bombay, 1962 (originally published in 1936).

Noman, Muhammad, *Muslim India: Rise and Growth of the All India Muslim League*, Kitabistan, Allahabad, 1942.

Nurullah, Sayyid and J. P. Naik, *History of Education in India during the British Period*, Macmillan, Bombay, 1943.

Padmasha, Dr., *Indian National Congress and the Muslims 1928–1947*, Rajesh, New Delhi, 1980.

Page, David, *Prelude to Partition: the Indian Muslim and the Imperial System of Control, 1920–1932*, Oxford University Press, Delhi, 1982.

Pakistan Historical Society, *A History of the Freedom Movement, 1707–1947, Vol. III, 1906–1936, Part I, 1906–1928*, The Society, Karachi, 1961.

———, *A History of the Freedom Movement, 1707–1947, Vol. III, 1906–1936, Part II, 1928–1936*, The Society, Karachi, 1963.

Pardaman Singh, *Lord Minto and Indian Nationalism 1905–1910*, Chugh Publications, Allahabad, 1976.

Parvate, T. V., *Gopal Krishna Gokhale*, Navajivan, Ahmedabad, 1959.

Perry, Sir Erskine, *The Indian Decisions (Old Series), iv, Supreme Court Reports*, Law Printing House, Bombay and Madras, 1912.

Pirzada, Syed Sharifuddin (ed.), *Foundations of Pakistan: All India Muslim League Documents, 1906–1947*, National Publishing House, Karachi, n.d. Volume I: 1906–1924.

Pollen, John, *Omar Khayyam, Faithfully and Literally Translated (from the Original Persian)*, East and West, London, 1915.

Qaddusi, Irshad-Ul-Haq, *Sir Agha Khan*, Ferozsons, Lahore, 1969. In Urdu.

Qassimali Jairazbhoy, Al-Haji, *Muhammad: "A Mercy to all the Nations"*, Luzac, London, 1937.

Qureshi, L. H., *The Muslim Community of the Indo-Pakistan Sub-Continent (610–1947): A Brief Historical Analysis*, Mouton, The Hague, 1962.

————, *The Struggle for Pakistan*, The University of Karachi, Karachi, 1965.

Rahman, Fazlur, *Islam*, Wiedenfeld and Nicolson, London, 1966.

Rahman, Matiur, *From Consultation to Confrontation: A Study of the Muslim League in British Indian Politics, 1906–1912*, Luzac, London 1970.

Razzaqi, Shahid Husain, *Sayyid Ameer Ali*, Idara-i-Saqafat-i-Islamia, Lahore, 1970. In Urdu.

Rizvi, S. Athar Abbas, *A Socio-Intellectual History of the Isna 'Ashari Sh'is in India (16th to the 19th Century A.D.), Vol. I*, Munshiram Manoharlal, New Delhi, and Ma'arifat Publishing House, Canberra, 1986.

Sen, S. P. (ed.), *Dictionary of National Biography*, Institute of Historical Studies, Calcutta, 1972, Volume I, A–D.

Setalvad, Chimanlal H. *Recollections and Reflections: An Autobiography*, Padma Publications, Bombay, n.d. (?1946).

Shafi Mian Muhammad, *Some Important Indian Problems*, Model Electric Press, Lahore, 1930.

Shahnawaz, Jahanara, *Father and Daughter: A Political Autobiography*, Nigarishat, Lahore, 1971.

Slater, Leonard, *Aly: A Biography*, W. H. Allen, London, 1966.

Smith, W. Cantwell, *Modern Islam in India: A Social Analysis*, Ashraf, Lahore, 1963. A reprint of the London 1946 rev. ed.

Special Golden Platinum Jubilee Day Number, Ismailia Association for Tanganyika, Dar-es-Salam, n.d.

Templewood, Lord, *Nine Troubled Years*, Collins, London, 1954.

Templewood, Viscount, *The Unbroken Thread*, Collins, London, 1949.

The Insistent Claims of Indian Reforms: Speeches at a Banquet in London on 7 March 1919, Philip Lee Warner, London, 1919.

Wasti, S. Munir, *Four Historical Essays*, The Author, Karachi, 1985.

Wasti, S. Razi, *Lord Minto and the Indian Nationalist Movement, 1905–1910*, Clarendon Press, Oxford, 1964.

Williams, L. F. Rushbrook (ed.), *Great Men of India*, The Home Library Club, Bombay, n.d.

Young, Gordon, *The Golden Prince*, Hales, London, 1955.

Zakaria, Rafiq, *Rise of Muslims in Indian Politics: An Analysis of Developments from 1885 to 1906*, Somaiya Publications, Bombay, 1970.

Unattributed

————, *Aga Khan, H.H.: A Sketch of His Life and Career,* G. Natesan, Madras, n.d.

————, *Eminent Musalmans,* G.A. Natesan, Madras, n.d. (?1926).

————, *His Highness the Aga Khan, G.C.S.I, G.C.V.O., G.C.I.E.,* Selwyn and Blount, London, 1924.

————, *Indian Leaders of Today,* The Educational Publishing Company, Karachi, 1942.

Articles

A Correspondent, "A Life Fully, Richly Lived", *Dawn* (Karachi), 2 November 1977.

————, "Contribution in the Field of Education", *Dawn,* 2 November 1977.

————, "The Aga Khan III as seen through His Writings" *Dawn,* 2 November 1977.

A Muslim Correspondent, "What Muslim India Thinks", *The Civil and Military Gazette* (Lahore), 4 December 1933.

Abbasi, Fida Ahmad, "His Highness Sir Agha Khan So'im", *Hurryat* (Karachi), 11 July 1977. In Urdu.

Ahmad, Nazir, "Recollections of Visits to the Aga Khan", *Dawn,* 15 July 1957.

Ahmad, M. Saleem, "From Simla to Dacca", *The Morning News* (Karachi), 14 August 1972.

Alam, Sayyid Masud, "Sir Agha Khan Marhum", *Jang* (Karachi and Lahore), 17 June 1969. In Urdu.

Algar, Hamid, "The Revolt of Agha Khan Mahallati and the Transference of the Ismaili Imamate to India", *Studia Islamica,* Vol. XXIX, 1969.

Ali, Bahadur, "Women's Role in Society stressed", *Dawn,* 2 November 1977. Stressed by the Aga Khan.

Ali, Rahmat, "Contributions à l'étude du problème Hindou-Musalman", *Revue des Etudes Islamiques,* Vol. 6, 1932.

Ali, Shokat, Letter, *Sun* (Karachi), 17 January 1977.

Allana, G., "A Citizen of the World", *Dawn,* 3 February 1954.

Alwari, S. Rajabali, Letter, *The Morning News* (Karachi), 14 February 1977.

Arif, "Prince Aga Khan", *Dawn,* 3 February 1954.

Asani, Ali S., "The Khojas of Indo-Pakistan: The Quest for Islamic Identity", *Journal of the Institute of Muslim Minority Affairs,* (London), No. I, 1987.

Asiaticus, "India: The Present Outlook", *National Review,* March 1910.

Badakhshani, Mir Baz Kkan, Letter, *Dawn,* 3 June 1977.

Baker, Robert L., "The Aga Khan: Muslim Pontiff", *Current History,* September 1935.

Baqir, M. Raza, Letter, *Dawn,* 8 July 1977.

————, Letter, *The Pakistan Times* (Lahore), 12 July 1977.

Carnegie, David J., "Weighing the Aga Khan in Diamonds: Natural Colour Photographs", *The National Geographic Magazine,* March 1947.

Chirol, V., "India in Travail", *Edinburgh Review,* July 1918.

————, V., Letter, *The Times,* 15 October 1928.

Chowdhuari Najmul Haq, Letter, *Star of India* (Calcutta), 20 April 1934.

Dacawala, Salim Sadruddin, Letter, *The Morning News,* 7 August 1977.

Dadashi, M. Yaqub, "Seven Decades of Splendour and Service to Islam", *Dawn*, 3 February 1954.

Damani, Nizamuddin N., Letter, *Dawn*, 22 May 1977.

Desnavi, S. M. S., "The Aga Khan's Services to India", *Star of India*", 10 March 1934.

Duchesne, A. E., "Race, Creed and Politics in India", *Imperial and Asiatic Quarterly Review*, April 1909.

——, A. E., "The Indian Muhammedans and the Reforms", *Empire Review*, May 1909.

Elliot, C. A., "Lord Morley's Indian Reforms", *The Nineteenth Century*, February 1909.

——, C. A., "The Indian Councils Act", *Empire Review*, June 1909.

Fontera, Richard, "Mr. Gandhi and the Round Table Conference", *Political Science Review*, April 1966.

Fazy, R., "Les Mémoires de l'Aga Khan", *Asiatische Studien*, Vol. 9, 1955.

Frank, Rana Bashir Ahmad, Letter, *Star of India*, 27 July 1935.

——, Letter, *Star of India*, 19 September 1935.

Fraser, A. H. L., "Lord Morley's Indian Reforms: The Proposals Examined", *Empire Review*, March 1909.

Gilani, A. M. Abdullah, Letter, *Dawn*, 11 July 1977.

Haq, Ekramul, Letter, *Star of India*, 26 December 1933.

Hasan, Syed M., "H. H. the Aga Khan", *The Muslim Times* (London), 24 October 1935.

Hasan, Syed Yaqub, "Aik 'azim mudabbar Muhammad Ali Jinnah ka bemisal kardar: Agha Khan Marhum ke ta'assurat", *Nawa-i-Waqt* (Lahore), 14 December 1972. In Urdu.

Hoodbhoy, Peer Muhammad, "Lady Ali Shah", *Dawn*, 3 February 1954.

Ismail, Hasan, Letter, *Dawn*, 14 May 1977.

Jafri, Rais Ahmad, "Hindu-Muslim ittehad ke liye Sir Agha Khan ki Masa'i", *Al-Zubair* (Bahawalpur), no. 2, 1970. In Urdu.

Jivani, Haider Ali H., "Practical Visionary", *Dawn*, 3 February 1954.

Johnson, William, "Review of Aga Khan's *India in Transition*", *Asiatic Review*, October 1918.

Khaliquzzaman, Chaudhri, "Dynamic Leadership", *Dawn*, 3 February 1954. Of the Aga Khan.

Khan, Hidayatullah, "Sir Agha Khan Marhum", *Mashriq* (Lahore), 2 November 1975. In Urdu.

Laithwaite, Sir Gilbert, "The Aga Khan", in E. T. Williams and Helen M. Palmer (eds.), *The Dictionary of National Biography, 1951–1960*, Oxford University Press, London, 1971.

Lasi, Sadruddin, Letter, *Dawn*, 26 June 1977.

Le Chatelier, A., "Aga Khan", *Revue du Monde Musalman*, Volume I, 1906.

Lokhandwalla, S. T., "The Bohras: A Muslim Community of Gujarat", *Studia Islamica*, No. 3, 1955.

Madelung, W., "Ismailiyya", in *The Encyclopaedia of Islam*, new ed., Leiden, Vol. IV, 1978.

Mansuri, G. H., "His Title to Fame", *Dawn*, 3 February 1954.

Mazumdar, Vina, "Sir Herbert Hope Risley and Indian Constitutional Reform, 1906–1909", *Patna University Journal*, January 1963.

Minault, Gail and David Lelyveld, "The Campaign for a Muslim University, 1898–1920", *Modern Asian Studies*, April 1974.

Mitra, S. M., "India in 1813 and 1913", *Fortnightly Review*, April 1914.

Morris, H. Stephen, "The Divine Kingship of the Aga Khan: A Study of Theocracy in East Africa", *Southwestern Journal of Anthropology*, 1958.

Mujahid, Sharif Al, "A Versatile Personality of Great Distinction", *Dawn*, 2 November 1977.

———, "Aga Khan III: An Appreciation", *Pakistan Pictorial* (Islamabad), May–June 1980.

———, "Devoted to the Service of Islam", *The Pakistan Times* (Lahore), 2 November 1977.

———, "The Late Aga Khan and Islam", *Dawn*, 23 January 1958.

Nehru, Jawaharlal, "His Highness the Aga Khan", *Modern Review*, November 1935.

Pardaman Singh, "The Early Years of the All India Muslim League, 1906–1910", *Bengal Past and Present*, No. 87, 1968.

Rahman, Matiur, "The Foundation of the All India Muslim League", *Journal of the Pakistan Historical Society* (Karachi), July 1970.

Parwaz, Ashiq Ali, "Agha Khan Marhum", *Mashriq*, 11 July 1975. In Urdu.

Rajabali, Shaukatali, Letter, *Dawn*, 4 November 1977.

Sareen, T. R., "The Simla Deputation", *Quarterly Review of Historical Studies* (Calcutta), Vol. I, No. 2. 1972.

Sarmasati, M. A., Letter, *Dawn*, 21 July 1977.

Shahzada, Muhammad Yusuf, "His Royal Highness Sir Sultan Muhammad Shah Agha Khan Marhum", *Jang* (Lahore), 2 November 1977. In Urdu.

Shakeb, Sabir Husain, "Agha Sultan Muhammad Shah", *Nawa-i-Waqt*, 2 November 1977. In Urdu.

Shallvani, Pir M. V., Letter, *Dawn*, 4 November 1977.

Sherwani, Latif Ahmad, "Aga Khan's Services to Muslims", *Dawn*, 14 July 1957.

Smith, C. Ryder, "The Aga Khan and the Khojas", *International Review of Missions*, April 1936.

Soomroo, Faiz Muhammad, "The Late Aga Khan's Appraisal [of Jinnah], *The Morning News*, 11 September 1964.

Tabani, M. Saleem, Letter, *Dawn*, 20 June 1977.

Tripathi, Amales, "Morley-Minto Reforms", *Bengal Past and Present*, July–December 1963

———, "Morley-Minto Reforms", *Bengal Past and Present*, January–June 1964.

———, "Morley-Minto Reforms", *Bengal Past and Present*, January–June 1965.

Towheed, M., Letter, *Star of India*, 7 April 1934.

Tritterton, W. R., "The Aga Khan", *Daily Herald*, 2 December 1930.

Verjee, Jimmy, "The Story of the Ismailis", *Dawn*, 23 January 1958.

Wasti, S. Razi, "Foundation of the London Branch of the All India Muslim League", *Journal of the Research Society of Pakistan* (Lahore), January 1965.

———, "One of the Greatest Muslim Leaders", *The Pakistan Times*, 2 November 1977.

Young, G., "Unknown Story of Aly Khan", *Coronet* (Boulder, Colo., USA), November 1954.

Zikri, Adiba, "Simla and Its Significance for the Muslims", *Dawn* (Karachi), 14 August 1973.

Unattributed

—— "Aga Khan vs. Mr. Jinnah", *The Tribune* (Lahore) 24 January 1939. Editorial comment.

—— "The Aga Khan", *The Times*, 12 July 1957 The leading article.

—— "The Aga Khan", *The Times*, 12 July 1957. The obituary notice.

—— "The Aga Khan", *The Times*, 17 July 1957 Tributes to him.

—— "The Aga Khan: Cochin Press Tribute", *Star of India*, 4 March 1936. Reproduced from the *Lokaprasan*, a weekly of Trichur.

—— "The Aga Khan and Communalism", *The Tribune*, 14 February 1934. Editorial Comment.

—— "The Aga Khan and Mr. Jinnah", *The Tribune*, 8 January 1934. Editorial comment.

—— "The Aga Khan as Prime Minister", *The Tribune*, 19 February 1934. Editorial comment.

—— "The Aga Khan or Mr. Jinnah", *The Tribune*, 28 February 1934. Editorial comment.

—— *Aligarh Magazine*, Aligarh, Special Aligarh Number, 1953–54, 1954–55.

—— "Biographies (with Portraits) of Their Highnesses, the Present and the Two Preceding 'Aga Sahibs' of Bombay, the Chiefs of the Khojas and Other Ismailians . . .", *Asiatic Quarterly Review*, July 1894.

—— "H. H. the Aga Khan", *Indian Review*, November 1916.

—— "India in Transition", *Spectator*, 29 June 1918.

—— "Misgivings about India: The Aga Khan and Turkish Extremists", *The Civil and Military Gazette*, 10 January 1924.

—— "Muslims and Their Claims", *The Englishman* (Calcutta), 19 November 1906.

—— "Simla Deputation", *Economist*, 6 October 1906.

—— "The All India Muslim Conference", *The Tribune* (Lahore), 25 March 1932. Editorial comment.

—— "The Indian Reforms and the Muslims", *The Times*, 5 October 1909.

—— "The Muhammedan Memorial", *The Times*, 1 October 1906.

—— "Who Pulled the String?", *The Tribune* (Lahore), 12 April 1931.

Official Documents

All India Muslim Conference, *Report of the All India Muslim Conference held at Delhi on 31 December, 1928 and 1 January, 1929, compiled and published by authority by Hafizur Rahman*, Aligarh, n.d.

East African Muslim Conference, *Proceedings of the East African Muslim Conference*, Mombasa, 1945.

——, *Combined Report of the 2nd East African Muslim Conference and the Annual General Meeting of the East African Muslim Welfare Society*, Mombasa, 1946.

Great Britain, Government of, *East India (Advisory and Legislative Councils . . .)*, HMSO, London, 1908. 2 volumes. Cd. 4426, 4435, 4436.

——, Government of, *East India (Executive and Legislative Councils): Regulations, etc. for giving effect to the Indian Councils Act of 1909*, HMSO, London, 1909. Cd. 4987.

——, *Report of the Royal Commission on the Public Services in India*, HMSO, London, 1917. Cd. 8382.

——, *Report on Indian Constitutional Reforms*, HMSO, London, 1918. Cd. 9109.

——, *Royal Commission on the Public Services in India, Appendix to the Report of* the Commissioners, *Volume VI: Minutes of Evidence Relating to the Indian and Provincial Civil Services Taken at Bombay from the 1st to the 12th March 1913*, with Appendices, His Majesty's Stationery Office, London, 1914, Cd. 7579.

————, *Joint Select Committee on the Government of India Bill, Vol. II: Minutes of Evidence*, His Majesty's Stationery Office, London, 1919.

————, *Indian Round Table Conference: 12th November 1930–19th January 1931: Proceedings*, His Majesty's Stationery Office, London, 1931. Cmd. 3778.

————, *Indian Round Table Conference (Second Session): 7th September 1931–1st December 1931: Proceedings*, His Majesty's Stationery Office, London, 1932. Cmd. 3997.

————, *Indian Round Table Conference (Third Session) (17th November, 1932–24 December, 1932)*, His Majesty's Stationery Office, London, 1933. Cmd. 4238.

————, *Joint Committee on Indian Constitutional Reform (Session 1932–33), Volume II C, Minutes of Evidence together with Appendix D*, Parliamentary Paper HL 79 (II C), HC 112 (II C), London, 1934.

————, *Joint Committee on Indian Constitutional Reform (Session 1933–34), Volume I (Part I), Report*, His Majesty's Stationery Office, London, 1934. H.L.6 (I, Part I), H.C.5 (I, Part I).

India, Government of, *Abstract of the Proceedings of the Council of the Governor General of India Assembled for the Purpose of Making Laws and Regulations*, Calcutta, Vol. XLII, 1903.

————, *Abstract of the Proceedings of the Council of the Governor General of India Assembled for the Purpose of Making Laws and Regulations*, Calcutta, Vol. XLIII, 1904.

————, *India in 1928–1929*, Calcutta, 1930. Prepared by John Coatman.

League of Nations, *Conference for the Reduction and Limitation of Armaments: Verbatim Record (Revised) of the Fourteenth Plenary Meeting, Friday, February 19th. 1932, at 10 a.m.*, Geneva, 1932.

————, *Official Journal, Special Supplement No. 101, Records of the Special Session of the Assembly Convened in Virtue of Article 15 of the Covenant at the Request of the Chinese Government*, Geneva, Volume I, 1932.

————, *Official Journal, Special Supplement No. 102: Records of the Special Session of the Assembly Convened in Virtue of Article 15 of the Covenant at the Request of the Chinese Government*, Geneva, Volume II, 1932.

————, *Official Journal, Special Supplement No. 104: Records of the Thirteenth Ordinary Session of the Assembly, Plenary Meeting, Text of the Debates*, Geneva, 1932.

————, *Verbatim Record of the Thirteenth Ordinary Session of the Assembly of the League of Nations, Twelfth Plenary Meeting, Monday, October 17th., 1932, at 10.30 a.m.*, Geneva, 1932.

————, *Verbatim Record of the Fifteenth Ordinary Session of the Assembly of the League of Nations, Twelfth Plenary Meeting, Thursday, September 27th., 1934, at 10 a.m.*, Geneva, 1934.

————, *Verbatim Record of the Sixteenth Ordinary Session of the Assembly of the League of Nations: Sixth Plenary Meeting, Friday, September 13th., 1935, at 10.30 a.m.*, Geneva, 1935.

————, *Verbatim Record of the Seventeenth Ordinary Session of the Assembly of the League of Nations: Tenth Plenary Meeting, Tuesday, September 29th., 1936, at 3.30 p.m.*, Geneva, 1936.

————, *Official Journal, Special Supplement No. 166: Records of the Special Session of the Assembly Convened for the Purpose of Considering the Request of the Kingdom of Egypt for Admission to the League of Nations (May 26th.–27th., 1937)*, Geneva, 1937.

————, *Verbatim Record of the Eighteenth Ordinary Session of the Assembly of the League of Nations, Second Plenary Meeting, Monday, September 13th., 1937, at 5 p.m.,* Geneva, 1937.

————, *Verbatim Record of the Eighteenth Ordinary Session of the Assembly of the League of Nations, Third Plenary Meeting, Tuesday, September 14th., 1937, at 10.30 a.m.,* Geneva, 1937.

————, *Verbatim Record of the Eighteenth Ordinary Session of the Assembly of the League of Nations, Ninth Plenary Meeting, September 28th., 1937, at 10.30 a.m.,* Geneva, 1937.

————, *Verbatim Record of the Eighteenth Ordinary Session of the Assembly of the League of Nations, Fourteenth Plenary Meeting, Wednesday, October 6th., 1937, at 5 p.m.,* Geneva, 1937.

Theses

Adkisson, Laura M., *Great Britain and the Kemalist Movement for Turkish Independence, 1919–1923,* Texas, Ph.D., 1958.

Ahmed, Sufia, *Some Aspects of the History of the Muslim Community in Bengal, 1884–1912,* London, Ph.D., 1960.

Bahadoor Singh, *Communal Representation and Indian Self-Government,* Oxford, B. Litt., 1944.

Case, Margaret Harrison, *The Aligarh Era in Muslim Politics in North India, 1860–1910,* Chicago, Ph.D., 1970.

Dhillon, Anup SingH, *India in the League of Nations and the International Labour Organization,* Harvard, Ph.D., 1935.

Dyer, M. G., *The End of World War I in Turkey, 1918–1919,* London, Ph.D., 1973.

Haroon, E. M., *All India Muslim League, 1906–1918;* Punjab, M. A., 1966.

Kaminsky, Arnold Paul, *Policy and Paperwork: The Formation of Policy in the India Office, 1883–1909, with special reference to the Permanent Under-Secretaryship of Sir Arthur Godley,* California (Los Angeles), Ph.D., 1975.

Khakee, Gulshan Gulam Ali, *The Dasa Avatara of the Satpanthi Ismailis and the Imam Shahis of Indo-Pakistan,* Harvard, Ph.D., 1972.

Koss, S. E., *"His Master's Voice": John Morley at the India Office,* Columbia, Ph.D., 1966.

Koymen, O., *A Comparative Study of Anglo-Turkish Relations c. 1830–70 and 1919–39,* Strathclyde, Ph.D., 1967.

Louis, M. C., *Indian Muslims and the Khilafat Movement, 1911–1927,* Western Australia (Perth), M. A., 1969.

May, Lini S., *Muslim Thought and Politics in India after 1857,* Columbia, Ph.D., 1963.

McManus, Gayle Constance, *The Viceroy's Imperial Council for the Purpose of Making Laws and Regulations 1892–1909,* Queensland, Ph.D., 1976.

Montgomery, A. E., *Allied Policies in Turkey from the Armistice of Mudros, 30 October 1918, to the Treaty of Lausanne, 24 July 1923,* London (Birkbeck College), Ph.D., 1969.

Qureshi, M. Naeem, *The Khilafat Movement in India, 1919–1924,* London, Ph.D., 1973.

Rahim, Hamshad, *The Aga Khan and the Khojas of India,* University of Chicago, M.A., 1958.

Riaz, Syed Muhammad, *The Khilafat Movement,* Aligarh, Ph.D., 1973.

Rizvi, Janet Mary, *Muslim Politics and Government Policy: Studies in the Development of Muslim Organization and its Social Background in North India and Bengal, 1885–1917,* Cambridge, Ph.D., 1969.

Ryland, R. S., *The Making of the Government of India Act, 1919*, Duke, Ph.D., 1970.
Saran, P., *The Imperial Legislative Council of India, 1861–1920*, Agra, Ph.D., 1959.
Taunk, Bengali Mal, *The Role of the Khilafat Movement in Indian Politics, 1919–1924*, Agra, Ph.D., 1963.
Watts, J. F. C., *The Viceroyalty of Lord Irwin, 1926–1931, with special reference to the Political and Constitutional Developments*, Oxford, D.Phil., 1973.

Periodical Publications

Asiatic Review, London.
Bombay Chronicle, Bombay.
Civil and Military Gazette, The, Lahore.
Comrade, Calcutta.
Daily Express, London.
Daily Herald, London.
Daily Sketch, London.
Dawn, Karachi.
East African Standard, Nairobi.
Edinburgh Review, Edinburgh.
Evening Standard, London.
Ismaili, Bombay.
Listener, London.
Mombasa Times, The, Mombasa.
Morning Post, The, London.
Muslim Times, The, London.
National Review, London.
Nineteenth Century and After, The, London.
Pakistan Horizon, Karachi.
Pakistan Observer, Dacca.
Rangoon Gazette, The, Rangoon.
Sunday Express, London.
Sunday Post, Nairobi.
Star of India, Calcutta.
Tanganyika Standard, Dar-es-Salaam.
The Indian Annual Register, Calcutta.
The Times, London.
The Times of India, Bombay.
Zanzibar Times, The, Zanzibar.

INDEX

Abbas, Shah, 790, 1420
Abbasi, Qazi Ali Haider, 854
Abbasi, R.Z., 922
Abbasids, 138, 210–11, 636, 774, 1257, 1309
Abd-un-Nur, Thabit Bey, 1051
Abdali, Ahmad Shah, 565, 1255, 1420
Abduh, Shaikh Muhammad, 119
Abdul Aziz, Shah, 158
Abdul Hamid, Sir, 1065
Abdul Hamid II, Sultan: replaced by national government, 32–3; Aga Khan's appeals on behalf of, 133, 405, 714, 1352–3; reign, 531, 534, 571–2, 1347; imprisonment, 1353; biography, 1420–1
Abdul Wahed, Haji Sulem, 742
Abdullah, S.M., 1108
Abell, Sir George, 45
Abingdon, Lord, 684, 1421
Abraham, the Prophet, 52, 1364, 1367
Abu Bakr, Caliph: example, 123, 207, 210; election, 635–6, 1363; great grand daughters, 1257; biography, 1421

Abu Musa, 211
Abu Nuwas, 1129
Abu Obaidah, 635
Abyssinia, Italian invasion, 77, 79, 1241, 1391, 1393–5
Acland, F.D., 680
Adamson, Sir Harvey, 499, 1421
Adrianople: Turkish reoccupation, 130, 482, 487, 1356; British policy, 134, 484; Turkish territory, 682, 757; population, 683; Treaty of Lausanne, 1359
Afghanistan: Aga Khan I's exile in, 4–5; Ismaili community, 22; invasions, 31, 777; government, 49, 537; Aga Khan's proposals, 54, 239, 242, 670, 671; Turkish question, 133; League of Nations, 139, 1039–43, 1070; self-determination, 141; buffer region proposal, 242, 243; borders, 274; rail links, 275; Muslim population, 321; Amir, 356; relationship with India, 573, 578–9, 580; British policy,

700, 701, 712, 884; health, 724–5; status, 764, 1032; relationship with Persia, 1041–2
Africa: Aga Khan's interest in, 45–6, 871; Muslim population, 127–30, 178, 765, 1186, 1195–1207, 1222–30, 1275, 1314–29
Aga Hall, Bombay, 5
Aga Khan I (Hasan Ali Shah, grandfather), 4–6, 199–200, 202
Aga Khan II (Agha Ali Shah, father), 6–7, 200, 202
Aga Khan III (Sultan Muhammad Shah): family, 3–7; historical background, 22–46; birth, 6, 7; childhood, 7–10, 199–201, 1330–3; father's death, 7; mother's influence, 8–10, 200; education, 9–10, 166, 200, 858, 1330–4; travels, 10, 201–2, 1334; appearance, 868, 929; health, 104, 295, 473, 609, 786–9, 856, 1023, 1294, 1302, 1309, 1333; marriages, 7, 13, 16, 18; children, 13;

statesmanship, 46–74; humanitarian concerns, 47, 90–2, 106–10, 160, 177, 178–9; in search of world peace, 75–80, 178–9; conciliator, 80–6; democratic values, 86–92, 177; educational ideals, 47–8, 92–106; social reforms, 106–14; Islamic modernism, 114–30, 180; world of Islam, 130–48; view of British Empire, 148–66, 179, 202–3, 233–4; love of poetry, 166–9; religious convictions, 172–5; on the concept of God, 1044–5, 1300, 1302, 1314, 1361–2, 1364–7, 1410–12, 1413–14; Diamond Jubilee, 18; Pakistani citizenship, 18; Iranian citizenship, 18; Platinum Jubilee, 19; publication of *Memoirs*, 19; achievements and legacy, 175–98; death, 19; burial, 19–20; honours, 10–11, 13, 15, 18–19; writings – *India in Transition*, 30, 61, 64, 86–7, 530–611, 666, 848, 1169; *Memoirs*, 19, 172, 1330–1406, 1408

Aga Khan IV (Prince Karim): birth, 17, 180; appointment as Imam, 19–20; his education, 180–1; institutions, 181, 186–9, 195; his views on education, 181–3, 191; Islam, 102–4, 190–2, 196–8; Islamic architecture, 192–6; Islamic civilization, 183, 190–2; journalism and the press, 189–90; social and economic development, 184–7; on Prophet Muhammad, 197–8

Aga Khan Award for Architecture, 195
Aga Khan Education Services, 189
Aga Khan Foundation, 181, 187–8
Aga Khan Fund for Economic Development, 181, 187–8
Aga Khan Health Services, 188–9
Aga Khan Programme for Islamic Architecture, 195
Aga Khan Rural Support Programme, 188
Aga Khan Students' Union, London, 1278
Aga Khan Trust for Culture, 181, 195
Aga Khan University, 181, 183–4, 188
Agabob, S.S., 504
Agra, Muslim history, 1338
agriculture: Indian, 107–8, 334, 366–7, 827–8, 1113–14; education, 107–8, 177, 313–16, 322, 1100–1, 1113–14; East African, 108, 1190; finance, 314–17; irrigation, 968; Egyptian, 1028
Ahmad, Bashr, 1065
Ahmad, Haji Rashid, 956, 1014, 1066, 1108
Ahmad, Hakim Nasiruddin, 1065

Ahmad, Maulana Sayed, 339
Ahmad, Maulvi Anees, 837
Ahmad, Nur, 1014, 1065
Ahmad, Sir Sayyid Sultan, 853, 881, 1065
Ahmad, Sir Sultan, 862
Ahmad, Zahur, 837, 1014
Ahmad Khan, Nawab Aziz, 1066
Ahmad Khan, Sahibzada Aftab, 259
Ahmad Khan, Sardar Sahibzada Sultan, 853, 880
Ahmad Khan, Sir Sayyid: Aga Khan's meeting, 11, 1334; MAO College, 11, 13, 115, 256–7, 361; views, 23–4, 114, 115–16, 118, 119, 1105, 1300; regard for British, 148–9, 154; influence, 156, 177, 179, 383, 535, 641, 1118, 1300, 1338; life, 268; biography, 1473
Ahmad Khan, Sir Shafa'at: Round Table Conferences, 16, 854, 862, 882, 922; Joint Committee, 37, 993, 994; All India Muslim Conference, 837, 841, 1011–12, 1108–9; Hoare dinner (1931), 883; National League speech (1933), 933, 939; biography, 1473
Ahrars, 150
Ahsan, Raghib, 1014
Aiyar, Sir C.P. Ramaswami, 853, 881, 993, 1372
Aiyar, Sir P.S. Sivaswami, 415

Ajmal Khan, Hakim
Muhammad, 259,
339, 382, 837, 1421–2
Ajmere-Merwara, 949,
954
Akbar, Emperor, 356,
546, 564–5, 566,
1273, 1422
Akbar Ali, Raja, 1065
Ala, Hussein, 1133
Alamut, 3
alcohol, 109, 1211, 1366
Alexander, A.V. (later
Lord), 43, 1389, 1422
Alexander II, Tsar, 531,
1422
Alexander III, Tsar, 531,
1422
Alexander the Great,
555, 1171
Ali ibn Abi Talib,
Caliph: grave, 7; Shia
belief, 20–1, 116;
example, 210;
tradition, 138, 773;
Prophet on, 324;
Khilafat, 635, 1416;
Ulu'l-amr Minkum,
1416–17; biography,
1422–3
Ali, Amjad, 1065
Ali, Asaf, 1065
Ali, Asghar, 1108
Ali, Khurshid, 1014,
1108
Ali, Maulana
Muhammad:
relationship with Aga
Khan, 14, 90, 389,
640; Khilafat
Movement, 34, 638,
640; editor of
Comrade, 90, 389,
1060; All India
Muslim Conference,
836–7, 841; Round
Table Conference,
853, 1372; death, 853;
on Irwin, 1379
Ali, Mubarak, 1066
Ali, Muhammad, Prime

Minister of Pakistan,
1307
Ali, Nawab Jamshed,
1108
Ali, Dr Zaki, 1183–8
Ali Imam, Sayyid Sir:
Nehru Report, 35,
822; Simla
deputation (1906),
259; Muslim League,
290; on Viceroyalty,
706; Round Table
Conference, 881;
biography, 1423
Ali Khan, Nawab
Muhammad
Ibrahim, 1014
Ali Khan, Nawab Sayyid
Sirdar, 259
Ali Khan, Nawab Sidiq,
1065
Ali Khan, Raja
Ghazanfar, 1108,
1109
Ali Khan, Sahibzada
Mumtaz, 922
Ali Khan, Shaffat, 1385
Ali Khan, Sir Ghulam
Muhammad, 339,
1425
Ali Shah, Sirdar Iqbal,
1159–61
Aligarh, Muhammadan
Anglo-Oriental
(MAO) College: Aga
Khan's interest in, 11,
103, 104–5, 177, 324,
493, 496, 1334–5;
Ahmad Khan's work,
13, 23, 115, 256, 361;
establishment, 23,
115, 256, 361;
development into
university, 104–5, 361,
1103, 1213;
influence, 257, 329,
361, 1225; George V's
visit, 345, 1100, 1103;
objectives, 325–7,
1100–1; trustees,
397–8; role, 1101–2
Aligarh, University of:

establishment, 2, 92,
177, 179, 750, 1111,
1311, 1334–5; origins,
23, 102–6, 182, 213,
235–6, 272, 335–6,
345, 361–3, 378–80,
383, 396–400, 494,
496–7, 1116, 1344;
funding, 213–14,
396–7, 1100, 1103,
1345; Constitution
Committee, 379;
charter terms, 396;
chair of Science and
Philosophy, 1044; Aga
Khan's Pro-
Chancellorship, 1099;
Aga Khan's visit and
address (1936),
1099–1104;
influence, 1114–15,
1225, 1292–3, 1311,
1335; African Muslim
students, 1202; Aga
Khan's speech
(1946), 1220;
achievement, 1345–6
Aligarh Movement,
24–5, 114, 152
Aligarh Old Boys'
Association, 1311–12
All India Khilafat
Conference, 66, 642,
685
All India Muhammadan
(Muslim) Educational
Conference
(Congress): Aga
Khan's presidency, 2,
11–12, 17, 122, 204,
214n, 1112, 1298; Aga
Khan's involvement,
11–12, 13, 96, 118,
1213, 1345; Dacca
meeting (1906), 27;
role, 99, 1114–15,
1117; creation, 115;
Aga Khan's speech
(1902), 204–14, 397,
410; Aga Khan's
speech (1911),
377–82; Aga Khan's

speech (1936), 1112; Nagpur meeting (1910), 1345

All India Muslim Conference: Aga Khan's role, 2, 16, 67–9, 118, 176; Delhi (1928–29), 16, 36, 52, 61n, 67, 88, 827–8, 829–41, 849, 944, 945, 951–3, 1368–9; League relationship, 17, 68–70, 887, 890, 1011, 1108, 1109; memorandum to Joint Committee (1933), 17, 943–56, 1015, 1055; origins, 67, 944, 1368; Executive Board, 88–9; Iqbal's presidency, 117, 841; relationship with British, 157; work, 887; Delhi (1933), 945, 953–5; Aga Khan's address to Executive Board, 1010–14; Conference Cabinet, 1010; role, 1058

All India Muslim League: Aga Khan's presidency, 2, 12–14, 28, 122, 176, 303, 442, 463–7, 495, 498, 1266, 1343; creation, 12, 27–8, 57, 256, 328–9, 442, 464–5, 489, 494, 497, 943–4, 1005, 1105, 1343; memorandum (1933) to Joint Committee, 17, 943–56, 1015, 1055; relationship with Conference, 17, 68–70, 887, 890, 1011, 1108, 1109; Lucknow Pact, 29–30; split (1924), 35, 753, 756, 806; status

(1928), 35–6; elections (1937–45), 38; Allahabad session (1930), 40, 64–5, 68; World War II, 41, 158; elections (1945), 42–3; Cabinet Mission plan, 43–4; Indian Constitution policy, 66; split (1927), 67; Muslim University project, 105; Iqbal's presidency, 117; Aga Khan's involvement, 118, 463–6, 753; wakf-alal-aulad, 124, 337; relationship with British, 158; Amritsar Conference, 290; Third Annual Session, 328; headquarters, 340; role, 360, 489, 887, 890, 1213, 1225; Indian self-government policy, 461; Congress relationship, 1005, 1105–6, 1193; history, 1005–6

All-India Services, 990

All Parties Conference, 35, 822, 976

All Parties Convention (1929), 35

Allama theory of knowledge, 126

Allana, Haji Ismail Haji, 743

Aloomi, Mowlana Mohamed Hussain, 1202

Altrincham, Lord, see Grigg

Alwar, Maharajah of, 852, 880

Aly Khan, Prince, second son of Aga Khan III, 13, 19–20, 180, 941, 999, 1056

Amanullah Khan, 177

Ambedkar, Dr B.R.:

Round Table Conferences, 853, 862, 879, 881, 922, 1372; Joint Committee, 993; biography, 1423–4

Ameer Ali, Sayyid: Muslim representation efforts, 12, 28, 58–9, 290, 306, 329, 1339, 1343; Khilafat Movement, 14–15, 32, 34, 136, 640, 768, 770–1, 772, 1352; Bengal work, 24; views, 114, 118–19, 124, 356; Turkish issues, 131, 633, 643–4, 684; influence, 169, 176, 177; The Spirit of Islam, 169, 1258, 1339; London Muslim League, 295, 337, 463, 489n, 495; biography, 297, 1339; Morley-Minto reforms, 302, 329, 1343; All India Muslim League, 332, 337, 360, 463; London mosque project, 362; Balkan Wars charity, 401, 402; Aga Khan's letter (1913), 463–6; Savoy dinner, 689; Red Crescent appeal, 782; death, 837

Ameer Ali, Waris, 1070

Amery, Leo, 615, 1049, 1424

Ampthill, Lord, 473, 479, 616, 684, 1424

Amr ibn al-As, 208, 1424

Amritsar: All India Muslim League Conference, 290; violence, 687

Amyn, Prince, second

grandson of Aga Khan III, 18, 20
anarchists, 607–8
Anatolia: German claim, 131, 407, 485; railway, 274; Greek presence, 711, 763; horrors, 733, 763; Turkish control, 1350, 1353, 1359
Andrews, C.F., 795, 1424–5
Aney, M.S., 35, 1065
Anglo-Persian Oil Company, 936
Anglo-Russian Convention (1908), 31, 696, 777
Angora (Ankara), Grand National Assembly, 15, 136, 714, 736, 759, 770, 772–3, 1355
Anik, A.S.M., 684, 1070
Anjudan, 3
Anjuman-i-Islamia Hazara, 150
Anjuman-i-Islamia High School, Bombay, 737
Annual Register, The, 849
Ansari, Dr M.A., 640, 1353
Anwari, 1036, 1425, 1128
Arab: science, 126, 1283, 1299; history, 235; commercial history, 113; nationalism, 1349, 1350–1, 1354
Arab League, 1193, 1212–13, 1235
Arabia, 765–7, 871, 936, 1032, 1088, 1349
Arabic: literature, 97, 200, 233, 322, 483, 1087, 1332, 1334; script, 101; language, 143, 146–8, 166, 395, 417, 426, 440, 447, 590, 932, 938, 1272–5, 1332

Arabiyyah Jamiyyat, Karachi, 1290
Arabs in East Africa, 1197, 1201, 1203, 1204–5, 1206, 1224, 1317
Aras, Rūstū, 1140
Archer, William, 615
architecture, 192–5, 1298
Arcot, Prince of, 339, 1425
Aristotle, 1360
armaments, 1298
Armenia, 131, 485
Arnold, Matthew, 1052
Arnold, T.W., 480, 484, 1425
art, 145, 171, 179, 867, 1257
Arundel, Sir A.T., 295
al-Ash'ari, Abul Hassan, 121, 211, 1425
Ash'arite school, 116
Ashton, Leigh, 1133
Asiatic Review, The, 939
Asoka, King, 546, 728, 1425
Asquith, Herbert, 130, 391, 1346, 1356
Asquith, Margot, 856, 1426
Assam: Chief Commissionership, 29; Cabinet Mission plan, 43; Muslim representation, 257, 304, 387, 389; reform proposals, 1106
Associated Press of India, 748, 995, 1091, 1167
Astor, Lord, 1307
Aswan, Aga Khan's tomb, 19–20
Atal, Pandit Amar Nath, 922
Atatürk, see Mustafa Kamal Pasha
Atia, Ismail Ibrahim, 496, 499, 504
Atkinson, L.P., 1017

atomic, see nuclear
Attlee, Clement, 45, 158, 955, 1368, 1379, 1403
Auchinleck, Sir Claude, 1402, 1426
Augustus, Emperor, 123, 235, 555, 1426
Aurangzeb, Emperor, 546, 564–5, 1273, 1426
Australia: self-government, 375, 695; defence, 540; votes for women, 593; Quetta earthquake relief, 1073
Austria: taxation, 559; government, 576; German influence, 578; Aga Khan's plans, 870; economic crisis (1931), 1379
Avebury, Lord, 295, 363
Avenol, M., 1155
Averroes, 1360–1, 1471
Azad, Abul Kalam, 39
Azam, Muhammad, 496, 499
Al-Azhar University, 3, 1197, 1202, 1205, 1317
Aziz, Syed Abdul, 837, 841

Ba Maw, Dr, 994
Babar, Emperor, 834, 1273, 1426–7
Bacon, Francis, 1299, 1427
Badayuni, Maulana Abdul Majid, 837
Badayuni, Abdul Qadir, 1108
Badru Mbogo, Prince, 1199, 1205, 1319, 1327–8
Badruzaman, Maulvi, 1065
Bagehot, Walter, 575
Baghdad: rail links, 274;

culture, 382; history, 1257

Bahawalpur, 1099

Bahl, K.N., 685

Bahrein, oil revenue, 1193

Baig, Abbas Ali, 517, 615, 939

Bajpai, Mr, 862

Baker, Colonel, 505

Bakhsh, Haji Rahim, 1013, 1014, 1061, 1108

Bakhtiar Shah, Shahzada, 258

Baldwin, Stanley, 808, 809, 1358, 1379, 1387, 1427

Balfour, Arthur, 523, 615, 1350

Balfour Declaration, 1350

Balkans: wars, 32, 401–2, 403, 466, 481–2; Aga Khan's plans, 84, 870; Russian activity, 224

Ballantine, E.W., 601

Baloch, Mir Muhammad, 837

Baluchistan: reforms, 36, 836, 849, 948, 952, 954; Pakistan, 40; Aga Khan's plans, 53, 62; politics, 275; Muslim representation, 305, 1386; Quetta earthquake, 1073–85

Banerjee, K.B., 504

Banerjee, Surendranath, 157, 589, 1427

Bangalore: Aga Khan I's home, 6; Indian Institute of Science, 591–2

Bangladesh, 18, 139, see also Pakistan East-banking, 314–17

Bansda, Raja Saheb of, 474

Baptista, Joseph, 795, 799

Barnes, George S., 615

Baroda, Maharajah Gaekwar of: Indian movement, 275; constitutional proposals, 279–80; views on education, 318, 369, 383, 545; South African issues, 474; views on economy, 792; Round Table Conferences, 852, 880, 922, 1372; Indian White Paper, 997; Diamond Jubilee, 1072; London dinner speech (1935), 1072; biography, 1427

Baroda, size of, 555

Baron, Bernhard, 1392

Barooha, Sarijut Chandradhar, 853, 881

Basu, Bhupendranath, 412, 560, 615, 689

Basu, J.N., 853, 880

Bavaria, model, 63, 819, 823, 843, 1113

Bayazid Bistami, 1361, 1428

Bayley, Sir Charles, 615

Bazlur-Rehman, Dr, 1174

Beaconsfield, Lord, 407, 408, 535, 637, 700, 1439

Beaman, Sir F.C.O., 646, 1428

Beaverbrook, Lord, 14, 1357, 1358, 1428

Beg, Mirza Shujaat Ali, 259

Begum Aga Khan, see Andrée Carron, Yvette Labrousse

Beirut university, 1205, 1225, 1229, 1335

Belgium: World War I,

536; agriculture, 828; peace policy, 1236; colonies, 1236

Benares, Hindu University, 95, 235, 415

Benares, Maharajah of, 350

Benares Hindu University Act (1915), 414–15

Beneš, Eduard, 1090

Bengal: partition, 25–6, 818; repeal of partition, 29, 384, 386–92, 843, 1095; Muslim representation, 29–30, 37, 73–4, 252, 257, 304, 305, 389, 877, 904, 912, 1058, 1107, 1338, 1341, 1375, 1386; Cabinet Mission plan, 43; Aga Khan's proposals, 53, 55, 61, 65, 466, 549, 561, 819; Persian language, 146; history, 356, 565–6; size, 372; Provincial Service, 422; terrorist activities, 490, 984; Gokhale's views, 526; education, 584, 589; budget control, 679; jute industry, 792, 980–1, 1019; Aga Khan's message to Muslim population, 927–8; electorate, 948, 955; second Chamber proposal, 986; press, 1017, 1020; Aga Khan's speech on, 1019–22; Communal Award, 1023

Bengalee, Shapurjee, 518

Bengali language, 435, 590

Bengali people, 63, 273, 818

Benn, Sir Ernest, 860, 1428

Benn, William Wedgwood (later Lord Stansgate), 852, 880, 1371, 1476

Bennett, Arnold, 858, 1035

Bennett, F.N., 684

Bennett, R.B., 941

Bennett, T.J., 295, 517–18, 615, 648, 660, 680

Benthall, Sir Edward, 881, 999

Bentinck, Lord William, 413

Bérenger, M., 911

Berlin, Conference (1884–5), 45

Berridge, Sir Thomas, 615

Betterton, Sir Henry, 941

Bewoor, G.V., 1066

Bey, Ahmed Jevdet, 770

Bey, Husain Jahyad, 770

Bey, Tevfik Rüstü, 911, 1041

Bhadbhade, Raghunath Gangadhar, 417

Bhanji, Jivabhoy, 496, 499, 504

Bharat, 1273, 1397, 1403

Bhavanagar: Maharajah of, 474, 545; government, 555

Bhopal, Nawab of: Round Table Conferences, 852, 861, 880, 919, 922, 1372, 1374, 1376; Eastern Federal Union Insurance Company, 1026; Aligarh University, 1100, 1115; Gandhi meetings, 1250, 1382,

1401; biography, 1428

Bhopal, Nawab of, Begum, 401, 1428–9

Bhownaggar, 225

Bhownagree, Sir Mancherjee M., 295, 615, 684, 689, 794, 1429

Bhurgari, S.M., 684

Bhutan, Aga Khan's proposals, 54, 580

Bhutto, Sir Muhammad Shah Nawaz Khan, 853, 881

Bigge, Sir A.J., 295, 391

Bihar: Hardinge's plan, 29; Aga Khan's proposals, 53, 549; history, 356; education, 584; electorate, 948, 954–5; second Chamber proposal, 986; earthquake (1934), 1080; reform proposals, 1106

Bijapur, kingdom, 565

Bikaner, Aga Khan's plans, 561

Bikaner, Maharajah of: tribute to Aga Khan, 80; education policy, 545; Aga Khan's career proposal, 550; Imperial War Conference speeches, 557–8; Sinha banquet, 613–24; speech (1919), 616–24; Nehru Report, 814; Round Table Conferences, 852, 880, 1372; Indian White Paper, 997; Peace Conference, 1351

Bilgrami, Nawab Sayyid Hussain, 256

Binyon, Laurence, 1133

Birdwood, Sir George, 295

Birkenhead, Lord, 34, 821

Birla, 158

Bismarck, Herbert von, 542

Bismarck, Otto von: Jinnah comparison, 171, 1403; influence, 394, 1247; on German government, 542, 556, 824, 1130; workload, 844; decision making, 1259; biography, 1429

Blanesburgh, Lord, 941

Blomberg, Werner von, 76

Blunt, W.S., 149

Bodley, Mr, 575

Bolivia, Paraguayan dispute, 909

Bolshevism, 162, 531, 578, 698–9, 712

Bomanji, S.R., 615

Bombay: Aga Khan I's home, 5–6, 185–6; Hasanabad mausoleum, 6; *Khoja* school, 7; Legislative Council, 7; Gandhi-Jinnah talks, 41–2; Cabinet Mission plan, 43; Aga Khan's proposals, 53, 549, 561; bubonic plague (1897), 127; Social Reform Conference, 280; Muslim representation, 304; Aga Khan's speech (1910), 320; Muslim community, 323–4; education, 371, 584, 584; status, 389, 650, 818; Aga Khan's speech at the Madrasah-i-Anjuman-i-Islam, 393–4; Aligarh University funding, 397; Indian Civil

Service, 419, 1386;
University, 424, 514;
Mehta's influence,
515–16, 716, 718;
women voters, 662,
664; electorate,
678–9; budget
control, 679; Ismaili
community, 723;
textile industry, 792;
Aga Khan's speech
(1927), 805;
economic future,
807–9; history,
809–11; Sind status,
878, 1057, 1375,
1386–7; Hindu-
Muslim riots, 903;
Lamington's
governorship, 1069;
reform proposals,
1106; Karachi
relationship, 1386
Bombay Chronicle, 720
Bombay Gazette, 1336
Booth, J.R.T., 1066
Borden, Sir Robert, 615
Bose, Sir Jagadis
Chandra, 411, 592,
689
Bose, S.C., 822
Bose, S.P., 1066
Bossom, Alfred, 1133
Botha, Louis, 604, 1429
boycott movement, 803
Boyle, Sir E., 689
Brabourne, Lady,
1097–8
Brabourne, Lord, 998,
1055, 1097–8, 1429
Brahmins, 600, 675,
1362
Brahmo Samaj, 595, 602
Brassey, Lord, 575, 615,
1429–30
Bray, Sir Denys de S.,
941, 1075, 1430
Breslau (German
warship), 1348
Brest-Litovsk, Treaty of,
1350

Briand, Aristide, 84,
896, 1162–5, 1430
Bridges, E.J., 684
Bright, John, 515
Britain:
Army race relations,
230, 270
Balkan policy, 130–5,
484–5
Bombay history,
809–11
Cabinet Mission
(1946), 43–4,
1389, 1400, 1402
Church of England,
1269, 1363
Commonwealth,
1191–2, 1256
Crown colonies,
1236–7
economic crisis
(1931), 1378–9
electoral reform, 563
Empire, 148–66, 266,
309–10, 460, 638,
704, 713, 842,
1063, 1086, 1178,
1349
engineering industry,
780–1
government of India,
24–5, 201–3,
240–2, 513–14,
559–60, 602–8,
704–5, 717, 777–9,
845–7
Governors General
and Viceroys of
India, 1419
health, 788
history, 285
ignorance of Islam,
135
India-Pakistan
relations, 1280–1
Indian self-
government, 48–9,
1378, 1388–9
Ismaili community,
22
League of Nations,
1394–5

Middle Eastern
policy, 161–2,
485–7, 523, 534,
539, 579, 691–3,
698–703, 766,
1349–51, 1354
monarchs, 1418
Muslim attitudes to,
885
naval power, 276
parliamentary
government, 543,
575, 576
peace policy, 1235
position after World
War II, 1191
Prime Ministers, 1418
Quetta earthquake
relief, 1072, 1073
relationship with
Islamic world,
1086–8
relationship with US,
1235
Secretaries of State
for India, 1419
South African policy,
92
trade and commerce,
935–8, 1113
Turkish policy, 636–7,
681–6, 688,
712–13, 720–2,
731–3, 734–5,
750–1, 753–4, 758,
762–7, 1346–7,
1350, 1355–9
university education,
739–40
unrest, 365, 1356
votes for women, 594
withdrawal from
India, 45
World War I, 1346–9
World War II, 41
British Indian
Delegation, 177, 851,
881–2 962–94, 995,
1003, 1007, 1029,
1057, 1063, 1372,
1374

Brodrick, Lord, *see* Midleton
Brooke-Popham, Sir Robert, 1049
Brown, Frank, 1336, 1430
Brown, Major, 801
Browne, Edward G., 145, 1035, 1037, 1430
Brunyate, Sir J., 689
Bryce, Lord, 616
Buckland, C.E., 295, 462
Buddha, 86, 234, 1231, 1383, 1430
Buddhists, 291, 900–1, 1362, 1381
Budrudin, Tayyabji, 716, 718
Buganda, Kabaka of, 1279
Bulgaria: German influence, 578; history, 1224–5, 1335
Bulgarians, 484
Bunting, Sir Percy, 295
Burke, Edmund, 376, 624, 920, 1431
Burma: Aga Khan's visit, 18, 1024–30; Ismaili community, 22, 1278; government, 53, 1030; Aga Khan's proposals, 55, 549, 679–80, 817–18, 819, 820; separation, 63; Indian community, 80–1, 82, 500–4, 1027–8; Upper, 266–7; politics, 275; Buddhism, 291; Muslim community, 493–9; education, 498; status, 847; commercial relations with India, 1027–30; independence, 1249
Butler, Sir Harcourt, 105, 153, 370, 584, 1344, 1431
Butler, M.S.D., 417

Butler, R.A., 921, 941, 955, 1344
Byrt, A.H., 1066

Cabinet Mission, 43–4, 1389, 1400, 1402
Cadell, P.R., 808, 1431
Cadogan, Major Edward, 941, 955
Caesar, Julius, 123, 235, 555, 1431
Cairo: city growth, 3; Conference (1945), 1192; Government Colleges, 1202; history, 1298
Calcutta: Aga Khan I's exile in, 5; capital of India, 29, 387, 1095; Madrassah, 256; riots (1910), 344, 390; university, 371, 390, 588; Research Institute, 592
Calcutta Club, 601
Caliphate, *see khilafat*
Caliphate Empire, 1246
Calvin, John, 1398
Campagnac, C.H., 994
Campbell Bannerman, Sir Henry, 604, 627
Canada: Ismaili community, 22; status of Indian community, 473, 491; Dominion status, 695, 1341; peace policy, 1235; economy, 1287; government, 1374
cancer, 724–5
Canning, Lord, 556, 1247, 1431–2
Cantlie, Dr James, 505
career planning, 101
Carlyle, Thomas, 483
Carmichael, Lord, 615, 624, 632, 689
Carnegie, Andrew, 1432
Carnot, Lazare, 245, 1432
Carnot, Marie François, 608, 1432

Carr, Sir Hubert, 853, 879, 881, 922, 994, 1432
Carr, Lady, 941
Carron, Andrée, Begum Aga Khan, 16, 18, 999, 1004, 1006, 1023, 1175, 1177
caste issues: and race, 52, 106–7, 156, 271, 291, 318, 815; Hindu-English relations, 52, 271; Indian Army, 230, 352–3; Hindu representation, 291, 675–6, 815; effects of education, 318; Marriage Bill, 669; *see also* Brahmins, Depressed Classes, race relations, Untouchables
Castillo Najera, M., 899
Castlereagh, Lord, 1247, 1432
Cater, Sir Norman, 1076, 1082, 1084
Cavendish-Bentinck, Lord H., 615
Cawnpore, events (1931), 864
Central India, Aga Khan's proposals, 55, 820
Central Indian Horse, 486
Central Provinces: Cabinet Mission plan, 43; Bihar merger plan, 53, 549; Aligarh University funding, 397; status, 818; reform proposals, 1106
Ceylon: Aga Khan's proposals, 54, 580; independence, 1249
Chadwick, Sir Burton, 1050
Chamber of Princes, 964, 1401
Chamberlain, Austen: Sinha banquet, 616;

Indian policy, 617, 618, 619; Locarno Treaty, 896; Aga Khan reception, 941; Joint Committee, 955, 1387; National Government, 1379
Chamberlain, Joseph, 515, 523, 1123
Chamberlain, Neville, 941, 1432–3
Chanak, 134, 732, 1356–7
Chand, Nanak, 685, 922, 1065
Chanda, Premjee, 504
Chandavarkar, Sir Narayan, 411, 412, 473, 476, 718, 1433
Chandragupta, 728
Chari, Sir Krishnama, 854, 955, 993
Charlemagne, 285, 1433
Charles, Sir Havelock, 615
Charles II, King, 809
Charter Act (1833), 606, 616, 846, 1071
Chatani, Mr, 1353
Chatterjee, Sir Atul, 941
Chaubal, Mahadev Bhaskar, 416, 447, 456, 584, 1433
Chaudhri, Abdul Matin, 1108
Chaudhri, D.K. Lahiri, 1065
Chchattari, Nawab Sir Ahmad Said Khan of, 853, 881, 885, 1065, 1102, 1108, 1433–4
Chelmsford, Lord: Montagu discussions, 30, 609; criticisms of, 619–20; Turkish policy, 714, 720, 721, 1353; Dominion status policy, 846; biography, 1434; see also Montagu-Chelmsford Report

Chenevix-Trench, Sir Richard, 854, 922, 942
Chesterfield, Lord, 616
Chetwode, Sir Philip, 1081
China: war with Japan, 79, 85–6, 1396; threat to India, 239, 275, 549–50; buffer region proposal, 242, 243; borders, 242, 274, 646, 539–40, 900; economy, 265; Reform movement, 265; Muslim population, 321; unrest, 365; government, 537; education, 581; Aga Khan's proposals, 871; dispute with Japan, 900–2, 909, 1393; trade, 935; scientific education, 1212, 1291; world power, 1236, 1277
Chingiz Khan, 212, 1232, 1434
Chinoy, Fazulbhoy M., 473, 479
Chinoy, Rahim, 742
Chinoy, Sultan, 1175
Chintamani, C.Y., 853, 881
Chiragh Ali, 116, 118
Chirol, Sir Valentine: Indian Unrest, 350, 352; Royal Commission on Public Services in India, 416, 430, 446, 453, 455–6; 'India in Travail', 609; views on Indian federalism, 823–4; biography, 1434
cholera, 810
Chota Nagpur, 29
Chotani, Seth, 710
Chowdhury, Abdul Bari, 496, 499

Chowdhury, Sayyid Nawab Ali, 259, 1343
Christ, Jesus, 507, 1232, 1361, 1364, 1367, 1380, 1383
Christianity: relationship with Islam, 75, 156, 289, 357, 1187, 1364–5; Renaissance education, 98; Uganda education, 102; missionaries, 115, 461, 1195–6, 1224; comparison with Islam, 24, 59, 119, 120, 165, 289, 1299, 1364–5; in England, 288, 326, 1410–12; World War I, 572; in India, 628; scientific education, 1116–17, 1291–2; position in Africa, 1223–4; messages of peace, 1231–2; in Middle Ages, 1247; miracles, 1299; mysticism, 1362; fundamentalism, 1364; monks, 1381
Churchill, Winston: Joint Committee, 159, 957–61; Aga Khan's opinion of, 171, 1397, 1398; Sinha banquet, 616; Aga Khan reception, 941; government (1951), 1344; World War I strategy, 1348
Civil and Military Gazette, 756, 779, 913, 999, 1008, 1016, 1059, 1219
Civil Marriage Bill, 560
Clarke, Tom, 941
class issues: democratic representation, 87
Clemenceau, Georges, 171, 1351, 1397

Clive, Lord, 845, 1434–5
Coatman, John, 862
Cobbold, John D., 685
Cochin, education, 545
Cocks, Mr, 955
Colebrooke, Lord, 616
College of Science, Aligarh, 100, 1115
Collins, M.V.H., 1065–6
colonialism, 1288, 1298
colonies, 1236–7
commerce, see industry and commerce
commercial education, 99, 100–1, 333
commercial travellers, 938
Commonwealth, 1191–2, 1256
Communal Award, 37, 60, 68, 998, 1001–2, 1015, 1023
communism, 843, 1288–9, 1382–3
Comrade, 90, 389, 1060
Conference for the Reduction and Limitation of Armaments, Geneva, see Disarmament Conference
Conference of Ruling Princes (1917), 621
Confucius, 86, 901
Congress, see Indian National Congress
Connaught, Duke of, 10, 201, 341, 566, 707, 964, 1435
Conrad, Joseph, 858, 1435
Conservative party, 243, 1048, 1356, 1358–9, 1377, 1379
conservatism, 551
Constantine I, King of Greece, 33
Constantinople: British policy, 131, 133, 633, 733; Muslim refugees, 401–2; Muslim attitude, 635, 1352;

population, 682; restoration to Turkey, 713–14, 757; Turkish conquest, 1290–1; Turkish control, 1350, 1352, 1353, 1356; imperial régime, 1351; Treaty of Lausanne, 1359
Constantinople Agreement (1915), 32
Constituent Assembly, 44–5
Constitution, Indian: Aga Khan's broadcast, 66; Gaekwar of Baroda's proposal, 279–80; Constitutionalist Party, 294; Gokhale and Mehta's proposals, 551; revision question, 748, 805; Aga Khan on, 813–16, 817–21, 823–4, 825, 871, 887, 903–5, 918, 919–21, 1091, 1117, 1193, 1376, 1387; Nehru Report, 814–16, 817–22; Memorandum for Round Table Conference, 876–9; Simon Commission, 903, 991–2; making of, 940–1, 943–55; Muslim League and Muslim Conference Memorandum (1933), 943–55; Joint Memorandum (1933), 962–93, 1388–9; Government of India Act (1935), 1071, 1091, 1388–9; see also Joint Committee, Muslim representation, Round Table Conferences

Constitutionalist Party, 294
co-operative societies, 333–4
Cooch Behar, Maharajah of, 474
Cook, Sir Joseph, 615
Corbett, Sir Geoffrey, 862
Corfield, C.L., 922
Cotton, Sir Henry, 295
cotton industry, 808, 811, 974, 1294
Council of Peers, 1086–8
Coupland, Sir Reginald, 29
cow sacrifice, 52, 462, 833–4
Cowasjee, B., 504
Cowasji, N.M., 994
Cox, H.V., 615, 696
Cox, Sir Percy, 761, 1435
Craddock, Sir Reginald, 941–2, 955
Craik, Sir Henry, 615, 648, 673, 677, 680
Cranworth, Lord, 472
Crawford, Lord, 616
Credit-Anstalt Bank, 1379
Crewe, Lord, 29, 391, 616, 619, 680, 778, 1435–6
Crewe Committee, 664–5
cricket, 462, 601, 867, 872, 1415
Crimean War, 637, 1247
Cripps, Sir Stafford, 41, 43, 158, 1389, 1436
Cripps Mission (1942), 1388, 1389
Cromer, Lord, 537, 538–9, 615, 699, 1436
Cromwell, Oliver, 269, 1436
Cross, Lord, 1008, 1436–7
Cross-Lansdowne reforms, 1341

Crostwaite, Sir Charles, 295
Cummings, H.R., 1165
Currimbhoy, Fazalbhoy, 394
Currimbhoy, Mahomedbhoy, 395, 473, 478
Curtis, Lionel, 30, 818, 823–4, 825–6, 1437
Curzon, Lady, 390
Curzon, Lord: relationship with Aga Khan, 11, 171, 1019, 1336, 1397; on British rule in India, 262, 574, 617–18, 846; Viceroyalty, 264–5, 346, 537, 920, 1069, 1214; Bengal partition scheme, 389–91, 818; Imperial Cadet Corps, 436; Sinha dinner, 615; Turkish policy, 733, 1359; education policy, 1111; biography, 1437
Cutch, Maharao of, 883
cycling, 201
Cyprus Convention, 407
Czechoslovakia, 1113, 1151–2

Dacca, 1265, 1268, 1274, 1311
Dacca, University of, 18, 100, 139, 388, 1264–6
Dadabhoy, Sir Maneckji, 862, 881, 1008, 1061, 1437
Dadachanji, Khan Bahadur Kersaspji, 474
Daily Express, 734, 738, 751, 763, 842, 1358
Daily Herald, 856
Daily Mail, 471, 734, 738, 751, 763
Daily Mirror, 734
Daily Nation, The, 189
Daily Sketch, 866, 1410

Dalhousie, Lord, 241, 556, 1437–8
Damascus, history, 1257, 1290
Dani, V.J., 411
Dante, 1052, 1438
Danyee, Abdeenbhoy Peerbhoy, 394
Dar-es-Salaam: Aga Khan's speech (1946), 82, 1239; Aga Khan's visit (1945), 1206–9
Dar-es-Salaam Cultural Society, 1209, 1231
Dar-ul-Islam, 142, 1258
Darbhanga, Maharajah of, 413, 853, 881
Das, Durga, 1065
Das, J.R., 504
Das, Sardar Jarmani, 854
Dastur, Sir Hormazdiar and Lady, 1175
Dastur, Pheroz Hosang, 473–4
Dasturs, 1257
Datt, A.C., 1065
Datta, Dr S.K., 881
Daud, Ahmad Mulla, 496, 499, 504
Daudpotta, Dr, 1175
Davam, Hakim Muhammad, 743
Davenport, W. Bromley, 685
Davidson, J.C.C., 921, 942, 955
Dawlatchand, Mansukhlal, 504
Dawn, 1266, 1270, 1294, 1300–1, 1303, 1306, 1312
Dawson, Sir Philip, 942
Dayam, Khan Bahadur Hakim, 742
Dean, B.C.L., 1081
Deccan: Muslim League, 284; Hindus, 564
Defence of India Act, 562
Dehlavi, Ali

Muhammad Khan, 1016, 1438
Delbos, Yvon, 1144
Delhi: capital of India, 29, 384, 391, 1095; Waliullah seminary, 115; Durbars, 222, 227, 247, 268, 328, 389, 391, 466, 525, 726, 888; All India Muslim League Third Annual Session, 328, 339–40; MAO Educational Conference (1902), 377, 397, 410; All India Muslim Conference (1928–29), 827–8, 829–41; status, 948–9, 954; history, 1298; Muslim history, 1338
Delhi Muslim Association, Aga Khan's speech (1935), 1060–1
Delvi, Mr, 411
democratic values, 86–92
Deoband School, 152
Depressed Classes, 461, 668, 675–6, 815, 877, 879, 1372, see also Untouchables
Derby, Lord, 932, 939, 942, 1357, 1387, 1438
Déroulède, M., 575
Desai, Balubhai J., 799, 1065
Dewani, 566, 644
Dewraj, Mukhi Hasanbhai Laljee, 1175
Dhalla, Count Fatehali, 1319
Dholpur, Maharajah Rana of, 852, 880
Diamond Jubilee, Aga Khan's, 18, 1219, 1223, 1227, 1239
Diamond Jubilee

Insurance Company, 186

Diamond Jubilee Investment Trust (Diamond Trust), 186, 1408

Dickens, Charles, 200, 858, 1439

Dikson, J.B.B., 685

Din, Mian Muhammad Shah, 259

Dinath, M.A., 1213

disarmament, 84–5, 892–9, *see also* world peace

Disarmament Conference, 2, 16–17, 76, 77, 892–9, 908, 924–6, 1048, 1089, 1213, 1233, 1239, 1390–2

Disraeli, Benjamin, *see* Beaconsfield

Divine Grace, 1405

Dixon-Johnson, C.F., 685

Douglas-Pennant, Violet, 942

Dow, H., 1066

Doyle, Sir Arthur Conan, 849, 1439

du Cane, J.P., 696

Du Maurier, George, 629

Dufferin, Lady, 278, 569, 594–5

Dufferin, Lord, 278, 846, 1439

Duke, Sir William, 615, 689, 1439–40

Dumasia, Navroji, 1336

Dupré, M., 907

Durban, Aga Khan's speech (1945), 1215–17

Dutt, P.K., 862

Dutt, R.B.D., 1066

Dwarkadas, Jamnadas, 685, 797

Earle, Sir Archdale, 689, 1440

East Africa: Ismaili community, 10, 22, 81–2, 746, 802, 1189; Indian community, 10, 81, 472–3, 488, 491, 720, 744–6; race relations, 82, 91, 92, 163–4, 491, 744–6, 748, 754–5, 1210, 1239, 1404–5; education, 101–2, 1197–8, 1201–2, 1204, 1229–30; agriculture, 108, 1190; Muslim population, 125, 128–30, 1195–99, 1201–3, 1204–7, 1223–8, 1404–5; press, 189; Aga Khan's visits, 1189–1209, 1222–39

East African, The, 189

East African Muslim Conference, 18, 128, 129, 1195–1200, 1201–3, 1204–5, 1223, 1226–8, 1229–30

East African Muslim Welfare Society, 130, 1199, 1314–29

East African Standard, 50n, 1189, 1194, 1240

East and West, 859, 871–2, 900–2, 925, 9311–2, 1034–5, 1040, 1051, 1067, 1086–8, 1131–2, 1139, 1147–8, 1173–4, 1210–11, 1245–9, 1298–1300

East India Company: control of India, 24, 308, 338, 1340; early history, 271, 295, 1047; in Bengal, 566, 644; Charter Acts, 606; relationship with Rulers, 620, 620; in Bombay, 809–11

Eastern Federal Union Insurance Company, 1025

Ebbisham, Lord, 942

Ebuz-Ziya, Velid Bey, 770

economic issues: Islamic principles, 65, 864, 932–3, 939; world peace, 86; Africa, 91; 'enabling environment', 186–7; Indian budget, 216–22, 223–32; banking, 314–17; capital for development, 317–18; Indian National Debt, 374; consumerism, 872–3, 1288; exchange rate, 874; share-holding, 874; capital investment, 1287–9; economic crisis (1931), 1378–9; *see also* industry and commerce, taxation

Ede, Chuter, 1289

Eden, Anthony, 79, 1052, 1149, 1241, 1395, 1440

Edinburgh Review, Aga Khan's articles: (1914), 480–92, 498; (1923), 761–7

education: Aga Khan's, 9–10, 166, 200, 858, 1330–4; Aligarh Movement, 23–4; Indian administration, 47–8, 175; Aga Khan's views on, 75, 91, 107, 175, 364–82, 393–4, 580–6, 666, 872, 874–5, 1112–18, 1337, 1344–5; commercial, 99, 100–1, 333, 1113; agricultural, 107, 177, 313–16, 322,

1113–14; girls, 111–12, 394, 582, 585, 741, 1112, 1117, 1211–12, 1216–17; African Muslims, 128–9, 1197–8, 1201–2, 1211–12, 1216–17, 1222; Muslim, 177, 322, 116–17, 1220, 1291–3; Muslim education in India, 204–14, 738–41, 836, *see also* Aligarh; primary education in India, 217, 312, 314, 333, 370–1, 380–1, 383, 465, 583–6, 597, 832, 836, 1112, 1117–18, 1337; technical and scientific in India, 218, 312–13, 322, 394, 586, 832, 1114, 1115, 1220, 1291; improvement in India, 231, 333–4, 369–73, 545; university education in India, 311–13, 371–2, 587–92, 740, 832; literacy, 312, 368–9, 538, 581–2, 981–2, 1337; secondary education in India, 333, 371, 586, 832; school attendance, 367–8, 545; scholarships, 394; schools in Burma, 498; funding, 585–6, 1117, 1204–5, 1229; career teachers, 1114–15; College of Technology proposal, 1115–16; religious, 1116–17; East African Muslim Welfare Society's work, 1316–17, 1319–20, 1322–3, 1325,

1327–9; *see also* universities
Education Commission (1882), 388
Edward VII, King, 201, 203, 331, 341–2, 377, 566, 1440
Edward VIII, 726–30, 829, 1095, 1097, 1100, 1440
Edwardes, S.M., 1441
Egerton, Sir Philip Grey, 615
Egypt: Aga Khan's visit, 19; Ismaili community, 21; sovereignty, 141, 764–5, 1032; Ikhwan, 142, 1258; army, 220; unrest, 365; literature, 483; Muslim population, 535; Khedive, 535; administration, 536, 539, 571, 573, 695; British relations, 936; agriculture, 1028; history, 1128, 1232, 1255; League of Nations membership, 1139–46; Palestine conference, 1169; African Muslims, 1198
Egyptian Mail, 1249
Einstein, Albert, 167, 873, 1036, 1441
elections: (1937), 38; (1945), 42
Elgin, Lord, 201, 1441
Eliot, George, 858, 1441
élites, 190–2
Elles, Sir Edmond, 225
Ellesmere, Lord, 942
Elliot, Major, 942
Ellison, Grace, 761, 763, 1441–2
Elphinstone, Mountstuart, 615, 810, 845, 1442

Emden (German warship), 1348
Empire Exhibition, Glasgow, 1162–6
Empire Review, 155
empires, 819
Engels, Friedrich, 1287, 1382, 1442
England: Aga Khan's visits, 10, 135, 201; Revolution, 269; role of Crown, 279; religion, 326, 1269, 1363, 1410–12; Indian Muslim youth, 458–9; press, 481; young Indians, 490–1, 1346; *see also* Britain
English: language, 95, 166, 189, 238, 358, 589, 1197–8, 1332; literature, 97, 322, 1334
Esher, Lord, 696
Esher Committee, 161–2, 692–6, 698, 705
Ethiopia, *see* Abyssinia
Europe, United States of, 1163–4
Evening News, 734, 738, 751, 763
Evening Standard, 14, 787
External Capital Committee, 978
Ezra, A., 615

Fakhruddin, Sahibzada, 1014
Faraday, Michael, 873, 1442
Farquharson, Margaret, 939, 1086
Farsi, 166, *see also* Persian
fascism, 1397, 1398
Fatima, daughter of the Prophet, 20–1, 1422
Fatimids, 3
Fazl-i-Hussain, Mian Sir, 1061, 1108, 1109

Fazlul Haq, Abul Kasem, 853, 881, 1014, 1020
Feetham, Richard, 672
Fell, Sir Godfrey, 697
Fergusson, Sir James, 7
Fergusson College, 516
Firdausi: Lady Ali Shah's appreciation of, 9, 1332; Aga Khan's opinion of, 168, 1036–7; millenium of birth, 1034, 1038, 1051–3; influence, 1129; biography, 1442
Fiscal Commission, 739
Fiscal Convention (1919), 974
Fisher, Herbert Albert Laurens, 456, 615
Fitzgerald, Edward: translation style, 168, 1037; Aga Khan's opinion of, 200, 519–20, 1035, 1037–8; quoted, 1385; biography, 1443
Foot, Isaac, 852, 880, 942, 955, 961
football, 867, 873
Foroughi, M., 911
Foster, Sir George E., 615
Fox, Charles James, 920, 1443
Framjee, Dosabhoy, 518
France: Aga Khan's visits, 19; Ismaili community, 22; Ankara treaty (1921), 33; Syria, 131, 407, 485, 766, 1349; Chanak withdrawal, 134, 732; Revolution, 269, 538, 1171; Muslim population, 321; spiritual devotion, 326; unrest, 364–5; Moroccan policy, 403; Paris Commune,

485; government, 543, 575; universities, 588; anarchism, 608, 705; Second Empire, 694; Turkish policy, 714–15, 721; health, 788; Disarmament Conference, 896; commerce, 1113; position after World War II, 1191; peace policy, 1235–6; colonies, 1236; Jerusalem claim, 1351
franchise: extension (1919), 31; female, 112–14, 118, 159, 593–4, 597–8, 645–7, 655, 662, 664, 668–9, 672, 676–7, 946, 948; Aga Khan's proposals for India, 552, 563, 659, 667–8; universal, 598; qualifications for, 678; response to White Paper proposals, 981–4
Franco-German War, 1247
Franks, George, 1017
Fraser, Sir Ian and Lady, 1279
freedom of will, 121, 211–12
Fremantle, Sir Edmund R., 685, 1443
French: language, 166, 420, 426, 439, 1332; literature, 434–5, 1334
Frere, Lady, 354
Fryer, Dr, 809–10
Fulton, Sir Robert, 615
Furdonjee, Naoroji, 518
Fyzee, Asaf A.A., 1068, 1173, 1175–7

Gainford, Lord, 615
Gait, Sir Edward, 593, 1443
Gallagher, Mr (tutor), 1331

Gandhi, Mahatma (M.K): Round Table Conferences, 16, 37, 71–2, 881, 976, 1371, 1379–80, 1384–7, 1388; Khilafat Movement, 34, 1351, 1380; worship of portrait, 39; 1942 disturbances, 41; imprisonment, 41; talks with Jinnah, 41–2; Muslim Conference influence, 68; meeting with Aga Khan (1946), 74, 1250, 1382–3, 1401; relationship with British, 158, 717, 1380; World War I, 158, 506, 508; relationship with Aga Khan, 171, 1091, 1380–3, 1384–5; South African activities, 475, 478, 795, 796, 1380; relationship with Muslim community, 755, 1384; on race relations, 776–7; illness, 1091, 1381; teachings on moral force, 1217; political philosophy, 1250–1, 1380–3, 1398; influence, 1336, 1396; Congress leadership, 1351, 1396; civil disobedience campaign, 1371; relationship with Jinnah, 1401; biography, 1443
Ganghji, Count A.H., 1319
Ganny, Yacoob Abdul, 504
Garcia d'Orta, 810
Garth, Sir Richard, 625

Garvin, Mr, 621Q
Geddes, Sir Eric, 616
Geneva: League of
  Nations, 1153, 1391;
  United Nations, 1391
Geneva Institute, 1233
Genghis Khan, 212,
  1232, 1434
George III, King, 1235
George V, King:
  Coronation Durbar
  (1911), 29, 391–2,
  726; Muslim subjects,
  149–50, 151, 355;
  Coronation
  celebrations in
  Lahore, 151;
  succession to throne,
  341; tour of India as
  Prince of Wales, 342,
  378, 566, 1093–4;
  visit to India (1911),
  344–5, 351, 377–8,
  382–3, 390–2, 413,
  566–7, 588, 727, 1095;
  loyalty to, 501, 566–7,
  621; health, 829–30,
  843, 1373; Aga Khan's
  tributes to, 843–4,
  1093–5, 1096–8;
  declaration on
  Indian status, 964;
  Silver Jubilee, 1071;
  death, 1093;
  relationship with Aga
  Khan, 1346; Round
  Table Conferences,
  1373; crisis (1931),
  1379; biography, 1444
George VI, King, 1235,
  1444
German: language, 166,
  420, 426, 435, 439;
  literature, 434–5
Germany: Aga Khan's
  visit, 10–11, 201; Aga
  Khan's proposals, 84,
  870; claims to
  Turkish territory, 131,
  407, 485, 508, 540;
  defence, 222, 227;
  Anatolian Railway,

274; borders, 275;
  unification, 285,
  579–80; Empire,
  309–10; religion,
  326; World War I,
  508, 546–7, 579,
  1099–1100, 1346–9;
  Prussian political
  development, 532,
  563; Bismarck's views
  on government, 542,
  1130; federalism,
  546, 556, 561, 823–4;
  Imperial
  government, 558;
  Middle Eastern policy,
  573; constitutional
  government, 576;
  army, 693–4;
  agriculture, 828;
  Imperial policies,
  830; commerce, 1113;
  League of Nations,
  1167, 1234, 1247,
  1391, 1394, 1396;
  Tanganyika question,
  1169; peace policy,
  1236; recovery, 1303;
  refugee problem,
  1306, 1307;
  militarism, 1415
al-Ghazali, 1364
Ghaznavi, Sir Abdul
  Halim: Joint
  Committee, 37, 993,
  994, 1020; Muslim
  Conference, 837,
  841, 1013, 1014, 1108,
  1109; Round Table
  Conferences, 853,
  881, 918, 922, 1020;
  views on finance, 932,
  939; Trojan horse
  image, 1062, 1065;
  tributes to Aga Khan,
  1063–5, 1109;
  biography, 1444
Ghiasuddin,
  Muhammad, 1065
Ghose, Arabinda, 430
Ghosh, Dr Rash Begari,
  412

Ghosh, Sudhir, 158
Ghulamhussain,
  Jafferbhoy, 685
Ghulamhussain,
  Muhammadbhoy,
  685
Ghuznavi, Sir Abdul
  Halim, see Ghaznavi
Gibbon, Edward, 200,
  1290, 1444
Gide, André, 168, 1037,
  1445
Gidney, Sir Henry:
  Round Table
  Conferences, 853,
  879, 881, 922, 1372;
  Joint Memorandum
  (1933), 966n, 984,
  989n, 993, 994; New
  Delhi dinner (1935),
  1065; biography, 1445
Gillman, Sir Webb, 697
Ginwala, Sir Padanji,
  881
Giri, V.V., 881
Gladstone, William
  Ewart, 405, 515, 637,
  700, 703, 1280, 1445
Glancy, Sir Reginald,
  854, 942
Glasgow, Empire
  Exhibition, 1162–6
Glasgow Herald, 1164–6
Gleeve, J.T., 1327
Gleichen, Lord Edward,
  685, 1445
Glenconner, Lord, 616
Godbole, K.V., 922
Godley, Sir Arthur, 390
Goeben (German
  warship), 1348
Goethe, Johann
  Wolfgang von, 1129
Gohar, Ali, 150
Gokhale, Gopal
  Krishna: relationship
  with Aga Khan, 158,
  170, 525–6, 1336–7,
  1338; budget speech
  (1904), 232n; on
  government of India,
  276, 317, 513, 551,

577, 813, 920;
influence, 277, 503,
517; work on
education, 367, 370,
381, 516, 545, 583;
Royal Commission
on Public Services in
India, 416, 445, 456;
education, 418;
South African
negotiations, 470,
502, 796; Imperial
Legislature, 515;
death, 525, 626; Aga
Khan's tribute to,
525–6; political
testament, 527–9,
548; on Muslim
representation, 614,
661; Mehta's
influence, 716;
renunciation, 717,
718; relationship with
Muslim community,
755; King's advice to,
1094; successor,
1351; biography,
1445–6
Gokuldas, Narotum
Morarji, 411, 414,
473, 479
Golconda, kingdom,
565
golf, 200–1, 787, 867,
872, 1166, 1411
Gopaljee, Shamjee, 504
Gordon Memorial
College, Khartoum,
102
Gour, Sir Hari Singh,
993, 994, 995, 997,
1446
Gourlay, W.R., 615
Government of India
Act (1858), 24, 308,
703
Government of India
Act (1919), 648–80,
689, 846, 990, 992,
1005
Government of India

Act (1935), 38, 1071,
1388–9
Graham-Little, Sir
Ernest, 942
Granville, Lord, 1280,
1446
Gray, Basil, 1133
Great Indian Peninsula
Railway, 811
Greece: conflict with
Turkey, 33, 132, 133,
482, 710, 711–12,
733, 759–60, 763,
777, 1349, 1355–9;
classical science, 126,
165, 1283, 1299;
influence on West,
178, 1132; classical
history, 235;
government, 576;
English support,
1351; classical
culture, 1360
Greek language,
classical, 417, 426,
447
Greenwall, Harry
James, 844
Grey, Sir Edward, 472,
1346, 1446
Grierson, Sir George,
590, 1446
Griffin, E.H., 685
Grigg, Sir Edward (later
Lord Altrincham),
1358, 1423
Guani, M., 1142, 1149
Gujerati: language, 53,
549, 590; race, 55,
819, 820
Gujjar, Bai Nanibai, 413
Gulbenkian, Nuber,
1051, 1133
Gunwala, Sir Padamji,
942
Gupta, Sir Krishna, 517,
697
Gurkhas, 272, 273
Gwalior: size of, 555;
Maharajah of, 557,
622, 1447; Aga Khan's
plans, 561

Gwiazdowski, M., 907
Gwyer, Sir Maurice, 942
Gwynne, H.A., 942

Habib, M.S., 1014
Habib, S.M., 1108
Habib, Syed, 837
Habibullah Khan of
Afghanistan, Amir, 52,
350–1, 1447
Habibullah Bahadur,
Nawab of Dacca, 841,
1014, 1270–1
Hafez, Sayyid Abdul,
1014, 1108
Hafiz: Lady Ali Shah's
appreciation of,
9–10, 1332; Aga
Khan's opinion of,
166–8, 172, 1035–7,
1128–30, 1132;
influence, 1132,
1361; biography, 1447
Hague Conferences,
893
Haile Selassie, 77
Hailey, Sir Malcolm,
151, 854
Hailsham, Lord, 880,
921
Hajee, I.S., 1175
Haji, S.I., 742
Hajibhai,
Mahomedbhai, 742
Hakim, Abdul, 752
Hakimji, Alibhoy, 504
Haksar, Colonel K.N.,
853, 880
Haldane, Lord, 616,
693, 1447
Hali, Khwaja Altaf
Hussain, 152
Halim, Professor, 1102
Hambro, M., 1149
Hamid, Abdul, 685
Hamid, Shaikh Abdul,
685
Hamilton, Lord
George, 10, 389, 523
Hamilton, Sir Robert,
852, 880
Hammick, Sir Murray,

416, 428, 456, 615, 1448
Harbottle, Sir J.G., 685
Hardie, Keir, 391
Hardinge, Lady, 569
Hardinge, Lord: Bengal partition repeal, 29, 386–8, 391; Aligarh University project, 105; Viceroyalty, 353, 459, 490, 547, 846, 888; great-grandfather, 413; Benares University, 415; South Africa policy, 475, 477–8; Balkan War policy, 486; Aga Khan's defence of, 522–4; university policy, 588; Sinha dinner, 612, 615; approach to Indian self-government, 619–20; appreciation of Muslim position, 1344; biography, 1448
Harington, Sir Charles, 1356, 1357, 1448
Harley, Sir Malcolm, 942
Haroon, Haji Seth Abdullah, 837, 841, 1013–14, 1066, 1108, 1448
Haroon, Yusuf, 1066
Haroon al-Rashid, Caliph, 1064–5
Harper, K.S., 994
Harries, T.W., 685
Harris, H. Wilson, 942
Harris, Lord, 200, 462, 517, 601, 1449
Hart Davies, T., 295
Harvard University, 180–1, 195
Hasan, eldest son of Ali, 138, 173, 773, 1365, 1422
Hasan, Sir Ali, 547
Hasan, Badrul, 1108
Hasan, K.B. Zafar, 1065

Hasan, Sayyid Wazir, 295, 340, 464, 466
Hasan al-Basri, 1257, 1449
Hasan Imam, 1353
Hasnain, S.G., 1065
Hassa, buffer region, 242
Hassan, Dr S.G., 1319
Hassan, K.M., 1065, 1319
Hassanali, Kamdia Kassamali, 1175
Hastings, Warren, 256, 845, 1449
Haughton, Colonel S.G.S., 1084
Hayat Khan, Malik Umar, 259
Hayat Khan, Nawab Muhammad, 1108
Hayat Khan, Nawab Sir Umar, 862, 939, 942
Hayat Khan, Sir Sikandar, 39, 40
health: Aga Khan's advice on, 75, 109, 786–9, 1414–15; African clinics, 130; medical education, 188–9; Indian standards, 538, 581–2; cancer, 724–5; cholera, 810; influenza epidemic, 1233; diagnosis, 1297; sanitation, 1298
Heaton, Joseph John, 417, 455
Hejaz, 682
Henderson, Arthur, 76, 852, 880, 899, 1391–2, 1450
Henschel, Lady, 1165
Herbert, Sir Alan, 1252–3
Herbert, C.G., 922
Herbert, Sir Dennis, 942
Hewett, Sir John, 622
Hidayat Husain, Hafiz,

837, 853, 881, 922, 1006, 1014, 1450
Hidayatullah, Sir Ghulam Husain, 742, 853, 881, 1108
Highet, J.C., 1081
Hill, Sir Claude, 689, 1450
Hinawy, Mbarak Ali, Liwali, 1223, 1229, 1318, 1319
Hindenburg, Paul von, 1348
Hindi, 39, 95, 146–7, 177, 589, 1273
Hindu-Muslim relations: electoral representation issue, 26–30, see also Muslim representation in India; riots, 34; Aga Khan's approach, 50–1, 65–6, 75, 343–4, 462, 755, 805–6, 903–5, 1119, 1167, 1219; cow sacrifice, 52, 462, 833–4; differences, 65, 288–9, 863–5; social mixing, 156–7, 271; role of education, 318; Calcutta riots (1910), 344; history, 564–5; in Bikaner, 614; in Hyderabad, 614; Constitution aims, 864–5, 1376; Bombay riots, 903; Congress-League agreement (1916), 1105–6; in South Africa, 1215–15; British Indian delegation, 1374–5, 1378, 1384–6
Hindus: politics, 23; caste issues, 52, 156, 230, 271, 291, 318, 815; extremism, 57; education, 95, 1116–17, 1212;

agitation, 155–6; conception of the family, 310; universities, 410–11; work for depressed classes, 461; holy places, 483; Indian self-government, 536–7, 1378; status of women, 592, 596, 602; scientific education, 1116–17, 1212, 1291; culture, 1132, 1157, 1345; philosophy, 1360

Hindustani, 566, 589, 1273, 1274

Hisham bin Abdur Rahman, 1257, 1450

Hisham ibn Abdul Malik, 123, 235

Hitler, Adolf, 1004, 1246, 1248, 1390, 1398, 1450–1

Hoare, Lady Maud, 883, 942

Hoare, Sir Samuel (later Lord Templewood): Disarmament Conference, 76; Round Table Conferences, 852, 880, 883–4, 921, 1372, 1387; Joint Committee, 940–1, 961; Aga Khan's tributes to, 940–1, 942, 996, 1055–6; Silver Jubilee dinner, 1071–2; relationship with Aga Khan, 1390; biography, 1477

hockey, 200

Hogg, John J., 685

Hogg, Malcolm, 645, 1451

Holland: Queen of, 728; peace policy, 1236; colonies, 1236

Holland, W.E.S., 627

Horne, Sir Robert, 1088, 1451

Horniman, B.G., 473, 479, 799

Horridge, Lady, 942

horses: Aga Khan's grandfather's influence, 199–200; racing, 199–200, 601, 856, 940, 941, 1072, 1092, 1166; Aga Khan's riding, 201, 786, 856, 1331; Aga Khan's love of, 867, 1062, 1065, 1415; Empire Exhibition, 1166

Huda, Abdul, 571

Hudson, Sir Havelock, 696

Hughes, W.M., 615, 910

Humayun, 1273

Hume, Allan Octavian, 157

Hungary, Aga Khan's proposals, 84, 870

Husain, second son of Ali, 123, 150, 1257, 1422, 1451–2

Husain, Mahmud, 1265–6

Husain, Mushir-ud-Dawlah Mamtaz-ul-Mulk Khalifa Sayyid Muhammad, 259

Husain, Mushtaq, 259

Husain, Nawab Mehdi, 837

Husain, Sayyid Karamat, 259

Husain, Sharif, 1350

Husain, Wajahat, 922

Husain, Yacoob, 685

Husain, Zahid, 1293

Husain Khan, Nawab Abul, 1065

Husain Khan, Nawab Bahadur Sayyid Amir, 259

Husain Khan, Nawab Sarfraz, 259

Husain Mian, Mawlana, 1014

Hussain Imam, Syed, 1014, 1065

Hutcheson, Captain, 496

Hutchison, Lord, 942, 955

Hydari, Nawab Sir Muhammad Akbar: Round Table Conferences, 853, 880, 919, 922, 1372; tribute to Aga Khan, 941; Joint Committee, 955, 993, 995; biography, 1451–2

Hydari, Lady, 942

Hyderabad: Usmanistan plan, 40; Aga Khan's plans, 55, 559, 561, 820; government, 553; Hindu-Muslim relations, 614

Hyderabad, Nizam of: refugee relief appeal, 401; status, 554–5, 557, 577, 591; on Morley-Minto Reforms, 621; Oosmania University, 832; views on Indian constitution, 997; Aligarh University, 1115; poetry, 1383

Hymans, M., 907

Hyndman, H.H., 266–8, 1452

Hythe, Lord, see Brassey

Ibn-i-Ahmad, 295

Ibn Rushd, 1360–1, 1471

Ibn Saud, 1349

Ibn Sina, 182

Ibrahim, Sir Currimbhoy, 324, 395, 1066, 1098

Ibrahim, Ramzanali, 1175

Ihtisham Ali, Munshi, 259

Ijma', 116–17, 122, 1183–4
Ijtihad, 116–17, 122, 1184
Ikhwan, 142, 1258
Ikramullaa, M., 1066
Imad-ul-Mulk, Nawab, 382
Imam, history, 20–1
Imamjan, A.K., 496, 499
Imperial Agricultural College Research Institute, 314
Imperial Cadet Corps, 219, 228–31, 246, 352, 436
Imperial College of Agriculture, 108, 1114
Imperial Conferences, 562
Imperial Gazetteer of India, 367, 809
Imperial General Staff, 696
Imperial Indian Citizenship Association, 795
Imperial Legislative Council, 11, 29, 57, 246, 254, 491, 498, 561, 656, 1266, 1336
Imperial Service Troops, 225–8, 231
Imperial Titles Act, 280
Inchcape, Lord, 616
income tax, 216–17, 949, 986–7
India:
 Aga Khan's proposals, 59–61, 176, 541–7, 871
 boycott movement, 803
 British policy, 160–2
 British rule, 24–5, 202–3, 240–2, 249–50, 266–74, 285–6, 338–9, 365, 407–8, 492, 513–14, 538, 556, 602–8, 704–5,

777–9, 845–7, 1063, 1402–3
 British withdrawal, 45, 1249
 budget, 216–22, 223–32
 caste system, 106–7, *see also* caste
 Census (1901), 224, 355–6
 central government reform proposals, 559–63
 Central Legislature, 877, 878, 946, 954, 1107
 civil disobedience campaign, 1371
 Civil Service, 175, 281, 372, 416–56, 526, 630–1, 689, 988–9, 1369, 1375
 Constitution, *see* Constitution
 constitutional deadlock, 1180
 Council of State proposal, 30–1
 criticism of League of Nations, 1089–90
 defence, 224–5, 238–47, 539–41, 894–5, 897, 966–8, 1241–2
 Dominion status, 50, 162, 613, 694–5, 813–16, 846–7, 964, 996, 1054, 1193, 1368, 1376, 1388
 economy, 374, 827–8, 968–72
 educational system, 93–4, 217–18, 231, 580–6
 Executive Council, 28, 291–2, 294, 349
 federalism, 2, 36–7, 52–3, 61, 64, 71, 176, 546–7, 548, 577, 662–3, 670, 679–80, 823,

842–3, 945–6, 1168–9, 1376, 1387–9
 Forestry Service, 418
 Free States, 176
 future role, 1237
 health, 538, 581–2, 724–5, 788–9
 Imperial Legislative Council, 11, 29, 57, 246, 254, 491, 498, 561, 656, 1266
 Indian Legislative Assembly proposal, 30–1
 Indian proposals for new constitutional order, 962–93
 industry, 203, 780–1, 792–3, 894
 Ismailism, 7, 21, 138, 432
 judges, 255, 949–50, 953–4
 man-power, 375–6
 Medical Service, 418
 military budget, 142, 164, 218, 523, 777–8
 Muslim attitude to British rule, 153–4, 1105
 Muslim population, 140, 206, 298, 321, 355–6, 407, 487–9, 535–6, 863–5, 886–8, 937
 Muslim representation, *see* Muslim representation
 mutiny (1857), 22, 155, 272, 1105
 nationalism, 348, 886, 1388
 Pakistan relations, 1280–1
 Police Service, 418, 984, 988–9
 press, 263, 481, 836, 1017
 Princely States, *see* Princely States

Princes, 919, 961, 964, 1168, 1193, 1372, 1378
proposed defence, 966–8
proposed federal finance, 986–7
proposed federal legislature, 981–84
proposed financial safeguards, 968–72
proposed fiscal convention, 972–5
proposed provincial constitutions, 984–6
proposed public services, 988–91
Provincial Civil Service, 419, 422–3, 427, 453–6
provincial elections (1937), 38
provincial reorganisation, 547–54, 650, 652
question of commercial discrimination, 976–81
Quetta earthquake (1935), 1072, 1073–85
reform scheme (1917), 543–4
role of Viceroyalty, 563–70, 602, 729–30
self-government, 48–50, 1220, 1249, 1277
Simon Commission, 34–5, 36, 54, 813, 821–2, 842, 959, 976–7, 980, 991–2, 1368, 1370, 1373
size of Muslim community, 298, 937
social mixing, 156–7, 271, see also caste

issues, race relations
Special Department of Education, 418
status of women, 592–8
trade, 934–5
transference of power, 1403
Turkish policy, 131–2, 133, 135
two-nation theory, 61
unrest, 365, see also riots
women's vote, 159
World War II, 1388, 1389
India Act (1919), 31, 34
India Office, 605, 659–60, 687
Indian Air Force, 1402
Indian Army: Muslims in, 27, 230, 295, 1375; Aga Khan's proposals, 218–19, 560, 562; Imperial Cadet Corps, 228–31, 352; race relations, 352–3; role in World War I, 523, 713; Maharajah of Bikaner's views, 619–20; Esher Committee, 693; Round Table Conference proposals, 955, 965–8; division between India and Pakistan, 1241, 1397, 1402; role in World War II, 1402
Indian Census, 724
Indian Central Committee, 850
Indian Christian Conference, 35
Indian Councils Act (1861), 25
Indian Councils Act (1892), 25

Indian Councils Act (1909), 28–9, 303
Indian Field Ambulance Corps, 505, 1346
Indian Independence Act (1947), 45
Indian Institute of Science, 591–2
Indian Liberal Federation, 157
Indian National Congress: Round Table Conferences, 16, 1371; Bengal partition issue, 26, 29; Lucknow Pact, 29–30; support for Khilafat Movement, 33–4; Nehru Report, 35, 54–5, 62, 813–16, 1368; elections (1937), 38; elections (1937–45), 38–9; flag, 39; police stations, 39; World War II, 41; 'quit India movement', 41; elections (1945), 42–3; Cabinet Mission plan, 43–4; Hindu extremism, 57; Joint Memorandum rejection (1933), 73, 1389; foundation, 155; role, 155–6; civil disobedience campaign, 155–6, 1371; relationship with British, 157–8, 267, 276–7; Curzon's policy towards, 390; Aga Khan's meetings (1910), 497; Calcutta (1890), 513; Dufferin's policy towards, 846; independence movement, 849; relationship with Muslim League,

1005, 1105–6, 1193;
Muslim membership,
1105, 1338, 1339,
1340; resignation of
Ministries, 1180;
problems with
Muslim
representation,
1337–40; Jinnah's
relationship with,
1342–3, 1369–70,
1399; Swaraj
interpretation, 1385;
rejection of Cabinet
Mission plan, 1403
Indian Overseas
Association, 794
Indian Reforms Act
(1935), 74
Indian Social Reformer,
443, 522–3
Indian Statutory
Commission, *see*
Simon Commission
Indian Tariff Board,
780, 977–8
Indian Volunteers
Committee, 505–9
Indigent Moslem Burial
Fund, 1070
Indo-British
Association, 618,
620, 623, 630
Indo-China, 1237
Indonesia, 142, 1237,
1258, 1300
Indus Provinces, 61
Industrial Promotion
and Development
Company, 187
Industrial Promotion
Services, 187
industry and
commerce:
development, 203;
education and
training, 333–4,
739–41; Aga Khan's
anxieties about India,
792–3, 807; East
India Association
meeting (1928),

807–11; tariffs, 562,
874; Joint
Memorandum
(1933), 976–81;
Burmese-Indian
relationship,
1027–30; Indian
backwardness, 1113;
Pakistan, 1286–9;
capital investment,
1287–9; Aga Khan's
family investments,
1294
inoculation, 127
insurance, 123–4, 186,
937, 1025–6
Inter-caste Marriages
Bill, 669
International Sirat
Conference, Karachi,
196
Iqbal, Sir Muhammad:
Round Table
Conferences, 36, 117,
881, 912–13, 922;
Pakistan origins, 39,
40, 62, 64–5; Muslim
League, 64–5, 68,
117; views, 114,
116–17, 118–19, 178;
use of Persian, 146;
regard for British,
150–2; Muslim
Conference, 837,
841, 912, 1012–13;
Muslim culture, 1035;
poetry, 1205, 1274;
biography, 1452
Iran: Aga Khan's visit,
19, 1276–7; Ismaili
community, 22;
dependency status
(1908), 31; culture,
144–5, 1127–8;
independence, 486;
tourism, 1088; oil
revenue, 1193;
history, 1255, 1309;
philosophy, 1360; *see
also* Persia
Iran Society, 1127,
1132–7

Iraq: Ismaili
community, 22;
League of Nations
membership, 911;
new kingdom, 936,
937
Ireland: political
violence, 608; Home
Rule, 816; peace
policy, 1235
iron and steel industry,
780–1, 808
Iron Curtain, 1246
Ironside, Sir Edmund,
1083
Irwin, Lord: Viceroyalty,
828; declaration on
Dominion status, 847,
920, 964, 1367–8;
Round Table
Conferences, 921,
1370–1, 1379;
London reception
(1933), 942; Joint
Committee, 955, 957
Isfahan, history, 1298
Islam:
African Muslims,
1198
Aga Khan's call to
Islamic world
(1934), 1031–3
Aga Khan on
religious revival,
1183–8
birth of, 1360
brotherhood, 1040,
1110, 1111, 1140,
1187, 1213, 1222,
1314, 1384, 1407,
1408, 1416
Christianity
comparison, 24, 59,
119, 120, 165, 289,
1299, 1363–5,
1410–12
continuity, 234
conversion, 129
diversity and unity,
1407
doctrine of necessity,
211–12

economic attitudes, 65, 116, 864, 932–3, 939

education, 97–9, 460–1, 1116–17

fundamentals of, 1363–7

Holy Places, 592, 682, 1351

idea of creation, 1365

in British Empire, 460–1

Judaism comparison, 1364–5

missionary activities, 1226, 1316

mysticism, 1332, 1362

pan-Islamic ideal, 75, 141–3, 483–4, 570–2, 765–6, 1187, 1314

principles, 1363–7

religion of nature and reason, 97–8, 115–16, 119–21, 125, 171, 182–3, 1290–3, 1299–1300

response to Turkish situation, 483–4, 712–13, 737

social customs, 104

status of women, 210–11, 592, 595

teachings of peace, 1232, 1235

tolerance, 165, 1108, 1261, 1268–9, 1282–3, 1404–5

unity of Islamic world, 138, 140, 141–2, 178, 357, 1011

see also Islamic, Muhammad, Muslim, Quran, Shia, Sunni

Islamic civilisation and culture, 764–5, 859, 871, 931, 934–5, 951, 953, 1011, 1031–2, 1067, 1086–8, 1101, 1110, 1173–4, 1186, 1273–5, 1282–3, 1290–1, 1298, 1360, 1366–7

Islamic Culture Society, Mombasa, 1230

Islamic Research Association, Bombay, 89, 1067–8, 1173–7

Islington, Lord, 416, 456, 615, 689

Ismail, A.K., 1202

Ismail, Chaudhri Muhammad, 1014

Ismail, Imam, 21

Ismail, Sir Mirza Muhammad, 853, 880, 922, 955, 993, 1372

Ismail Khan, Haji Muhammad, 259

Ismail Khan, Nawab Muhammad, 841

Ismaili, 1064, 1132, 1174, 1289

Ismaili Women's Association of Karachi, 1295

Ismailism: Aga Khan's Diamond Jubilee, 18, 1219, 1225, 1239; Aga Khan's Platinum Jubilee, 19, 1300–1, 1302, 1407, 1408; Aga Khan's position, 20, 122, 127, 432, 773, 1303, 1364, 1408; origins, 21; Shia Islam, 21, 130; communities, 21–2, 81–2, 130, 1219; Prince Karim's succession, 181; Aga Khan's visits to Ismaili communities, 201–2, 802; Aga Khan's speech (1951), 1278–9; Aga Khan's speech (1954), 1302; Pakistani citizenship, 1302–3; foundation, 1416; position of

'Ulu'l-amr Minkum, 1416

Ismay, Lord, 45

Ismet Pasha (later Inünü), 15, 134, 757, 770–1, 772–4, 1452–3

Israel, creation of, 1284

Ispahani, M.H., 615, 685, 689, 751, 752, 1017

Istanbul, history, 1298, see also Constantinople

Italian language, 166, 450–1

Italy: invasion of Abyssinia, 77, 79, 83, 1241, 1391, 1393–5; Chanak withdrawal, 134, 732; anarchists, 269, 608; King of, 728; Aga Khan's plans, 870; League of Nations, 1234, 1247, 1391; peace policy, 1236

Ittla'at, 1276, 1277

Ivanow, W., 1174, 1175

Iyengar, A.S., 1066

Iyengar, Rangaswami, 881, 994

Iyer, Ranga, 1066

Jackson, Sir Henry, 942

Jacob, Sir Claud W., 696

Jacobson, S., 1065

Jadhav, B.V., 853, 881

Jafar, Ahmad Ibrahim Haroon, 1066

Ja'far al Askari, 1042

Ja'far al-Sadiq, Imam, 21

Jafri, S.N.A., 1066

Jahangir, Emperor, 565, 1273, 1453

Jaipur, 997

Jairazbhoy, Al-Haji Qassim Ali, 1044

Jam Sahib, 960–1

Jamal, Abdul Karim, 496, 499, 504

James, F.E., 1065

Jami, 1036, 1037, 1453
Jamil Khan, Hakim, 841, 1065
Jammu and Kashmir, Maharajah of, 852, 880, 922, 997, 1372
Jamnagar, Maharajah of, 225, 1372
Janjira: Aga Khan's plans, 561; Nawab of, 810, 1099
Jaora, 1099
Japan: invasion of Manchuria, 77; war with China, 79, 85–6, 1396; army, 218, 244; expansionism, 275; government, 280, 576; war with Russia, 365; regeneration, 381–2, 394, 461, 532, 539; taxation, 559; health, 725; exports, 792–3; Aga Khan's proposals, 871; dispute with China, 900–2, 909, 1393; cotton industry, 974; development, 1032; League of Nations, 1234, 1247, 1391; peace policy, 1236; recovery, 1303, 1306–7
Jaunpuri, Karamat Ali, 24
Java, 1032
Jayakar, M.R.: Nehru Report, 35; Privy Councillor, 157; South African issues, 799; Round Table Conferences, 881, 922, 1372; Joint Committee, 993, 994, 995, 997
Jeans, Sir James, 167, 1036, 1453
Jehangir, Sir Cowasji, 473, 474, 853, 881, 922, 1372
Jehangirabad, Raja of, 397, 398

Jeejeebhoy, Sir Jamsetjee, 1098
Jejeebhoy, Byramji, 797
Jenkins, Sir John, 391, 547
Jenkins, Lady Lawrence, 689
Jenkins, Sir Lawrence, 271, 1453
Jersey, Sarah, Lady, 595
Jerusalem, 1269, 1351
Jesuits, 1331–2
Jews, 165, 265, 288, 326, 1284, 1354, 1362, see also Judaism
Jezira, 744
Jezirul-al-Arab, 738
Jijibhoy, Sir Jamsetji, 473, 477
Jinnah, Muhammad Ali: Round Table Conferences, 16, 36, 68, 853, 881, 1371n, 1372, 1374, 1385–6, 1388, 1399; League election victories, 38; opposition to 1935 constitution, 39; Pakistan origins, 40, 42, 1342–3; on Congress revolt (1942), 41; talks with Gandhi (1944), 41–2; London talks (1947), 44; India partition policy, 66, 1342–3, 1369–70, 1382, 1397; Muslim League, 67, 806, 1005, 1109, 1399–1400; influence, 156; World War II, 158; Aga Khan's tribute to, 170–1, 1243, 1262, 1302, 1397; London Muslim League, 462; South African issues, 798; Quaid-i-Azam, 1255–6, 1258, 1259, 1267–8; death, 1262, 1302; memorial, 1262; relationship

with Aga Khan, 1342; relationship with Congress, 1342–3, 1369–70, 1399; career, 1396–7, 1398–9; comparison with Mussolini, 1397–8, 1401; relationship with Gandhi, 1401; acceptance of Cabinet Mission plan, 1402–3; biography, 1453
Jinnah League, 67, 806
Jivanjee, Yusufali A, Karimjee, 1319
Jodhpur, government, 550, 997
Joglekar, Rao Bahadur Ramchandra Narayan, 417, 455, 1453–4
Johannesburg, Aga Khan's speech (1945), 1210–13
Johnson, William, 609
Joint Free Conference, 850
Joint Memorandum (1933), 73, 943–56, 1004, 1015, 1055–6, 1063, 1388–9
Joint Select Committee on the Government of India Bill (1919), 648–80, 778
Joint Select Committee on Indian Constitutional Reform (1933), 17, 60, 68, 159, 169, 177, 835, 918, 920, 940, 943–56, 957–61, 1007, 1015, 1020, 1054–5, 1057–9, 1387–9
Jones, Field, 800
Jones, Morgan, 942
Jones, T.F. Gavin, 853, 881
Joseph, Pothan, 1017

Joshi, N.M., 35, 853, 881, 922, 993, 994, 1066
Jowitt, Sir William, 852, 880
Jubilee Insurance Company, 186
Judaism, 59, 289, 1132, 1362, 1364–5, *see also* Jews
Junagad, 225, 1099

Kabiruddin, Kazi, 411, 742
Kaderbhoy, Adamali E., 1319
Kaderbhoy, A.H., 1226, 1227, 1315–16, 1319
Kaderbhoy, K.T., 479
Kafayat Ali, Mian, 39, 40
Kajiji, Mr Justice, 742, 743
Kak, Pandit Ramchandra, 922
Kalameah, Muhammad, 496, 499, 504
Kalema, King, 1315
Kalyanwala, Dr D., 685
Kapurthala: education, 545; government, 555
Karachi: Aga Khan's birthplace, 7, 1302; speech (1954), 82n; commerce and industry, 739; proposed Research Institute, 1220; capital city, 1260, 1310; Bombay relationship, 1386
Karim, Prince, *see* Aga Khan IV
Karimjee, Abdulkarim Y.A., 1319
Karimjee, Abdullah, 1315, 1319
Karimjee, Tayabali H.A., 1319
Karslake, Major-General, 1075, 1081–2, 1084
Kashmir: Pakistan plan,

40; Aga Khan's proposals, 55, 561, 820; Muslim representation, 73; size, 554; India-Pakistan relations, 1281; *see also* Jammu
Kassamali, Seth Hussainali, 1066
Kathiawar, Aga Khan's proposals, 55, 820
Keeling, E.H., 1051, 1133
Keith, Professor, 665
Kelkar, N.C., 922, 994
Kenny, Mr (tutor), 1331, 1333
Kenya: committee, 15; Ismaili community, 81–2, 802, 1189; education, 102, 1189–90, 1325; agriculture, 108; building programme, 130; Indian rights, 159, 163–4; British policy, 163–4; press, 189; race relations, 744–6, 748, 754–5, 777, 1313; development, 1189–90; mosques, 1326
Kershaw, Sir Louis, 942, 1065
Khairuddin Pasha, 119
Khalid ibn al-Walid, 208, 1454
Khallikote, Raja of, 922
Khan, Agha, 504
Khan, Gulsher, 837
Khan, Muhammad Israel, 504
Khan, Sir Muzamilullah, 1064–5, 1102
Khan, Obaid-ur-Rahman, 1102
Khandalawalla, D.N.D., 1175
Khaqani, 1036, 1454

Khartoum, University of, 102
Khatav, G., 473
Khayal, Naseer Husain Khan, 259
Khayyam, Umar, 200, 519–20, 1035, 1087, 1413, 1479
khilafat (Caliphate): Aga Khan's anxieties for future of, 2, 14–15, 130; Aga Khan's appeal to Turkey, 15; abolition, 15, 34, 136; Indian Muslim attitude to, 31–4, 640–2, 770–1, 1351; Aga Khan's defence of, 118, 122–3, 483; Aga Khan's campaign, 118, 134–5, 136–8, 178, 768–70, 775; Shia view, 116, 122, 637, 1416–17; Sunni view, 116, 637, 768–70, 1351, 1416–17; origins, 635–6, 1363; arguments in support of campaign, 638–9; Montagu's position, 720, 1351; *see also* Abu Bakr, Ali, Umar, Uthman
Khilafat Movement, 14n, 15, 32, 33–4, 135–6, 155, 635, 640–2, 1351–3
Khojas, 7, 21
Kidwai, Mushir Husain, 685, 1066, 1108
Kifayatullah, Maulana Mufti, 837, 841
Al-Kindi, 183
Kinloch-Cooke, Sir Clement, 942
Kipling, Rudyard, 1383–4
Kirman, Governorship, 4
Kisch, Sir Cecil, 942

Kitchener, Lord, 245, 505, 1336, 1346, 1347, 1454
Ko Ba Oh, 496, 499, 504
Kolahpur, Maharajah of, 557
Komura, Marquis, 382
Koran, *see* Quran
Korea, Raja of, 880
Kotwal, K.P., 685
Krishna, Sir Balchandra, 410, 411, 414
Krofta, M., 1151
Kropotkin, Prince Peter, 1250, 1454–5
Kruger, Paul, 470, 688, 798
Kurdistan, 131, 485

Labour Government, 963
Labrousse, Yvette, Begum Aga Khan, 18, 19–20, 1206, 1214, 1307
Lahore, 151, 273; Resolution, 40–1, 1018
Lake, Lord, 644, 1455
Lakha, Count Hassan Kassim, 1319
Lall, Sir Sundar, 415
Lall, T., 615
Lamington, Lord: mosque project, 344; Sinha banquet, 615; Riff appeal, 782; on private enterprise, 808; National League reception, 885; Royal Central Asian Society, 1051; Aga Khan's tribute to, 1069–70; Iran Society, 1127, 1133; biography, 1455
Lancashire cotton industry, 808, 811, 973, 974
Lancers, 9th, 270
land reform, 118

Land Revenue and Agricultural Department, 313
landowners, representation, 304–5
languages: national language of Pakistan, 146–8, 1272–5; local Indian, 372; in education, 589–91, 832, 872, 932, 938; *see also* Arabic, English, Persian, Urdu
Lansbury, George, 1379
Lansdowne, Lord, 224, 365, 661–2, 798, 1455
Lari, Z.H., 1312
lascars, 356
Latif, C.A., 295
Latif, Sayyid Abdul, 39, 40
Latif Khan, Nawab Abdul, 24
Latifi, Alma, 862
Latin language, 417, 426, 447
Latthe, A.B., 854
Lausanne, Treaty of (1923), 15, 33, 134, 136, 179, 753, 757–60, 761, 1359
Laval, Pierre, 1090
Law, Andrew Bonar, 133–4, 615, 731–2, 1358, 1455
Law, Sir Edward, 222n
Law, Dr Narendra Nath, 853, 881
Lawley, Sir Arthur, 615
Lawrence, Lord, 243, 1456
Lawrence, D.H., 168, 1037, 1456
Lawrence, H.S., 742
Lawrence, Mr (tutor), 1331
Lawrence, Sir Walter R., 615
League of Nations: Aga Khan's role, 2, 76, 77–9, 870, 1213,

1233, 1239, 1247, 1390; Aga Khan's presidency, 17, 79–80, 1147–50, 1191; Aga Khan on, 83, 896–9, 900–2, 1147–8, 1163; Afghanistan membership, 139, 1039–43, 1070; British policy, 162, 694; Arab status, 767; race relations, 784; role, 896–9, 1233–4, 1280; Special Session (1922), 900–2; Turkish membership, 906–7; Aga Khan's speeches (1932), 908–10, 911, 914–15; Iraqi membership, 911; finances, 914–17; Aga Khan's speech (1935), 1089–90, 1393; Wells on, 1123; Aga Khan's speech (1936), 1124–6; Egyptian membership, 1139–46; Aga Khan's speeches (1937), 1147–8, 1151, 1153, 1155–7; Geneva headquarters, 1153; origins, 1163, 1233, 1247; end of, 1170, 1191, 1234, 1239, 1247; Covenant, 1247; appeasement, 1396
Leigh, Lord, 615, 942
leisure, 874
Lenin, V.I., 1004, 1287, 1382, 1456
Leonardo da Vinci, 1299, 1456
Lester, Sean, 907
Lewis, W.H., 1066
Liaquat Ali Khan, 44, 1456
Liaquat Ali Khan, Begum, 1260
Liaquat Hayat Khan,

Nawab, 919, 922, 955, 993, 1457

Liberal party, 244, 282, 365–6, 481, 562, 803, 1356, 1379

Liberalism, 114, 551, 562, 1123

Lim Chin Tsong, 504

Liman von Sanders, General, 1348

Linlithgow, Lord, 955, 1387, 1457

Listener, The, 875

literacy, 312, 368–9, 538, 581–2, 981–2, 1337

literature: Aga Khan's views on East-West knowledge, 145; Aga Khan's education, 200; in education, 336, 872; Aga Khan's reading, 858; Aga Khan's enjoyment of, 867; Oriental, 1159–61; *see also* Arabic, English, French, German, Persian, Sanskrit

Lithgow, Sir James, 1165

Litvinov, Maxim, 76, 77, 1234, 1241, 1394, 1457

Liwali, the, 1199, 1206, 1223, 1226, 1229, 11230

Lloyd, Lord, 1048, 1394, 1457

Lloyd George, David: pro-Greek policy, 33, 763, 1350, 1358–9; Turkish policy, 33, 638–9, 643, 1350, 1352; Khilafat Movement response, 34, 639, 1353; comparison of Kaiser to Prophet, 159–60, 507; Aga Khan's opinion of, 159–60, 171, 1397, 1398; land campaign, 481; on 'ramshackle empires', 589, 847; on self determination, 604; opinion of Hitler, 1246; Chanak crisis, 1356–7; fall of government, 1357–9; biography, 1458

Lloyd George, Major G., 942

Locarno, Treaty of, 896

Lockhart, Laurence, 1133

London: Treaty of (1915), 32; Aga Khan's lecture (1911), 51; speech (1951), 82n; mosque project, 143, 344, 361–2, 1182, 1412; mission, 1412

London Mosque Fund, 1070

London Muslim League: Aga Khan's involvement, 2, 176, 466, 489n, 495, 1214; campaign for Muslim representation, 13, 28, 360; status, 14; Aga Khan's address (1913), 51, 458–62; Aga Khan's letter (1909), 294–5; Aga Khan's speech (1909), 298–301; Ameer Ali's presidency, 337, 489n; crisis (1913–14), 480

Londonderry, Lord, 942

Long, Walter, 616

Lothian, Lord, 852, 880, 921, 942, 955

Lucknow: All India Muslim League, 340; Balkan War meetings, 409

Lucknow Pact, 29–30, 37, 665, 674, 677, 1214

Ludendorff, Erich von, 693, 1458

Luther, Martin, 1398

Lyautey, Marshal, 732, 1458

Lyon, P.C., 615

Lyttleton, Oliver, 1313, 1458

Lytton, Lord, 256, 1072, 1102, 1458

Ma Saw Sa, Dr, 994

Macaulay, Lord, 412, 784, 940, 1273, 1459

MacDonald, Alister, 1165

MacDonald, Ramsay: Communal Award, 37, 60; on Hindu Indian nationalism, 348–9; Royal Commission on the Public Services in India, 416, 438, 444, 450, 456; Round Table Conferences, 852, 880, 921, 1371, 1377, 1387; Disarmament Conference, 925; National Government, 1379, 1387; biography, 1459

McDougall, Rev., 685

Macedonia: Turkish loss, 408; Anglo-Turkish relations, 459

Mackenzie, Sir George, 295

McMahon, Sir A.H., 1460

MacMahon letters, 1350

Macmillan, Lord, 1050

Macpherson, Lord Thomas, 1279

Madanjit, V., 504

Madariaga, M. de, 1041

Madge, Walter Culley, 416, 435, 449, 450, 456

Madras: Cabinet Mission plan, 43; Aga

Khan's proposals, 53,
549; Muslim
representation, 304;
status, 389; Balkan
War meetings, 409;
non-Brahmans, 552;
women voters, 664;
Muslim community,
750–2; reform
proposals, 1106
Magliano, Teresa
(second wife of Aga
Khan), 13, 15
Mahallat, Lords of, 3
Mahasabha, Hindu, 16,
55, 62, 71–2, 159,
1109, 1376, 1386
Mahmoud Fakry Pasha,
899
Mahmud, Agha, 496,
499
Mahmud, Mir Maqbul,
922, 942, 1108
Mahmudabad,
Maharajah of: views
on Indian
independence, 153;
electoral plan, 304;
educational work,
379, 397, 398; refugee
appeal, 401; Muslim
League, 1005;
biography, 1459
Mahomedbhoy,
Husenali, 742
Mahrattas, 56, 63, 273,
356, 565, 566, 667,
675, 728, 818,
819–20, 847
Mahratti language, 53,
549, 590, 809
Majid Khan, Abdul, 259
Makerere College,
Kampala, 102, 1197,
1198, 1201–3, 1206,
1224
Malabari, Behramji
Merwanji, 595,
1459–60
Malak, Mawlana H.M.,
259
Malan, Dr D.F., 797

Malaviya, Pandit Madan
Mohan, 414, 881,
1386
Malcolm, Sir John, 810,
845, 847, 1460
Mall, Muhammad Haji
Solayman, 504
Mamun, Abul Abbas
Abdullah al, 212,
1460
Manchester Guardian, 34
Manchuria, Japanese
invasion, 77
Mandlik, N.V., 394
Manifesto (1927), 87
Mansoor, Dr, 1066
Mansur al-Hallaj, 1361,
1447–8
Mant, Sir Reginald, 942
M.A.P., 199
marriage, 118, 314, 868
Married Women's
Property Act (1882),
595
Marshall Plan, 1248
Marten, Sir Amberson,
808
Marx, Karl, 1250, 1287,
1382, 1383, 1397,
1460
Mary, Queen, 341–2,
351, 377–8, 382–3,
727, 829, 1460
Masaryk, Thomas,
1151–2
Massachusetts Institute
of Technology, 195
Massey, H.J., 615
Matheson, General Sir
Tornquhil, 1075
Mathur, M.S., 1066
Matsuoka Yosuke, 77
Maududi, Abul 'Ala,
117
Maugham, W.
Somerset, 1406
May Report, 1379
Mayo, Lord, 313
Mayurbhanj, Maharajah
of, 615
Mazharuddin, Maulvi,
837, 1014, 1108

Mecca, 684, 767, 1257,
1349, 1411
Mecklai, Ali
Muhammad, 1068,
1175–7
medicine, 1298, *see also*
health
Medina, 684, 767, 1257
Mehemet Ali, 1146
Mehr Shah, Nawab Sir
Sayyid, 881, 1108
Mehta, C.B., 1098
Mehta, C.V., 742
Mehta, Sir Homi, 942
Mehta, Sir Manubhai,
853, 880, 919, 922,
955, 993
Mehta, Sir
Pherozeshah: Aga
Khan's relationship
with, 27, 57, 170, 479,
502, 512, 716, 1337;
death, 170, 512; Aga
Khan's tributes to,
170, 512–17, 716–18;
South African issues,
473, 474–6, 502, 794;
Aga Khan's visit to
Burma, 503, 504;
Gokhale's testament,
525, 548; views on
Indian constitution,
551, 813, 920;
biography, 716,
1460–1
Menon, V.P., 45
Merchant, Gulamali G.,
1175
Mesopotamia: German
position, 131, 485;
British position, 131,
162–3, 407, 408, 485,
523, 534, 539, 691–2,
695, 766; Aga Khan's
views, 239, 242,
698–703; buffer
region proposal, 242;
Turkish territory, 682
Meston, Sir James, 113,
645–6, 689, 1461
Mexico, oil, 702

Middle Eastern Defence Organization, 1354
Middleton, Lord, 363
Midleton, Lord (Lord Brodrick–, 389, 648–9, 671, 677, 679–80
migration, 1120
Mildmay, Lord, 942
Milikoff, Loris, 531
Mill, John Stuart, 1334
Milner, Lord, 783–5, 1461
Mi'mar: Architecture in Development, 195
Minto, Lady, 353–4
Minto, Lord: Muslim deputation to (1906), 2, 12, 26–7, 58, 249–56, 290, 303, 329, 348, 497, 943, 1006, 1266, 1340–3; sympathy for Muslim cause, 28, 58, 1343; Aga Khan's friendship with, 158; London mosque project, 344; Aga Khan's tribute to, 346–54; letter to Ruling Chiefs, 369; opinion of Sinha, 617; approach to Indian self-government, 619, 846; successor, 1344; biography, 1461; *see also* Morley-Minto Reforms
Mir Hasan, Shams-ul-Ulema Mawlawi, 152–3
Mirza, Muhammad Aziz, 340, 495
Mitha, Sir Sulaiman Cassum, 1016
Mitra, Sir Bhupendra Nath, 853, 942, 1075, 1462
Mitter, Sir P.C., 853, 881
Moazzam, Muhammad, 1014

Mobeds, 1257
Mody H.P.: South African issues, 473, 479, 798; biography of Mehta, 716; Round Table Conferences, 853, 881, 942, 1372
Mogul, *see* Mughal
Mohamed, Varas Ahmedbhoy, 1175
Mohammed Ali Club, Cairo, 601
Mohani, Maulana Hasrat, 841
Moi, Daniel Arap, 185n, 186n
Moloney, M.J., 1066
Molony, W. O'Sullivan, 685
Mombasa: Institute for Technical Education, 102; Aga Khan's visits, 802, 1223–30
Mombasa Times, 802
Mongol invasions, 1256, 1283
Montagu, Edwin Samuel: memories of Lady Ali Shah, 8; approach to Indian self-government, 30, 574–5, 609, 619–20, 654, 694–5, 818, 843; Montagu-Chelmsford Report, *see* Montagu-Chelmsford Report; Turkish policy, 33, 714, 720, 721, 1351, 1353; resignation, 33; Indian Khilafat Movement, 34, 1351; criticisms of, 162; on Hardinge, 522; proposals submitted to, 548; Aga Khan's tribute to, 612–14; re-appointment, 622; speech at Sinha dinner, 628–32; Joint Select Committee,

648, 680; on Punjab unrest, 670; on referendum proposal, 671; on communal representation, 677, 679; Aga Khan's speech at dinner in honour of, 687–9; Lancashire deputation to, 973; biography, 1462
Montagu-Chelmsford Report, 30, 53, 59, 64, 113, 609, 627, 646, 687, 693, 701, 717, 871, 888, 976, 988, 1057, 1353
Montford Scheme, 943–4, 1105
Montreux Convention, 1359
Moolla, Muhammad Ebrahim, 504
Moonje, B.S., 853, 881
Moore, Arthur, 1066
Moplah outbreaks, 984
Morarji, Ratansi D., 797
Morison, Sir Theodore, 367, 416, 450, 456, 685, 1462
Morley, John (later Lord): Aga Khan's battle with, 12, 58–60, 176, 1343; plans for electoral reform, 28, 58–60, 290–2, 308, 347, 351; Muslim delegation to, 296; pledges to Muslims, 299–300; Viceroy's Executive nomination, 349; response to unrest, 366, 488; on Indian economy, 374; reversal of Bengal partition, 391; taxation policy, 539; attitude to appointment of Indians, 550, 1342;

on manners, 599–600; Indian self-government policy, 619, 846, 1341; relationship with Indians, 626; Savoy dinner, 689; political strategy, 1003; biography, 1462–3; *see also* Morley-Minto Reforms

Morley-Minto Reforms, 14, 28, 58, 60, 170, 176, 293, 302, 303–6, 324, 328–30, 337, 492, 514, 526, 619, 621, 846, 943, 1340–3

Morning Post, 734

Morocco: Riff, 139, 782; Muslim population, 321, 535; French policy, 403; literature, 483; crisis (1906), 547; development, 1032; history, 1255

Morvi, Aga Khan's proposals, 561

Morvi, Maharajah of, 941

Moses, the Prophet, 1364

mosques: building, 128, 130, 143, 344, 361–2, 800, 1182, 1197, 1205, 1412; use of, 836; schools, 1197, 1205; East African Muslim Welfare Society's work, 1316, 1321–2, 1323–4, 1326–7

Motamar-al-Alam-al-Islami, 1272, 1275

motoring, 201

Mountbatten, Lord, 45, 158, 1400, 1403

Moussadek, Dr, 1284

Muawiyah, Caliph, 123, 235, 635, 1290, 1463

Mudaliar, Ramaswami, 853, 881, 922, 1372

Mughal emperors, 95, 146, 267–8, 271, 356, 564–5, 589, 728, 810, 1171, 1255, 1273, 1340

Muhammad, the Prophet, 116, 182, 1364, 1383; teachings, 104, 114, 1031, 1044–5, 1222; *hadith*, 116, 122, 1274; Lloyd George's Kaiser comparison, 159–60, 507; companions, 209; example, 197, 210, 322, 1031; ceremonial tradition, 234; exhortations on knowledge, 322, 324; on education, 336; on position of women, 592, 1295; women followers, 592–3, 1295; succession, 635–6, 1363, 1407; Aga Khan's descent from, 857, 1360; trading career, 934; Jairazbhoy's biography of, 1044–5; religious authority, 1363; last words, 1366; interpretations of message, 1407

Muhammad, Allibhoy, 499

Muhammad Ali, Albanian leader, 581, 1463

Muhammad Khan, Mirza Ali, 394, 462, 799

Muhammad Khan, Raja Sher, 853, 881, 1014, 1108

Muhammad Mehdi, first son of Aga Khan, 13

Muhammadan Anglo-Oriental (MAO-College, *see* Aligarh

Muhammadan Anglo-Oriental Educational Conference, 214n, *see also* All India Muhammadan Educational Conference

Muhammadi, Ismail Ahmad, 496, 499

Muhayyuddin Khan, Ahmed, 259

Muhsin-ul-Mulk, Nawab: Aga Khan's friendship, 11, 1334, 1338; All India Muslim League, 12, 27, 57, 329, 464, 494, 497, 1343; Simla Deputation (1906), 58, 259, 464; influence, 116, 1205, 1213, 1338–9; religious convictions, 119, 1300; work for Muslim education, 177, 1292, 1300; death, 177, 329; biography, 1463

Mukerjee, Ashutosh, 371

Mulla, Muhammad Ibrahim, 496, 499

Mumtaj, Hafiz Muhammad Sidiq, 1065

Mungaldas, Tribhovandas, 411

Muniwarabad Charitable Trust, 185

Muqtadari, Abdus Samad, 1014

Murtaza, Maulana Sayyid, 841, 1014, 1066

Musa al-Kazim, 21

Musa Khan, Haji Muhammad, 340

Musafaradin, Shah of Iran, 11, 1332

Muscat, Sultans of, 1255

music, 1257

Muslim countries, economic

conditions, 1185–6, 1192–3, 1286–9, 1309
Muslim Educational Conference, Bombay (1904), 12, 233–6
Muslim empires, 1255–7
Muslim League, see All India Muslim League, London Muslim League
Muslim representation in India: Bill of Muslim Rights (Simla deputation 1906), 26–7, 249–60, 272–3, 303, 329, 348; separate electorates, 27, 28, 29, 304–6, 803, 849–50, 877, 1311; Muslim League, 27–8, 328–9, 464–5, 756, 943–4; electoral college scheme, 28, 290; Indian Councils Act (1909), 28–9, 303–6, 328; provincial councils, 28–9; Lucknow Pact, 29–30, 37, 665, 674, 677, 1214; Communal Award (1932), 37, 37, 60, 68, 998, 1001–2, 1015, 1023; Aga Khan on, 272–3, 288–92, 298–301, 328–9, 464–5, 545, 614, 748–9, 755, 803, 830–2, 863–5, 1015, 1106–7, 1337–9; communal representation, 614, 661, 667–8, 1001, 1107; Nehru Report, 814–15, 817, 944; All India Muslim Conference (1928–29), 849–50, 944, 1369; Central Legislature, 877, 878, 946, 954, 1107;

Provincial Legislatures, 947–8, 1107
Muslim University, see Aligarh
Mussolini, Benito: Aga Khan's opinion of, 171, 1397–8, 1401; Locarno Treaty, 896; invasion of Abyssinia, 1391, 1393–5; biography, 1463–4
Mustafa Kamal Pasha (Atatürk): victories against Greeks, 15, 33, 711, 1355–6, 1357; liberation of Turkey, 33, 763–4, 774; Treaty of Lausanne, 134, 757; educational reforms, 177; relationship with Sultan, 714; religious policy, 722, 769; relationship with Britain, 763–4; leadership, 1349; military organization, 1355, 1357; biography, 1464
Mustapha El-Nahas Pasha, 1143
Al Mutannabi, 1129
Muzaffar Khan, Nawab, 1065
Muzammillullah Khan, Muhammad, 259
Mysore: Aga Khan's proposals, 55, 561, 578, 820; government, 553; size, 554
Mysore, Maharajah of, 415, 545

Nabiullah, Sayyid, 259
Nadir Shah, 565, 1255, 1464
Nadwaht-ul-'Ulema, 152–3
Nagpur, 53, 497, 556, 1345

Naidu, Sarojini: Round Table Conference, 16, 72, 881, 1380, 1383–4; Aga Khan's opinion of, 170, 1383–4; Montagu dinner, 689; South African issues, 799; biography, 1464
Nail, Sir Joseph, 942
Nair, Sir Sankaran, 301, 1464, 689
Nairang, Ghulam Bhik, 1066
Nairobi: Enabling Environment Conference, 185–7; mosque stone-laying ceremony, 800–1; Aga Khan's visit, 1189
Najmudeen, Dr, 1226, 1318–19
Nall, Sir Joseph, 955
Naoroji, Dadabhai, 266, 717, 1464–5
Napoleon I, 84, 870
Napoleon III, 694
Naranji, Lalji, 799
Nariman, G.K., 504
Natal, Indian community, 112, 471, 1215–17
Natal Indian Congress, 1215–17
Natarajan, K., 443, 447, 474, 479, 799
Nath, Raja Narendra, 853, 881
Nathu, Rao Bahadur Keshowji, 411
Nation Printers and Publishers, 189
National Government, 963
National League of Britain, 151, 931–3, 1086
National Muhammadan Association, 7, 24
National Review, 261, 583–4, 729
nationalism: Aga Khan's

views, 80–1; Sindhi, 148; Indian, 348–9, 886, 1388; dangers of, 1278; Arab, 1349, 1350–1, 1354; need for peace, 1415

Native States, *see* Princely States

nature: Islam as a natural religion, 97–8, 115–16, 1290–3, 1298–1300; Aga Khan's enjoyment of, 171, 866–7, 1414; spiritual values, 171, 179; Islamic architecture, 194–5; Western philosophy, 1298–1300

Nauman, Muhammad, 1066

Naumani, Maulana Shibli, 152

Navy League, 1048–50

Nawanagar, Maharajah of, 852, 880

Nawaz, Begum Shah, 854, 882, 922, 994, 1372

Nawaz Khan, Major Ahmed, 1066

Nazerali el-Africi, Sultanali, 1303, 1318

Nazerali, Count V.M., 1319

Nazimuddin, Khwaja, 1017

Negrin, M., 1148

Nehru, Jawaharlal: call to Muslims, 38; transfer of authority, 44; London talks (1947), 44; relationship with Mountbatten, 45, 158; relationship with Aga Khan, 1336; relationship with Jinnah, 1399

Nehru, Pandit Motilal: All Parties Conference, 35, 822,

976; Aga Khan's relationship with, 1336; *Autobiography*, 1371; influence, 1396; relationship with Jinnah, 1399; biography, 1465

Nehru Report, 35, 37, 54–5, 62–3, 176, 813–16, 817–22, 944, 976

Neogy, K.C., 854, 922

Nepal: Aga Khan's proposals, 54, 580; government, 280, 537

New Delhi, 63, 1008, 1062, 1110

New Statesman, 34

New Zealand: self-government, 374; votes for women, 593; peace policy, 1235

Nicholas II, Tsar, 265, 591, 1465

Nicholson, Lord, 523

Nicholson, R.A., 145, 1035, 1133, 1176, 1465

Nietzsche, Friedrich Wilhelm, 1397

Nightingale, Florence, 170, 1383

Nissim, Meyer, 799

Nizam-ud-Daulah, 6, 200

Nizami, 1036, 1037, 1128, 1465

Nizami, Khwaja Hasan, 1066

Noman, Muhammad, 1108

Noon, Sir Firoz Khan, 841, 1108, 1165, 1265, 1465–6

North-West Frontier Province: autonomy plan, 36; Pakistan, 40; Cabinet Mission plan, 43; Aga Khan's proposals, 53, 62; defence, 225; Muslim representation, 305,

1106–7, 1386; independent tribes, 356; reforms, 836, 849, 952, 1057; proposed status, 878, 1057

Northcliffe, Lord, 720, 722, 1357, 1466

Northcote, Lord, 201, 1466

Northumberland, Duke of, 680

Norton, Roger, 1279

Noyce, W.F., 504

nuclear: energy, 1220, 1298; weapons, 1246, 1259, 1298

Nuhu Mbogo, Prince, 1315

Nurmohamed, A.H., 1318–19

Nurul Amin, 1265, 1466–7

Nur-ul-Haq, 1017

Observer (Nairobi), 1222

O'Dwyer, Sir Michael, 151, 696

oil, 163, 701–2, 936, 1192

Oman, buffer region, 242

Omar, *see* Umar

Orange, H.W., 370

Orient Club, 601

Orissa: Lieutenant Governorship, 29; Cabinet Mission plan, 43; history, 356; electorate, 954–5; reform proposals, 1106

Ormsby-Gore, Major, 648, 680, 689

Osmania University, 591, 832

Othman, *see* Usman

Ottoman Empire, 31–2, 130–2, 636–7, 759, 936, 1255, 1348–9, 1350–1

Oudh: Kings of, 555, 565–6; status, 556, 825

Pacifico, Don, 469
Padshah, Sayyid Muhammad, 881, 1014, 1108, 1109
Pahlavi dynasty, 790
Paisa Akhbar, 149, 150
Pakistan:
  Aga Khan's family investments, 1294
  Aga Khan's visits, 18–19, 1254–71, 1286
  capital city, 1260, 1310
  citizenship, 1302–3
  Communal Harmony Week, 1268
  creation, 2, 139, 1225, 1243, 1249, 1256, 1262, 1277, 1300, 1343, 1400, 1403
  defence, 1241–2
  East, 139, 148, 1264, 1267–9, 1311, *see also* Bangladesh
  economy, 110, 1286–9, 1294
  education, 100, 1264–5, 1291–3
  India relations, 1280–1
  Islamic State, 124, 1254–5, 1267–71
  language, 145–8, 1272–5
  Muslim League, 1304
  origins, 39, 40–4, 58, 62, 64–5, 179, 1059, 1339, 1397
  refugee problem, 1306–8
  women, 1260
Pakistan Horizon, 1289
Pakistan Institute of International Affairs, 19, 1254, 1286, 1289, 1309–10

Pakistan Muslim League, 1304
Pakistan National Movement, 1018
Pakistan Observer, 1270, 1271
Palestine: problem of, 682, 766, 936, 1167; British presence, 695, 936, 1351; Zionism, 1070, 1350; cultural influence, 1132; Round Table Conference, 1169–70; Grand Mufti, 1170; creation of Israel, 1284; Balfour Declaration, 1350
Palmer, George, 685
Palmer, Julian A.B., 685
Palmerston, Lady, 595
Palmerston, Lord, 5, 469, 637
Pan-Islamic movement, 274
pan-Islamism, 75, 141–3, 481, 483–4, 570–2, 765–6, 1011, 1187, 1314
Panandikar, G.V., 742
Pande, Major, 922
Panikkar, K.M., 923
Panna, Maharajah of, 474
Pannir Selvam, A.T., 853, 879, 881
Papacy, 1247, 1363
Paraguay, Bolivian dispute, 909
Parekh, Gokuldas K., 411
Parikh, J.M., 517
Parlakimedi, Raja of, 853, 881
Parmoor, Lord, 616, 685, 1467
Paroo, Count Kassamali R., 1319
Parsis: status of women, 8, 602; World War I, 8;

origins, 11; social mixing, 271, 600; education, 429; Mehta's role, 718; distinguished families, 1008; Round Table Conferences, 1372
Parwez, Ghulam Ahmad, 114, 117–18, 118, 178
Passive Resistance Movement, 471
Patel, Esmail Muhammad Hoosein, 504
Patel, Sardar Vallabhbhai, 39, 1180, 1396, 1467
Patel, V.J., 479, 584, 1371n
Pathak, Pandit P.N., 923
Pathan, Ghyasuddin, 1304
Pathan rule, 146
Patiala, Maharajah of, 621, 622, 814, 853, 880, 997, 1372
patriotism and loyalty, 284–7, 317, 336, 339, 506, 516, 531, 589, 594, 603, 610, 717, 718, 721, 802, 864, 1028, 1095, 1106, 1215, 1278, 1302–3
Patro, Sir A.P., 853, 881, 922, 994
Pattani, Lady, 942
Pattani, P.D., 411
Pattani, Sir Prabhashankar, 853, 880, 923, 993
Patterson, Sir Stewart, 942
Paul, K.T., 853
Paul, Saint, 234, 1467
peace, *see* world peace
Peel, Lord, 852, 880, 921, 955
Peel Committee, 987
Peerbhoy,

Ebrahimbhoy Adamji, 259

Peerbhoy, Sir Adamji, 398

Pemba, 491, 1327–9

Peninsular and Oriental (P&O) Company, 811

Pentland, Lord, 550

Percy, Lord Eustace, 942, 955

Percy Committee, 987

Persia: Aga Khan's proposals, 54, 84, 670, 671, 871; disorder, 132, 365, 704; independence, 141, 764, 1032; British position, 163, 698, 702; government, 206; buffer zone proposal, 242, 243; borders, 274; Muslim population, 321, 459, 535, 712; status, 403, 486–7, 535, 578; monarchy, 537; relationship with India, 573, 579–80; Pahlavi dynasty, 790; travel books, 859; economy, 936; relationship with Afghanistan, 1041–2; history, 1128, 1130, 1171; see also Iran

Persian: language, 9, 143, 146–7, 420, 426, 439–40, 451, 590, 932, 938, 1273–4, 1332; literature, 9, 97, 140, 166–8, 200, 233, 322, 417, 434–5, 483, 1034–8, 1087, 1128–31, 1332, 1334; script, 101, 832

Persian Gulf, 491

Persian Society, 1070

Peter the Great, 591, 1467

Pethick-Lawrence,

Lord, 43, 158, 880, 1389, 1467–8

Petit, Sir Dinshaw, 473

Petit, Jehangir B., 477, 795, 797, 798–9

Petrie, Sir David, 1066

Pflügl, M., 907

Phillips, Morgan, 1392

Phillott, D.C., 685

Phipps, Henry, 314

Pickford, Miss, 955

Pickford, Sir Alfred, 1165

Pickford, Mary, 942

Pickthall, Marmaduke, 685, 1467–8

Pillai, G.P., 923

Pillay, A.M., 504

Pindari, 566

Piracha,F.H., 1066

Platinum Jubilee, 19, 1300–1, 1302–3, 1407, 1408–9

Plato, 1360

poetry: Aga Khan's love of Persian, 166–8, 1034–8; religious significance, 172, 179, 867; Western, 200; in education, 872; see also Persian literature

Poincaré, Raymond, 33, 1357

Polak, H.L., 794

Politis, Nicolas, 910, 1145

Pollen, John, 517, 519–20, 646, 1468

Poona: Aga Khan I's home, 6; Gandhi's imprisonment, 41; Municipality, 516

Portsmouth, Lord, 616

Portugal: Ismaili community, 22; government, 575; Indian rule, 784, 809–10; colonies, 1236

Portuguese language, 938

poverty, 106–7, 118, 269, 394, 581, 1337

Powar, B.I., 923

Power, Sir John, 942

Pradhan, S.R., 35, 822

Pragji, Hanaraj, 414

Pranjpe, 411

Prasad, Rajendra, 39

Prasad, Sir Sukhdeo, 922

Prashad, Pandit Mahadev, 414

press, role of, 89–90, 189–90, 263, 836, 1017

Press Act, 514

Pretoria, Aga Khan's visit (1945), 1214

Princely States (Native States, Protected States): Nehru Report, 62; Muslim representation, 62, 73; military role, 219–22, 224–5, 560; education, 369, 539, 545; Indian Civil Service, 420; government, 537, 553; health, 539; Aga Khan's proposals, 554–8, 559–60, 577–8; Muslim-Hindu relations, 614; representation, 1168

Princes Association, 961

Princes' Chamber, 964, 1401

private property, 874

Privy Council, 17

Public Services Commission, 877

Punjab: Muslim representation, 29–30, 37, 73, 252, 304, 305, 877, 904, 912, 1058, 1106–7, 1338, 1341, 1375, 1386; Pakistan, 40; Cabinet Mission plan, 43; Aga Khan's proposals, 53, 61,

549; language, 146;
Government, 150,
151; Imperial Service
Troops, 225; politics,
273; Sikh population,
291; Aligarh
University funding,
397; education, 584;
unrest, 670, 705, 984;
Communal Award,
1023
Punjab Unionist Party,
153
purdah: female
enfranchisement,
113, 114, 646, 655,
669, 672, 676–7;
origins, 211, 676;
social life, 595;
disappearance of,
602; property rights,
669
Pushkin, Alexander,
1129

Qa'ani, 168, 1037, 1128,
1131, 1468
Qajar, Shah
Muhammad Ali, 6
Qayyum, Nawab
Sahibzada Sir Abdul,
153–4, 841, 853, 881,
1014
Quaid-i-Azam, see
Jinnah
Quaid-i-Azam Memorial
Fund, 100, 1262
Quetta: Aga Khan's
proposals, 549; British
position, 700;
earthquake, 1072,
1073–85
Quran: teachings,
116–18, 120, 127,
206, 1366;
interpretations of,
116–17, 119, 122,
1300, 1362–4, 1366;
references to natural
phenomena, 97,
119–20, 125–6, 1185,
1261, 1290–3, 1300;

freedom of will, 121,
211; language of,
147, 483, 1274;
English translation,
169; on knowledge,
97, 125–7, 182–3,
1185, 1297, 1300; on
women, 210; on
importance of trade,
934; on 'Kalam', 1020;
importance of, 1411;
verse on light, 1362
Qureshi, Shoib, 35, 822,
862, 923

race relations: Aga
Khan's work, 75,
1239; East Africa, 82,
91, 92, 163–4, 491,
744–6, 748, 754–5,
1210, 1239, 1404–5;
South Africa, 91–2,
334–5, 468–79, 491,
794–9, 1210–11,
1215–16; India, 164,
230, 270–1, 532–3,
599–602, 776–7;
Mesopotamia, 534;
Kenya, 744–6, 748,
754–5, 1313; British
Imperialism, 783–5;
see also caste issues
racing, 199–200, 856,
940, 941, 1072, 1092,
1166
Rafi, Muhammad, 1065
Rafiuddin Ahmad, Sir,
259, 287n, 411, 413,
1468
Raghavia, T., 854, 880
Rahim, Sir Abdur: Joint
Committee, 37;
Simla deputation
(1906), 259; Royal
Commission on
Public Services, 456;
Joint Memorandum,
985n, 993; Joint
Committee, 994, 995,
997; New Delhi
dinner (1934), 1004;
Muslim Conference,

1014; Delhi Muslim
Association, 1061;
New Delhi dinner
(1935), 1064, 1065
Rahim, Mulla Abdur,
496, 499, 504
Rahimtulla, Sir
Ibrahim, 473, 477,
742, 828, 837, 841
Rahman, Dr Abdul,
797, 799
Rahman, Sir Abdur,
1066
Rahman, Khalilur-,
1014
Rahman, S.A., 504
Rahman, V.M. Abdur,
496, 499, 504
Rahman Khan,
Habibur, 259
Rahmat Ali, Chaudhri,
39, 40, 62, 65, 1018
railways: effects in
India, 268–9, 273;
meeting of Indian
and Russian, 274–5;
capital investment,
317; history of
construction, 811;
Bavarian, 823; Joint
Committee
proposals, 950, 981
Rajagopalacharia, C.,
41, 1065
Rajkumar Colleges, 436
Rajpipla, Maharajah of,
1072
Rajput States, 555, 577
Rajputana: Aga Khan's
proposals, 55, 820;
Imperial Service
Troops, 225
Rajputs, 271, 272, 273
Ramji, Manmohandas,
473, 474
Rampur, Nawab of, 401,
1099, 1468
Ramzanali, Alijah
Sabzali, 1066
Rana, Dr M.A., 1195,
1319
Ranade, Mahadev

Govind, 418, 716, 718, 813, 1468–9
Ranadive, R.K., 923
Rankeillour, Lord, 942, 955
Rao, B. Shiva, 853, 881
Rao, Madhava, 923
Rao, M. Ramachandra, 853, 881
Rashiduddin, Sahibzada Muhammad, 837, 1014
Rathbone, Eleanor, 942
Rau, P.R., 1066
Rauf, Sayyid Abdur, 259
Rayleigh, Lord, 725, 1469
Raza Ali, Sayyid, 1014
Raza Shah, 177, 790
Reading, Lord: Khilafat Movement 34; Greco-Turkish policy, 132, 710, 714, 751; Viceroyalty, 704, 729, 755; Aga Khan's tribute to, 706–8; Aga Khan's telegram to, 710; Round Table Conferences, 852, 880, 921, 1372, 1376; Dorchester dinner, 942; Joint Committee, 955; White Paper, 957; biography, 1469
Reay, Lord, 515
Red Crescent Society, 15, 139, 401, 402, 404, 486, 782, 1070
Red Cross, 505
Red Shirt movement, 904
Reddiar, S. Ramnath, 504
Reed, Sir Stanley, 473, 479, 798, 807–9, 1469–70
Rees, Sir J.D., 295, 615, 648, 674, 680, 689
referendum proposal, 657–8, 660–1, 669–70, 673–4
Reform Act (1918), 563, 604
refugees, 401–2, 405, 1306–8
Rehman, Dr Bazlur, 1175
Reid, Sir Marshal, 615
religion and spiritual values: religious evolution of India, 586; physical beauty, 787; in Kenya, 802; spiritual happiness, 866–8, 1414–15; religious freedom, 872, 876, 878; in Bengal, 1020, 1021; East and West, 1051; religious tolerance, 1107–8, 1282–3; religious education, 1116–17; Islamic revival, 1183–5, 1213; in South Africa, 1215–16; spiritual forces, 1127; Persian culture, 1130, 1257; ideals behind League of Nations, 1162; unity of Muslim peoples, 1187; medieval, 1247; in Turkey, 1255, 1351; in Baghdad, 1257; position of women, 1257, 1295; in Pakistan, 1260–1, 1286, 1303; dangers of religious fervour, 1278; Islamic ideals, 1286; and nature, 1299; spiritual being, 1309; science and magic, 1359–60; religious experience, 1361; power of love, 1361–2; religious authority, 1363–4; monotheism, 1364–5; duties of man, 1366–7; political influence, 1392, 1398; influence for good, 1404–5; Divine Grace, 1405; Ismaili principles, 1408–9, 1416–17; concept of religion, 1410–12
religions, 289–91, 1062–3, 1410–12
Renaissance, 98, 1171, 1291, 1298
research, 94–5
responsible government, 536–8, 574–6, 606, 649–52, 654, 656, 779, 815, 846, 852, 918, 921, 940, 975, 991–2, 997, 999, 1054–5, 1107
Restrepo, M., 907
Reuters Agency, interview with Aga Khan, 341–2
Rewa, Maharajah of, 853, 880, 1372
Reynolds, R.V., 685
Ribblesdale, Lord, 616
Richmond, J.R., 1166
Riff, 139, 782
riots: (1910), 344, 390; (1927–32), 34, 56, 903
Ripon, Lord, 329, 700, 1470
Ritchie, Philip C.T., 685
Ritz Hotel, 16, 928–9, 1372, 1380
Robert Missionary College, Constantinople, 1225, 1335
Roberts, Charles, 615
Roberts, Sir Herbert, 616
Rockefeller, John D., 1470
Roman Catholicism, 1363, see also Christianity
Rome, classical: influence on Muslim world, 165;

achievements, 178;
government, 202;
influence on
European education,
235; fall of Empire,
819, 1171, 1360;
period of peace, 1232,
1246
Ronaldshay, Lord, 295,
344, 416, 453, 456
Rookshah, Aga Shah,
742
Ross, Sir Denison, 145,
1035, 1038, 1052,
1133, 1470
Ross, Sir Ronald, 873
Rothermere, Lord, 14,
1356–7
Rothschild, Lord, 1350
Round Table
Conferences: Aga
Khan's involvement,
2, 16, 36–7, 60, 70,
122, 159, 177, 835,
857, 861, 919–21,
1029, 1091, 1266;
sessions (1930–32),
16–17, 36–7, 70, 71–2,
851–4, 861, 876–86,
888, 912–13, 918,
944, 970, 1006, 1015,
1020, 1054, 1056,
1091, 1371–80,
1384–7; committees,
16; Jinnah's
involvement, 16, 36,
68; Gandhi's role, 16,
37, 71–2; Iqbal's
involvement, 36, 117;
Muslim Conference
influence, 68;
Zafrullah Khan's
influence, 169–70;
memorandum for
(1931), 876–9;
Minorities
Committee, 879, 976;
Consultative
Committee, 904;
Prime Minister's
declaration, 963;
King's address, 1095

Rowlatt Committee,
619, 670
Roy, Gordon, 685
Roy, M.R., 882
Royal Asiatic Society of
London, 1176
Royal Central Asian
Society, 1051, 1070
Royal Commission on
the Public Services in
India, 13, 159, 416–56
Royal Indian Navy, 560,
562, 1047–8, 1402
Royal Navy, 1394–5
Rumbold, Lady, 1051
Rumbold, Sir Horace,
1051, 1470–1
Rumi, Jalaluddin: Lady
Ali Shah's
appreciation of, 9,
1332; Aga Khan's
opinion of, 172,
1036–7; quoted by
Aga Khan, 727;
influence, 1128,
1361; mysticism,
1364; biography, 1471
Rushbrook-Williams,
L.F., 854, 922
Russell, Lord, 852
Russell, Sir Guthrie,
1079, 1081
Russia: Aga Khan's visit
(1912), 13; fall of
Tsar, 138, 688; threat
to India, 218, 224,
239–45, 684; army,
218; Balkan policy,
224, 485; Tibetan
plans, 224;
revolution, 265, 274,
578–9; borders, 275;
Muslim population,
321; war with Japan,
365; Turkish territory,
407, 1347; education,
436; Tsarist rule, 531,
608, 696, 830, 936,
1063; democratic
government, 537;
Slavs, 737; USSR's
membership of

League of Nations,
1148; World War I,
1347–8, 1350, 1412
Ryrie, Sir Granville, 907

Sa'adi, 323, 928, 1036,
1128, 1157, 1471
Sadiq, Mufti
Muhammad, 837,
1014
Sadiq, Muhammad, 837
Sadiq, Shaikh Ghulam,
259
Sadiq, Shaikh
Muhammad, 837
Sadler, Sir Michael, 689
Sadruddin, Maulvi, 685
Sadruddin, Pir, 21
Sadruddin, Prince,
third son of Aga Khan
III, 17, 19–20
Safavi period, 1130
Sahni, J.N., 1065
Sahni, R.B. Dayaram,
1066
Said Khan, Nawab Sir
Ahmad, 841
St Jean de Maurienne
Agreement (1917), 32
Sait, H. Essak, 1066
Sait, Sir Haji Ismail, 752
Sait, R.A. Basak, 1065
Sakina, 123, 1257
Salam Khan, Munshi
Abdus, 259
Salim, Sultan, 636–7,
639
Salimah, Begum, 181
Salimpur, Raja of, 1108
Salimullah Khan,
Mawlawi Haji
Muhammad, 1118
Salimullah Khan,
Nawab of Dacca, 27,
57, 1266, 1268, 1343,
1471
Salisbury, Lord, 10, 657,
701, 955, 1247
salt tax, 216, 755, 987
Samaldas, Lalubhoy,
411, 478

Samji, Alijah Abdulla
Hasan, 1175
Samuel, Sir Herbert,
615, 942, 1379,
1471–2
Sandhurst, Lord, 616
Sandler, M.R.J., 1040,
1149
Sandow, Eugene, 786,
1472
Sandwich, Lord, 616
Sangli, Chief Sahib of,
853, 880
Sankey, Lord, 852, 880,
921, 942, 1371, 1472
Sanskrit: language, 417,
426, 440, 447, 549,
1345; literature, 97,
322, 336
Sapru, Tej Bahadur: All-
Parties Conference,
35, 822; Round Table
Conferences, 71,
853, 881, 884, 919,
922, 1371n, 1372,
1376, 1377; British
honours, 157; South
African issues, 794,
796; Aga Khan's
tributes to, 883, 995,
997; tribute to Aga
Khan, 941; British
Indian Delegation,
994, 995, 997; Privy
Council, 1072;
London dinner
speech (1935), 1072;
education policy,
1112; on Hafiz,
1129–30; biography,
1472
Saran, Munshi Iswar,
1065
Sarila, Raja of, 880, 922
Sastri, Srinivasa: Round
Table Conferences,
71, 854, 882, 1372,
1376; Privy
Councillor, 157; East
African issues, 163,
745, 748, 754;
biography, 1472

Satara, 556
Satchu, A.C., 1226, 1319
sati, 46–7
Satyagraha, 155–6
Satyamurti, S., 1066
Saudi Arabia, oil
revenue, 1193
Sayani, Rahmatullah
M., 7
Sayyid Ahmad Khan, *see*
Ahmad Khan
Sayyid Khan, Nawab Sir
Muhammad Ahmed,
1013
science: education,
99–100, 118, 218,
873, 1212, 1220;
Islamic approach,
125–7, 1031–2, 1212,
1290–3, 1298–9; Aga
Khan's proposals,
873–4; future
possibilities, 1220; *see
also* technology
Scientific Society, 115
Scindhia: Maharajah,
225, 247; defeat, 356
Scott, Rev Dr, 473
sects, sectarianism, 773,
1107, 1173, 1184,
1210, 1258, 1314,
1364, 1407, 1408,
1416–17
Seddon, C.N., 923
Selborne, Lord, 680
Sen, P.C., 504
Sen, S.C., 1066
Sen, U.N., 1065
Sepahbodi, M., 1041
Serbia, World War I,
536
Setalvad, Sir Chimanlal,
157, 797–8, 854, 882,
1372, 1375
Seth, Haji Sattar, 1108
Seth, Kanwar
Bisheshwar Dayal,
854, 882
Seth, M., 685
Seth, N.C., 689
Sethna, Sir Phiroze:
Round Table

Conferences, 854,
882, 1372; Joint
Committee, 993, 994,
995, 997; biography,
1473
Sèvres, Treaty of, 15, 32,
132, 134, 135, 179,
638, 708, 710, 711,
735–6, 759, 763, 774,
1172, 1353, 1355
Shadman, Sayyid F.,
1052, 1133
Shafa'at Ahmad Khan,
see Ahmad Khan
Shafi, Mian Sir
Muhammad: Round
Table Conferences,
16, 70, 853, 862, 881,
1372, 1385; Muslim
League, 67, 339, 806,
1005; Simla
deputation (1906),
259; Muslim
Conference, 837,
841; New Delhi
dinner (1935), 1065;
influence, 1343;
biography, 1473–4
Shafi Daudi, Maulana
Muhammad: Muslim
Conference, 837,
1012, 1013, 1014,
1108; Round Table
Conferences, 881;
New Delhi dinner
(1935), 1066;
biography, 1474
Shafi League, 67, 806
Shah, Abul Hasan, 3
Shah, Agha Jangi, 7
Shah, Fath Ali, Qajar
emperor, 3–4
Shah, Hasan Ali, 4
Shah, Khalilullah, 3–4
Shah, Khwaja Yusuf, 259
Shah, Lady Ali, 8–10,
17–18, 200, 999,
1056, 1332, 1334
Shah, Muhammad, 4, 5
Shah, Muhammad Ali, 6
Shah, Nadir, 3
Shah, Nur, 7

Shah, Sayyid Allahdad, 259
Shah, Shahabuddin, 7
Shah, Sirdar Amjad Ali, 859
Shah, Sirdar Ikbal Ali, 859
Shah Jehan, 565, 1273, 1474
Shah of Iran, 10, 11, 535, 790
Shahzadi Begum (first wife of Aga Khan), 7, 13
Shakespeare, William, 483, 1129, 1474
Shams-ud-Deen, Honourable, 1195–6, 1199–1200, 1203
Shamsuddin, Abbas, 1332
Shamsuddin, Aga, 1332, 1334
Shamsuddin, Pir, 21
share-holding, 874
Sharfuddin, Mawlawi, 259, 837
sharia, 115, 123
Sharifi family, 1349
Shat-ul-Arab, buffer region, 242
Shaukat Ali, Maulana: Aga Khan's aide, 106, 382, 1345; Khilafat Movement, 155; Muslim Conference, 836–7, 841, 1108; Round Table Conferences, 882, 1385; New Delhi dinner (1935), 1065
Shaw, George Bernard, 1252–3
Shephard, Sir H.H., 462
Sheppard, W.D., 615
Shia Islam: origins, 20–1; relationship with Sunni Islam, 75, 115, 116, 118, 122, 141; khilafat, 116, 118, 122, 178, 483, 637, 1416–17; Persians,

133, 712; Bombay community, 324; final reconciliation between Sunni and Shia, 118, 122, 1416–17; see also Ismailism
Shirinbai, Mrs, 394
Shirzi, Khaleel, 751
Shivaji, 728
Shujauddin, Dr Khalifa, 956
shura, 118
Siam, Aga Khan's plans, 670
Siddiqi, Abdul Qadir, 841
Sikh League, 35, 822
Sikhs: electoral representation, 30, 37, 291, 818; Simon Commission, 35; Round Table Conferences, 37; relationship with British, 271, 272, 273; religious history, 565
Simla: deputation to Viceroy (1906), 2, 12, 26–7, 58, 249–60, 290, 303, 329, 497, 943, 1006, 1266, 1340–3; Conference (1945), 42
Simon, Sir John (later Lord), 34, 79, 616, 850, 921, 1368, 1379
Simon Commission (Indian Statutory Commission), 34–5, 36, 54, 813, 821–2, 842, 959, 976–7, 980, 991–2, 1368, 1370, 1373
Simpson, Sir John Hope, 15
Simur, Raja of, 222n, 232n
Sind: status in relation to Bombay, 36, 73, 835–6, 849, 878, 904,

1015–16, 1057–8, 1375, 1386–7; Pakistan, 40; Cabinet Mission plan, 43; Aga Khan's proposals, 53, 61, 62, 549, 820; self determination, 63; Muslim representation, 73, 252, 304, 1106, 1369, 1386; language, 146; Sindhi nationalism, 148; Provincial Civil Service, 422
Sind, University of, 192
Sindhi nation, 56, 847
Singh, Baldev, 44
Singh, Buta, 993, 994, 999
Singh, Raja Sir Hari, 689
Singh, Sardar Mangal, 35, 922
Singh, Sardar Sampuran, 853, 882
Singh, Sardar Tara, 922
Singh, Sardar Ujjal, 854, 882
Singh, Sir Jawahar, 1065
Singh, Sir Partab, 550
Sinha, Lord: relationship with Minto, 349; banquet in honour of, 612–32; Aga Khan's tribute to, 612–14; peerage and appointment as Parliamentary Under-Secretary of State, 615, 632; Maharajah of Bikaner's tribute to, 616–24; speech (1919), 624–8; Joint Select Committee on the Government of India Bill, 648, 665, 680, 689; Peace Conference delegate, 1351; biography, 1474–5
Sinhji, Digvijaya, 922

Sino-Japanese dispute, *see* China, Japan
Sircar, Sir Nripendra Nath, 922, 994
Sirhindi, Shaikh Ahmad, 115
Sivaji, 565
Sivaya, V.N., 504
slavery, 118, 310
Sly, Frank George, 416, 442, 456, 1475
Smith, E.F.H., 685
Smith, H.B. Lees, 852, 880
Smith, Sir James Dunlop, 615
Smith, Vincent, 564, 1475
smoking, 109, 1211
Smuts, Jan, 604, 615, 795, 941, 1247, 1475
Smyrna, 32, 132, 733, 763, 1353, 1356, 1358
Snell, Lord, 880
Sobhani, Maulana Azad, 837
socialism, 90–1, 531–2, 1060–1, 1287, 1397
Somalis, 1197, 1198, 1201, 1203, 1204–5, 1206, 1224, 1229, 1317
Somjee, Rai Gulamhusein Bundally, 1175
Sonawalla, Alarakhia, 1175
Soorty, Muhammad Goolam Hoosein, 504
Sorabji, R.K., 923
Sorel, Georges, 1397
South Africa: Ismaili community, 22; Indian community, 81, 91–2, 96, 334–5, 468–79, 794–9, 1215–17; race relations, 91–2, 334–5, 468–79, 491, 794–9, 1210–11, 1215–16; education, 101, 1211–12,

1216–17; poverty, 109; Indian rights, 159, 324, 334–5, 468–79, 794–9; war, 365; self-government, 374, 604, 695; Aga Khan's work, 502, 503–4; Kruger regime, 688; Aga Khan's proposals, 871; Aga Khan's visit (1945), 1210–17; peace policy, 1235
South America, 937–8, 1113, 1234, 1236
South Asiatic Federation, 54, 544, 554–5, 573–4
Southborough, Lord, 113, 630, 645–6, 655–6, 689, 1475–6
Southborough Report, 645, 668, 674
Soviet Union: Aga Khan's opinion, 91; economy, 110, 1287–9; League of Nations membership, 1148, 1234, 1394; position after World War II, 1191, 1238; role of women, 1217; peace policy, 1238; science and technology, 1298, 1300; *see also* Russia
Spain: Ismaili community, 22; Islamic rule, 128, 165, 233, 382, 1196, 1205, 1223, 1232; Moroccan rebels, 139, 782; Christian intolerance, 165, 1282–3; literature, 483; government, 575, 1247
Spanish language, 938
Spectator, 169, 1116
spelling reform, 1252–3

Spinoza, Baruch, 167, 1128, 1362, 1476
spiritual: forces, 144, 1127–8, 1405; values, 171–5, 866, 872, 1408–9; *see also* religion
Spoor, Benjamin Charles, 648, 677, 680
sports: Aga Khan's interest in, 200–1; Indian and English relationships, 601, 728, 860; Aga Khan's activities (1925), 786–9; Aga Khan's enjoyment of, 867; Aga Khan's proposals, 872–3; Aga Khan's advice, 1415
Sra Shwe Ba, 994
Srinivasan, M.R. Rao Bahadur, 854, 882
Stalin, Joseph, 1382
Stamfordham, Lord, 616
Stanley, Sir John, 615
Stanley, Oliver, 852, 880
Stansgate, *see* Benn
Stanton, A.W., 685
Star of India, 90, 928, 939, 1017–18, 1026, 1032, 1092, 1102, 1108, 1111, 1118, 1167, 1168
steel industry, 780–1, 808
Stein, Sir Aurel, 1051
Stephens, Percy, 685
Stevenson, Sir Daniel, 1165
Stewart, Sir Findlater, 942
Stewart, Sir John, 1165
Stewart-Sandeman, Sir Nairne, 942
Storrs, Sir Ronald, 1051
Strakosch, Sir Henry, 942
Strangman, Sir Thomas, 808

Stresemann, Gustav, 84, 896, 1162–5, 1476
Subbarayan, Mrs, 854, 882, 1372
Suez Canal, 1395
Sufism, 1364
Suhrawardy, Sir Abdullah, 1014
Suhrawardy, Sir Hasan, 1182
Suhrawardy, Husain Shaheed, 841, 956
Suhrawardy, Mahmud, 1108
Sulaiman, Muhammad, 1065
Sunday Express, 779
Sunday Post, 1222, 1249
Sunni Islam: origins, 20–1; relationship with Shia Islam, 75, 115, 116, 118, 122, 141; *khilafat,* 116, 118, 122, 136–7, 141, 178, 483, 637, 768–70, 1351, 1416–17; Bombay community, 324; principles, 1363–4; final reconciliation between Sunni and Shia doctrines, 118, 1416–17
Sunthralingam, O., 685
Surve, D.A., 854, 922
suttee, 310
Swahili language, 189
Swahilis, 1197, 1201, 1204–5, 1206, 1224
Swaraj, 63, 72, 132, 285–6, 708, 814, 817–18, 964, 998, 1064, 1385
Sweden, government, 576
Swedish Match Company, 977
Switzerland: Aga Khan's wartime residence, 18; Aga Khan's home, 19; languages, 96; Confederation, 551,

589, 649, 651, 656; universities, 588; referendum, 660, 669, 673
Sydenham, Lord, 488, 621, 648, 670–1, 680
Sykes, Sir Frederick, 807, 808, 809, 1476
Sykes-Picot Agreement (1916), 32, 1350
Syria: Aga Khan's visit, 19; Ismaili community, 21; French rule, 131, 407, 485, 766, 1349; Turkish loss, 540, 682; Umayyad period, 1232

Tagore, Rabindranath, 157, 570, 590
Tahzib-ul-Akhlaq, 115–16
Taj-ud-Daulah, Princess, 180
Talbot-Rice, Professor D., 1133
Talhah ibn Ubaidullah, 1257, 1476–7
Tambe, S.B., 854, 882
Tamerlane, 1232, 1477
Tamil language, 53, 549, 590
Tanganyika: Indian community, 81, 1167, 1169; Aga Khan's visit (1945), 91, 1190, 1206–9; agriculture, 108–9, 1190; Muslim population, 129, 1206–7; building programme, 130; German transfer question, 1169; economy, 1208–9; administration, 1225; schools, 1319–20; mosques, 1321–2
Tanganyika Muslim Association, 1206–7
Tanganyika Standard, 1206, 1208, 1240
Tanganyika Tribune, 1249

Tartar Muhammadans, 265
Tata, Sir Dorab J., 474
Tata, Jamsetji Nasarwanji, 411, 592
taxation: salt tax, 216, 755, 987; income tax, 216–17, 949, 986–7; education and health funding, 538–9; representation and, 551; Aga Khan's proposals for India, 559, 562; Round Table Conference proposals, 949, 972–5
Tayebji, Badruddin, 236n, 395, 716, 755
Tayebji, Daoodbhoy Salehbhoy, 837
technology, 99–100, 127, 195; technical education, 218, 1100, 1264–5
Telang, 418, 718
Telugu language, 53, 549, 590
Templetown, Lord, 942
Templewood, Lord, *see* Hoare
tennis, 787, 867, 873, 1331, 1415
Tewfiq Pasha, 1346–7
Thackeray, William Makepeace, 200, 858, 1477
Thakersey, Sir Vithaldas, 411, 414, 473
Thakurdas, Sir Purshotamdas, 473, 479, 882, 922, 994
Thom, Captain, 800
Thomas, J.H., 852, 880, 942
Thombare, Y., 955, 993
Thomson, Sir J.J., 873, 942, 1051, 1477
Thoreau, Henry David, 1380
Thrace: Turkish control, 130, 131,

132, 134, 1356, 1359; Aga Khan's campaign for Turkish control, 634–5, 682, 1352–3; Bonar Law on, 733
Tibet: Aga Khan's proposals, 54, 580, 670; Russian policy, 224; buffer region proposal, 242; borders, 274
Tilak, Bal Gangadhar, 717, 718, 1460, 1478
Times, The, 12, 14, 34, 62, 69, 73, 113, 133–4, 165, 190, 290, 299, 320, 358, 460, 470, 480–2, 522, 633, 640, 645, 711, 713, 731, 772, 781, 782, 783, 803, 805, 809, 816, 847, 850, 861, 865, 886, 903, 956, 1023, 1035, 1071, 1074, 1075, 1119, 1120, 1169, 1241, 1250, 1282, 1313, 1352, 1356
Times of India, The, 51, 273, 343, 361, 473, 619, 734, 736, 746, 753, 775, 792, 807, 827, 995, 1001, 1009, 1016, 1054, 1059, 1064, 1108, 1111, 1172, 1176, 1220, 1336
Tirpitz, Alfred von, 693
Titterton, W.R., 1413
Tiwana, Allah Bakhsh, 1108
Tiwana, Sir Umar Hayat Khan, 697
Tolstoy, Leo, 405, 737, 1036, 1380, 1381
Topan, Sir Tharia, 754
Toynbee, A.J., 770–1
trade, importance of, 75, 874, 934–9, *see also* industry

Transferred Departments, 984
Transvaal Muslim League, 1210, 1213–14
travelling, importance of, 75, 872
Tripoli, Turkish loss, 32, 408
Tripoli War, 403
Trotsky, Leon, 1478
Tucker, Booth, 689
Tunis, French rule, 570
Turkestan, Chinese, 239, 242, 274
Turkey: territory, 2, 130–6, 407, 534, 540, 634–5, 682, 712, 762–7, 1255, 1350–5; *khilafat, see khilafat*; future of, 14, 178; Grand National Assembly, 15, 136; Ottoman Empire, 31–2, 130–2, 636–7, 759, 1255, 1348–9, 1350–1; World War I, 32–3, 164, 510–11, 535–6, 570–1, 578, 637–8, 762, 1346–9; Sultanate, 32–3, 34, 136, 482, 535, 637, 1349; Young Turks, 33, 130, 485, 534, 571, 572, 711, 1346–7, 1349; Greek conflict, 33, 132, 133, 482, 710, 711–12, 733, 759–60, 763, 777, 1355–9; Aga Khan's proposals, 84, 871, 1354; self-determination, 141; secular state, 142, 1258; government, 206, army, 218, 1355–6, 1357; poetry, 233; borders, 274; Muslim population, 321, 404–6, 459, 535; unrest, 365; Balkan Wars, 403–8, 459,

481–2, 484, 487; refugees, 405; Anglo-Turkish relations, 459–60; government, 537; Pan-Turanian movement, 572–3; post-war future, 633–5; British policy, 636–7, 681–6, 688, 712–13, 720–2, 731–3, 734–5, 750–1, 753–4, 758, 762–7, 1346–7, 1350, 1355–9; national state, 757–8; press, 770; League of Nations membership, 906–7; literature, 1088; recovery, 1303, 1306–7; Aga Khan's influence, 1346–7; *see also* Lausanne (Treaty of), Sèvres (Treaty of)
Turkish Relief Fund, 498
Turner, Sir Montagu, 217, 1478
Tyabji, Badruddin, 517, 1478–9
Tyabji, S.A.S., 994
Tyebji, Faiz B., 1175
Tyebji, Saif, 1175

U Ba Pe, 994
U Ba Thein, 504
U Chit Hlaing, 994
U Hpay, 502, 504
U Kyaw Din, 994
U May Oung, 502, 504
U Po Oh, 504
U Shwe Tha, 994
U Thein Maung, 994
Udaipur, 997
Uganda: education, 102; building programme, 130; Aga Khan's visit (1945), 1190; economy, 1209; schools, 1322–3; mosques, 1323–4
Ulu'l-amr Minkum, 1417
Umar ibn Abdul Aziz, Caliph, 1257

Umar ibn al-Khattab, Caliph: model ruler, 123; reign, 207, 382; death, 208–9, 635; example, 210–11; Khilafat succession, 635; in Jerusalem, 1269; biography, 1479

Umayyads, 635, 1232, 1256, 1257, 1290–1, 1309

unemployment, 836, 984

Union of Soviet Socialist Republics (USSR), *see* Soviet Union

United Nations (UN, UNO), 83–4, 1225, 1235, 1241, 1248, 1280

United Press of India, 1219

United Provinces: Government schools, 39; Cabinet Mission plan, 43; status, 95; language, 146; Muslim representation, 304; Aligarh University funding, 397; Aga Khan's proposals, 549, 825; proposed reforms, 986, 1106

United States: Ismaili community, 22; South American policy, 243; power, 276; civil war, 285; immigration, 358; government, 558, 564, 576, 649, 671; Central American influence, 578; languages, 589–90; anarchism, 608; Aga Khan's broadcast to, 863–5; Disarmament Conference, 893, 894, 896–7; relationship with

Islamic world, 1086–8; commerce, 1113; League of Nations, 1163, 1167, 1233–4, 1247; position after World War II, 1191; role of women, 1217; relationship with Britain, 1235; peace policy, 1235; economy, 1287–9; science and technology, 1298, 1300

universities: Indian standards, 93–4, 311; Simla deputation proposals, 253–4; University movement, 378–80; graduate unemployment, 984; East African education, 1197, 1202, 1205, 1225–6, 1229; South African education, 1216

University Movement, 404, 410

Untouchables, 106–7, 291, *see also* Depressed Classes

Urdu, 19, 39, 53, 95, 143, 145–8, 179, 465, 549, 589, 590–1, 832, 932, 938, 1273–5; script, 101, 832; promotion of, 214n; literature, 1088

Uthman ibn Affan, Caliph, 208, 635–6, 1479

usury, 65, 116, 864, 932

Vambéry, Arminius, 571, 1479

Varjivandas, Sir Jugmohandas, 411

Varjivandas, Tribhovandas, 411, 414

Vaux, Major, 736

Venizelos, Eleutherios, 33, 576, 1350, 1479

Venkatagiri, Kumara Raja of, 942

Verma, Mr, 1066

Versailles, Treaty of (1919), 83, 858, 1172, 1351

Viceroyalty, 563–70, 602, 729–30, 1419

Victoria, Queen: Aga Khan's visit to Windsor, 10, 201; death, 11, 150; Proclamation (1858), 149, 278, 347, 550, 616, 620, 624, 846; attitude to India, 341, 566; interest in education, 378; Native States policy, 556; biography, 1479–80

Vijayaraghavacharya, Sir T., 942

Vimadalal, J.J., 411, 413

Vincent, Mr and Mrs, 942

Völcker, Dr J.A., 313, 1480

Wacha, Sir Dinsha Edulji, 716

Wadia, H.A., 478, 794

Waghorn, Lieutenant, 810

wakf-alal-aulad, 124, 337

Waldegrave, Lady, 595

Walid, 123, 235

Waliullah, Shah, 114–15, 118–19, 178

Ward, Sir Joseph, 615

Wardlow-Milne, Sir John, 942

Wavell, Lord, 42–5, 1402, 1403, 1480

Webb, M. de P., 471

Wedderburn, Sir William, 157, 360, 626

Wedgwood, Commander, 689

Weir, Lord and Lady, 1166

Wells, H.G., 689, 858, 1110, 1120–3, 1480

West, Sir Raymond, 295

Westminster Gazette, 478

Wheeler, Sir Henry, 942

White, H. Graham, 880

White Paper (1933), 940, 944–56, 957, 995–9

Whitehead, A.N., 167, 1036, 1480–1

Wigram, Clive, 616

Wilhelm II, Kaiser: Aga Khan's meetings, 10–11, 201; Lloyd George's comparison with Prophet, 159–60, 507; influence, 265; German opinion of, 547; Turkish alliance, 762; biography, 1481

Wilkinson, E., 1133

Williams, Garfield, 371

Willingdon, Lady, 8, 750, 1078

Willingdon, Lord: relationship with Lady Ali Shah, 8; Governor of Bombay, 550, 551, 584; encouragement of sport, 601; Sinha banquet, 615, 617; Governor of Madras, 750; Indian policies, 847, 999, 1055–6; relationship with Aga Khan, 1059; Quetta earthquake relief, 1073–4, 1078; biography, 1481

Wilson, Sir Robert, 1165

Wilson, Woodrow: boundary policies, 84, 870; principles, 138, 613; hopes for future, 539; League of Nations, 1163, 1233, 1247; Aga

Khan's meeting, 1351; biography, 1481

Wingate, R.E.L., 1065

Winterton, Lord, 921

women: emancipation of, 110–14, 118, 177, 597–8; education, 111–12, 394, 582, 585, 591, 1117–18, 1211–12, 1216–17; status of, 210–11, 592–8, 602, 1257, 1295–6; Indian suffrage, 645–7, 655, 662, 664, 668–9, 672, 676–7, 946, 948; East African communities, 1206; role in Pakistan, 1260

Wood, Sir Charles, 47, 310

Wood, Sir C.E., 854, 882

Woodburn, Sir J., 271

Woodroffe, James T., 646

Wordsworth, William, 1037, 1131, 1481

World Economic and Monetary Conference, 909

world government, 85

World Islamic Conference, 150

world peace: Aga Khan's campaign, 75–80, 178–9; Aga Khan's proposals, 870–1, 874–5, 1120; Aga Khan's speech (1933), 924–6; Aga Khan's lecture (1946), 1231–8; Aga Khan's article (1947), 1245–9; Islamic ideal, 1366; need for, 1415

World War I: Ottoman Empire break-up, 32–3; Indian support for Britain, 48, 158, 505–8, 695, 830, 1346; Aga Khan's support for Allies,

505–8, 856–7, 1346; Turkish entry on German side, 510–11, 637, 762; effects on race relations, 532–3; Turkish defeat, 570–1; role of women, 594; Turkish peace treaty, 760; economic effects, 934–5, 969, 1100; Indian expenditure, 969; George V's response to, 567, 1094–5, 1096; origins of League of Nations, 1162–3, 1247; horrors of, 1171, 1233, 1245–6; Aga Khan's Turkish negotiations, 1346–9

World War II, 40–1, 74, 158, 1171, 1178, 1233, 1234, 1246

Worley, Sir Arthur, 999

Wright, H. Seppings, 685

Wynne, Sir Treverdyn, 615

Yakub, Sir Muhammad: Muslim Conference, 70, 837, 841, 890–1, 1014, 1108, 1109; Joint Committee, 942, 956; speech on Aga Khan's achievements, 1006–7; New Delhi dinner (1935), 1062, 1063–5; Aligarh University, 1102; biography, 1481–2

Yamin Khan, Sir Muhammad, 1014, 1065, 1102, 1108

Yar Jang, Nawab Mehdi, 854, 922, 939

Yasmin, Princess, granddaughter of Aga Khan III, 19

Yate, C.E., 615
Yazid, Caliph, 635
Yemen, Ismaili
community, 22
Young, Sir Hilton, 942
Young, J.W., 923
Young Turks, 33, 130,
485, 534, 571, 572,
711, 1346–7, 1349
Younghusband, Sir
Francis, 151
Yule, Colonel H., 809
Yusuf, Muhammad, 841
Yusuf Ali, Abdullah:
Joint Committee, 60,
956; interpretations
of Quran, 119, 169,
1116; translation of
Quran, 169; Sinha
banquet, 615; Muslim
Conference, 841,
1014; National
League meeting

(1933), 939; Muslim
Educational
Conference, 1345;
biography, 1482

Zafrullah Khan, Sir
Muhammad: Round
Table Conferences,
16, 36, 70, 169, 854,
862, 882, 922, 1372,
1385; Joint
Committee, 37, 60,
169, 956, 993, 994;
Aga Khan's tribute to,
169–70, 1110–11;
National League
meetings (1933),
933, 939; on Islamic
principles, 939;
biography, 1482–3
Zaidi, B.H., 923
Zaki-ud-din, 1066
Zamindar, 150

Zand, Karim Khan, 3,
790
Zanzibar: Indian
community, 472, 488,
491; Aga Khan's visit
(1945), 1190;
mosques, 1327
Zetland, Lord, 852, 880,
942, 955, 1073–5,
1483
Ziauddin Ahmad, Sir,
942, 1014, 1065,
1102, 1108, 1483–4
Zill-us-Sultan, 6
Zionism, 1070, 1349,
1350
Zoroaster, 1257, 1365
Zoroastrianism, 11,
1257, 1362, 1365
Zulfiqar Ali Khan,
Nawab Sir
Muhammad, 1343,
1483
Zürich Technological
School, 100